SND

SOCIETY OF NEWSPAPER DESIGN

TEN YEAR ANNIVERSARY

1 9 7 9 1 9 8 9

TENTH EDITION

THE BEST OF NEWSPAPER DESIGN

ANNUAL AWARDS COMPETITION

SOCIETY OF NEWSPAPER DESIGN

1 9 8 8 1 9 8 9

Distributor to the book trade in the United States and Canada
Rizzoli International Publications, Inc.
597 Fifth Avenue
New York, N.Y. 10017

Distributor to the art trade in the United States
Letraset USA
40 Eisenhower Drive
Paramus, N.J. 07653

Distributor to the art trade in Canada
Letraset Canada Limited
555 Alden Road
Markham, Ontario L3R 3L5, CANADA

Distributed throughout the rest of the world by
Hearst Books International
105 Madison Avenue
New York, N.Y. 10016

PBC INTERNATIONAL, INC.
One School Street
Glen Cove, N.Y. 11542

ISSN 1040-4732

ISBN 0-86636-117-0 (Hardbound)

ISBN 0-86636-116-2 (Softbound)

Cover design by Karen Smith
U.S. News & World Report

printing and binding by Toppan Printing Co.
(H.K.) Ltd. Hong Kong

Printed in Hong Kong
10 9 8 7 6 5 4 3 2 1

ACKNOWLEDGMENTS

Tenth Edition

Randy Stano, SND Competition Committee chairman, director editorial art and design, *The Miami Herald.*

Dierck Casselman, Tenth Edition chairman, assistant managing editor, *The Detroit News.*

C. Marshall Matlock, Tenth Edition on-site chairman, assistant professor, Newhouse School of Communications, Syracuse University.

At The Detroit News

Robert H. Giles, editor, publisher and president.
Dale Peskin, news editor/design.
Laura Varon, graphics editor.
Felix Grabowski, graphics editor.
Marla Camp, graphics editor.
Michele Fecht, graphics reporter.
David Pierce, graphics artist.
Pat Sedlar, graphics artist
Mary Harris, news copy desk slot.
Marcia Hart, administrative manager.
Terry Dobson, administrative supervisor.
Also: Pegie Stark, professor,
School of Journalism, University of Florida.

At The Miami Herald and el Nuevo Herald

David Griffin, designer for *National Geographic,* editing images for the Tenth Edition book.

Jim Price, organizing and categorizing Tenth Edition book images.

Assisting in book production:
Steve Rice, assistant managing editor for graphics.
Jackson Dykman, graphics editor/editorial art.
Tiffany Grantham, editorial artist.
Liz Heisler, editorial artist.
Ricardo Martinez, editorial artist.
Pam Swischer, editorial artist.
Herman Vega, editorial artist.

From the Society

Stephen Cvengros, Ninth Edition chairman and deputy design director, *Chicago Tribune.*

Jim Jennings, Eleventh Edition chairman and graphics editor, the *Lexington (Ky.) Herald-Leader.*

Alan Jacobson, Twelfth Edition chairman and design director, *The Virginian-Pilot and The Ledger-Star.*

Rob Covey, SND president, art director, *U.S. News & World Report.*

Nanette Bisher, SND 1st vice-president, Eighth Edition chairman and assistant art director, *U.S. News & World Report.*

David Gray, SND treasurer and assistant managing editor, the *Providence Journal-Bulletin.*

Robin Fogel, Tenth Edition reporter, chief page designer, *The Philadelphia Inquirer.*

Nancy Tobin, Tenth Edition reporter, SND secretary, design director, *Asbury Park (N.J.) Press.*

Jacqueline Combs, Tenth Edition reporter, SND 2nd vice-president, graphics editor, *Chicago Tribune.*

John Goecke, Tenth Edition volunteer worker, design director/news, *Detroit Free Press.*

At Syracuse University

Edward Stephens, dean, Newhouse School.
Judith Van Nostrand, assistant dean, Newhouse School.
Rosanna Grassi, assistant dean, Newhouse School.
Tony Golden, Newhouse photo professor and Tenth Edition portrait photographer.
David Sutherland, Newhouse photo professor and Tenth Edition candid photographer.
Cathy Dowhos, Newhouse student and coordinator of entry sorting.
Sam Babbage, student assistant to Professor Matlock.

Syracuse University students:
Dave Allen, Jackie Avin, Bob Baker, Rick Conant, Maria E. Devletoglou, Michael Flam, Scott Goldman, Ilene J. Locke, Catherine O'Mara, Ken Paulsen, Jim Rife,Don Sena, Keith Shaw, Lee Ann Schmidt.

Also: Barbara Hines, Tenth Edition database coordinator and professor, School of Journalism, Howard University.

Contents

JUDGES

Russ Ball, senior illustrator, *Albuquerque Journal.*

Lucy Bartholomay, art director, *Boston Globe.*

Rob Covey, art director, *U.S. News & World Report;* SND president.

Robert H. Giles, editor, publisher and president, *The Detroit News.*

Judy Griesedieck, staff photographer, *San Jose Mercury News.*

David Griffin, layout editor, *National Geographic.*

Ken Raniere, design editor/production coordinator, *The A.D. Times*, Allentown, Pa.

Steve Rice, assistant managing editor/ graphics, *The Miami Herald.*

John Rumbach, managing editor, *The Herald*, Jasper, Ind.

Jose Diaz de Villegas Sr., art director, *El Nuevo Dia*, San Juan, Puerto Rico, and director for Latin American Region of SND.

Melissa Farlow, staff photographer, *The Pittsburgh Press*.

Mario R. Garcia, associate director, Poynter Institute for Media Studies, St. Petersburg, Fla.

Howard I. Finberg, assistant managing editor, *The Arizona Republic*; chairman of SND's Technology Committee.

John Kascht, free-lance illustrator and illustrator/designer, *The Washington Times*.

Jennie Palmer, editor, *The Gastonia (N.C.) Gazette*.

Therese Shechter, art director, *Financial Times of Canada*, Toronto.

Bonnie Timmons, free-lance illustrator, Philadelphia.

Tom Trapnell, editorial art director, *Los Angeles Times*.

Foreword

When it came time to issue a call for entries to this year's Society of Newspaper Design competition, we were worried.

The Society had decided to change the contest to a calendar year. The Tenth Edition would judge entries printed over just nine months: May 1988 through January 1989. Judging would be in March, not June.

How could we tell SND members so they would remember? Could we keep the number of entries from dropping off?

I turned for help to one of Detroit's best-known communicators and paraphrased one of her better-known messages.

Take it, Aretha.

What you want, baby you know I got it;
What you need, you know I got it.
All I'm askin'
Is for a little respect in the newsroom.

Not a little confusion followed. Who's asking for respect? Who's got it to give? What is "it" that "I" got that "you" want?

I saw it two ways.

In one version, graphics people are telling editors that they have "it": the ability to seize readers' attention with imaginative presentations, strong visuals and clean design. To get "it," editors need to show graphics people a little respect.

In another version, graphics people are telling Tenth Edition judges that they have "it": work worthy of an award. All they're asking is for recognition: something printed, signed and ready for framing. Something to display on the desk, some respect in the newsroom.

One way or another, the message got through.

Participation in the contest dropped only slightly. There were more than 7,150 entries to the Tenth Edition, about 700 fewer than last year. The surprise was the decline in the number of awards.

Although 77 publications won awards, just 23 fewer than in the Ninth Edition, the awards were given at about half the rate of previous contests — a total of 337 awards were made.

As we watched this develop during the weekend of judging, we wondered why: A shorter contest year meant fewer opportunities for prize-winning work? Fewer large news stories? Earlier deadlines meant less time to edit entries? Judges simply were hard-assed?

Perhaps the real reason is a combination of all of the above. The 18 judges, all highly respected and accomplished and with vast amounts of newspaper experience among them, uniformly found that many entries were repetitive or imitative; many ideas were stale.

From the start of judging that weekend in March in Syracuse, N.Y., their standards were high, and they maintained them as they continued their work. They found that they were looking for the original, the simple, the straightforward presentation. It took imagination and restraint to win their respect.

The introduction and the lead-ins for the chapters that follow are designed to illuminate the judging process, whenever possible using quotes from the judges themselves. The hope here is that the Tenth Edition book is educational and inspirational, a touchstone to newspaper design in 1988 and a directional sign for design in the years to come.

My thanks go to the judges who worked long hours and walked many miles between entry-laden tables over three days of judging. And thanks, too, to the legions of SND officers and members, Syracuse University faculty and students and colleagues at *The Detroit News* who volunteered their time and talent to organize, execute and report on the contest; and to the graphics and design staffs at *The Miami Herald* and *U.S. News & World Report*, who helped produce this book.

— Dierck Casselman
Tenth Edition chairman
Assistant managing editor
The Detroit News

Introduction

An overview: respect, restraint and renewal

After a decade of dominant art and cosmic colors, megagraphics and tortured typography, the twists and turns of newspaper design are leading back to basics

A theme for the Society of Newspaper Design's tenth competition emerged on the second day of judging.

Eighteen judges had spent the previous day looking at thousands of newspaper pages. Just after 8 a.m., the 12 core judges gathered to look at thousands more. Several chatted about the competition. Several chewed on continental breakfast. Several surveyed the tables of tearsheets that awaited. Robert H. Giles, executive editor of *The Detroit News*, went a separate way. He unfolded *The New York Times* and began to read.

At an exercise in looking at newspapers, Giles was compelled to read one. It was a private moment, a solitary interlude between print and person.

"Good newspaper design begins with good reading," Giles would say later.

As it turned out, the other judges agreed. Entries that showed respect for reading — and restraint in design — won the year in newspaper design.

Respect for reading? Restraint in design? What's going on here?

After a decade of dominant art and cosmic colors, megagraphics and tortured typography, the twists and turns of newspaper design are leading back to basics.

"The age of experimentation is over," declared judge Jose Diaz de Villegas, art director of San Juan's *El Nuevo Dia*. "Newspapers that have been going for effect are forgetting something very important: People have to read the page."

Diaz and the other judges took a dim view of work intended to impress rather than inform. They eliminated entries that put form before function, design before content. The victims included overpowering color, overplayed photos and uninformative graphics.

The judges also put a premium on originality. Dozens of look-alike shuttle graphics, dinosaur illustrations and Freddy Krueger photos were cut quicker than you can say cliche.

"I'm troubled by all the imitation," lamented judge Mario Garcia, associate director of The Poynter Institute. "It is obvious that too many designers are picking up the SND book and saying 'Gee, let's do that.' There are few newspapers willing to set a standard, develop a personality, and distinguish themselves from the field."

There were notable exceptions. In each category, the judges recognized distinctive work that presented information in readable, restrained and original ways.

In the news categories, they singled out *The Orange County Register* for its comprehensive road map to the 1988 election and the *Detroit Free Press* for its innovative news page design.

In informational graphics, they were impressed with *The Detroit News* for newsy graphics that worked as sidebars, enhancing reporting and guiding readers through events.

In features, they cited the originality of *The Boston Globe's* ArtsEtc. section, the distinctive illustrations of *The Washington Times'* life! and Books sections and *The Washington Post's* imaginative Health and Food sections. In magazines, they noted the high quality of information and design of *The New York Times*, *The Washington Post* and *The Boston Globe.*

And in the art and photography, where three of the four Gold Awards were won, they praised David C. Turnley's photographs in the *Detroit Free Press* of Armenia after the earthquake, John Kaplan's photographs in *The Pittsburgh Press* of a young man's journey through the court system and Sam Hundley's portfolio of illustrations in Norfolk's *Virginian-Pilot and Ledger-Star.* The fourth Gold went to John Kascht for his page designs in *The Washington Times.*

Judges agreed that winning entries shared common qualities.

- Each had clear concepts. "How much do readers need to know?" asked Howard Finberg, assistant managing editor of *The Arizona Republic.* "The best designs answered the question."
- Each were precisely executed. "I looked for detail," said Ken Raniere, free-lance illustrator and design editor of *The A.D. Times* in Allentown, Pa. "Scale, frame of reference and technique count."
- Each presented information simply and precisely. "The slogan for this year's judging was R-E-S-P-E-C-T," said Therese Shechter, art director of the *Financial Times* of Canada. "It should be R-E-S-T-R-A-I-N-T."
- Each was thoroughly edited. "Where's the lead? Where's the nut graph? Where's the editing?" Rob Covey, SND president and art director of *U.S. News & World Report*, repeatedly asked.
- Each was honest and original. "The best resource is here," said Lucy Bartholomay, art director of *The Boston Globe Magazine*, pointing to her head.

Failure to meet those standards resulted in the most notable — and most discussed — consequence of the competition. Of the 7,150 entries this year, 336 — or 4 percent — received awards. That's the lowest percentage in the history of an SND competition that usually bestows 10 percent of its entries with awards.

As the numbers became obvious early in the contest, Competition Committee Chairman Randy Stano reminded judges that they were voting for Awards of Excellence and that medal discussions would come later.

"We had an ongoing discussion about fair and appropriate standards," said John Kascht, who judged illustrations and features page design. "I wish that everyone who entered could know how deliberate the judges were. All but a few pages were looked at more than once. We shuffled entries into categories that seemed more appropriate. We edited entries to give them a better chance."

In the end the judges' message was this: They were setting a new agenda for newspaper design.

"A statement is being made here," said Garcia. "We are establishing a new standard for newspaper design. Good enough isn't good enough anymore."

Not all judges were comfortable with the numbers. " 'High standards' is a nice way to put it," judge Bonnie Timmons said. "Hard-assed judging might be more accurate. I think it would not have hurt to have been a little less selective. I hate to squelch a lot of new talent that could have been represented."

Garcia recognized that the standard set may not be popular.

"I imagine the immediate reaction will be anger by a lot of people," Garcia said. "Everybody wants to win. I saw awards of excellence from the features sections that would have been Silvers or Golds two years ago."

And, after all, isn't that the point of the SND competition? That each of the nine editions has helped establish direction, expand horizons and lift expectations.

The Tenth Edition is an argument for newspaper design. It is meant to provoke ideas and discussion. It should be looked at, studied and read.

So follow judge Giles' example. Find a quiet corner, turn the pages of this book, and read.

— Dale Peskin

Chapter 1

Four Gold Awards and news judges' award for design

Sam Hundley

The Virginian-Pilot and The Ledger-Star

Illustration portfolio

"What I try to do is stress the idea. I approach my job as a problem-solver. Illustration is really a way of thinking, rather than just drawing.

"I usually average three illustrations a week. My deadlines vary greatly. The important thing is having the extra time to think. Execution doesn't take very long. I work with pastels, I kind of smear them with my hands. They are easy to work with.

David C. Turnley

Detroit Free Press

Photostory

"I don't remember who called whom first because we were both thinking the same thing. But as soon as the earthquake hit, everyone agreed: Turnley needed to go to Armenia. The problem was how.

"David was finally able to get a ride with a French medical relief team. He was held up in Turkey for a day, and then got into Armenia. He was there about a week.

"Transmitting photos was really impossible. And getting film out was as difficult as getting into the country. All together, there were four film shipments. The first went out with a pilot on the same French medical team, the second with a television cameraman, the third with Tom Hundley a reporter for the *Chicago Tribune* who is based in Detroit. The fourth shipment David brought out himself when he went to Moscow.

"The film ended up getting here about the same time. There were 100-150 rolls of film. Photo editor Marcia Prouse made the first edit; photo director Mike Smith and I made the final edit.

"A special report was definitely the best way to go with it. Having Sunday fall on Christmas was good timing. It made the story even more touching. I recommended the extra space; editor Heath Meriwether approved it. John Goecke, design director/news, and I did the design.

It took about two days from film to production.

"We put together the special section while David was starting on a monthlong project in Moscow. That project ran a few weeks later."

— Randy Miller
Deputy managing editor/
graphics
Detroit Free Press

John Kascht

The Washington Times

Page-design portfolio

"I think John has done a tremendous job pushing the format of the page. He primarily does this through the use of illustration. I think he's been very successful integrating typography with illustration. The whole page is like a package. It goes very well together.

"John works very closely with the editor of the section. He does have a lot of freedom in terms of what he can do on that page.

"The basic format of the page was designed two years ago during the paper's redesign. We're in a good position here. The art department has a lot of say in how the paper looks. We have a presence in each section. They realize here that what we do is important for the paper. I think part of that is because the paper is relatively new. We've never been a service department. I think it was important that we established ourselves early."

— Joe Scopin
Assistant managing editor/
photo and design
The Washington Times

John Kaplan

The Pittsburgh Press

Photostory

"I was intrigued that this young suspect was more than a statistic.

"In general the media rarely humanizes crime stories that aren't big news. This case certainly didn't involve famous or influential people. Nevertheless, I've always felt lives are equally valuable whether or not they yield power or influence.

"In society's eyes, Woodson's label had instantly changed from personable young father to dangerous accused murderer. I wanted to learn more about the man behind the stereotype.

"It was my idea to follow Rodney's case. I talked to his attorney to ask if I could follow through with the story. My goal was neither to attract sympathy for Woodson nor to condemn him before his trial. I wanted to follow him through the legal system and show how his family was attempting to cope with their crisis.

"I worked for more than a year on the story. I faced so many roadblocks along the way. It was canceled three times by the family and twice by the paper.

"It's hard to convince editors that a huge amount of space is warranted for a story that seems to have little news value. It also was the first time a criminal trial had been photographed in Pennsylvania. It took a lot of legal wrangling. It's the most challenging assignment I've ever done.

Rodney Woodson, the subject of Kaplan's story, is serving a five-year sentence for voluntary manslaughter. Kaplan has started a small bank account for Woodson's two children.

Detroit Free Press

News judges' award for extraordinary and innovative design in all news categories

"Perhaps our biggest advantage is that we have no restrictions — no set story count, no minimum number of items, no guidelines for what must appear above the fold.

"Instead, Randy Miller, deputy managing editor for graphics, instills in everyone involved that we are starting from scratch each day. We ask ourselves one simple question: What elements will best serve the reader?

"Call it common sense. Call it customer obsession. Call it whatever you want. But too few papers fail to think about how best to present news to their readers. Putting a story at the top of the page with a big headline often isn't enough.

— John Goecke
Design Director/News

"When you try to do that much with a page, and have that much freedom, it has to be done by designers. That's another thing that sets us apart. Our designers decide how our pages look — all the pages, not just the front."

— Randy Miller
Deputy Managing Editor/
Graphics

"We want our front page to always convey the excitement we feel about the news. With the design desk always trying to shrewdly hook the reader, we think our pages should never be bland or uninspired. And to tell you the truth, this philosophy for page one makes newspapering a helluva lot more fun at the Free Press than at most places. And it pays off for readers."

— Heath Meriwether
Executive Editor

GOLD AWARD
PHOTOJOURNALISM
PHOTO STORY
Detroit Free Press
Photographer
David C. Turnley

COMMENT
Detroit Free Press

DETROIT FREE PRESS — SUNDAY DEC. 25, 1988

WHEN THE CLOCKS STOPPED

David Turnley, a Free Press photographer stationed in Paris, traveled with relief workers to the site of the Armenia earthquake. He filed these impressions from the scene Dec. 15, his second day there.

BY DAVID C. TURNLEY

SPECIAL REPORT: THE ARMENIAN EARTHQUAKE

A city of weariness

SPECIAL REPORT: THE ARMENIAN EARTHQUAKE

At graveyards after tragedy, toasts and tears

GOLD AWARD
PHOTOJOURNALISM
PHOTO STORY
Detroit Free Press
Photographer
David C. Turnley

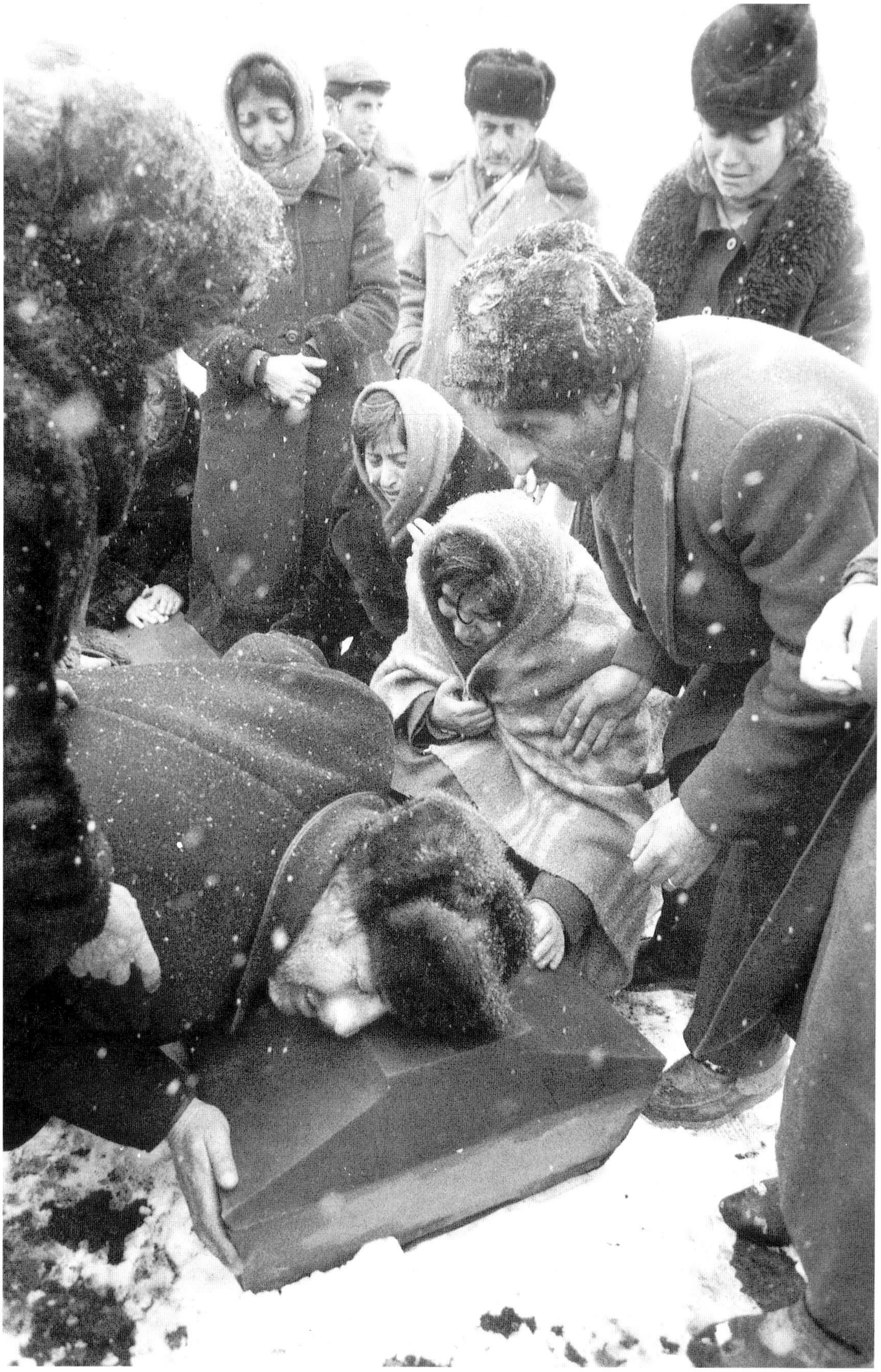

GOLD AWARD
PHOTOJOURNALISM
PHOTO STORY
The Pittsburgh Press, Sunday Magazine
Photographer
John Kaplan

GOLD AWARD
PHOTOJOURNALISM
PHOTO STORY
The Pittsburgh Press, Sunday Magazine
Photographer
John Kaplan

GOLD AWARD
ART AND ILLUSTRATION
PORTFOLIO OF WORK
The Virginia-Pilot and The Ledger-Star
Norfolk, Virginia
Designer
Sam Hundley
Illustrator
Sam Hundley
Art Directors
Bob Lynn, Bill Pitzer
Editors
Ann Hoffman, Marian Anderfuren,
David Loomis

SUNDAY JULY 10, 1988 — The Virginian-Pilot — THE LEDGER-STAR — SECTION C

■ GEORGE TUCKER/C2
■ BOOKS/C4
■ EDITORIALS/C6

Commentary

PENTAGATE

Are consultants corrupt? Possibly. Is the system defective? Certainly. When will U.S. weapons-buying be fixed? When Congress dismantles the false pretenses on which the system always has been based.

Staff illustration by SAM HUNDLEY

By Edward Luttwak

Before the consultant witch hunt goes much further, we might pause to wonder why "waste, fraud and abuse" scandals persist in the Pentagon year after year, in spite of the regiments of auditors, bookkeepers and investigators added to the payroll since 1981, the dozens of laws and hundreds of regulations enacted since then, and a whole series of "procurement reforms."

Two explanations are possible: Either Pentagon officials, defense-industry executives and the consultant tribe are naturally inclined to dishonesty; or else there is something fundamentally wrong with the system — a defect so basic that it has remained quite untouched by all the varied reforms of the past two decades.

A comparison with the (pre-Gorbachev) Soviet economy is instructive. Alongside thieves, murderers and rapists, one would find in Soviet jails those guilty of "economic crimes": the man who repaired cars in his spare time, the farmer who sold cucumbers from his garden, the taxi driver who worked extra hours to pick up extra fares.

An economic system built on the false pretense that it provided all these necessary goods and services punished those who recognized reality and sought to fill the gaps.

Exactly in the same manner, our defense purchasing system is built on a false pretense: that military products are commodities — identical, precisely defined goods traded in open markets.

A few important Pentagon purchases really are commodities — chiefly gasoline, diesel and jet fuel — and they can in fact be bought like commodities: by arms-length, open-market purchasing.

Some other items — boots and blankets, uniforms and stationery — are too varied to be actual commodities, but they too resemble the idealized "goods" traded in the idealized markets of economic textbooks, simply because they can be described very precisely. Hence these items, too, should only be purchased in the free-market way, by public tenders and competitive bidding.

But most of the $80 billion of Pentagon "procurement" and almost all the $36 billion spent on research and development buys neither commodities nor textbook "goods" — but aircraft, missiles, warships, armored vehicles and military electronics of all kinds.

None of those things is a standard item traded every day on open markets, and none of them can actually be described precisely in a request for competitive bids.

But under the false pretense on which the entire system is based, thousands of laws and regulations compel defense officials to act as if weapons and weapon projects were just like soy beans, boots and blankets. The result hovers between absurdity and crime.

The problems begin with the very statement of what is wanted.

Instead of "600 tons, fuel oil No. 2," or at least a 20-page tender document for boots or blankets that an industry cost accountant can read down to the last cent, Pentagon contracts for major weapons run to millions of pages.

But that mass of detail hardly defines the product, because so many weapons include untried exotic materials, designs never attempted before, and unproven engineering methods. And during the 10 or 15 years that will pass between the start of research work and the beginning of production, thousands of changes in the specifications will be required.

Some of those "change orders" are caused by the tendency of technology-fixated military bureaucracies to add what are called "bells and whistles" in the trade, nice-to-have extras that are often technically exciting, and which may or may not be tactically significant in combat.

Other change orders, by contrast, are the beneficial results of the same emphasis on technology that is the hallmark of our military establishment.

Either way, those changes make nonsense of the original cost estimates on which the winning bid was supposedly based — estimates that were little more than guesses in the first place.

Thus the Pentagon officials who first comply with the letter of the law by issuing mountainous contracts, written out by hordes of clerks in spurious detail, must next pretend to take seriously the bids

Please see **PENTAGON,** *Page* **C2**

Mr. Luttwak, a former defense consultant, now is with Georgetown University's Center for Strategic and International Studies in Washington, D.C.

Pari-mutuel: Poll shows race-track wagering is a favorite in the fall

But softness in support could make campaign a rerun of 1978 race

BONNIE V. WINSTON
INSIDE VIRGINIA

Joe Baldacci is no Johnny-come-lately to the business world. A self-made success who built an empire in the concession and catering business around Richmond, Baldacci moved into the world of auto racing with the ownership of Southside Speedway, a small oval in burgeoning Chesterfield County that draws such weekend crowds that it creates traffic jams.

The speedway will close in October, its prime suburban location to be taken over by a shopping center. Baldacci plans to reopen in a more rural setting, and with legalized horse racing and betting looming as a possibility in Virginia, he's thinking about diversifying. He has options on land in both Dinwiddie and New Kent counties that he envisions being easily transformed into a race track. Already he is discussing a possible partnership with an outfit that owns horse and dog tracks across the country.

But Baldacci assumes what even proponents of horse racing and pollsters refuse to take for granted — that voters will approve pari-mutuel betting this November when the question is posed in a statewide referendum. "We made the conscious decision to run hard and run scared," said Jeff Gregson, director of Virginians for Horse Racing. "History is against us."

A survey last month of 828 Virginia voters by Mason-Dixon Opinion Research Inc. found that 53 percent of those polled said they support pari-mutuel betting, while 37 percent opposed it. Another 9 percent were undecided.

But, according to the pollster, support for legal betting is less firm than the opposition. With November likely to see a high voter turnout for the presidential election, the pari-mutuel question is really up in the air. A "different electorate" will be voting in the fall, said the pollster, "one that might be more inclined to shift positions as the election draws closer."

Baldacci admitted in a recent interview that he was mistaken in 1978, the last time the question of legalizing pari-mutuel betting was put to Virginia voters.

"I thought it was going to pass then," Baldacci said. "I had studies all prepared. I was ready to open a track then."

Polls taken one month before the '78 election showed supporters of horse racing with a 19-point lead. On election day, however, pari-mutuel was defeated 52 percent to 48 percent.

A majority of voters in Norfolk, Virginia Beach, the Richmond area and Northern Virginia backed the gambling proposal. But that support was offset by overwhelming disapproval in many rural portions of Virginia, as well as in Portsmouth and Chesapeake.

The latest Mason-Dixon poll reflects these same trends, with the greatest opposition to betting registered in rural Southwest and Southside Virginia, while voters in Hampton Roads, metropolitan Richmond and Northern Virginia form the strongest base of support.

The two most-talked-about sites for

Please see **RACING,** *Page* **C2**

Bonnie Winston covers Virginia politics and government from Richmond for The Virginian-Pilot and The Ledger-Star.

Staff illustration by SAM HUNDLEY

Staff illustration by SAM HUNDLEY

WEDNESDAY/THURSDAY JANUARY 11/12, 1989 — The Virginian-Pilot — The Ledger-Star — SECTION E

Health & Fitness

■ ONGOING EVENTS/E4
■ ZOOM/E6

Staff illustration by SAM HUNDLEY

LETHAL LEGACY

Life is a cruel guessing game for children of parents with Huntington's Disease, an incurable brain disorder. Do they have it or don't they? Geri decided to find out for sure

By Susan Ager
Knight-Ridder News Service

THEY MADE THE decision in bed one chilly autumn night in 1986. She had always wanted to know for sure; guessing drove her crazy.

Results from the new blood test could be like a promise of happiness-ever-after from a fortune teller, but more potent, based in science, not superstition.

If she were found free of the gene for the disease, they could pursue the life they wanted: another child, a house on a lake, a modest boat, California vacations, a college education for B.J. — the candied hopes of the young.

If that were not to be, Geri hoped to accept her fate with some grace, not deny it, run from it, rage against it as her mother had.

Randy told himself her family's tragic legacy would not touch them. But he knew his wife needed proof, and so did a private corner of his own mind.

At bedtime some nights, he would touch her softly and say, "Geri, this is getting scary," but neither ever suggested turning back.

Each of Kaye Wieske's six children, including Geri, grew up with a 50-50 chance of inheriting Huntington's Disease — an incurable, largely untreatable brain disorder that has been passed without malice through generations of the family tree.

"You either won the toss of the coin or you lost it at conception," Gerry Wieske told his children frankly.

For 25 years, they have watched him care for his wife, their mother, transformed by Huntington's Disease first into a shrew who broke every knickknack her kids gave her, then into a recluse who slept all day and rarely changed her clothes, and finally into a mute, withered woman, gagged and bound to a body and mind that no longer work.

It has been described as a combination of Alzheimer's disease and cancer, but it is worse: Its victims linger for decades, all too able to recall their healthy pasts and recognize the disease's devastation.

Until 1986, life for children of parents with Huntington's Disease could only be a cruel guessing game. The disease often does not appear until between the ages of 35 and 45, after life's major choices have been made, and after many have borne children, a new generation at risk.

Those at risk are obsessively vigilant for hints — a bobbled glass, a bungled word, an emotional overreaction — that could be early symptoms of the disease. Or that could mean nothing at all.

Five years ago, scientists found a genetic marker — a red flag that signaled the presence of the defective Huntington's gene. A test for the marker became available experimentally two years ago. By analyzing DNA from the blood of those at risk and some of their relatives, doctors could, with 99 percent certainty, free people from a lifelong burden of worry — or confirm that the worst is in store for them.

The pioneering decision made by Geri Harville, 30, and her husband, Randy, 34, could within a generation become routine as thousands of young people choose to know their medical fates through predictive tests for other inherited adult disorders, including some forms of Alzheimer's disease and cancer.

Advocates say the new test allows healthy people to make wiser decisions about their lives, based on information, not suspicion. But cynics wonder whether it might not decimate young lives more than it empowers them.

Among her siblings, only Geri lived close enough to a testing center to be eligible for the program. And only she was sure she wanted to know.

Beginning on a misty day in mid-April 1987, Geri would make six visits to Johns Hopkins Hospital in Baltimore, an easy two-hour drive from her home in Harrisburg, Pa. Three times, Randy would accompany her.

In tiny, windowless, fluorescent-lit rooms, researchers would put her through a repetitive, frustrating battery of questions and behavioral and intelligence tests. Psychiatrists would poke at the couple's psyches and their marriage, to make sure they were strong enough to handle even bad news.

They would wait 18 months for the verdict.

Dr. Susan Folstein, 44, a psychiatrist and clinical director of the Huntington's Disease project at Johns Hopkins, is glad the test is available, but worries that those who choose it cannot know its potency, as she does. She deliberately makes it tough for them to go on.

"In the abstract, people might say the ones who are affected are the ones who really should know, because they're the ones whose children will be at risk, and they're the ones responsible for not passing this on. But, gee —" she swallows hard, her eyes moistening. "They sure do suffer.

If Geri was found to have the Huntington's Disease gene, she hoped to accept her fate with some grace, not deny it, run from it, rage against it as her mother had.

"They suffer so much, it seems hardly fair that they'll be suffering for years ahead of time."

Geri's father took her shopping to buy her first bra. Her three older sisters taught her about menstruation. And when she was 16 and met 22-year-old Randy Harville, she bought a book by a woman gynecologist who, with no reassuring hugs, answered her questions about sex and birth control.

Geri's mother taught her little except the thousand details of Huntington's Disease. Even then, she learned only by watching her mother lose control — first of her emotions, then of her body, in classic pattern.

"She would throw things," Geri remembers aloud, curled on the sofa. "You know how kids buy you little odds and ends — glasses and cups and saucers and little statues and stuff? She had a ton of that stuff, and she broke every piece she had over a five- to 10-year period.

"Whatever the upset was, she'd get in where she couldn't control her anger and had to break something. She'd break windows, too, making a big scene. It was always 2 in the morning," and the police would come. In Utica, Mich.; St. Clair Shores, Mich.; and Mount Clemens, Mich.; where the Wieske kids grew up, their house had a reputation.

"She'd have typical depression things: sleep all day, awake all night. I know what it is now, but I didn't understand it then. Our mother was really the only mother we knew that was in bed when we got home from school. It was really hard, because other kids noticed it, too. And they often said things. I got into a fist fight once with a girl who said she was crazy.

"I was really furious, because I knew my mother wasn't crazy. There was just something going on, and it wasn't her fault. But people didn't want to bother with it. She was different, so she was crazy."

"Even when I would go with her to the beauty shop, the beauticians would ask me, 'How does she want her hair?' because her glasses were half-cocked and there was clearly something wrong with her. But that would make me furious, and I'd say, 'She's got a mouth! Ask her!'"

Geri looks up suddenly, her eyes wide. "She was a good mother, though," she says. "I have really loving memories of her."

But there are just three:

"I can remember when I was about 10 having a tremendous ear infection, and her sitting up nights with me with my head in her lap."

And: "I used to sit up late and watch TV with her. We used to watch all these stupid old movies together: Fred Astaire and Ginger Rogers, Danny Kaye, Bob Hope and all those old corny movies. She liked all those guys."

And the earliest memory, before anything was wrong: "I was really small, and I can remember her washing the dishes in the kitchen, and she was singing."

Sometimes it is hard for Geri to untangle the love, the pity, the anger she feels for her mother. Sometimes it is even hard for her to separate her mother's personality from her own.

She has screamed at B.J., her 7-year-old son, and heard her mother screaming at

Please see DISEASE, Page E2

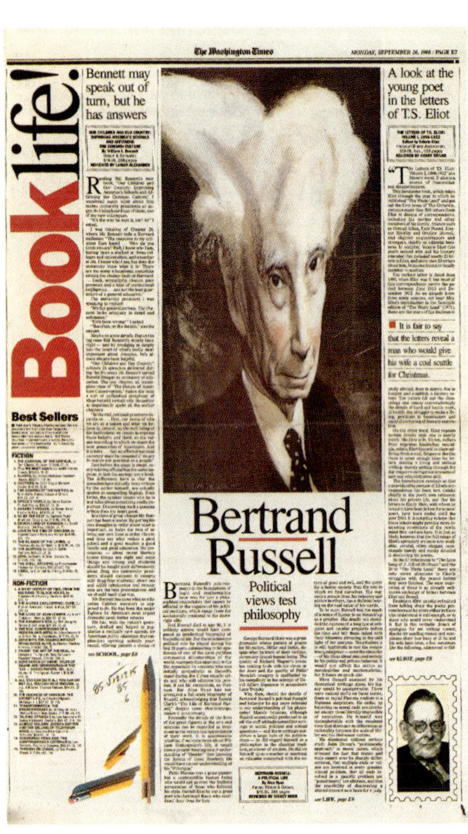

The Washington Times — MONDAY, SEPTEMBER 26, 1988 / PAGE E7

Book life!

Bennett may speak out of turn, but he has answers

A look at the young poet in the letters of T.S. Eliot

It is fair to say that the letters reveal a man who would give his wife a coal scuttle for Christmas.

Bertrand Russell

Political views test philosophy

Best Sellers

PAGE E6 / MONDAY, SEPTEMBER 5, 1988 — The Washington Times

Book life!

Self-satisfied New Yorker is no longer, alas, the talk of the town

YEAR OF CHANGE

EJ KAHN JR.

赤龍舟圖

A rosy view of China's actions in Africa

Touted author strikes out on convoluted

Best Sellers

GOLD AWARD

FEATURE PAGE
DESIGN PORTFOLIO
CIRCULATION 100,000-249,000

The Washington Times

Designer
John Kascht

Illustrator
John Kascht

Art Director
John Kascht

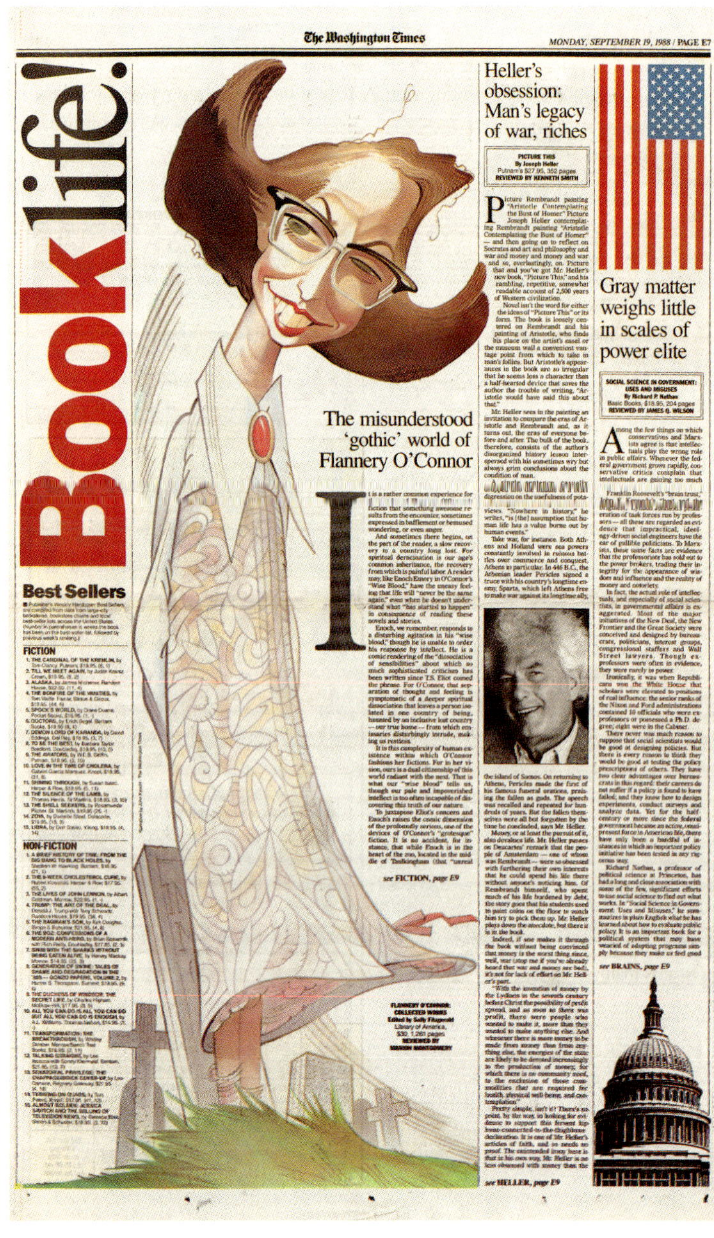

The Washington Times — MONDAY, SEPTEMBER 19, 1988 / PAGE E7

Book life!

Heller's obsession: Man's legacy of war, riches

PICTURE THIS
By Joseph Heller
Putnam's $27.95, 352 pages
REVIEWED BY KENNETH SMITH

Gray matter weighs little in scales of power elite

The misunderstood 'gothic' world of Flannery O'Connor

Best Sellers

FICTION

NON-FICTION

see FICTION, page E9

see HELLER, page E9

see BRAINS, page E9

The Washington Times — MONDAY, OCTOBER 3, 1988 / PAGE E7

Book life!

Vann and Vietnam as seen through a '60s time warp

What we have here is two books in a single symbiosis. One book is a biography of the legendary John Paul Vann, the other is a history of the Vietnam War or at least major parts of it. "A Bright Shining Lie: John Paul Vann and America in Vietnam" will be bought and read, and probably will sell well as a biography. This is just as well, because what Neil Sheehan has produced here is good biography and bad history.

Those of us who have known Mr. Sheehan personally over the years, and have followed from afar his seemingly endless travail on the manuscript of this book, assumed that he was writing a biography of Vann as a metaphor for the war itself. Vann's career, his personality, the events of his life were to be used to personify the war with all its contradictions of genius and folly, ambitions and idealism, good intent and evil result.

A BRIGHT SHINING LIE: JOHN PAUL VANN AND AMERICA IN VIETNAM
By Neil Sheehan
REVIEWED BY DOUGLAS PIKE

Best Sellers

FICTION

NON-FICTION

The obscure composer of beloved concerto

MAX BRUCH: HIS LIFE AND WORKS
By Christopher Fifield
George Braziller $30, 351 pages
REVIEWED BY PAUL HUME

When I was a teen-age voice student in Chicago, my great teacher Else Harthan Arendt (Max Reger had been her father's secretary) included in many of her recitals the "Ave Maria" from "The Cross of Fire" ("Das Feuerkreuz") by Max Bruch.

The text of the oratorio, which Bruch completed when he was 50, was by Walter Scott, and the "Ave Maria" is not the familiar Latin text, but an impassioned German translation of a dramatic scene in which the singer cries out "Norman! Norman!" The "Ave Maria" is very much the high point in vocal beauty of the entire oratorio and well worth the time and attention of any of today's leading sopranos. (There is, for those lucky enough to own it, a recording made by Joan Hammond around 1953.)

When you say "Max Bruch," you are saying the name of a man who wrote one of the most popular works ever placed in the repertoire of violin concertos: the Concerto No. 1 in G Minor. Recent Schwann catalogs have listed as many as 21 recordings of the concerto, played by such giants as Jascha Heifetz, Yehudi Menuhin, Isaac Stern, Zino Francescatti, Salvatore Accardo, Fritz Kreisler, Arthur Grumiaux, Nathan Milstein, Itzhak Perlman, Ruggiero Ricci and Pinchas Zukerman. It was the first concerto to be recorded by the rising young star Joshua Bell. In point of fact, the Bruch G Minor Concerto has been in the active repertoire of almost every major and minor violinist.

And would you believe it, Bruch sold the rights to the concerto to a publisher for 250 talers. He never got another cent for this work, the royalties from which, according to "Max Bruch: His Life and Works,"

see VANN, page E9

see BRUCH, page E9

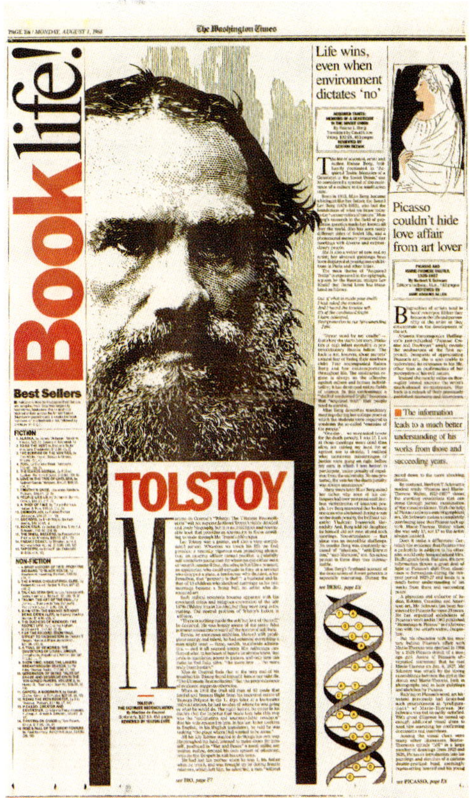

The Washington Times — MONDAY, AUGUST 1, 1988

Book life!

Best Sellers

FICTION

NON-FICTION

TOLSTOY

Life wins, even when environment dictates 'no'

Picasso couldn't hide love affair from art lover

The information leads to a much better understanding of his works from those and succeeding years.

see PICASSO, page E8

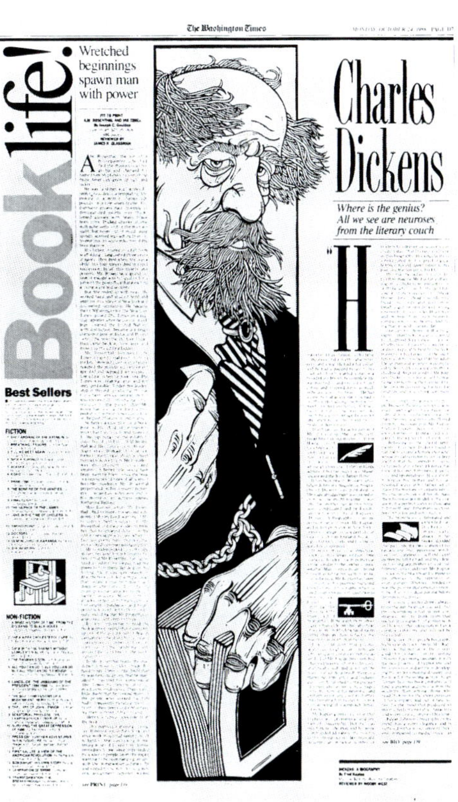

The Washington Times

Book life!

Best Sellers

FICTION

NON-FICTION

Wretched beginnings spawn man with power

Charles Dickens

Where is the genius? All we see are neuroses from the literary couch

NEWS JUDGES' AWARD FOR DESIGN

Detroit Free Press

Designers

Randy Miller, John Goecke, Deborah Withey, Andrew Hartley, Lee Yarosh, Wayne Kamidoi

SPECIAL REPORT: THE ARMENIAN EARTHQUAKE

COMMENT

Detroit Free Press

DETROIT FREE PRESS — SUNDAY, DEC. 25, 1988

WHEN THE CLOCKS STOPPED

A soldier and his family stand near a fire in the streets of Leninakan; their apartment building was destroyed.

David Turnley, a Free Press photographer stationed in Paris, traveled with relief workers to the site of the Armenia earthquake. He filed these impressions from the scene Dec. 15, his second day there.

By DAVID C. TURNLEY

INSIDE: DEVELOPMENT

■ A day-care center is being designed right into a local office building. Page 6.

Monday, Nov. 14, 1988

BUSINESS MONDAY

Detroit Free Press

SECTION C

Advertising, Page 2
The week ahead, Page 3
Detroit Equity 50, Page 7
Call Business: 222-8784

INSIDE INFORMATION

No blue light special here

Where there's smoke, there's Lido!

Take my car ... please

A dog's life is spared

Joe Gagnon, consumer gladiator

HIGH PROFILE

BONUS AT THE BORDER

Analysts see a benefit for Michigan if there is a Canadian-American Free Trade Agreement

Developer's quarry is a vista of opportunity

Norman LoPatin, left, and his father, Larry LoPatin, plan a resort complex near Petoskey.

BOWL GAME RESULTS — SPORTS, SECTION D

IRISH NO. 1
Notre Dame wins Fiesta over W. Virginia, 34-21
MIAMI 23
NEBRASKA 3
FSU 13
AUBURN 7
UCLA 17
ARKANSAS 3
CLEMSON 13
OKLAHOMA 6
SYRACUSE 23
LSU 10

METRO FINAL

Snow likely. High 30, low 15. Wednesday: Mostly cloudy. Details, Page 2A

Detroit Free Press

On Guard For 157 Years

TUESDAY, January 3, 1989. For home delivery call 222-6500. 20 cents

THE ROSE BOWL

FINALLY, IT'S BO'S SHOW

U-M dispels its hex with rosy 22-14 win

PASADENA, Calif. — He was running for all of them, for this Michigan team, and for every Michigan team that has ever come out here and had its face smeared with California egg. Someone grabbed his feet. He broke free. Someone wrapped around his thigh. He yanked loose. He ran through the linemen and through the linebackers and through the hands and arms and bodies, breaking free as the ghosts of Wolverines past screamed in a collective voice: "GO! GO! NEVER STOP!"

MITCH ALBOM

See ALBOM, Page 11A

- Not everyone loves bowl games. Page 3A.
- Rose Parade draws big crowd. Page 11A.
- Photostory, 16D.

University of Michigan's Wolverines mob Chris Calloway, who caught a six-yard pass for a touchdown Monday in the third quarter of U-M's 22-14 Rose Bowl victory over the University of Southern California.

Alleged bomber's bag said to be found

By DUANE NORIYUKI

See FLIGHT 103, Page 15A

Overloaded ferry sinks; 65 drown

See SINKING, Page 15A

Chevy chief hoping to retire on top

By JANET BRAUNSTEIN

See CHEVROLET, Page 11A

AUTO SHOW 1989

- Where: Cobo Hall
- When: Saturday through Jan. 15
- Hours: 2 p.m. to 10:30 p.m. Mon. through Fri., noon to 10:30 p.m. Sat. and Sun.
- Admission: $5 for adults under 65; free for kids under 12 with adult or those 65 and over; $1 for kids under 17 not with adult.

McNamara says county now has fighting chance

By DAVID McHUGH

See McNAMARA, Page 15A

Wayne County Executive Ed McNamara

INSIDE TODAY

Livonia driver forced off road, knifed by man

By L. CAROL RITCHIE

See KNIFING, Page 15A

FEMININITY FACTOR

Assertive women find a bias

THE WAY WE LIVE, 1B

A KICK, A TWIRL

Scientific knowledge helpful in many jobs

SCIENCE/MEDICINE, 1C

I'M SORRY — AGAIN

Monaghan apologizes to Gibson

SPORTS, 1D

METRO FINAL

Mostly cloudy, windy. High 56, low 37. Wednesday: Partly cloudy. Details, Page 2A

Detroit Free Press

SPRINGLE AVENUE STANDOFF

TUESDAY, October 18, 1988. For home delivery call 222-6500. 20 cents

Besides being nice to look at, the Fisher Building, opened in 1928, is good to look out of.

FISHER AT 60

Birthday bash will celebrate lovable edifice

By JEANNE MAY

See FISHER, Page 4A

2 cops, mentally ill man slain

An officer and an EMS worker rush a stretcher Monday to the east side apartment where a Detroit man held police at bay for seven hours, shooting two to death, before he was killed.

Barricaded resident poured gas in building

By MARGARET TRIMER, DEBORAH KAPLAN AND BRIAN FLANIGAN

See STANDOFF, Page 12A

THE VICTIMS

LT. JAMES SCHMIT

OFFICER FRANK WALLS

CHARLES KNOWLES

Man's mental problems on record since 1969

By DAVID McHUGH

See KNOWLES, Page 12A

INSIDE

- Officials: Mentally ill not usually violent. Page 3A.
- Slain officers were cut of same blue cloth. Page 12A.
- Michigan law seeks to balance rights. Page 12A.
- Threat of fire caused police to break policy and rush gunman. Page 13A.

INSIDE TODAY

3 share Nobel Prize for medicine

2 U.S. researchers, British professor cited for treatments

Sir James Black — Gertrude Elion — George Hitchings

A special Comment section examines the man, the myth and what his lost meant to a generation.

YOUR MONEY

A personal financial guide to planning, saving and investing

Business, 1C

METRO FINAL

Detroit Free Press

On Guard For 157 Years

SUNDAY

November 13, 1988

57 held in abortion protest

Pro-choice activists confront group blocking Livonia clinic

Theater's new face to debut

Big money, hopes ride on renaissance

The main staircase in the Fox Theatre, which will reopen Saturday after a multimillion-dollar renovation.

ROSE BOWL BOUND!

Bush must act or face crash, economists say

Town in fear over possible child snatcher

COMING UP

THE REOPENING

THIS WEEK

INSIDE TODAY

IN SPORTS

FOOTBALL

Oklahoma State's Sanders gets Heisman

HOCKEY

Wings clipped in Quebec, 6-4

SUNDAY FEATURES

MAGAZINE

How ordinary people became war heroes at home

TRAVEL

It's time to think warm: Caribbean special section

ENTERTAINMENT

Stevie Wonder hits the Fox (with Keith Richards next)

THE WAY WE LIVE

A debate rekindled: Who is a Jew?

METRO FINAL

Detroit Free Press

SUNDAY

December 4, 1988

CRACK WAR

NO WINNERS

Sales flourish despite arrests

Many are arrested, but most soon go free

U.S. probes Meese role in McGoff prosecution

Ex-attorney general denies interceding

INSIDE TODAY

Israel returns hijackers, crew to Soviet Union

TAKING REQUESTS

Rose Bowl is shaken, but unhurt in quake

NEWS JUDGES' AWARD FOR DESIGN

Detroit Free Press
Designers
Randy Miller, John Goecke, Deborah Withey, Andrew Hartley, Lee Yarosh, Wayne Kamidoi

INSIDE: BOOKS

■ Richard Bach takes flight in new book, but cruises slowly. Page 11C.

Sunday, Nov. 13, 1988

BUSINESS

Detroit Free Press

SECTION C

NYSE, **Page 6**
AMEX, **Page 7**
Mutual funds, **Page 8**
Call Business: 222-8765

PERSONAL FINANCE

Since the stock market almost melted down, you may have shied away from any investment more exotic than the basic savings account. This section is designed to help you, a year later, readjust your strategy.

Illustration by Deborah Withey

MAKING YOUR MONEY WORK HARDER

Higher interest rates, risk and diversification: Keys to reaching your goals

By Rick Ratliff
FREE PRESS BUSINESS WRITER

You can almost hear it snoring. It's your money, and it is tucked inside your warm, dark bank account. Every now and then it yawns and stretches, and you reap a little interest.

Maybe it's time to wake that money up.

If you are like many other people, soon after the market crashed in October 1987, you abandoned stocks for investments more readily convertible to cash. And that probably was a move appropriate to uncertain times.

A year has passed, however. Maybe it's time to ask whether there's more your money could be doing, whether building more risk, more diversification and higher interest rates into your portfolio is needed to make your money achieve your goals.

This personal finance section is designed to help you determine whether your money should be doing more to meet your objectives. It may help you explore diversified alternatives to your investment status quo.

Think about it. Are your kids going to college in a few years? Do you have what you need for a comfortable retirement? And what about all those major purchases you haven't made yet — a house, perhaps, or a new refrigerator?

It is important to determine how much risk you are comfortable with and to pick a good investment adviser who can help you map your strategy. And anyone who thinks a certificate of deposit is a certificate of deposit should think again. Interest rates can vary widely depending on the amount of deposit, length of the investment and other terms of the account.

"These days, people are cautious," said Joseph Giordano, a Rochester certified planner. "Since the crash in October, they are more cautious of the person they're doing business with."

Caution is understandable given the horror stories of Oct. 19, 1987, he said.

"A client of mine was dealing with a broker who knows she doesn't have a lot of money to play with," Giordano said. "He put $25,000 in an up-and-coming company at $10 a share. Now the stock is worth 12.5 cents a share. Her $25,000 is now worth less than $350."

Nevertheless, stocks can still be good investments, but you have to determine how you want to use them. There are myriad choices not only of individual stocks but also of mutual funds.

And what about real estate, extended warranties, tax planning strategies, employe stock options, and payroll deduction savings and pension plans?

John Findling, vice-president and Ann Arbor branch office manager for Shearson Lehman Hutton, said most of his clients have plenty of ready cash. "We suggest a three-month backlog of cash to meet their monthly needs," he said. "Most people exceed that by 50 percent."

Findling said there are two kinds of post-crash investors. "There's the investor who stayed with the market after it crashed in 1987," he said, "and the one who bailed out." He said the person who stayed on the market is often doing better than "the

See GOALS, Page 5C

2 *Using a 401(k) retirement plan as a tax-deferred savings account will get tougher.*

3 *Twelve ways to save on your 1988 taxes. Our savvy bushy-tail tells how to squirrel it away from the tax man.*

4 *Financial planning — it's for every person who earns a paycheck, no matter how big or how small.*

5 *Value is the key when searching for a stock to purchase, not just the price-to-earnings ratio.*

Chapter 2

Overall design

Nine newspapers in four circulation categories received awards; no awards were given in three other categories.

What gives?

■ Small news hole: "Many newspapers seem like vehicles for advertising. There is no commitment for space," said one judge.

■ Lack of attention past the section covers: "I would like to see someone reinvent the inside of news sections," another judge said.

■ Poor use of color: "There is a difference between using color and really utilizing it," said one judge.

Judges praised the winners for their consistency, fine typography and good use of visual elements and for their seeming respect for art direction: a sophisticated, imaginative approach to presentation with attention to detail and to content.

"Art departments finally seem to be making positive inroads into decision making processes affecting news presentation," said judge Mario Garcia.

NORGES STØRSTE MORGENAVIS

Aftenposten

Verdens eldste, men ung av sinn SIDE 19

Utflagget kaptein ble rik reder

LES A-MAGASINET

NORSKE BISTANDS-PROSJEKTER SLAKTES

Feilslått milliard-hjelp til Tanzania

PALME-DRAPET

Fengslet i lukket rett

Nå skal Armenias døde begraves

Sorgen følges av vrede

ANNONSER

TIPS-TELEFON: 02/33 60 00

2 POLITIKK

Aftenposten

Når krukken er tom

U-hjelp

O julesaldoen senket seg

Fortsatt krenkelser i Sovjet

AKTUELL KOMMENTAR

Pensjon - sparing eller tildeling?

UTLAND 9

Hanoi-retrett fra Kampuchea

VERDEN RUNDT

AKTUELL PROFIL

«En mann av folket» gikk til topps

KOMMENTAR

Gorbatsjovs ideologiske opphørssalg

AWARD OF EXCELLENCE

OVERALL DESIGN

Aftenposten

Oslo, Norway

Designer

Staff

CLASS OF 2000
Santa or not, they're ready

BESS MYERSON NOT GUILTY
Ex-Miss America acquitted in divorce-fix scheme

DETROIT GOES 0-1-1
Wings the Blues; Pistons fall

METRO FINAL

Detroit Free Press

FRIDAY
December 23, 1988

On Guard For 157 Years

1st black named to new cabinet
Bush also selects conservationist to head EPA, fills 3 other posts

NEW TEAM MEMBERS

Fontes gives thanks, but is he in over his head?

FLIGHT 103

A CHRISTMAS TRAGEDY

Probers look for bomb clues

Anonymous call claims jumbo jet was blown up

Bess Myerson found innocent of alimony plot

INSIDE TODAY

Crash victim sought a new life in Europe

MORE INSIDE

MICHIGAN'S DEAD

INSIDE:

COMMENT

Detroit Free Press

SECTION E

DETROIT'S DEADLY EPIDEMIC

WHY DID TANEEA HAVE TO DIE?
Vengeful hail of bullets haunts family, friends

"I've personally had about four cases this year where teenagers . . . injured or killed an innocent bystander. If you look at the arguments . . . somebody bumped somebody, somebody stepped on somebody's foot . . . they aren't even worth a fistfight."

AWARD OF EXCELLENCE

OVERALL DESIGN

Detroit Free Press

Designer
Staff

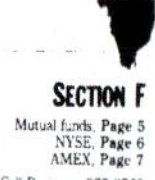

INSIDE: FINANCE

BUSINESS

Detroit Free Press

SECTION F

BABY BELLS BEGIN TO GROW UP

PAUL LIENERT
Auto Insider

Saturn girds for challenge

Long-distance rates decline as expected but confusion rises

5 years of telephone deregulation

Dow Chemical seeks respect through growth

Tarnished platinum gets its luster back

"I don't see a lot of the variables that have served us well going south."

THE SECOND FRONT PAGE

MORE LOCAL NEWS:
■ Richard Thompson sworn in as Oakland County prosecutor. Page 8C.

Detroit Free Press

• Page 3A
Wednesday, Dec. 21, 1988

Lottery extra: Tuesday's number, 604, was drawn once before.

GEORGE WALDMAN/Detroit Free Press

Richard Reid, 20, left, and Derivon Reid, 17, appear at their arraignment Tuesday in 46th District Court in Southfield.

2 arraigned in abduction of teens

Possible tie to 2 other cases probed

BY GEORGEA KOVANIS
Free Press Staff Writer

Two New York men were charged Tuesday with the gunpoint abduction and robbery of two 15-year-old Detroit youths from Northland mall.

Richard Reid, 20, and Derivon Reid, 17, were arraigned before Magistrate A. Kay Stanfield Brown in Southfield's 46th District Court on two counts each of kidnapping, armed robbery and using a firearm while committing a felony.

The Reids, who told the court they moved to New York state three months ago from Washington, D.C., and that they had lived in the Detroit-Ohio area before that, both shook their heads as Brown read the charges.

Richard Reid said he heard the charges but added, "They're all fake."

The Reids apparently are brothers, police said, but officers still are trying to confirm their identities. Derivon Reid carried several driver's licenses with different names, Southfield Detective Robert Diegel testified.

Meanwhile, police in Southfield and two other Oakland County communities continued to probe possible connections between the Northland incident and two weekend kidnapping-robberies. In one, a 30-year-old Royal Oak man was critically wounded.

Police in Bloomfield Township and Madison Heights said there is a good chance the weekend abductions in their communities are related.

Southfield police testified that the Reids abducted the youths about 11:30 a.m. Monday as they left a McDonald's restaurant and forced them into a dark blue Mercedes, drove them around Southfield and Troy for 1½ hours and released them unharmed at Square Lake and Adams roads. Police originally said the youths had been dropped off at Big Beaver and Adams roads.

The Reids were arrested in a Northland parking lot that afternoon when they returned to exchange a pair of shoes taken from the victims, said Southfield Officer Gary Conat.

Police said they recovered three pairs of shoes, a sweater, and a hat that were stolen from the victims and found a fully loaded, 9mm automatic handgun that was wrapped in a towel and placed on the Mercedes' engine block.

The Reids are being held on $500,000 bond each in the Southfield jail. A preliminary examination is

See KIDNAPPING, Page 18A

Court dumps non-resident ban at parks in Dearborn

BY DAWSON BELL AND DENNIS NIEMIEC
Free Press Staff Writers

LANSING — A Dearborn ordinance that barred non-residents from city parks cannot be enforced because it discriminates against blacks and would allow unreasonable police searches, the state Court of Appeals said in a ruling released Tuesday.

Opponents of the ban hailed the ruling, which upheld a 1986 decision by Wayne County Circuit Judge Marvin Stempien, as a victory for civil rights.

Dearborn Mayor Michael Guido said Tuesday he would recommend the City Council agree to fund an appeal of the court's ruling.

"The ordinance was passed because of overcrowding . . . that concern was allayed during the last couple of summers," said Guido. "A referendum is a powerful voice and the majority of our citizens voted for it."

The parks ban, enacted by the voters in 1985, created a major controversy, provoked a black boycott of Dearborn merchants and revived memories of past racial discrimination in the nearly all-white city. The ordinance was challenged by lawyers for the NAACP and the American Civil Liberties Union (ACLU) shortly after it went into effect but before enforcement began.

Detroit NAACP President Arthur Johnson said he hoped hard feelings would not be revisited in the wake of the appeals court decision.

"This is a significant case and a significant victory," Johnson said. "It establishes the right of any citizen to visit a public park.

"But we're not interested in the small, narrow victory of saying 'We did it to Dearborn,' " he said. "We're dealing with rights of citizenship and equality . . . a sense of community."

Howard Simon, executive director of the Michigan ACLU, said the decision is historic because it reduces the burden of proof in discrimination cases.

"People who are victims of civil rights violations now only have to show that a local law has a discriminatory impact, even if they can't show the intent was discriminatory," said Simon.

Stempien, in the decision affirmed by the appeals court, said Dearborn's ordinance was unconstitutional because it had "an unlawfully disparate

See DEARBORN PARKS, Page 18A

SUSAN WATSON IS ON VACATION

THE POWER OF MUSIC

Clark Sisters bring cheer to Children's Hospital

Jennifer Heliste, 6, who was awaiting surgery, and her mother, Shirley, of Troy listen to the Clark Sisters gospel group Tuesday at Children's Hospital.

Above, the Clark Sisters, from left, Dorinda, Twinkie and Karen, serenade Jessica Boik, 3, of Canton. Left, the sisters join hands and recite a prayer after singing to children getting ready for surgery.

Photos by Pauline Lubens

Icy retreats jump-start souls frazzled by city life

BY DAVID HACKER
Free Press Staff Writer

TRAVERSE CITY — How do you spell relief?

To some, who've fled to northern Michigan from downstate, you spell it W-I-N-T-E-R.

Today is when this serious season begins, with the winter solstice at 10:28 a.m., and the year's longest day of darkness.

As silly as it sounds, there are some who *like* to ice fish, to ski out the back door, to shovel snow, to drive in a turtle-like pace in blizzards on snow-packed roads and to breathe air so cold it turns words brittle.

Take Charley and Alice Hansen, who've been married for 22 years, and their daughters Stacey, 17, and Erica, 14. The Hansens moved to Traverse City a year and a half ago from Grosse Pointe Woods. Charley Hansen, 44, works as a printer for Gwen Frostic's Presscraft Papers in Benzonia. It's a 35-mile commute for him, a 45-minute drive in nice weather, an hour or longer in bad weather.

"I'm never in a hurry anymore," he said. Last winter, just months after moving, Charley Hansen had open-heart surgery and was off work for three months.

See WINTER, Page 4A

Nobody admits telling Landers of child's abuse

BY JACK KRESNAK
Free Press Staff Writer

No Detroit area parents came forward Tuesday to admit they had chained their 17-year-old daughter to a bed frame in a basement to keep her from hurting herself or others because of her addiction to drugs and alcohol.

That was the word from the state Department of Social Services, where protective services workers said they half-expected a phone call from the writer of a letter to Ann Landers that was published in Tuesday's Free Press.

The letter, signed "Needing Guidance in Detroit," was supposedly written by a man concerned because his daughter had been behaving strangely and violently since she began using drugs four years ago. To punish her behavior, he said he shackled the girl to a bed in the basement of their Detroit area home, where she was left for three months.

See DSS, Page 4A

Meals on Wheels gifts fuel young appetites for giving

BY JEANNE MAY
Free Press Staff Writer

The students at Plumbrook Elementary School in Sterling Heights look like the cast of "The Brady Bunch," but they know Christmas isn't all Santa Claus and Nintendo cassettes.

The second-, third-, fourth- and fifth-graders gave up their school Christmas gift exchange and donated the money to Meals on Wheels. At an assembly Tuesday, they handed over $609 to the program. That's enough for 128 hot meals.

The students also made cards and favors to go along with the meals — carefully crayoned angels, a snowman made of cotton pasted to construction paper, elaborate drawings of Christmas scenes, some decorated with sparkles. They signed their names, and they're hoping they get letters from some of the people who eat their food.

Meals on Wheels is a federal program, but it doesn't cover food on holidays. The Area Agency on Aging 1-B raises money for holiday meals in Livingston, Macomb, Monroe, Oakland, St. Clair and Washtenaw counties.

Fourth-grade teacher Pat Sarven started the school program two years ago with just one other teacher. More teachers signed on last year, still more this year.

"My personal philosophy is children are remembered at Christmas, but the adults aren't," she said. "Our children here have a home and all the food they want and all the amenities, and I think they should know that everyone doesn't."

The students have learned the lesson well.

Like Giacomo Garris, 9, who wants to be a doctor when he grows up: "I just wanted to make the people happy, the poor people. Like one day they're out of work and they run out of money and they get broke."

And Jessica Spurner, 9: "We have to help so they get good food."

And finally 10-year-old Laura Bench, who spoke volumes in just eight words: "It's not fair. We should give them meals."

Tax-deductible donations may be sent to Area Agency on Aging 1-B, 29508 Southfield Road, Southfield 48076. People who would like to help deliver meals may call the holiday meals coordinator at 569-0333, between 8:30 a.m. and 5 p.m., Mondays through Fridays.

Vera Bozinovski, 9, a fourth-grader at Plumbrook Elementary School in Sterling Heights, holds a sign telling how much second- through fifth-graders raised for a Christmas gift donation for Meals on Wheels.

WILLIAM ARCHIE/Detroit Free Press

INSIDE:
■ Bob Talbert gets an earful from an angry Roy Orbison fan. Page 11B.
Wednesday, Dec. 21, 1988

THE WAY WE LIVE

Detroit Free Press

SECTION B
Bookmarks, **Page 3**
Television, **Pages 8-9**
Feature Page, **Page 11**
Call The Way We Live: 222-6610

JAMES RICCI

Sexual angst tests father of girls

According to a Parade Magazine poll this week, two-thirds of teenage boys have had sex, which is unsettling news to a father of teenage girls.

I doubt there's a more profound ambivalence than a father's toward the sexuality of his adolescent daughters.

There's a ton of irony in this. A father plays a determining role in his girls' eventual development into sexually capable beings, young women with high regard for themselves and a capacity for affection and intimacy with men. He is his daughters' first, innocent lover. His cuddling and stroking and twirling their hair around his finger during bottle-feeding and "Sesame Street" presage the young men who await them for the mating dance in the unimaginable future.

Things change as they get older, of course. He is more tentative and judicious about his hugs as he comes to feel the incipient form of a woman in his arms. But his affectionate relationship with them becomes a special point of pride as it endures the inevitable bad weather systems that sweep through the teen years. Not for him the destructive contentiousness of uncomprehending father and defiant daughter.

Then one Saturday evening there is a caller at the door.

It is Don Giovanni, tickling his mandolin and crooning, "Deh! vieni alla finestra," and slyly anticipating his next conquest.

Only with difficulty is a father able to discern the figure of a 16-year-old boy with moussed hair drooping over his forehead, his weight shifting from one penny loafer to the other.

Because he is enlightened and has faith in his daughter's judgment, he greets the boy with a smile, like a fellow man. But the handshake he gives him is extra firm and carries a subliminal message: "Feel the strength, kid." Almost despite himself, he implants the subtle notion that he is a threat, even if he can't be there in the backseat of the car. It is the hapless, unsaid blessing he sends her off with.

What does he fear, exactly?

That she will become prematurely pregnant, certainly, and her youth will thus collapse instantly, no matter how the situation is resolved.

That she will contract disease.

That she will expose herself to an unsalvable heartbreak because she invested herself before having attained a mature assessment of her great worth.

That she will become soured from having started too soon.

That she will become the love slave of a callow, posturing boy (but, a father wonders, is sex so powerful it can turn her mindlessly obedient after years of admonishing have failed to make her stop discarding clothes on the floor?).

Lastly, that — face it — she will learn, before he is altogether ready for her to, that there is male love more compelling than his.

A father must let go. Lay down a few theoretical rules, hope they have some force out there in the vibrant adolescent night, release her to begin her journey in strange lands.

So long as the trek leads back to his door by 11:30.

James Ricci appears Monday, Wednesday and Friday in the Free Press.

THE RITE TIME OF YEAR

LONG BEFORE MYRRH

Christian tradition credits the Magi with the first Christmas gifts, but holiday gift-giving was customary long before their Bethlehem trip. Believing that the winter solstice was a time when gods sparred with evil spirits, ancient people offered sacrifices of food and precious metals to give the gods an edge. Later, the practice broadened to giving gifts to friends and family.

Lacking American Express, ancient people stuck to simple presents — candles and clay figurines. But even then, glitter and sweets were part of the holiday scene. The kinds of gifts people gave conveyed their wishes for the coming year: sweet treats suggested harmony; gold, silver and copper accompanied wishes for wealth.

NORSE NOISEMAKING

Along with lighting fires, Norsemen blew horns and shouted to scare away witches and evil spirits at Yule time. But one night wasn't enough for their revelry. In the cold, dark North where there wasn't much else to do, they often partied for weeks.

OH, ROMAN TREE

Historians aren't sure who first had the idea of dragging trees indoors and hanging things from their branches; the custom seems to have developed in several cultures. Romans trimmed trees with trinkets and toys during Saturnalia. And today's shiny, glass balls may be reminders of the days when Druids celebrated by tying gilded apples on boughs.

BY NANCY ROSS-FLANIGAN
Free Press Science Writer

Holly and mistletoe, decorated trees.

Gluttony, hangovers, shopping sprees.

It's getting to look a lot like Saturnalia.

"Christmas," you say? Sure, that's what those things mean now, but many of the traditions — and excesses — we associate with Christmas and New Year's Day have ties to pre-Christian astronomical and agricultural rites. A program at Michigan State University's Abrams Planetarium traces the origins of some of these customs.

Winter solstice celebrations spawned many of today's holiday customs, says planetarium producer Doug Murphy. The solstice, which usually falls around Dec. 22, is the time when the sun is at its most southerly position, directly over the Tropic of Capricorn. This year, the winter solstice comes at 10:28 a.m. today in Detroit.

The name "solstice," which means "sun stops," is a clue to why ancient people got a bit wild and crazy around that time of year. It marks the first day of winter — the turning point when days stop getting shorter and begin to stretch out again.

Early Romans merged solstice festivities with Saturnalia, seven days of revelry that honored Saturn, the god of agriculture.

Norsemen had similar celebrations, Yule and Up-helly-aa, marked by noise and merriment. And the Teutons and Celts held mid-winter agricultural rites.

Long before shopping malls and eggnog, people managed to celebrate too much during the holidays. When the fourth-century Greek, Libanius, described Roman winter rituals, he could have been writing about modern America at holiday time: "Everywhere may be seen carousals and well-laden tables . . . The impulse to spend seizes everyone . . . People are not only generous toward themselves, but also toward their fellow-men. A stream of presents pours itself out on all sides."

■ MORE RITES TO REMEMBER, 3B.

NORSE NOSHING CAME FIRST

Even Santa's cookie and milk snack may have ancient antecedents. During Yule, Norse people set out full meals as offerings to the hearth gods.

DATE OF CHRISTMAS

The very date of Christmas has more to do with celestial and seasonal observances than with historical record. Dec. 25 was borrowed from Mithraism, a religion that originated in Persia and spread to Rome, where it later rivaled Christianity.

Mithra was a sun god who traveled the sky in a chariot, judged the world and kept order in the cosmos. His birthday, which coincided with the winter solstice on old calendars, was Dec. 25. On that date, Romans celebrated the "Birthday of the Unconquered Sun."

Early Christians didn't commemorate Christ's birth, believing the practice to be sacrilegious. When they finally decided to celebrate, around 320 AD, no one knew the real date of Christ's birth. Dec. 25 was chosen, historians say, to channel the excitement of pagan mid-winter festivals into more pious pursuits.

ANCIENT LOG LOVERS

The first Yule logs probably burned in Norse bonfires. At the solstice, Norsemen set fire to ships, symbolizing the death of the old sun and the coming of a new season. Teutons and Celts held winter agricultural rites, invoking magic and ritual to bring back light and growth. They brought huge logs to their hearths, made wishes and lit the logs with the remains of last year's log.

STEPHEN SCHUDLICH/Special to the Free Press

THE CARP CHRONICLES — **BY RICHARD GUINDON**

I SEE WHERE YOUR BELOVED PRESIDENT IS LEAVING US WITH A 50 BILLION DOLLAR SAVINGS AND LOAN BAIL-OUT.

YOU'RE SUCH A NINNY! IT ALL WORKS OUT ON CHRISTMAS EVE, IN CASE YOU DIDN'T KNOW!

"YOU SEE, BERT THE COP FINDS JIMMY STEWART ON THE BRIDGE AND HE GOES..."

GEORGE, WHERE THE DEVIL HAVE YOU BEEN? THE WHOLE TOWN'S LOOKING FOR YOU!

BERT, LOOK, ZUZU'S PETALS! I'M ALIVE AGAIN!

BOTTOM LINE: STICKING TO THE SPEED LIMIT

You're a normal, car-crazed teenager, right? So would you drive any vehicle with a bumper sticker that reads: IF I'M DRIVING IRRESPONSIBLY CALL MY PARENTS: — followed by their phone number? You would if you were Albuquerque entrepreneur Fred Stangle because Stangle, 17, sells them.

Stangle wondered how he could help reduce teen accident statistics after a friend was hurt in an accident caused by speeding.

The idea occurred to Stangle that nothing affects teenagers more than public humiliation: "If they had to have this sticker on for two or three weeks for the privilege of driving the car, they'd change their driving habits."

Stangle suggests that parents threaten their teen with the sticker as a first step. If that doesn't work, slap the sucker with a sticker, says Stangle.

Each sticker has space to write in a phone number with heavy black marker. Stickers are $2 apiece or three for $5. To order, write Fred Stangle, P.O. Box 11633, Albuquerque, N.M. 87192. Specify whether the call should be made to "Dad," "Mom" or "Parents."

By Mari Jackson Levin

FRIDAY: The Christmas spirit burns brightly — in, on and all around Metro Detroit homes 1D

WINGS TIE 4-4 Battered team catches Blues **1F**

PISTONS LOSE Knicks knock off Detroit 88-85 **1F**

BERMAN How we unload loser gifts **1C**

Flurries — Low tonight 36° — High Saturday 43° — Details, page 10F

Friday December 23, 1988

The Detroit News

15¢

GOOD DAY BRIEFLY IN THE NEWS

Wayne Fontes gets a 3-year contract.

Dream comes true for Lions coach

13 injured in GM plant fire

'E.T.' star ends rehab

Bandit has the yule spirit

2 die in light plane crash

INSIDE ...

THE TRAGEDY OF PAN AM FLIGHT 103

Sabotage suspicion grows

When Pan Am Flight 103 crashed to the earth, it left a large black crater and rows of charred houses amid the village of Lockerbie, Scotland.

TERRORISM: Cockpit tapes reinforce theory a bomb destroyed jetliner

THREAT: Few knew of Dec. 5 call

VICTIMS: Each fateful tale adds to storm of tragedy

WAIT: Lip-biting sorrow, then a miracle

'Bess Mess' defendants cleared

Bush picks 4 more for Cabinet

ON SATURDAY'S RELIGION PAGE: Some city churches plan what may be their last Christmas masses

AWARD OF EXCELLENCE

OVERALL DESIGN

The Detroit News

Designer

Staff

Illustrator

Staff

Photographer

Staff

Art Director

Staff

■ Carlyle's Christmas 3C ■ Pet Doctor 3C

The Detroit News Friday, December 23, 1988

Accent

Section C

BERMAN

Dealing with the gifts that keep on giving

For cheap grins, we imagine what the world would be like if these 10 publicity hogs hadn't been born

IT'S A

Wonderful Life

By Michael McWilliams

R.I.K.'s: The right mix of pasta and pampering

By Sandra Silfven

RESTAURANT REVIEW

92

Super Sports

■ Inside

☐ Iowa QB has knee surgery/2E
☐ Tigers appoint Amaro scout/2E
☐ Murray-Wright stops Cass Tech/6E
☐ Gator's not a big draw for MSU/12E

■ NBA / NHL scoreboard

The Detroit News
Wednesday, December 21, 1988

Sports

Section E
☐ Focus on Sports/2E
☐ Classified/13E
☐ Comics/14E
☐ Weather/16E

Shelby Strother

Humility returns to sports vogue

Wings' wonder fuels win

Yzerman's brilliance colors Blues losers, 6-3

By Cynthia Lambert

Wingswatch

Pistons' reserves too hot for Heat to handle

By Terry Foster

Pistonswatch

U-M does number on NMU

By Jim Spadafore

SUPER BOWL XXIII ODDS

Bengals favored in Super Bowl

NEWS IN BRIEF

MADD to protest bond reduction plea

Warehouse being made into a home

STERLING HEIGHTS

Band members aim to strike right note for new president

GEORGE WEEKS

Election's over, so politicians seek huge raises

OUTTAKES

THE LOTTERIES

■ 3 ticket-holders split $179 million Lotto jackpot 6B

The Detroit News
Friday, December 23, 1988

Metro

Section B

George Cantor

Bowl games have a high zzzzz factor

8 cops face trial in drug raid

By Constance Prater

Getting dressed up for the show

Dodak to get $30,000 office

By Dennis B. Mulqueen

Barrow rigged poll in his favor, Young allies say

By N. Scott Vance

The desperate elderly

2,000-3,000 walk Detroit's streets homeless and hungry, study finds

By Don Tschirhart

Did life of your party drink too much? You could be liable

NEWS FOCUS

For the Record

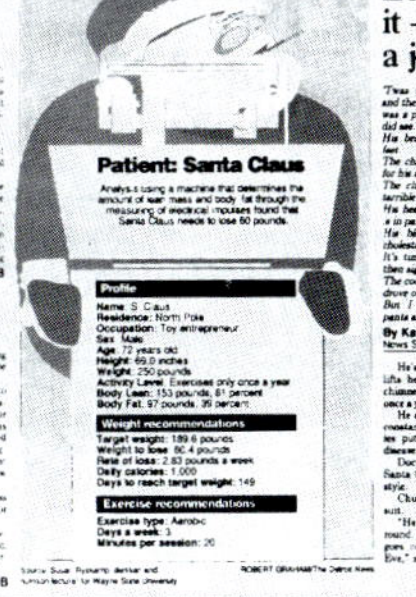

Patient: Santa Claus

Let's face it — Santa's a jolly mess

AWARD OF EXCELLENCE

OVERALL DESIGN

The Hartford Courant

Designer

Staff

The Hartford Courant

SPORTS

SECTION B

Pistons move to within victory of title

NBA Finals

Lyle, Gilder Nicolette in 3-way tie

U.S. Open scoreboard

Orioles decelerate Sox, 8-4

INSIDE

THE YEAR OF THE UMP

Suddenly, major league umpires no longer enjoy anonymity

Local news

Students honored at Special Education Learning Center.

Page D3

INSIDE CONNECTICUT

Connecticut Living

Electronics wizards open up new audio-video frontiers.

Page E1

Sports

Pistons head for LA with 3-2 lead in series.

Page B3

Sports Final

The Hartford Courant

Subpoenas are issued in defense probe

Jury widens contractors investigation

Key figure in probe now UTC adviser

Crafts denies he killed his wife

Ex-Nazi officials received U.S. help

L'Ambiance disaster spurs safety bills

Other partners could offer alternate bid for Whalers

Index

Mecham acquitted of charges involving huge campaign loan

The Hartford Courant

BUSINESS

SECTION E

SUNDAY JUNE 12, 1988

Tony Bacewicz/ The Hartford Courant

Joseph Friedman, left, and his brother Daniel Friedman, developers of 180 Allyn Street: "We wanted to build a big building," Daniel Friedman said.

Tony Bacewicz/ The Hartford Courant

Anthony F. Cutaia, Cutter Realty Group chairman: "If I die tomorrow, this project will be built."

Two buildings, two lofty visions for downtown

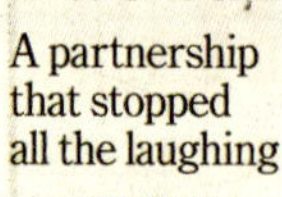

A partnership that stopped all the laughing

By SEAN HORGAN
Courant Staff Writer

When they started planning the 180 Allyn Street office tower four years ago, the brothers Friedman were viewed as a couple of kids taking an improbable shot at the big time.

Nobody seemed to take them very seriously.

Editorial cartoons poked fun at their relative youth — Joseph, who was working as a mortgage banking correspondent in Washington, D.C., for Aetna Life & Casualty Co., was 30, and Daniel, who was selling securities, was 27.

The established Hartford real estate community, stealing a line from "Butch Cassidy and the Sundance Kid," kept asking, "Who are these guys?"

Daniel Friedman, chairman of the Oakleaf Development Corp., said owners of some of the parcels needed to complete the site treated the brothers in a patronizing manner. Even after the site was assembled, their own architect said he wasn't sure the project would happen.

"We had in the general business plan to assemble this particularly large site, and of course we were met by every banker and lawyer we talked to with: 'Sure you are,' " said Friedman.

But the site bordered by Church, Allyn and High streets was indeed assembled for $9.35 million in August 1986. Plans now call for a $225 million building, with 1.06 million square feet of office space, 60,000 square feet of retail and parking for about 1,200 cars — that would be taller than anything now standing in New England.

"We wanted to build a big building," Friedman said. "We felt it was time somebody built a tall building on spec, one that would not be institutionally backed."

Today there remains some argument whether the 46-story, 801-foot tower will outduel its major competition — Cutter Financial Center and The Tower at Society Center — to make its way to the skyline. But few people are laughing at the Friedmans anymore.

Part of the reason for that is that Tishman

See Partnership, Page E2

ON HARTFORD'S HORIZON

Question remains: Who will build the tallest skyscraper in New England?

Immense project no undertaking for fainthearted

By SEAN HORGAN
Courant Staff Writer

As planned, it will rise above Hartford and every other building in New England.

But, the Cutter Financial Center seems to have been greeted with more skepticism by the city's real estate and development community than any of the other large projects on tap.

Perhaps it's the fact that Cutter — with its 59 stories and 1.25 million square feet of space, its $350 million price tag, its planned mixed-use that includes retail and high-priced condominiums and its location smack in the middle of downtown — is the most ambitious of an ambitious group of projects.

It would be the tallest building in New England, eclipsing the 800-foot-high John Hancock Tower in Boston by 78 feet.

Perhaps it's that developer Anthony F. Cutaia, chairman of Stamford-based Cutter Realty Group and the visionary of the project, is not a native of Hartford and is tackling the project without a high-profile development partner.

Whatever the reasons, Cutaia doesn't understand or agree with the skeptics.

"There's no question that there's a lot of people out there that wish it were them and they turn around and say, 'Why isn't it me?' " Cutaia said. "There will always be doubters. I can't respond to the doubters. All I can tell them is just watch it. It'll be there. If I die tomorrow, this project will be built."

Cutaia's insistence is understandable, considering the financial investment — $23 million for the land alone — and the obvious personal and emotional investment. Cutaia even has about $5 million of his own money in the project, he said.

After all, this is a massive project. The tower, which will have a skin of red brick with white brick and limestone accents, will have 102 condominiums on the top 14 floors, about 20,000 square feet of retail and underground parking for 1,232 cars.

It was designed by the Farmington-based architectural firm of Russell Gibson von Dohlen Inc. and will be built by Providence-based Gilbane Building Co.

See Developer, Page E2

DATA WATCH

Dow Jones average

The Dow Jones average of 30 industrials rose 8.36 points to 2,101.71 Friday, finishing the week with a net gain of 30.41.

Gold prices

Gold prices were $449.10 in the Friday settlement price on the New York Commodity Exchange, down $15.70 from a week ago.

Advest stock index

The Advest Stock Index, published Sunday in The Courant, is an indicator of Connecticut companies' weekly market performance.

Producer price index

Wholesale prices rose a moderate 0.5 percent in May, supporting beliefs that inflation is accelerating but not dangerously.

Insurers lobbying hard against antitrust suits

By DIANE LEVICK
Courant Staff Writer

Attorneys general around the nation, who are about to announce whether they will join antitrust lawsuits against insurance companies, have been lobbied aggressively by insurers urging them not to participate.

Campaigns by Aetna Life & Casualty Co. and Cigna Corp. have been among the most extensive, as the insurers try to convince attorneys general that the federal lawsuits filed by eight states in March are meritless. Cigna and Aetna are among the more than 30 defendants.

In some states, trial attorneys, insurers' foes on tort reform, also have lobbied the attorneys general — asking them to participate in the litigation.

Attorneys general "are taking a very close look at the evidence and they're feeling incredible pressure from companies like Cigna that have been going on a roadshow trying to convince people not to file," said George W. Sampson, assistant attorney general in the antitrust bureau of the New York attorney general's office.

Officials of the insurance companies and the attorneys general offices said they do not consider the contact to be pressure — Cigna does not even call it lobbying — but both sides acknowledged the meetings and letters were insurers' initiatives.

The lobbying was spurred by lawsuits filed in U.S. District Court in San Francisco that accuse insurers

See Insurers, Page E2

The Hartford Courant

ARTS/ENTERTAINMENT

SECTION G
SUNDAY
JUNE 12, 1988

Atheneum opens doors to once-despised decor

By OWEN McNALLY
Courant Staff Writer

Victorian decorative arts and furnishings traditionally have received short shrift from art museums.

The Wadsworth Atheneum hopes to right this slight with a king-size, bazaarlike exhibition of Victoriana that opens today and runs through Jan. 8, 1989.

Ranging from an elegantly crafted Japanese-style folding screen from 1887 to a broken-down couch covered in its original upholstery from 1863, the 150-object exhibit creates a colorful, almost flea-market kind of atmosphere.

"It's really all about the fun and excitement of Victoriana," says William Hosley, the museum's curator of American decorative arts, during a whirlwind tour of the exhibits before they were installed.

"No one is going to come away from this exhibition without finding some things they like a lot, or some things they just think are trash," Hosley says as he gestures toward shelves packed with Victorian wares and a small contingent of modern items that make up the exhibition called "Victorians and Moderns: New Acquisitions and Old Treasures."

Chronologically, the Atheneum's overview of American decorative arts sweeps from the 1840s well past 1901 — the year of Queen Victoria's death — and into the 1930s, the modernist, anti-Victorian period.

Exhibits by the "moderns" — a small fraction of the overall exhibit — include a Bauhaus-inspired chair and desk designed by the famous architect Frank Lloyd Wright; a streamlined, digital clock and pen holder, which originally was made as a gift for Connecticut Gov. Wilbur L. Cross; and other sleek-looking objects representing the then new wave in decorative arts of the 1920s and 1930s.

In marked contrast with these lean, spare modernist works — objects that rejected the ornate, corpulent look of Victoriana — the exhibit also includes anti-modernist works from the 1920s and '30s. Looking backward rather than forward in time, these traditionalist furnishings embraced simpler rustic or colonial designs and themes.

Hosley likes this counterpointing of styles against one another — Victorian played against modernist, anti-modernist pitted against modernist.

But Victoriana is obviously the heart and soul of the show for him as he highlights the

See Wadsworth, Page G6

■ This piece, left, known as Paul Revere pottery, was made for the Helen Storrow family; Storrow founded Paul Revere pottery. Rookwood pottery, below left, from Cincinnati, is an example of art pottery that became quite fashionable for a time.

Photos by Brad Clift / The Hartford Courant

Class, gloss, glitz

Victorian style

■ This folding screen is vintage 1887 and is done in the textbook style of Japanese decoration. It is oil painted on pine.

O'Neill plays poised for run on Broadway

By FRANK RIZZO
Courant Staff Writer

They're not the kind of plays that normally would be the toast of Broadway.

There's little spectacle, and nobody is dressed as a cat, performs on roller skates or wears a half-mask and swings from a chandelier.

Two plays by Eugene O'Neill are about to open on Broadway after a sellout run at the Yale Repertory Theatre in New Haven. One is a 3¾-hour play about tragic relationships in an American family. The other is warm human comedy, but one that has been performed routinely by community theaters throughout the country for decades.

Yet "Long Day's Journey Into Night" and "Ah, Wilderness!" have all the makings of this summer's biggest theatrical events on Broadway.

When the plays were performed in repertory from March through May in New Haven, both were immediate sellouts, making them the biggest hits ever at the Rep.

"Everyone thought they'd do well," says Arvin Brown, who directed "Ah, Wilderness!" "But it became this avalanche, really."

Subscriptions to Yale Rep increased 40 percent after last July's announcement that the plays would be presented. Benjamin Mordecai, Yale Rep's managing director, says season ticket subscribers grew from 5,500 to 7,500 on the basis of the O'Neill plays. And when single-show tickets went on sale in February, they sold out immediately.

Mordecai attributes the success of the Yale run to a combination of factors.

This year marks the 100th anniversary of the birth of O'Neill, arguably the best playwright this country has produced, and the first American playwright of major stature to be accorded a centennial observance.

Then there were the talents involved, Mordecai says. Both plays reunite Jason Robards and Colleen Dewhurst, who were a sensation on Broadway in the early '70s with a production of O'Neill's "A Moon for the Misbegotten." That production was staged by the foremost stage director of O'Neill, José Quintero. Quintero also is directing "Long Day's Journey Into Night."

Brown, who scored a Broadway triumph in Long Wharf Theatre's production of "Ah, Wilderness!" in the late '70s, returned to stage that play with Robards and Dewhurst, along with George Hearn and Elizabeth Wilson, who also have worked with Robards and Dewhurst over the years.

"There is a sense of family coming together again," Brown, artistic director of Long Wharf Theatre in New Haven, says of the talents involved. "There is a tremendous amount of excitement in seeing these people work together again in O'Neill, especially Colleen and Jason. There's a special kind of magic when they come together again to do O'Neill, and as they get older and bring new levels of experience to the parts. It just gets richer and richer.

"But if you want to know what hit me the hardest as a member of an audience, it was during 'Ah, Wilderness!' 's first performance. Seeing Jason taking Colleen around the shoulders and watching them kiss and seeing them going off together at the end of the play, I realized that those two people embodied 30 years of American theater history, and of Eugene O'Neill's history."

Will a hit in New Haven translate into big box office on Broadway?

So far Broadway ticket sales have been going "very well," according to producer Ken Marsolais. The plays, which also will be performed in repertory on Broadway, have been extended through Sept. 16. (Robards leaves for a film commitment then.) Extending the run beyond that with a replacement for Robards is a possibility, says Marsolais, depending on the reviews that the shows receive this month and ondemand for tickets.

The production also is scheduled to play the Kennedy Center in Washington, D.C., in November "with as many of the original cast [from this production] as we can," Marsolais said. "If Jason is available, he will join us."

Taking the two shows to the Soviet Union also is a possibility, "but it's all on tenuous ground at the present time," Marsolais said last week.

Marsolais says this "Long Day's Journey" won't be hurt by the fact that the play ran just two years ago on Broadway starring Jack Lemmon.

"I think there's an audience out there waiting to see Colleen and Jason together again in an O'Neill play because of the success of 'A Moon for the Misbegotten,'" he says.

He adds that the epic family tragedy "Long Day's Journey" has been selling over "Ah, Wilderness!" by a 3:1 ratio.

Brown believes the two plays' being presented in

See Rep's, Page G5

■ Yale Repertory's Eugene O'Neill celebration moves to Broadway this week. A poster sold at the Rep hails O'Neill's centennial.

University Theatre

Audiences are discovering Hanks is serious, too

By SID SMITH
Chicago Tribune

Tom Hanks is going on about a favorite subject. Money.

"Am I big box office? I guess so, I hope so," he says. "It's good if I am, but I wouldn't out-and-out lay claim to that. Supposedly, I am. But nothing I've done has really gone over the roof or entered into the national consciousness.

"The only movie that got into supermegagrosses was 'Splash,' my first success," he continues. "My salary's OK these days. But it's not growing by leaps and bounds.

"Maybe if I had muscles," he adds, a dig at Sylvester Stallone's reputedly seismic fee for "Rambo III."

Hanks's co-star Elizabeth Perkins loves her role, Page G10.

Perhaps Hanks should make a "Rambo" takeoff, it's suggested.

"Yeah, now what would we call it?" he asks, pausing only a second, just enough to set up the punchline: "How about 'Crambo'?"

Clearly, Hanks is much like the guy he so often plays: glib, slyly smart-aleck, ever amiable and bubbling with non-stop, rat-a-tat-tat fraternity blather. He would be at home at the ballpark, swilling beers around a beach campfire, playing poker all night or childishly charming a diffident career woman at a yuppie watering hole. (Too late for the latter: Hanks wed his longtime friend, actress Rita Wilson, on April 30.)

But there's a deeper, richly subterranean side to Hanks the man and actor that Hollywood is getting closer to unearthing. His talent is more than that of a lickety-split funny man. In the underrated "Nothing in Common," Hanks portrayed an aggressive, lightning-quick advertising genius with a mix of comedy and realism that rivals (and, in an odd way, almost foreshadowed) Holly Hunter's television producer in "Broadcast News."

Like the film, his performance went largely unnoticed, to be followed by his more or less supporting work for Dan Aykroyd in "Dragnet" (a bit that "could have been funnier," Hanks now says). Some of Hanks' more resonant acting

See Tom, Page G4

The Hartford Courant

TRAVEL

SECTION F
SUNDAY
JUNE 12, 1988

The art of traveling with a partner without disagreements — and vacationing by yourself without bouts of the blues

TANDEM TOURS

SOLO FLIGHTS

Stories by
STEVE SILK / Courant Travel Writer

Illustrations by
PETER HOEY / Special to The Courant

Going it alone

It is the best way to travel, and the worst. For solo travelers, the highs of being your own boss and creating your own itinerary often are counterbalanced by the lows of dining alone in a sumptuous restaurant. Going it alone is a mixed bag at best.

Such a mixed bag, in fact, that relatively few choose to travel alone. Though it is usually more expensive (single hotel room rates are only nominally less than double rooms, and most tours and cruises levy a single surcharge), it's not the extra costs that prevent solo travelers from hitting the road.

Instead, it is often fear — of the unknown, or of loneliness — that keeps them home, according to Esther Watstein, an instructor at The Short Course in New Haven who has conducted numerous seminars for would-be single travelers. But the Stratford resident says there's no reason to be afraid. She tells those in her seminars to look at the trip as an adventure.

The trick to single travel is learning to minimize the lows and maximize the highs.

The highs are what can make solo travel so appealing. Free from worry about a companion's happiness, lone journeyers can dive into specialized interests and indulge themselves ad nauseam. Like impressionism? As a solo traveler, you can choose to visit every museum in Paris housing a Monet. If beaches are more your thing, spend an entire vacation sprawling on every stretch of sand on Maui.

You can luxuriate in whatever it is *you* want to do, says Sarah Maxson Medvitz, of East Granby, who teaches a course at The Learning Exchange titled Traveling Solo. "You're in charge. There's no negotiating."

In fact, anyone traveling to pursue specific interests should consider traveling alone if their partner doesn't share *exactly* the same ideas. Sure, going to 25 museums in Paris might sound like fun at home, but a less-than-totally-committed companion might balk after number 5.

The independent voyager's freedom to make travel dreams come true is well known to Medvitz, whose personal passion is chasing solar eclipses. Since few share her offbeat

See Vacationing, Page F8

Two for the road

When Bill Collins takes a trip, he craves spontaneity. His wife, Tish Gibbs, prefers a detailed itinerary. He loves traveling by car; she doesn't. Long wilderness hikes are just the thing for him; cruises are her idea of a perfect getaway. But in spite of their differences, Collins and Gibbs, of Norwalk, have discovered how to take mutually rewarding vacations together.

But for other couples, touring together is often a trip to vacation hell. One wants to go to the beach, the other to museums. One thinks vacation is the time to splurge on fine dining; the other thinks that fast food should do when time is limited. Such traveling twosomes pack the ingredients for arguments as effortlessly as they pack their clothes.

Their vacations can be stressful. One partner may feel dominated by the other. Arguments may flare up, especially when aggravated by the intensity of spending all day, every day together. Even little things can provoke disagreement: choosing a restaurant, a hotel or an activity. Travel can put a strain on any marriage or friendship.

Margot Biestman of Sausalito, Calif., traveled often with her husband. It was seldom easy. He liked to travel quickly from place to place; she preferred a slower pace. That was just one of the difficulties. Biestman's experiences resulted in a book, "Travel For Two: The Art of Compromise" (Pergot Press, $10.95).

Once, on a trip to Greece, Biestman's husband drove a rented car through a raging thunderstorm to reach the top of a remote mountain. It was a hair-raising trip, she says, made even worse when the windshield wipers broke. At the summit, the storm cleared, light splashed on hundreds of flowers and the views were incredible. "My husband looked at me and said, 'I wouldn't have missed this for anything in the world,' and I said, 'Nothing is worth this kind of fear.'

"We looked at each other and said 'We've got to do something about this.'"

What the Biestmans did was learn to

See Traveling, Page F9

Gettysburg guns to roar once again

By RANDY KRAFT
Allentown Morning Call

Gettysburg is about to be invaded again.

Thousands of tourists — no one is sure how many — will converge on this small south-central Pennsylvania town during the last weekend in June and first weekend in July to commemorate the 125th anniversary of the bloody battle that was a turning point in the American Civil War.

The total number of visitors those two weekends probably will be far greater than the estimated 172,000 Union and Confederate soldiers who clashed at Gettysburg July 1 to 3, 1863.

What promises to be the largest battle re-enactment ever held in North America will be June 24 to 26. Four engagements that took place at Gettysburg will be re-created on private farmland about six miles south of the actual battleground.

On July 1 to 3, more than 1,000 Civil War buffs portraying soldiers are expected to participate in a living history encampment and demonstrate military tactics, without engaging in mock combat, at Gettysburg National Military Park, the battlefields surrounding the town.

All motel rooms in the Gettysburg area have been booked for many months. Linda Sharrah of the Gettysburg Travel Council said bed-and-breakfast establishments also are full and "campgrounds are getting there." People who call the travel council about going those weekends are sent lists of all available accommodations within a 30- to 40-mile radius of Gettysburg.

Normally, Gettysburg gets about 1.5 million visitors a year. The travel council predicts 2.5 million will visit this year.

John Andrews of the National Park Service estimates the park will get 50,000 visitors a day during its 125th anniversary activities, but added, "It could be higher than that."

Gettysburg received up to 50,000 visitors a day during the 100th anniversary of the battle in 1963. Andrews said more people may come this year, because the 125th anniversary is on a weekend. The 100th anniversary was on weekdays.

This battle of Gettysburg is being billed as "The patriotic event of

See Gettysburg, Page F6

A battlefield too horrible to glorify

By RANDY KRAFT
Allentown Morning Call

The brave, weary eyes of the shining soldier — who forever keeps a vigil along the front line at Gettysburg — seem to beseech all who pass by: "Don't glorify what happened here. It was too horrible."

More men fell on the battlefield surrounding this small town in south-central Pennsylvania than in any other battle ever fought in North America, according to the National Park Service. There were more than 51,000 casualties at Gettysburg.

They fought and died at Culp's Hill, Devil's Den, Little Round Top, Bloody Run, on Seminary and Cemetery ridges. Even names as innocuous as the Wheatfield and Peach Orchard became synonymous with killing fields.

The battle, a turning point in the Civil War, was fought 125 years ago — July 1 to 3, 1863.

Gettysburg National Military Park, which covers almost 4,000 acres, looks like a surrealistic but oh-so-peaceful graveyard for giants. Heroic sculptures, obelisks, temples, towers and many other monuments seem to have been haphazardly dropped everywhere — in the middle of fields, in front yards, in forests, on isolated and heavily wooded hilltops.

Something about this place tugs at the soul. You may feel compelled to stand alone in the middle of Gettysburg's tranquil green and yellow fields on a hot afternoon and slowly walk up toward the low stone wall where the Union army waited on Cemetery Ridge — as 12,000 gallant Confederate soldiers marched on July 3, 1863, in what history remembers as Pickett's charge.

See 'Don't, Page F6

AWARD OF EXCELLENCE

OVERALL DESIGN

The Orange County Register

Santa Ana, California

Designer

Staff

Wednesday, September 14, 1988 — The Orange County Register — Thursday, September 15, 1988

Food

GRILLING ON

THE ROAD TO MOROCCO

By Kitty Morse
Special to the Register

Grilling evokes visions of backyard barbecues, juicy hamburgers and crispy chicken. It's fun, and more importantly, it's easy to do.

But what of a new idea? Turn to one of the world's most ancient cuisines for a fresh perspective. The next time you barbecue, why not try a North African twist. Put on your own backyard "mechoui," a traditional, Moroccan-style barbecue.

Grilling and barbecuing is an integral part of the Moroccan culinary tradition, and many Moroccan homemakers still rely on "canoons," small charcoal braziers, to cook their daily meals. Vendors hawk shish kebabs (also called by the French name "brochettes"), and grilled fish, the local version of fast food, in every marketplace or main square throughout Morocco.

When a celebration is called for, however, Moroccans prepare a mechoui (pronounced "mush-OO-ee") or whole roast lamb.

The best place to sample a mechoui and other grilled specialties is at a moussem in late summer or early fall. A moussem is an annual festival held to celebrate a bountiful harvest or to honor a local saint. It also serves as a sort of annual country fair for farmers who compete for awards for the best livestock or the most beautiful horse.

A week before the moussem is slated to begin, large tents sprout like mushrooms around a central quadrangle at a pre-selected site. This is where the highlight of the moussem will take place, a uniquely Moroccan display of horsemanship called a fantasias.

For several days, women are busy building cone-shaped mud ovens to bake bread, while men dig the pits for roasting the mechoui or whole roast lamb, the crowning meal at the conclusion of the moussem.

The buzz of commercial activity soon permeates the tent city. The bleeting of sheep almost drowns out the spirited bargaining sessions taking place inside the animal corrals, where herds of sheep, clusters of supercilious camels and docile mules await new owners.

At every street corner, itinerant vendors tempt the country folk with the latest Moroccan fashions. Children squeal with delight at riding the primitive wooden Ferris wheel. Spice vendors sit cross-legged behind neat pyramids of paprika in varying shades of crimson. Next to them, vegetable vendors boast of the

Please see MOROCCO/11

Elaine Isaacson/The Register

Moroccan zahlouk, a salad made of eggplant and tomatoes, goes well with meat dishes or as a dip for pita bread. Cumin and cilantro add an exotic touch to brochettes of kefta, right.

Photo at right by Ygnacio Nanetti and food styling by Tillie Clements/The Register. Ceramic platter by Denise Ford, courtesy of the Laguna Art Museum at South Coast Plaza

Pierogi: It's Polish pasta filled with lots of pride, hard work and goodies

JOE CREA

Soul food is in the eye — actually, palate — of the beholder. So many munchables flip my switches, but few haunt me so dreamily as pierogi.

Pierogi are one of Eastern Europe's dearest doughy delights. Poland's humble, crescent-shaped first cousins to ravioli are hauntingly good. Filled with wonderously earthy things — mushrooms, sauerkraut, potatoes or prunes, and often more exotic alternatives — each handmade pocket is simmered until tender and sauteed until golden brown. The result is a toothesome savory, at once bitey and tender, mellow and bursting with subtle or lively surprise.

Ah, but you don't find them so good anymore. Now they're machine-made. Play-Dough appealing. Insipid, pasty fillings.

Not so when they're fashioned by cooks true to honest tradition. When the women of the John Paul II Polish Center of Yorba Linda get rolling — literally, rolling yard after yard of dough for their beloved "little entrees" — there's no fudging on quality. And when the reason is the center's annual "Dozynki" or Harvest Festival (this Saturday and Sunday) and thousands of pierogi to be sold becomes the goal, pride grows into passion. And perspiration.

Suggest to a roomful of Polish women that some continental types don't exactly revere their fare as an equal to, say, French cuisine, and you're lucky if all you have to duck are some scornful glances. Levelheadedly, this crew took devil's advocacy in stride.

"They have not *tasted*, they've just *heard*," says Stella Dybas-Lento of Anaheim.

"Take the fillings for the pierogi," adds Jean Kaminski of LaMirada. "Some would say that the peasants only have sauerkraut and potatos. Maybe true. But we have the mushrooms and cheese and so forth, which

Please see CREA/11

Joe Crea is the Register's food editor. His column appears each week in the Food section.

A2 The Orange County Register Friday, September 16, 1988

Today

COUNTY

Ruling affects Westminster: Appellate justices in Santa Ana declare part of Proposition 62 unconstitutional, a relief for Westminster officials A1

Dannemeyer pursues memo: The Fullerton congressman says he filed suit against a San Francisco newspaper to find out who wrote a memo about him A3

Hams help out: Ham radio operators in Orange County help relay "health and safety" messages from areas hit by Hurricane Gilbert A18

Another Kraft trial delay: Judge Donald McCartin is dismayed when two panelists on the Randy Kraft jury ask to be excused for hardships B1

Woman released: A mentally impaired woman is released from jail a week after a judge allowed her to represent herself in court and gave her a 25-day jail sentence B1

Former POWs to meet: A Santa Ana man will be among the estimated 220 former POWs from Orange and Los Angeles counties expected to gather in Long Beach B1

Backlash on jail site: County supervisors are poised to reverse themselves and allow the sale of surplus land for an elementary school in Santa Ana B1

STATE

Political unknown nominated: Gov. George Deukmejian nominates state Auditor General Thomas W. Hayes to succeed the late Jesse Unruh as state treasurer A1

Six win lotto jackpot: Wednesday's $5.4 million top prize in the California lottery is split six ways, with each winner to receive a share A3

Dummy company investigated: The state Fair Political Practices Commission investigated an FBI dummy company used in the sting A3

Frozen head: Sixties drug guru Timothy Leary says he has signed up to have his head removed and frozen for possible resurrection after he dies A4

NATION

Handgun amendment dropped: In a victory for the pro-gun lobby, the House ...

Concord rally: Vice President George Bush accepts a sweatshirt at a Ygnacio Valley High School gathering in Concord on Thursday. The GOP presidential nominee said he hopes Oliver North is found innocent of charges in the Iran-contra affair A6

BUSINESS

SPORTS

SHOW

LAST WORD

WORLD

People

Comedian Goldberg is beaming up for 'Next Generation' of TV episodes

The word out of Star Fleet Command is that none other than **Whoopi Goldberg** has been tabbed for a recurring role next season on syndicated TV's "Star Trek: The Next Generation."

A deal is said to be all but official to have the comedian play the part of the intergalactic bartender Guinan, tending bar on the Enterprise's new cocktail lounge that it's calling Ten Forward (or "Ten-For" to the ship's crew). It's where the star-ship gang will unwind after a long day dodging alien life forms.

Once signed, the deal calls for Goldberg to appear in seven of the first 12 episodes of "Star Trek" next season. The show, a winner of three Emmy awards, begins production on its new season next week. New episodes are expected to hit the air by late November.

Goldberg

SIDESHOW/A LIGHTER LOOK

TODAY IN ORANGE COUNTY

TODAY IN HISTORY

TOMORROW IN THE REGISTER

HOW TO REACH US

The Orange County Register — Wednesday, September 14, 1988

Metro

Supervisors refuse sale of school site

Jail needs prompt board's vote to hang onto land in Santa Ana

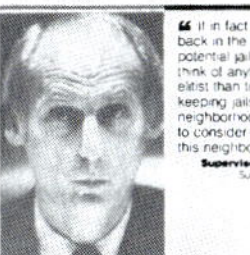

"If in fact this is going back in the hopper as a potential jail site, I can't think of anything more elitist than to talk about keeping jails out of neighborhoods and then to consider putting a jail in this neighborhood." — Supervisor Roger Stanton

Site controversy

Tempest on the rocks

A battle at the Top of the World

School district plan to sell land opposed

Teacher jailed for lewd conduct is fired

State to probe whether firm is using illegal scare ads to sell water purifier

BOB EMMERS

INSIDE

Marines, Irvine will try to ease helicopter noise over city

The Orange County Register — Wednesday, September 14, 1988

Sports

Dodgers shut out Braves

Tudor, two relievers combine on two-hitter

Mater Dei wide receivers coach Karen Frank, 32, shouts instructions from the sideline during game. Frank, the school's track coach, is in her first season as a football coach.

A NEW ROLE

Track coach Karen Frank joins Mater Dei football staff

'Invisible linebacker' now casting a shadow

Owens starts 1988 with several big plays

FREEWAY BOWL

Just one question on Rams: When does reality set in?

STEVE BISHEFF

Angels lose to Royals, are officially eliminated

IOC would ban drug-dealing athletes from Games for life

INSIDE

BUSINESS: **US trade deficit plummets**

ACCENT: **Building bodies, profits**

SPORTS: **KC puts Angels out for '88**

METRO: **OC won't sell land for school**

THE ORANGE COUNTY Register

WEDNESDAY EVENING — SEPTEMBER 14, 1988 — 25 CENTS

Gilbert pounds Yucatan Peninsula

16,000 flee coastal regions; Texans prepare to evacuate

Center stays calm in eye of media storm

Peruvian riches untapped

Archeologists say they've just begun

Jurors, 8 alternates named for Kraft trial

Bush aims election campaign at Hispanics at OC breakfast

Lasers replace bullets at OC training center

Death ends a My Lai nightmare

Homeless US veteran, haunted by 1968 massacre, slain

AWARD OF EXCELLENCE

OVERALL DESIGN

Gwinnett Daily News

Lawrenceville, Georgia

Designer

Lou Silverstein and Staff

D

"Dirty Rotten Scoundrels" and other funny films for the weekend 7D

Georgia Style

Going Out

Daily News, Friday, December 23, 1988

RON HUDSPETH

The Fox went to the Dogs

It was a "How 'Bout Them Dawgs" kind of evening at Kenny Rogers' annual Christmas show at The Fox. When Kenny, an Athens resident, introduced the University of Georgia string section as part of the evening's extravaganza, the entire audience began to bark, and a few brave souls even shouted, "Dooley for Governor!" If that wasn't enough, Barbara Dooley was there front and center, so Kenny asked her to stand and take a bow. There was only one problem during the show. Instead of a steady, but light stream of snow falling during the grand finale, an avalanche of snow fell on Rogers' head, causing the audience to howl. And are you looking for a place to live? Word I get is Rogers' farm near Athens is still up for sale. You can grab it for a cool $12.5 million.

Best parties

HUDCAPS: Looking for the hot New Year's Eve parties? You can bet Rupert's, the hottest club in town at the moment, will be packed. It's $25 a person at the door and the dress is black-tie optional. Another good bet is Gregg Allman at Center Stage. The $16 ticket will get you Southern rock and blues played like few can.

• • •

The Surf Club has an interesting concept for its party. It's black tie even though the room is a beach club concept and the price is $119.89 a person, which gets you Dom Perignon and some party favors. Easier on your pocketbook is Carey's Buckhead Longbranch where there is no cover charge, free champagne at midnight and music by Hank Gallups and his band.

They're back

There's nothing quite like a press release from the Harlem Globetrotters. The Globetrotters are due at The Omni Jan. 7 for their annual basketball show and for the umpteenth time, Red Klotz, the coach of the win-hungry Washington Generals, says "we've had it with losing. The Harlem Globetrotters may be in for some big surprises this year." At last count, the Globetrotters had beaten Klotz' team 6,276 straight times.

PEOPLE SPOTTER: Evel Knievel at Carey's Buckhead Longbranch ... Lewis Grizzard at Creekside ... Phil Niekro at the Gwinnett Skeeters ... Bobby Butler at Coach & Six ... Moses Malone at Jocks & Jills.

• • •

PULSE OF PEACHTREE: Gunther-Gebel Williams, the great wild animal trainer, will be making his last Atlanta appearance ever when the Ringling Brothers and Barnum & Bailey Circus comes to The Omni Jan. 25. Gebel-Williams is preparing to leave the ring after this season and take on a management role with the circus.

Please see OLD, page 5D

Today

Don't be afraid to fall 2D

Best bets for viewing on tube 8D

Comics give funny bone a tickle 9D

The return of Urban Cowboy

By Elizabeth Lee

Daily News staff writer

As the music of the Charlie Daniels Band blares from the speakers, a circle of dancers topped with cowboy hats and shod in shiny, pointed boots skates across the floor, two-stepping to the tune of the "Uneasy Rider '88."

Please see URBAN, page 6D

Gene Ivey of Snellville (top) dons a cowboy hat and shirt during a night out on the town. Couples at Miss Kitty's Saloon and Dancehall (left) swing their partners, while boot-clad dancers (above) do a line dance (also at Miss Kitty's).

Photos by Joe Gentry

"TORCH SONG TRILOGY"

Movie has powerful message

By Kathryn Cave

Daily News staff writer

Arnold Beckoff could be any other man in trouble with love. Except for the bunny slippers. And his full-time profession as a drag queen.

"Torch Song Trilogy," which is the story of several years in Arnold's heretofore romantically unfulfilled lifetime, could have been a sappy, overdone movie with heavy-handed overtones that hoped to beat into its viewing audience the message that gay life is much like everyday life. There is the search for companionship; for family; and for acceptance.

But its writer and star is much smarter than that. You don't get the audience you're trying to reach with a heavy hand. Laugh at yourself and the world laughs with you. And if you're Harvey Fierstein, they learn a little something along the way.

Chances are, however, those who go to see the movie based on the long-running, Tony Award-winning play will be those who have already received the message. Too bad. In an age of AIDS and scare sex, "Torch Song Trilogy" is blessedly dated. It hovers in the 1970s.

Instead, the message behind "Torch Song" is simpler than safe sex. It defines homosexuality in human terms — person to person, man to man, mother to son, son to father and lover to lover.

Alan (Matthew Broderick) portrays the protagonist's lover in "Torch Song Trilogy."

It starts with Arnold's mother, played by Anne Bancroft. The young mother (Ms. Bancroft ages a lot better than Jessica Lange does in "Everybody's All American" and does it in half the time) is searching for her young son, brushing past the tea set, past the doll-house and all the way to the closet where she finds him dressed in a feather boa and putting on lipstick.

Next scene: Arnold comes out of the closet, so to speak. Now Arnold (Fierstein) is getting paid for the very same thing posing as Virginia Hamm (not even the best of the bizarre monikers). He wisecracks through several Woody Allen-like sequences in which he breaks down the wall between audience and movie by giving his own interpretation of what's going on.

He also offers some tongue-in-cheek wisdom. To Arnold, there are three kinds of hopeless men: "Married. Just in for the weekend. And terminally straight."

Arnold has met them all. He's fallen for most of them.

When he meets Ed (Brian Kerwin) at a gay bar, it's a reminder of every straight meat market visited in the 1970s. Ed uses all the standard lines, sweeping a shy Arnold off his feet and into his bed. Arnold is ready to buy a bunny china pattern (his apartment is decorated with rabbits such as bunny stenciling, a bunny tea pot and just plain stuffed bunnies) when he finds out that Ed has another lover — a woman.

The movie rests more on the matter-of-factness to its content than on the acting skills of its participants. The acting, in fact, is almost overshadowed by the ease of the script. Fierstein eases us out of the uptight 1980s and back into the no-holds-barred 1970s with stellar writing. The actors, like Kerwin and Ms. Bancroft and Matthew Broderick as Arnold's

Please see FILM, page 4D

MOVIE SPOTLIGHT

'Burning Secret' offers subtle tale of coming of age

By Elizabeth Lee

Daily News staff writer

Film-ing a coming-of-age story can present some difficulties if you're trying to portray a 12-year-old boy who has no knowledge or understanding of sex and violence. There just aren't too many totally naive children around anymore.

Ms. Dunaway, Brandauer, and Eberts star.

Like other recent growing-up movies, "Burning Secret" solved that dilemma by journeying to an earlier, supposedly more innocent time — in this case, Austria just after World War I. The snow-covered mountains and elegant but stuffy resort hotel provide the setting for a woman (Faye Dunaway) to be seduced by a smooth-talking stranger (Klaus Maria Brandauer) and her son to learn something about adult passions and responsibilities.

The muted colors of the film and the quiet elegance of the settings match the subtle glances and small gestures that reveal the characters' emotions. For the most part, "Burning Secret" is marked by the subtle and understated, meaning the audience must pay close attention to catch the nuances of the film. Unfortunately, the dialogue in the movie — particularly some of Brandauer's remarks as he talks about the war's effect on him — doesn't measure up to the quality of the rest of the film.

"Burning Secret" focuses on the developing and

Please see SUBTLETIES, page 5D

Hawks stop Sonics 1C

SPORTS FINAL

GWINNETT

Daily News

Wednesday, December 21, 1988

Jackets down Richmond 1C

Willis returns to Hawks 1C

Indiana beats Kentucky 5C

Complete coverage inside

First day of winter

UGA courts Sheridan after Erk says no

Winter of '89 is coming in like a lamb

County's '89 budget goes public

Officials hear concerns over spending

Costs reach $5.5 million for design of center

Showers

ATLANTA TODAY

Sky show

Man dressed like Santa steals $695,000

Armenian Relief Fund

Bush aides battle to save HHS nominee

4 days until Christmas

The Score

NFL

Bengals 20
Redskins 17

Broncos 21
Patriots....... 10

See stories, page 2C

NBA

Cavaliers ... 120
Hawks 94

Knicks 117
Bullets 102

Sixers 119
Jazz.......... 107

Mavericks .. 104
Heat 87

Pistons 100
Hornets 91

Nets 100
Pacers 92

Warriors 123
Spurs 113

Bulls.......... 112
Bucks 93

Nuggets 114
Clippers...... 99

Sonics 141
Kings........ 111

See stories, page 8C

STATE FINALS

W. Robins .. 33
Brookwood 7

Thomasville . 12
Stephens Co. .. 7

R.E. Lee 17
Wash.-Wilkes 16

Clinch Co. ... 34
Palmetto 14

Scores 963-7252

FOOTBALL

'Report says Oklahoma on probation 3C

BASKETBALL

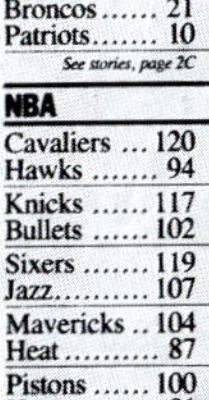

Tar Heels whip UCLA 6C

Cavaliers rout Hawks 9C

FOOTNOTES

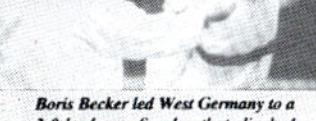

FOOTBALL

The Cincinnati Bengals clinched the AFC Central title with a 20-17 win over the Washington Redskins.

TENNIS

Boris Becker led West Germany to a 3-0 lead over Sweden that clinched the Davis Cup championship.

FALCONS-SAINTS

The Falcons hope to get their running game going again in their 1988 NFL season finale at New Orleans.

C SportsSunday

Daily News, Sunday, December 18, 1988

Demons bedevil Brookwood

Brookwood's Mark Lloyd (21) goes after a loose ball as Warner Robins' Kip Stokes (10) closes in.

Warner Robins wins AAAA championship

By Randy Fingeroot

Despite Brookwood's offensive and defensive woes, which saw the Broncos trail 13-0 at the half, Brookwood coach Dave Hunter felt his team was still alive.

"I thought we had a chance in the second half," Hunter said. "Then we had the bad play when Mickey (Haynes) got hurt, we made a couple mistakes and they got a couple big plays."

The third quarter was devastating to Brookwood. After receiving the kickoff, Brookwood moved from its 25 out to the 37, but on second down, Haynes was pressured and was

Please see BROOKWOOD, page 4C

Russell's recruiting ability is questioned

By Terry Doherty
Daily News staff writer

ATHENS — With Vince Dooley publicly stating his preference for the preservation of his current staff after his departure as Georgia's football coach, the impetus for the selection of Erk Russell as Dooley's successor is growing.

Russell has long ties to Georgia, and it's like-

■ Georgia Southern loses to Furman in NCAA I-AA championship game. Page 2C

vinced that Russell will be the next Bulldogs' coach raise an important question: How good a recruiter will Russell be?

As coach at Division I-AA's Georgia South-

athletes," said a member of the school's football program. "That's a negative."

Said a prominent alumnus, "How is Erk going to compete (as a recruiter)? That's the important question, especially right now.

"This is a must season. Gaps have got to be filled."

The questions become more pressing as each day goes by since Dooley's announce-

cal recruiting year, Georgia is already operating at a deficit.

The loss of outside linebackers coach Dicky Clark to an assistant's position at East Carolina leaves Georgia with three coaches who many privately agree are top recruiters: running backs coach Ray Goff, defensive coordinator Dale Strahm and receivers coach Bob Harrison. With Clark gone, recruiting coordi-

Please see RUSSELL, page 7C

BILL ZACK ■ *Point of View*

Cremins' face shows more than courtside acrobatics

ATLANTA

Please see CREMINS, page 7C

Inspired Georgia tops struggling Tech 80-69

By Denise H. Maloof

Please see GEORGIA, page 7C

B Local/State

Santa's helpers earn pat on back for holiday deeds 2B

Special people receive recognition.

Editorial/Forum, 9-11B

Daily News, Sunday, December 18, 1988

Shelter for battered women may open in January

By Kathy Norcross
Daily News staff writer

LAWRENCEVILLE — Gwinnett County Commissioners on Tuesday will consider approving a lease agreement that would establish a shelter for battered women in the county.

"It's a transfer of an existing shelter (building) in Gwinnett County," said Ann Granger, executive director for the metrowide Council on Battered Women. "The

construction will be completed on the shelter, and they hope to be open by the end of January, she said.

In addition, the council has requested an increase in the county's monetary contribution, she said. For the past four years, Gwinnett has provided $8,825 each year for the council, she said. This year, the council has requested $25,000, Ms. Granger said.

She said that they don't expect Gwinnett officials to provide all the funding, and the council has obtained two federal grants that are administered through the state

ter 24 hours a day.

Gwinnett's shelter will have 20 to 25 beds and be able to house 10 to 12 women with their children, she said.

The shelter would be the second available since Mary and Martha's Place opened in mid-October. It is a shelter sponsored by the Lawrenceville Baptist Association designed for battered women, which also accepts some homeless women, said Jerry Cruce, director of Christian Ministries for the association. That shelter can hold 16 people at a time. Since it opened, 45 women and children

finding employment, and each night at Mary and Martha's there is a devotion time. Irene Jordan has volunteered to live there for a year so that the shelter is staffed 24 hours a day, he said.

The council has worked with Mary and Martha's volunteers and trained them, Ms. Granger said, and will continue to support that shelter.

"There's never enough space," she said.

There are small shelters in Cobb, DeKalb and Clayton counties, Ms. Granger said.

Please see ORGANIZERS, page 4B

Maltbie's mile: Tough traveling in Lawrenceville

By Pat Murdock

Edge of pavement on Maltbie Street deteriorating.

Most agree Maltbie is everything a road shouldn't be. The dilemma is how to make it better.

"I use it all the time," City Councilman Mahlon Burson said. "It is not safe."

Burson has recently taken up the mantle of improving Maltbie Street and tried to rally his fellow councilmen to the cause.

George Black, Gwinnett's director of transporation, said it is difficult to imagine a county road ever falling into the same disrepair.

"I don't believe we have a road that narrow that runs through an industri-

Please see CITY, page 4B

A heavy truck straddles the center line as it heads down Maltbie Street.

Harris silent on bond trip, awaits probe

Petition seeks officials' resignations

By Mark Meltzer

Gov. Joe Frank Harris with glass water faucet given to him by Democrats as a reminder of controversial bond trip.

In an interview following the talk, Harris refused to say whether the members of the county commission should resign or whether the storm of protest over expenses incurred on the board's February trip to New York had drained the commissioners of their ability to govern.

"That's a matter that is presently being investigated by the grand jury and until there's something presented by them, I don't want to comment," Harris said.

Asked if he would resign if he was the commission chairman, Harris also declined to answer.

"I don't want to enter into it at all until the investigation has been completed," he said.

In his address, Harris said he agreed to speak to the Gwinnett Democrats in August of 1987 and chose the date for the talk about a month later. That was well before the commissioners' bond rating trip to New York or revelations of excessive spending on the trip, the cost of which was billed to county water and sewer customers.

The commission furor was at the top of everyone's agenda but Harris'. Attendees at the breakfast were asked to sign a petition calling for commissioners to resign, and the party sold T-shirts at the breakfast chiding the commission chairman with the slogan, "Lillian Webb's World Tour '88." A hand-blown glass design of a water faucet was created

Please see DEMOCRATS', page 4B

DATELINE GWINNETT

County to consider justice center contract

"Of course the building is not finished yet so we need to continue them working for a while."

— Jill Pylant

— Matt Kempner

Squeeze

■ *Crowds pack into Gwinnett Place mall Saturday on the last full weekend of shopping before Christmas.*

Donald wins council seat in Lilburn

LILBURN Michael Donald defeated Cas Robinson for the Post 4 council seat in a special election Saturday in Lilburn.

Although Robinson led two weeks ago, Donald won Saturday with 359 votes to Robinson's 238.

The voter turnout of 597 was considered "good" by city officials for a special election in the middle of the Christmas season. About 730 of the more than 3,000 registered city voters went to the polls in the first election.

Donald

Donald's successful efforts to stop some rezonings may have stuck in voters' memories when they went to the polls.

Donald led a movement in February by residents to defeat a zoning application that would have allowed a company to locate near the railroad tracks near Old Town Lilburn.

He later led opposition to a zoning change for a cement plant on Arcado Road near the railroad tracks.

— Connie Mulqueen

OUR TURN

Students speak out

Hot stuff
Cooks at The Californian win big with Hot Off the Press Chili/**D1**

Onward, Scout
Despite disability, Scout completes strenuous bike/**E1**

Water polo win
Monte Vista beats Valhalla as two powers meet in opener/**B1**

The Californian

WEDNESDAY
September 14, 1988

East County, San Diego

LMSV ST-LK
25 CENTS
VOL. 56, NO. 221

NEWS DIGEST

▲ Hurricane preparation

◄ A proper welcome

▲ To the rescue

▲ Marines arrive

INDEX

Injuries fatal to one Navy flier

Pilot, two civilians hurt in air crash remain hospitalized

Please see **CRASH,** Page **A2**

Shooting victim

Officer cleared in shooting

Stabbing, shooting mark drug sweep

Water shortage fear for 1989 prompts county action

AWARD OF EXCELLENCE
OVERALL DESIGN
The Californian
El Cajon, California
Designers
Ed Goodell, Manny Cruz
Karen Barnett, Gail Woynar
Editors
Jim Slusher, Ray Bordner,
Mary Kaye Ritz
Art Director
Alan Jacobson

The Californian

ACCENT ON THE ARTS **Lifestyles**

FRIDAY
September 16, 1988

PAGE **A7**

BRIEFLY

Lamplighters

"So Long on Lonely Street" continues at the Ben Polak Fine Arts Center, 8053 University Ave., La Mesa, with performances at 8 p.m. today and also on Sept. 17, 23 and 24, and at 2 p.m. Sept. 18 and 25. General admission tickets are $7 each. Call 464-4598 for more information.

▲ 'Hamlet'

Chula Vista's Park & Recreation Department's free Shakespeare Festival presents "Hamlet" at the Memorial Bowl, 373 Park Way, Chula Vista, through Oct. 8. Performances continue at 4 p.m. Saturday and Oct. 17, Oct. 24, and Oct. 1 and 8. The performance is presented in a modernized lanugage text. Kenneth Enright (above) portrays Hamlet (photo by P.N. Enright). The bowl is an open-air amphitheater; blankets or chairs are suggested for seating on the grass.

'Tribute'

Santee Community Theater's production of "Tribute," opens today for a four-week run at the media center of Cajon Park School, 10300 N. Magnolia Ave., Santee. "Tribute" is about Scottie Templeton, a 51-year-old charmer who finds his so-far perfect life in upheaval as he tries to make friends with a son alienated by years of neglect. Performances are at 8 p.m. Fridays and Saturdays through Oct. 8, and at 2 p.m. Sunday Sept. 25 and Oct. 9. Tickets are $6 for adults and $5 for seniors and youth through high school. Call 448-5673 for reservations.

▲ Lubovitch Dance

The Lar Lubovitch Dance Company will perform at 8 p.m. Sept. 30 and Oct. 1 at Symphony Hall, 1245 Seventh Ave., San Diego. The event is sponsored by the San Diego Foundation for the Performing Arts. Tickets, available through Ticketmaster (278-TIXS), range in price from $15 to $45. Lar Lubovitch, whose company's style epitomizes the "risky dancing" theme of this year's season, has forged a unique style of movement through the creation of more than 45 dances for his company and others.

▲ George Michael

George Michael brings his worldwide Faith tour to San Diego at 8 p.m. Oct. 11 at the San Diego Sports Arena. (This date is a change from the originally scheduled Oct. 9 show.) Michael has emerged as a popular pop star. His album "Faith," released four months ago, is becoming one of the year's best-selling albums. Tickets are available at Ticketmaster locations or can be charged by calling 278-TIXS.

Melodrama

An old-fashioned melodrama, "Fireman Save My Child," will premier at Magnolia Mulvaney's restaurant, 8861 Magnolia Ave., Santee, at 8 p.m. Oct. 5. A vaudeville showcase of San Diego talent will follow. The event will continue on Wednesdays through spring. Call 258-1558 for reservations and more information.

Masks aren't just for Halloween

"The Return of the Masks," an exhibit of the works of Los Angeles artist Joseph McLaughlin, is on display through September at the Tarbox Gallery, 1202 Kettner Blvd., San Diego. Gallery hours are 11 a.m. to 9 p.m. Tuesday through Friday and from 5 to 10 p.m. Saturday. Parking is available in the building annex. Call 234-5020 for more information.

By Karen Barnett
Californian Lifestyles editor

Masks are meant to be beautiful and fun, says artist Joseph McLaughlin. And seeing his stunning creations will make a believer of you.

Made from brilliantly colored feathers and plumes, quills, corn husks, glittering ornaments and sparkling jewels, from the whimsical to the exotic, no two are alike.

One of molded black leather features the skeleton of a bird's head curving over the forehead with a huge pear-shaped "diamond" just beneath it and another on the nose. Other jewels adorn the mask.

One is eight feet high with peacock feathers. Some have horns, some are half-masks, some are entire faces.

Another is "Tammy Faye" — namesake of the notorious wife of a notorious TV evangelist — her hair a mass of white, yellow and gold paper ribbon festooned with a cheap white lace bow. And of course the obligatory heavily made-up eyes.

There's one named "Diva" with elegant hair of pearls. And "Shirley," which the artist explained is "everybody's aunt from New Jersey."

"They're all my favorites," McLaughlin said expansively, waving an arm as though to embrace them all.

Feathers are most representative of his work, he said, although he uses all kinds of materials in his handmade masks, and they are as varied as they are beautiful. Some are to be worn; some are wall ornaments.

"You can talk about them all you want," McLaughlin said, "but to see them is incredible."

Although McLaughlin admits he came to his unusual career almost by accident, he brought an impressive background with him. He graduated from the Academy of Dramatic Arts in New York City and has degrees from the Fashion Institute of Technology and the Geological Institute of America. He worked as an assisant to Jean Schlumberger, a designer at the famous Tiffany's. That experience, he said, helped him develop his color sense.

Later, he opened two fashion accessory shops in Greenwich Village. After a friend brought him 12 masks to sell, he sold 11 of them the first day he displayed them. He realized how popular masks are and he was on his way to a new career.

"I wanted to do an art form, but I wanted a challenge and I wanted to be the best," McLaughlin said.

He also wanted to get out of the New York rat race, and by 1984 he opened a studio in Hollywood to make his masks. Soon, he said, his buyers were stars, celebrities and movie studios commissioning him to create his masks for special events and productions.

"My friend Larry Hagman told me to go to New Orleans to see the masks," said McLaughlin. "I went and realized how really good I am.

"I said to myself, 'Wow! Yeah, I'm good.'"

No lack of self-image here, but McLaughlin's words are backed up by sweet success. Some 18 art galleries carry his work, he said, among them the Smithsonian and the Palm Springs, Philadelphia and Brooklyn museums.

Most range in price from $100 to $500 but there are some that fetch even more, such as a dark helmet encrusted with Austrian crystals that boasts a price tag of $5,000.

"More and more people understand mask-making as an art force," he said. "Masks aren't just for Halloween. People are getting more intersted in art and there's more interest in arts and crafts."

McLaughlin sees his work as a marriage of the two, an art form that anybody and everybody can enjoy.

"We can relate to a mask instantly," he said, "because it's a face."

McLaughlin said most of all he would like people to see and enjoy his work.

"There's a lot of new expression going on in the world, and I'm happy to think I've contributed," he said.

The Tarbox Gallery, located on the north side of the Santa Fe Station, is tucked into the Galleria. Owner Ruth Tarbox, elegantly tall, slim and silver-haired, brings a grandmotherly warmth to her tiny gallery. She began in the business 18 years ago in La Jolla and has been at her present location four years.

Ron Dipping *The Californian*
This elaborate feathered mask is from a collection on display at the Tarbox Gallery.

Ron Dipping *The Californian*
Joseph Mclaughlin shows off one of his creations.

'Moon Over Parador': Comedy or message?

Richard Dreyfuss
"Moon Over Parador"

By Paul Sterman
Californian staff writer

MOVIE REVIEW
★ ★ *Ho hum*

The main problem with "Moon Over Parador," the erratic new comedy from director Paul Mazursky, is that this movie never quite makes up its mind what it wants to be.

Part of the film is a fast-moving and funny trip under the Paradorian sky, carving out its territory in splashy strokes of broad farce. About halfway through this journey, however, the film lurches off into the land of message-laden movie-making, attempting to treat its once-satirical themes with the greatest of seriousness. Snippets of slapstick suddenly turn into an arena for the socially conscious statement.

Some films can effectively incorporate such a mixed bag into their cinematic scope; "Moon Over Parador," however, can not. The film's inconsistency and indecision as to the tone it wants to adopt simply blunts any potential power it may have had had it stuck to one route or the other.

The plot of "Parador" revolves around the adventures of its troika of stars — Richard Dreyfuss, Raul Julia and Sonia Braga. Dreyfuss is a journeyman New York actor by the name of Jack Noah who is trying to make the pivotal career jump from soap operas to the stage, and has come to Parador to star in a grade-B movie — which is quite entertaining in its awfulness.

Things heat up when the dictator of this Latin American country dies of a heart attack, and corrupt henchman Roberto Strausmann (Julia), anxious not to let the public know of the death, recruits Noah to play the role of a lifetime — the dictator of Parador.

The request is not a typical casting call — it is made with a gun put to Noah's head; but at the same time it is clear that Strausmann is also playing upon the actor's thesbian sensitivities. Noah wants to show that he could play the dictator better than DeNiro could.

Braga, as the dead dictator's mistress, soon jumps on ship and goes along with the elaborate gag.

Up to this point, the movie moves along quite nicely. Displaying a light touch, it generates its share of inspired lunacy, and even manages to paint a subtle and rather poignant picture of the struggles endured by the Everyman Actor.

But the colors on this canvas soon change their hue, and the film goes badly astray in the process. The Dreyfuss role, which had been so rife with parody precisely because it was so preposterous, suddenly is turned into a character who now decides to genuinely try and affect political change in the country, attempting to transform corruption into noble platforms of progress. The abrupt leap in the movie's thematic direction veers too far off course to hold up.

The approach becomes heavy-handed and over-simplistic, the tone smug and self-congratulatory. The end result is a second half which plods along dully and slowly, dragging its feet while the audience members restlessly shuffles theirs.

As a whole package, however, the film does offer a fair amount of entertainment value and features some funny moments along the way. Lingering images that leap from the mind are the Dreyfuss character leading the nation in a session of aerobic exercises, and in another scene injecting a few lines

Please see **MOON,** *Page* **A11**

The Californian

SUNDAY
September 11, 1988

STATE NATION WORLD **Digest**

PAGE **A3**

Environmental groups defend firefighting policy

Associated Press

WASHINGTON — Major environmental groups, some of them no friends of the Reagan administration, have jumped to the defense of federal forest firefighting policies attacked by some western members of Congress.

Sen. Malcolm Wallop, R-Wyo., last week suggested that William Penn Mott, director of the National Park Service, be fired for following a "let it burn" policy in Yellowstone National Park.

Environmental spokesmen compared Wallop to "Alice in Wonderland," accused him of grandstanding and called his suggestion ridiculous.

Members of Congress who lead the committees overseeing the parks, also heavily critical of the administration at times, defended the firefighting policy.

"I applaud the president and the secretary (of the interior) for standing firm" against Wallop's suggestion, said Paul Pritchard, president of the National Parks and Conservation Association and a critic who has rarely applauded them for anything.

"Those who jump up in the midst of a major catastrophe and cry bloody murder and 'Off with their heads' remind me of Alice in Wonderland," Pritchard said.

Interior Secretary Donald P. Hodel, one of the three-member inspection team sent by President Reagan to Yellowstone over the weekend, has called the firefighting policy a "disaster."

The "disaster" remark was clearly intended as "hindsight," said spokesman Alan Levitt, and Hodel stands by an earlier statement that what the park service and other agencies "need now is our understanding of the difficulties they face and our support."

"There's been a lot of inaccurate information. Because of the drought, these fires are going to get away from you no matter what the policy is."
Tim Mahoney, Sierra Club

The Park Service since 1972 has followed a so-called "let it burn" policy which fights forest fires caused by humans and natural fires that threaten human lives and property, but lets most natural fires burn for the benefits they bring to forest regeneration.

A century of fuel buildup from suppressing fires — Yellowstone was declared a park in 1872 — are worsening fires today, some suggested.

"There's been a lot of inaccurate information passed around," said Tim Mahoney of the Sierra Club. Because of the drought, "These fires are going to get away from you no matter what the policy is."

Sen. Dale Bumpers, D-Ark., chairman of the national parks subcommittee of the Senate Energy and Natural Resources Committee, toured Yellowstone in August.

"I don't mind telling you I was glad to get out of there" because of the fire danger and the fuel buildup, said Bumpers on Friday. "There were as many trees on the ground as there were standing."

"The fire management policies of the Park Service and the Forest Service are sound, flexible and scientifically based. We support them," said a statement by George Frampton, president of the Wilderness Society.

"We think the calls for Mott to resign are ridiculous," said Robert SanGeorge, spokesman for the National Audubon Society in New York.

"Though we don't favor letting people's houses burn down, we're concerned that (calling for Mott's dismissal) would be the popular thing to do to respond to people who are concerned about their property," SanGeorge said. "Politics should not intrude on biology."

STATE

▲ Bentsen blasts 'popgun war'

SAN DIEGO — Democratic vice presidential candidate Lloyd Bentsen said Saturday that illegal narcotics flooded the nation while Vice President George Bush directed a botched "popgun war" against drugs. "The vice president talks tough on drugs, but while he has been talking, America has [illegible] at an outdoor rally attended by several hundred supporters. "The ultimate irony of the Reagan-Bush popgun war on drugs is the role of the vice president," Bentsen said. "They asked him to lead the battle, and he blew it."

◄ Wins suit

CHICO — George Neary, a rancher from the Chico area (shown in a file photo), has won a $7 million libel award from the University of California and three University of California at Davis veterinarians. Neary claimed the three veterinarians purposely falsified their reports about the 1978-79 death of 500 of the cattle on his ranch. This, he said, was after state veterinarians sprayed the animals with toxaphene to fight what they said was a feared outbreak of scabies mites.

Red Cross appeals for flood aid

LOS ANGELES — The consul general of Bangladesh appealed to Californians to fund Red Cross efforts to help her nation, which has been three-quarters submerged under flood waters that have killed hundreds. "The numbers affected are so large, the need so overwhelming that individuals may think they cannot help," consul general Nancy Bretzfield said in a statement released by the local American Red Cross. "But each and every person contributing to the Red Cross will have an impact," she said. At least 25 million of Bangladesh's 110 million people are homeless and more than 1 million of the flood victims have turned to the Red Cross or Red Crescent for help, said spokesman Ron Farina.

Swaggart draws small crowd

OAKLAND — Louisiana evangelist Jimmy Swaggart drew a crowd of about 2,000 to the Oakland Coliseum Arena, and 103 of the bunch stepped forward to pay $100 each for a handshake with the minister forced from the pulpit after charges of regularly visiting a prostitute. Swaggart returned to the pulpit in May, after a three-month suspension from the Assemblies of God denomination. He never confirmed or denied the prostitute charges, but in a televised service he apologized for having "sinned" and begged his family's and viewers' forgiveness.

NATION

▲ Boy in a bubble

PORTSMOUTH, N.H. — Sean Barrett, 5, of Dover, N.H., sits and holds his breath inside a soap bubble during the weekend Bubble Festival held at the Children's Museum.

▲ Florence claims life

NEW ORLEANS — Joseph Clark finds his lost dog Babes Saturday in the rubble left by Hurricane Florence in Bucktown, a suburb of New Orleans. The remnants of Florence pushed into Mississippi on Saturday as thousands of Gulf Coast residents returned home, happy to find little damage from 80 mph winds and sheets of rain. One death — that of an Alabama man who drowned Friday trying to secure a boat against the rising winds — was linked to the storm, which was downgraded a tropical depression by dawn Saturday.

Reagan pushes death penalty

WASHINGTON — President Reagan made a telephone call to a drug enforcement agent seriously wounded in the line of duty Friday and said the call makes him want to take on congressmen opposed to the death penalty in drug cases. Reagan described his telephone call to Bruce Travis, a special agent with the Drug Enforcement Administration who was shot during a drug arrest in New York City Tuesday night, as he ended a speech to the Federalist Society, a lawyers' organization. Reagan told the audience he had just received word of the shooting. "I had read some of the statements by the opposition in Congress to the death penalty amendment that was passed yesterday (expressing) sheer horror at the idea that we should be taking someone's life away in connection with drugs," Reagan said. "I would like to engage some of them in personal conversation. In fact, I'll go out of my way to do it."

Columnist Rowan out of hospital

WASHINGTON — Syndicated columnist Carl T. Rowan, who collapsed after speaking to a student audience, was released from Georgetown University Hospital Saturday after spending two nights there. Hospital officials said the cause of Rowan's collapse appeared to be heat and exhaustion. The columnist collapsed Thursday night after delivering a speech on the presidential election at American University.

Yellowstone closed

YELLOWSTONE NATIONAL PARK, Wyo. — The last hotels and campgrounds in fire-blackened Yellowstone National Park were closed as firefighters braced for high winds expected to create the worst wildfire conditions this summer. "Our weather for the next few days is really what everything is going to hinge on," U.S. Forest Service official Brian Avery said.

▲ Miss America crowned

ATLANTIC CITY, N.J. — Gretchen Carlson of Anoka, Minn., Miss America 1988, is crowned by former Miss America Kaye Lani Rae Rafko Saturday night. Carlson, a self-assured performer who wants to be a Harvard-trained lawyer, became the first classical violinist to win the Miss America crown in a close contest that needed two polls of the judges.

WORLD

Police clash with protesters

BUENOS AIRES, Argentina — Police fired rubber bullets and water cannons to break up an anti-government rally of 20,000 during a nationwide general strike. Labor leaders called for another work stoppage Monday. The clashes with police, vandalism, burning of cars and looting of stores resulted in dozens of injuries and arrests during the walkout Friday protesting spiraling inflation and unemployment. The unrest made the General Labor Confederation's 12th general strike strike against the nearly 5-year-old government of President Raul Alfonsin the most disorderly and bloody. Labor leaders and police blamed each other for the violence.

▲ Pope on pilgrimage

HARARE, Zimbabwe — Pope John Paul II, shown with Zimbabwean President Robert Mugabe, arrived in Harare today on the first leg of a pilgrimage to five black-ruled nations bordering racially-troubled South Africa. Before leaving Rome on the 10-day journey, the pontiff said he hopes he can help solve some of white-led South Africa's problems on a future trip there. His fourth journey to Africa and his 39th abroad will be to Botswana, Lesotho, Mozambique, Swaziland and Zimbabwe — all countries less than 20 years old that vehemently oppose South Africa but depend on it for economic survival. The Vatican said the pope was not snubbing South Africa and hoped to visit the country in the future.

▲ Novel flood protection

DHAKA, Bangladesh — A Dhaka resident has a novel way to protect his car. Dhaka's streets have gone under several feet of flood waters and boats have replaced autos as a means of transportation. The floods that inundate this poor, overpopulated nation with deadly regularity are a combination of man-made and natural phenomena. This year's deluge — the most devastating in memory — has claimed more than 600 lives by government count and more than 1,400 according to newspapers. It has submerged three-quarters of the country, spawning disease and destroying homes, roads, bridges, schools and food warehouses. From the air, Bangladesh looks like a large brown sea with atolls where the map shows cities, towns and villages.

PEOPLE

◄ Proud papa

Lorenzo Lamas, star of the prime-time soap opera "Falcon Crest," and his girlfriend, actress Daphne Ashbrook, have become the parents of a girl. Ashbrook gave birth to the couple's first child Tuesday in Los Angeles. They named her Paton Lee Lamas. Lamas, the son of film star Fernando Lamas, and Ashbrook met on the soap opera

◄ Wants protection

Roger Galbraith, accused of breaking into Chris Evert's home in West Palm Beach, asked that the second year of his probation be dropped, but the tennis star said he still writes her in apparent violation of his sentence. "I hope that they can have some sort of protection for me, like a restraining order," Evert said. The break-in was last June.

▲ On location

Actress Tyne Daly confers with producer-director Shari Cookson during taping in Los Angeles of an upcoming Lifeline Cable TV documentary, "Gangs: Not My Kid." It premieres Oct. 12.

Nearly killing herself

Olympic gymnast Cathy Rigby says that while she was competing in 1968 and 1972, she was nearly killing herself with bulimia, an eating disorder. "I was driven to impress other people," said Rigby to a Drury College audience. "With this attitude, it guaranteed I would feel good inside only if somebody else praised me." Rigby, an actress, singer and sports commentator for ABC-TV, said she eventually overcame the compulsion with the help of husband, Tom McCoy.

Successor to Sills

Beverly Sills' successor as general director of the New York City Opera will be conductor Christopher Keene, who served as the company's music director. The opera's board appointed Keene "with great enthusiasm," said Martin Oppenheimer, vice chairman of the board. Sills, 59, announced in May that she would resign effective Jan. 1 as general director of the nation's second-largest opera company.

The Californian

WEDNESDAY
September 14, 1988

Sports

SECTION **B**

FANFARE

▲ Fans in Phoenix

Burt Nye and Jim Chandler, both Phoenix residents, adjust their TV antenna in Sun Devil Stadium prior to Monday night's NFL game between the Phoenix Cardinals and the Dallas Cowboys. Despite an average ticket price of $38 — highest in the league — 67,139 fans attended the game. There were 5,036 no-shows.

End of ► the road

Sarah Fulcher, a 26-year-old distance runner, enters Anaheim Stadium during halftime of last weekend's game between the Los Angeles Rams and the Detroit Lions. Fulcher was completing a one-year marathon in which she covered 26 miles a day to help raise $3 million for the United State Fitness Academy. Her journey covered the perimeter of 35 states.

▲ Drive carefully

A bus leaving the main press center in Seoul, South Korea Monday, the area where most of the international print media is headquartered during the Olympics, is seen carefully making its way around security spikes located at one of the facility's exits. Heavy security is in force at all Olympic area sites. More/**B6**

▲ Cooling it

U.S. Olympic platform diver Wendy Williams cools her knee with ice bags after taking part in a training session with the U.S. team at the Olympic Swimming Pool in Seoul, South Korea. Williams has been suffering from tendonitis in her right knee.

▲ Grand slam

Jim Rice of the Boston Red Sox (center) is congratulated by teammates Mike Greenwell, right and Larry Parrish after hitting a grand slam home run off Baltimore Orioles pitcher Pete Harnish in the third inning Tuesday night at Fenway Park. More/**B2**

▲ Heavy hitter

Jose Canseco of the Oakland Athletics, hoping to become the first baseball player to hit 40 home runs and steal 40 bases in the same season, hit his 39th homer of the season against Texas last night. He later stole his 37th base.

Reuschel continues mastery of Padres

By Boyce Garrison
Californian correspondent

"It (Rick Reuschel's pitching performance) was nothing unusual. He pitches like that every time out. He would already have 20 wins if we'd scored some runs for him."
Giants manager Roger Craig

SAN DIEGO — Who needs youth, when experience and savvy get the job done?

San Francisco's 39-year-old right-hander, Rick Reuschel, continued his season and lifetime mastery over the Padres with a seven-inning, seven-hit performance, to give the Giants a 4-1 victory last night at San Diego Jack Murphy Stadium.

Reuschel improved his season mark to 18-8, and his record against San Diego to 4-1 in 1988. Lifetime, he owns a 19-8 advantage vs. the Padres.

"It was nothing unusual," said Giants manager Roger Craig. "He pitches like that every time out. He would already have 20 wins if we'd scored some runs for him. If I was a young pitcher, I'd follow him around and watch every move he makes. He's amazing."

A crowd of 10,477 saw the Padres take an early 1-0 lead, but Reuschel's offspeed pitching tamed the Padres' bats until he turned over the reigns to former Padre Craig Lefferts, who worked the final two innings for his eighth save.

"Our bats had a slight touch of the flu," said Padre manager Jack McKeon. "We'll get the doctor to take a look at them. They'll be all right, though."

The Padres got the run off Reuschel in the first. Marvell Wynne led off with a single to left center, then tagged up and went to second on Roberto Alomar's foul fly to the Padres' bullpen in left field. Carmelo Martinez followed with a sinking liner to Candy Maldonado in right field. Maldonado tried a basket catch, but dropped the ball for an error.

Wynne went to third on the play, then scored on John Kruk's single to right center. Reuschel got out of the inning by getting Keith Moreland to line out to third and Benito Santiago to ground out to third. The run was still earned, but that was it offensively for the Padres.

"I just let them put the ball in play," Reuschel said. "I got some great plays behind me; (Mike) Aldrete throwing the guy out at home. I either get 'em out or I don't get 'em out. Tonight I got 'em out."

After Padre starter Ed Whitson retired the first 10 batters, Robby Thompson ended the no-hitter by smashing a 3-2 pitch over the left center-field wall to even the score.

The Giants took the lead for good in the fifth. Ernest Riles led off with a single up the middle that almost took Whitson's head off. Riles scored the go-ahead run on Kirt Manwaring's double off the left field wall. With one out, Reuschel blooped a single to left to send Manwaring to third. Whitson loaded the bases by hitting Brett Butler, and gave up a sacrifice fly to Thompson to make it 3-1.

"The only bad pitch I made all night was to Thompson," Whitson said. "I hung a 3-2 slider to him and he hit it out."

Please see **PADRES**, Page **B4**

Michael Darden *The Californian*

Mike Nalu of Valhalla looks for a teammate to pass to while being guarded by Rich Calder of Monte Vista in Grossmont League water polo action Tuesday.

Monarchs hold off Valhalla in water polo opener

Californian staff report

WATER POLO

The teams favored to win the Grossmont League water polo championships opened the season against one another Tuesday afternoon.

The 3A Monte Vista Monarchs prevailed over the visiting 2A Valhalla Norsemen 13-8 in the nonleague battle of East County powers.

In other matches Tuesday, El Cajon Valley surprised Granite Hills 11-10 at Montgomery Middle School, Mount Miguel nipped Grossmont 12-11, and Helix fell to Mount Carmel 12-9. The El Capitan-Santana match was not reported.

Junior Mike Poulson led the Monarchs' offensive surge with six goals, while sophomore John Farinsky turned in a brilliant game in the Monte Vista nets with 16 saves.

Keith Saward and Mike Nalu each had three goals apiece to lead Valhalla.

Jason LeBlanc sparked El Cajon Valley's upset of Granite Hills with a five-goal scoring spree. Mackie Fujita added three tallies for the Braves, who were picked to finish third in the Grossmont 2A race.

Jake Gaeir copped high-point honors with seven goals for the Eagles, who are expected to challenge Monte Vista for the 3A league crown.

Mount Miguel junior Mike Vannoy scored with 20 seconds remaining to break an 11-11 tie. His goal came after the Foothillers had tied the game on Roger Mathews' goal with 1:30 left.

The Foothillers, who trailed 9-6 early in the fourth quarter, scored five goals during the final seven-minute period.

Kyle Newman had four goals to lead Mount Miguel, while Vannoy and Seth Eaton each had three. Rick Waite made 14 saves in the Matadors' nets.

Grossmont's Todd Yarbrough led all scorers with six goals.

Mount Carmel used a five-goal second period to pull away from host Helix.

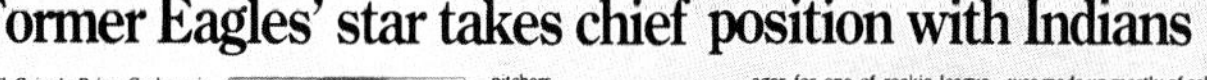

Former Eagles' star takes chief position with Indians

BILL DICKENS
Sports editor

El Cajon's Brian Graham is embarking on a new adventure in professional baseball.

"It's a promotion," said the 28-year-old Granite Hills graduate of his appointment to manage the Cleveland Indians' entry in the Florida Winter Instructional League.

This is a vote of confidence for Graham, who has been a minor league coach in the Cleveland organization for only two seasons. He assisted former major-league first baseman Mike Hargrove with the Indians' Class AA Eastern League team in Williamsport, Pa. this past summer. Graham and Hargrove worked together during the 1987 season in Kinston, N.C. of the Class A Carolina League.

In his rookie season as a manager, Graham will have a roster of 30 players and three coaches at his disposal. His coaches include former major-league pitcher Eric Rasmussen, who toiled for the Cardinals and Padres, and Bob Molinaro, who was an outfielder for the White Sox and Orioles.

"I'm looking at this as an opportunity to learn," Graham said in a telephone interview from his hotel room in Baseball City, Fla. "It's a new experience. I've always been an instructor. And now I'm the guy making the decisions."

The duties of an instructional league manager aren't exactly the same as those of a regular-season skipper.

"Winning and losing are always important when I'm involved," Graham said. "But our primary purpose down here is to develop players."

Graham is obligated to follow a masterplan designed by the Cleveland organization's upper management.

"The 30 players we have down here are basically our top minor league prospects," he said. "Fourteen of them are pitchers.

"Every player is down here working on some phase of the game. A pitcher might be learning how to throw a split-fingered fastball. Some other guys might be working on bunting, changing their batting stance, or improving their base-running."

Sometimes that means traditional baseball strategy must take a backseat.

"You might have a situation where a player wants to swing away, yet he's down here to work on his bunting. So you have him bunt.

"This is a people business," Graham said. "You are dealing with player development and people's lives as a manager. You have to be conscientious about every move you make and every decision you hand down."

Based on his rapid progression through the Indians' coaching ranks thus far, one gets the idea Graham could be around baseball for quite some time.

"Next year I'll either be a coach with our AAA team in Colorado Springs, Colo. (of Pacific Coast League), or a manager for one of rookie league teams," he said. "They haven't decided which way I'll go. But either way, I'll look at it as a promotion."

If given a preference, Graham said he'd opt for the AAA position.

"It's just one step from the big leagues," he said. "You can make a lot of contacts at that level."

And landing a job in a major-league dugout is what it's all about at this stage of Brian Graham's life.

Once a winner, always a winner. Or so it seems for Granite Hills graduate Donnie Carroll, who helped lead the Dodgers' Great Falls, Mont. rookie team to the Pioneer League championship this summer.

Carroll, the Dodgers' No.2 pick in the 1987 June draft, was the starting center fielder at Great Falls. Although he was used to hitting in the high .400s as a prep superstar, Carroll was pleased to finish his first professional campaign with a respectable .287 average.

"I was hitting over .300 before I went into a 1-for-18 slump the last 1½ weeks of the season," he said. "Our team was made up mostly of college-age players. I batted leadoff for 10 games, but most of the year I batted eighth or ninth in the order."

Carroll, who slugged only three doubles and one home run in 168 at-bats, was bothered by a hand injury part of the season.

"I messed up my hand sliding into second base," explained Carroll, who stole 25 bases in 70 games. "It was similar to the injury I had at the end of my senior year. But I still played every day. You can't afford to make excuses and miss games at this level."

Carroll and the majority of his Great Falls teammates were invited to participate in the Dodgers' winter instructional league in Mesa, Ariz., which began Monday.

"They (Dodgers' management) are comparing this Great Falls team to their 1968 rookie league team that (Steve) Garvey, (Ron) Cey, (Davey) Lopes and (Bill) Buckner played on," Carroll said. "But I don't feel any pressure from

Please see **DICKENS**, Page **B5**

AWARD OF EXCELLENCE

OVERALL DESIGN

The San Francisco Bay Guardian

Designer
John Schmitz

Art Director
John Schmitz

THE SAN FRANCISCO BAY

GUARDIAN

SEPT. 21, 1988/VOL. 22/NO. 49

THE NEWS, ARTS AND ENTERTAINMENT WEEKLY

Boz Scaggs, a.k.a. Presidio Slim

ON THE COVER:

FALL ENTERTAINMENT SPECIAL

BOZ SCAGGS' COUP

How the owner of Slim's recruited Bill Graham's ace club manager to grab a piece of the SF nightclub action

THE INSURANCE INITIATIVES:

CONSUMER REVOLT, INDUSTRY SCAMS

A no-nonsense guide to the most expensive campaign in California history

COMPUTER VIRUSES & HOW TO CURE THEM

Expert advice on protecting your computer from hidden disaster

THE $252 MILLION DRAIN

Exclusive: At least one out of five SF tenants pays rent to an out-of-town landlord, at a cost to the local economy of $252 million.

BY CRAIG MCLAUGHLIN

AT LEAST one out of every five San Francisco tenants pays rent to an out-of-town landlord, a Bay Guardian survey of rental property has concluded.

That's a conservative estimate, and probably far understates the true extent of out-of-town ownership of San Francisco rental property. Yet it still amounts to 42,000 checks every month.

At an average rent of $500 per month — and it's getting hard to find a studio in this town for that little — those checks represent $252 million that flee San Francisco every year for Bay Area suburbs, Southern California, Texas, even Hong Kong.

And unless rent controls are placed on vacant apartments, during the next ten years more than $158 million more every year will leave the city in the form of rent checks — much of it never to return.

Knowing how many of out-of-town landlords control San Francisco rental property is particularly important this election season because of the presence of a vacancy control initiative, Proposition U, on the November ballot.

In June, the Bay Guardian published the findings of a study by Community Economics, an Oakland consulting firm, that showed that continuing to allow landlords to jack up the rent on vacant apartments would cost San Francisco tenants $4.3 billion over the next nine years. The conclusions suggested that vacancy control could contribute more to the local economy every year than a downtown ballpark and the homeporting of the *USS Missouri* combined (see "The $4 billion rent control bonanza," Bay Guardian, 6/22/88).

CE director Joel Rubenzahl acknowledged that the study was limited in scope and many of the assumptions could potentially be challenged. "Some of our data and assumptions may be slightly off, and we encourage people to challenge and question them," he told the Bay Guardian at the time. "But the bottom line is, the numbers are so large that even if we're off by a huge amount in every assumption, the conclusion will almost certainly be the same."

When it published the results, the Bay Guardian echoed Rubenzahl's call for comments and criticisms, and the responses were not long in coming. Many critics questioned one of the main assumptions underlying the study's conclusions — that a significant part of the $4.3 billion that was shifted from tenants to landlords would be lost to the local economy.

One Bay Guardian reader wrote to say that the $4.3 billion dollar figure "is not a net cost to the San Francisco economy. That would only be the case if, among other things, all landlords are outside the San Francisco area, they reinvest zero percent of their revenues and none of their expenditures filter back to San Francisco."

There are other reasons why the huge transfer could hurt the local economy. One could argue, for example, that property owners are more affluent, have more savings and are more likely to tie up their money in stocks, bonds and other types of investments that slow down the flow of money around the community.

But the issue of outside ownership still remains. Owners that live in other towns are less likely to spend money in local restaurants, card shops, automobile

continued next page

THE LOCAL COST OF VACANCY DECONTROL

	1988	1989	1990	1991	1992	1993	1994	1995	1996	1997
Total number of tenants sending their rent checks out of town	42,000	42,000	42,000	42,000	42,000	42,000	42,000	42,000	42,000	42,000
Cumulative number of tenant moves since 1988	0	6,000	11,143	15,551	19,329	22,568	25,344	27,723	29,763	31,511
Tenants presumed to move this year	6,000	5,143	4,408	3,778	3,239	2,776	2,379	2,040	1,748	1,498
Average monthly increase in unit rents	$400	$400	$400	$400	$400	$400	$400	$400	$400	$400
Total yearly increase in rent	$28,800,000	$24,686,400	$21,158,400	$18,134,400	$15,547,200	$13,324,800	$11,419,200	$9,792,000	$8,390,400	7,190,400
Cummulative rent increase since 1988	$28,800,000	$53,486,400	$74,644,800	$92,779,200	$108,326,400	$121,651,200	$133,070,400	142,862,400	$151,252,800	$158,453,200

This chart shows that rent payments to out-of-town landlords will increase by $158 million over the next ten years if the city's policy of allowing unrestricted rent increases on vacant apartments continues. The chart relies on assumptions from an earlier Community Economics study of the cost of rent control — that an average tenant moves once every seven years, and that the average rent on a two-bedroom apartment jumps $400 when it becomes vacant and rent controls come off.

MICRO FILMS

By Zena Jones

Alice

Decorum and gentility have no place in Czech director Jan Svankmajer's version of Lewis Carroll's classic, as Alice (Kristyna Kohoutova) follows the White Rabbit via a garbage can elevator rather than down a tunnel. The sinister replaces the sweet as she finds jam jars full of tacks, animals who eat their own sawdust stuff-

ing and, in an eerily funny moment, a rat who starts a fire on Alice's head to cook a meal, which even she thinks is going too far. She finds the keys to her adventures in the drawer of an old writing desk, placed always in the oddest locations. When she drinks ink she shrinks, and turns into an animated look-alike doll; when she eats tarts she starts to grow, and so it goes, an *Alice* that is creative but bizarre, maliciously stripped of its Victorian veneer. For a while the animals, insects and antique toys are intriguing, but without Carroll's magic it all becomes repetitious and palls, and definitely isn't for the kiddies. (Roxie, SF.)

The Deceivers

Oh, no! It's blunted Remington Steele meets Minorpiece Theater, as director Nicholas Meyer's muddled movie neglects to provide a necessary explanatory Thuggee preface. What *is* a Thuggee, anyway? A recipient of a Thug? Far too many confusing moments later we learn they're a cult dedicated to strangling unwary travelers in 1825 India, and British officer Pierce Brosnan prepares to infiltrate their ranks and destroy them. But, since he's about as credible as a rhinestone instead of a Jewel in the Crown, it's hard to get involved, and the heavy emphasis on massacre turns the British do-nothing attitude, suttee rites and what should have been glorious scenery into the merely incidental. Also, the Thuggees, aka Deceivers, call upon their god Kali (and make it sound like "collie") so often one almost expects Lassie to appear. Well, the film *is* a dog, and as for the implication that Brosnan learns to kill and like it, did he have to make the movie his major victim? (Regency 3, SF; Century, Oakl.)

continued page 28

Hot tickets for fall theater: Doron Tavori in *Soul of a Jew*. **See page 32.**

Painter David Greenfield: Bridging cultures in the Middle East.

THE FUTURE OF *TV GUIDE*

Fox *TV Guide*? When Rupert Murdoch bought *TV Guide* from Walter Annenberg in August, the most influential mass publication on television fell to the man whose corporation also runs the Fox TV network and several TV stations. The possibility that Murdoch's imperial interests might affect *TV Guide*'s coverage has scattered advertisers and has sent thrills up the spine of competitors. (It's been many years since anyone dared launch a rival to the 17 million circulation — second highest in the nation — magazine in the U.S.)

Readers of serious reporting on TV are also watching closely. Walter Annenberg is Reagan's best buddy, but his magazine regularly reported independently and responsibly on TV. Famed for launching the investigation of the CBS documentary on Vietnam *The Uncounted Enemy*, the magazine also published more recently a definitive account of public TV's problems. Onetime network correspondent Liz Trotta also published in the *Guide* last February a revealing account of broadcast bias called, "Why the Network Didn't Want My Exclusive on Grenada." She charged that "executive producers want sensational pictures, and their threshold for boredom is low," and that a news elite fostered a "smart-ass school of journalism that views the world from the insulated premises of country houses, fancy restaurants and chauffeured limousines."

Let's see whether network owner Murdoch wants articles like that in his new acquisition. And if not, let's see if any of the eager competitors wants to fill that gap.

— *Pat Aufderheide*

ART AND POLITICS

It's a long way from San Francisco to Israel, but painter David Greenfield is working on making that distance shorter. He just returned from a six-month stay as the artist-in-residence at Ma'alot Tarshiha, an Israeli town of 8,000 Jews and Arabs. He spent much of his time teaching visual arts to non-Jewish teenagers and working to bring Arab and Jewish children together through the study of art.

Greenfield, a graduate of University of California at Santa Cruz, has dual citizenship with Israel, and served in the Israel Defense Force from 1975-77. "It was much different to travel as an artist rather than a soldier. . . . I would like to go back, because the country needs people with more of a vision," Greenfield says. In the meantime, he'll be continuing his painting, which has been shown in galleries across the U.S. as well as in Israel, and hopes to bring an exhibit of Israeli and Palestinian art to the U.S.

— *Jean Field*

AWARD OF EXCELLENCE

OVERALL DESIGN

The Express Line

Norfolk, Virginia

Designers

Michelle Gaps, Bill Pratt

Editor

Michael Bass

Art Director

Alan Jacobson

X8 THE EXPRESS LINE, PUBLISHED BY THE VIRGINIAN PILOT AND THE LEDGER-STAR, JANUARY 4, 1989

THE BOTTOM LINE . . . THE BOTTOM LINE . . . THE BOTTOM LINE . . . THE BOTTOM LINE . . . WHAT PEOPLE ARE SAYING ABOUT TODAY'S TOPICS

THE BOTTOM LINE

THIS 'DR. LOVE' LOSES HIS LICENSE

PAY A SENATOR, SAVE THE FUTURE

BUCHANAN SOCKS IT TO BRODER

HUMAN RIGHTS IS IN FASHION NOW

THE QUOTE OF THE WEEK

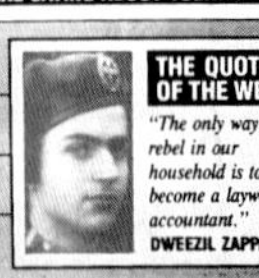

"The only way to rebel in our household is to become a lawyer or accountant."

DWEEZIL ZAPPA

ROAD WARRIOR

DON'T BELIEVE DRIVER POLLS

DR. LOVE FAILS BEDSIDE MANNER

BY KEVIN COWHERD

The Baltimore Evening Sun

FIRST QUESTION: HOW OFTEN DO YOU THINK ABOUT SEX?

NASA'S BLUEPRINT: ESTABLISH BASE ON MARS BY 2015

HOT AIR

PAYOLA

Say, brother, can you spare a dime for your senator?

BY MICHAEL BASS

Express Line Columnist

OTHER VOICES

HUMAN RIGHTS AN ISSUE

By Anthony Lewis

KEMP HAS BIG JOB

By A.M. Rosenthal

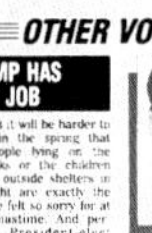

SPEAK FOR YOURSELF

By Patrick Buchanan

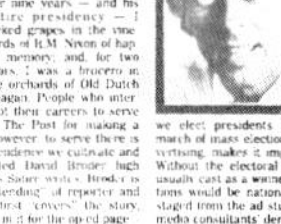

KEEP THE COLLEGE

By Edwin M. Yoder Jr.

THE EXPRESS LINE, PUBLISHED BY THE VIRGINIAN PILOT AND THE LEDGER-STAR, DECEMBER 28, 1988 X7

THE INSIDE LINE . . . THE INSIDE LINE . . . THE INSIDE LINE . . . THE INSIDE LINE . . . THE INSIDE LINE . . . A GUIDE TO THE GOOD TIMES AT HOME

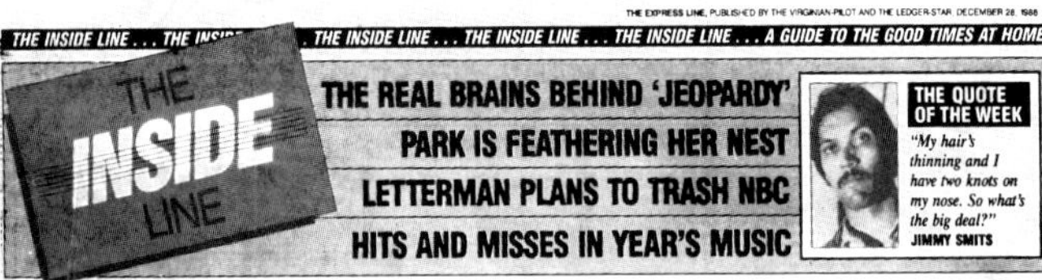

THE INSIDE LINE

THE REAL BRAINS BEHIND 'JEOPARDY'

PARK IS FEATHERING HER NEST

LETTERMAN PLANS TO TRASH NBC

HITS AND MISSES IN YEAR'S MUSIC

THE QUOTE OF THE WEEK

"My hair's thinning and I have two knots on my nose. So what's the big deal?"

JIMMY SMITS

STAR LINE

A SPACE FOR PARK

HE SMELLS FUNNY

LEGAL EAGLE

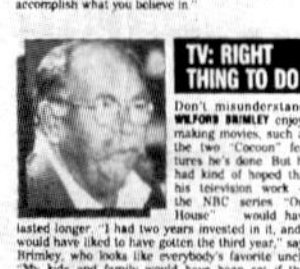

TV: RIGHT THING TO DO

THEY AIM TO TEASE

'Jeopardy' writers tickle brain cells

BY LEWIS BEALE

Los Angeles Daily News

THE TOP TEN

	Television Shows		Video Rentals
1	THE COSBY SHOW NBC	1	BEETLEJUICE Warner
2	A VERY BRADY CHRISTMAS CBS	2	THREE MEN AND A BABY Touchstone
3	A DIFFERENT WORLD NBC	3	E.T. THE EXTRA-TERRESTRIAL MCA
4	CHEERS NBC	4	ABOVE THE LAW Warner
5	ROSEANNE ABC	5	BILOXI BLUES MCA
6	WHO'S THE BOSS? ABC	6	COLORS Orion
7	GOLDEN GIRLS NBC	7	SHOOT TO KILL Touchstone
8	L.A. LAW NBC	8	THE SEVENTH SIGN RCA-Columbia
9	MURDER, SHE WROTE CBS	9	MOONSTRUCK MGM/UA
10	DEAR JOHN NBC	10	FUNNY FARM Warner

TV PRIME PICKS

ICE CAPADES WITH KIRK CAMERON

Thursday, 8 p.m., ABC

L.A. LAW

Thursday, 10 p.m., NBC

CINEMAX SESSIONS: ROY ORBISON & FRIENDS

Friday, 7 p.m., Cinemax

PERFECT STRANGERS

Friday, 8 p.m., ABC

MOVIE: THE SOUND OF MUSIC

Friday, 8 p.m., NBC

HAPPY NEW YEAR U.S.A.

Saturday, 10 p.m., PBS

DICK CLARK'S NEW YEAR'S ROCKIN' EVE

Saturday, 11:30 p.m., ABC

HAPPY NEW YEAR, AMERICA

Saturday, 11:30 p.m., CBS

TV LINE

DANSON CHEERS UP NBC EXECS

WEEK OF JAN. 4 - JAN. 10, 1989

V

THE EXPRESS LINE

EXTRA! EXTRA! SPECIAL YEAR-IN-REVIEW ISSUE

OREL FIXATION *Hershiser's 56 shutout innings was one of sport's remarkable numbers/***X10**

THUMBS UP *Siskel & Ebert list their 10 best flicks of the year/***X5**

HERE'S THE BEEF *Thin was out in '88 as television celebrated the year of the fatso/***X7**

'TIS THE SEASON TO BUY A NEW AUTOMOBILE/PAGE X17

TELEVISION

HEFTY ASSIGNMENT

There's good news and bad news for **TOM BOSLEY.** First, the good news: NBC has ordered an additional three segments of his "Father Dowling Mysteries." That means he can draw a steady paycheck without hawking Hefty trash bags. Now the bad news: Bosley will be stuck in Denver through March shooting the additional episodes. "That doesn't make my wife and kids — or me — very happy," says the 61-year-old actor. "My wife has to stay in L.A., because she can't take the altitude here. I'm missing my grandson's development. He's a year old. When I left at Thanksgiving, he was just beginning to crawl. And now he's running."

MORE TELEVISION NEWS, PAGE X7

MOVIES

WAKE UP TO MAKEUP

If Santa Claus were a movie mogul, **BETTE DAVIS** would ask him to put the role of cosmetics queen Helena Rubenstein under her tree. "There is a great book on her," says Davis. "But I cannot sell the idea to anybody because all the men say, 'Who is interested in a woman who made cosmetics?' " Well, just to play devil's advocate here, who *is* interested? "A million women, that's who," says the 80-year-old Davis. "And she is fascinating."

MORE MOVIE NEWS, PAGE X5

MUSIC

A BUM RAP

Fans of soul singer **JAMES BROWN** — the Hardest Working Man in Show Business — are working hard to get their hero out of prison. Brown is facing 15 months to six years in a South Carolina jail for leading a posse of cops on a car chase. "Six years is ridiculous," say rappers Van Silk and Melle Mel, the organizers of the Free James Brown Movement. "We want people to say this is wrong. Especially rappers." Letters of support can be sent to the Free James Brown Movement, c/o Guardian Productions, 161 W. 54th St., New York, N.Y. 10019.

MORE MUSIC NEWS, PAGE X5

NEWSMAKERS

INTRIGUING PEOPLE

The most intriguing people of 1988? According to People magazine, they include **ELIZABETH TAYLOR,** George Bush, Mike Tyson and Pakistan Prime Minister Benazir Bhutto. The magazine calls Taylor "the Cleopatra of our age," and notes that the 22-year-old Tyson "vanquishes all comers in the ring only to lose badly in love." Also on the People roster were Dodger pitcher Orel Hershiser and psuedo-Durham Bull catcher Kevin Costner. And two non-humans rounded off the list: Jessica Rabbit of "Who Framed Roger Rabbit," and the Phantom of "The Phantom of the Opera."

MORE NEWSMAKERS, PAGE X3

Illustrations by Jeff MacNelly

WAR ON SCUZZ

Dave Barry reveals 1988's obscure news

BY DAVE BARRY
Knight-Ridder Newspapers

EDITOR'S NOTE: DAVE BARRY is lieutenant governor of Indiana. His most recent story was on jute.)

JANUARY

1 — In postseason college football action, a series of shocking upsets in the Rose, Orange, Peach, Sugar, Pez, Spam, Wax Fruit and Complimentary Motel Shower Cap bowls results in the national championship being awarded to the Southwest Arkansas Community College Spittoon-Licking Weimaraners.

2 — The Federal Aviation Administration bans nose-picking on flights where the cabin lights are on. A Michigan supermarket shopper encounters Elvis in frozen foods.

3 — A massive unexpected blizzard caused by the Greenhouse Effect slams into Iowa and traps an estimated 3,000 leading presidential contenders; tragically, most of them are able to survive by eating non-essential aides.

7 — Toadlike Panamanian strongman and longtime U.S. ally Manuel Noriega, speaking on Panamanian national television, says that "anyone who wants to buy some drugs should call me," adding that "I will sell you some drugs" because "I am engaged in drug trafficking." Observant U.S. foreign-policy experts begin to suspect that "something fishy" might be going on.

15 — In Chicago, a team of surgeons announce that they have successfully fitted a 57-year-old man with the world's first artificial zit.

16 — Vice President George Bush's

> "FEB. 5 — ELVIS APPEARS AT K MARTS IN VERMONT AND ALABAMA."

Please see **BARRY,** *Page* **X2**

DO YOU WANT TO KNOW A SECRET?

BY LORENZO BENET
Los Angeles Daily News

CAN'T KEEP A SECRET? You're in good company. Here's a list of some of the worst-kept secrets of all-time. These are classics that have, much to somebody's chagrin, blundered into the headlines:

■ Debbie Reynolds, everybody's favorite girl next door, was the last one let in on the affair her husband, Eddie Fisher, was having with Liz Taylor.

> "POOR GARY HART COULDN'T KEEP HIS MONKEY BUSINESS TO HIMSELF."

Of course, Fisher got his years later when Richard Burton and Taylor fell in love on the set of "Cleopatra."

■ This year's Debbie Reynolds "I was the last to know" award goes to actress Julianne Phillips, Bruce Springsteen's jilted bride who never saw her third wedding anniversary before Springsteen started flaunting his affair with backup singer Patti Scialfa.

■ Imitation may be the sincerest form of flattery, but you can bet the folks at NASA weren't patting themselves on the back when the Soviets unveiled their look-alike version of the space shuttle.

■ There is a long and colorful history of presidential politicians messing around. But poor Gary Hart couldn't keep his Monkey Business to himself and subsequently lost out on a chance at the presidency.

■ Despite denials and "no comments" galore, did anyone not know that Cybill Shepherd and Bruce Willis were brawling on the set of ABC-TV's "Moonlighting?"

■ Lorimar did its darnedest to hide how it was going to sneak the "dead" Bobby Ewing back into the CBS-TV soap "Dallas" last season. Long before the big shower scene, there was talk of creating a Bobby twin or concocting a fake death scheme.

Scriptwriters settled on the dream sequence, and grocery-store tabloids reported it before the show was broadcast. Yawn.

■ Dan Quayle's secret about how relatives and friends helped him find a spot in the Indiana National Guard to avoid being drafted into the Army unraveled like toilet tissue thrown out of a window as Quayle made the rounds on the networks during the Republican Convention. It dominated the headlines in the weeks following, but, despite the news, Bush prevailed.

NEWSLINE . . . NEWSLINE . . . NEWSLINE . . . NEWSLINE . . . NEWSLINE . . . NEWSLINE . . . NEWSLINE . . . NEWSLINE . . . NEWSLINE . . . NEWSLINE

IN THE WORLD

Two brothers arrested in ecologist's slaying

RIO DE JANEIRO, Brazil — Federal police came closer to finding the murderer of Francisco Mendes (right) last week. Two men were arrested in connection with the slaying of the famed ecologist. Brothers Aleci and Oloci Alves da Silva were captured after a gun battle with police on their family ranch in Xapuri, the jungle town where Mendes was killed two weeks ago. The men are sons of Darly Alves da Silva, a cattle rancher who was angry over Mendes' campaign to save the Amazon rain forest.

MORE WORLD NEWS/PAGE 3

IN THE NATION

Professor is charged in plane bomb threat

ALBUQUERQUE, N.M. — A college lecturer was cleared of charges he made a bomb threat on an American Airlines flight after an 11-year-old boy admitted he wrote the note and left it on the aircraft, says an apologetic FBI. Charges against Peter W. Canning, a lecturer in literature at the University of California-Berkeley, were dropped last week after the boy told the FBI he wrote the note. Canning, 40, found the note on an American Airlines jetliner, gave it to a flight attendant and was arrested by the FBI.

MORE NATIONAL NEWS/PAGE 3

IN THE REGION

Nurse held in rape of comatose patient

PORTSMOUTH — A nurse has been charged with raping a comatose patient at Maryview Medical Center, where he worked part time. David Joseph Diraimondo of the 400 block of Twin Pines Road in Churchland was freed from Portsmouth City Jail after posting bail. He was arrested last week after nurses discovered evidence of the alleged incident and reported it to hospital officials. The 28-year-old victim remains in a coma. Her condition is "stable and unchanged," hospital officials said.

MORE REGIONAL NEWS/PAGE 3

Chapter 3

News design: Winning pages show strong influence of designers

"We wanted somebody to carry the ball a little bit farther."

The news judges concurred: News design is headed in a good direction.

After they'd viewed more than 1,100 entries, judges paused to discuss what they'd seen and the trends they'd singled out in the 76 winning entries.

Many judges said that they saw the strong influence of designers and that a long battle for newsroom recognition of designers appeared to be subsiding. They also said they'd looked for work from papers that had built upon that new strength.

"We wanted somebody to carry the ball a little bit farther," said judge Rob Covey. "That's what we were in search of: something that rose above the others."

"I kept looking for surprises or things that were out of the ordinary," added judge Steve Rice. "Something to say, 'Hey, this is really special. Stop here if you haven't stopped anywhere else.' I was looking for markers along the way, a kind of reaching out and pulling you in. A kind of visual banter."

In the case of several newspapers published outside the U.S., that something was an interesting combination of generous news hole and almost magazine-like stacking of advertisements toward the back of sections.

"I think they have a more generous news space, which helped make the impact," said judge Robert Giles. "I thought there was a nice mixing of their brief columns with their main news stories. I was particularly impressed with the interiors of those sections."

Two newspapers received Silver Awards:

■ *The Orange County Register* for presentation of its sustained campaign coverage. "It's impressively comprehensive and it's planned from March until November. That's a long period of time to sustain a style, look and approach," Covey said.

■ *The Miami Herald* for the design of a business page on the anniversary of the stock market crash.

The panel of news category judges also singled out the *Detroit Free Press* for special recognition for extraordinary and innovative design work in all news categories.

"I think they stood out as a group, as a whole newspaper, not in one particular area, so it was an excellent way to acknowledge their work," said judge Jennie Palmer.

— Robin Fogel

AWARD OF EXCELLENCE
FRONT NEWS SECTION
Aftenposten
Oslo, Norway

ROLEX
Bjerke
Karl Johansgt. 31 Oslo 02-42 20 44
Prinsensgate 21 Oslo 02-42 60 50
Nedre Torggt. 11 Drammen 03-89 30 77

Aftenposten

NORGES STØRSTE MORGENAVIS

Morgenutgave. Fredag 9. desember 1988. Uke 49. Nr. 572. 129. årg. Kr. 6,00. Fly/ekspr.: Vest-/Midt-Norge kr. 7,00. Nord-Norge kr. 8,00

En hel verden tilbyr hjelp

● Sovjetisk Røde Kors ba igår kveld om internasjonal hjelp til jordskjelvofrene i Armenia. En rekke land har team klare med leger, medisiner og utstyr. Titusener av mennesker ligger døde i ruinene, hvor mange er uklart. «Tallene er store og tragiske», heter det offisielt. Uoffisielle anslag går opp til 70 000 døde.

● Byen Leninakan med 290 000 innbyggere er hardest rammet, minst halvparten av bygningene ligger i grus. Alle høyblokker er knust. Fra restene av en skole trakk soldater ut 50 døde barnekropper. Jordskjelvet rammet i skoletiden med en styrke 14 ganger Hiroshima-bomben. **Side 3 og 4**

President Mikhail Gorbatsjov og fru Raisa avbrøt igår besøket i USA og dro hjem, slik at han kan koordinere hjelpearbeidet. Byen Spitakskij (t.h.) er blant de hardest rammede.

FOTO: TASS

1 Torskekrangel

Forskere og fiskere krangler igjen om kvoter og prognoser. Til tross for det eventyrlige torskefisket i Barentshavet, vil forskerne redusere neste års fangst-kvote. Havforskningsinstituttet har mistet sin troverdighet, mener fiskernes organisasjoner. Side 6

2 Det nye Schibsted

SCHIBSTED-GRUPPEN
AFTENPOSTEN · VERDENS GANG
CHR. SCHIBSTEDS FORLAG

Schibsted-gruppen blir fra 1. januar delt i et ansvarlig selskap og et aksjeselskap. Det blir morselskap for bl.a. A/S Aftenposten. Side 21

3 Vil til OL

Bob-kjørere i Norge? Visst finnes de. Bare 40—50 i tallet foreløbig, men blikket er festet på OL i 1992 — og i 1994. Side 27

4 Bjørnepappaen

Den franske filmskaperen Jean-Jacques Annaud har laget et psykodrama sett med en foreldreløs bjørnunges redde øyne. Nå har «bjørnepappaen» vært i Oslo, hvor han røbet stor forståelse for barns kjærlighet til bamser og teddybjørner ... Side 41

ANNONSER

Ring får nei til sykehusdrift

Regjeringen sier idag nei til sykehusdrift ved Ring Medisinske Senter i Oslo. Dermed er det duket for erstatningskrav mot Staten på over 20 millioner kroner, foruten en heftig politisk strid. **Side 7**

FOTO: KNUT SNARE

Når oppsigelse er et faktum

29 år gamle Kai Henning Olsen (bildet) er en av de mange som stiller opp på arbeidsformidlingen i Oslo. Aftenposten har undersøkt hva fagforeningene gjør for arbeidsløse medlemmer. **NæringslivMagasinet**

Brann ødela for 100 mill.

Siste side

AWARD OF EXCELLENCE

FRONT NEWS SECTION

USA Today

Designer

Staff

DEMOCRATS: BEHIND THE SCENES

ATLANTA ON TV

A LOOK AT HOW TV IS COVERING THE CONVENTION

Democratic royalty focus of 1st day

BY BRIAN DONLON AND GREG KATZ

ABC wins 1st Dukakis interview on a coin toss

JENNINGS: Producer got lucky

2 surprise guests on Jackson 'caravan'

Rival camps won't join for interviews

WALLACE: Program reshuffled

NBC 'news' squeezes out average folks

Jackson-Dukakis battle swamps shows

Ellerbee joins CNN for essays this week

STYLE ON THE DIAL

Neckwear makes the news

STAHL

— Liz Sparkin

Old guard, new faces

▶ 7:30 p.m.: Election of convention chair, House Speaker Jim Wright.

▶ 8:10 p.m.: Wright introduces ex-House Speakers Carl Albert and Tip O'Neill plus former Vice President Walter Mondale.

▶ 8:29 p.m.: Washington Gov. Booth Gardner speaks on "Democratic Party Tasks: Solving Problems of Real People for the 1990s."

▶ 9:24 p.m.: Texas State Treasurer Ann Richards delivers the keynote address.

▶ 9:14 p.m.: First-graders from the Class of 2000 and Garrison Keillor lead the pledge of allegiance.

▶ 10:34 p.m.: Former President Jimmy Carter addresses the convention.

Who to watch

Dukakis interviews aren't scarce

Omni center: A tight fit for delegations

Construction crews have worked weeks to get the Omni International Center into shape for the Democratic convention. A look inside the hall:

There's little room to roam

THE SUPERDOME

MOSCONE CENTER

DALLAS CONVENTION CENTER

$825,000 A DAY

BIRD'S EYE VIEW

ON THE CLOCK

BRAVE DRAWING

It will be family week for the Dukakis clan in Atlanta

ATLANTA DIARY

by Kitty Dukakis

GETTING READY TO GO

ON THE ROAD

THE WEEK AHEAD

EMOTIONAL ROLLER-COASTER

VIA SATELLITE — THE NATION'S NEWSPAPER — 50 CENTS

USA TODAY

NO. 1 IN THE USA... 5.3 MILLION READERS EVERY DAY

BASEBALL: TWINS' VIOLA WINS 20th

LATE TRADES

BEST FEMALE ATHLETE

DIVORCING THE BOSS

NOW FILED: PHILLIPS VS. SPRINGSTEEN

NEW RULES FOR CASHING CHECKS

CRACKDOWN ON COMPANY TRIPS

THURSDAY, SEPTEMBER 1, 1988

NEWSLINE

WEATHER · WALL STREET · LABOR DAY PLANS? · PUSH FOR DEMS · CENSUS UPDATE · NATION · ABROAD · WASHINGTON · TODAY'S DEBATE · MONEY · SPORTS · LIFE · WEEKEND EDITION

Luck, lessons save 94 lives

'There must be a God'

How crash occurred, 6A; air safety, 9A

Genes tied to another cancer

Solidarity edges toward recognition

COVER STORY

'You hope you weren't going to die'

USA SNAPSHOTS

Question of taxes

Defusing 'sticker shock'

Call 1-800-USA-0001 . . . And get 6th Anniversary Savings with USA TODAY

AWARD OF EXCELLENCE

FRONT NEWS SECTION

The Detroit News

Designers

Dale Peskin, Nancy Hanus,
Beth Reeber, Tim Finn

ACCENT: Dr. Etiquette helps give bad breath the brush-off 1C

DRIVER'S SEAT
GM exec Roberts on track at Navistar 1D

TIGERS FALL 5-3
Offense sputters; Royals hold on 1E

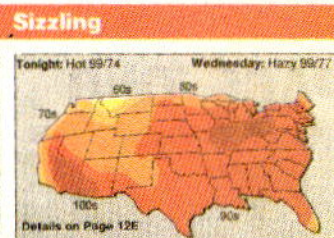

Tuesday
August 2, 1988

The Detroit News

15¢

BRIEFLY
IN THE NEWS

Pack up the cooler; the heat's back on

Female bishops approved

Farewell to formaldehyde

The trouble with Angels

Maybe Mickey will go bald

Today's primary

INSIDE

CARDINAL JOHN DEARDEN 10/15/07 - 8/1/88

A people's cardinal dies

"I am done. With God's help, I have kept my promise. This, I think, is all that I promised to do when I began this huge work."

Dearden years: Time of glory, grief

URBAN LEAGUE CONVENTION

Dukakis talk stresses civil rights

Court upholds ban on roadside sobriety tests

Thousands apply for prepaid tuition plan

IN WEDNESDAY'S FOOD SECTION: Flour power and the quesadilla revolution

NEWS
IN BRIEF

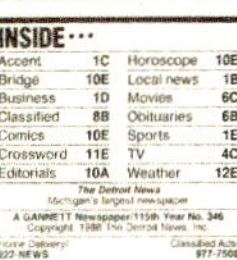

NASA works to fix Discovery fuel leak

U.S., Philippines set to resume talks

Teens kick up heels as dance ban ends

Carlucci challenges Soviets

Asks for proof of defensive military strategy

NEWS FOCUS
THE WEST BANK

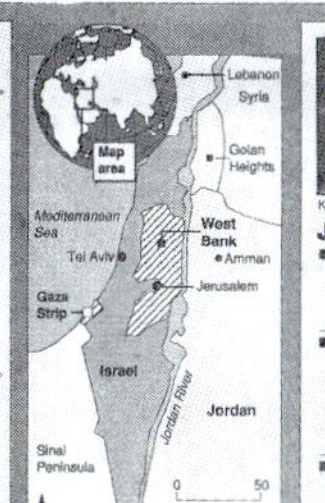

The West Bank

Jordan

Jordan's move puts peace in limbo

U.S., Israel left to deal with PLO

8 Arabs expelled from Jerusalem

Medically fit for job of president, Bush says

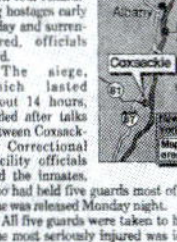

Guards freed as prison siege ends in N.Y.

Drive to crush Mafia is failing

Key official blames Italian bureaucracy

Burrowed in

AWARD OF EXCELLENCE

LOCAL NEWS SECTION

Star Tribune

Minneapolis, Minnesota

Metro/State news

Star Tribune Monday July 4/1988 **1B**

All fired up for the Fourth

Staff Photo by Brian Peterson

Fireworks from the Taste of Minnesota burst over the State Capitol and St. Paul Cathedral Saturday night.

St. Anthony Park is small-town enclave within urban setting

By Jean Hopfensperger
Staff Writer

For more than 30 years, residents of the St. Anthony Park neighborhood have held their own down-home July 4th bash. The highlight always is a ragtag parade down Como Av., consisting of kids pedaling crepe-paper-decorated bikes, an oompah polka band, local scout troops, budding baton twirlers and a school board member or politician perched on the back of a convertible.

This year, however, there is one contemporary addition. A lawn mower brigade, a group of men pushing their grass cutters, will perform drill team maneuvers in an attempt to make rain.

The parade is a throwback to the 1950s, and in some ways, so is the tiny St. Paul neighborhood that nudges Minneapolis. Designed originally as a suburban addition to Minneapolis and St. Paul, the neighborhood today is more like a small town, complete with its own theater company, arts forum, community gardens, thriving little downtown and dozens of community projects run by hundreds of volunteers.

And as the nation celebrates its independence today, so St. Anthony Park celebrates more than 100 years as one of the Twin Cities' most

Neighborhood continued on 4B

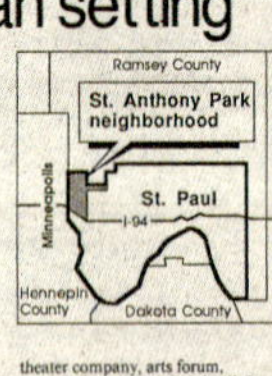

Staff Photo by Brian Peterson

Maya Verjovsky, 4, watched as Paul Carlson, 4, prepared his bicycle for St. Anthony Park's July 4th parade, a ragtag event that features residents of the St. Paul neighborhood and often gets a bit corny.

Poss' big-city skills, savvy benefit small city of Blaine

By Cheryl Johnson
Staff Writer

It was December 1985 when Don Poss, the man who built the Humphrey Metrodome, was last in the local headlines.

He was recommended as the man who could build Minneapolis' world-class convention center, the man who could make the city look good by bringing that project in on time and under budget, as he had done with the Metrodome in 1982 while executive director of the Metropolitan Sports Facilities Commission.

Poss passed and joined a private company.

Now the man whose high-profile resume includes a stint as vice president of Dolphin Inc., the Miami Dol-

Poss continued on page 3B

Don Poss

Flight instructor, student die in crash in Ham Lake

A flight instructor and his student were killed Sunday afternoon when their single-engine plane nose-dived into a swampy area in Ham Lake about 5 miles from the Anoka County Airport in Blaine.

"I was the first person here," said State Patrolman Paul Straka, "and there was nothing I could do for them."

The propeller and nose of the Piper Tomahawk was partially buried in the spongy soil. It took Straka and several other officers about two hours to cut away the twisted metal and remove the bodies.

The Anoka County Sheriff's Department said that the men's names would not be released until today because their relatives had not been contacted yesterday. They were in

Crash continued on page 4B

Barbara Flanagan

What may be the best Minnesota song yet is on the soundtrack of a new video to promote **Celebrate Minnesota 1990**, our first all-state homecoming party. The tune, **"This is a Production that is Home Made,"** is by **Art Novak**, creative director of **Martin/Bastian Inc.**, 1128 Harmon Place in Minneapolis.

Amateur singers join with the six-member group **Essentially Jazz** to sing it, and it's great. Just ask your favorite radio station to play it soon.

■

On the subject of parties, **Curt and Arleen Carlson's** golden wedding was a party to be remembered.

To begin, their children and grandchildren borrowed a 51-year-old Ford coupe, decorated it with flowers and tin cans, then parked it at the front door to give the Carlsons and some of the guests happy memories of their wedding 50 years ago on June 30, 1938.

In a car just like it, the newlywed Carlsons drove to **Yellowstone Park** for their honeymoon. Curt couldn't remember what kind of mileage he got, but Arleen recalled that they had pleasant weather.

At the outdoor dinner dance the Carlsons greeted some 200 guests on the terrace at the home of their daughter and son-in-law, **Barbara** and **Edwin (Skip) Gage**, who live down the road from them. Most of those invited were Minnesotans as well known as the Carlsons. Guests included **Lola** and **Gov. Rudy Perpich**; **Eleanor** and **Gov. Elmer L. Andersen**; **Rose** and **Jay Phillips**, who will celebrate their 71st wedding anniversary in August and who also brought long-distance greetings from two Californians — their son, **Morton**, and daughter-in-law, advice columnist **Abby Van Buren**; **Helen** and **George Wilson**, retired head of the **Billy Graham Association**, who passed along Graham's good wishes; **Eloise and Carl Pohlad**; **Virginia** and **Jim Binger**; **Sally** and **George Pillsbury**; **Joan** and **Don Stolz** of the **Old Log Theater**; the **Rev. David T. Scoates**, the Carlson family's pastor at **Hennepin Av. United Methodist Church**, and his wife, **Vonda Kay**, a former **Miss America**; **Margaret** and **DeWalt Ankeny Jr.**; **Luella** and **Dr. Stanley Goldberg**; **Mig** and **Dr. John Najarian**; **Cleo** and **Dick Enroth**, a former sportscaster fondly remembered as the "voice of the **Minneapolis Lakers**;" **Carol** and **Herb Bloomberg**, who created the **Chanhassen Dinner Theatre**; **Carol Ann** and **Harvey Mackay**; **Martha** and **Brooks Fields** of **Canterbury Downs**; **Bruce Dayton** and **Ruth Stricker**, director of **the Marsh** fitness spa in Minnetonka; **Karen** and **Stan Hubbard**; **Virginia** and **Harry Piper Sr.**; **Lorraine** and **Lester Malkerson**; **Shirley** and **Phil Harris**, and many, many more.

Swedes may have outnumbered Norwegians in the crowd because of the Carlsons' activities on behalf of Swedish-American organizations, but such Norskis as **Beverly** and **Arley Bjella** and **Sue** and **Carl Platou** had great fun, too.

The Carlsons' two daughters, **Marilyn Nelson** and **Barbara Gage**, and their husbands, **Dr. Glen Nelson** and **Edwin (Skip) Gage**, put together an evening that included serenades by **Cliff Brunzell** and the famous **Golden Strings** violin ensemble that used to play in the **Flame Room** of Carlson's old **Radisson Hotel** in Minneapolis; dinner under a tent decorated with fresh roses, pink ribbons and sparkling lights; and a finale of spectacular fireworks.

Before deciding to stage a fireworks display, the children and grandchildren alerted all of their neighbors that it would be noisy for a few minutes, but they promised not to do it again for another 50 years. The neighbors were agreeable.

Many people toasted the couple and told stories about them. Gov. Perpich summed it up when he noted that the Carlsons not only have been involved in efforts to make Minnesota a better place, but they also are responsible for more than 50,000 jobs at the **Carlson Companies**, a mega-firm that includes hotels, travel agencies and restaurants. Later this month at the **St. Paul Civic Center**, the Carlsons will celebrate the 50th anniversary of the company's founding. **Bob Hope** will headline the show at that event.

At the evening's end, before all of their guests had departed, the Carlsons got into the 1937 Ford and drove up the hill to their own home. The clatter of tin cans sounded as if 1938 was only yesterday.

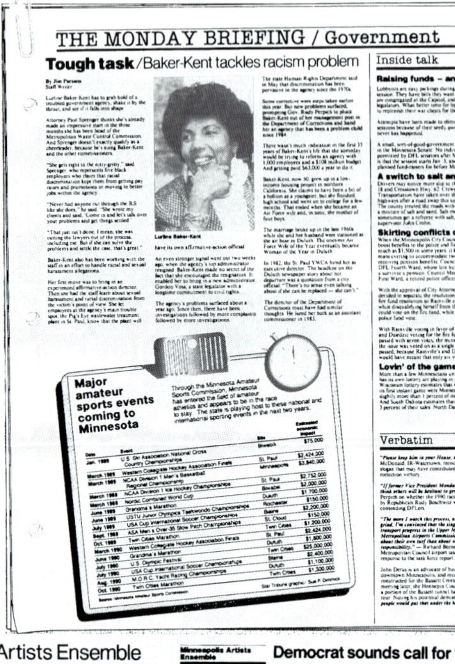

Metro/State news

Star Tribune Monday/December 5/1988

THE MONDAY BRIEFING / Government

Tough task / Baker-Kent tackles racism problem

By Jim Parsons
Staff Writer

Lurline Baker-Kent

Inside talk

Raising funds – and questions

A switch to salt and sand

Skirting conflicts of interest

Lovin' of the game

Verbatim

Major amateur sports events coming to Minnesota

Through the Minnesota Amateur Sports Commission, Minnesota has entered the field of amateur athletics and appears to be in the race to stay. The state is playing host to these national and international sporting events in the next two years:

Date	Event	Site	Estimated economic impact
Jan. 1989	U.S. Ski Association National Cross Country Championships	Biwabik	$75,000
March 1989	Western Collegiate Hockey Association Finals	St. Paul	$2,424,000
March 1989	NCAA Division 1 Men's Basketball Regional Championship	Minneapolis	$3,840,000
March 1989	NCAA Division 1 Ice Hockey Championships	St. Paul	$2,752,000
March 1989	Nordic Combined World Cup	Biwabik	$2,000,000
June 1989	Grandma's Marathon	Duluth	$1,700,000
June 1989	USTU Junior Olympics Taekwondo Championships	Rochester	$150,000
July 1989	USA Cup International Soccer Championships	Blaine	$2,200,000
Sept. 1989	ASA Men's Over-35 Slow Pitch Championships	St. Cloud	$150,000
Oct. 1989	Twin Cities Marathon	Twin Cities	$1,200,000
March 1990	Western Collegiate Hockey Association Finals	St. Paul	$2,424,000
June 1990	Grandma's Marathon	Duluth	$1,800,000
July 1990	U.S. Olympic Festival	Twin Cities	$25,000,000
July 1990	USA Cup International Soccer Championships	Blaine	$2,400,000
Aug. 1990	M.O.R.C. Yacht Racing Championships	Duluth	$1,100,000
Oct. 1990	Twin Cities Marathon	Twin Cities	$1,300,000

Source: Minnesota Amateur Sports Commission

Star Tribune graphic / Sue P. Dimmick

Artists Ensemble premieres 'Portrait'

A review

Minneapolis Artists Ensemble

Review: The ensemble gave expert performances of works by Hummel, Grieg and Rossini as well as the premiere of a deftly written work by Laura Karpman, inspired by the late jazz bassist Jaco Pastorius.

Democrat sounds call for 'real' issues

Associated Press

Democrats must make the "real" issues clear if they are to win presidential elections, West Virginia Attorney General Charlie Brown told 900 Minnesota DFLers at the annual Hubert H. Humphrey Day Dinner.

Brown, considered one of the emerging leaders of the Democratic Party,

6 escape carbon-monoxide fumes from furnace

Sixth in family dies of injuries from N.D. crash

AWARD OF EXCELLENCE
LOCAL NEWS SECTION
The Orange County Register
Santa Ana, California
Designer
Staff

B2 The Orange County Register Friday, May 20, 1988

Orange County Life

COMMUNITY CLOSE-UP: DANA POINT

NEWSMAKER

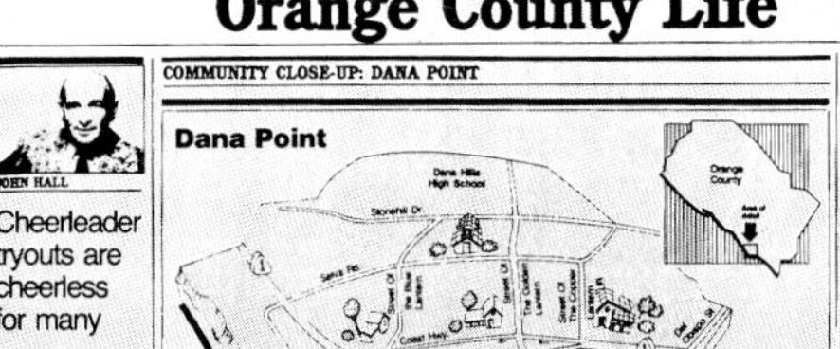

JOHN HALL

Cheerleader tryouts are cheerless for many

Official still has hope for river project

CURIO

ORANGE COUNTY BRIEFLY

B section The Orange County Register Friday, December 23, 1988

Metro

BOB EMMERS

Illuminating traditions of Christmas

I love Christmas because Christmas is a time to observe traditions. For instance, in our house we just finished observing the annual Untangling of the Christmas Tree Lights.

First, of course, we had to get the Christmas tree. Getting the Christmas tree is a ritual that women just don't understand.

We were driving home. "Let's stop at Vons and pick up a tree," Betty said.

"WHAT!" I shouted, nearly swerving into a bunch of carolers. "Get a Christmas tree at a SUPERMARKET??"

When I was a kid my father would take me over to Tait's farm. We'd pay the man a fee, then hike up the mountain in the snow and scout through the forest until we found the perfect tree. It was like a Currier and Ives print. I explained all this to Betty.

"So?" she said.

"So that's WHY I don't want to go to any stupid SUPERMARKET for a TREE," I explained. "At least if I go to one of those tree lots I can have the illusion of stalking the tree. Like when I was a kid. But you go to a supermarket and getting a tree has all the romance of buying a can of peas. See what I mean?"

"*Stalking* the tree?" is all she said.

In the end we did stop at a lot and I got to walk around and get real nostalgic, although this was somewhat difficult inasmuch as the attendants wore shorts and sunglasses and called each other dude. We took a tree home.

Now, there's one thing I just don't understand about relationships between men and women. ... Well, there are any number of things I don't understand about relationships between men and women, but what I'm specifically talking about in this case is WHY IS IT ALWAYS THE MAN'S JOB TO PUT UP THE TREE AND THE LIGHTS? You do all the hard work, then the woman comes by and tosses a couple red balls and some tinsel on the tree and takes credit for the whole thing. It's just not fair.

I got out my Christmas tree tools — machete, pliers and hammer — and set to work on getting the tree into one of those stands with the four little screws that you screw in to hold the tree up. You screw in one screw a little and then another one, and after about half an hour you finally have the tree straight. Whereupon the whole stand immediately falls apart. Whoever invented the damned thing ought to be condemned to 30 years of listening to the world's worst Christmas song ever recorded, Elvis singing "Oh, Come All Ye Faithful" in Latin.

Sweating and cursing, I finally got the tree upright and into the living room. "It looks great," Betty said sweetly. "I guess you'll make it straight later. ..." Fortunately, I was carrying no blunt instruments at the time.

I got the lights out. The lights, of course, were wadded up in a giant ball. It doesn't matter how carefully you put them away after last Christmas, they always come out wadded up. A half hour later I had them untangled and laid out neatly on the floor. The dogs chose this precise moment to run into the living room, jump all over me, run through the lights, pick up the lights, bite the lights, turn the lights into a huge wad once again.

Curses. Barks. Shouts. Screams. Yips. Dogs running. People running. Doors slamming. More curses. General mayhem. Bob vowing never again to put up Christmas lights. Betty speaking in soothing tones.

I got the lights untangled again and strung them on the tree. I only knocked the tree over once. Finally, I was done. I reached down and plugged in the lights. ...

It's amazing. It really is. They're just colored lights hung on a dead pine tree.

Then why is it that every year when I turn them on, they bring tears to my eyes?

Bob Emmers is a Register columnist. His column appears Sundays, Mondays, Wednesdays and Fridays.

New tactic in battle over Aegean Hills

Mission Viejo Co. offers to pay for citywide vote on annexation

By Cheryl Downey
The Register

MISSION VIEJO — The Mission Viejo Co. offered Thursday to underwrite the cost of an advisory election to determine whether city residents want to annex Aegean Hills.

The company, which designed and built Mission Viejo, strongly opposes any change in the city's borders.

But the City Council, which is under no obligation to hold such an election, rejected the idea of calling one at a recent council meeting.

Two councilmen have accused the company of trying to control city political decisions through its involvement in the issue. The Register reported Wednesday that the company had asked its employees to help circulate petitions against the annexation.

An advisory election, Councilman Robert Curtis said, "would simply be an opportunity for the Mission Viejo Co. to wage a very expensive, negative and slanted campaign against the people of Aegean Hills."

Curtis grew up in Mission Viejo but lived in Aegean Hills before he moved back to the city to run for the council. Before his successful candidacy, he had been active in efforts to merge Mission Viejo and Aegean Hills — a pie-slice of land next to Mission Viejo that is home to 7,000 people.

"It's an effort to manipulate the political process, to delay the annexation proposal and to garner opposition to the proposal through a heavily funded and distorted campaign," Curtis said. "Other residents would not be able to match the financial resources of the Mission Viejo Co. Our residents would not receive a fair analysis of the issue with which to make an informed decision."

Wendy Wetzel, the company's spokeswoman, said the company certainly would participate in the election, if it were held.

"We would expect it to be an opportunity for a thorough airing of all issues, which has not been done to this point," she said.

Harvey Stearn, president of the company's California division, made the offer to pay for a November advisory election in a news release. Wetzel said the offer was directed at the City Council.

In the release, Stearn said the company had a difference of opinion with the council members.

"They apparently believe that a majority of Mission Viejo residents wouldn't object to their decision to expand and add to the community. And our polls tell us that the majority of Mission Viejo residents simply want to preserve their community the way it is," Stearn said.

Curtis said he believed the council probably would reject the company's offer. Mayor Norm Murray

Please see ELECTIONS/8

A glasnost goodbye

Ken Steinhardt/The Register

Soviet student Anya Stzunnikova, 12, and Debbie Mosman, 21, of Buena Park say their goodbyes Thursday after a brown-bag lunch at Costa Mesa's Shiffer Park. Anya was part of a group of 40 visitors from the Soviet town of Troitsk who were completing a three-day trip to Orange County. Costa Mesa families played host to the group. Earlier Thursday, the visitors got a whirlwind tour of holiday-decorated South Coast Plaza/9

$50,000 reward offered

Inmate's family seeks clues to how he died

By Dan Weikel
The Register

The family of a young man who died in the Orange County Jail infirmary offered $50,000 of its $300,000 civil settlement Thursday as a reward for information that might explain or link others to the death.

Saying there still are many unanswered questions, relatives of Arthur Oviedo offered the money at a news conference held to announce the $450,000 settlement of two wrongful-death suits against Orange County.

The Oviedos, of Santa Fe Springs, will receive $300,000 from the county, and Frank Wilcox of Darien, Conn., will get $150,000 for the death of his father, John Frank Wilcox.

Wilcox, 71, and Oviedo, 25, died 14 days apart in January 1987 after being placed in a medical-observation cell with Jerry Thomas Pick, a mentally ill inmate who had fought with other prisoners.

Pick, 26, is awaiting trial in Orange County Superior Court on two counts of murder. He is accused of strangling Oviedo with a shoestring Jan. 31, 1987, and inflicting mortal injuries to Wilcox on Jan. 17, 1987.

Members of the Oviedo family said Thursday that they are not convinced Pick acted alone. They suspect sheriff's deputies could have placed Oviedo in the medical-observation cell with Pick as punishment or that other inmates or jail staffers might have killed him.

"I don't think they have been fair in their investigation," said Susan Oviedo, Arthur Oviedo's sister. "I think he might have been put into the situation for retaliation for some reason."

Kevin McDermott, the attorney representing the Oviedo and Wilcox families, said the $50,000 reward will be given for information

Please see REWARD/8

Enrollment goes up 1.7% in OC schools

But 10 of the districts show declines for '88-'89

By William H. Kossen
The Register

Enrollment in Orange County public schools this fall rose 1.7 percent, to 350,909, an increase for the fifth straight year but below the peak of 376,304 reached in 1975, according to figures obtained this week from the county Department of Education.

Although 18 school districts posted enrollment gains over the past year, 10 experienced declines.

The increase of 5,940 students was concentrated largely in Santa Ana and in southern and eastern Orange County.

The northern and western parts of the county generally had stable or declining enrollment, although most of the school districts serving Anaheim and Fullerton posted gains.

Private-school enrollment increased by nearly 6 percent, from 39,442 to 41,699, according to the county figures.

The public-school enrollment figures are monitored closely by administrators because they determine the amount of state funding that local districts receive.

The biggest gainers were Santa

Please see SCHOOLS/8

Christmas Day

Banks
- Many banks and savings and loans will be closed Saturday; all will be closed Monday.

Government offices
- Federal offices closed Monday.
- State offices closed Monday.
- County offices closed Monday
- City offices:

Fullerton closed Saturday through Jan. 2.
Tustin closed at noon today through Monday.
Buena Park, Cypress, Garden Grove, Irvine, Placentia, San Juan Capistrano, Santa Ana and Stanton closed today and Monday.
Other cities' offices will be closed Monday only.

Schools
- Closed.

Postal service
- No mail delivery Monday.

Register delivery
- Morning edition only Monday. Evening subscribers will receive the morning paper.

Trash pickup
- Customers in Orange are asked to put their refuse out as usual; residential trash collection in all other areas will be one day late.

The Register

INSIDE

Officials believe pets discovered in freezer died of natural causes

By Carroll Lachnit
The Register

The 22 animals found last week in a Yorba Linda woman's freezer apparently died of natural causes, the county's chief of veterinary services said Thursday.

"In some animals, there were obvious causes of death," Dr. Nila Kelly said. "In none of the animals did we find any unnatural causes of death."

The results of toxicological tests being performed on some of the animals will take about six weeks to complete, she said. The animals are being examined by Los Angeles County veterinary pathologists.

Police investigating possible child endangerment discovered the frozen carcasses of 11 puppies, three cats, six kittens, a bird and a turtle in a freezer at the home of Patricia Lynn Monte on Dec. 14.

An officer also found 13 live dogs and seven live cats, which were in good condition when taken to the county Animal Shelter, Kelly said.

Police went to the home in response to a call from the county Social Services Agency, which reported possible child endangerment there.

Brea police would not say what conditions might have endangered Monte's 11-year-old son.

He was taken from the home and Monte was arrested on suspicion of child endangerment.

She was released Dec. 15 on her own recognizance.

Her son was released from county protective custody Monday, said Bob Theemling, deputy director of children's services. The roster did not indicate whether the boy was returned to his mother or to another relative, he said.

The animals have been released to Monte and members of her family, Kelly said.

"There are no signs of abuse, and we don't have the legal means or reasons to keep them," she said.

The dead cats and a representative sample of the dead puppies are undergoing necropsies, Kelly said. So far, pathologists have not found sure causes of death, but there also is no sign of abuse, she said.

She said that because the puppies died within hours of birth, "We may never have a definitive cause of death."

"There were no obvious signs of struggle or abuse," she said.

The kittens died of a common, highly contagious upper-respiratory infection, she said.

The wild bird apparently left the nest before it could fly and died

Please see ANIMALS/8

AWARD OF EXCELLENCE
SPORTS SECTION
Gazette Telegraph
Colorado Springs, Colorado
Designer
Dan Cotter

C18 GAZETTE TELEGRAPH SUNDAY, NOV. 27, 1988

OUTDOORS

Nebraska, where all signs point to . . . Pheasants

Appearances deceiving on dreary weekend hunt

Season format, antler restrictions renewed

Commission seeks sales tax, higher license fees

NOTES

Bighorn sheep society offers safari to Wyoming refuges

SPORTS

SUNDAY, NOV. 13, 1988 GAZETTE TELEGRAPH • SECTION C

SCORES

COLLEGE FOOTBALL

Cougars shoot down Air Force

Falcons won't go bowling

Mistakes doom CU in loss to NU

RALPH ROUTON

Bad luck catches up with AFA

DeBerry can't blame attitude

INSIDE

HIGH SCHOOLS

VOLLEYBALL

Coronado claims state crown

FOOTBALL

Fountain is only area survivor

SOCCER

Palmer drops heartbreaker

AWARD OF EXCELLENCE

SPORTS SECTION

The Orange County Register

Santa Ana, California

Designer

Staff

C12 The Orange County Register Thursday, Sept. 29, 1988

THE SEOUL 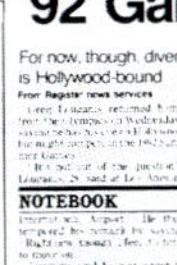 OLYMPIC GAMES

TODAY'S KEY EVENT

Women's 100-meter hurdles

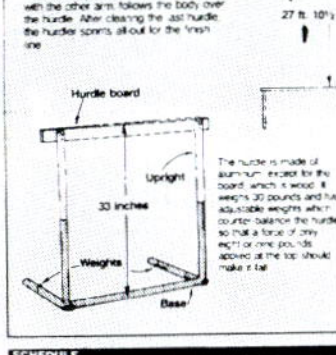

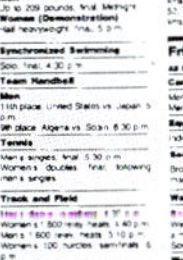

'92 Games? Louganis might

For now, though, diver is Hollywood-bound

From Register news services

NOTEBOOK

Diver Greg Louganis shows his two gold medals after returning to Los Angeles on Wednesday.

Abbott savors victory

Winter of rest next for Angels' draftee

By John Strege
The Register

US pitcher Jim Abbott leaps in celebration after the final out of the gold-medal clinching 5-3 victory over defending champion Japan.

Another US-USSR showdown

Americans, Soviets meet in water polo semifinal

By Michele Himmelberg
The Register

Gray not charged in taxi incident

C section | The Orange County Register | Sunday, November 27, 1988

Sports

Irish have Trojans' number

MARK WHICKER

Holtz works his mind magic once again

LOS ANGELES — Obviously, it's time to unleash Lou Holtz on the rest of the world.

All week the Notre Dame coach convinced the most interviewed, televised and idolized college football team in the land that it was none of the above ... that the Fighting Irish players were actually ignored, discriminated against, underrated ... that hardly anyone outside their gleefully pie-eyed cheering section in the Coliseum expected them to win.

"Coach kept telling us that we were No. 1 and USC No. 2, and how come we were four-point underdogs?" defensive end Frank Stams said later. "He said nobody was giving us any respect, that, basically, no one had all year."

Then how come the polls ... ah, never mind.

You can't beat mind control, especially when it meshes with Rodney Peete control and line-of-scrimmage control. It all came together for Notre Dame on Saturday and simultaneously landed on Peete, who walked out of the Coliseum with his left shoulder in a sling and USC's national-title hopes in a dumpster. The Fighting Irish, 27-10 victors here, now win it all if they beat West Virginia in the Fiesta Bowl on Jan. 2.

Hey, guys, what about the Fiesta Bowl?

"Can't comment," Stams said.

"I can't talk about the Fiesta Bowl," said cornerback Stan Smagala, grinning.

Holtz warmed up Friday night by suspending running back Tony Brooks and receiver Ricky Watters for continual tardiness to meetings and meals. (The players couldn't comment on that, either, at least not to any meaning-

Please see WHICKER/8

Rick Rickman/The Register

USC lineman Brent Parkinson offers a hand to hard-hit QB Rodney Peete during Saturday's 27-10 loss.

After USC mistakes open the way, No. 1 Notre Dame runs away, 27-10

By Steve Grimley
The Register

LOS ANGELES — The USC Trojans had the flashy numbers Saturday afternoon at the Coliseum. They ran more plays (84-50), piled up more yards (356-253) and made more first downs (21-8) than Notre Dame.

But the most important number still belongs to the Irish today — No. 1.

Notre Dame took advantage of second-ranked USC's dominance in another significant category — turnovers — and mixed in a couple of big plays to defeat the Trojans, 27-10, before 93,829.

It was the sixth consecutive Notre Dame victory over the Trojans in college football's longest-standing intersectional rivalry, and this one could lead to the ultimate payoff for the Irish. They will take an 11-0 record into the Fiesta Bowl on Jan. 2 against unbeaten West Virginia in what essentially will be the national championship game.

The Trojans head for the relative anonymity of the Rose Bowl with a 10-1 record, no chance for a ninth national title and a month to ponder what might have been.

What might have been if:

■ They had not committed four turnovers in the first half, including an interception returned for a Notre Dame touchdown by Stan Smagala with 41 seconds left in the half.

■ They had not broken down defensively on two plays, one a 65-yard scoring run by Irish quarterback Tony Rice.

■ They had scored a touchdown instead of a field goal in the third quarter when they had a first-and-goal at the Notre Dame 4-yard line.

■ They had protected quarterback Rodney Peete more effectively.

You get the picture. USC ran up and down the field, outgaining Notre Dame, 254-7 — that's right, 7 yards — from late in the first quarter through the third quarter. However, the Trojans kept finding a way to avoid getting into the Notre Dame end zone.

Although the Irish offense was virtually invisible for much of the second and third periods, Notre Dame avoided the turnover pitfall that undermined the Trojans. The Irish made only one mistake, a harmless second-quarter fumble by Rice.

When USC had to settle for a field goal and a 20-10 deficit late in the third quarter, the dormant Notre Dame offense suddenly came to life for a 70-yard touchdown drive to clinch it.

Forget about how it looked, Notre Dame coach Lou Holtz said. Look at the scoreboard.

"I think this team is underrated, even though we're No. 1," said Holtz, whose team was a four-point underdog coming into the game. "I've read articles that people have sent me all year saying we're lucky against this team or that team. Our football team is prettier

Please see IRISH/10

Patrick Tehan/The Register

Notre Dame coach Lou Holtz, left, watches his team run out the clock in beating USC, 27-10.

Peete separated from goals

Injured QB sees Heisman, national championship dreams shattered

STEVE BISHEFF

LOS ANGELES — Not only was he suffering from broken dreams and shattered hopes, but, in all likelihood, a separated left shoulder.

Hey, bring back the measles and the laryngitis.

After all the trials and tribulations, after all the illnesses and medications, it came down to a nice, warm, healthy, sun-splashed afternoon of opportunity.

Only Rodney Peete couldn't capitalize on it.

He tried. Oh, how he tried, playing the second half with more pain and discomfort than he cares to admit. But maybe the law of averages, as well as that overpowering Notre Dame defense, finally caught up to him.

USC lost more than just a football game on the way to absorbing that 27-10 drilling at the hands of Lou Holtz's impressive Irish here Saturday. It blew its shot at the national championship. And Rodney Peete lost whatever chance he still had at the Heisman Trophy.

"This is a tough loss to take," admitted Peete. "The seniors on this team now have to leave never having beaten Notre Dame. That's really tough to take right now."

It is a measure of this quarterback, however, that even at his darkest, most depressing hour, a ray of light — or maybe we should say a ray of courage — would come shining through.

Peete was injured just before halftime, injured more seriously than anyone in the crowd of 93,829 realized. "Yeah," admitted Erik Affholter, his best buddy and favorite receiver, who was pretty banged up himself, "I think he probably separated his shoulder a little bit."

You don't separate your shoulder a little bit. You either separate it or you don't. And all the evidence pointed to the Trojans' All-America senior playing the final 30 minutes, taking all those vicious hits, dealing with all the obvious pain, while playing with an injury that would have kept almost any other quarterback in football on the sideline.

Immediately after the play on which he was injured, a second-quarter sack by the Irish's omnipresent defensive end, Frank Stams, Peete staggered off the field, his left arm sagging noticeably, one hand tucked against his stomach.

As the rest of the Trojans sprinted into the dressing room, Rodney walked off slowly with the trainer. And while he returned and showed no apparent ill effects in the final two periods, he rarely was allowed to roll out and constantly threw the ball away, rather than attempt to scramble for extra yardage.

Afterward, as he addressed the

Please see BISHEFF/9

USC'S TURNOVERS

Chris Covatta/The Register

USC tailback Aaron Emanuel watches as Notre Dame's Frank Stams recovers his fumble, one of four Trojans turnovers.

No. 1: Fumble

At second-and-7 from its 30 with 4:01 left in the first quarter, USC committed its first turnover as tailback Aaron Emanuel was hit on the second play after Notre Dame's first touchdown and fumbled. Irish defensive end Frank Stams recovered at the USC 19, marking only the sixth fumble lost by USC all season. Five plays later, Mark Green scored and Notre Dame had a 14-0 lead with 1:49 left in the first quarter.

No. 2: Interception

Early in the second quarter, at second-and-8 from his 42, USC quarterback Rodney Peete was intercepted by strong safety George Streeter. Streeter returned the ball 23 yards to the USC 42, where Peete made possibly a touchdown-saving tackle. Two plays later, the Irish committed their only turnover of the game, as quarterback Tony Rice fumbled at the USC 22.

No. 3: Fumble

On their deepest drive yet into Notre Dame territory, the Trojans lost the ball with 7:25 left in the second quarter. Tailback Ricky Ervins fumbled at the Irish 19-yard line, and Notre Dame defensive tackle George Williams recovered. Four plays later, Notre Dame was forced to punt.

No. 4: Interception

Having cut the deficit to 14-7 and taken over at midfield after a Notre Dame punt, the Trojans suffered one of the worst stings of the day with 41 seconds left in the half. On first down, Peete scrambled to his left and passed toward John Jackson, who appeared to slip as the ball was thrown. Cornerback Stan Smagala intercepted and went 64 yards for a touchdown.

Reports of Gretzky-Ftorek rift spread as Kings lose to Flames

By Lisa Dillman
Special to the Register

CALGARY — Once again, another big event was overshadowed by ongoing reports regarding Kings coach Robbie Ftorek's handling, or mishandling, of star center Wayne Gretzky.

The focus, seemingly, should have been on this matchup between the top two teams in the league, the Kings and the Flames. Calgary, playing tight defensive hockey, won the game, 4-1, on Saturday night before a sellout crowd of 20,002 at the Saddledome and also put a stop to Bernie Nicholls' 10-game goal-scoring streak.

But news of a widening rift between Gretzky and Ftorek dominated the postgame interviews. The first hint of trouble came earlier this month in a column in a Toronto newspaper when the Kings played in Montreal. The latest problem, according to newspapers here and in Detroit, arose during the Kings' 8-3 victory over the Red Wings on Wednesday.

Ftorek benched Gretzky for almost 7½ minutes during the third period. Before the benching,

Please see KINGS/6

INSIDE

The SportsLine, (714) 953-7723

Pistons rebound to capture Round 1 against Lakers, 102-99

By Don Greenberg
The Register

AUBURN HILLS, Mich. — It was tough to figure out which was more upsetting to Coach Pat Riley after his Lakers lost, 102-99, to Detroit on Saturday night before 21,454 at The Palace: Was it the bonus basket the Pistons received between the second and third periods, or was it the late pounding on the offensive boards administered by Dennis Rodman?

Call it a jump ball. Riley was steamed about both after Detroit ended the Lakers' three-game winning streak and took Round 1 of the regular-season series between the contestants in last season's NBA Finals.

Joe Dumars hit a basket at the halftime buzzer. Rookie referee Gary Benson was emphatic in signaling the basket was no good and the Pistons had a 52-49 halftime lead. But when the prime-time CBS audience tuned in for the start of the third quarter, Detroit had a 54-49 advantage.

Riley said Ed T. Rush, the lead official, explained that the other veteran in the three-man crew,

Please see LAKERS/4

AWARD OF EXCELLENCE

BUSINESS SECTION

Aftenposten

Oslo, Norway

Illustrator

Peter Vider

Art Director

Tor Bugge

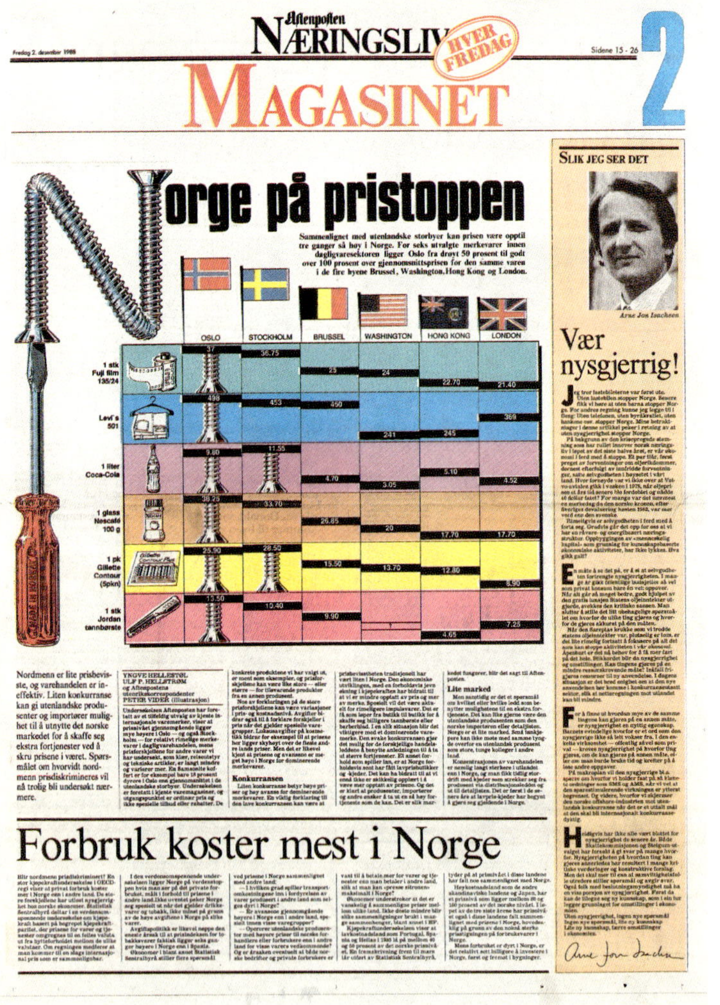

Aftenposten
NÆRINGSLIV
HVER FREDAG
MAGASINET
2

Fredag 2. desember 1988

Sidene 15 - 26

Norge på pristoppen

Sammenlignet med utenlandske storbyer kan prisen være opptil tre ganger så høy i Norge. For seks utvalgte merkevarer innen dagligvaresektoren ligger Oslo fra drøyt 50 prosent til godt over 100 prosent over gjennomsnittsprisen for den samme varen i de fire byene Brussel, Washington, Hong Kong og London.

	OSLO	STOCKHOLM	BRUSSEL	WASHINGTON	HONG KONG	LONDON
1 stk Fuji film 135/24	37	36.75	25	24	22.70	21.40
Levi's 501	498	453	450	241	245	369
1 liter Coca-Cola	9.80	11.55	4.70	3.05	5.10	4.52
1 glass Nescafé 100 g	38.25	33.70	26.85	20	17.70	17.70
1 pk Gillette Contour (5pkn)	25.90	28.50	15.50	13.70	12.80	8.90
1 stk Jordan tannbørste	13.50	10.40	9.90	[illegible]	4.65	7.25

Nordmenn er lite prisbevisste, og varehandelen er ineffektiv. Liten konkurranse kan gi utenlandske produsenter og importører mulighet til å utnytte det norske markedet for å skaffe seg ekstra fortjenester ved å skru prisene i været. Spørsmålet om hvorvidt nordmenn prisdiskrimineres vil nå trolig bli undersøkt nærmere.

YNGVE HELLESTØL
ULF P. HELLSTRØM
og Aftenpostens utenrikskorrespondenter
PETER VIDER (illustrasjon)

Konkurransen

Lite marked

Forbruk koster mest i Norge

SLIK JEG SER DET

Arne Jon Isachsen

Vær nysgjerrig!

18

NÆRINGSLIV MAGASINET

Fredag 11. november 1988 Aftenposten

Advarer mot EF-debatt

— Finn Kristensen er et aktivum for Norge! Jens P. Heyerdahl d.y. slår ut med hendene og fastslår på sitt avslepne riksmål at næringsministeren har bredere støtte for sitt forslag om et statlig investeringsfond i næringslivet enn det som er kommet til uttrykk i pressen.

ULF PETER HELLSTRØM
FRIDE FREDERSEN (foto)

Man kan ikke forvente at jeg skal svare på om jeg liker Bjørn Bettum eller ikke.

Mange bedriftsledere er positive til Finn Kristensens forslag om et statlig investeringsfond.

Jeg har vært i en konstant kampsituasjon overfor rikspolitikere.

TEKNOLOGI

Tilbake til etikken

ROLF L. LARSEN

Etikk, sikkerhet, helse og miljø er kommet på programmet hos flere bedriftsledere og teknologer. Og ungdommen søker igjen til teknologiutdannelse. I økende grad også kvinner.

Nordisk Teknologiår 1988 nærmer seg slutten. Her i landet har det båret frukter, mener mange. Året har øket folks kunnskaper om teknologi, gitt bedre forståelse for teknologiens betydning for samfunnet og det enkelte menneske, og har engasjert til debatt.

Hat—kjærlighet

Etikk

Ungdom

AWARD OF EXCELLENCE

OTHER NEWS SECTION

The Orange County Register

Santa Ana, California

Designer
Pam Marshak

Photographers
Paul E. Rodriguez,
Bill Alkofer

Art Director
Tom Porter

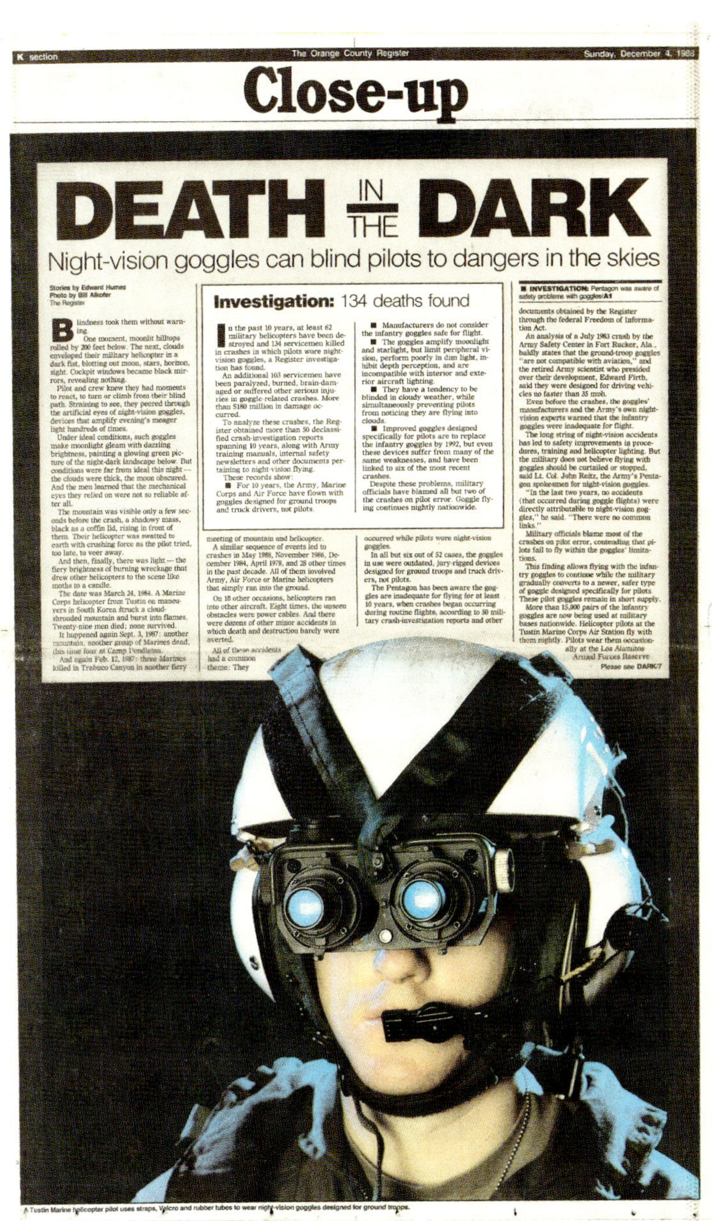

K section The Orange County Register Sunday, December 4, 1988

Close-up

DEATH IN THE DARK

Night-vision goggles can blind pilots to dangers in the skies

Stories by Edward Humes
Photo by Bill Alkofer
The Register

Blindness took them without warning.

One moment, moonlit hilltops rolled by 200 feet below. The next, clouds enveloped their military helicopter in a dark fist, blotting out moon, stars, horizon, sight. Cockpit windows became black mirrors, revealing nothing.

Pilot and crew knew they had moments to react, to turn or climb from their blind path. Straining to see, they peered through the artificial eyes of night-vision goggles, devices that amplify evening's meager light hundreds of times.

Under ideal conditions, such goggles make moonlight gleam with dazzling brightness, painting a glowing green picture of the night-dark landscape below. But conditions were far from ideal this night — the clouds were thick, the moon obscured. And the men learned that the mechanical eyes they relied on were not so reliable after all.

The mountain was visible only a few seconds before the crash, a shadowy mass, black as a coffin lid, rising in front of them. Their helicopter was swatted to earth with crushing force as the pilot tried, too late, to veer away.

And then, finally, there was light — the fiery brightness of burning wreckage that drew other helicopters to the scene like moths to a candle.

The date was March 24, 1984. A Marine Corps helicopter from Tustin on maneuvers in South Korea struck a cloud-shrouded mountain and burst into flames. Twenty-nine men died; none survived.

It happened again Sept. 3, 1987: another mountain, another group of Marines dead, this time four at Camp Pendleton.

And again Feb. 12, 1987: three Marines killed in Trabuco Canyon in another fiery meeting of mountain and helicopter.

A similar sequence of events led to crashes in May 1988, November 1986, December 1984, April 1978, and 28 other times in the past decade. All of them involved Army, Air Force or Marine helicopters that simply ran into the ground.

On 18 other occasions, helicopters ran into other aircraft. Eight times, the unseen obstacles were power cables. And there were dozens of other minor accidents in which death and destruction barely were averted.

All of these accidents had a common theme: They occurred while pilots wore night-vision goggles.

In all but six out of 52 cases, the goggles in use were outdated, jury-rigged devices designed for ground troops and truck drivers, not pilots.

The Pentagon has been aware the goggles are inadequate for flying for at least 10 years, when crashes began occurring during routine flights, according to 50 military crash-investigation reports and other

■ INVESTIGATION: Pentagon was aware of safety problems with goggles/A1

documents obtained by the Register through the federal Freedom of Information Act.

An analysis of a July 1983 crash by the Army Safety Center in Fort Rucker, Ala., baldly states that the ground-troop goggles "are not compatible with aviation," and the retired Army scientist who presided over their development, Edward Firth, said they were designed for driving vehicles no faster than 35 mph.

Even before the crashes, the goggles' manufacturers and the Army's own night-vision experts warned that the infantry goggles were inadequate for flight.

The long string of night-vision accidents has led to safety improvements in procedures, training and helicopter lighting. But the military does not believe flying with goggles should be curtailed or stopped, said Lt. Col. John Reitz, the Army's Pentagon spokesmen for night-vision goggles.

"In the last two years, no accidents (that occurred during goggle flights) were directly attributable to night-vision goggles," he said. "There were no common links."

Military officials blame most of the crashes on pilot error, contending that pilots fail to fly within the goggles' limitations.

This finding allows flying with the infantry goggles to continue while the military gradually converts to a newer, safer type of goggle designed specifically for pilots. These pilot goggles remain in short supply.

More than 15,000 pairs of the infantry goggles are now being used at military bases nationwide. Helicopter pilots at the Tustin Marine Corps Air Station fly with them nightly. Pilots wear them occasionally at the Los Alamitos Armed Forces Reserve

Please see DARK/7

Investigation: 134 deaths found

In the past 10 years, at least 62 military helicopters have been destroyed and 134 servicemen killed in crashes in which pilots wore night-vision goggles, a Register investigation has found.

An additional 103 servicemen have been paralyzed, burned, brain-damaged or suffered other serious injuries in goggle-related crashes. More than $180 million in damage occurred.

To analyze these crashes, the Register obtained more than 50 declassified crash-investigation reports spanning 10 years, along with Army training manuals, internal safety newsletters and other documents pertaining to night-vision flying.

These records show:

■ For 10 years, the Army, Marine Corps and Air Force have flown with goggles designed for ground troops and truck drivers, not pilots.

■ Manufacturers do not consider the infantry goggles safe for flight.

■ The goggles amplify moonlight and starlight, but limit peripheral vision, perform poorly in dim light, inhibit depth perception, and are incompatible with interior and exterior aircraft lighting.

■ They have a tendency to be blinded in cloudy weather, while simultaneously preventing pilots from noticing they are flying into clouds.

■ Improved goggles designed specifically for pilots are to replace the infantry goggles by 1992, but even these devices suffer from many of the same weaknesses, and have been linked to six of the most recent crashes.

Despite these problems, military officials have blamed all but two of the crashes on pilot error. Goggle flying continues nightly nationwide.

A Tustin Marine helicopter pilot uses straps, Velcro and rubber tubes to wear night-vision goggles designed for ground troops.

L16 The Orange County Register Sunday, January 15, 1989

REMEMBERING REAGAN

Reagan arrives at El Toro Marine air station in August 1984. Sen. Pete Wilson is at left.

Carpeting that bears the presidential seal dominates the Oval Office in the White House.

Speech writer Ken Khachigian of San Clemente and the president review a text.

Home away from home

Orange County was fertile ground for the Reagan Revolution, and he visited often — 63 times in 25 years.

First as governor, then as president, Reagan knew he could count on Orange County residents — for votes, money and, more importantly, for political soulmates.

Reagan might be buffeted by world events and the attacks of his critics, but whenever he needed the applause of a partisan audience, he could count on Orange County supporters to roll out the red carpet, turn out a crowd, and cheer him on.

Orange County will remember him.

Smooth sailing with county and California partisans on the day before Election Day 1988. From left are congressional candidates Christopher Cox and Dana Rohrabacher, Gloria Deukmejian, Gov. George Deukmejian and Rep. Robert Dornan of Garden Grove.

The Reagans depart from an April 1, 1988, library fund-raiser in Coto de Caza.

Reagan uses Mile Square Park in Fountain Valley to kick off his 1984 re-election campaign. About 50,000 people attended the Sept. 3 event. 'You ain't seen nothin' yet,' Reagan said.

AWARD OF EXCELLENCE
FRONT PAGE DESIGN
Syracuse Herald-Journal, Herald American
Syracuse, New York
Managing Editor
Tim Atseff

ACCENT: What area blacks think about Jesse Jackson's call for African-American designation 1C

WINGS WIN
Hat trick sinks Blues 4-2 1D

TRADE TALK
Will Probert, Klima go? 1D

McWHIRTER
Bakkers' guest star: Satan 1C

Rain
Low tonight 30°
High Friday 33°

Thursday
January 5, 1989

The Detroit News

15¢

GOOD DAY
BRIEFLY IN THE NEWS

Security misses 1 fake bomb, bags 3

Case of fire-brewed beer

Lotto birds of a feather

Rare crane is shot down

Reagan to say farewell

Vietnam memorial saved

Mom sentenced for abuse

INSIDE...

Pounds of news, gallons of coffee
By Jon Pepper

PULL-AWAY SECTION

AUTO SHOW

THE AFTERMATH: "We, as well as the fish, are awaiting them."

Khadafy warns U.S.

Jet fighters clash

Libyan leader asks Soviets for warships to fight off 'attack'

INSIDE:

Woman may have been alive when locked in freezer
By Jim Mitzelfeld

State beats S. Africa stock law
By Dennis B. Mulqueen

Heart-lung transplant patient dies
By Kathleen Bohland

IN FRIDAY'S ENTERTAINMENT SECTION: An art gallery for every taste

AWARD OF EXCELLENCE
FRONT PAGE DESIGN
The Detroit News
Designer
Dale Peskin
Illustrators
Marty Westman, David Pierce
Researchers
Michele Fecht, Laura D. Varon
Art Director
Felix Grabowski
Graphics Editors
Felix Grabowski, Laura D. Varon

HOMETOWN VOICES: An Air Force proving ground/B8 METRO: The area's best, brightest Christmas lights/B1 WEATHER: Flurries today/A2

SUNDAY

Syracuse Herald American

DECEMBER 18, 1988

THE POST-STANDARD

FINAL EDITION

$1.25

Frantic shoppers, drivers race as Christmas finish line looms

Jean Klauden of Eastwood looks for her car in the Shoppingtown lot Saturday.

CLASH IN THE ADIRONDACKS

A view of the Adirondacks high peaks from Mt. Marcy, the highest point in New York state.

2nd Indian fugitive finds haven

Hatcher in Onondaga Nation after fleeing charges in N.C.

Rift stalls funds for lake cleanup

Police probe: Did a ring return from the grave?

A woman who survived 10 days trapped in the rubble of Leninakan is carried out on a stretcher Saturday.

Quake's other toll: political stability

Customer service - 470-0050

S.U. SUSPENDS MICHAEL OWENS: Sports/D1 MYERSON CRIES AFTER ACQUITTAL: State/B3 HOLIDAY FLURRIES: Weather/A2

SYRACUSE HERALD-JOURNAL

CITY EDITION

DECEMBER 23, 1988 30 cents

Three die in blaze

North Syracuse home burns

TERRORIST THREAT KEPT SECRET; PARENTS ANGRY

Anguished dad: 'This is murder'

In grief and rage, some parents said their children died in Wednesday's plane crash because of a bad decision by the U.S. government.

Federal officials had warned airports, airlines and an embassy about a terrorist threat to blow up a Pan Am flight.

But the government warning said the public shouldn't be told.

"I cannot imagine what kind of madman would pursue a policy like that," said Daniel Cohen of Port Jervis, Orange County, whose daughter died in the crash.

"This is murder and there are two parties to it," he said. "One is the terrorists, certainly. Either the U.S. government or the airlines is a murderer, too."

His daughter, Theodora, 20, was a Syracuse University drama student.

At least 280 people were killed when Pan Am

Village's Christmas canceled

'There's nothing you can do'

THE VICTIMS of FLIGHT 103

Good evening

Some rain

SYRACUSE HERALD-JOURNAL

SUBURBAN EDITION

DECEMBER 21, 1988 30 cents

WALKING ON THE EDGE IN FASHION

SU graduate Betsey Johnson no flash in pan.

Lifestyle/D1

LEGISLATORS STAND UP YOUNG, PIRRO

Assemblyman-elect only one to attend City Hall session.

Metro/B1

NEWSMAN MAX ROBINSON DIES AT 49

He was first black to anchor network news on television.

Obituaries/B4

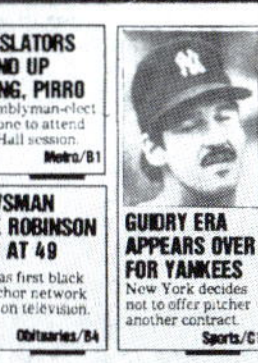

GUIDRY ERA APPEARS OVER FOR YANKEES

New York decides not to offer pitcher another contract.

Sports/C1

Entering Robeson County, home of a deadly DA and sudden death

By Matthew Spina
Staff Writer

LUMBERTON, N.C. — The DA once held the record for sending people to death row. When he ran for judge this year his opponent, a Lumbee Indian, turned up dead. So did the man accused of killing him.

The sheriff appointed his son chief drug investigator. When $100,000 of drugs disappeared from an evidence locker, no one was convicted.

The son killed a drug suspect, also an Indian. When the inquest was held, the son was cleared of wrongdoing.

Indians are afraid of the criminal justice system in Robeson County, home to 55 percent of North Carolina's Native Americans.

They are especially afraid of Joe Freeman Britt, the DA who for 18

■ JUSTICE, Page A12

Hoping to make MONY

Prominent investors to buy part of Towers

By Adriel Bettelheim
Staff Writer

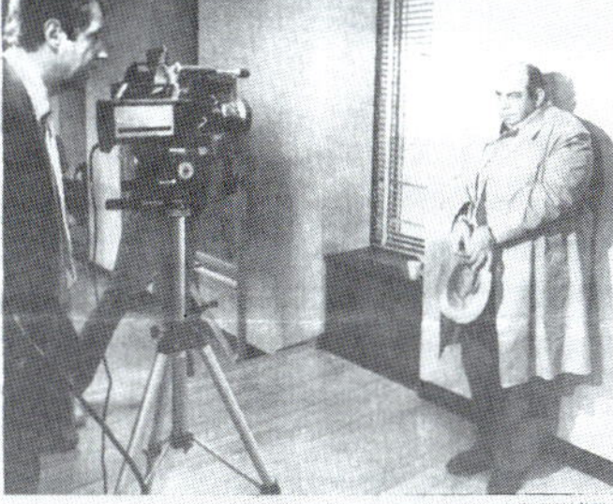

Syracuse police Lt. David Owens, left, videotapes gambling suspect Nicholas LaPenta.

Police hold 14 in raid

$8 million city gambling ring cracked, cops say

By John Doherty
Staff Writer

■ POLICE, Page A13

Winter makes a hot entrance

A Sterling nuke site could threaten water supply

Where the sites are

Aides trying to salvage Sullivan's chances

Good evening

Colder

AWARD OF EXCELLENCE

FRONT PAGE DESIGN

Aftenposten

Oslo, Norway

Designer

Kjell Iversen

NORGES STØRSTE MORGENAVIS

Flest for private sykehus

● Nordmenn flest mener at private bør få adgang til å drive både sykehus og skoler. Flertallet er størst når det gjelder privat sykehusdrift. Blant dem som har tatt standpunkt, sier 62 prosent ja. I gruppen trygdede og pensjonister er forholdet mellom tilhengere og motstandere 63 mot 37 prosent.

● 55 prosent sier ja til private skoler. Størst er flertallet blant dem som har lengst utdannelse (62 mot 32 prosent). Blant dem som har kortest utdannelse, er motstanderne i flertall. Dette fremgår av en ny meningsmåling Opinion A/S har foretatt for Aftenposten tirsdag og onsdag. SIDE 10

Ulykkene Sovjet fortiet

Tre hemmelige atomulykker i Sovjet, i 1957, 1967 og 1978, er avslørt av sivile satellitter og andre kilder. De to første førte til enorm radioaktiv forurensning. Den siste ble avverget i siste liten. Moskva tier ennå om ulykkene i Kysjtym i Ural, som inntraff i et anlegg for produksjon av atomvåpen. Anlegget er utvidet og i drift. SIDE 23

Bush viser mer omsorg

FOTO: REUTER/UPI

George Bush signaliserer større innsats for USAs fattige og vanskeligstilte i sin tid som president. 68 prosent av amerikanerne ser med optimisme frem til å ha Bush som sin leder de neste fire år. Washington feiret maktskiftet i hele natt, bl.a. med ni ball. Og idag er det åpent hus i presidentboligen. SIDE 2 (leder) OG 12

ANNONSER

1. SEKSJON		2. SEKSJON	
Reiselivet	14	Eiend.mark. forts.	33
Kunngjøringer	18	Underv. - instr.	38
Motet - Furn.st	18	Båt - Bil - Fly	38
For samlere	18	Stillingsmark.	39
Religiøse møter	18	Underholdning	40
Eiend. markedet	19		
Dødsfall	21		

KRISTIN REDDET AV LILLESØSTERS BENMARG

Tilbake til livet

FOTO: KNUT SNARE

Frisk efter akutt blodkreft

Kristin Bockelie fra Asker (t.h.) er endelig frisk, takket være benmarg fra lillesøster Marianne. To ganger har Kristin (22) fått knallhard behandling for leukemi. Cellegift hjalp ikke. Redningen ble transplantasjon av benmarg fra Marianne. Idag er Kristin kurert.

Rikshospitalet er eneste sykehus i landet som kan overføre benmarg fra en person til en annen. Det er et dyrt og drastisk inngrep, men resultatene er gode, sier overlegene Dagfinn Albrechtsen (t.v. under) og Stein A. Evensen. Men Norge mangler et fast tilbud for slike transplantasjoner. SIDE 10

FOTO: KNUT SNARE

Stille norsk hjelp USA - Arafat

Flere ganger har Norge i all stillhet formidlet viktige politiske budskap fra PLO og dets leder Yasir Arafat (bildet) til USA. Denne hemmelige norske innsatsen for fred i Midt-Østen ble avbrutt for et år siden. SIDE 12 OG 25

FOTO: NPS

Adopsjonsskandalen: Stjålne barn til Norge?

Fem advokater er arrestert i sitt hjemland Ecuador, mistenkt for å ha kidnappet 30 barn. En av de mistenkte har bistått norske adopsjonsmyndigheter, og tilsammen 13 barn har kommet til Norge ved hjelp av denne advokaten. Foreløbig kjenner ingen til om noen av disse barna er kommet til landet på ulovlig vis, og de norske adoptivforeldrene er i så fall totalt uskyldige. SIDE 8

Politiet skal oppspore skattesyndere på flukt

Aksjon «Ære og samvittighet» er Oslo-politiets offensiv for å oppspore folk som har gått i dekning for å slippe unna skatt, bidrag eller gjeld. Politiet har en liste på 127 skatterømlinger som leker gjemsel med kemner og kreditorer. En av dem hadde 50-årslag da politiet kom. Han godtok forelegget ute i trappen. — Vi finner mange, sier politiet. SIDE 8

AWARD OF EXCELLENCE
FRONT PAGE DESIGN
The Sacramento Bee
Sacramento, California
Designer
Edward Canale

FACES OF THE TRAGEDY

Day of anguish, few answers

Pupils return for lessons in healing

'Military hang-up' gripped angry killer

A short life full of hate

Super Bowl advertisers plan a dazzling offense

Federal sentencing system upheld

Ueberroth feels out governor's race

AWARD OF EXCELLENCE
FRONT PAGE DESIGN
The Detroit News
Designers
Dale Peskin, Nancy Hanus
Illustrator
Staff
Researchers
Graphics Staff

SPECIAL NFL PREVIEW The lesson for '88 Lions is clear: Learn to win 1D

FOUL BALL Owners guilty of collusion 1G

The Detroit News

BRIEFLY

Can Tigers repeat as boys of September?

'Let's get out of here'

94 survive jet crash in Dallas; 13 killed

Terrified survivors scrambled to safety

Escape from Flight 1141

Jefferson's school plan would freeze teacher salaries

Walesa calls for end to strikes

SURVIVAL: THE CRASH OF FLIGHT 1141

"You're hoping you weren't going to die. It's getting smoky, and you're just trying to get the hell out of the plane."

Penn Waugh
Passenger

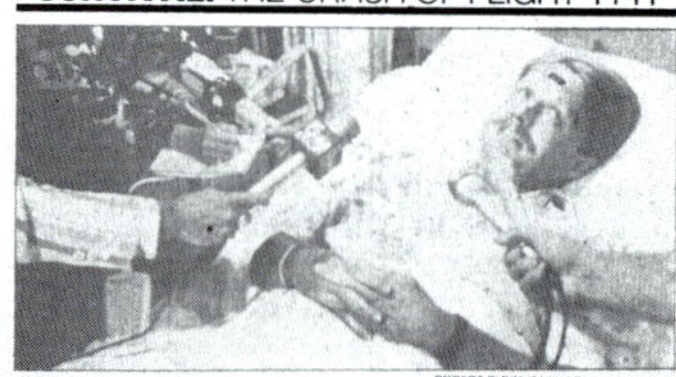

ROBERT BUNCH/United Press International

Norman Newcity of Kennesaw, Ga., broke his ankle when he jumped from the wreckage.

"When I finally got up to where I could see an opening in the top of the plane . . . we could climb that wreckage and there was a little hole up through the top. Personally, I think the Good Lord left it there."

Dennis Selvage
Passenger

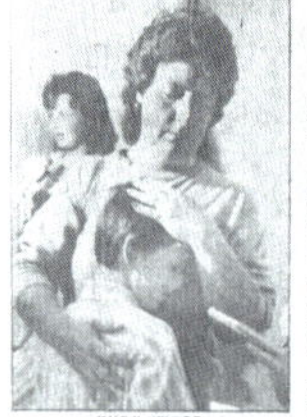

DALE G. YOUNG/The Detroit News

Sheila Blair hugs son Guy, who flew from Dallas to Detroit Wednesday.

Relief follows anguish at Metro Airport

By Howard Warren
News Staff Writer

LOCAL REACTION

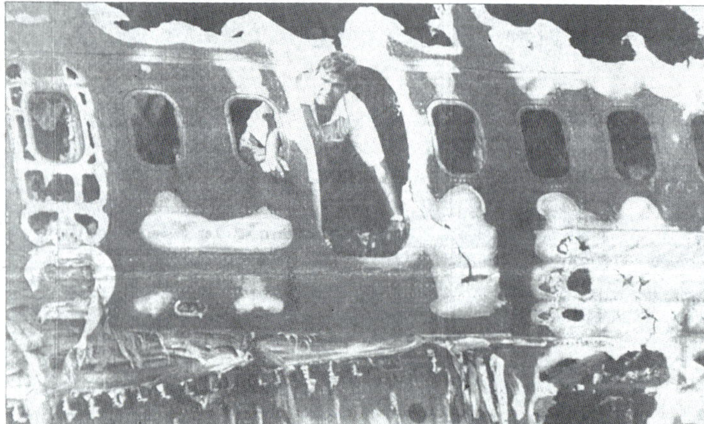

A rescue worker looks through an emergency exit door of the Delta 727 jetliner that crashed after takeoff at the Dallas-Fort Worth International Airport on Wednesday.

GLEN ELLMAN/Associated Press

Survive

Passengers fought flames, terror jumping to safety

From page 1A

Planes must be made less fire hazardous, senator says

By Anne Willette
Gannett News Service

SAFETY

Delta praised for response; Northwest is criticized

By Rebecca Powers
News Staff Writer

HANDLING DISASTER

KEN HAWKINS/UPI

Delta spokesman William Berry announces the death toll Wednesday.

AWARD OF EXCELLENCE

FRONT PAGE DESIGN

Syracuse Herald-Journal

Syracuse, New York

Managing Editor

Tim Atseff

SYRACUSE

HERALD-JOURNAL

DECEMBER 22, 1988 — CITY EDITION — © 1988 The Herald Company — 30 cents

Crash of Pan Am Flight 103

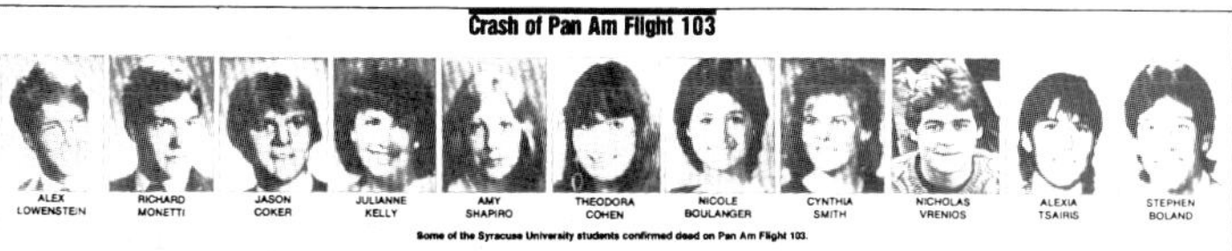

Some of the Syracuse University students confirmed dead on Pan Am Flight 103.

SABOTAGE SUSPECTED

SU, Oswego State, Colgate and Cornell students die in air crash

Sky was raining bodies

Editor's note: *Herald-Journal staff writer Steve Carlic arrived at Lockerbie, Scotland, this morning and filed this report.*

■ THE SKY, Page A11

A huge crater was gouged out of the earth in Lockerbie, Scotland, when Pan Am Flight 103 crashed Wednesday.

Syracuse mourns its loss

By Hart Seely and Dan McGuire
Staff Writers

LIST OF LOCAL STUDENTS KILLED
Page A12

■ SABOTAGE, Page A10

With all hope gone, grief was all they had

By Dan McGuire
Staff Writer

■ WITH ALL, Page A11

SU students mourn at a vigil Wednesday evening at Hendricks Chapel.

LIGHTS OFF	**SOMBER VIGIL**	**WHY PLAY?**	**EGGERS' PAIN**	**A WARNING**
Mayor, county executive ask that holiday lights be doused in respect for dead. **A11**	Dick Case reports, shares the grief of SU students at prayer service. **A12**	Bud Poliquin wonders why a basketball game had to be played. **A13**	Grieving chancellor calls the crash the worst tragedy in SU history. **A13**	U.S. embassy told diplomats of bomb threats against Pan Am flights. **A14**

THE TRAGEDY OF FLIGHT 103

The sky was raining bodies

Syracuse Herald-Journal, Thursday, December 22, 1988 — A11

"We've learned in past years as a community to celebrate the successes of the university; and now we must share what is perhaps the most difficult of human experiences, the mourning of our children."

— Syracuse Mayor Thomas Young

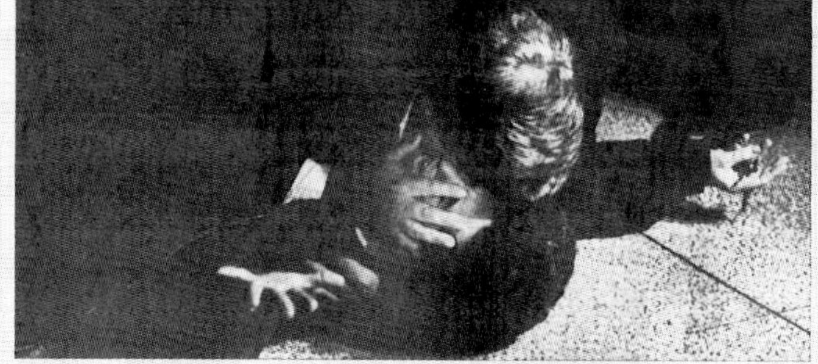

A man at Kennedy International Airport tries to comfort a grief-stricken woman whose child was aboard Flight 103.

The sky was raining bodies

Residents of town describe the horror as plane came down

■ THE SKY
Continued from Page A1

— *Herald-Journal news services contributed to this report.*

Jumbo jet's wreckage is strewn across the Scottish countryside around Lockerbie. The aircraft smashed into the village, setting bungalows afire and killing 22 people on the ground.

Turn off holiday lights: Young

By Margaret LeBrun
Staff Writer

With all hope gone, only grief was left for relatives at JFK

■ WITH ALL
Continued from Page A1

Quake relief checks were aboard plane

The Associated Press

747 disasters

AWARD OF EXCELLENCE
SPORTS FRONT PAGE DESIGN
The Miami Herald
Illustrator
Phill Flanders
Editors
Paul Anger, Mike O'Malley
Director of Editorial Art and Design
Randy Stano

SUPER BOWL PREVIEW

Sports Special

Friday, January 20, 1989 — The Miami Herald — Section F

ACCENT ON OFFENSE

Maybe this is the year for a shootout

BOB RUBIN

Conventional wisdom says teams reach the Super Bowl on defense. But conventional wisdom also said Dan Quayle on the ticket would destroy George Bush's presidential hopes, the Oakland A's would kill the Dodgers in the World Series and Mike and Robin would live happily ever after.

Conventional wisdom has been taking it in the chops lately, and the cold streak continues in the pro football venue. The Cincinnati Bengals' defense is good, and the San Francisco 49ers' defense is very good, but what catches the eye as the teams approach Sunday's rendezvous in Joe Robbie Stadium are their offenses, which were ranked No. 1 and 2 in the NFL during the regular season. The only other Supe that matched the top two attacks was four years ago, when the No. 1-ranked Dolphins lost to the No. 2 49ers, 38-16.

Cincinnati quarterback Boomer Esiason is the league MVP, a big, strapping blond kid with an arm and mouth like a machine gun. San Francisco quarterback Joe Montana has thrown six touchdown passes in his past two games, performances that rank among the finest in his Hall-of-Fame decade as a pro.

Delicious thought: The Super Bowl just might enjoy a shootout.

The Bengals have been versatile to the point of schizophrenia on offense, displaying starkly different personalities this season. Early in the year, they played airball well enough for Esiason to finish atop the quarterback rankings. But about midseason they started to bump and grind, and because

Turn to RUBIN / *15F*

INSIDE THE SPECIAL

PHILL FLANDERS/Miami Herald Staff

AWARD OF EXCELLENCE
SPORTS FRONT PAGE DESIGN
Gazette Telegraph
Colorado Springs, Colorado
Designer
Dan Cotter
Photographer
Mark Reis

SPORTS

THURSDAY, JULY 7, 1988 — GAZETTE TELEGRAPH — SECTION C

BASEBALL

Cardinals' Smith, A's Canseco are fans' favorites

LEADING VOTE-GETTERS

NBA

Nuggets sign Davis, release Dunn, Evans

Walter Davis

GOLF

Saiki rallies to win second Ladies title

Smith can't shake early round, opponent's putter

■ Chip Beck chases million-dollar mark/**C7**

A CLOUD OF DUST

SKY SOX

Rain can't dampen Springs' zany show

Zuvella, Lovell hit first homers

See **SKY SOX**/C5

INSIDE

SKY SOX
Colo. Springs 13, Las Vegas 10

RALPH ROUTON: Many NFL players have interesting avocations, some of which will lead to careers after football./**C3**

SOCCER: Benefits of the 1994 World Cup being played in the United States may reach to Colorado Springs./**C7**

OLYMPICS: Kennedy McKinney stuns ex-champ Michael Collins at the Boxing Trials./**C7**

BASEBALL
American League
Cleveland 8, Oakland 6
Detroit 7, Seattle 6
California 5, Toronto 4 (10)
Minnesota 8, Boston 1
Chicago 4, Baltimore 1
Milwaukee 4, Kansas City 2
Texas 4, New York 2
National League
San Francisco 2, Chicago 0
New York 5, Cincinnati 4
Atlanta 3, Philadelphia 2
Montreal 4, Houston 2
Los Angeles 7, St. Louis 3
Complete report/C4

Business begins on C8

FOOTBALL

Broncos plan around two starters

Air Force tackle has leg amputated

AWARD OF EXCELLENCE
SPORTS FRONT PAGE DESIGN
Dayton Daily News
Dayton, Ohio
Designer
Ted Pitts
Photographer
Bill Waugh
Art Director
Ted Pitts

Sun., Jan. 22, 1989 **Dayton Daily News** 1 - W

A SPECIAL 8-PAGE WRAP-AROUND SUPER BOWL SECTION

W

OFFENSE
Ickey Woods
The high-impact, light-stepping rookie running back grows up and gains ground in Cincinnati/**3W**

SUPER SUNDAY
CINCINNATI vs. SAN FRANCISCO
JANUARY 22, 1989
SUPER BOWL XXIII

DEFENSE
Tim Krumrie
Playing ugly takes on a whole new meaning for the Bengals' outstanding nose tackle/**5W**

BILL WAUGH/STAFF PHOTOGRAPHER

BOOMER AND SAM
What a difference a year makes

By Marty Williams
STAFF SPORTS WRITER

MIAMI — No two people in the Cincinnati Bengal organization have more reason for gloating than Head Coach Sam Wyche and quarterback Boomer Esiason.

But unless there is a sudden transformation within the next few hours, even a victory over San Francisco in today's Super Bowl would not bring an "I told you so" to either man's lips.

In the chaos and destruction of the team's 4-11 record in 1987, Wyche and Esiason seemed to stand almost alone. They were the most visible targets and and they took almost all of the direct hits.

But that was then and this is now. The '88 Bengals are 14-4 and only one victory away from completing a miracle.

The same tactics that made Wyche Wicky-Wacky last season have suddenly made him creative and innovative. The same coach that everyone wanted to fire is now a source of civic pride in Cincinnati.

And the same quarterback who could do nothing right is the National Football League's Most Valuable Player.

The irony of all this is not lost on either man, but so far they have been able to withstand the temptation to thumb their noses at the one-time critics who are now fighting for room on the bandwagon.

"The problem with gloating," Wyche said, "is there's always next year. When teams don't have a good year they say wait til next year. When you have a great season, you have to be careful about next year. This one's going to be hard to top."

According to Wyche, the difference between 4-11 and 14-4 is not nearly as big as the numbers indicate. "It shows how big the swing is and how quickly the pendulum operates. And it can show the importance of things over which you have no control, such as injuries and the way the ball bounces.

"If the record is bad," he added, "the coach is assumed to have done a bad job. If the record is good, you assume the coach did a good job. And frankly, sometimes there's no difference. Sometimes the guy with the poorer record did the better job."

Wyche paused and searched his memory banks for more evidence. Then he continued, "Look at Cleveland this year. To me, Marty Schottenheimer was the Coach of the Year. I think he did the best job of any coach in the league. He was the guy who had the most to overcome (including the loss of his top three quarterbacks) and he did it. He put his team in the playoffs. But now he's no longer working for the Browns (Schottenheimer quit because of postseason differences with owner Art Modell)."

The volatile Esiason has surprised most of his critics by the way he recovered from last season. There were those who thought he wouldn't handle success any better than he handled adversity.

"I did a lot of thinking during the offseason," he explained, "and I went to training camp determined to give my full concentration to football. I think what happened to us last year hardened us to some extent and helped us put things in perspective. There's a fine line in this business and you have to stay right on it. You can't let yourself go too far one way when things are bad and you can't go too far the other way when things are good."

SEE BOOMER/**3D**

AWARD OF EXCELLENCE
SPORTS FRONT PAGE DESIGN
The Dallas Morning News
Designer
Bob Shema
Photographer
David Woo
Art Director
Ed Kohorst

Thursday, August 25, 1988 © 1988, The Dallas Morning News **The Dallas Morning News** Section F

FOOTBALL '88
THE COWBOYS

Herschel Walker: Focal point of offense and franchise

By Bernie Miklasz
Staff Writer of The Dallas Morning News

In the gospel according to Tex Schramm, the Cowboys are now Herschel Walker's team. It's the buzz phrase of the 1988 season, a homage to the running back who the Cowboys will rely on as they move into a new generation.

"It's up to him to make this team as good as it's going to be," said Schramm, the Cowboys' president. "Tony Dorsett has been traded. The offense has been redesigned. The path has been cleared for Herschel. And we are looking to him to lead us."

Herschel — and he is one of the few sports superstars whose first name carries instant recognition — has had the Cowboys' star pinned squarely on his breast, more than any player since Roger Staubach.

Take a look around. There he is, posed bare-chested, on the cover of the 1988 Cowboys Yearbook. There he is, on the front flap of the Cowboys' 1988 ticket brochure and '88 calendar. His name is blared on every radio and TV promotion.

Herschel has been asked to play The Hero for a franchise that crashed — and is slowly recovering — after 20 years of success.

He has been asked to sell tickets, kiss babies, sign autographs, smile for snapshots, and become the living symbol of the new, enthusiastic image that the Cowboys are peddling. He is the darling of the Cowboys' board of directors, a sweet-natured commodity to be packaged and merchandised.

"They are trying to keep the tickets going and Herschel has become their public relations machine," said Cowboys cornerback Everson Walls. "He's a nice guy. Very nice. But he's a human being. Human beings aren't perfect."

On the field, the Cowboys also have turned their lonely eyes to Herschel. They have rewritten the offensive playbook in his name.

Please see WALKER on Page 9F.

Joey Guy, 6, from Thousand Oaks, Calif., isn't the only one who looks up to Cowboys superstar Herschel Walker.

The Dallas Morning News: David Woo

FOOTBALL 1988

Sports Special

Thursday, September 1, 1988 · The Miami Herald · Section F

TICKET TO A

SUPER SEASON

BIG NAMES, BIG GAMES MAKE IT A SCHEDULE FOR FANS TO SAVOR

UM Coach Jimmy Johnson

FSU Coach Bobby Bowden

MIAMI VS. FSU
SATURDAY

Will the winner of the season opener emerge as the eventual national champion? Don't bet against it. Will the winning coach be the leading candidate for coach of the year? Absolutely. This one isn't just big. It's *huge*.

BEARING DOWN
SUNDAY

The struggling Bears have a less frightening look for the Dolphins in the season opener at Soldier Field.

Chicago Coach Mike Ditka

ROAD TRIPS
SEPT. 17

No letdowns: UM plays at No. 10 Michigan, and FSU plays at No. 4 Clemson.

ERIC THE GREAT
SEPT. 25

Is that Dolphin run defense really improved? There won't be any way to hide the truth after Miami goes to Indianapolis to face Eric Dickerson and the Colts.

SHOWDOWN WITH THE IRISH
OCT. 15

Maybe the friendly confines of South Bend, with the ghosts of Knute and the Gipper and Touchdown Jesus, will help the Fighting Irish of Notre Dame get some revenge against Miami, a team that has beaten them four times since 1982.

Notre Dame Coach Lou Holtz

VINNY UPDATE
OCT. 30

What's the skinny on Vinny? Testaverde and the Dolphins find out in Tampa.

KELLY'S HEROES
NOV. 14

Since the arrival of Buffalo Jim, the Bills are no longer the jokes of the AFC East. When Kelly and Co. ride into town, the Dolphin defense had better be at full strength. And the Bills' defense is rekindling memories of the old Bermuda Triangle. A quarterback could get lost in the middle of Bruce Smith, Shane Conlan and Cornelius Bennett.

Buffalo QB Jim Kelly

MIAMI AT LSU
NOV. 19

A wild one on the road: Former University of Miami assistant Mike Archer and his 17th-ranked LSU Tigers play host to Miami.

FLORIDA AT FLORIDA STATE
NOV. 26

As Keith Jackson might say, "*Hooooo*, boy, there's gonna be some leather a'poppin' and some fur a'flyin' when these two state rivals get to mixin' it up. These teams don't like each other."

FSU RB Sammie Smith

Florida RB Emmitt Smith

HEISMAN TROPHY ANNOUNCEMENT
DEC. 3

Florida's Smiths might not be kin, but Sammie of FSU and Emmitt of Florida have one thing very much in common — they can run the football better than most. Who'll win the Heisman? Probably a guy named Smith.

BERNIE'S BACK
DEC. 12

Bernie Kosar vs. Dan Marino. That's as hot a quarterback matchup as December ever brings. And the Browns are the team many believe will be back at Joe Robbie Stadium for the Super Bowl.

Cleveland QB Bernie Kosar

ORANGE BOWL CLASSIC
JAN. 2

You can expect to see Oklahoma or Nebraska after they play Nov. 19 in Norman.

SUPER SUNDAY
JAN. 22

Dolphins owner Joe Robbie and his stadium will serve as hosts for Miami's sixth Super Bowl. The game returns to Miami for the first time since Pittsburgh beat Dallas, 35-31, in 1979.

This will be the first of many Super Bowls at JRS. You can bet on it.

Dolphins owner Joe Robbie

PHILL FLANDERS Miami Herald Staff

DOLPHINS: HE ISN'T BIG, BUT YOU DON'T WANT TO TOY WITH TROY STRADFORD IN THE OPEN FIELD. Page 3F

DAVE BARRY: PENALTIES, REPLAYS AND OTHER JOYS OF A 12-MONTH FOOTBALL SEASON. Page 6F

AWARD OF EXCELLENCE
SPORTS FRONT PAGE DESIGN
The Miami Herald

Illustrator
Phill Flanders
Editors
Paul Anger, Mike O'Malley
Director of Editorial Art and Design
Randy Stano

AUGUST 31, SEPTEMBER 1, 1988 · The Virginian-Pilot The Ledger-Star · SECTION G

FOOTBALL 1988

SPORTS SPECIAL

THE PROS
*Sizing up the Redskins, plus the NFC and AFC races/***G2-3**

THE COLLEGES
*Preview of state, region and ACC teams, plus TV listings/***G5-12**

THE PREPS
*High-school notebook and team-by-team analysis/***G14-15**

Staff illustration by SAM HUNDLEY

Doug Williams

From low lows to high highs, Redskin quarterback has persevered

"Ten years ago I wondered how long I'd play. Now I'm at a point where whatever happens, I'm going to be happy."

By Jim Ducibella
Staff writer

WASHINGTON — The triumphs and tragedies of Doug Williams' life float from town to town and time to time on a river of his tears.

Down the modest streets of his home in Zachary, La. — just mentioning its name can stir his emotions — his friends drive by, honk the horn, and keep going, pleasantly oblivious to his fame.

Tears flowed with the sudden death of his first wife in April, 1983, 11 weeks after their daughter was born, and the assumed interment of his career four months later when he made a bitter departure from the Tampa Bay Buccaneers and joined the USFL's Oklahoma Outlaws.

When the USFL folded two years later, 27 NFL teams passed on Williams. He was prepared to become an assistant coach at Southern University near Zachary.

Telephone calls from Joe Gibbs and Bobby Beathard changed those plans, and Williams instead became a Redskin.

Last November the tears flowed again, outside Gibbs' office the day Williams was yanked as starting quarterback — temporarily, it turned out.

The tears flowed inside San Diego's Jack Murphy Stadium last January when his left knee buckled and he collapsed in terrible pain early during Super Bowl XXII, then were wiped away at Disneyland, where Williams promised he'd go in a commercial he made seconds after being named the game's MVP.

Since then, he hasstarted the Doug Williams Foundation, which endowed 10 Washington-area students with $1,000 college scholarships; sponsored 50 handicapped kids to training camp for a day; sponsored a busload of kids to D.C.'s Lorton Prison as part of a "Youth-on-the-Rise" program, "to show them what it's all about and to try and get them going in the right direction;" and completed so many public-service announcements the Redskins lost count months ago.

"It's best time of my career, my life," Williams said two weeks before starting his 11th professional season. "Ten years ago I wondered how long I'd play. Now I'm at a point where whatever happens, I'm going to be happy.

"If I don't play another down, people are going to know who Doug Williams is. Every preseason magazine, there's a picture of Doug Williams. They've done three or four TV specials on Doug Williams. Now, Doug Williams is etched in stone. I'm not saying there's a place in Canton, but a lot of people know who Doug Williams is."

By the way, Williams made good on the promise to do Disneyland. He brought his daughter Ashley and eight nieces and nephews, who complained that he spent too much time signing autographs.

They would have had the same gripe had they come to training camp at Dickinson College. Autograph seekers never had to look far for Williams, and never had to fear being turned away.

"I saw some rookie going out the back door one day here," Williams recalls from a shed near the practice field at Dickinson College. "I said, 'What you doing going out the back door?' He said he didn't want to sign autographs. I told him, 'There's going to be a day when nobody wants your autograph.' Never go through the back door again.' I'd never walk through a group of kids and not give them an autograph."

No surprise there. Doug Williams is true to his word, which partly explains

Please see **DOUG**, *Page* **G4**

AWARD OF EXCELLENCE
SPORTS FRONT PAGE DESIGN
The Virginian-Pilot and The Ledger-Star
Norfolk, Virginia

Designer
Sam Hundley
Illustrator
Sam Hundley
Art Directors
Bob Lynn, Bill Pitzer

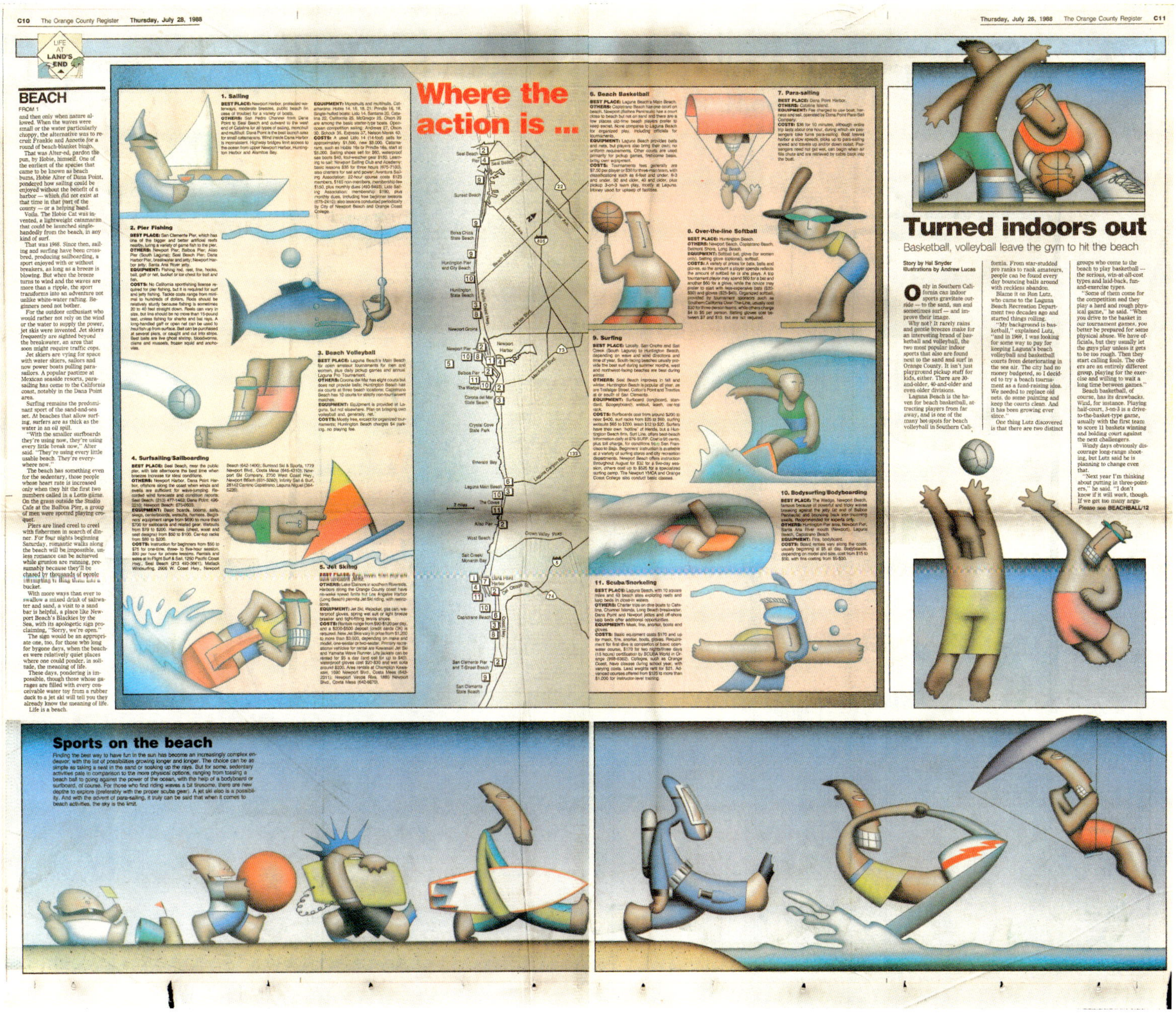

C10 The Orange County Register Thursday, July 28, 1988

Thursday, July 28, 1988 The Orange County Register C11

LIFE AT LAND'S END

BEACH

Where the action is ...

1. Sailing

2. Pier Fishing

3. Beach Volleyball

4. Surfsailing/Sailboarding

5. Jet Skiing

6. Beach Basketball

7. Para-sailing

8. Over-the-line Softball

9. Surfing

10. Bodysurfing/Bodyboarding

11. Scuba/Snorkeling

Turned indoors out

Basketball, volleyball leave the gym to hit the beach

Story by Hal Snyder
Illustrations by Andrew Lucas

Sports on the beach

Sports

Dodgers lose game, 2-1, but win trip

MARK WHICKER

Surf is the new turf for sports enthusiasts

LIFE AT LAND'S END

Rambis agrees to contract terms with Charlotte expansion team

Wallyworld a fun place again

AWARD OF EXCELLENCE
SPORTS FRONT
PAGE DESIGN
The Orange County Register
Santa Ana, California

Designer
Staff
Illustrator
Andrew Lucas

VOL. 3, NO. 44 HAMPTON·ROADS AUG. 22, 1988

RETURN OF THE HOSPITAL REGULATORS
PAGE 3

THE GROWTH OF A GOURMET GROCERY
PAGE 4

BUSINESS WEEKLY

COMPUTERS: FLAT IS WHERE IT'S AT
PAGE 6

A COSTLY SETTLEMENT FOR TWO THRIFTS
PAGE 10

Privacy on the Job

Drug testing, computer surveillance, telephone eavesdropping — employers are looking deeper into their workers' lives. It helps fight theft and lowers risks, but how far is too far? Courts and Congress are drawing the line.

PUBLISHED AS PART OF THE VIRGINIAN-PILOT AND THE LEDGER-STAR

AWARD OF EXCELLENCE
BUSINESS SECTION
FRONT PAGE DESIGN
The Virginian-Pilot and The Ledger-Star
Norfolk, Virginia
Designer
Sam Hundley
Photographer
Jamie Francis
Art Directors
Bob Lynn, Bill Pitzer
Editor
Chris Kouba

AWARD OF EXCELLENCE
BUSINESS SECTION
FRONT PAGE DESIGN
The Virginian-Pilot and
The Ledger-Star
Norfolk, Virginia
Designer
Sam Hundley
Illustrator
Sam Hundley
Art Directors
Bob Lynn, Bill Pitzer
Editor
Chris Kouba

VOL. 4, NO. 11 HAMPTON·ROADS JAN. 2, 1989

BUSINESS WEEKLY

HOW DEFENSE SPENDING IS RETREATING
PAGE 12

THE PORT'S PLAN TO CONTINUE ITS BOOM
PAGE 14

WHAT'S WRONG WITH RETAIL SALES?
PAGE 18

HIDDEN GAINS FOR HOME BUILDERS
PAGE 23

FORECAST 1989
Holding recession at bay for one more year?

PUBLISHED AS PART OF THE VIRGINIAN-PILOT AND THE LEDGER-STAR

HAMPTON·ROADS

BUSINESS WEEKLY

BANKS STEP UP THE BATTLE FOR DEPOSITS
PAGE 3

THE OUTLOOK FOR MORTGAGE MAKERS
PAGE 4

HARSH WORDS ON THE TOPIC OF ILLITERACY
PAGE 6

WEIGHING A PARTNERSHIP'S PROS AND CONS
PAGE 8

Dishonesty is more common, and more costly, than you might think
DID YOU HIRE A **LIAR?**

Sun., Jan. 29, 1989

The Asbury Park Press

ECONOMY 2

Personal Finance

INVESTING

Is The Party Over?

Per Capita Annual Income*

Unemployment Rate**

Key: United States; New Jersey; Monmouth County; Ocean County

INSIDE

Ocean and Monmouth counties continue to be popular retirement areas, but for now, the supply of housing exceeds demand. — page 2

Owners of small businesses in four downtown shopping districts are concerned about local and national issues. — page 6

Area economists don't expect much movement in either mortgage interest rates or home-buying activity through most of 1989. — page 8

New Jersey CPAs offer advice on how to cut your use of credit cards and save more of your income during 1989. — page 25

Decade may end on sour financial note

AWARD OF EXCELLENCE

BUSINESS SECTION
FRONT PAGE DESIGN

The Asbury Park Press

Neptune, New Jersey

Designer
George Frederick
Illustrator
George Frederick

SILVER AWARD

BUSINESS SECTION
FRONT PAGE DESIGN

The Miami Herald

Designer
Ana Maria Lense, Randy Stano
Illustrator
Ana Maria Lense
Editor
Bob Stickler
Director of Editorial Art and Design
Randy Stano

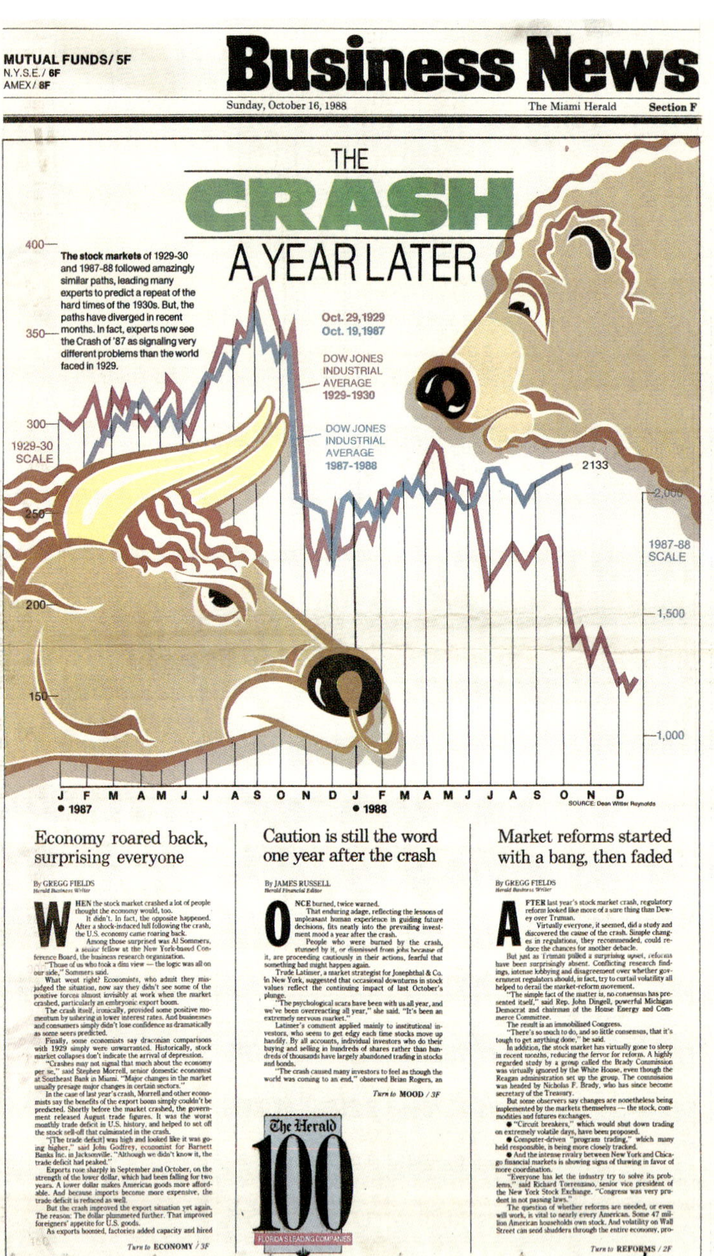

MUTUAL FUNDS/ 5F
N.Y.S.E./ 6F
AMEX/ 8F

Business News

Sunday, October 16, 1988 — The Miami Herald — Section F

THE CRASH A YEAR LATER

Economy roared back, surprising everyone

By GREGG FIELDS

Caution is still the word one year after the crash

By JAMES RUSSELL

Market reforms started with a bang, then faded

By GREGG FIELDS

The Herald 100

The Detroit News
Monday, January 23, 1989

Business

Section D

OUTLOOK '89: SPECIAL REPORT

Consumer Outlook

A few bumps, but mostly smooth sailing ahead

4 banks plan to increase lending in city this year

By Steve Kaskovich

Rising costs on Main Street

INSIDE

- Investment fears send Wall Street off to a slow start — 20
- Experts urge U.S. firms to plot trade-trade strategy — 20
- Sears joins K mart, Wal-Mart in battle of discount giants — 30
- Airline travelers face higher fares, tighter security — 30
- Costly savings and loan crisis becomes taxpayers' problem — 40

State's farmers learned some withering lessons in drought of 1988

By Bill Vlasic

AWARD OF EXCELLENCE

BUSINESS SECTION
FRONT PAGE DESIGN

The Detroit News

Designer
Kehrt Reyher
Illustrator
Marty Westman
Art Director
Felix Grabowski

Close-up

THE TIES THAT BIND

Solidarity is key for uprooted Mexicans in US

IMMIGRATION REFORM TOUCHES LIVES ON BOTH SIDES OF THE BORDER

The Road that leads to La Habra

Unity: Border crossings continue

AWARD OF EXCELLENCE
OTHER NEWS SECTION
FRONT PAGE DESIGN
The Orange County Register
Santa Ana, California

Designer
Pam Marshak
Photographer
Paul E. Rodriguez

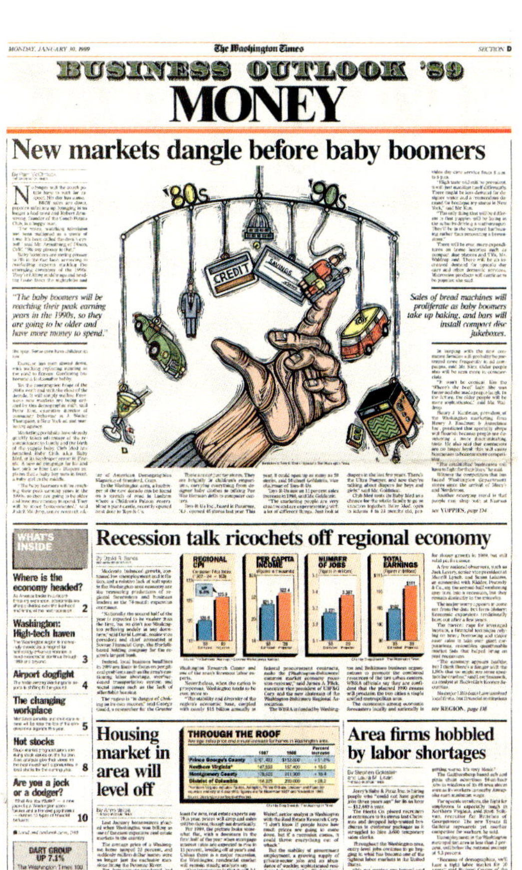

The Washington Times

BUSINESS OUTLOOK '89

MONEY

New markets dangle before baby boomers

Recession talk ricochets off regional economy

Housing market in area will level off

THROUGH THE ROOF

Area firms hobbled by labor shortages

AWARD OF EXCELLENCE
BUSINESS SECTION
FRONT PAGE DESIGN
The Washington Times

Designer
Greg Groesch
Illustrator
Terry E. Smith
Art Director
Greg Groesch

AWARD OF EXCELLENCE
OTHER NEWS SECTION
FRONT PAGE DESIGN
The Orange County Register
Santa Ana, California

Designer
Pam Marshak
Art Director
Tom Porter
Sculptor
Katrena Ann Earnest

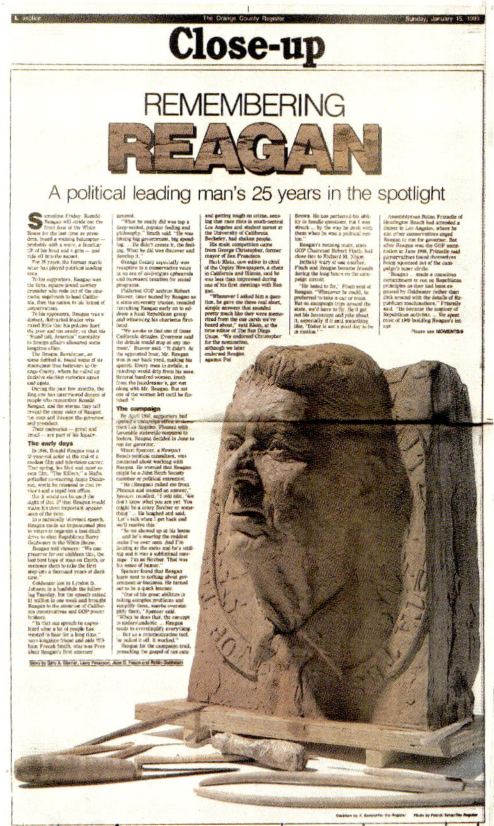

Close-up

REMEMBERING REAGAN

A political leading man's 25 years in the spotlight

AWARD OF EXCELLENCE

INSIDE NEWS, SPORTS OR BUSINESS SECTION PAGE DESIGN

The San Diego Union

Designer
Randy Wright
Art Director
Randy Wright

ELECTION 88

Sunday, October 23, 1988 The San Diego Union A-9

Voter's guide to auto insurance

After years of legislative inaction and feuding between the insurance industry and trial lawyers, Californians now face five complex insurance-related initiatives on the Nov. 8 ballot. Here are their key points.

PROP. 100 Good driver | PROP. 101 Polanco | PROP. 103 Voter Revolt | PROP. 104 No-fault | PROP. 106 Lawyer fee

"Proposition 103 provides rate cuts and the kind of insurance reform that lasts long into the future."
– Consumer Activist Ralph Nader

"Proposition 106 is needed to protect victims from having 40 percent or more of their awards ripped off by lawyers."
– Assemblyman Tom McClintock R-Thousand Oaks

"Proposition 100 was written by and for consumers to reduce insurance premiums for good drivers everywhere."
– Atty. Gen. John Van de Kamp

"The key to success is not regulation. The key to success is a good no-fault law. This is a good no-fault law."
– Law Prof. Jeffrey O'Connell

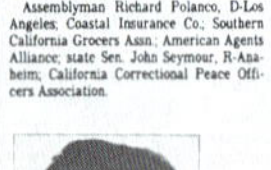

"Neither the trial lawyers nor the insurance industry supports Proposition 101. It tells me we are on the right track."
– Assemblyman Richard Polanco

6A · THURSDAY, SEPTEMBER 1, 1988 · USA TODAY

THE MIRACLE OF FLIGHT 1141

Dallas crash refuels fire debate

Anxious kin kept vigils

How 94 people escaped

List of dead, survivors

AT THE CRASH SITE: A priest and emergency services personnel confer Wednesday against a backdrop of the charred skeleton of the Delta Air Lines Boeing 727 that crashed.

Passenger praises the pilot for doing 'an excellent job'

727 a popular 'workhorse'

Delta's 'good' image secure

Who flies 727s

AWARD OF EXCELLENCE

INSIDE NEWS, SPORTS OR BUSINESS SECTION PAGE DESIGN

USA Today

Designer
John Sherlock
Illustrators
Bill Baker, John Sherlock, Jeff Dionise, Sam Ward, Julie Stacey
Art Director
Lynn Perri

New York Newsday

MONDAY, JULY 4, 1988 • QUEENS • 25 CENTS

U.S. DOWNS IRAN JETLINER

'A Terrible Tragedy'

But Reagan Defends Action as Proper

290 Die In Mistaken Attack On Gulf Plane

Tugboat crewmen, in film broadcast by Iranian TV, raise their fists in anger after recovering bodies of commercial jetliner victims.

Coverage Begins, Pages 2-3

AWARD OF EXCELLENCE
BREAKING NEWS
The Downing of Iran Air Passenger Plane
New York Newsday
Designer
Jeff Massaro
Photographer
Wire Services
Art Director
Bob Eisner
Researchers
Staff
Editors
Robert E. Keane,
Pamela S. Robinson

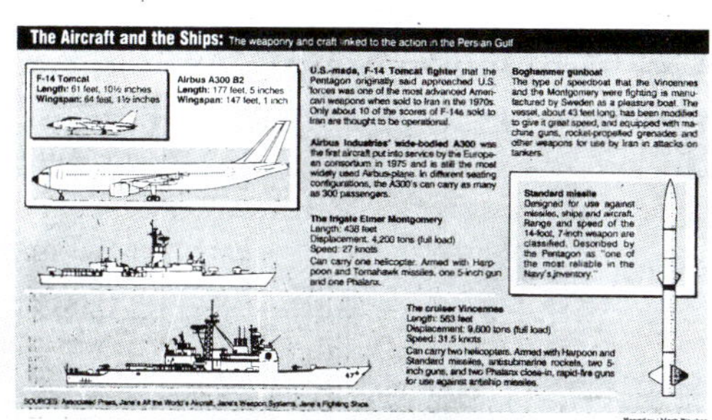

The Aircraft and the Ships: The weaponry and craft linked to the action in the Persian Gulf

High Tech and High Risk

Technology has increased naval danger

By Ford Fessenden

Iran's state television repeatedly flashed this composite image of the downing.

Iran Claims 'Massacre'

Please see IRAN on Page 12

Please see TECHNOLOGY on Page 12

COLORADO SPRINGS GAZETTE TELEGRAPH

MONDAY JULY 4, 1988

PERSIAN GULF

U.S. downs Iran jetliner; 290 die

Civilian flight mistaken for attacking F-14

"... a terrible human tragedy."

HOLIDAY

Portion of Gold Camp Road closed to motorists today

MILITARY

Soviet team flies into Pueblo to inspect Pershing rockets

Army depot wide open to 10 observers

July 4th events

AWARD OF EXCELLENCE
BREAKING NEWS
The Downing of Iran Air Passenger Plane
Gazette Telegraph
Colorado Springs, Colorado
Designer
Lee Freeman
Illustrator
Scott Hiestand
Art Director
Scott Hiestand

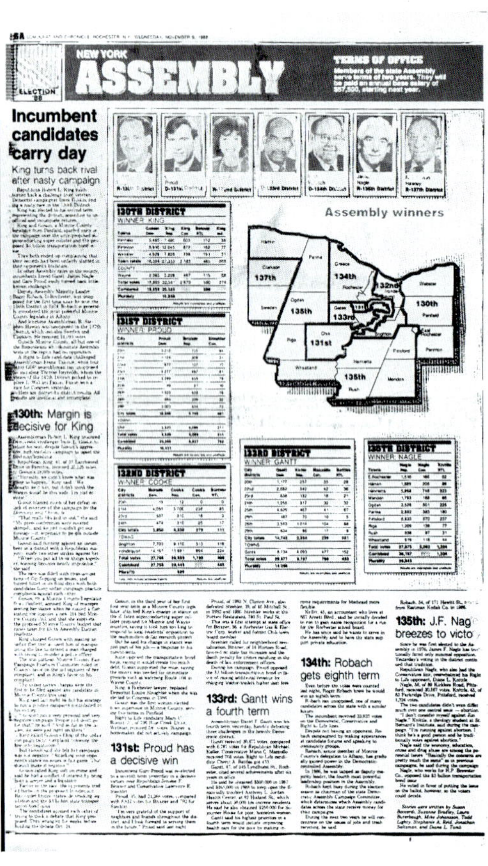

NEW YORK ASSEMBLY

TERMS OF OFFICE

Incumbent candidates carry day

King turns back rival after nasty campaign

130th DISTRICT

131st DISTRICT

Assembly winners

130th: Margin is decisive for King

132nd DISTRICT

133rd DISTRICT

135th DISTRICT

131st: Proud has a decisive win

133rd: Gantt wins a fourth term

134th: Robach gets eighth term

135th: J.F. Nagle breezes to victory

AWARD OF EXCELLENCE
BREAKING NEWS
National Election Results
Democrat and Chronicle
Rochester, New York

Designer
Joe Gibbs
Illustrator
David Cowles
Managing Editor
Joette Rhiele
Art Director
Ray Stanczak

WHERE TO FIND IT

IN OTHER NEWS...

Democrat and Chronicle

Bush bashes Duke, but loses New York

METRO EDITION

Moynihan says win sets Senate record

Dukakis loss is bitter end to bitter race

AT A GLANCE

Electoral votes

Cooke keeps Assembly seat by 689 votes

Voters reject criticisms of Quattrociocchi

Bond issue wins approval of N.Y. voters

Slaughter rolls to re-election

INSIDE

AWARD OF EXCELLENCE
BREAKING NEWS
National Election Results
Dayton Daily News
Dayton, Ohio

Designer
Kevin Riley
Illustrator
Ted Pitts
Photographers
Bill Garlow, Ty Greenlees,
Laura Shagory
Art Director
Ed Henninger

Dayton Daily News

ELECTION SPECIAL Pullout section Pages 5-12

Dayton, Ohio, Wednesday, Nov. 9, 1988

The First Cox Newspaper

It's President Bush

Winner faces challenges, hostile Congress in January

President-elect George Bush and his wife, Barbara, celebrate his victory in Houston

The electoral vote by state

Meyer claims upset victory over Norris in clerk race

Horn pulls out key win for GOP

ELECTION '88: AT A GLANCE

NATION

MONTGOMERY COUNTY

GREENE COUNTY

MIAMI VALLEY

Warmer

AWARD OF EXCELLENCE
BREAKING NEWS
National Election Results
San Jose Mercury News
Designers
David Yarnold and Staff
Illustrator
David Miller
Photographer
Staff
Art Director
Mark Wigginton

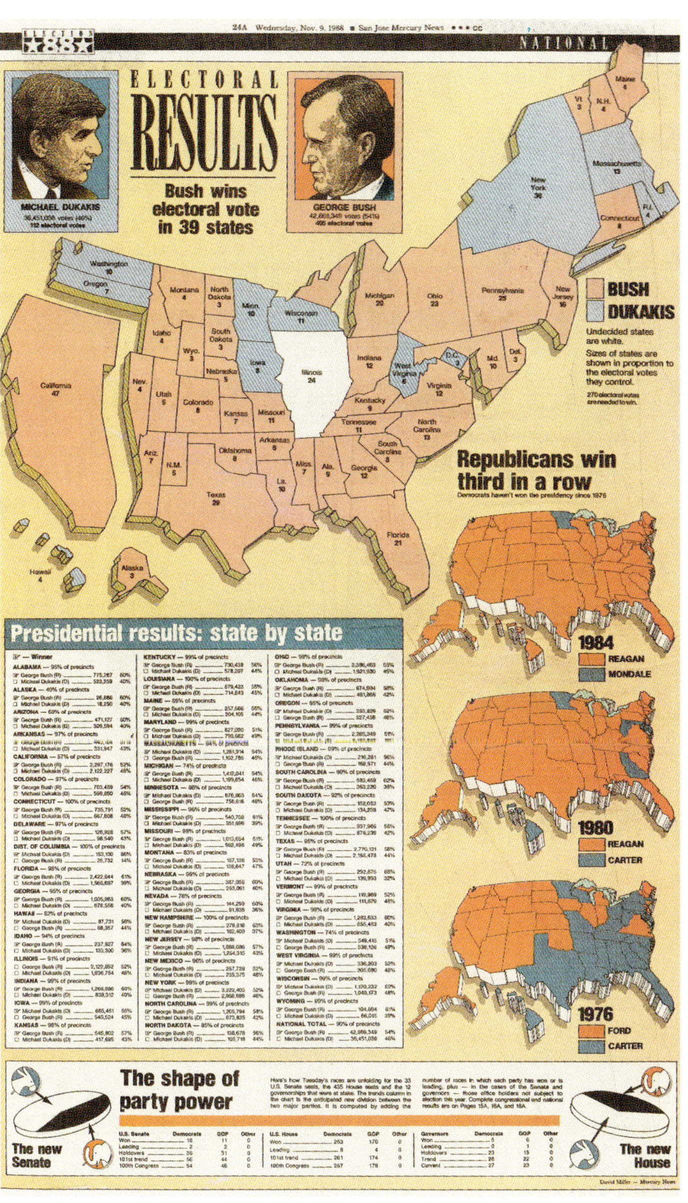
24A Wednesday, Nov. 9, 1988 San Jose Mercury News

NATIONAL

ELECTORAL RESULTS

Bush wins electoral vote in 39 states

MICHAEL DUKAKIS

GEORGE BUSH

BUSH

DUKAKIS

Republicans win third in a row

Presidential results: state by state

1984 REAGAN MONDALE

1980 REAGAN CARTER

1976 FORD CARTER

The shape of party power

The new Senate

The new House

WINNERS, LOSERS, WHAT IT MEANS: 17 FULL PAGES IN TWO SECTIONS

San Jose Mercury News

Bay Area favors Dukakis; state goes GOP

It's Bush in a breeze

Wilson re-elected to Senate in a rout

Demos retain Congress

Bush faces tough issues, hostile Congress

3 insurance issues decisively defeated

TV reports blasted

Cigarette tax passes despite costly attack

AWARD OF EXCELLENCE
BREAKING NEWS
National Election Results
The Hartford Courant
Designer
Staff

Former Yale head Kingman Brewster dies. Page A1.

Election '88 Special

The Hartford Courant

Bush easily beats Dukakis; Lieberman claims victory

Victor calls for healing

Weicker doesn't concede

Senior senator faces the specter of defeat

Built-in advantages helped Bush in race

Democrats keep control of state legislature

BUSINESS: Thanksgiving feast to carry higher price tag 1C

EATERY FOLDS Vannelli Detroit closes doors 1B

STILL PERFECT 3-0 Pistons beat 76ers 116-109 1E

BERMAN Dicey time in Lake Tahoe 1D

55° 45°

Wednesday November 9, 1988

The Detroit News

20¢

IN MICHIGAN, exit poll gives vice-president close win; confusion mars voting; lines long at Metro precincts

Bush wins it

HOW: Dukakis fails in key Midwest states

DAY OF DECISION AT A GLANCE

GIVE 'EM HELL MIKE

TURNOUT: Judge lengthens polling hours

THE VOTE

MICHIGAN: Bush racks up big independent vote

ABORTION: 'Pro-life' forces victorious in emotional battle

RIEGLE: Landslide victory gives senator his third term

INSIDE

IN THURSDAY'S SCIENCE SECTION

AWARD OF EXCELLENCE
BREAKING NEWS
National Election Results
The Detroit News
Designers
Dale Peskin, Nancy Hanus, Beth Reeber, Tim Finn, Joe Gray

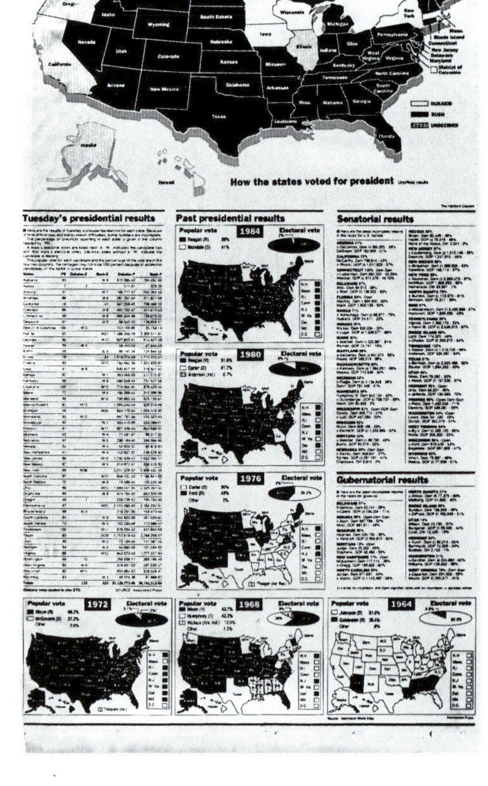
Election '88 Special ★ The nation

How the states voted for president

Tuesday's presidential results

Past presidential results

1984 1980 1976 1972 1968 1964

Popular vote

Electoral vote

Senatorial results

Gubernatorial results

AWARD OF EXCELLENCE
BREAKING NEWS
National Election Results
The Hartford Courant
Designer
Staff

SATURDAY JANUARY 21, 1989

THE SUN

SPORTS FINAL

VOL. 304 NO. 57 BALTIMORE, MARYLAND 25 CENTS

Bush becomes president, urging unity amid diversity

Dignity and easy grace mark Ronald Reagan's final hours in office

Bush stretches hand to nation, both parties

THE INAUGURATION OF THE PRESIDENT

Speech's placating style sets Bush apart already

INSIDE

AWARD OF EXCELLENCE
BREAKING NEWS
The Presidential Inauguration
The Baltimore Sun
Designer
Staff
Art Director
Richard D'Agostino

The Daily Telegraph

FRIDAY, DECEMBER 23, 1988

US was warned of air attack

Anti-terror squad chief heads disaster inquiry

An air of unreal normality

Air bomb threat kept from public

Boy saved by good turn as family dies

Fighter crashes

THE LOCKERBIE DISASTER

A policeman with the cockpit section of Pan Am's Boeing 747, which was found in a field at Tundergarth, three miles east of Lockerbie

Fatal flaw? The Boeing 747 is immensely strong but, as the crash of an Air India jumbo in 1985 showed, it can be vulnerable to a knowledgeable terrorist. In that case a bomb was apparently placed in the forward luggage hold. When it exploded, it destroyed the aircraft's vital electronic centre, instantly disrupting the controls and communications

Plane good as new after refit, says Pan Am

24 mechanical problems

Investigators sift wreckage for clues

Town also had worst rail crash

Tragedy shows the Commons at its best

COMMONS SKETCH

AWARD OF EXCELLENCE
BREAKING NEWS
EDITOR'S CHOICE
National/International
The Daily Telegraph
London, England

THE CLAPHAM JUNCTION DISASTER

'When I shut my eyes tonight I'll hear the train coming up behind me'

Disaster scene: rescuers swarm over the trains. Ambulances stand ready for survivors. The first crash happened at 8.13am. Within seconds a third train hit the wreckage

Worst rail crash for twenty years

WHAT THE SIGNALS MEAN

AND HOW THEY WORK

Timetable of events leading to the tragedy

Doctors airlifted in by police helicopter

MAJOR COLLISIONS 1967-87

End of the day: the heavy lifting gear moves in

THE CLAPHAM JUNCTION DISASTER

'We were rolling and tumbling...I thought the world was going to end'

Blood-stained Gregg Ford escaped from the front coach of the Bournemouth train

Death and destruction on the Monday morning ride to work

Inquiry into overcrowding urged

AWARD OF EXCELLENCE
BREAKING NEWS
EDITOR'S CHOICE
National/International
The Daily Telegraph
London, England

AWARD OF EXCELLENCE
BREAKING NEWS
EDITOR'S CHOICE
Local/Regional
Detroit Free Press
Designers
John Goecke, Randy Miller

TRADING PARTNERS

BATTLE FOR THE EAST

OREL TEST PASSED

METRO FINAL

Detroit Free Press

THURSDAY

On Guard For 157 Years

SEOUL '88

Detroit to lose more than a third of Catholic churches

TV COVERAGE

FAA finds 200 safety violations

HIGHLIGHTS

Cardinal Szoka announces plan to close 43 parishes

At the cape, shuttle fans await final countdown

ON TV

Jazz world mourns death of Detroit's J.C. Heard

INSIDE TODAY

REQUIEM OR REBIRTH?

PROPOSED CHURCH CLOSINGS/MERGERS

LEGEND

ASSUMPTION OF THE BLESSED VIRGIN MARY (WEST)

CORPUS CHRISTI

HOLY GHOST

MOTHER OF CONSOLATION

OUR LADY OF SORROWS

RESURRECTION

ST. ANDREWS

ST. ANTHONY (LITHUANIAN)

ST. BENEDICT THE MOOR

ST. BONIFACE-ST. VINCENT

SILVER AWARD
SPECIAL NEWS TOPICS
Campaign '88
The Orange County Register
Santa Ana, California
Designers
Pam Marshak and Staff
Illustrator
Andrew Lucas
Art Director
Bill Dunn

Marine sentenced to death

Charlotte stings Clippers

The Orange County Register

CAMPAIGN 88

Bush crushes Dukakis; Prop. 103 stuns foes

KEY RESULTS

OC: Voters help give Bush, Wilson victories

Auto insurance: 103 wins against $70 million campaign

Tobacco: Tax increase on cigarettes passes, 3-2

Guards: Observers at polls investigated

M section — The Orange County Register — Sunday, March 6, 1988

Close-up

Super showdown

Sixteen states hold primaries Tuesday, and four will have caucuses. Democrats will compete in 20 races for 1,307* delegates, while Republicans face off in 17 contests – two are not binding – for 712 delegates. There will be 4,160 total Democratic delegates, with 2,081 needed to nominate, and a total of 2,277 Republican delegates, with 1,139 needed to nominate.

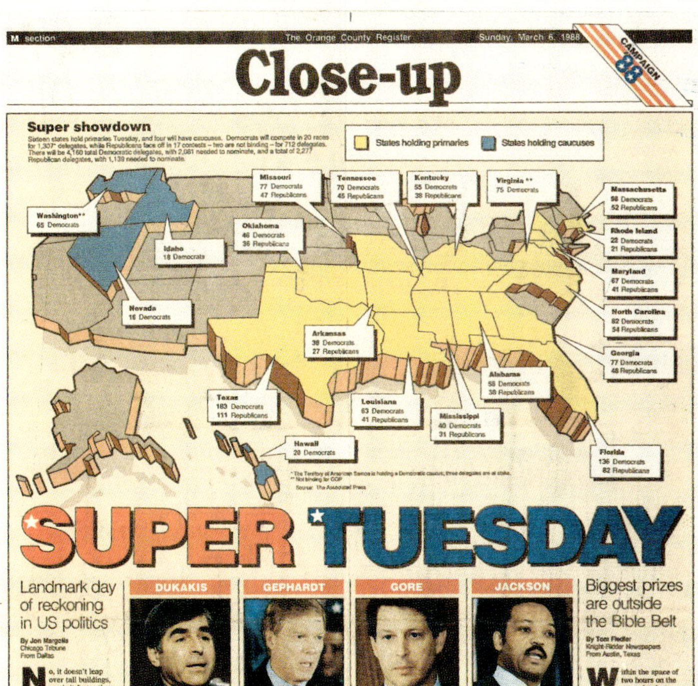

SUPER TUESDAY

Landmark day of reckoning in US politics

By Jon Margolis
Chicago Tribune
From Dallas

No, it doesn't leap over tall buildings, nor is it faster than a speeding bullet.

But it is Super Something — bigger, broader, more expensive and perhaps more confusing than anything in the tangled history of US presidential politics. And after being pondered and analyzed for two years, it is just about here.

DUKAKIS — The Massachusetts governor is expected to sweep his own state and neighboring Rhode Island on Super Tuesday. His goal is to win Southern delegates rather than statewide victories.

GEPHARDT — The Missouri congressman has built his campaign on economic nationalism. He is expected to do well in his home state, but needs a strong showing to offset Dukakis' strength in the North.

GORE — The Tennessee senator's candidacy is predicated on coming in first or second throughout the South. Gore bypassed Iowa and all but ignored New Hampshire to concentrate on the South.

JACKSON — He is expected to win the vast majority of black votes in the South and could be the biggest Democratic winner on Super Tuesday. That would make him a major power broker at the convention.

BUSH — The vice president, who represented Texas in Congress, has more money and better organizations in Super Tuesday states than his rivals. Bush's aides said he intends to win every Southern state.

DOLE — The Kansas senator hopes to stay alive in the South. Dole is betting that a respectable showing there will enable him to beat George Bush when the contests move into the Middle West.

KEMP — The New York congressman is running out of money and time. How he fares in the South will depend on what kind of turnout Pat Robertson generates.

ROBERTSON — The former television evangelist is a wild card in the South. Because many of his core supporters, evangelical Christians, have not participated in the nominating process, his strength is hard to gauge.

Biggest prizes are outside the Bible Belt

By Tom Fiedler
Knight-Ridder Newspapers
From Austin, Texas

Within the space of two hours on the same day last month, rival Democrats Albert Gore Jr. and Richard Gephardt campaigned in Austin, hopped in waiting jets and zipped away to similar shows in Florida.

The day before, Massachusetts Gov. Michael Dukakis, another contender for the ...

Please see LANDMARK/2
Please see PRIZES/2

Sunday, October 30, 1988 — The Orange County Register — L section

ELECTION GUIDE

Close-up

VOTING — NATIONAL

OC crucial to winning in California

Story by Larry Peterson
Illustration by Andrew Lucas
The Register

For Republican presidential nominee George Bush and Democratic nominee Michael Dukakis, California is the "Big Spin."

In a winner-take-all gamble for California's 47 electoral votes, both candidates have bet more of their campaigns on this state than on any other.

The heavy play appears to be paying off for the GOP — this month for the first time in the campaign Bush moved ahead of Dukakis in statewide polls. He did so, voter surveys suggest, because of a television advertising blitz hammering Dukakis as soft on crime, national defense and taxes, and by beating him in a televised debate Oct. 13.

...

McCarthy. Wilson, with President Reagan as his drawing card, netted $450,000 at an Irvine fund-raiser in August and McCarthy has campaigned in the county frequently.

But, like Bush and Dukakis, Wilson and McCarthy have relied heavily on television advertising and contacts with the news media to reach the state's 13 million registered voters.

...

Please see CAMPAIGNS/10

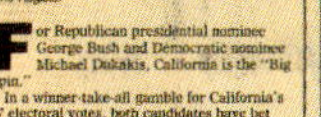

Election at a glance

Polls open: 7 a.m. to 8 p.m.
Number of precincts: 2,397
For polling place, election information, call 567-7600
First returns (absentee ballots) available 8:30 p.m.
Additional returns expected to be available starting at 9:30 p.m.
Final count due to be completed at 4 a.m.
Registered voters: 1,183,166
Republican: 650,348
Democrat: 410,644
American Independent: 12,020
Libertarian: 6,209
Peace and Freedom: 2,683
Miscellaneous other: 961
Non-partisan: 100,321
Predicted turnout: 80 percent

Source: Orange County registrar of voters

President: Race is similar to '60 campaign

By Larry Peterson
The Register

The 1988 presidential campaign has been compared — in some ways aptly — to the 1960 race between Richard Nixon and John Kennedy.

This year, as in 1960, a Republican vice president, George Bush, is running in his own right after serving eight years under a popular president. And a Massachusetts presidential candidate, Michael Dukakis, and a vice-presidential running mate from Texas are on the Democratic ticket.

...

Please see PRESIDENT/3

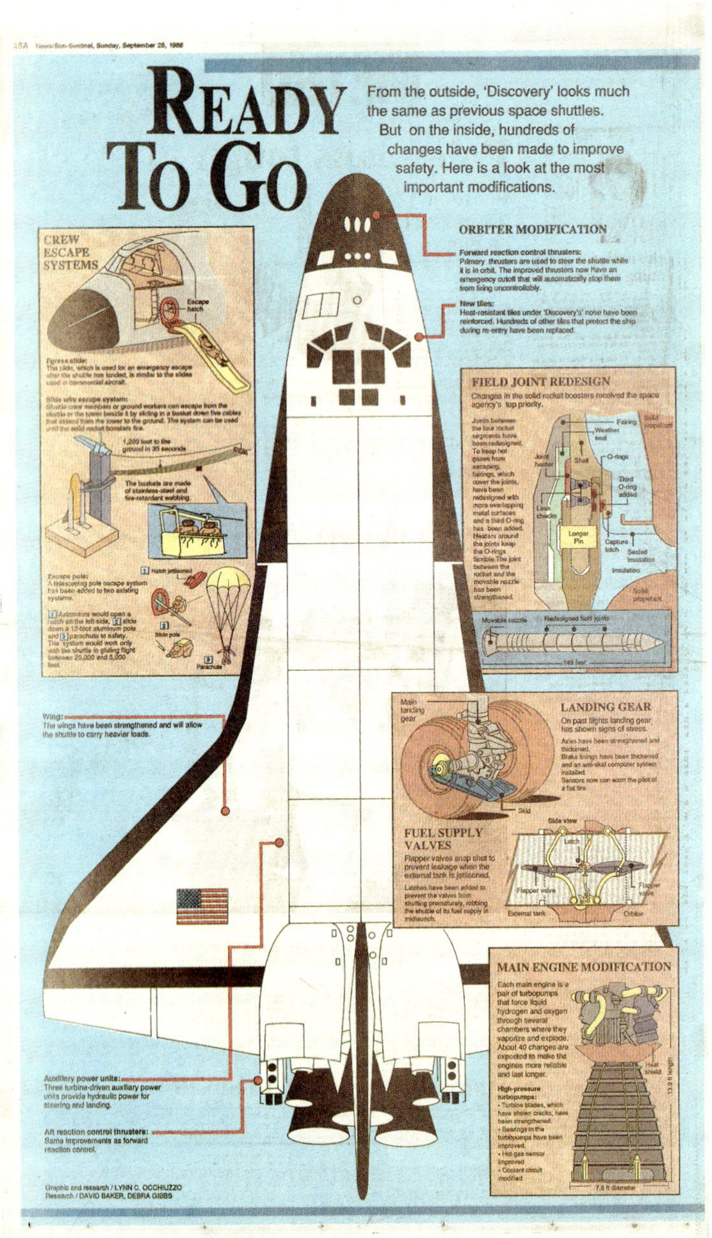

28A News/Sun-Sentinel, Sunday, September 25, 1988

READY TO GO

From the outside, 'Discovery' looks much the same as previous space shuttles. But on the inside, hundreds of changes have been made to improve safety. Here is a look at the most important modifications.

AWARD OF EXCELLENCE
SPECIAL NEWS TOPIC
Launch of Space Shuttle Discovery
News / Sun-Sentinel
Ft. Lauderdale, Florida

Designers
Bill McDonald, Diann Slattery
Illustrators
Lynn Occhiuzzo, Jeff Jamison
Photographers
Elliot Schechter, Bob Mack, Arnold Earnest
Researcher
Debra Gibbs
Graphics Coordinator
David Baker

METRO: Pembroke Park may lose police protection. 1B.

SPORTS: Red Sox wallop Indians, clinch tie for AL East. 1C.

Sun-Sentinel

SOUTH BROWARD FINAL

Friday, September 30, 1988 25 cents

U.S. rediscovers space

INSIDE

THE LAUNCH

Matt Sell, an 8th-grader at Christa McAuliffe Middle School in Boynton Beach, scans the sky for *Discovery* on Thursday. Throughout South Florida, people paused to watch America's return to space. **13A**

The shuttle's redesigned booster rockets pass the test. **12A**

Families of *Challenger* crew watch with sorrow, joy. **13A**

DIGEST

Sun-Sentinel wire services

U.N. soldiers win Nobel Prize

OSLO, Norway — Soldiers on the front lines of the United Nations' 40-year quest for peace won the 1988 Nobel Peace Prize on Thursday.

The Nobel Committee said the U.N. peacekeeping troops built greater faith in the United Nations, which "has come to play a more central part in world affairs."

The award could bolster new U.N. peacemaking efforts to oversee shaky truce agreements in the Persian Gulf and Afghanistan.

Please see story, 14A

Lotto jackpot at $9 million

TALLAHASSEE — This week's state Lotto jackpot was boosted to $9 million on Thursday, making it the largest first-week prize offered since the game began in April, Lottery Secretary Rebecca Paul said.

The big-money prize started the week at $7 million.

On Monday, Dennis Glover of Temple Terrace claimed a $35.8 million jackpot.

Hirohito bleeding won't stop

TOKYO — Japanese Emperor Hirohito clung to life on Thursday, but palace officials appeared to make the first admission that doctors could lose the fight to save him.

The Imperial Household Agency has stubbornly refused to disclose any real details of the ailments that have left Hirohito bedridden and fed by intravenous drips for 10 days.

The deeply conservative bureaucrats who control every aspect of royal life have been repeatedly criticized by the government and press for their attitude.

But on Thursday, Kenji Maeda, the agency official acting as palace spokesman, told a routine news briefing: "Doctors have determined that the bleeding has not stopped."

INDEX

Vol. 29, No. 124

WEATHER

70s
80s
90s
Rain
Thunderstorms

Today's forecast: Mostly sunny with a high about 90.
Details: Page 2A.

LOTTERY

Florida Lottery winning numbers selected on Thursday night.

CASH 3: 6-6-2

"America is back in space. . . I think I had my fingers crossed like everybody else." — President Reagan

Staff photo/BOB MACK and ELIOT J. SCHECHTER

Discovery's flawless, breathtaking launch on Thursday sent the space shuttle, and the nation's emotions, soaring into orbit. After a minor delay because of winds, liftoff came at 11:37 a.m.

Long wait over; new era begins

By DON MELVIN
Staff Writer

CAPE CANAVERAL — With that magnificent roar that has not been heard in more than 2½ years, the shuttle *Discovery* put the United States back into space on Thursday morning as an anxious nation sighed its relief.

NASA officials hugged and kissed each other as the orbiter lifted off at 11:37 a.m. and again when the solid rocket boosters — which had been blamed for the *Challenger* explosion that derailed the space program — fell harmlessly on schedule into the Atlantic Ocean two minutes and four seconds later.

"It was a great day for me and a great day for America," said an exultant Forrest McCartney, Kennedy Space Center director. "Just as it was when we launched the first shuttle and everybody stood tall, everybody stood tall today."

The launch was nearly scrubbed because high-altitude winds were blowing in a different direction from what National Aeronautics and Space Administration officials had anticipated for this time of year.

In the end, NASA did what Rear Admiral Richard Truly, associate administrator for space flight, only the day before had vowed not to do: waive one of the tough new weather restrictions.

Six hours after liftoff, the five-man crew accomplished the main mission of its flight by releasing a $100 million satellite that will give NASA nearly constant communication with future shuttle missions.

The shuttle began its ascent slowly, trailed by a 600-foot plume of orange flame and billowing clouds of white smoke. Within about 30 seconds, the magnificent roar of the engines shook the ground three miles away and the shuttle picked up speed.

About 50 seconds into the flight, the spaceship disappeared behind a small cloud, only to emerge a minute later as a tiny speck in the sky.

"We've worked so hard to get to this point," said Gerald Smith, manager of

SEE DISCOVERY / 12A

Spectators cry, pray, get giddy

By ROBERT McCLURE
Staff Writer

TITUSVILLE — For just a moment after *Discovery* soared skyward, spectators peering east from the Max Brewer Causeway lost sight of the space shuttle in a low-level cloud.

For a very long couple of seconds, *Discovery* was nowhere to be seen.

At long last, it speared through the top of the cloud.

Wildly, the crowd whooped, yelled and whistled.

"All the way, U.S.A! All the way, U.S.A!" they chanted.

Some thanked God. Some cried. All rejoiced.

"I got goose bumps all over. It's unbelievable, it's unbelievable," said Theresa Lowe of Pascagoula, Miss. "That is something I'll remember the rest of my life."

"I'm so excited. I didn't expect it to be this exciting," said Allyson O'Steen, a junior at Clemson University in South Carolina, who drove down on a whim.

Veteran shuttle watchers Virginia and George Adams of Margate, who had seen the *Challenger* explode, were particularly relieved.

"I didn't take a breath of air for 72 seconds," said Virginia Adams, referring to her reaction in 1986. "I thought this launch was fantastic."

Moments after the launch, her husband said: "The timing was just right. A little longer and it would have been too cloudy. Seeing it made me want to jump up and down."

"It's a milestone in history," said

SEE SPECTATORS / 15A

Weekly Review Special Report

What's the BIG DEAL?

A voter's guide to free trade

By TERRANCE WILLS
Gazette Ottawa Bureau

Free trade with the U.S. has become the biggest issue in the Nov. 21 election.

Culture has been major concern.

Can we work in U.S.?

Cheaper U.S. goods?

Why it's a big deal

Why business likes it

Why there's opposition

What about subsidies?

Escaping U.S. penalties

Is energy threatened?

U.S. wine should be cheaper.

Opinions differ on what could happen to Canadian water.

What happens to water?

What do farmers think?

Rules on investment

The culture question

AWARD OF EXCELLENCE

SPECIAL NEWS TOPIC
EDITOR'S CHOICE
National/International
The Gazette
Montreal, Canada

Designer
Julien Chung
Illustrator
Paul Gamboli
Art Director
Lucy Lacava
Editors
Brian Kappler, Bryan Demchinsky

ON HARTFORD'S HORIZON

Developers stretch skyline to fit dreams

Continued from Page 1

floodlit at night, imparting a glow on the skyline that would be visible for miles. The developers estimate they also would bring to downtown about 10,000 more workers.

On an oversized wall map in her windowless bunker of an office, Williams' staff has plotted 20 lesser projects in the planning stages for downtown and its increasingly active periphery.

"We're really under siege," said Williams, whose tenure as director started in 1980, at the outset of the boom. Perpetually harried, she is not complaining. "It's an exciting time."

More than the skyline of the city's compact central business district is changing. The latest round of activity goes beyond the construction of office buildings:

- I-84, a deep wound carved through the middle of the city nearly 30 years ago, is to be covered with decks that would hide the highway with two small parks and, possibly, stores and a parking garage. The project is part of the reconstruction of I-84 and I-91.
- Pratt Street, a once-fashionable lane of jewelers and furriers, is being renovated by a partnership of Aetna Life & Casualty Co. and developers David T. Chase and Richard H. Gordon. By early next year, the street is to be paved with bricks as a pedestrian mall that planners expect will be the main thoroughfare from the Civic Center to the stores of Main Street.
- The first downtown hotel to be built since the Sheraton-Hartford Hotel opened in 1975 is under construction on Asylum Street, behind the brick Queen Anne facade of the century-old Goodwin building. The 125-room, suites-only hotel will be part of the 30-story Goodwin Square office-and-hotel complex.
- After 20 years of talking about what might be, the renovation of Union Station is nearly complete. City officials are optimistic the old brownstone landmark, which is to house the popular Hot Tomato's restaurant, a bar and a food court, can be the cornerstone of an entertainment district. Three nightclubs are across the street and a fourth is around the corner.
- Construction is to begin this summer on a riverfront park immediately south of the downtown, including the first stage of a river walk that will stretch from Windsor to Wethersfield. State transportation officials say, however, they do not have enough money to carry out plans to cover I-91 with two pedestrian plazas and rejoin downtown with the Connecticut River.
- City officials are working on plans for a $100 million convention center north of the highway, on land that has been vacant since the bulldozers of urban renewal rumbled through in the late 1950s.
- More people would be able to live downtown or nearby. Linden Court at City Park, the first new luxury condominiums downtown since the Bushnell Plaza tower was completed in 1969, is to be constructed south of Bushnell Park, between Linden Place and Elm Street. The city council in April approved the first phase of the project, a 29-story tower with 202 condominiums.

The top floors of Cutter Financial Center, on the north side of the park, are to be occupied by 102 luxury condominiums. Charter Oak Square, a 214-unit apartment building, is ready to open at Main Street and Charter Oak Avenue, on downtown's southern periphery, where restaurants have opened in historic, rehabilitated buildings. Renaissance Place, a 19-story office-and-housing complex proposed for a site nearby, on Prospect Street, would have 87 condominiums.

While the plans for the three big office towers have grabbed the headlines, the development group behind City Park, MONY/Capitol Joint Venture, predicts developers are ready to turn their attention to housing.

"My feeling about downtown Hartford is it has arrived at a point in its life where housing will be in demand and continue to be in demand for 10 years," said Howard W. Nannen, a former city planner who is a partner in MONY/Capitol. "Our project is just the tip of the iceberg."

Nannen said his group's research shows a demand in the downtown area for nearly 1,000 units of middle- and upper-income housing. Housing is crucial to enlivening the downtown, city officials say.

Hartford rewrote its downtown zoning regulations in 1984, the same year the city council adopted a downtown development plan amid concerns the central business district would never be more than a high-rise office park.

A key component of the new code was a requirement that all new buildings downtown have street-level stores or restaurants, an attempt to make the streetscape lively for pedestrians.

The goal was to make Hartford a "24-hour city," or at least one that didn't roll up all the sidewalks at 6 p.m.

A design review board was created to advise the city council, which is the zoning authority in Hartford. The regulations also created a two-step approval process that provides months of comment and review.

As a result of the city's review, every downtown high-rise proposal has seen major design changes.

Massive parking garages were forced underground in plans for Cutter Financial Center and 180 Allyn Street because city officials feared the garages would have a deadening effect on the street.

City officials also persuaded Gordon to abandon plans to build glass-skinned office towers at Main and State streets, near the Old State House.

Instead, he built State House Square — a retail-and-office complex clad in a brown granite more sympathetic to its historic surroundings. It also has a major addition to downtown retailing, a 72,500-square-foot mall, the Pavilion at State House Square.

While the city has been more assertive in regulating the design of proposed buildings, its attitude on regulating against an overbuilt Hartford has been laissez-faire.

"As a practical matter, I think the problem solves itself," said I. Charles Mathews, chairman of the council's planning, development and zoning committee.

Mathews said he does not expect lenders to finance a building unless several tenants have agreed to lease space. He said, "The financial institutions will govern whether a project is doable."

Guest, hired from Cincinnati in 1986 to oversee the reorganization of all community development and planning functions, is not so confident.

In reality, the council is in no position to prevent the downtown from being overbuilt. It already has approved two of the big three: Cutter Financial Center and 180 Allyn Street.

As a matter of legal right, developers can build 10 square feet of office or retail space for every square foot of land in a given parcel downtown.

The city has a stronger say when developers seek the city council's permission to exceed size restrictions.

Knowing that 80 percent of local property taxes are generated by office towers and other commercial property, the council has been reluctant to discourage developers who wish to build big buildings.

The ability of developers to finance their skyscrapers is likely to remain the biggest factor limiting growth.

"The other limiting factor is traffic," Mathews said. And here, Mathews and Guest agree, the city needs to be more active.

According to a national traffic engineering journal, Hartford has the 19th-worse traffic congestion of any metropolitan area with 1 million people. It ranks ahead of Philadelphia, Cleveland, Baltimore, Kansas City, Cincinnati, Milwaukee, St. Louis and Miami.

The city is building a computer data base on all downtown buildings and the traffic they generate, but, for now, the city generally relies on traffic studies commissioned by developers.

The Tower at Society Square, the 45-story office building proposed by Society for Savings in the heart of downtown, seems likely to force the issue. The site is across from the Old State House, bordered by Pratt, Main and Asylum streets.

The bank wants to build a 1,000-car parking garage beneath the building (870 spaces now and the rest in a later phase) that Williams said will make gridlock commonplace on Asylum Street and spill over to several key intersections.

"The challenge for Society will be the issue of where to park the cars," Williams said. "Society is going to force us to do something on traffic."

The city is re-examining its downtown zoning regulations with an eye toward measures that might encourage more parking on the periphery of downtown.

The other issue increasingly drawing the attention of planners is the pressure downtown land values are placing on the neighborhoods around downtown, particularly to the south.

Developers are looking at South Main Street and the blocks south of Bushnell Park as potential office sites.

"What we have to be concerned about is the transition from neighborhoods to that downtown skyline," Guest said. "We have a very walkable downtown, a relatively good pedestrian atmosphere."

With the exception of the vacant tracts north of I-84, Guest said, the city planning department hopes to prevent the central business district from sprawling beyond its traditional borders — I-84 to the north, Asylum Hill to the west, Bushnell Park to the south and the river to the east.

"The core is still very small and very tight. To me, that's a characteristic of Hartford that ought to be valued," Guest said. "We ought to manage how we allow that to grow."

How we created the skyline photographs:

In an effort to show readers a realistic facsimile of what Hartford's skyline could look like in the future, we wanted to overlay the proposed new buildings onto Hartford's present skyline.

To do this, The Courant used a computerized photographic process known as digital color-imaging.

We first took aerial photographs of Hartford's skyline. After selecting the best angles from these photographs, we also made photographs of the developers' three-dimensional scale models at the same angles.

The proposed buildings in the photographs do not have architectural detail because the models show only size and shape. In some cases, the building details have not been decided.

The photograph of each model and the aerial were entered into a computer through the use of a laser scanning device. Then a computer operator was able to overlay the pictures of the models onto the present skyline by combining these scanned images.

This new computer technology allowed us to create a vision of the skyline as it might look a few years from now.

Photo illustration by Linda Shankweiler, Tony Bacewicz / The Hartford Courant and Jon G. Barrientos / Newsday (Copyright 1988, The Hartford Courant)

Nine buildings included in project

The nine buildings, identified by number in the map, key and chart and profiled below, are not the only projects contemplated for downtown Hartford and vicinity. Other projects were excluded because too few details were available, their application status was unclear or they were outside the central business district. The subdued color of the new buildings was added to highlight them from the original skyline.

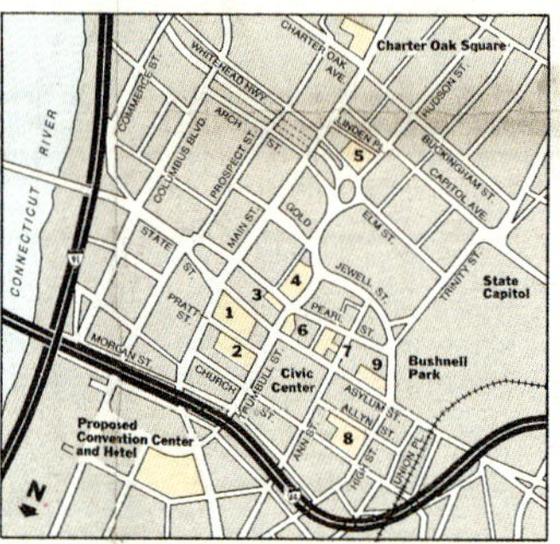

Key to graphics

PROPOSED AND PARTIALLY CONSTRUCTED(*) BUILDINGS

1. The Tower at Society Center
2. Aetna Realty Investors Building* (site includes Pratt Street Renovation)
3. 100 Pearl Street*
4. Cutter Financial Center
5. City Park
6. CityPlace II*
7. Goodwin Square*
8. 180 Allyn Street
9. World Trade Center of Hartford

EXISTING MAJOR BUILDINGS

10. One Commercial Plaza
11. Travelers Corp.
12. One Financial Plaza (Gold Building)
13. CityPlace
14. Hartford Civic Center

Graphics by Linda Shankweiler / The Hartford Courant

FEET: 900, 800, 700, 600, 500, 400, 300, 200, 100

10. One Commercial Plaza - 349 feet, 29 stories

11. Travelers Corp. - 527 feet, 34 stories

12. One Financial Plaza - 335 feet, 26 stories (Gold Building)

13. CityPlace - 535 feet, 38 stories

1 The Tower at Society Center

Asylum and Main streets

Height: **700 feet**
Stories: **45**
Square feet: **770,000**
Estimated cost: **$150 million**
Developer: **Gerald D. Hines Interests, Houston, Society for Savings**
Architect: **Cesar Pelli & Associates, New Haven**
Builder: **unknown**
Main financer: **unknown**
Tenants announced: **Society for Savings (200,000 square feet)**
Parking spaces: **870 (phase 1)**
Status/completion date: **Mid-1991**

2 Aetna Realty Investors Building

242 Trumbull St.

Height: **116 feet**
Stories: **eight**
Square feet: **240,000 square feet office; 80,000 square feet retail.**
Estimated cost: **$50 million**
Developer: **Aetna Life & Casualty Co., David T. Chase, Richard H. Gordon.**
Architect: **Russell Gibson von Dohlen Inc., Farmington**
Builder: **Development Consultants Inc.**
Main financer: **Aetna Life & Casualty Co.**
Tenants announced: **Aetna Realty Investors and other Aetna divisions for 220,000 square feet.**
Parking spaces: **None on site**
Status/completion date: **Under construction; spring 1989**

3 100 Pearl Street

100 Pearl St.

Height: **220 feet**
Stories: **17**
Square feet: **291,243**
Estimated cost: **$45 million**
Developer: **Pearl Street Associates Limited Partnership, Hartford**
Architect: **Jeter Cook & Jepson, Hartford**
Builder: **Fusco Corp., New Haven**
Main financer: **Bank of Boston Connecticut**
Tenants announced: **Mechanics Savings Bank (60,000 squarefeet), Bank of Boston Connecticut (30000 square feet), and the Farley Co. (12,000 square feet)**
Parking spaces: **283**
Status/completion date: **Under constructon, with a summer 1988 completion**

4 Cutter Financial Center

111 Pearl St.

Height: **878 feet**
Stories: **59**
Square feet: **1.25 million**
Estimated cost: **$350 million**
Developer: **Cutter Realty Group, Stamford**
Architect: **Russell Gibson von Dohlen Inc., Farmington**
Builder: **Gilbane Builders, Providence, R.I.**
Main financer: **not available**
Tenants announced: **United Bank & Trust Co.**
Parking spaces: **1,232**
Status/completion date: **Final plans approved; financing incomplete**

5 City Park

30 Linden Place

Height: **330 feet**
Stories: **29**
Units: **202 condominiums.**
Estimated cost: **not available**
Developer: **MONY/Capitol Joint Venture of Hartford**
Architect: **Fletcher Thompson Architects and Engineers, Bridgeport**
Builder: **Associated Construction Co., Hartford**
Main financer: **not available**
Parking spaces: **300**
Status/completion: **Final plans approved; construction to begin late this year.**

6 CityPlace II

185 Asylum St.

Height: **270 feet**
Stories: **18**
Square feet: **296,587**
Estimated cost: **$60 million**
Developer: **Urban Investment Development Co., Hartford**
Architect: **Jeter Cook & Jepson, Hartford**
Builder: **Walsh Construction Co., Trumbull**
Main financer: **Bank of Boston Connecticut will provide construction financing**
Tenants announced: **none**
Parking spaces: **300**
Status/completion date: **Under construction with July 1, 1989, expected completion date**

7 Goodwin Square

Asylum and Haynes str

Height: **522 feet**
Stories: **30**
Square feet: **350,000 square feet of offices, 125 hotel rooms**
Estimated cost: **$100**
Developer: **Fusco Corp., New Haven, and Keith Corp., Glastonbury**
Architect: **Skidmore, Owings & Merrill, Washington D.C.**
Builder: **Fusco Corp., New Haven**
Main financer: **State of Connectic fund**
Tenants a **Halloran, Hagarty; 75,000 s both (21. leased).**
Parking s
Status/co **Under con Offices to 1989; ho Sept. 1, 1**

The 1.1 million square feet of office space is being constructed in four projects (100 Pearl Street, the Aetna Realty Investors Building, Goodwin Square and City-Place II), with about 400,000 square feet of that space committed to tenants.

That means within 18 months or so, about 700,000 square feet of new, as-yet-uncommitted office space will be coming on the market. Hartford real estate experts concede chances are slim those buildings will be more than 60 percent leased by the time construction is completed.

Developers say Hartford is a "kick-the-tires town," where tenants prefer to see the buildings before committing to space.

They point to the construction of Xerox Centre, Metro Center and State House Square as examples of speculative projects that were built with only a modicum of pre-leasing, but were saved when various insurance companies agreed to take large blocks of space.

"If you look at the last few buildings, they were basically built spec," Russell said. "Metro was built, and then along came Cigna. Look at State House Square. Things were starting to get a little tight there, and then along comes Connecticut Mutual. If you look at the buildings Richard Gordon did, and then along comes Travelers."

William Farley, president of the Farley Co. real estate brokerage firm and a partner in the 100 Pearl Street project, said there is about 750,000 square feet of empty office space downtown now. Farley said the Hartford market would need about a year to absorb that existing space, and another year to absorb the 700,000 square feet of new space expected within 18 months.

Developers, however, still say the demand exists, albeit not enough to handle all that has been proposed.

"I'd say there is a good 3.5 million square feet that could be built and filled within the next three to eight years," said Daniel Friedman, chairman of Oakleaf Development Corp.

But what makes Farley and others nervous about the market's ability to fill the space are the huge shadows cast by the three largest development proposals — the 180 Allyn Street project by Oakleaf Development Corp. and Tishman Realty & Construction Co. of New York, the Cutter Financial Center by Cutter Realty Group of Stamford and The Tower at Society Center by Hartford-based Society for Savings and Houston-based Gerald D. Hines Interests.

The Cutter and Oakleaf projects represent more than a combined 2 million square feet of office space, with the Society tower offering 800,000 more. The remainder of the proposed 9.9 million square feet would come from other smaller and mid-sized projects.

The consensus around the city is that, at most, only two of the larger projects will be built. Most say the order probably will be Society, Oakleaf and then Cutter.

Russell offers a different and more disturbing scenario.

"I would want some odds, but I think every one of these buildings will get built," he said. "The market can't support it because they're all coming on at the same time. They say, 'Well, if we can get into the ground six months earlier than the others . . .' That's baloney. A tenant is willing to wait six months for another building for leverage to get a better rent."

But, regardless of which buildings become reality, the Hartford market will be deluged with new space. "Like anything else, markets can come back," Russell said. "But I see a market that could be overbuilt for years to come."

The engine that has driven the Hartford market to its current frenzied state has been the financial services industry, led by the banks and, of course, the insurance companies — both of which have benefited from a strong regional economy.

"The real growth started in the late 1970s and right at the turn of this decade, really started to move," Farley said. "The insurance companies started it, and then the banks followed on somewhat the same track. We've also had three other waves of growth — a series of reinsurance firms, software and hardware people and, in the past 18 months, out-of-state mortgage lenders."

Given the expansion of the insurance industry in the last five years, it is easy to see how the major companies have gobbled up space as if they were sitting at an all-you-can-eat buffet.

"The insurance industry in the past several years has exhibited what seems to be an insatiable appetite for space," said Anthony Caruso, executive director of the Hartford Downtown Council. "I guess some developers look at it as if the service industry will continue with business as usual, resulting in their building being leased up in a reasonable period of time. Then, there are some that are a little more cautious."

Insurance officials say consolidations will result in less need for office space, and what pockets of business expansion that do occur will happen in the suburbs.

And for good reason. In most cases, the suburbs are cheaper, provide easier access for the work force and expand the labor pools in one of the tightest labor markets in the country.

"In the last five months, we've actually given up 100,000 square feet in Farmington. We have no space search going, and that is very unusual for us," said Mills of Travelers. "We have recently acquired 160,000 square feet in State House Square. That's going to hold us for a while. We're not likely to be in the market for space for at least the next three years."

That time frame still leaves a window of opportunity for the larger projects scheduled to be completed between late 1990 and 1992. But there is no guarantee that the insurance companies will be looking for downtown space then, either.

Travelers currently leases 1.25 million square feet in the downtown area, having added an average of 100,000 square feet a year during the last six years.

Another industry mentioned by developers as a possible suitor for all of the new space is the banking industry, particularly if interstate banking finally is enacted in Connecticut in the next two years.

Not so, say the local bankers.

"We have not fully digested the impact of the Shawmut merger," Paul J. McDevitt, a senior vice president for determining space needs at Connecticut National Bank, said of the merger last year between his bank and Boston-based Shawmut Corp.

CNB occupies about 750,000 square feet in the downtown and across the river in East Hartford. "However, I do not see that our space requirements will increase significantly in the near term," McDevitt said.

A Connecticut Bank and Trust Co. spokesman also said that bank is not looking for additional space downtown in the coming years.

The out-of-state banks should have an impact. The question remains whether the giant New York banks will create their presence in the Hartford market by consuming some of the small or medium-sized Hartford banks, or whether they will take space on their own. If they choose the latter, there also is some question whether that space will be downtown or in the suburbs.

"If they start from scratch, they aren't going to start by leasing 200,000 square feet and filling it up," McDevitt said. "They'll lease 40,000. And some will come to Hartford, while others might go to New Haven or even a place like Meriden."

So, what will happen if it is left to existing businesses to fill the huge amount of new space built here?

"There are some areas that are growing at astounding rates, like the legal side, the accounting and, in some parts, banking," Russell said. "I'm bullish on that part of the market, and there is going to be a definite need downtown. Now, the question is how to quantify how much. That's where I run into problems."

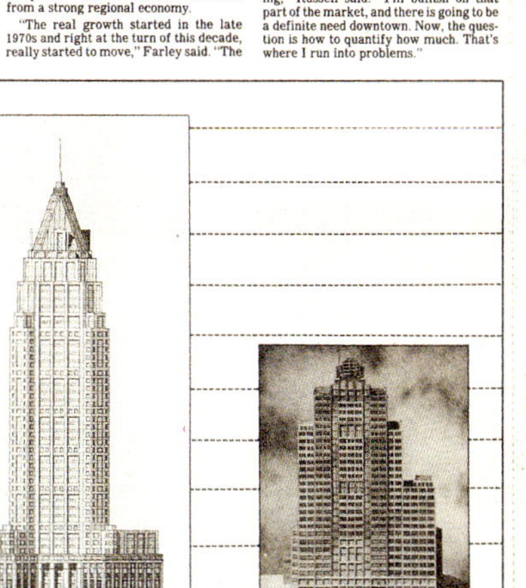

180 Allyn Street

180 Allyn St.

...eet
....69 million ...cluding ...million ...fice space, ...re feet of
...t: $225
...kleaf ...Corp., ...man ...struction

Architect: **Skidmore, Owings & Merrill, New York**
Builder: **Tishman Realty & Construction Co., New York**
Main financer: **Under negotiation**
Tenants announced: **None.**
Parking spaces: **1,200**
Status/completion date: **Final plans approved, site cleared; financing being assembled**

9 World Trade Center of Hartford

Asylum and Ford streets

Height: **405 feet**
Stories: **27 stories**
Square feet: **569,000**
Estimated cost: **not available**
Developer: **Chase Enterprises, Hartford**
Architect: **Russell Gibson von Dohlen Inc., Farmington**
Builder: **not selected**
Main financer: **unavailable**
Tenants announced: **Connecticut World Trade Association**
Parking spaces: **784**
Status/completion date: **Application for preliminary zoning approval is pending.**

Home
Regional Market abloom with colorful cultivators.
Page J1

Northeast magazine
Five inspiring cases of people who improved their health.
Inside Hometown

Sports
Risen Star wins Belmont; Whalers draft left winger.
Page C1

Sports Final

The Hartford Courant

ESTABLISHED 1764. DAILY EDITION. VOL. CLI NO. 163 — SUNDAY, JUNE 12, 1988 — 15 SECTIONS — FINAL — COPYRIGHT 1988, THE HARTFORD COURANT CO. $1.25

Tax fight erupts

Democrats feud about calling for increased levies

By JAMES McCARTNEY
Knight-Ridder Newspapers

See Democrats, Page A9

FUTURE This is how Hartford could look in the next five years. This view, taken from the fifth floor of the State Capitol, shows proposed buildings superimposed on the current skyline. The tallest buildings, from left, are: 180 Allyn Street, Goodwin Square, the existing CityPlace, The Tower at Society Center and Cutter Financial Center.

Downtown's daring rise

Tall talk in a towering urban market

By MARK PAZNIOKAS
City Hall Bureau Chief

PRESENT In the same view, CityPlace dominates the skyline.

ON HARTFORD'S HORIZON

THE BEGINNING — Hartford settlers created the early streetscape of Front Street, Farmington Avenue and Wethersfield Avenue, but a lot has happened since. Hartford's past is the blueprint for understanding what the city is today. **Page A12**

THE DEVELOPERS — Anthony F. Cutaia, a seafarer in an ocean of naysayers, and Daniel and Joseph Friedman, boys wonder, are developers of the two biggest projects on the boards. **Page E1**

TOMORROW — A look at the future of the city and its user-friendliness, a poll on attitudes toward Hartford and a daylong diary of the downtown.

See Developers, Page A10

Hopefuls refining support

By DAVID LIGHTMAN
Washington Bureau Chief

See Bush, Page A8

When construction dust settles, will the offices remain empty?

By SEAN HORGAN
Courant Staff Writer

See Building, Page A11

City housing chief turns memory into motivation

By PAUL BRADLEY
Courant Staff Writer

See Housing, Page A12

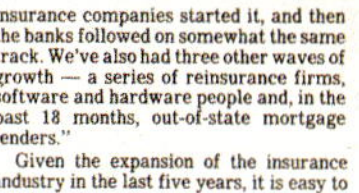

AWARD OF EXCELLENCE

SPECIAL NEWS TOPIC
Editor's Choice
Local/Regional
The Hartford Courant

Designers
Linda Shankweiler, Randy Cox, Marty Petty

Illustrator
Linda Shankweiler

Photographers
Brad Clift, Shana Surek, Tony Bacewicz

Art Director
Linda Shankweiler

Editor
Stephanie Summers

Chapter 4

Features design: seeking new ways to be distinctive

"News pages are getting a features look, so features pages are moving toward broad, general topics and a distinctive visual emphasis."

Subtle colors framed in white, original designs, mixed patterns — the best of 1989's features sections are as fresh as the season's spring fashions.

And nobody wore them better than *The Boston Globe*, *The Washington Post* and *The Washington Times*.

The *Globe*, *Post* and *Times* dominated the feature categories, winning 29 of the 74 awards, including six of the nine Silver Awards. Originality, use of color, white space, typography and illustration distinguished them from the bulk of the 2,200 entries.

Features judges were impressed by the use of white space as an organizational device in the *Globe*'s ArtsEtc. section; the subtle colors and varieties of typography in the *Post*'s Food sections; and the vivid illustrations that anchored the *Times*' life! and Book sections.

"Features pages are becoming the new magazines," observed judge Jose Diaz de Villegas, art director of San Juan's *El Nuevo Dia*. "News pages are getting a features look, so features pages are moving toward broad, general topics and a distinctive visual emphasis."

Judges also agreed that they looked for original ideas and restraint in design in assessing the entries.

"A lot of papers are reacting to what won in previous years," said judge David Griffin, layout editor of *National Geographic*. "Enough of that."

"Be yourself," advised judge Lucy Bartholomay, the *Globe*'s art director. "Set high standards, develop original ideas, then base the design on content. Don't overdue. Honest designs are the best designs."

COMMENT

Detroit Free Press

SPECIAL REPORT

THE TROUBLES

Northern Ireland struggles to find normalcy in chaos as 20-year conflict rekindles

Some are wary of Church of God's relaxed rules

SILVER AWARD

OPINION COMMENTARY, VIEWPOINT, EDITORIAL, NEWS ANALYSIS SECTION

Detroit Free Press

Designers

John Goecke, Randy Miller, Wayne Kamidoi

Photographer

David C. Turnley

JFK 25 YEARS

Over tragic November weekend, TV grew up

PERSPECTIVE

A SPECIAL REPORT

Remembering JFK

How the Camelot fable has shaped America in the 25 years since his assassination

"I believe the times demand invention, innovation, imagination, decision. I am asking you to be new pioneers on that New Frontier."

The day Kennedy died: Triumph, then tragedy

AWARD OF EXCELLENCE

OPINION, COMMENTARY, VIEWPOINT, EDITORIAL, NEWS ANALYSIS SECTION

The Arizona Republic

Phoenix, Arizona

Designers

Steve Anderson, Howard I. Finberg

PERSPECTIVE

SPECIAL REPORT

A NEW PHOENIX RISES

Downtown sports new skyline, but will it create a city's soul?

Politics
Editorials
Opinion-Commentary

THE SUN
Perspective

SECTION P
SUNDAY NOVEMBER 27, 1988

RESTRUCTURING THE SCHOOLS

IN CHICAGO

Radical reform tackles bureaucracy head-on

By Kathy Lally

Starting over in Chicago

Key elements of the new school plan:

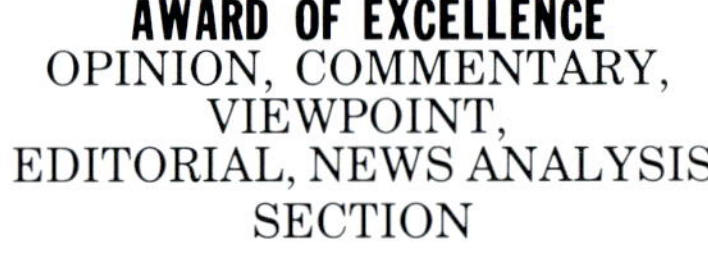

AWARD OF EXCELLENCE
OPINION, COMMENTARY, VIEWPOINT, EDITORIAL, NEWS ANALYSIS SECTION
The Baltimore Sun

Designers
Tony Deferia, Charles R. Hazard
Illustrators
Tony Deferia, Charles R. Hazard
Art Directors
Tony Deferia, Charles R. Hazard
Editor
Bill Salganik

REFOCUSING ON ECONOMIC REALITY

The post-election dollar is shaky, but don't expect the ceiling to cave in (just yet).

By Stephen E. Nordlinger

Currency traders (in Tokyo and elsewhere) will give us an early reading on George Bush's handling of the deficit.

It's time to bring back the orphanage

By Lois G. Forer

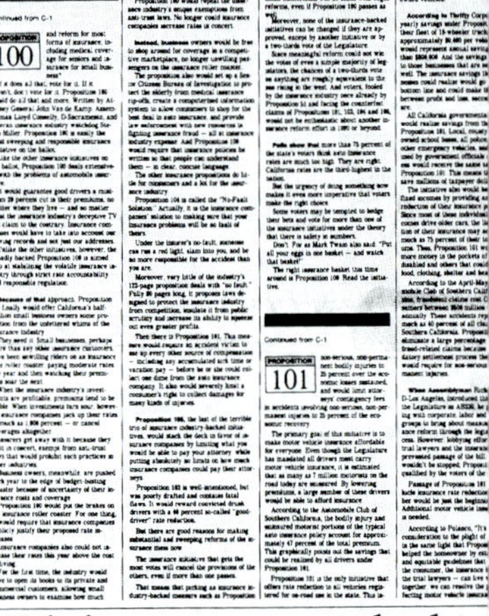

THE GREAT CA[...] INSURANCE WA[...]

PROPOSITION 100

PROPOSITION 101

This is no way to make law

Whatever happened to representative government?

By Robert J. Caldwell

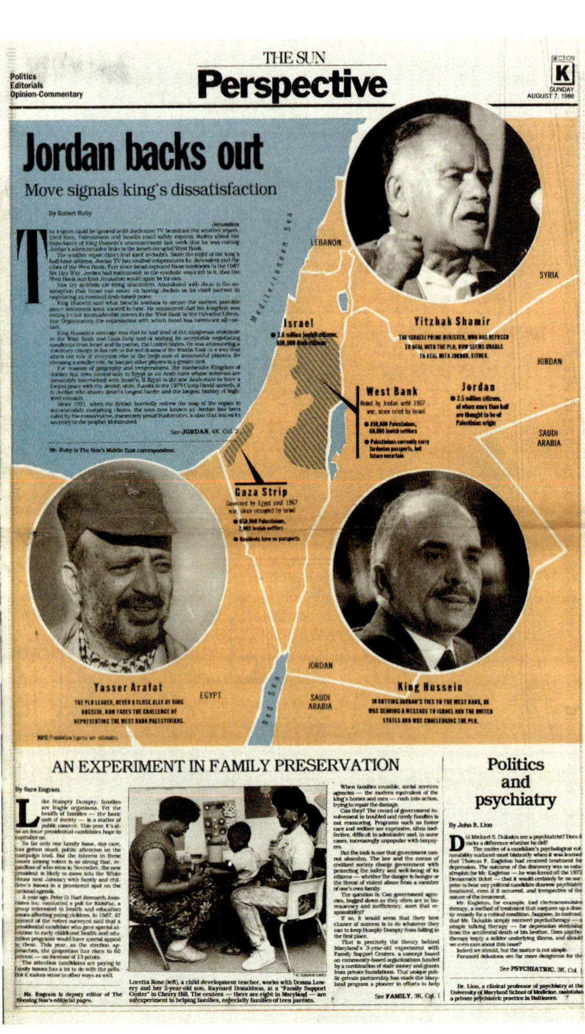

Politics
Editorials
Opinion-Commentary

THE SUN
Perspective

SECTION K
SUNDAY AUGUST 7, 1988

Jordan backs out

Move signals king's dissatisfaction

By Robert Ruby

AN EXPERIMENT IN FAMILY PRESERVATION

By Sara Engram

Politics and psychiatry

By John B. Imbert

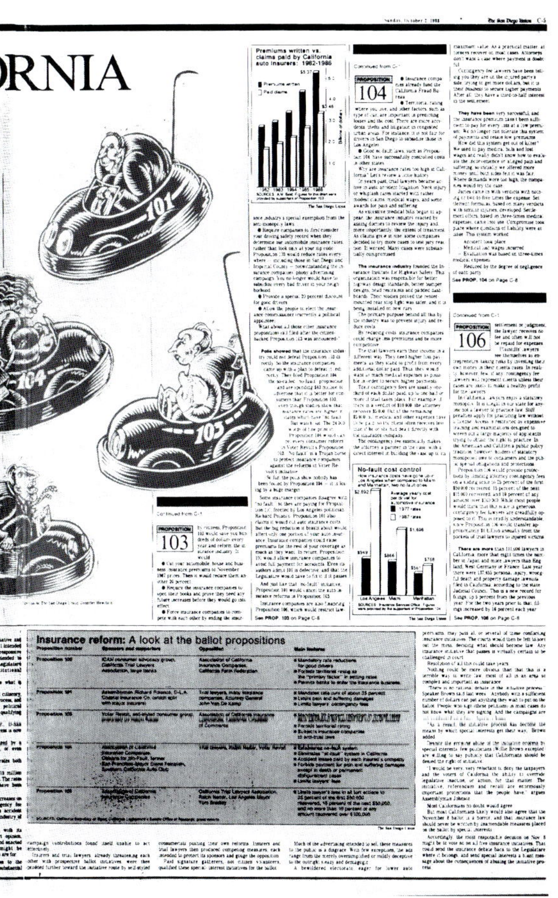

ORNIA

Insurance reform: A look at the ballot propositions

AWARD OF EXCELLENCE
OPINION, COMMENTARY, VIEWPOINT, EDITORIAL, NEWS ANALYSIS SECTION
The San Diego Union
Designers
Ken Marshall, Bill Evans
Art Director
Ken Marshall

COMMENTARY

Who are the real censors?

Seeking salvation for Africa's soul

Politics reshaped by degrees

Taking on the enemy with a carrot

AWARD OF EXCELLENCE
OPINION, COMMENTARY, VIEWPOINT, EDITORIAL, NEWS ANALYSIS SECTION
The Washington Times
Designers
Alex Hunter, Robin Applestein
Illustrator
Alex Hunter
Art Director
Alex Hunter

Opinion

He restored the American dream

The Reagan Record

The first successful, two-term presidency in a generation changed America and the world

Fiscal goals only partly achieved

The last Reagan budget:
It leaves Bush a persuasive case for no new taxes

COMMENTARY

Where militarism flourishes

De-deification . . . and vindication

Lost in farm aid shuffle

sonido

13

EL NUEVO DIA, DOMINGO 17 DE JULIO DE 1988

por SYLVIA M. LAMOUTTE

ESPECIAL PARA EN GRANDE

El guitarrista Leo Brower se destaca de manera importante entre los compositores jóvenes de Cuba

Ilustración por JOSE DIAZ DE VILLEGAS, HIJO

La rica tradición musical de América Latina ha tenido una expresión culta tan importante como su música popular y folclórica

NO TODO ES TANGO Y RUMBA

INTRODUCCION

ARGENTINA

POR FAVOR PASE A LA PAGINA SIGUIENTE

AWARD OF EXCELLENCE
LIFESTYLE/FEATURE SECTION
El Nuevo Dia
San Juan, Puerto Rico
Designer
Jose L. Diaz de Villegas, Sr.
Illustrator
Jose L. Diaz de Villegas, Sr.
Art Director
Jose L. Diaz de Villegas, Sr.

hobbies

EL NUEVO DIA, DOMINGO 23 DE OCTUBRE DE 1988

9

Ilustración por STANLEY COLL

¡RRRABIA!

por EDWIN P. BURGOS D.V.M.

ESPECIAL PARA EN GRANDE

LOS ANIMALES TRANSMISORES

Aunque el perro es considerado como el mayor transmisor de la rabia a los humanos, en los últimos años los gatos han superado a los caninos en el número de casos de rabia reportados

POR FAVOR PASE A LA PAGINA SIGUIENTE

ORANGE COUNTY

LIFE

Los Angeles Times

Thursday December 22, 1988

ALL IN JEST

Clowns Love to Play the Fool—and Why? For the Smile of a Child

Just clowning around, from left: Jerry Coleman, Ryan Cody, Vicki Murrell, Carolyn Deiss and Nick De Long, and on bottom, Leo Gentleman.

A makeup kit—the key, some clowns say, to a total change in their personalities.

Got some spare change? Captain Leo wants to test his entrepreneurial skills.

INSIDE

The agonies and the ecstasies of the workplace get a pretty thorough going over at some special seminars on office survival. 3

For serious celebrants, the week's parties and the views and the caus-es were all—well, just plain breath-taking 4

If it's the thought and not the gift that really counts at this time of the year, this list is going to leave a few well-known people cringing 5

AWARD OF EXCELLENCE
LIFESTYLE/FEATURE SECTION
Los Angeles Times, Orange County Edition
Costa Mesa, California
Designer
Chuck Nigash
Art Director
Chuck Nigash

ORANGE COUNTY

LIFE

Los Angeles Times

Saturday September 17, 1988

At Aliso Beach, as was true all along the county's coastline, Labor Day weekend litterers did their worst, and groundskeeper Sabrina Schmitt gets an early start in cleaning up.

The Mop Squad

Summer's End Is When Vacation Begins for the Beaches' Trash Brigade

The early bird gets pick of the litter, as this gull finds at Aliso Beach.

INSIDE

Books & Authors: Theodore Taylor has no trouble shifting gears from children's books to some pretty heavy adult fare. Page 3

Family Life: How often do you prepare a formal meal—with stemware, good china and background music—just for the family? Page 5

Horses: Olympic gold medalist Melanie Smith will be demonstrating her winning ways at a clinic in Costa Mesa. Page 7

On the Waterfront: "Amazing" is the word most used for a busy doctor who rules the waves in yacht-racing circles. Page 8

AWARD OF EXCELLENCE
LIFESTYLE/FEATURE SECTION
The Orange County Register
Santa Ana, California
Designers
G. W. Babb, Katherine Garraty, Gwen Wong, Steve Elders

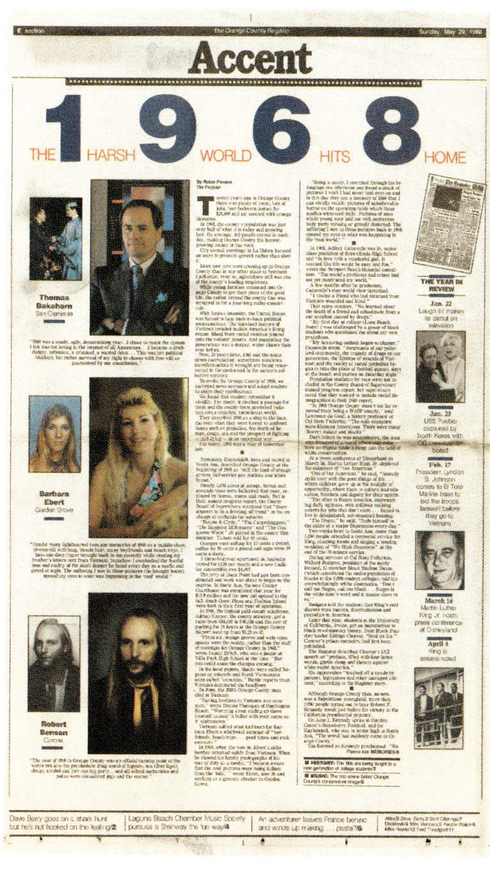

Accent

1 THE 9 HARSH 6 WORLD 8 HITS HOME

Thomas Bakehorn

Barbara Ebert

Robert Benson

THE YEAR IN REVIEW

E section | The Orange County Register | Sunday, September 4, 1988

Accent

A LOOK INSIDE

Vietnam today

REPORTER'S JOURNAL

A former resident of Saigon finds a once-bustling city has turned dull

Dave Barry sees cash value in theories on Grand Unification, so count him in/4

A rapist tries to explain why he did what he did and how it all began/9

A study on emotional life shows little has changed with men and women/10

AWARD OF EXCELLENCE
LIFESTYLE/FEATURE SECTION
The Orange County Register
Santa Ana, California
Designers
G. W. Babb, Katherine Garraty, Gwen Wong, Steve Elders

AWARD OF EXCELLENCE
LIFESTYLE/FEATURE SECTION
The Washington Times
Designer
William Castronuovo, Paul Watts
Art Directors
William Castronuovo, Joe Scopin

life!
The Washington Times

Robert F. Kennedy

House and garden special section/7

life!

Advice: Dating complaints/11

The Washington Times

NEXT STOP, THE NEW UNION STATION

Sunday New York Newsday October 9, 1988

PART II
ENTERTAINMENT

ROLLING SOLO

Keith Richards makes the album he hoped he'd never have to: one without the Stones. Pages 4-5

Theater: Word Games for the Stage From Richard Foreman. Page 13
Art: At the Brooklyn Museum, the Beauty of Cleopatra's Egypt. Page 19
Part III / Travel: A Spectacular Voyage on the Yangtze River.

AWARD OF EXCELLENCE
ENTERTAINMENT
SECTION
Newsday
Long Island, New York
Designer
Cynthia Currie
Art Director
Gary Rogers
Editor
Caroline Miller

Sunday Newsday January 22, 1989

PART II
ENTERTAINMENT

MAESTRO

Christoph von Dohnanyi has created a symphony of virtuosity and velvet, and added a little muscle. The result: The Cleveland Orchestra may be the finest in the country. Pages 4-5

Movies: Oscar, Meet Felix, Europe's Entry in the Awards Game. Page 3
Theater: The Dream's the Thing for Playwright Larry L. King. Page 13
Part III / Travel: Freeway Fever — Wheeling Around Los Angeles.

SILVER AWARD
ENTERTAINMENT SECTION
The Boston Globe

Designer
Various

Illustrator
Various

Art Director
James Pavlovich

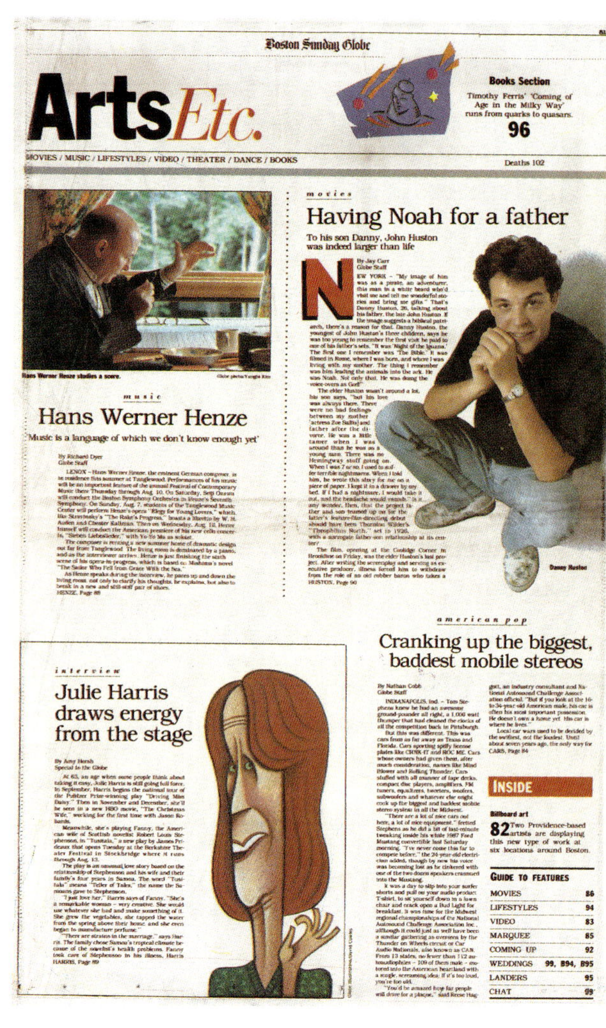

Boston Sunday Globe

Arts*Etc.*

MOVIES / MUSIC / LIFESTYLES / VIDEO / THEATER / DANCE / BOOKS

Books Section
Timothy Ferris' "Coming of Age in the Milky Way" runs from quarks to quasars.
96

Deaths 102

movies

Having Noah for a father

To his son Danny, John Huston was indeed larger than life

music

Hans Werner Henze

'Music is a language of which we don't know enough yet'

interview

Julie Harris draws energy from the stage

american pop

Cranking up the biggest, baddest mobile stereos

INSIDE

Billboard art
82 Two Providence-based artists are displaying this new type of work at six locations around Boston.

GUIDE TO FEATURES

MOVIES	86
LIFESTYLES	94
VIDEO	83
MARQUEE	85
COMING UP	92
WEDDINGS	99, B94, B95
LANDERS	95
CHAT	99

Arts*Week*

A SELECTIVE GUIDE TO ACTIVITIES FOR THE WEEK OF MAY 22-28

SUNDAY BEST

BOSTON AREA

FAMILY AFFAIR

THE REGION

Yo-Yo Ma

critic's choice

'Life and Fate' at ART

Lilac Sunday

THE BOSTON SUNDAY GLOBE · OCTOBER 16, 1988

Books

Reading about reading
Children's Corner surveys books for adults about books for youngsters.
108

SHORT TAKES

Anna and Sigmund Freud in 1938.

A spirited biography of Anna Freud

The 'Silver Fox' of nuclear politics

Graham Greene mines familiar territory

Graham Greene

AWARD OF EXCELLENCE
ENTERTAINMENT
SECTION
The Boston Globe
Designer
Miriam Campiz
Art Director
Miriam Campiz

COVER STORY

3
THE HARTFORD COURANT
THURSDAY OCTOBER 27, 1988

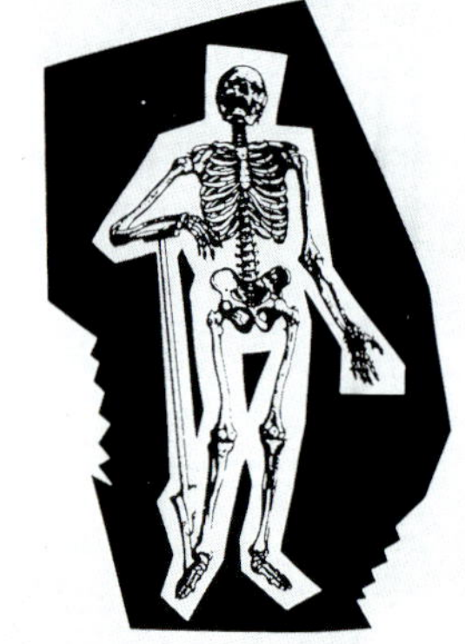

Adults taking over a children's holiday

Kids still get in on the fun, but grown-ups are celebrating Halloween in a big way

By FRANK RIZZO
Courant Staff Writer

Screams used to be so simple.

For Halloween, kids would dress up as ghosts, witches and goblins, wave goodbye to their parents, grab their double-strength shopping bags and go trick-or-treating by the pale light of the autumn moon.

Now Halloween, that all-American holiday, has been overwhelmed by sicko acts that are more terrifying than Freddy Krueger's worst nightmare.

Reports of dastardly deeds, such as tampering with candy, have tainted what was once a fun-scary night. Reality has driven a stake through Halloween's heart, snuffing out its playful spirit and leaving in its place a modern gothic tale.

Halloween, as we have known it, is dead.

Many parents now don't let their kids roam the streets in costume, or they limit their trick-or-treat time or accompany their children on their excursions.

In a national survey of more than 1,400 respondents conducted by Wendy's restaurants, 64 percent of parents say they plan on accompanying their children trick or treating, 55 percent will screen their treats and 19 percent will give private Halloween parties.

Now adults have appropriated the holiday for themselves.

"In the last four years, I have seen more adults than ever before coming in [for Halloween-related purchases]," says Keith Busiere, manager of Pelican's, a clothing and accessory boutique at 942 Main St. in Hartford. "I think more adults just want to be a kid again."

Some of that surge has to do with the fact that baby boomers now make up a lot of those adults, he says.

Adults make up 90 percent of the business at Fierberg's Costume Shop in Hartford. "In the past 10 years, I have seen it turn into a real adult holiday," says Joshua Jacobson, owner of the store. "For some adults, it's their favorite holiday."

Still, kids are not entirely out of the picture, Jacobson says. "Halloween is now a dual holiday," he says. "Kids are still celebrating, though they're doing it more at parties instead of trick-or-treating."

This year is especially festive for adults because the holiday falls on a Monday night. Parties, charity balls and special events geared specifically for adults looking for a night on the town are planned from Friday through Monday, making it a long weekend of revelry.

"Halloween in Hell II: Nightmare on Allyn Street" is a public costume party to be held Saturday night at the Hartford Arts Center, 94 Allyn St. Presented by Artworks Gallery, Company One and Real Art Ways, the annual event has grown over the years and attracts as many as 400 celebrants. (Information: 525-5521.)

"Kids are increasingly being pushed out [of celebrating the holiday] by the threat of going out at night, which leaves it open for the adults," says Paul Brenner, marketing director for Real Art Ways.

Brenner also points out one aspect of the holiday's spirit that specifically appeals to Hartford-area adults.

"I think that people in a city like Hartford are more likely to celebrate Halloween because it gives them an opportunity to take off their corporate garb and let loose," says Brenner. "In a costume, they don't mind how they look when they dance."

Though more stylish than ghoulish, a "Dress for Excess" party is planned for Saturday at the Wadsworth Atheneum in Hartford. Invitees are asked to dress in a period costume (but extravagance from any era will do) in celebration of the museum's "Fashion Before the Deluge: Paris/Vienna 1900-1914." (Information: 278-2670.)

And more than 900 are expected to attend the Connecticut Sports Club's 14th annual masquerade ball Friday at the Parkview Hilton in Hartford. (Information: 285-0097).

Several radio stations are planning bashes that attract hundreds of fans. WKSS (95.7 FM) is having an invitation-only party at the Treadway Hartford Hotel in Cromwell Monday. WTIC (96.5 FM) will hold its fifth annual Halloween Ball at the Parkview Hilton on Saturday. More than 1,500 are expected for that sold-out event.

And it looks as if every nightclub and restaurant in the area is planning at least one Halloween party — and in many cases several — during the weekend. Acts range from bands playing the oldies to punkish bands such as Closetful of Fear (at the Night Shift in Naugatuck Monday night) and Gidget Goes to Hell (at Katina's in Hadley, Mass.).

There are even events for adults planned during daylight hours.

There will be a 45-minute tour of historic burying grounds at noon Monday, sponsored by the Connecticut Historical Society. Conducted by William Hosley, Ancient Burying Ground conservation manager, the tour begins at the Gold Street entrance to the Ancient Burying Ground. (Information: 236-5621).

At the movies, adults can check out "Halloween 4" for the gore, "Alien Nation" for the neat makeup, "Dead Ringer" for double suspense and "A Nightmare on Elm Street 4" for Freddy. All four movies are rated R.

But kids haven't been left out entirely from the festivities.

Throughout the state, dressing up at events at schools, libraries and clubs are planned, offering an alternative to going out at night.

Some examples:

On Saturday at 1 p.m., there is a children's Halloween costume party at the Hungerford Outdoor Education Center in the Kensington section of Berlin. (Information: 827-9064).

The Hartford Public Library, 500 Main St., is showing spooky films such as "Halloween Is Grinch Night," "Winter of the Witch" and "Georgie" today at 3:30 p.m. A Halloween gathering is planned at the library Saturday at 2 p.m. (Information: 293-6074.)

Gertrude Blanks will tell spooky stories at the Connecticut Historical Society Sunday at 3 p.m. at the society's headquarters at 1 Elizabeth St. in Hartford. "Ghosts and Goblins in Connecticut: A Halloween Party" will be an educational experience as well as a fun event, organizers say. (Information: 236-5621).

The American Indian Archaeological Society in Washington will present an evening of scary stories for children between the ages of 6 and 12 Monday at 6:30 p.m. (Information: 868-0518.)

The readings for children, says Diana McCain, public information officer of the Connecticut Historical Society, have increased in popularity over the past few years.

"I think parents are looking for things to do with their kids," she says. "Parents are eager to take their kids to these events which they can enjoy as well."

Christine Ermenc, director of education at the Connecticut Historical Society, says that Halloween is not dead so much as redefined to include more celebrants, both young and old, parents as well as their children.

"It's a hard holiday to kill," says Ermenc

AWARD OF EXCELLENCE
ENTERTAINMENT SECTION
The Hartford Courant
Designers
Patti Nelson, Linda Shankweiler
Art Director
Patti Nelson

AWARD OF EXCELLENCE
ENTERTAINMENT SECTION
The Toronto Star
Designer
Kam Wai Yu
Photographer
Dick Loek

Friday
Watch art 'come to life' at Yale gallery

Saturday
Hartford Stage begins previews of Shakespeare

Sunday
Auto buffs, take a spin to car show

These and other best bets, Page 16

The Hartford Courant

CALENDAR

YOUR ENTERTAINMENT GUIDE FOR THE WEEK OF SEPT. 29- OCT. 5, 1988

PRINCE

ROCK'S SEXY EVANGELIST

PAGE 3

Illustration by BUDDY HICKERSON / Special to The Courant

AWARD OF EXCELLENCE
ENTERTAINMENT SECTION
The Hartford Courant
Designers
Patti Nelson, Linda Shankweiler
Art Director
Patti Nelson

THE TORONTO STAR, FRIDAY, OCTOBER 14, 1988 E3

COVER STORY

ROM adds robotics to prehistoric debate

CHRISTOPHER HUME

Forget everything you ever heard about dinosaurs. They weren't the stupid, lumbering creatures we were told. Far from it. If contemporary scientific thinking is correct, dinosaurs were quick, agile animals with strong social instincts and "a brain large enough to dream."

It's not surprising that after decades in the doldrums, dinosaurs are hotter than ever. Icons of pop culture, scientifically very sexy, the "terrible lizards" have never looked better.

Or more alive.

On Thursday, when the Royal Ontario Museum opens the doors to *Dinosaurs*, Toronto will get a first-hand glimpse at just what the mighty creatures *really* might have looked like. The three-month celebration (Oct. 20 to Jan. 2) will change the way we think about these mysterious and fascinating beasts.

The highlights of this eclectic festival of prehistory are four computer-controlled dinosaur robots that blink, growl, stamp their feet and sway their heads from side to side, as well as a superb and authoritative exhibition of dinosaur art dating back nearly 150 years.

In addition, the ROM has pulled a few skeletons from its own closets for the occasion. The main entrance, for example, is now graced with the reassembled superstructure of a 12-foot giant ground sloth.

But it's the robots that'll get people buzzing. Three of the four are half size and still they stand 10 feet tall. Covered in rubber skin, all painted and unfolded, they are startlingly realistic.

So are their movements. Each is mounted on a platform from which it doesn't move, so activity is limited. But what they lack in scope they make up for in verisimilitude. Their gestures are convincing.

Confronted with the spectacle, my two young companions, girls aged 4 and 7, were frightened at first but then delighted. The eldest ended up "feeding dinner" to the Triceratops, which obligingly opened its gaping mouth, and both chose one for a pet.

"Are they real," each girl asked in turn. I explained that they weren't but, for an instant, when the Pachycephalosaurus leaned down over me and rolled its eyes, I wasn't sure. In case you've forgotten, Pachycephalosaurus is the one with a 10-inch-thick skull beautifully designed for head-butting.

The other favorite was Parasaurolophus, the crested plant-eater that might have been a prototype for the monster(s) in *Alien(s)*. Ironically, only the high-tech Tyrannosaurus Rex failed to impress. For some reason, its skin has been left smooth and, well, rubbery. It looks like something you'd expect to find in some tacky stall at the CNE.

But what hits you most about this Tyrannosaurus is how it differs from the way it used to be portrayed. For instance, the tail on the model T. Rex moves up and down. For decades, the hulking predator was depicted dragging its tail behind it.

As newly interpreted, the huge carnivore comprises mainly head, legs and teeth. He may have hunted in packs and cruised at speeds of 3 to 5 miles per hour, tail raised well off the ground.

"Tyrannosaurus Rex was really a great big bird," declares renegade paleontologist and artist Robert Bakker. "Birds *are* dinosaurs. They evolved from close relatives of Tyrannosaurus . . . It's not coincidence that the rear end of a turkey looks startlingly like

CONTINUED ON E4

CHARLES KNIGHT'S 1897 painting was ahead of its time — a crisp, clear study of two agile Dryptosaurus predators fighting to the death.

The Dinosaur exhibit at the ROM, 100 Queen's Park runs daily (except Christmas and New Year's Day) from Oct. 20 to Jan. 2, 1989, with several lectures, screenings and other special events scheduled throughout the run at both the museum and McLaughlin Planetarium. Phone 586-5549 for details.

DEINONYCHUS: 1969 drawing by Robert Bakker put him at odds with "Ivy League big heads.".

PROTOCERATOPS: 1975 sculptural rendering by ROM show's curator, Sylvia Czerkas.

ROBERT BAKKER: "To me, anatomy and art are the same thing."

ROBOT REX: Only Tyrannosaurus failed to impress.

What's ON

Listings are published free of charge. Information must be received by 1 p.m. the Friday before date of publication. Write What's On, The Toronto Star, One Yonge St., Toronto M5E 1E6. We regret that we cannot take listings over the telephone, but late changes can be phoned in between 10 a.m. and noon Mondays at 869-4485.

SUNDAY SEPTEMBER 4, 1988

The Virginian-Pilot The Ledger-Star

SECTION G

■ YOUR HOROSCOPE/G14
■ ON BROADWAY/G15

The Daily Break

With September upon us, the cultural season can't be far behind. Consult our listings, beginning on page G7, to find out what's ahead in music, dance, theater, film, visual arts and lectures.

ARTS CALENDAR 1988 · 1989

SUNDAY OCTOBER 2, 1988

The Virginian-Pilot The Ledger-Star

SECTION G

■ ON BROADWAY/G7
■ YOUR HOROSCOPE/G8

The Daily Break

the man who would be

KING OF CABLE

With his new TV channel about to debut, mogul Ted Turner declares 'total war' on the networks

Ted Turner, above, says his new channel will rely heavily at first on his library of classic films, including a two-part showing of "Gone With the Wind" Monday and Tuesday nights.

MUSIC

Riding high, Bruce Hornsby has his feet on earth

Bruce Hornsby and The Range perform Tuesday and Wednesday at Chrysler Hall.

TELEVISION

WTKR hoping to ride pricey reruns of 'Cosby' to the top of the ratings

Media: WAVY makes news with Tawana Brawley coverage **G9** ■ **Music:** Willett Hall goes Broadway **G4**

Art: Chrysler adds Mayan ceramics **G10** ■ **Travel:** Industry rebounds in wake of Hurricane Gilbert **G11**

AWARD OF EXCELLENCE
ENTERTAINMENT SECTION
The Virginian-Pilot and The Ledger-Star
Norfolk, Virginia

Designers
Peter Dishal, Sam Hundley, Craig Shapiro

The Washington Times

Food life!

SECOND HELPINGS

Chip cookies are still fresh after 50 years

A star is reborn

A MORE GENTLE ERA CALLS FOR MOM'S OLD-FASHIONED MEATLOAF

AWARD OF EXCELLENCE
FOOD SECTION
The Washington Times

Designer
Richard Slusser

Photographer
Glen Stubbe

Art Directors
Dolores Motichka, William Castronuovo

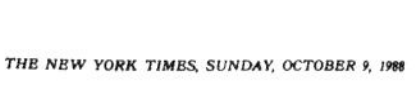

THE NEW YORK TIMES, SUNDAY, OCTOBER 9, 1988 XX 15

Coping With the Costs

The dollar is up this year, but so are prices. Still, there are ways to cut a few corners

By STEVE LOHR

The United States dollar, after two years of behaving like a punctured balloon, has actually gained a bit in value against the major European currencies this year. But what should be good news for American travelers in Europe — an increase in the value of the dollar of roughly 10 percent since the beginning of 1988 — has not worked its way into lower prices for dollar spenders because of inflation in the booming European travel business.

Rising international tourism, fueled by deregulation of airline travel and the growth of inexpensive fares worldwide, means that hotels, restaurants and shops have generally increased their prices in Europe by more than the dollar has regained in value this year. And there is enough demand for their services and wares for them to get away with the price increases. For example, luxury hotels and Michelin-starred restaurants in Europe typically report that they are seeing fewer Americans these days, but that gap is more than offset by increased bookings by visitors from Japan, land of the rising yen.

Yet high costs in Europe have certainly not kept American travelers at home. Air passenger traffic from America to Europe is up 10 percent so far this year. "The Americans are still coming," says David Kyd of the International Air Transport Association, the world airline trade group in Geneva. "They are philosophical about the dollar. Americans may be staying at cheaper hotels and restaurants perhaps, but they still want to travel to Europe."

American visitors, travel agents say, are also saving money by trimming their vacations to Europe. More and more, people will stay in a country for 5 days instead of 7 or spend 10 days on a swing through a few countries instead of 2 weeks. In both cases, assuming a steady daily spending rate, the reduction in cost is 30 percent.

The high yearly price increases in dollar terms, which American travelers in Europe absorbed during the previous two years, were no longer a feature of 1988. Still, despite the mild rebound this year, the dollar has dropped more than 40 percent since autumn 1985 against the West German mark and in lesser amounts against other currencies.

The State Department's per diem travel allowances provide a reliable guide to costs abroad; they are what the United States Government will reimburse its employees to cover moderately priced food, lodging and incidental expenses in different cities.

Between October 1987 and October 1988, the allowance for London has gone from $171 a day to $197 — a 15 percent increase. In Munich, the allowance rose from $132 to $155, up 17 percent. The biggest percentage jump among cities in the European survey was Madrid, up 23 percent, from $128 to $158. Even prices in some of the least expensive cities advanced sharply. The daily allowance for Athens rose 12 percent, though at $94 it remains the favorite major European city of the thrifty. Yugoslavia is also a prime destination for the budget-conscious, with a per diem of $112 in Belgrade.

In other major cities — Amsterdam, Dublin and Geneva, for instance — the price increases were less than 10 percent. And in Paris and Rome, costs, by the State Department's reckoning, agreeably behaved as they should during a period when the dollar rose — they fell. In Paris, the allowance fell from $180 a day to $162, a 10 percent decline; in Rome, it was down 6 percent.

Though bargains in Europe may be increasingly scarce, they can still be found on selected items. Theater in London's West End, for example, is still cheaper than on Broadway, though the gap has narrowed in recent years. The average ticket price in London is $22.56, according to the Society of West End Theater. By contrast, the average Broadway ticket was $31.10 last year, reports the League of American Theater Directors. A half-price ticket booth (with a $1.77 booking fee) is at Leicester Square near Charlie Chaplin's statue. The booth sells tickets for evening performances weekdays from 2:30 to 6:30 P.M. Matinee tickets are sold Wednesdays, Thursdays and Saturdays from noon.

STEVE LOHR is a correspondent in the London bureau of The New York Times.

Per Diem Travel Expenses

The State Department's current per diem allowance for Federal employees traveling abroad on business. The rates are intended to cover food and lodging at moderately priced establishments, as well as tips, taxes and laundry. The allowances are compared with those of October 1985, the year of the dollar's most recent high against European currencies.

City	Oct. 1985	Oct. 1988
Amsterdam	75	157
Athens	67	94
Budapest	73	116
Dublin	113	164
Geneva	90	135
Lisbon	65	120
London	124	197
Madrid	94	158
Munich	71	155
Paris	112	162*
Rome	87	136
Stockholm	137	183
Vienna	104	137

*Adjusted downward from $180 in September 1988 after less expensive restaurants were figured into meal allowances.

The New York Times/Oct. 9, 1988

When shopping, go to a country's strength and chances are the prices will be attractive — in short, goods that a nation is renowned for exporting purchased at the source, before all the middlemen have put their margins into the price tag. Ireland, for example, is surprisingly expensive for a country whose per-capita income is only two-thirds the European Community average. But woolens are an excellent buy, almost irresistibly so. I recently spotted a Donegal tweed sport coat, fully lined, for $145 at the duty-free emporium at Dublin airport. Except for the color, it was the same jacket, with the same label inside, that I had purchased for about $200 eight years ago in one of Manhattan's better men's stores.

To keep costs down, there are a few general guidelines. At the top of the cautionary list is to send friends and relatives postcards instead of calling them on the phone from a hotel. Phone calls from hotels are regularly twice or three times the normal rate. A recent 15-minute call from a hotel in Goteborg, Sweden, to New York added more than $90 to the bill. One is tempted to say that the way to keep expenses down while traveling in Europe is to avoid Scandinavia altogether.

Jean-Luce Huré

The manager, chef and wine steward at the Ritz Espadon in Paris show off their $44 fixed-price menu.

Partly because wages are kept high in service industries, in the name of egalitarian socialism, the result is poor value for the money in many Scandinavian hotels. Not long ago, I paid $180 a night for a Copenhagen hotel room that was a tiny, modular-construction number with all the charm and comfort of a World War II submarine berth.

BUT while hotel and restaurant prices are steep, public transportation and other services are efficient and inexpensive in keeping with the strong socialist tradition of the Nordic nations. For example, the excellent bus service from Arlanda airport to central Stockholm costs about $5.85, but the taxi fare for the same trip can run more than $40.

In most countries, buses and subways are far cheaper than taxi rides the same distance. But there are bargains: a two-mile ride costs $1.20 in Lisbon, $1.32 in Athens.

Buses, however, offer both a scenic and democratic tour of Europe's great cities. In Paris, a single ticket costs roughly 78 cents, while a two-day ticket, with unlimited rides on buses or the city's subways, is priced at $8.90. One favored ride is on the 52 bus, which starts at the Opéra de Paris, proceeds down to l'Eglise de la Madeleine, then along the back of Elysée Palace, past the police guarding the Republic, up to the Arch of Triumph and then through Avenue Victor Hugo, and finally down to Champs de la Pompe.

One-day travel cards in Dublin and London also offer bargains. Dublin Bus's pass, for unlimited city travel, is $1.30. London Transport's Travelcard, $3, allows unlimited travel on buses and underground after 9:30 A.M. weekdays and all day Saturday and Sunday.

Finding accommodations outside the larger cities can not only save money but also provide a more relaxing, distinctive experience than staying in a large urban hotel. The small towns outside Florence offer moderately priced lodging and proximity not only to Florence but to a number of ancient sites in the area. At Greve in Chianti, which is 17 miles from Florence and 25 miles from Siena, three-star hotels charge roughly $50 a night for a double room. In addition, Italian country-home accommodations can be arranged through Agriturist (651-2342 in Rome), for less than $30 a night excluding breakfast. In Budapest, the practice of staying in private homes instead of hotels is highly developed. These arrangements can be set up by a travel agent, and typically cost $10 a night.

If you plan to rent a car in Europe, it is often cheaper to arrange it from the United States through the car-rental company, a travel agent or airline. The price of reservations made at home can be drastically less than renting the same car in the country where you will be driving. In Munich, a Ford Escort hired from Avis for seven days with unlimited mileage is $356, if it is reserved in West Germany. But a week's reservation with unlimited mileage for the same Ford Escort made through Avis from outside Germany costs $211.

ANOTHER budget-stretching tactic is to eat at fine restaurants for lunch rather than dinner. At Le Gavroche (43 Upper Brook Street, London; 408 0881) the fixed-price lunch (served between noon and 2 P.M. Monday through Friday) is $32.50 a person, while the fixed-price dinner costs $71.40 a person. Similarly, Dublin's Le Coq Hardi (35 Pembroke Road; 689-070) offers lunch (served between 12:30 P.M. and 2 P.M. Monday through Friday) at $19.65 a person. An à la carte dinner averages nearly $43 a person.

On the Continent, where eating well is deemed a right, the tradition of first-rate, affordable food thrives, from the French brasserie to the Greek taverna. In the tavernas of Athens, such as the Pergoula (Markou Moussourou Street; 9234-062) or O Manitsas (93 Grigori Kousidou Street at Terma Zografou; 7794-891), meals for two, including a carafe of the local barrel wine, will typically cost between $13 and $26.

But perhaps Europe's biggest bargain is its rich cultural history on display to everyone, from the ruined Greek temples and theaters of Sicily to Napoleon's Arch of Triumph in Paris to the British Museum's Rosetta Stone, all free to those willing to go and see. ■

Jonathan Player

A tour in an open-topped bus can be a bargain in London. This one is approaching St. Paul's.

What Your Dollar Will Buy in 10 Cities in Europe

	Amsterdam	Athens	Dublin	Geneva	London	Madrid	Munich	Paris	Rome	Vienna
Taxi Two-mile ride	$5.50 11 guilders	$1.40 200 drachmas	$3.87 2.55 Irish pounds	$8.66 13 Swiss francs	$7.15 4 pounds	$2.08 260 pesetas	$5.09 9 marks	$6.60 40 francs	$2.05 2,700 lire	$4.00 50 schillings
Luxury Hotel One night, double room with tax and service	$237 475 guilders Amstel	$144 20,550 drachmas Intercontinental Athenaeum	$191 128.50 pounds Berkeley Court	$320 480 Swiss francs Richemond	$378 211.80 pounds Inn on the Park	$582 72,800 pesetas Villa Magna	$246 435 marks Vier Jahreszeiten	$396 2,400 francs Crillon	$252 330,850 lire Hotel Excelsior	$288 3,600 schillings Imperial
Moderate Hotel One night, double room with tax and service	$167 335 guilders Schiller	$77 10,950 drachmas Chandris	$121 79.54 pounds Buswells	$186 280 Swiss francs Hotel Warwick	$181 101 pounds Basil Street Hotel	$58 7,300 pesetas G. H. Colón	$153 270 marks Excelsior	$83 500 francs Hotel de l'Elysée	$167 220,000 lire Hotel Quirinale	$151 1,890 schillings Hotel Europa
Dinner For two with tax and tip but not drinks	$55 110 guilders Martinn	$70 10,000 drachmas Premiere	$32 21.28 pounds Patrick Guilbaud	$133 200 Swiss francs Perle du Lac	$134 75 pounds Belvedere	$94 11,766 pesetas El Cenador del Prado	$121 218 marks Sabitzer	$73 440 francs Le Train Bleu	$84 110,000 lire Passetto	$80 1,000 schillings Zu den Drei Husaren
Cup of Coffee In a hotel coffee shop or restaurant	$1.38 2.75 guilders Schiller	$1.96 280 drachmas Chandris Hotel	$1.38 91 pence Buswells	$1.33 2 Swiss francs Hotel Warwick	$2.41 1.35 pounds Basil Street Hotel	$2.40 300 pesetas G. H. Colón	$1.70 3 marks Excelsior	$2.97 18 francs Hotel de l'Elysée	$1.90 2,500 lire Quirinale	$2.72 34 schillings Hotel Europa

Based on exchange rates offered by Deak International at midday, Oct. 3, 1988. All figures above $10 rounded off to the nearest dollar.

The New York Times

Travel

Sunday, November 27, 1988

Section 5

CORRESPONDENT'S CHOICE

Settings for the Season

West Germany Candle-lit mass at Cologne Cathedral.

Mexico A posada staged at San Miguel de Allende.

Italy A Roman holiday in the Piazza Navona.

France A wood-burning world outside Paris.

Canada Powder and ice in British Columbia.

England A feast in five courses at the Savoy.

Eight Times correspondents from Rio to Rome describe a favorite place – plaza or church, mountain or forest – to spend the holidays. Pages 14 and 15.

On the Slopes Of Sarajevo

A week's trip costs $800, with nary a duck fajita in sight. By Clifford D. May. Page 17.

What's Doing in London 10
The city of Johnson and Dickens is all aglow for Yule shopping and celebrating. By Sheila Rule.

Shopper's World 12
In Florence, the visitor can wear out plenty of shoe leather while looking over the array of elegant footwear. By Frances Mayes.

Prey to the Travel Bug 27
It started with insomnia before a class trip. The best prescription is a valid passport. By Thomas Swick.

Where Eagles Soar

Northeastern California, a rugged region that celebrates independence, is a perfect habitat for the bald eagle. By Cheryll Aimée Barron. Page 8.

SILVER AWARD
TRAVEL
SECTION
The New York Times

Designer
Michel Valenti

Art Director
Michel Valenti

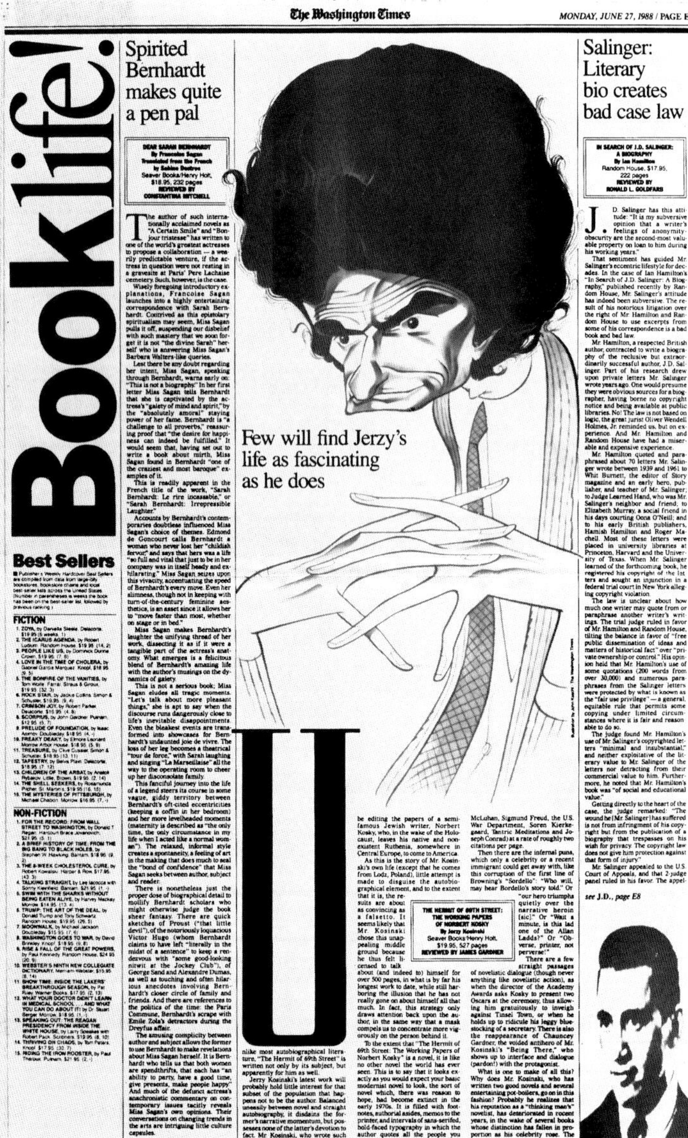

The Washington Times MONDAY, JUNE 27, 1988 / PAGE E7

Book life!

Best Sellers

■ Publisher's Weekly Hardcover Best Sellers are compiled from data from large-city bookstores, bookstore chains and local best-seller lists across the United States. (Number in parentheses is weeks the book has been on the best-seller list, followed by previous ranking.)

FICTION

1. ZOYA, by Danielle Steele. Delacorte. $19.95 (6 weeks, 1)
2. THE ICARUS AGENDA, by Robert Ludlum. Random House. $19.95 (14, 2)
3. PEOPLE LIKE US, by Dominick Dunne. Crown. $19.95 (7, 6)
4. LOVE IN THE TIME OF CHOLERA, by Gabriel Garcia Marquez. Knopf. $18.95 (9, 5)
5. THE BONFIRE OF THE VANITIES, by Tom Wolfe. Farrar, Straus & Giroux. $19.95 (32, 3)
6. ROCK STAR, by Jackie Collins. Simon & Schuster. $19.95 (9, 4)
7. CRIMSON JOY, by Robert Parker. Delacorte. $16.95 (4, 8)
8. SCORPIUS, by John Gardner. Putnam. $12.95 (5, 7)
9. PRELUDE OF FOUNDATION, by Isaac Asimov. Doubleday. $18.95 (4, -)
10. FREAKY DEAKY, by Elmore Leonard. Morrow Arbor House. $18.95 (5, 9)
11. TREASURE, by Clive Cussler. Simon & Schuster. $18.95 (13, 11)
12. TAPESTRY, by Belva Plain. Delacorte. $18.95 (7, 12)
13. CHILDREN OF THE ARBAT, by Anatoli Rybakov. Little, Brown. $19.95 (2, 14)
14. THE SHELL SEEKERS, by Rosamunde Pilcher. St. Martin's. $19.95 (16, 15)
15. THE MYSTERIES OF PITTSBURGH, by Michael Chabon. Morrow. $16.95 (7, -)

NON-FICTION

1. FOR THE RECORD: FROM WALL STREET TO WASHINGTON, by Donald T. Regan. Harcourt Brace Jovanovich. $21.95 (5, 1)
2. A BRIEF HISTORY OF TIME: FROM THE BIG BANG TO BLACK HOLES, by Stephen W. Hawking. Bantam. $18.95 (9, 2)
3. THE 8-WEEK CHOLESTEROL CURE, by Robert Kowalski. Harper & Row. $17.95 (43, 3)
4. TALKING STRAIGHT, by Lee Iacocca with Sonny Kleinfield. Bantam. $21.95 (1, -)
5. SWIM WITH THE SHARKS WITHOUT BEING EATEN ALIVE, by Harvey Mackay. Morrow. $14.95 (13, 4)
6. TRUMP: THE ART OF THE DEAL, by Donald Trump and Tony Schwartz. Random House. $19.95 (26, 5)
7. MOONWALK, by Michael Jackson. Doubleday. $15.95 (7, 6)
8. WASHINGTON GOES TO WAR, by David Brinkley. Knopf. $18.95 (9, 8)
9. RISE & FALL OF THE GREAT POWERS, by Paul Kennedy. Random House. $24.95 (20, 9)
10. WEBSTER'S NINTH NEW COLLEGIATE DICTIONARY. Merriam-Webster. $15.95 (8, 14)
11. SHOW TIME: INSIDE THE LAKERS' BREAKTHROUGH SEASON, by Pat Riley. Warner Books. $17.95 (2, 13)
12. WHAT YOUR DOCTOR DIDN'T LEARN IN MEDICAL SCHOOL . . . AND WHAT YOU CAN DO ABOUT IT! by Dr. Stuart Berger. Morrow. $18.95 (1, -)
13. SPEAKING OUT: THE REAGAN PRESIDENCY FROM INSIDE THE WHITE HOUSE, by Larry Speakes with Robert Pack. Scribners. $19.95 (8, 10)
14. THRIVING ON CHAOS, by Tom Peters. Knopf. $17.95 (30, 7)
15. RIDING THE IRON ROOSTER, by Paul Theroux. Putnam. $21.95 (2, -)

Spirited Bernhardt makes quite a pen pal

DEAR SARAH BERNHARDT
By Francoise Sagan
Translated from the French by Sabine Destree
Seaver Books/Henry Holt, $18.95, 232 pages
REVIEWED BY CONSTANTINA MITCHELL

The author of such internationally acclaimed novels as "A Certain Smile" and "Bonjour tristesse" has written to one of the world's greatest actresses to propose a collaboration — a wearily predictable venture, if the actress in question were not resting in a gravesite at Paris' Pere Lachaise cemetery. Such, however, is the case.

Wisely foregoing introductory explanations, Francoise Sagan launches into a highly entertaining correspondence with Sarah Bernhardt. Contrived as this epistolary spiritualism may seem, Miss Sagan pulls it off, suspending our disbelief with such mastery that we soon forget it is not "the divine Sarah" herself who is answering Miss Sagan's Barbara Walters-like queries.

Lest there be any doubt regarding her intent, Miss Sagan, speaking through Bernhardt, warns early on: "This is not a biography." In her first letter Miss Sagan tells Bernhardt that she is captivated by the actress's "gaiety of mind and spirit," by the "absolutely amoral" staying power of her fame. Bernhardt is "a challenge to all proverbs," reassuring proof that "the desire for happiness can indeed be fulfilled." It would seem that, having set out to write a book about mirth, Miss Sagan found in Bernhardt "one of the craziest and most baroque" examples of it.

This is readily apparent in the French title of the work, "Sarah Bernhardt: Le rire incassable," or "Sarah Bernhardt: Irrepressible Laughter."

Accounts by Bernhardt's contemporaries doubtless influenced Miss Sagan's choice of themes. Edmond de Goncourt calls Bernhardt a woman who never lost her "childish fervor," and says that hers was a life "so full and vital that just to be in her company was in itself heady and exhilarating." Miss Sagan seizes upon this vivacity, accentuating the speed of Bernhardt's every move. Even her slimness, though not in keeping with turn-of-the-century feminine aesthetics, is an asset since it allows her to "move faster than most, whether on stage or in bed."

Miss Sagan makes Bernhardt's laughter the unifying thread of her work, dissecting it as if it were a tangible part of the actress's anatomy. What emerges is a felicitous blend of Bernhardt's amazing life with the author's musings on the dynamics of gaiety.

This is not a serious book; Miss Sagan eludes all tragic moments. "Let's talk about more pleasant things," she is apt to say when the discourse runs dangerously close to life's inevitable disappointments. Even the bleakest events are transformed into showcases for Bernhardt's undaunted joie de vivre. The loss of her leg becomes a theatrical "tour de force," with Sarah laughing and singing "La Marseillaise" all the way to the operating room to cheer up her disconsolate family.

This fanciful journey into the life of a legend steers its course in some vague, giddy territory between Bernhardt's oft-cited eccentricities (keeping a coffin in her bedroom) and her more levelheaded moments (maternity is described as "the only time, the only circumstance in my life when I acted like a normal woman"). The relaxed, informal style creates a spontaneity, a feeling of art in the making that does much to seal the "bond of confidence" that Miss Sagan seeks between author, subject and reader.

There is nonetheless just the proper dose of biographical detail to mollify Bernhardt scholars who might otherwise judge the book sheer fantasy. There are quick sketches of Proust ("that little devil"), of the notoriously loquacious Victor Hugo (whom Bernhardt claims to have left "literally in the midst of a sentence" to keep a rendezvous with "some good-looking nitwit at the Jockey Club"), of George Sand and Alexandre Dumas, as well as touching and often hilarious anecdotes involving Bernhardt's closer circle of family and friends. And there are references to the politics of the time: the Paris Commune, Bernhardt's scrape with Emile Zola's detractors during the Dreyfus affair.

The amusing complicity between author and subject allows the former to use Bernhardt to make revelations about Miss Sagan herself. It is Bernhardt who tells us that both women are spendthrifts, that each has "an ability to party, have a good time, give presents, make people happy." And much of the defunct actress's anachronistic commentary on contemporary issues tacitly reveals Miss Sagan's own opinions. Their conversations on changing trends in the arts are intriguing little culture capsules.

see SARAH, page E9

Few will find Jerzy's life as fascinating as he does

THE HERMIT OF 69TH STREET: THE WORKING PAPERS OF NORBERT KOSKY
By Jerzy Kosinski
Seaver Books/Henry Holt, $19.95, 527 pages
REVIEWED BY JAMES GARDNER

Unlike most autobiographical literature, "The Hermit of 69th Street" is written not only by its subject, but apparently for him as well.

Jerzy Kosinski's latest work will probably hold little interest for that subset of the population that happens not to be the author. Balanced uneasily between novel and straight autobiography, it disdains the former's narrative momentum, but possesses none of the latter's devotion to fact. Mr. Kosinski, who wrote such effective novels as "The Painted Bird" and "Being There," purports to be editing the papers of a semi-famous Jewish writer, Norbert Kosky, who, in the wake of the Holocaust, leaves his native and nonexistent Ruthenia, somewhere in Central Europe, to come to America.

As this is the story of Mr. Kosinski's own life (except that he comes from Lodz, Poland), little attempt is made to disguise the autobiographical element, and to the extent that it is, the results are about as convincing as a falsetto. It seems likely that Mr. Kosinski chose this unappealing middle ground because he thus felt licensed to talk about (and indeed to) himself for over 500 pages, in what is by far his longest work to date, while still harboring the illusion that he has not really gone on about himself all that much. In fact, this strategy only draws attention back upon the author, in the same way that a mask compels us to concentrate more vigorously on the person behind it.

To the extent that "The Hermit of 69th Street: The Working Papers of Norbert Kosky" is a novel, it is like no other novel the world has ever seen. This is to say that it looks exactly as you would expect your basic modernist novel to look, the sort of novel which, there was reason to hope, had become extinct in the early 1970s. It is filled with footnotes, authorial asides, memos to the printer, and intervals of sans-serifed, bold-faced typography in which the author quotes all the people you might expect him to quote (Roland Barthes, Walter Benjamin, Marshall McLuhan, Sigmund Freud, the U.S. War Department, Soren Kierkegaard, Tantric Meditations and Joseph Conrad) at a rate of roughly two citations per page.

Then there are the infernal puns, which only a celebrity or a recent immigrant could get away with, like this corruption of the first line of Browning's "Sordello": "Who will, may hear Bordello's story told." Or "our hero triumphs quietly over the narrative heroin [sic]." Or "Wait a minute, is this lad one of the Allan Ladds?" Or "Obverse, printer, not perverse!"

There are a few straight passages of novelistic dialogue (though never anything like novelistic action), as when the director of the Academy Awards asks Kosky to present two Oscars at the ceremony, thus allowing him gratuitously to inveigh against Tinsel Town, or when he holds up to ridicule his leggy bluestocking of a secretary. There is also the reappearance of Chauncey Gardner, the voided antihero of Mr. Kosinski's "Being There," who shows up to interface and dialogue (pardon!) with the protagonist.

What is one to make of all this? Why does Mr. Kosinski, who has written two good novels and several entertaining pot-boilers, go on in this fashion? Probably he realizes that his reputation as a "thinking man's" novelist, has deteriorated in recent years, in the wake of several books whose distinction has fallen in proportion as his celebrity rose. The

see JERZY, page E9

Salinger: Literary bio creates bad case law

IN SEARCH OF J.D. SALINGER: A BIOGRAPHY
By Ian Hamilton
Random House, $17.95, 222 pages
REVIEWED BY RONALD L. GOLDFARB

J. D. Salinger has this attitude: "It is my subversive opinion that a writer's feelings of anonymity-obscurity are the second-most valuable property on loan to him during his working years."

That sentiment has guided Mr. Salinger's eccentric lifestyle for decades. In the case of Ian Hamilton's "In Search of J.D. Salinger: A Biography," published recently by Random House, Mr. Salinger's attitude has indeed been subversive. The result of his notorious litigation over the right of Mr. Hamilton and Random House to use excerpts from some of his correspondence is a bad book and bad law.

Mr. Hamilton, a respected British author, contracted to write a biography of the reclusive but extraordinarily successful author, J.D. Salinger. Part of his research drew upon private letters Mr. Salinger wrote years ago. One would presume they were obvious sources for a biographer, having borne no copyright notice and being available at public libraries. No! The law is not based on logic, the great jurist Oliver Wendell Holmes, Jr. reminded us, but on experience. And Mr. Hamilton and Random House have had a miserable and expensive experience.

Mr. Hamilton quoted and paraphrased about 70 letters Mr. Salinger wrote between 1939 and 1961 to Whit Burnett, the editor of Story magazine and an early hero, publisher, and teacher of Mr. Salinger; to Judge Learned Hand, who was Mr. Salinger's neighbor and friend; to Elizabeth Murray, a social friend in his days courting Oona O'Neill; and to his early British publishers, Hamish Hamilton and Roger Machell. Most of these letters were placed in university libraries at Princeton, Harvard and the University of Texas. When Mr. Salinger learned of the forthcoming book, he registered his copyright of the letters and sought an injunction in a federal trial court in New York alleging copyright violation.

The law is unclear about how much one writer may quote from or paraphrase another writer's writings. The trial judge ruled in favor of Mr. Hamilton and Random House, tilting the balance in favor of "free public dissemination of ideas and matters of historical fact" over "private ownership or control." His opinion held that Mr. Hamilton's use of some quotations (200 words from over 30,000) and numerous paraphrases from the Salinger letters were protected by what is known as the "fair use privilege" — a general, equitable rule that permits some copying under limited circumstances where it is fair and reasonable to do so.

The judge found Mr. Hamilton's use of Mr. Salinger's copyrighted letters "minimal and insubstantial," and neither exploitative of the literary value to Mr. Salinger of the letters nor detracting from their commercial value to him. Furthermore, he noted that Mr. Hamilton's book was "of social and educational value."

Getting directly to the heart of the case, the judge remarked: "The wound he [Mr. Salinger] has suffered is not from infringment of his copyright but from the publication of a biography that trespasses on his wish for privacy. The copyright law does not give him protection against that form of injury."

Mr. Salinger appealed to the U.S. Court of Appeals, and that 2-judge panel ruled in his favor. The appel-

see J.D., page E8

AWARD OF EXCELLENCE
OTHER FEATURE
SECTION
The Washington Times
Designer
David Bartlett
Art Director
Joe Scopin

Washington**Weekend**

Baby boomer offspring are finding 'It's just so much fun to go downhill fast'

Ski slopes resound with a new generation

By A.R. Hogan
SPECIAL TO THE WASHINGTON TIMES

Downhill skiing has snowballed into a family affair.

"Lots of baby-boom folks dropped out of skiing when they had children because most ski areas weren't catering to families and kids much until about the last five years," said Viki Fleckenstein, a member of the 1980 U.S. Ski Team, which competed in the Olympics at Lake Placid, N.Y. "But now, almost all the major ski resorts cater to families. There is steady growth.

"It's a great sport to do together as a family. You can grow and learn together. It's one of the very few activities you can do as a family for a lifetime," said Ms. Fleckenstein, 33, who supervised a "Family Ski Center" display at the Baltimore Ski and Travel Show earlier this month. "I've done it with my own parents, and with my little 6-year-old niece."

"It's just so much fun to go downhill real fast. It's like gliding, like floating," said Sarah Morton, 11, of Silver Spring. Her father introduced her to skiing two years ago. "The only thing I don't like is when you have to walk around, or ride up in the lift, and the skis and stuff are really heavy."

When Barbara Norkus joined the Ski Club of Washington, D.C., a decade ago, she recalls that most club members were single. "But as we've all grown older, we've met people in the ski club, gotten married, and had children. Now everybody's taking their children on ski trips," said Mrs. Norkus, a secretary in Crystal City. "The parents intend to get their children on skis as soon as the little ones start walking."

"Little kids love to ski 'cause they get to go real fast," explained Paul M. Maraschiello, 45, a Bethesda public relations specialist and avid skier for two decades. "Jessie just loves to zip right along," he said of his 8-year-old daughter, a skier for four years.

"When you share an experience with your kids, it enriches them and makes for group solidarity," Mr. Maraschiello said. "Plus, if you have a zillion dollars and start early enough, your kid could win a gold medal in the Olympics."

Added Mrs. Norkus, "It's a great way to get kids active early, to show them there's nothing to be afraid of in being athletic. You're on a difficult run and you see all these little 3-year-olds whizzing by you. They have no fear."

"As a cocky 13-year-old, I didn't think I needed any lessons," recalled economist Arthur A. Morton, 41, of Silver Spring.

Mr. Morton debuted inauspiciously on the Contintental Divide on a slope near his native Denver.

"I went straight down the slope [instead of zigzagging], not knowing any better. The Ski Patrol came racing after me, and told me they would kick me off the slope for the day if I did that again. I did, and they did."

In recent winters, Mr. Morton hired ski instructors to teach his daughter, Sarah, and 9-year-old son, Joey. "It's near insanity to expect to learn how to ski on your own, and it's best not to teach someone close to you either," he explained.

"The instructor took Joey on

W4 NOVEMBER 24, 1988 WASHINGTON WEEKEND THE WASHINGTON TIMES

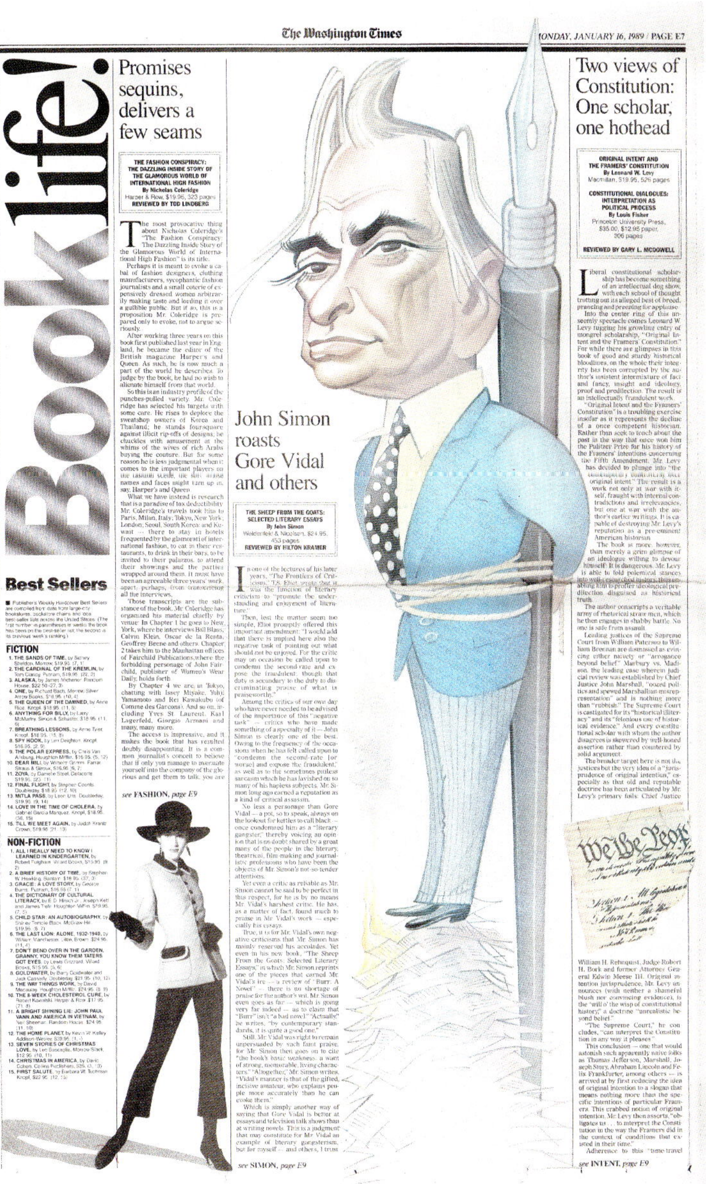

The Washington Times MONDAY, JANUARY 16, 1989 / PAGE E7

Book life!

Promises sequins, delivers a few seams

John Simon roasts Gore Vidal and others

Two views of Constitution: One scholar, one hothead

Best Sellers

FICTION

NON-FICTION

see FASHION, page E9

see SIMON, page E9

see INTENT, page E9

AWARD OF EXCELLENCE
OTHER FEATURE SECTION
The Washington Times
Designer
John Kascht, Paul Watts
Illustrator
John Kascht
Art Director
John Kascht, Joe Scopin

MIDTOWN: Bar and grill is a welcome addition to 18th Street. 7

SCULPTURE: Jeff Kirk's stoneware at Jackie Chalkley Gallery. 17

COUNTRY: Steve Sanders talks about joining the Oak Ridge Boys. 30

WashingtonWeekend

SPLATTERED!
Combat makes warriors see red, then yellow, then blue 4

AWARD OF EXCELLENCE
OTHER FEATURE SECTION
The Washington Times
Designer
David Bartlett
Art Director
Joe Scopin

NATIONAL WEEKLY EDITION

The Washington Post

VOLUME 5, NO. 52 OCTOBER 17–23, 1988 $1.50

A Year After Black Monday

POLAND'S FOUNDERING ECONOMIC REFORM

THE CANDIDATES AND THE ENVIRONMENT

THE ELECTION: A 50-STATE POLL

AWARD OF EXCELLENCE
OPINION, COMMENTARY,
VIEWPOINT,
EDITORIAL,
NEWS ANALYSIS
PAGE DESIGN

The Washington Post National Weekly

Designer
Marty Barrick
Photographer
Bill O'Leary
Art Director
Michael Keegan

COMMENT

Detroit Free Press

JFK 25 YEARS

Jacqueline Kennedy, widow of President John F. Kennedy, is handed the American flag that covered her husband's casket at his final resting place in Arlington National Cemetery on Nov. 25, 1963. Right, Detroiters mob Kennedy on a downtown street during his only visit to Michigan as president, in October 1962.

TONY SPINA/Detroit Free Press

Eyewitnesses to the tragedy can't forget

BY MARTIN MERZER
Knight-Ridder Newspapers

DALLAS — It has been 25 years now, and he is 71 years old and retired. But Dr. M.T. Jenkins still remembers so very much about that day.

He remembers a call over the hospital intercom, and he remembers sirens, wailing so loudly and for too long. He remembers the surprisingly tall man, a victim of gunshot wounds, sprawled on a table in Trauma Room One.

Most of all, Jenkins remembers a woman. "She looked so drawn and so white and so wide-eyed."

He remembers that this woman, her suit splattered with blood, cupped her hands in front of her, the way a priest creates a vessel of flesh as if to protect a soul.

He remembers that this woman did not relax her grip for a very long time as the doctors worked on her husband.

And now, this doctor who thought he had seen it all realized the enormity of what was happening. Later, they would call it the "Crime of the Century."

John Fitzgerald Kennedy, the 35th president of the United States, the hope and inspiration of a new generation of Americans, was on that table in Trauma Room One at Parkland Memorial Hospital.

And he was dead.

Nov. 22 marks the 25th anniversary of the assassination of Kennedy. For many Americans, as they go about their routine chores, it will be a day of reflection.

"The biggest difference now is there is so much concern with things and not much else," says David Pearson, a Miami public relations executive who served as an aide in the Kennedy administration. "Then, there was much more of a concern with ideas.

"Kennedy was the catalyst of our time. It's like our life was capsuled into those three years, and everything after that was an anti-climax. We need to keep looking for another Kennedy. We need a vision."

Jenkins, Pearson and scores of other Americans became unwitting footnotes to history on Nov. 22, 1963. They played small roles in a sweeping drama, and what they saw and experienced changed them forever.

It is possible to reconstruct much of the story through some of the people entrapped in the nightmare: the doctor, the government aide, a

See KENNEDY, Page 4B

West Virginians cherish memories of 'their' JFK

BY BILLY BOWLES
Free Press Southern Bureau

FAYETTEVILLE, W. Va. — After 25 years, the memory of John Kennedy does not fade, not for Charles Garvin Jr., now retired from the circuit court bench. In 1960, Judge Garvin recessed a trial so the jurors could meet Kennedy as he came through Fayetteville stumping the West Virginia hills and hollows for votes.

And not for Thomas Evans, a retired high school principal in Beckley, W.Va. A black man in an overwhelmingly white state, a Republican among Democrats, Evans says he was immediately attracted to Kennedy because, "The things he was talking about were the things people wanted to hear."

John Kennedy touched a chord in West Virginians that reverberates today, and apparently they touched a chord in him.

In "The Making of the President, 1960," his book on the campaign, Theodore White wrote that Kennedy reacted to the poverty and suffering of West Virginia's poor, "with the emotion of original discovery."

As the anniversary of Kennedy's assassination approaches, the bond between president and people is nowhere more evident than in West Virginia.

Richwood

Jim Comstock, editor of the West Virginia Hillbilly, is judging student exhibits at a social studies fair in the Richwood Junior High School gymnasium when a

See WEST VIRGINIA, Page 7B

A generation he inspired still mourns

BY JANE DAUGHERTY
Free Press Staff Writer

Classes were just changing at Largo Junior High School that relentlessly sunny Friday when Principal Morgan Fitzgerald's voice rasped over the loudspeaker. He said something like, "Boys and girls, we have just heard some terrible news from Dallas. President Kennedy has been shot. . . . We don't know much more, but he has been rushed to a hospital."

Tears streamed down hundreds of Clearasil-dabbed faces even before the news got worse that day. The dean of girls stood on the porch of the little house on campus that served as her office and the school clinic and silently hugged students as she urged them to go on to the next class.

In eighth-grade conversational Spanish, the usually gruff Mr. Short, his face an ashen mask of composure, shooed us into the little booths with headsets and turned on the day's lesson. It was either "En la Biblioteca" or "Albondigas, no te dije?" I forget. But the rest of that nightmare day seems as vivid as yesterday. My stomach felt exactly the same as it had two years earlier when I learned my 34-year-old father had died suddenly.

The fear was almost paralyzing. What would happen to us? What would the Soviets do? The Soviets were very much on the minds of many American school children after the Cuban missile crisis, only a year before. In Florida's public schools, we had spent hours in civil defense drills learning to "duck and cover" under our desks on command and memorizing megatonnage and the lethal levels of roentgens, or whatever they called those units of death from the A-bomb. We had seen more films of the horrors of Hiroshima and Nagasaki than any 14-year-olds should see: clinical poses of flash-burned bodies, clothes melted into children's skin, buildings imploding at ground zero.

If that was our reality, Jack Kennedy was our naive hope. The vigor, the promise that he embodied for so many of us had been contagious. Some of it was superficial: Girls

See HERO, Page 5B

At Hyannis Port, Mass., John Kennedy abandons the cares of his office and relaxes with Jacqueline and Caroline.

AWARD OF EXCELLENCE
OPINION, COMMENTARY,
VIEWPOINT,
EDITORIAL,
NEWS ANALYSIS
PAGE DESIGN

Detroit Free Press

Designer
Wayne Kamidoi
Art Director
John Goecke

8G DETROIT FREE PRESS/SUNDAY, DECEMBER 25, 1988

SPECIAL REPORT: THE ARMENIAN EARTHQUAKE

DAVID C. TURNLEY/Detroit Free Press

Some of those injured by the earthquake wait for their train to leave Leninakan for Yerevan where they are to be treated, above; in some cases, patients were sent on to Moscow. Below, patients at Yerevan Republic Hospital.

Stacks of wooden caskets are seen at nearly ever street corner in the city of Leninakan more than a week after the earthquake that all but wiped out the city of 250,000. Some people are so overwhelmed by the destruction that they seem to have lost their memories.

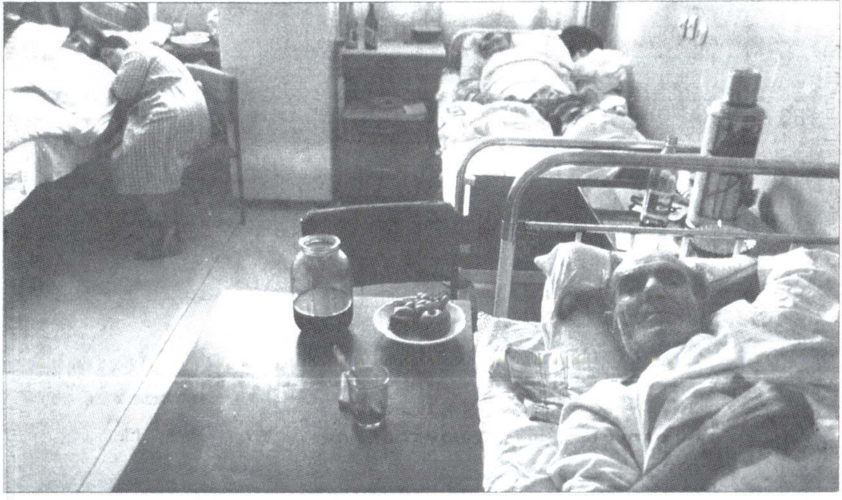

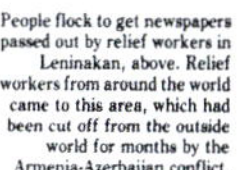

People flock to get newspapers passed out by relief workers in Leninakan, above. Relief workers from around the world came to this area, which had been cut off from the outside world for months by the Armenia-Azerbaijan conflict.

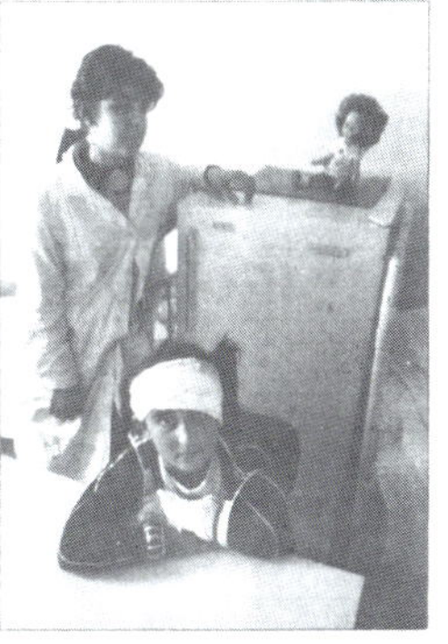

A young earthquake victim from Spitak receives treatment at the hospital in Yerevan, above. A man wearing war medals carries his ration of bread in the streets of Leninakan. Red eyes are to be seen everywhere in the city.

AWARD OF EXCELLENCE
OPINION, COMMENTARY, VIEWPOINT, EDITORIAL, NEWS ANALYSIS PAGE DESIGN
Detroit Free Press
Designer
Randy Miller
Photographer
David C. Turnley

SPECIAL REPORT: THE ARMENIAN EARTHQUAKE

COMMENT

Detroit Free Press

DETROIT FREE PRESS — SUNDAY, DEC. 25, 1988

WHEN THE CLOCKS STOPPED

DAVID C. TURNLEY/Detroit Free Press

A soldier and his family stand near a fire in the streets of Leninakan; their apartment building was destroyed.

David Turnley, a Free Press photographer stationed in Paris, traveled with relief workers to the site of the Armenia earthquake. He filed these impressions from the scene Dec. 15, his second day there.

BY DAVID C. TURNLEY
Free Press Staff Photographer

LENINAKAN, USSR — This city looks like the image you might have of a city the day after the nuclear bomb explodes.

Leninakan, one of three cities hit hardest by the earthquake that killed an estimated 55,000 Armenians, is a picture of destruction.

Clocks on buildings in the middle of town are stopped at about 11:30 — the time the earthquake hit on Dec. 7 and all but wiped out a city of 250,000.

You see homeless families sitting around fires in the middle of the street, where they spent the night. You see relief workers, the military and civilians working day and night to find survivors. You see coffins on nearly every street corner.

I watched Dec. 15 as an engineer stood on top of the debris that had been the building where his family lived. Armenian civilians digging into the rubble to find his wife uncovered her body and placed it into a wooden coffin. He knelt and threw himself on top of it, crying.

Red eyes are everywhere. Everyone has been awake either trying to find others or just surviving since the earthquake. Some people seem to have lost their memories.

It's striking how so many foreign relief organizations have descended on this region of the USSR that for so many months was cut off from the rest of the world because of the Armenia-Azerbaijan conflict.

Western workers are arriving in cargo planes and being given visas and complete access. The hotel is full of people from all over the world — journalists and relief workers.

There are all sorts of problems. The airport, used to 10

See ARMENIA, Page 4G

Levon Hekimian, 36, left, holds a picture of his wife and children moments before rescue workers found his wife's body in the debris of their nearby apartment building; his five-year-old son also perished. The body of a woman found in a collapsed building in Leninakan lies covered on a stretcher, below. Below left, a young victim from Spitak is treated at Yerevan Republic Hospital.

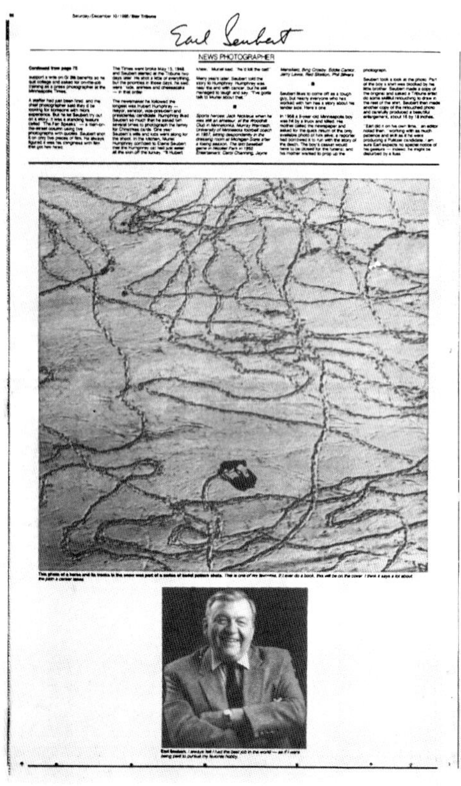

Earl Seubert

NEWS PHOTOGRAPHER

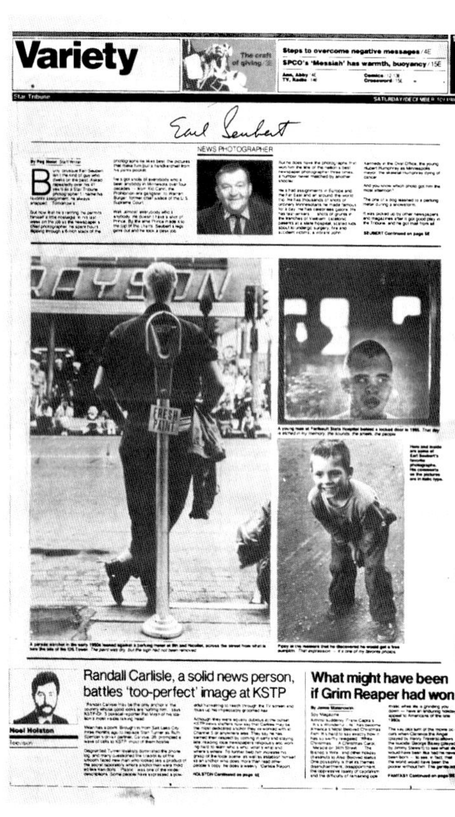

Variety

Star Tribune

Earl Seubert

NEWS PHOTOGRAPHER

Randall Carlisle, a solid news person, battles 'too-perfect' image at KSTP

Noel Holston

What might have been if Grim Reaper had won

AWARD OF EXCELLENCE
LIFESTYLE/FEATURE
PAGE DESIGN
Star Tribune
Minneapolis, Minnesota
Designer
Todd Grande
Art Director
Todd Grande

THE BIG STORY

Marching to the MUSIC

'What are the brass players doing?'

WHERE TO SEE THE BANDS

AWARD OF EXCELLENCE
LIFESTYLE/FEATURE
PAGE DESIGN
The Advocate and Greenwich Time
Stamford, Connecticut
Designers
Amelia Bellows, David Elkinson
Photographer
John Voorhees
Art Directors
Amelia Bellows, David Elkinson

BLIJDORP IN PERSPECTIEF

NRC HANDELSBLAD

DONDERDAG AGENDA

14 tot 21 juli 1988

The Washington Post

JANUARY 13, 1989

'Aliens Stole My George Winston Tapes!' Story, Page 686

Weekend

CAT LOVERS

EXPOSED!

They Know It's Wrong, But They Can't Help It

'Cats Just Don't Like You — I Hate That!' An Opposing View

AWARD OF EXCELLENCE
LIFESTYLE/FEATURE
PAGE DESIGN
The Washington Post
Designer
Richard P. Whiting
Photographer
Jesper Jorgensen
Art Director
Richard P. Whiting
Editor
Roger Piantadosi

AWARD OF EXCELLENCE
LIFESTYLE/FEATURE
PAGE DESIGN
NRC Handelsblad
Rotterdam, Netherlands
Designer
Willem van Zoetendaal
Art Director
Willem van Zoetendaal

Göteborgs-Posten

SÖNDAG

DEL 2

Killar och vänskap sexinformation, mamma, trista lördagar, snart nian, och sista nattbussen. Ett samtal om livet i Lerum när man är

14

AWARD OF EXCELLENCE
LIFESTYLE/FEATURE
PAGE DESIGN
Goteborgs-Posten
Gothenburg, Sweden
Designer
Ulf Johanson
Photographer
Lars Soderbom

AWARD OF EXCELLENCE
ENTERTAINMENT
PAGE DESIGN
Dagens Nyheter
Stockholm, Sweden
Designer
Maria Osterberg
Photographer
Hasse Persson

DAGENS NYHETER.

SÖNDAG

Söndagen den 16 oktober 1988

DEL 2

Tjurridning är höjdpunkten på rodeon i Pendleton. Det gäller att hålla sig kvar i åtta sekunder.

Foto: HASSE PERSSON

O, rodeo

Rodeo, världens kanske tuffaste sport, lockar stor publik i USA.
50 000 kom till Pendleton, Oregon, för att se tjurridning.

Sjömansbiff och citronmyssja mums för miljöpartist **11**

Clint Eastwood har bytt revolvern mot Charlie Parkers saxofon **2**

محفوظ

Mahfouz

Nya Nobelspråket **7**

Det finns flera miljoner fotograferande och fotointresserade personer i Sverige. Anhöriga och vänner till alla dessa får i år inga problem med att fundera ut den lämpliga julklappen: det blir givetvis en stillvideo!

Denna modernitet, beskriven som stillbildens motsvarighet till de rörliga bildernas video, var ett publikknipande inslag på årets gigantiska fotomässa i Köln. DN:s Eric Dyring, som rapporterar från detta "kaos av bild, ljud, teknik och PR" på sid 11, fick bland annat se just årets julklapp till fotografins vänner: en japansk stillvideo bestående av kamerahus, två zoomobjektiv och en telesändare, som säljs i ett paket. Priset ligger på över 100 000 kronor, men då ingår bärrem — sägs det. Kruxet blir väl att skriva julklappsvers på detta hårda paket, ty vad rimmar på stillvideo?

Se där något att grubbla på under dagens höstfriska promenad.

KURT PERSSON
DN SÖNDAG

AWARD OF EXCELLENCE
ENTERTAINMENT
PAGE DESIGN
NRC Handelsblad
Rotterdam, Netherlands
Designer
Willem van Zoetendaal
Art Director
Willem van Zoetendaal

AWARD OF EXCELLENCE
ENTERTAINMENT
PAGE DESIGN
The Boston Globe
Designer
James Pavolvich
Illustrator
David Cowles
Photographer
Suzanne Kretter
Art Director
James Pavlovich

charting the best RECORDS of 1988

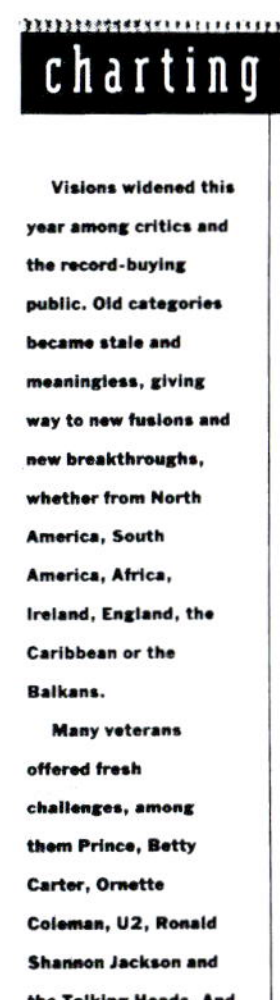

Visions widened this year among critics and the record-buying public. Old categories became stale and meaningless, giving way to new fusions and new breakthroughs, whether from North America, South America, Africa, Ireland, England, the Caribbean or the Balkans.

Many veterans offered fresh challenges, among them Prince, Betty Carter, Ornette Coleman, U2, Ronald Shannon Jackson and the Talking Heads. And though there was constant talk about retro rock and other nostalgia-centered music, this was ultimately a year of new vision and new faces — Tracy Chapman, Toni Childs, Hothouse Flowers, Sugarcubes, K. D. lang, Ziggy Marley, Shinehead, Public Enemy, 10,000 Maniacs, Big Dipper — and the list goes on, as you'll see from our critics' Top Tens.

Jimmy Page, "Outrider" (Geffen) A blast-off album from Led Zeppelin's Jimmy Page, who can still be the meanest, most feedback-savvy guitarist around. A great car stereo record.

R.E.M., "Green" (Warners) The lyrics traffic in obscure fables, but the beguiling melodies are among the band's best. An album that grows with repeated listens.

In Tua Nua, "The Long Acre" (Virgin) Irish rock was a big story this year. Dublin's In Tua Nua offered sweeping power, grace and a shoot-for-the-heart singer in Leslie Dowdall.

Keith Richards, "Talk Is Cheap" (Virgin) The glue behind the Rolling Stones turned up in a solo setting and just did his thing. Raw, basic rock 'n' roll, funk and soul.

Obed Ngobeni, "My Wife Bought a Taxi" (Shanachie) Say hello to the free-spirited dance music of Zulu Jive, with hints of reggae, synth-pop, guitar rock and soul music. A joyful brew.

AC/DC, "Blow Up Your Video" (Atlantic) The hit single, "Heatseeker," was just the tip of this metal onslaught. A throwback to their "Back in Black" album and even "Powerage."

Prince, "Black Album" (bootleg) The most bawdy, pelvis-spinning music of Prince's career. Too bad a failure of nerve kept him from releasing it commercially.

Wagoneers, "Stout and High" (A&M) Buddy Holly meets the Everly Brothers in 1988. A fresh perspective on rockabilly and country music. Ancient and new at the same time.

Julia Fordham, "Julia Fordham" (Virgin) Tracy Chapman, Anita Baker and Toni Childs were brilliant, but so was Fordham with her mysteriously enchanting mix of rock, New Age and jazz.

Ziggy Marley, "Conscious Party" (Virgin) The official coming-of-age of Bob Marley's son. Producers Chris Frantz and Tina Weymouth of the Talking Heads brought out Ziggy's best.

— **Steve Morse**

This was a year in jazz with no dominant artist(s) and no real surprises or striking developments. The balance suggests reassessment and transition. Big bands seemed to get more attention than usual with a flurry of releases including the chart-topping effort by Diane Schuur with the Count Basie Orchestra and solid albums by Illinois Jacquet, George Gruntz, Julius Hemphill and, on the local front, the Either/Orchestra. So much for trends.

The year-end list includes mind-ticklers and simple dance tracks, avant-noise-punk-jazz as well as suit-and-tie tradition. So it goes.

Henry Threadgill "Easily Slip Into Another World" (RCA/Novus) and **The Wynton Marsalis Quartet "Live At Blues Alley"** (CBS) offer two distinctive views of tradition. For Threadgill it serves as a jumping-off point into the future; Marsalis wants to explore some of what jazz's compulsive need to move on left behind. **Jesus (Chucho) Valdez "Lucumi"** (Messidor), is a luminous, lyrical solo album by this Cuban pianist better known in the US as the leader of Irakere.

Ronald Shannon Jackson's "Texas" (Caravan of Dreams), and the dark, often brutal **Last Exit's "Iron Path"** (Virgin) deliver what jazz rock fusion once promised: raw power and intelligence, music for the feet and the mind. To be played loud. Drummer **Jack De Johnette's Special Edition "Audio Visualscapes"** (MCA Impulse) offers a perhaps more subtle, elegant blend of fusion but just as moving and challenging. **Kip Hanrahan's "Days and Nights of Blue Luck Inverted"** (Pangaea) is an elusive, insightful, surprising musical collage.

South African pianist **Chris McGregor Brotherhood of Breath's "Country Cooking"** (Virgin), both spiritual and worldly, often suggests a ragged version of Abdullah Ibrahim's Ekaya. **Charlie Haden Quartet West "In Angel City"** (Verve) goes down easy, like fine brandy and with some of the same results.

Completing the list: **Anthony Braxton**'s insightful readings of Thelonious Monk's music on **"Six Monk Compositions (1987)"** (Black Saint).

— **Fernando Gonzalez**

1. The Feelies, "Only Life" (A&M): The pursuit of an ideal — minimalism, Velvet Underground pulses, Beatles melodies — is transposed to a modern world. Nervous, tranquil sounds find a resting ground.

2. The Pogues, "If I Should Fall From Grace With God . . ." (Island): More Irish/trad mayhem and heartfelt roots music, sung from the gutters of Irish London, and, also, from the outskirts of any world. Eclectic, wild-eyed guys; not dilettantes. Raw power.

3. Midnight Oil, "Diesel and Dust" (Columbia): Australia's raging guintet of righteousness puts out their best LP yet: stick-like-glue melodies coupled to victims-who-fight-back lyrics. And lots more.

4. Prince, "Lovesexy" (Warner Bros.): The usual cornucopia of pop/funk, mind/body delights played off against the spectre of the unreleased, much bootlegged, "Black Album." Both win.

5. U2, "Rattle & Hum" (Island): The big project that mostly works. Elevation and moderation, celestial heights and serious grandeur.

6. Steve Earle, "Copperhead Road" (Uni): Hard-worn, well-thought out country-rock sentiments and the best feel-good rock 'n' roll you can imagine.

7. Big Dipper, "Craps" (Homestead): Elliptical, direct, haunting and re-assuring: "Hey Mr. Lincoln, Mr. Lincoln, the drinks are on us." Thoughts — however oblique — that won't quit.

8. Hothouse Flowers, "People" (Polygram): The strongest Van Morrison-esque rock 'n' roll to emerge from the Emerald Isle.

9. Pere Ubu, "Tenement Year" ((Enigma): Pretty much what you would hope for a decade-plus down the dusty pike: still off-center, but rock 'n' roll centered, avant-cool.

10. Mofungo, "Bugged" (SST): *Their* most pop album, sans sacrifice, compromise or edge. Mofungo has come to peace with agitation and enticement.

— **Jim Sullivan**

1. Opera: Britten: "Paul Bunyan" (Virgin Classics); runner up: Auber: "La Muette de Portici" (EMI)

2. Early Music: Ancient Airs and Dances: Paul O'Dette, lute (Hyperion)

3. Early Instruments: Schubert: "Great" Symphony in C, the Orchestra of the Age of Enlightenment, Sir Charles Mackerras, conductor (Virgin Classics)

4. Symphonic: Mendelssohn: Scottish Symphony and Die Erste Walpurgisnacht: The Cleveland Orchestra, conducted by Christoph von Dohnanyi (Telarc); Faure: Pelleas et Melisande and other works: The Boston Symphony Orchestra, Seiji Ozawa, conductor (DG)

5. Piano: Scarlatti Sonatas: Dubravka Tomsic (Vienna Master Series); runner-up Beethoven: Diabelli Variations: Michael Oelbaum (Bridge)

6. New Music: Lou Harrison: Piano Concerto (with Keith Jarrett) and other works (New World Records)

7. Reissue: Artur Schnabel plays Mozart (Arabesque, 4 CDs); Astrid Varnay sings Wagner (Deutsche Grammophon, 2 CDs)

8. Vocal: Janet Baker sings Schubert with pianist Graham Johnson (Hyperion; volume 1 of a projected complete series of Schubert's songs); runner-up: Songs of America: Jan deGaetani, mezzo-soprano, with pianist Gilbert Kalish (Nonesuch)

9. Local Performers: Marimolin, violinist Sharan Leventhal and marimbist Nancy Zeltsman in music by Thomas Oboe Lee, Robert Aldridge, Scott Wheeler, Les Thimmig, Amelia Rogers and Lyle Mays (GM); James Maddalena and Sanford Sylvan in principal roles in "Nixon in China" (Nonesuch)

10. Light music: "Show Boat" conducted by John McGlinn (EMI); "Night and Day: Joan Morris and William Bolcom perform songs of Cole Porter" (Omega)

— **Richard Dyer**

AWARD OF EXCELLENCE
ENTERTAINMENT
PAGE DESIGN
The Boston Globe

Designer
Miriam Campiz
Art Director
Miriam Campiz

MAY 29, 1988 — Boston Sunday Globe — B Section

Arts*Etc.*

Books Section After two years in court, Ian Hamilton's biography of J. D. Salinger is finally in the stores. **B15**

MOVIES / MUSIC / LIFESTYLES / VIDEO / THEATER / ART / BOOKS — Home & Garden B18

music

Retro Rock is flying high

Oldies' resurgence fueled by videos, anniversary releases and summer tours

lifestyles

The swing set is having a ball

conversations | marian christy

Matlin: a star's sign of the times

movies

The 'Big' story: a simple plot, a chaotic past

INSIDE

B8 Movies and events at this year's film festival ranged from the sublime to the ridiculous.

B7 Laser discs may be the wave of the future.

GUIDE TO FEATURES

ARCHITECTURE	B10
ART	B2
RECORDINGS	B4
LIFESTYLES	B13
LANDERS	B55
CHAT	B55
WEDDINGS	B56

AWARD OF EXCELLENCE
ENTERTAINMENT
PAGE DESIGN
The Boston Globe
Boston
Designer
Rena Sokolow
Art Director
Rena Sokolow

AWARD OF EXCELLENCE
ENTERTAINMENT
PAGE DESIGN
The Toronto Star
Designer
Kam Wai Yu

WHAT'S ON

MOVIES: Waits hits the Big Time 10
MUSIC: Canada's great hip-hop hope 13
STAGE: Spectacle is fit for Sun King 11
LPs: T.O. singer's sensational debut 16

THE STAR'S GUIDE TO ENTERTAINMENT IN TORONTO THIS WEEKEND AND NEXT WEEK

THE TORONTO STAR
FRIDAY, NOV. 18, 1988

SECTION B
PAGES B1-B20

Marcel Marceau

Shhh!

A MOMENT OF SILENCE, PLEASE, FOR THE MIME WHO WON'T SHUT UP : B3

WHAT'S ON

POSTERS: Up against the wall 18
MOVIES: Wonderful, warmed-over Willow 6
MUSIC: Meet the Meat Puppets 10
FORUM: What's on at Ontario Place 17

THE STAR'S GUIDE TO ENTERTAINMENT IN TORONTO THIS WEEKEND AND NEXT WEEK

THE TORONTO STAR
FRIDAY, MAY 20, 1988

SECTION E
PAGES E1-E24

BOPHA
RESIST
ARREST

South African policemen -- the whites and blacks who enforce apartheid -- use the term "bopha" to mean "arrest." But for the people in the townships, the word has come to mean "resist." Bopha! is also the name of a South African play that opened last night at TWP Theatre: D3

Starring in Bopha! are (from top) Aubrey Moalosi Molefi, Aubrey Radebe and Sydney Khumalo.

AWARD OF EXCELLENCE
ENTERTAINMENT
PAGE DESIGN
The Toronto Star
Designer
Kam Wai Yu
Photographer
Dick Loek

Friday
Opening 'Love Letters' at Long Wharf
Saturday
Elizabeth Swados brings Broadway to West Hartford
Sunday
Belle epoque fashions Dress up Wadsworth Atheneum
These and other best bets, Page 16

The Hartford Courant
CALENDAR
YOUR ENTERTAINMENT GUIDE FOR THE WEEK OF OCT. 27-NOV. 2, 1988

NEW HAUNTS
THE CHANGING FACE OF HALLOWEEN
PAGE 3

Inside CLUBS 27 DINING OUT 7 EXHIBITS 23 ON THE SCREEN 11 RADIO 27 RECORD REVIEWS 5 SHOWTIMES 10 SOUND CHECK 4 VIDEO 31 WEEK AHEAD 15

Friday
Get sidetracked with Santa in Essex
Saturday
The hip side of yuletide at RAW
Sunday
'H.M.S. Pinafore' calls at New London
These and other best bets, Page 14

The Hartford Courant
CALENDAR
YOUR ENTERTAINMENT GUIDE FOR THE WEEK OF DEC. 15 - DEC. 21, 1988

O COME, ALL YE FAITHFUL
Christmas music to fill churches
PAGE 3

Inside CLUBS 24 DINING OUT 7 EXHIBITS 20 ON THE SCREEN 9 RADIO 24 RECORD REVIEWS 5 SHOWTIMES 8 SOUND CHECK 4 VIDEO 27 WEEK AHEAD 12

AWARD OF EXCELLENCE
ENTERTAINMENT PAGE DESIGN
The Hartford Courant
Designer
Patti Nelson
Illustrator
Anthony Russo
Art Director
Patti Nelson

AWARD OF EXCELLENCE
ENTERTAINMENT PAGE DESIGN
The Hartford Courant
Designer
Linda Shankweiler
Illustrator
Linda Shankweiler
Art Director
Patti Nelson

MAY 22, 1988
Boston Sunday Globe
Arts Etc.
MOVIES / MUSIC / LIFESTYLES / VIDEO / THEATER / ART / BOOKS
Books Section
Tom Hayden's autobiography recalls what a long, strange trip it was.
109
Hobbies 112

performing
The last dance
'It's time to turn in the pink satin slippers for a pair of practical shoes'

Gayle Maronek.

Anne Jackson, Eli Wallach and friend.

theater
The Actors Enclave
Its members are seeking a friendly environment away from the commerce of Broadway

lifestyles
Our changing sexual behavior

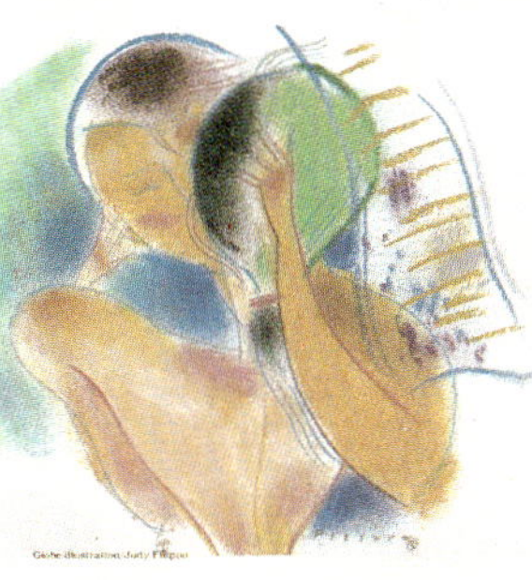

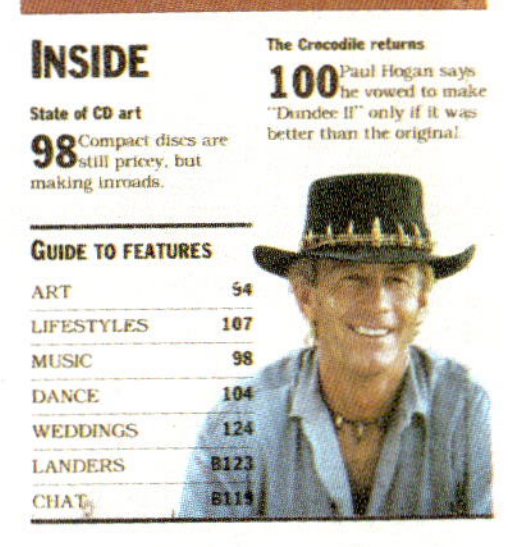
INSIDE
State of CD art
98 Compact discs are still pricey, but making inroads.
The Crocodile returns
100 Paul Hogan says he vowed to make "Dundee II" only if it was better than the original.
GUIDE TO FEATURES
ART 54
LIFESTYLES 107
MUSIC 98
DANCE 104
WEDDINGS 124
LANDERS B123
CHAT B111

SILVER AWARD
ENTERTAINMENT PAGE DESIGN
The Boston Globe
Designer
Judy Filippo
Illustrators
Peter Freed, Tom Landers
Art Director
James Pavolvich

The Washington Post

On the Fridge: Sausage without preservatives 10

Also On the Fridge: Quick Manhattan Clam Chowder 10

Food

TODAY'S RECIPES

The Discerning Chow Hound

Discriminating Consumers And Their Pet Foods

RICHMAN'S TABLE

Vegetarian Self-Defense

THE GUEST BOOK

Yesterday's Harvest

Is It Soup Yet?

Well, It Could Be After Just a Few Minutes in the Microwave

Cooking and Loving It

Traci Weingarten Is at Home in Her Kitchen

AWARD OF EXCELLENCE
FOOD
PAGE DESIGN
The Washington Post
Designer
Nancy Brooke Smith
Illustrator
Patrick Blackwell
Art Director
Nacy Brooke Smith

The Washington Post

Winter's finest moment: Nantucket's bay scallops 3

Richman's Table: Moors and Christians in New Jersey 8

Food

12 Wine: Sampling two of Saint-Emilion's best

14 Updating the health-claim labeling controversy

AWARD OF EXCELLENCE
FOOD
PAGE DESIGN

SILVER
TYPOGRAPHY
The Washington Post
Designer
Nancy Brooke Smith
Art Director
Nancy Brooke Smith

AWARD OF EXCELLENCE
FOOD
PAGE DESIGN
The Dallas Morning News
Designer
Doug Stanley
Art Director
Ed Kohorst

Food Sunday

The Dallas Morning News

ENTERTAINING

Get On The Stick

Having a party? Check our list of hors d'oeuvres that can stand up to the heat, from kebabs to jalapeno turnovers.

Page 2

TECHNIQUES

Why Clarify Butter?

Clarifying removes solids that burn, allowing you to cook at higher temperatures without scorching. And lobster wouldn't be the same without it.

Page 4

FOOD HISTORY

Happy Birthday, Velveeta

This year, the familiar yellow brick celebrates 60 years of melting moments.

Page 6

The Washington Post

Flashes in the Pan: Julia Child at the Smithsonian 3

Nutrition: Does your child get enough protein? 8

Food

TODAY'S RECIPES

A Sense of Direction

Finding a Place for Novel Products in the Old Dominion

RICHMAN'S TABLE

Divided by Pizza Philosophy

Italians and Americans Disagree on Their Vision of the Pie

The Adventures of Autumn

Harvesting Exotic Fruits and Vegetables

Awash in a Sea of Garbage

Practical Steps to Help Stem the Tide of a Growing Crisis

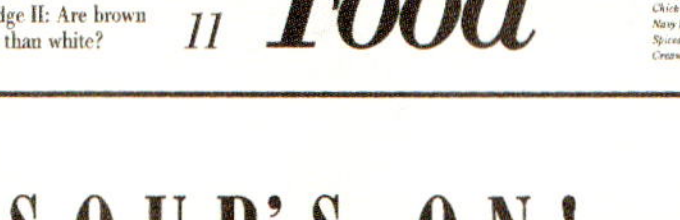

The Washington Post

On the Fridge: Any bargains at the salad bar? 11

On the Fridge II: Are brown eggs better than white? 11

Food

TODAY'S RECIPES

SOUP'S ON!

Warm & Hearty Flavors for the Cold & Blustery Season

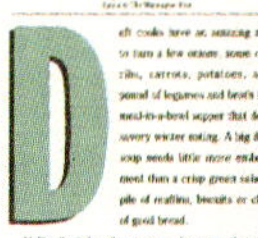

To Market, To Market

What the U.S. Must Learn About Exporting

Down Paths Of Nostalgia

Three Cookbook Authors Return to Their Roots

RICHMAN'S TABLE

Not by Ravioli Alone ...

Attitude Counts as Well

AWARD OF EXCELLENCE
FOOD
PAGE DESIGN
The Washington Post
Designer
Nancy Brooke Smith
Illustrator
Gary Head
Art Director
Nancy Brooke Smith

The Washington Post

On the Fridge: Figuring the fat calories 3

A positive message from first cholesterol conference 21

Food

TODAY'S RECIPES

RICHMAN'S TABLE

The Baker Also Rises

Maeve Barnes Conquers With Can-Do Approach

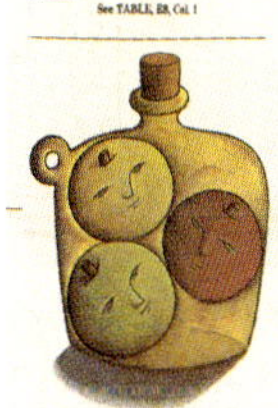

Saluting Cider

A Seasonal Winner in All Its Many Guises

Bringing Up Baby

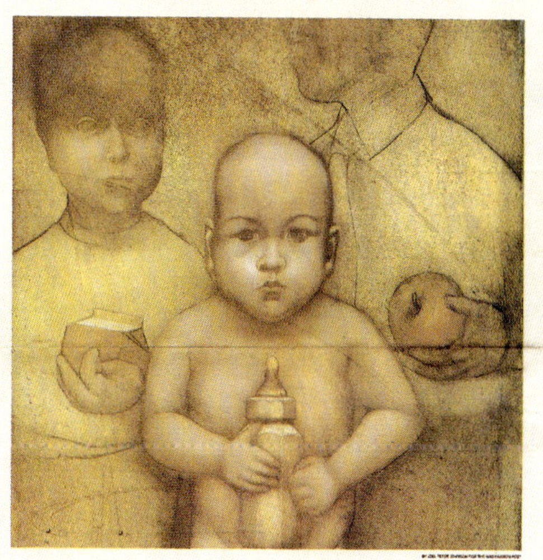

Into the Mouths of Babes: Sound Strategies for Feeding Infants

Healthful Meals at the Day Care Center

... And Learning Nutrition at School

SILVER AWARD
FOOD
PAGE DESIGN
The Washington Post
Designer
Nancy Brooke Smith
Illustrator
Joel Peter Johnson
Art Director
Nancy Brooke Smith

AWARD OF EXCELLENCE
FASHION
PAGE DESIGN
Chicago Tribune
Designer
Margaret Carsello
Photographer
Bob Fila
Art Director
Margaret Carsello

Wednesday, December 21, 1988, Los Angeles Herald Examiner B3

High Style

Bogner's "Falmenca" suit with embossed nylon cavalry-style jacket in orchid and black two-way stretch wool pants.

Bogner's high-flying "Sambis" jacket in olive and black crinkle nylon with ribbed waistband paired with the "Doma" pants in leopard print two-way stretch wool.

Bogner's "Estee" suit, black crinkle nylon bomber jacket with white piping and white crinkle nylon pants with elasticized bottom.

Franz Moser-Boy's neon bright jumpsuit and vest, and Bolle glasses, all from Vail West in Beverly Hills.

Fashion goes downhill

By Gaile Robinson

At 3,000 feet the drivers are cursing the perilous road conditions and the skiers are rejoicing.

The early snowfalls have all the local ski resorts up and running. Mount Waterman boasts the most snow at 4 feet. Mount Baldy has 2 feet of the white stuff, and Bear Mountain is supplementing its scant 4 inches with snow of their own making.

Part of the hazardous driving conditions are due to the skiing zealots racing to the summit for the first pre-Christmas snows in three years.

Of the more than 1 million skiing enthusiasts in Southern California, 350,000 of them, claims Ski Industries of America, find the time to use their lift tickets at least 10 times a year.

Like any worthwhile recreational activity, boating, for instance, skiing can be expensive. The first outing is cheap — a pair of rented skis and boots and a day's worth of lessons. Then the insidious lust for your own equipment takes over — skis, boots, a rack for the car and poles.

Then a burning desire for waterproof pants and a new parka, not to mention the air fares, lift tickets, the run-side accommodations and resort-scale per diems. The ski-rabid and the passing fanciers alike have boosted the annual take of the ski industry to the billions.

Smelling a trend-heavy, fashion-conscious, money-making proposition, the apparel industry is hard at work to get its share of the billion-dollar pie.

For years, the prevailing fashion on the slopes was anything that would provide warmth, usually resulting in a Michelin-man silhouette.

The advent of film-coated fabrics like Gore-Tex, which provide waterproofing and breathability (allowing body vapors to evaporate), and the polyester insulations like Du Pont's Thermolite, have given ski-wear garments a thinner profile and more flexible constructions.

While the American manufacturers are spending time developing new materials, the European ski-wear designers, Bogner from Germany, Colman from Italy and Steinebronn from Austria, have been creating top-flight styles for the slopes.

With details borrowed from the couture runways, their ski wear sports high-waisted stretch jacquard pants, Tyrolean embroidery motifs on jackets and jumpsuits, op art prints in a rainbow of neon colors and fur trims. Their fittings, industrial zippers, leather-covered buttons, elastic waistbands and drawstrings are all more state-of-the-art than American products.

The constructions are more adept as well. "They have an empirical understanding of the sport the Americans just don't have," says Jeff Wilk, owner of the Beverly Hills ski shop Vail West. "The constructions are more flattering, the workmanship is better and so are the materials."

The one bright spot on the American ski-wear scene was brought to the slopes by the snow boarders. Dressed in brilliant Day-Glo colors, they are latter-day surfers and skateboarders who have taken their act to the snow scene.

Their clothes are unique blends of swimwear's bright colors and the skateboarders' eclectic pattern mixes. Graffiti, animal and op art prints in pain-threshold green, screaming orange, ultra violet and chlorine blue are their not-to-be-missed colors of choice.

Their vivid hues have permeated the traditional ski-wear business. "There is an incredible craving for neon," says Anne Stables of the ski-wear manufacturer Roffe. "Any form, slice or part of neon drives the sales, very often regardless of the styles."

Especially prevalent in children's ski wear, the neon colors make the obligatory fashion statement and wayward offspring easy to spot.

The children's ski business is growing as parents who discovered the sport in its glory days of the '70s are bringing their families back to the mountain. Vail, once a hotbed of singles' snow action, is now gearing its business for families.

"Skiing is very positive," says Wilk. "It's a crime-free area, it's great exercise, the air is clean and the food's good in the restaurants."

Which is not something you can say about spending an afternoon in the Panorama City mall.

Maybe it's time to reconsider your weekend plans. After all, Bear Mountain is only 2½ hours away.

Serus' "Masque" of ventilated neoprene in ultra violet.

Roffé Lite's splash print nylon shell in neon green and black stretch pants with black and white check gaiters, the eclectic mix for snow-boarders.

AWARD OF EXCELLENCE
FASHION
PAGE DESIGN
Los Angeles Herald Examiner
Designer
David Limrite
Art Director
Mike Gordon

The Washington Times

TUESDAY, NOVEMBER 22, 1988 / PAGE E7

Fashionlife!

Karl Lagerfeld

The savior of Chanel introduces his own line to America

By Marie Moniz Hammons

A la Chanel, bob haircut is 'in' again

Lagerfeld's Chanel look for spring: Feminine, flattering and very wearable

see KARL, page E8

AWARD OF EXCELLENCE
FASHION
PAGE DESIGN
The Washington Times

Designer
John Kascht
Illustrator
John Kascht
Art Director
John Kascht

Sunday Star-Ledger

FALL PREVIEWS

SEPTEMBER 11, 1988/SECTION 10

FASHION
BEAUTY
STYLE

It's farewell to the frill and bon voyage to the bubble as fall takes on a more sophisticated look.

Perry Ellis Portfolio greets autumn with the sophisticated wool jacket, $225; 100 percent silk shirt, $160, and plaid trousers in a blend of wool and nylon, $160, at Bloomingdale's, Short Hills

P A N T S
WITH PANACHE

AWARD OF EXCELLENCE
FASHION
PAGE DESIGN
The Star-Ledger
Newark, New Jersey

Designer
Bernadette Germain
Illustrator
Maning Obregon
Photographer
Jennifer Lawson
Art Director
Bernadette Germain
Assistant Photo Editor
Beverly Long
Section Editor
Linda Fowler

SILVER AWARD
HOME/REAL ESTATE
PAGE DESIGN
The Boston Globe

Designer
Lisa L. Chune
Illustrator
Blair Thornley
Art Director
Lisa L. Chune

THE BOSTON GLOBE FRIDAY, JULY 1, 1988 **63**

At home

Automobiles 69

The Boston Globe

At a city auction house or under a tent in the country, the same caveats apply

Let the bidder BEWARE

By Janice Byrd
Special to the Globe

To a newcomer, attending an auction may seem akin to being an outsider at a meeting of a secret society where everyone else knows the lingo, the high sign and rules of the game. Often in these halcyon days of summer, vacationers – with time to kill and money to burn – find themself under the auction tent and then wonder what to do next.

Whether the auction is being held at a large city auction house or in a tent in the country there are important guidelines to follow before you bid. These preliminary procedures usually take more time than the actual bidding, but as with a jockey excercising a race horse or a runner stretching his

AUCTIONS, Page 66

Blair Thornley illustration

SINGLE FILE

Lisa Chune illustration

The bittersweet revenge

By Ron Gasbarro
Special to the Globe

Because I work at home, a couple of days can go by where I see no one else but the woman behind the counter at the newstand.

The other day, however, I had several things planned that would take me away from the house. I had an appointment for a haircut. Really exciting. This was followed by a meeting at a company where I was taking on a free-lance writing project.

After that, since I was going to be "out that way," I thought I would pop into Sears.

The day would be a good one. I

SINGLE FILE, Page 66

Globe staff photos/Joanne Rathe

Lillian and Donald Stokes observe the wildlife that frequents their 5-acre backyard in Carlisle. Far right, small birds at one of the many feeders on their property.

WILDLIFE AND THE LANDSCAPE

By Carol Stocker
Globe Staff

CARLISLE – You don't need to safari to Africa or the Everglades to see Nature. Man and wildlife can find happiness together in the suburbs.

Landscaping to promote wildlife is of growing interest in eastern Massachusetts, where the merciless building boom has rendered any little patch of wilderness or unspoiled coastline the ultimate possession among many homeowners.

Few people know as much about attracting backyard wildlife as do Lillian and Donald Stokes, authors of the "The Bird Feeder Book, An Easy Guide to Attracting, Identifying, and Understanding Your Feeder Birds" ($8.95) and their well-known six-volume "Stokes Nature Guides" series ($9.95 and $10.95), published by Little, Brown.

In 4½ years the Stokes have cleared parts of their once totally wooded 5-acre property to provide a varied habitat that has enticed 40 types of birds to nest there. These include chickadees, crows, song sparrows, brown thrashers, mockingbirds, catbirds, tree swallows, tufted titmice, wrens, red-winged blackbirds and yellow-throated warblers. If you count the birds sighted visiting the tally reaches 115 species.

During a recent interview, a giant pileated woodpecker flew into the yard and began prospecting for carpenter ants around piles of logs and a standing dead birch tree.

A comical looking bird more than a foot long from head to tail, he sported a flaming red crest reminiscent of Walter Lantz's Woody Woodpecker. The matching red mustach over his drillhammer beak was evidence of his masculinity.

The Stokes were on the second-story deck of their house, which doubles nicely as a wildlife observation platform, and reached for their ever-present binoculars. After 10 minutes, the bird slowly flapped off into deep woods, a pterodactyl-like silhouette with its long neck, small rectangular head and large body.

The pileated 'pecker's visit was tes-

STOKES, Page 67

At home's Alfresco features focus on making the most of outdoor spaces.

8/City Living NY NEWSDAY, THURSDAY, SEPTEMBER 22, 1988

A CURVACEOUS SOFA BY ZANOTTA WITH DETACHABLE CUSHIONS THAT CAN BE REPOSITIONED IN DIFFERENT CONFIGURATIONS

MILAN from Page 7

end to create a chaise longue. Take four. The bolsters and cushions are positioned in an S-shape so that two people can sit facing one another for a private tete-a-tete.

A second flexible piece by Zanotta forms a slinky S-shaped curve, like a playful serpent. The sofa's line of cushions detach from one side of the frame and may be quickly hooked on to the opposite side, thus expanding the seating possibilities.

"There is new technology that allows us to do this today," said Gualtierotti, one of the love seat's designers, pointing to what's known as "toroidal rings" attach the cushions to the metal fra allows your own movements to l the way the furniture is going to l

Another va on the same theme can be seen in Italian storage units. Mondo, a tw old company, introduced a unit th adaptation of an ancient Chinese

BIEFFEPLAST'S NESTED COFFEE TABLES, RIMMED WITH A METAL FENCE, LOOK LIKE A FREE-STANDING GEOMETRIC SCULPTURE. AT RIGHT, FOR DRIADE, BOREK SIPEK DEVISED A NEW LOOK FOR THE TRADITIONAL TUFTED CHESTERFIELD SOFA: HIS VERSION SPROUTS WOODEN WINGS.

ade of elm that has been stained a
d, the elements of the piece stack
r to form a staircase — change
nponents around and the stairs
osition. For Acerbis, designer
Bellini made a pyramid-shaped
alled "Square Wave." Placed
the wall, it looks like a solid nose unit. But put it in the center
room and its four shelves swivel
xis, creating a wild windmill ef-

s and drawers are alternately
and convex to create further vice. "The idea was to make it a
e in the room, like a monument,
hitecture," said Bellini. "Instead
rdered frame, it's dynamic and

— generally thought of as stable
f furniture — also incorporated
ible motif. Axil's bed was in a
state of flux: Its cushions (at-
to the frame by sliding steel
uld be moved together to form a
ard or positioned diagonally.
e, three pear-shaped tables slid
the beds' edges, serving as night
telephone tables or even break-
ys. Arflex' bed folds up slightly
orner to form a butterfly-shaped
And at Oggioni, the beds' black
headboard slides forward to
pillows. If a couple has a spat,
pull down a leather arm rest,
also serves to split the bed in

notable flexible examples in-
B & B Italia's black lacquer
with a rotating glass top that
a table, and Orsenigo's black
TV cart. The piece comes with
drop shelf that accommodates a
tachable side shelf pockets hold
and tapes.
offered a startling twist on the
y introducing a chair that doesn't
a chair. Designed by architect
otta, it forms a flat pyramidal
ut when weight is applied to the
he material is pressed down and
becomes a seat.
ritten statement, Botta said his

Please see MILAN on Page 13

MILAN IN MOTION

SEVERAL SUPPLIERS TRIED TO HUMANIZE THEIR FURNITURE. A COLUMN OF DRAWERS BY STILLWOOD IS TOPPED BY A MIRROR THAT RESEMBLES A FACE.

PHILIPPE STARCK'S ALUMINUM TABLE IS INSCRIBED WITH A CLOWN FACE. THE TOP TILTS SO THAT ITS OVAL FORMS THE CLOWN'S HEAD, WHILE THE PEDESTAL BECOMES THE BODY.

PHOTOS BY DARWIN DAVIDSON

NEWSDAY, THURSDAY, SEPTEMBER 22, 1988 NY City Living/9

AWARD OF EXCELLENCE
HOME/REAL ESTATE
PAGE DESIGN
Newsday
Long Island, New York

Designer
Jacqueline Segal
Photographer
Darwin Davidson
Art Director
Bob Eisner

THE BOSTON GLOBE FRIDAY, JUNE 17, 1988 43

At home

Comics 50, 51
TV & Radio 52, 53

The Boston Globe

AN AMERICAN CRAFTS SHOWCASE

By Janice Byrd
Special to the Globe

WEST SPRINGFIELD – In the past 20 years, hand-made crafts have come of age in America, and as the popularity of these hand-made, often one-of-a-kind objects has grown, so has the quality of the workmanship.

Since the 1960s, when there was a resurgence of interest in the arts and crafts movement, artists have been experimenting and fine-tuning their craft. No longer are these hand-made works considered the poor relations of the fine arts community. Instead of being plain, homespun and earthy, like some of their early prototypes, these contemporary crafts are sophisticated, imaginative and innovative.

They are highly prized by a decorative arts market – gallery owners and serious art collectors. And (starting each day at 11 a.m.) from next Friday through Sunday, some 6,000 of them, along with 30,000 members of the general public are expected to visit the fifth American Craft Council (ACC) Fair held at the Eastern States Exposition here to see, and buy, the works of these gifted craftsmen.

Getting a chance to show your wares at the fair

CRAFTS, Page 46

Kari Lonning's baskets (above); Jerri Finch's "Fan Dance" wall hanging (below); and Stephen Daniel's ginko chair, (right).

Next week, the Eastern States Exposition in West Springfield is the place to be if you're interested in the decorative arts, hand-crafted variety. But don't expect to see the plain or the homespun. Fine points of imagination and sophistication are the rule here.

When you want that secure feeling

The professional approach

By Lora Sharpe
Special to The Globe

A boa constrictor is the home security system for the heroine Madame Bodot in Tomi Ungerer's children's story "Crictor."

Not only does the boa of the same name frighten the burglar who has the temerity to trespass in the Bodot lair, but he wraps him up for the authorities.

While a boa constrictor may be your children's idea of the perfect security system, it probably isn't yours or the local humane society's. I mean, who's willing to sacrifice the livestock to keep the rumblies from the boa's tummy and the boa from hugging little Jimmy?

The more practical means is electronic. The contemporary electronic avenues are paved with microcomputer chips. And those chips can do everything from turning on the lights and alarm in a house to sounding a siren and verbally warning an intruder from the premises.

While home security systems may once have been the province of the rich or the victimized, they are increasingly sought by the average American before a burglar finds his TV or VCR.

Moreover, home security systems are within range of almost everyone's budget. If you can afford the TV and VCR, you can probably afford a system.

ALARMS, Page 45

Or doing it on your own

By Michael Alexander
Special to the Globe

Imagine that you have just returned home from a tough day at the office. You open the front door, step inside and immediately sense that something is not quite right. Then it hits you: the TV set, VCR and many other of your possessions are gone. You have been robbed. It's a scene that will greet one in four homeowners this year, according to the FBI.

You can protect your home and person from burglars and all of the other things that go bump in the night and day. If you can afford it, your best bet is to have a professional install a security system.

If you can't, buy a system, and do it yourself. That is what more homeowners than ever are doing these days, if sales of over-the-counter security systems are any indication. By the time 1990 rolls around, consumers will spend $2.7 billion on do-it-

DO-IT-YOURSELF, Page 47

AWARD OF EXCELLENCE
HOME/REAL ESTATE
PAGE DESIGN
The Boston Globe

Designer
Lisa L. Chune
Art Director
Lisa L. Chune

AWARD OF EXCELLENCE
HOME/REAL ESTATE
PAGE DESIGN
Los Angeles Herald Examiner

Designer
David Limrite
Photographer
Chris Gulker
Art Director
Mike Gordon

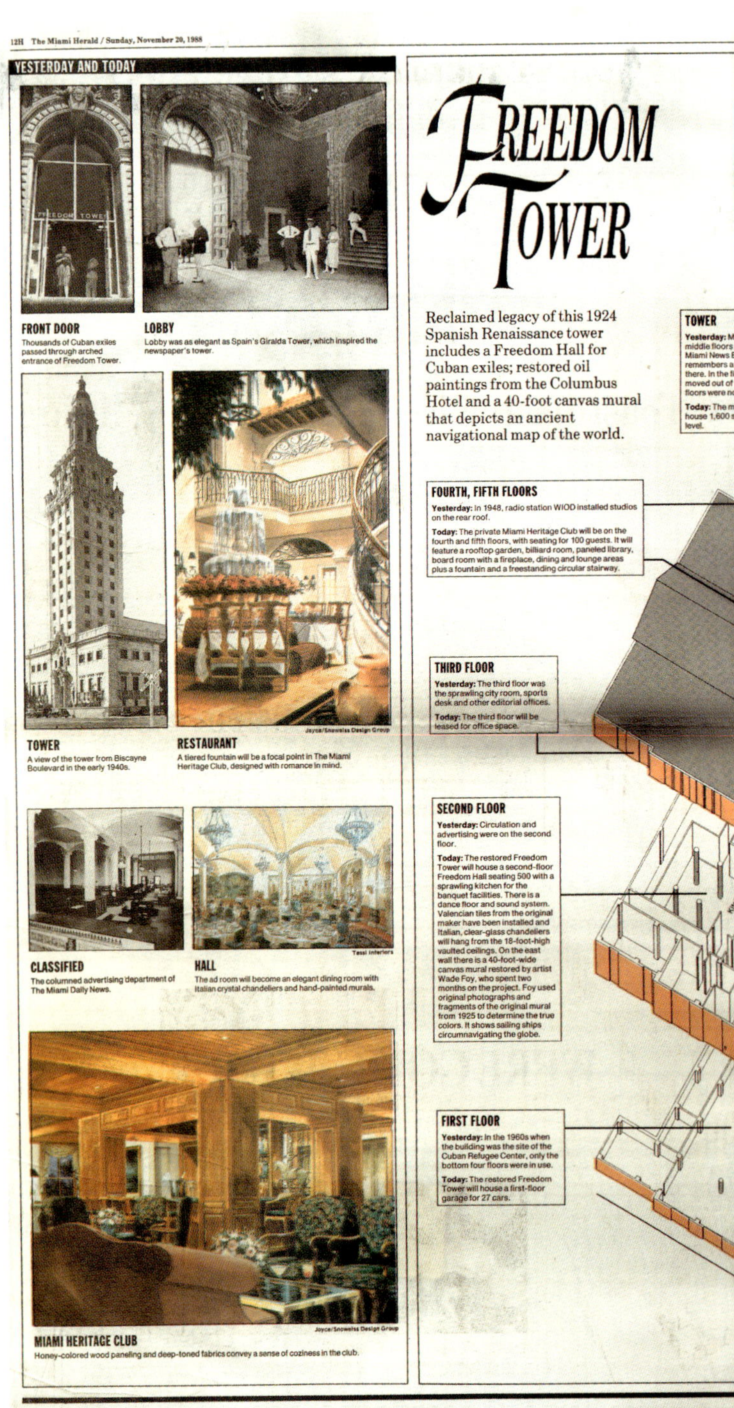

Sunday, November 20, 1988 / The Miami Herald 13H

Landmark salvage effort is reclaiming a city's past

TOWER / from 1H

Each floor is different

Building is stronger today

FREEDOM HALL

Left, view in the lobby as you look north. Plaster caps, top right, are on second-floor, now Freedom Hall, columns; bottom right are wall decorations.

DETAILS FROM INSIDE MIAMI HERITAGE CLUB

Material samples used by designers Joyce/Snoweiss Design Group.

FROM THE BAR/LOUNGE

COMPLEMENTS
Taupe, cream and teal complement wood moldings.

WARMTH
Chairs will be upholstered in a warm burgundy fabric.

SIT ON IT
Tapestry will cover arm chairs in The Miami Heritage Club.

TABLES, BARS
Sand-colored marble will top tables and bars.

FROM THE RESTAURANT

CARPET
Leafy patterned carpet chosen for club and restaurant.

SPANISH
Fabric with a Spanish motif selected for banquettes.

ATMOSPHERE
Print in burgundy and teal conveys clubby atmosphere.

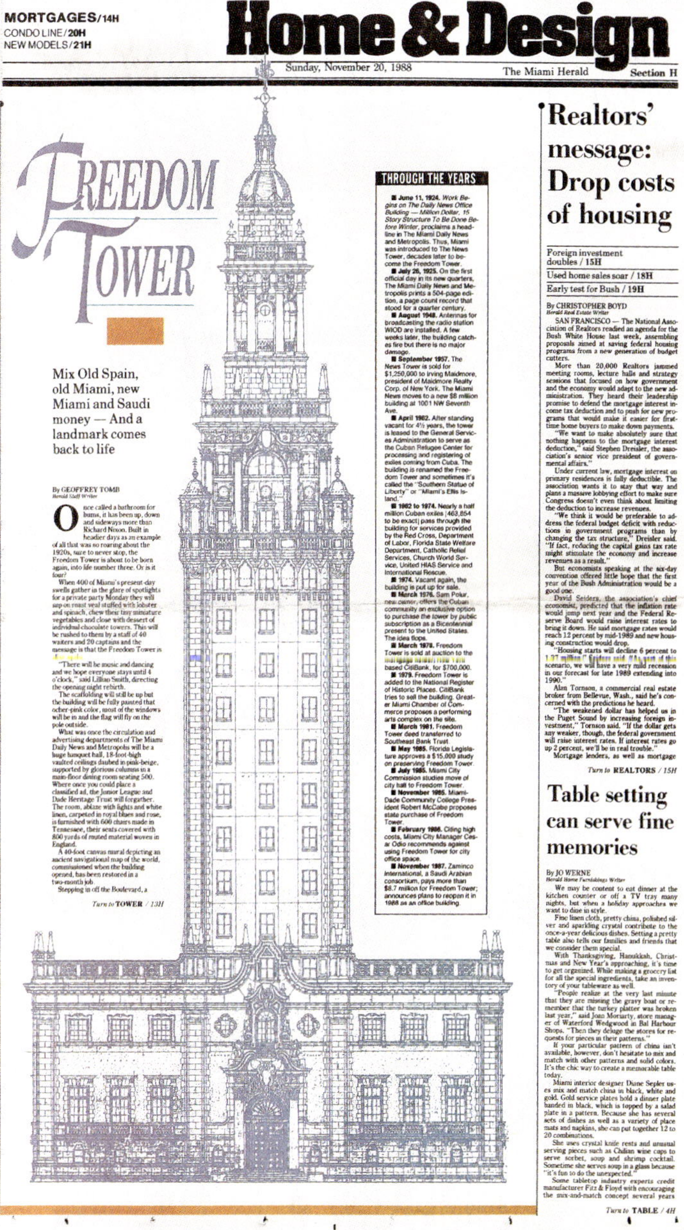

MORTGAGES/14H
CONDO LINE/20H
NEW MODELS/21H

Home & Design

Sunday, November 20, 1988 — The Miami Herald — Section H

Freedom Tower

Mix Old Spain, old Miami, new Miami and Saudi money — And a landmark comes back to life

By GEOFFREY TOMB

Turn to TOWER / 13H

THROUGH THE YEARS

Realtors' message: Drop costs of housing

Foreign investment doubles / 15H
Used home sales soar / 18H
Early test for Bush / 19H

By CHRISTOPHER BOYD

Turn to REALTORS / 15H

Table setting can serve fine memories

By JO WERNE

Turn to TABLE / 4H

AWARD OF EXCELLENCE
HOME/REAL ESTATE
INSIDE FEATURE
PAGE DESIGN
The Miami Herald

Designers
Pam Swischer, Liz Heisler, Herman Vega

Illustrator
Pam Swischer

Researchers
Pam Swischer, Geoffrey Tomb

Editors
Wayne Markham, Max Roberts

Director of Editorial Art and Design
Randy Stano

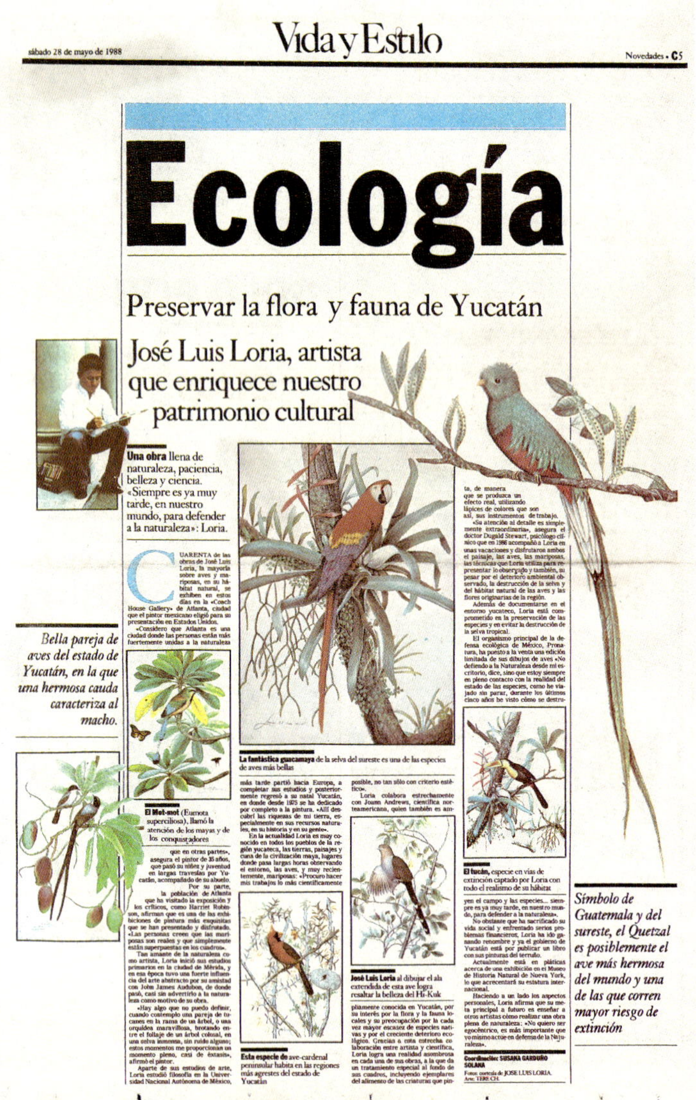

sábado 28 de mayo de 1988

Vida y Estilo

Novedades • C5

Ecología

Preservar la flora y fauna de Yucatán

José Luis Loria, artista que enriquece nuestro patrimonio cultural

Una obra llena de naturaleza, paciencia, belleza y ciencia. «Siempre es ya muy tarde, en nuestro mundo, para defender a la naturaleza»: Loria.

Bella pareja de aves del estado de Yucatán, en la que una hermosa cauda caracteriza al macho.

Símbolo de Guatemala y del sureste, el Quetzal es posiblemente el ave más hermosa del mundo y una de las que corren mayor riesgo de extinción

AWARD OF EXCELLENCE
TRAVEL
PAGE DESIGN
Novedades
Mexico City, Mexico
Designer
Teresa Chaurria
Illustrator
Jose Luis Loria
Art Director
Claudio Rodriguez Alvarez

INSIDE:

A salute to winners of the Free Press Writing Award contest. Page 7.

Sunday, May 15, 1988

TRAVEL

Detroit Free Press

SECTION J

Ask Away, Page 6
Diversions, Page 8
Books and Authors, Page 9
Call Travel: 222-6521

50 GREAT SUMMER VACATIONS

By Rick Sylvain
FREE PRESS TRAVEL EDITOR

AWARD OF EXCELLENCE
TRAVEL
PAGE DESIGN
Detroit Free Press
Designer
Andrew Hartley
Illustrator
Bonnie Timmons
Art Director
Deborah Withey

14 XX THE NEW YORK TIMES, SUNDAY, NOVEMBER 27, 1988

CORRESPONDENT'S CHOICE

Eight Settings for the Holiday Season . . .

West Germany

Midnight mass at Cologne's great Gothic cathedral

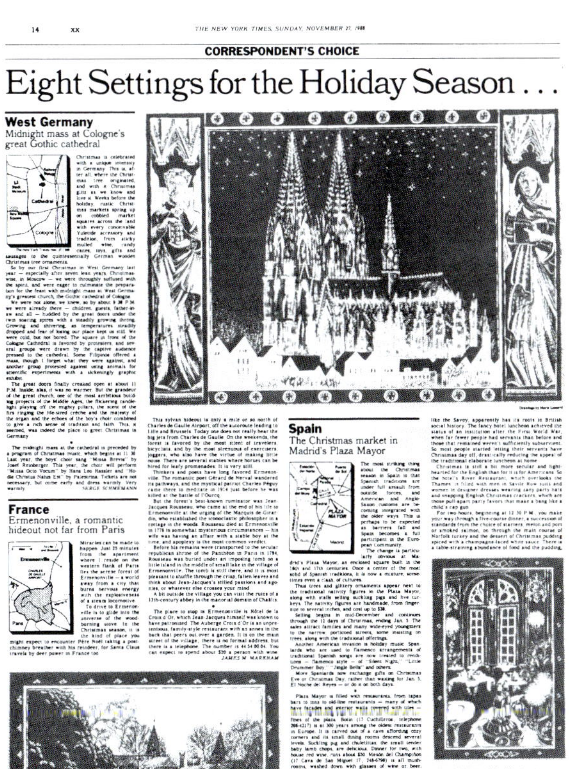

France

Ermenonville, a romantic hideout not far from Paris

Spain

The Christmas market in Madrid's Plaza Mayor

England

Christmas luncheon at the Savoy Hotel

THE NEW YORK TIMES, SUNDAY, NOVEMBER 27, 1988 XX 15

CORRESPONDENT'S CHOICE

. . . From Rio's Heights to Rome's Heart

Italy

When the Romans reclaim the Piazza Navona

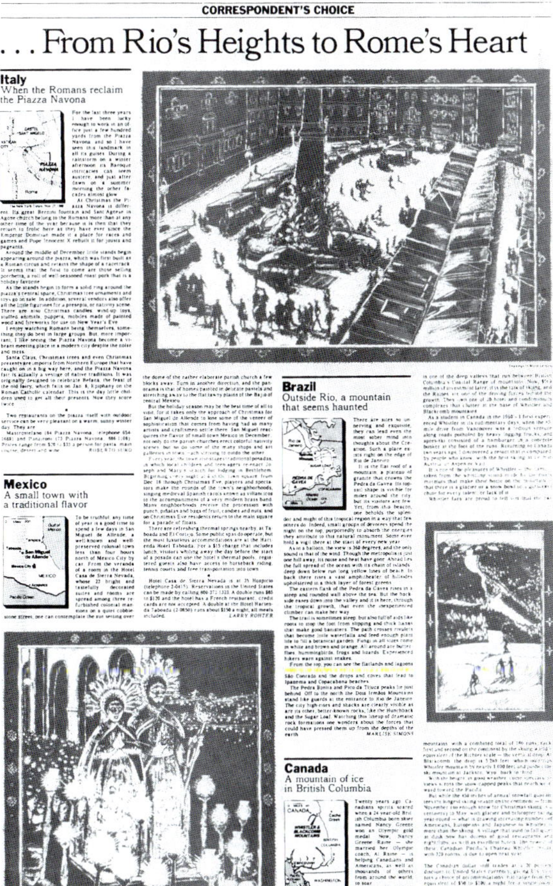

Mexico

A small town with a traditional flavor

Brazil

Outside Rio, a mountain that seems haunted

Canada

A mountain of ice in British Columbia

AWARD OF EXCELLENCE
TRAVEL
PAGE DESIGN
The New York Times
Designer
Michael Valenti
Illustrator
Marie Lessard
Art Director
Michael Valenti

The Boston Globe
SUNDAY, DECEMBER 25, 1988

TRAVEL

Hobbies A68

Elephants, zebras, giraffes, Cape buffalo and ostriches — they provide a pulse-quickening spectacle for visitors to Amboseli National Park in Kenya.

On safari

AN ALBUM OF WILD THINGS

AMBOSELI NATIONAL PARK, Kenya — You are the one in the zoo.

Your car, or your van, or your 4-wheel-drive vehicle is the cage.

It is your protection and your vantage point for a day, or, if you are fortunate, a week or more.

The animals see a lot of creatures like you, being ported around and wearing those strange sun visors or safari

KENYA, continued on next page

photographs by Janet Knott

AWARD OF EXCELLENCE
TRAVEL
PAGE DESIGN
The Boston Globe
Designer
Aldona Charlton
Photographer
Janet Knott
Art Director
Aldona Charlton

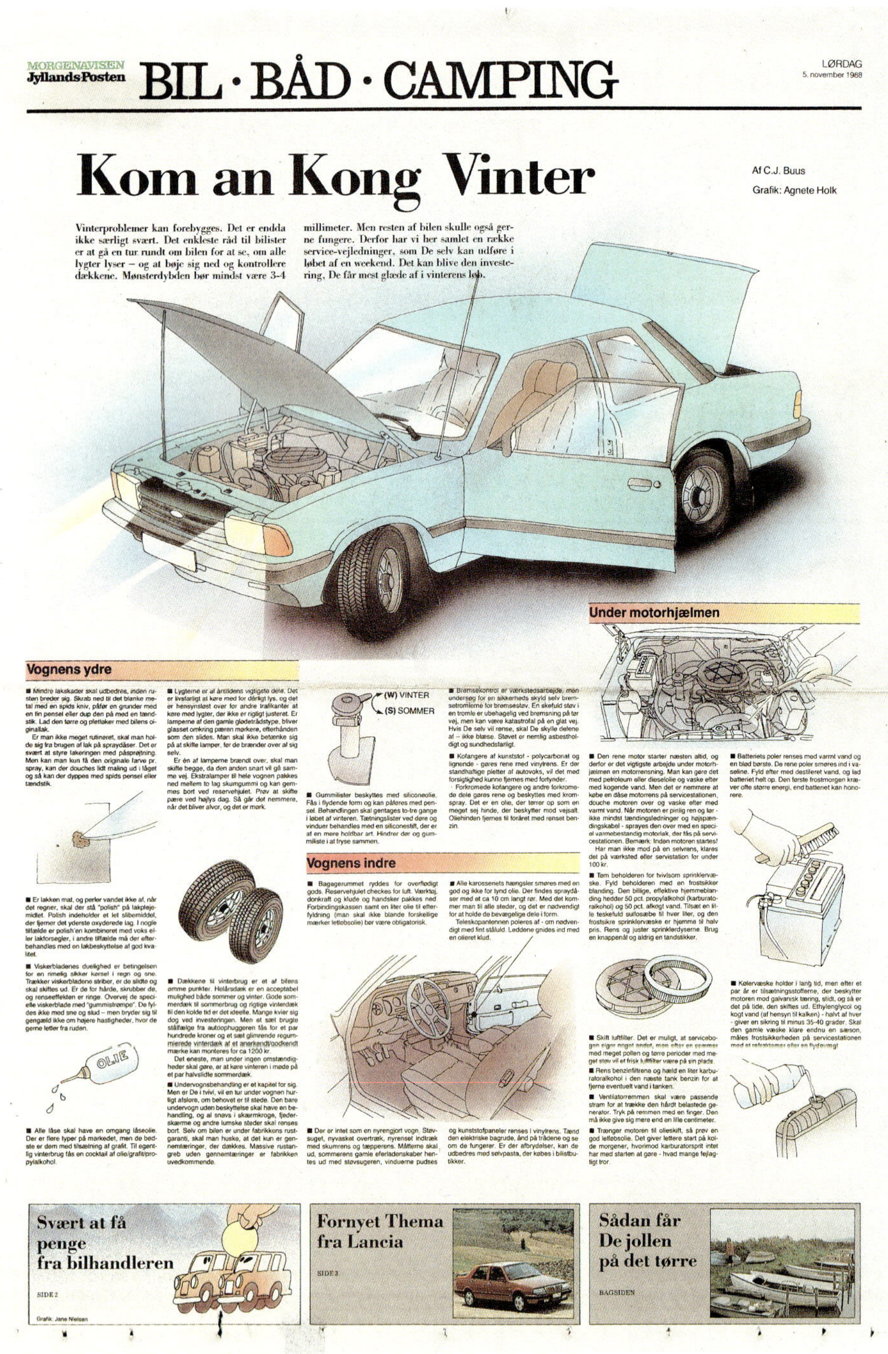

MORGENAVISEN Jyllands-Posten

BIL · BÅD · CAMPING

LØRDAG
5. november 1988

Kom an Kong Vinter

Af C.J. Buus

Grafik: Agnete Holk

Vinterproblemer kan forebygges. Det er endda ikke særligt svært. Det enkleste råd til bilister er at gå en tur rundt om bilen for at se, om alle lygter lyser – og at bøje sig ned og kontrollere dækkene. Mønsterdybden bør mindst være 3-4 millimeter. Men resten af bilen skulle også gerne fungere. Derfor har vi her samlet en række service-vejledninger, som De selv kan udføre i løbet af en weekend. Det kan blive den investering, De får mest glæde af i vinterens løb.

Vognens ydre

■ Mindre lakskader skal udbedres, inden rusten breder sig. Skrab ned til det blanke metal med en spids kniv, påfør en grunder med en fin pensel eller dup den på med en tændstik. Lad den tørre og pletlaker med bilens originallak.

Er man ikke meget rutineret, skal man holde sig fra brugen af lak på spraydåser. Det er svært at styre lakeringen med påsprøjtning. Men kan man kun få den originale farve pr. spray, kan der douches lidt maling ud i låget og så kan der dyppes med spids pensel eller tændstik.

■ Er lakken mat, og perler vandet ikke af, når det regner, skal der stå "polish" på takplejemidlet. Polish indeholder et let slibemiddel, der fjerner det yderste oxyderede lag. I nogle tilfælde er polish'en kombineret med voks eller lakforsegler, i andre tilfælde må der efterbehandles med en lakbeskyttelse af god kvalitet.

■ Viskerbladenes duelighed er betingelsen for en rimelig sikker kørsel i regn og sne. Trækker viskerbladene striber, er de slidte og skal skiftes ud. Er de for hårde, skrubber de, og renseeffekten er ringe. Overvej de specielle viskerblade med "gummistrømpe". De fyldes ikke med sne og slud – men bryder sig til gengæld ikke om højere hastigheder, hvor de gerne letter fra ruden.

■ Alle låse skal have en omgang låseolie. Der er flere typer på markedet, men de bedste er dem med tilsætning af grafit. Til egentlig vinterbrug fås en cocktail af olie/grafit/propylalkohol.

■ Lygterne er af årstidens vigtigste dele. Det er livsfarligt at køre med for dårligt lys, og det er hensynsløst over for andre trafikanter at køre med lygter, der ikke er rigtigt justeret. Er lamperne af den gamle glødetrådstype, bliver glasset omkring pæren mørkere, efterhånden som den slides. Man skal ikke betænke sig på at skifte lamper, før de brænder over af sig selv.

Er én af lamperne brændt over, skal man skifte begge, da den anden snart vil gå samme vej. Ekstralamper til hele vognen pakkes ned mellem to lag skumgummi og kan gemmes bort ved reservehjulet. Prøv at skifte pære ved højlys dag. Så går det nemmere, når det bliver alvor, og det er mørk.

■ Dækkene til vinterbrug er et af bilens ømme punkter. Helårsdæk er en acceptabel mulighed både sommer og vinter. Gode sommerdæk til sommerbrug og rigtige vinterdæk til den kolde tid er det ideelle. Mange kvier sig dog ved investeringen. Men et sæt brugte stålfælge fra autoophuggeren fås for et par hundrede kroner og et sæt glimrende regummierede vinterdæk af et anerkendt/godkendt mærke kan monteres for ca 1200 kr.

Det eneste, man under ingen omstændigheder skal gøre, er at køre vinteren i møde på et par halvslidte sommerdæk.

■ Undervognsbehandling er et kapitel for sig. Men er De i tvivl, vil en tur under vognen hurtigt afsløre, om behovet er til stede. Den bare undervogn uden beskyttelse skal have en behandling, og al snavs i skærmkroge, fjederskærme og andre lumske steder skal renses bort. Selv om bilen er under fabrikkens rustgaranti, skal man huske, at det kun er gennemtæringer, der dækkes. Massive rustangreb uden gennemtæringer er fabrikken uvedkommende.

■ Gummilister beskyttes med siliconeolie. Fås i flydende form og kan påføres med pensel. Behandlingen skal gentages to-tre gange i løbet af vinteren. Tætningslister ved døre og vinduer behandles med en siliconestift, der er af en mere holdbar art. Hindrer dør og gummiliste i at fryse sammen.

■ Bremsekontrol er værkstedsarbejde, men undersøg for en sikkerheds skyld selv bremsetromlerne for bremsestøv. En skefuld støv i en tromle er ubehagelig ved bremsning på tør vej, men kan være katastrofal på en glat vej. Hvis De selv vil rense, skal De skylle delene af – ikke blæse. Støvet er nemlig asbestholdigt og sundhedsfarligt.

■ Kofangere af kunststof - polycarbonat og lignende - gøres rene med vinylrens. Er der standhaftige pletter af autovoks, vil det med forsigtighed kunne fjernes med fortynder.

Forkromede kofangere og andre forkromede dele gøres rene og beskyttes med kromspray. Det er en olie, der tørrer op som en meget sej hinde, der beskytter mod vejsalt. Oliehinden fjernes til foråret med renset benzin.

Vognens indre

■ Bagagerummet ryddes for overflødigt gods. Reservehjulet checkes for luft. Værktøj, donkraft og klude og handsker pakkes ned. Forbindingskassen samt en liter olie til efterfyldning (man skal ikke blande forskellige mærker letløbsolie) bør være obligatorisk.

■ Alle karosseriets hængsler smøres med en god og ikke for tynd olie. Der findes spraydåser med et ca 10 cm langt rør. Med det kommer man til alle steder, og det er nødvendigt for at holde de bevægelige dele i form.

Teleskopantennen poleres af - om nødvendigt med fint ståluld. Leddene gnides ind med en olieret klud.

■ Der er intet som en nyrengjort vogn. Støvsuget, nyvasket overtræk, nyrenset indtræk med skumrens og tæpperens. Måtterne skal ud, sommerens gamle eferladenskaber hentes ud med støvsugeren, vinduerne pudses og kunststofpaneler renses i vinylrens. Tænd den elektriske bagrude, ånd på trådene og se om de fungerer. Er der afbrydelser, kan de udbedres med sølvpasta, der købes i bilistbutikker.

Under motorhjælmen

■ Den rene motor starter næsten altid, og derfor er det vigtigste arbejde under motorhjælmen en motorrensning. Man kan gøre det med petroleum eller dieselolie og vaske efter med kogende vand. Men det er nemmere at købe en dåse motorrens på servicestationen, douche motoren over og vaske efter med varmt vand. Når motoren er pinlig ren og tør - ikke mindst tændingsledninger og højspændingskabel - sprayes den over med en speciel varmebestandig motorlak, der fås på servicestationen. Bemærk: Inden motoren startes!

Har man ikke mod på en selvrens, klares det på værksted eller servistation for under 100 kr.

■ Tøm beholderen for tvivlsom sprinklervæske. Fyld beholderen med en frostsikker blanding. Den billige, effektive hjemmeblanding hedder 50 pct. propylalkohol (karburatoralkohol) og 50 pct. afkogt vand. Tilsæt en lille teskefuld sulfosæbe til hver liter, og den frostsikre sprinklervæske er hjemme til halv pris. Rens og juster sprinklerdyserne. Brug en knappenål og aldrig en tandstikker.

■ Skift luftfilter. Det er muligt, at servicebogen siger noget andet, men efter en sommer med meget pollen og tørre perioder med meget støv vil et frisk luftfilter være på sin plads.

■ Rens benzinfiltrene og hæld en liter karburatoralkohol i den næste tank benzin for at fjerne eventuelt vand i tanken.

■ Ventilatorremmen skal være passende stram for at trække den hårdt belastede generator. Tryk på remmen med en finger. Den må ikke give sig mere end en lille centimeter.

■ Trænger motoren til olieskift, så prøv en god letløbsolie. Det giver lettere start på kolde morgener, hvorimod karburatorsprit intet har med starten at gøre - hvad mange fejlagtigt tror.

■ Batteriets poler renses med varmt vand og en blød børste. De rene poler smøres ind i vaseline. Fyld efter med destilleret vand, og lad batteriet helt op. Den første frostmorgen kræver ofte større energi, end batteriet kan honorere.

■ Kølervæske holder i lang tid, men efter et par år er tilsætningsstofferne, der beskytter motoren mod galvanisk tæring, slidt, og så er det på tide, den skiftes ud. Ethylenglycol og kogt vand (af hensyn til kalken) - halvt af hver - giver en sikring til minus 35-40 grader. Skal den gamle væske klare endnu en sæson, måles frostsikkerheden på servicestationen med et refraktometer eller en flydevægt

Svært at få penge fra bilhandleren

SIDE 2

Grafik: Jane Nielsen

Fornyet Thema fra Lancia

SIDE 3

Sådan får De jollen på det tørre

BAGSIDEN

AWARD OF EXCELLENCE
SCIENCE/TECHNOLOGY
PAGE DESIGN

Morgenavisen Jyllands-Posten
Aarhus, Denmark

Designer
Agnete Holk
Illustrator
Agnete Holk

AWARD OF EXCELLENCE

SCIENCE/TECHNOLOGY
PAGE DESIGN

Detroit Free Press

Designer
Michele Vernon-Chesley

Illustrator
David Cutler

Art Director
Deborah Withey

SCIENCE & MEDICINE

Detroit Free Press

Tuesday, Oct. 25, 1988

INSIDE: CLASSIFIED

SECTION C

CURIOSITIES

Freezing doesn't make water clean

DAVE CUTLER/Special to the Free Press

MIND VS. MATTER

As researchers gain exciting insights into how the brain works, some still believe it must be more than the sum of its parts

EUREKA!

Quake predictor studied

Comets and extinctions

The swirling hot Sun

THINK AGAIN

"We are involved with mathematics all the time," says Joel Schneider.

Kids can see the fun in figures

AN ODE OF SORTS TO THE OAKS

GALERIA

POR DENTRO

MARTES 1 DE NOVIEMBRE DE 1988 / EL NUEVO HERALD

CIENCIA ESPACIAL

Por Rolando Millas

Una isla en el espacio

EL TERCER OJO

La parasicología lo sitúa en la llamada glándula pineal, y cree podría ser la sede de las facultades extrasensoriales, el foco neurálgico emisor de la energía síquica.

NURI DUCASSI / El Nuevo Herald

WITHOUT A CLUE — MYSTIC PIZZA — ALIEN NATION

El eterno personaje de Sherlock Holmes en un filme superaburrido

Without a Clue resulta un desperdicio de talento para dos buenos actores a la deriva.

Ofrece un recital en París la actriz argentina Marucha Bo

AWARD OF EXCELLENCE

SCIENCE/TECHNOLOGY
PAGE DESIGN

el Nuevo Herald
Miami, Florida

Designer
Nuri Ducassi

Illustrator
Nuri Ducassi

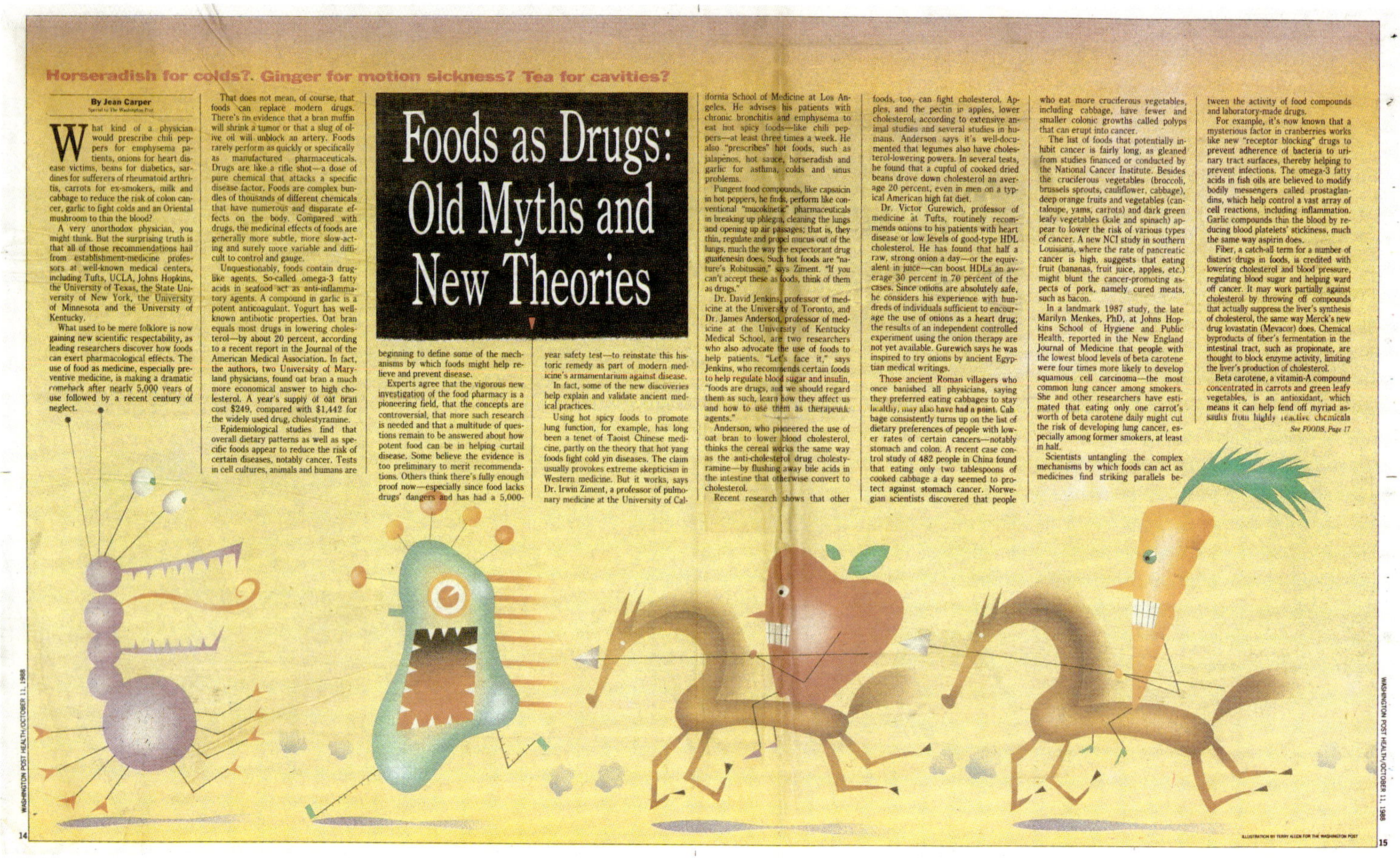

Horseradish for colds?. Ginger for motion sickness? Tea for cavities?

Foods as Drugs: Old Myths and New Theories

By Jean Carper
Special to The Washington Post

What kind of a physician would prescribe chili peppers for emphysema patients, onions for heart disease victims, beans for diabetics, sardines for sufferers of rheumatoid arthritis, carrots for ex-smokers, milk and cabbage to reduce the risk of colon cancer, garlic to fight colds and an Oriental mushroom to thin the blood?

A very unorthodox physician, you might think. But the surprising truth is that all of those recommendations hail from establishment-medicine professors at well-known medical centers, including Tufts, UCLA, Johns Hopkins, the University of Texas, the State University of New York, the University of Minnesota and the University of Kentucky.

What used to be mere folklore is now gaining new scientific respectability, as leading researchers discover how foods can exert pharmacological effects. The use of food as medicine, especially preventive medicine, is making a dramatic comeback after nearly 5,000 years of use followed by a recent century of neglect.

That does not mean, of course, that foods can replace modern drugs. There's no evidence that a bran muffin will shrink a tumor or that a slug of olive oil will unblock an artery. Foods rarely perform as quickly or specifically as manufactured pharmaceuticals. Drugs are like a rifle shot—a dose of pure chemical that attacks a specific disease factor. Foods are complex bundles of thousands of different chemicals that have numerous and disparate effects on the body. Compared with drugs, the medicinal effects of foods are generally more subtle, more slow-acting and surely more variable and difficult to control and gauge.

Unquestionably, foods contain drug-like agents. So-called omega-3 fatty acids in seafood act as anti-inflammatory agents. A compound in garlic is a potent anticoagulant. Yogurt has well-known antibiotic properties. Oat bran equals most drugs in lowering cholesterol—by about 20 percent, according to a recent report in the Journal of the American Medical Association. In fact, the authors, two University of Maryland physicians, found oat bran a much more economical answer to high cholesterol. A year's supply of oat bran cost $249, compared with $1,442 for the widely used drug, cholestyramine.

Epidemiological studies find that overall dietary patterns as well as specific foods appear to reduce the risk of certain diseases, notably cancer. Tests in cell cultures, animals and humans are beginning to define some of the mechanisms by which foods might help relieve and prevent disease.

Experts agree that the vigorous new investigation of the food pharmacy is a pioneering field, that the concepts are controversial, that more such research is needed and that a multitude of questions remain to be answered about how potent food can be in helping curtail disease. Some believe the evidence is too preliminary to merit recommendations. Others think there's fully enough proof now—especially since food lacks drugs' dangers and has had a 5,000-year safety test—to reinstate this historic remedy as part of modern medicine's armamentarium against disease.

In fact, some of the new discoveries help explain and validate ancient medical practices.

Using hot spicy foods to promote lung function, for example, has long been a tenet of Taoist Chinese medicine, partly on the theory that hot yang foods fight cold yin diseases. The claim usually provokes extreme skepticism in Western medicine. But it works, says Dr. Irwin Ziment, a professor of pulmonary medicine at the University of California School of Medicine at Los Angeles. He advises his patients with chronic bronchitis and emphysema to eat hot spicy foods—like chili peppers—at least three times a week. He also "prescribes" hot foods, such as jalapeños, hot sauce, horseradish and garlic for asthma, colds and sinus problems.

Pungent food compounds, like capsaicin in hot peppers, he finds, perform like conventional "mucokinetic" pharmaceuticals in breaking up phlegm, cleaning the lungs and opening up air passages; that is, they thin, regulate and propel mucus out of the lungs, much the way the expectorant drug guaifenesin does. Such hot foods are "nature's Robitussin," says Ziment. "If you can't accept these as foods, think of them as drugs."

Dr. David Jenkins, professor of medicine at the University of Toronto, and Dr. James Anderson, professor of medicine at the University of Kentucky Medical School, are two researchers who also advocate the use of foods to help patients. "Let's face it," says Jenkins, who recommends certain foods to help regulate blood sugar and insulin, "foods are drugs, and we should regard them as such, learn how they affect us and how to use them as therapeutic agents."

Anderson, who pioneered the use of oat bran to lower blood cholesterol, thinks the cereal works the same way as the anti-cholesterol drug cholestyramine—by flushing away bile acids in the intestine that otherwise convert to cholesterol.

Recent research shows that other foods, too, can fight cholesterol. Apples, and the pectin in apples, lower cholesterol, according to extensive animal studies and several studies in humans. Anderson says it's well-documented that legumes also have cholesterol-lowering powers. In several tests, he found that a cupful of cooked dried beans drove down cholesterol an average 20 percent, even in men on a typical American high fat diet.

Dr. Victor Gurewich, professor of medicine at Tufts, routinely recommends onions to his patients with heart disease or low levels of good-type HDL cholesterol. He has found that half a raw, strong onion a day—or the equivalent in juice—can boost HDLs an average 30 percent in 70 percent of the cases. Since onions are absolutely safe, he considers his experience with hundreds of individuals sufficient to encourage the use of onions as a heart drug; the results of an independent controlled experiment using the onion therapy are not yet available. Gurewich says he was inspired to try onions by ancient Egyptian medical writings.

Those ancient Roman villagers who once banished all physicians, saying they preferred eating cabbages to stay healthy, may also have had a point. Cabbage consistently turns up on the list of dietary preferences of people with lower rates of certain cancers—notably stomach and colon. A recent case control study of 482 people in China found that eating only two tablespoons of cooked cabbage a day seemed to protect against stomach cancer. Norwegian scientists discovered that people who eat more cruciferous vegetables, including cabbage, have fewer and smaller colonic growths called polyps that can erupt into cancer.

The list of foods that potentially inhibit cancer is fairly long, as gleaned from studies financed or conducted by the National Cancer Institute. Besides the cruciferous vegetables (broccoli, brussels sprouts, cauliflower, cabbage), deep orange fruits and vegetables (cantaloupe, yams, carrots) and dark green leafy vegetables (kale and spinach) appear to lower the risk of various types of cancer. A new NCI study in southern Louisiana, where the rate of pancreatic cancer is high, suggests that eating fruit (bananas, fruit juice, apples, etc.) might blunt the cancer-promoting aspects of pork, namely cured meats, such as bacon.

In a landmark 1987 study, the late Marilyn Menkes, PhD, at Johns Hopkins School of Hygiene and Public Health, reported in the New England Journal of Medicine that people with the lowest blood levels of beta carotene were four times more likely to develop squamous cell carcinoma—the most common lung cancer among smokers. She and other researchers have estimated that eating only one carrot's worth of beta carotene daily might cut the risk of developing lung cancer, especially among former smokers, at least in half.

Scientists untangling the complex mechanisms by which foods can act as medicines find striking parallels between the activity of food compounds and laboratory-made drugs.

For example, it's now known that a mysterious factor in cranberries works like new "receptor blocking" drugs to prevent adherence of bacteria to urinary tract surfaces, thereby helping to prevent infections. The omega-3 fatty acids in fish oils are believed to modify bodily messengers called prostaglandins, which help control a vast array of cell reactions, including inflammation. Garlic compounds thin the blood by reducing blood platelets' stickiness, much the same way aspirin does.

Fiber, a catch-all term for a number of distinct drugs in foods, is credited with lowering cholesterol and blood pressure, regulating blood sugar and helping ward off cancer. It may work partially against cholesterol by throwing off compounds that actually suppress the liver's synthesis of cholesterol, the same way Merck's new drug lovastatin (Mevacor) does. Chemical byproducts of fiber's fermentation in the intestinal tract, such as propionate, are thought to block enzyme activity, limiting the liver's production of cholesterol.

Beta carotene, a vitamin-A compound concentrated in carrots and green leafy vegetables, is an antioxidant, which means it can help fend off myriad assaults from highly reactive chemicals

See FOODS, Page 17

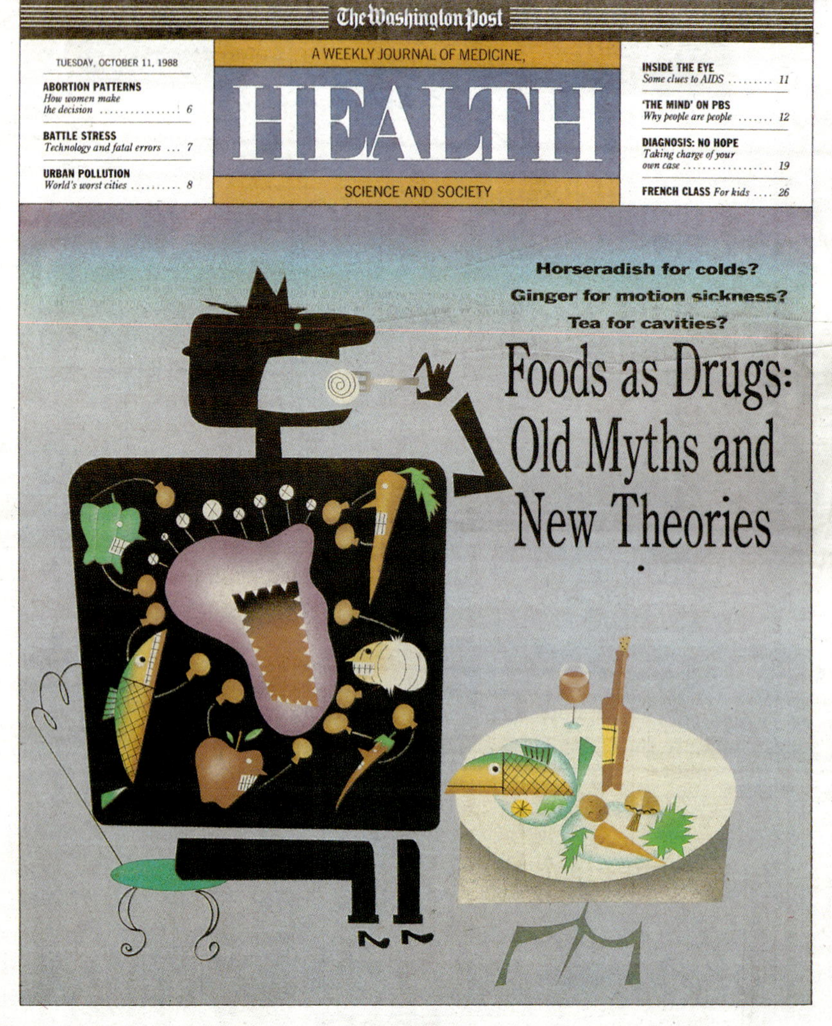

The Washington Post

A WEEKLY JOURNAL OF MEDICINE,

HEALTH

SCIENCE AND SOCIETY

TUESDAY, OCTOBER 11, 1988

Horseradish for colds?
Ginger for motion sickness?
Tea for cavities?

Foods as Drugs: Old Myths and New Theories

AWARD OF EXCELLENCE
SCIENCE/TECHNOLOGY
PAGE DESIGN
The Washington Post
Designer
Alice Kresse
Illustrator
Terry Allen
Art Director
Alice Kresse

THE SUN

INDUSTRY/TECHNOLOGY

A GUIDE TO AMERICA'S HIGH TECH BELT

Manufacturing's malaise may have bottomed out locally

By PAUL KONSTADT
Sun Staff

Manufacturing should remain on the underside of the Massachusetts Miracle in 1989, say the economists who watch such things.

Even as the high tech boom has reverberated back and forth through the hills surrounding Boston, manufacturing has shrunk under the inevitable pressures of outside competition, and the biggest question is now whether the downtrend has bottomed out.

Please see INDUSTRY/B6

Computer makers sort themselves out after slowdown

By MICHAEL O'CONNELL
Sun Staff

As the 1980s come to a close, the computer industry finds itself in a certain amount of turmoil.

Vendors and customers alike are confused about which industry standards will take hold. Demand in the United States is flat, and Europe is showing signs of slowing down, too.

Then there's the once-proud minicomputer sector, a Massachusetts stronghold, that's being squeezed from the bottom by

Please see COMPUTERS/B6

INSIDE

The Big Players
A look at eight of the region's largest employers and where they are headed in the near future. 2

Corporate Directory
Thumbnail sketches of hundreds of local companies, detailing what they do and who's in charge. 8

THE BIG SNEEZE

NEW ADVANCES IN TREATING ALLERGIES

By Robin Marantz Henig

The Science of Allergies

Sneezy, Drippy and Dopey

Hay Fever Remedies

SILVER AWARD
SCIENCE/TECHNOLOGY
PAGE DESIGN
The Washington Post
Designer
Alice Kresse
Illustrator
Alice Kresse
Researcher
Bettmann Archives
Art Director
Alice Kresse

AWARD OF EXCELLENCE
SCIENCE/TECHNOLOGY
PAGE DESIGN
The Sun
Lowell, Massachusetts
Designer
Mitchell J. Hayes
Illustrator
Bob Dahm
Art Director
Mitchell J. Hayes
Editor
Chromwell Schubarth

AWARD OF EXCELLENCE
SCIENCE/TECHNOLOGY
PAGE DESIGN
The Washington Post
Designer
Alice Kresse
Illustrator
Randy Lyhus
Infographic
Alice Kresse
Art Director
Alice Kresse

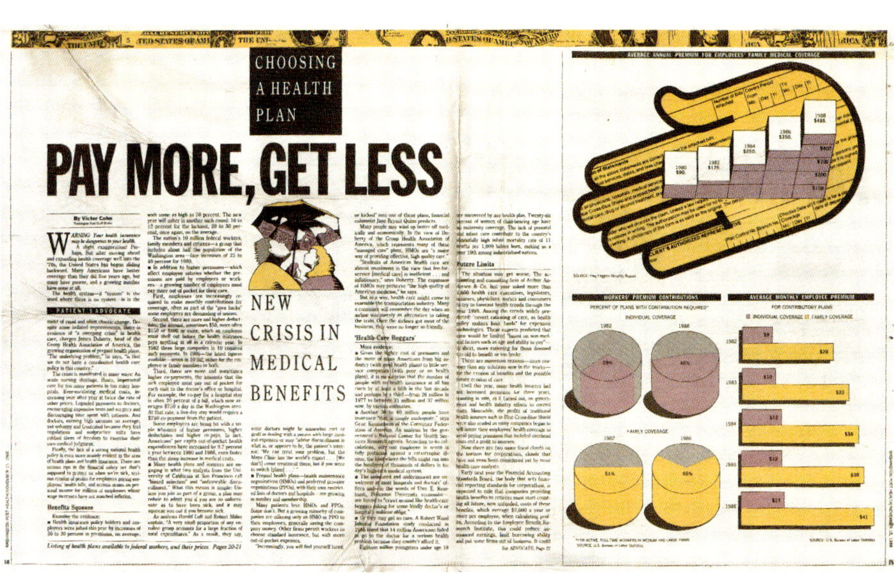

CHOOSING A HEALTH PLAN

PAY MORE, GET LESS

NEW CRISIS IN MEDICAL BENEFITS

By Victor Cohn

AVERAGE ANNUAL PREMIUM FOR EMPLOYEE'S FAMILY MEDICAL COVERAGE

WORKERS' PREMIUM CONTRIBUTIONS

AVERAGE MONTHLY EMPLOYEE PREMIUM

The Washington Post

A WEEKLY JOURNAL OF MEDICINE, SCIENCE AND SOCIETY

HEALTH

CHOOSING A HEALTH PLAN

PAY MORE, GET LESS

NEW CRISIS IN MEDICAL BENEFITS

DAGENS NYHETER.

SÖNDAG

Söndagen den 28 augusti 1988

DEL 2

Foto: LEIF ENGBERG

En sprinter på upploppet

Koreas språng mot den världsekonomiska eliten pågår som bäst. Leif Engbergs bild av säkerhetspolisen på OS-stadion i Söul kan stå som symbol. DN:s Ingvar Oja porträtterar människorna och landet bakom undret.

4–7

한국 KOREA

Tonårsgrupperna slår tillbaka 8

Foto: JOSE AZEL/Contact

I Floridas turistmarker 13

Foto: ULF SIRBORN

Framgång för John Norum 2

So-Wol Kim tog livet av sig 31 år gammal 1934 som olycklig och missförstådd poet utan uppskattning. I dag är han en av Koreas populäraste diktare och varje korean kan delar av hans verk utantill. I Sverige översatte Martin Strindlund en av hans böcker förra året. Dikterna är spröda och ömtåliga. De handlar om kärlek och känslor. På tröskeln till OS i Söul presenterar DN Söndag några människoöden i Sydkorea. Men först några rader av So-Wol Kim. Dikten Längtan:

Tätnande skymning.
Molnet över bergåsen smälter ihop med mörkret.
Varför längtar jag så efter henne i dag?
Hon kommer ju inte. Det är inte rätta kvällen.
Min otåliga väntan är fåfäng.
Månen är uppe, och vildgässen snattrar i skyn.

FREDRIK ROOS
DN SÖNDAG

DN Söndag — DAGENS NYHETER Söndagen den 28 augusti 1988

한국 KOREA

Sydkoreas bönder en armé av tjänstemän

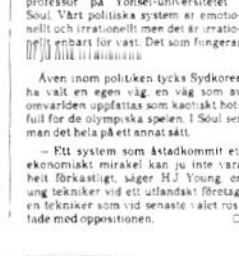

"Moderna tider"

Inget att frukta

Chock för väst

Tron på OS

Här är man van vid mer våld än nöden kräver

Den unga studenten på Yonsei-universitetet, radikalismens förhållande till Nordkorea.

"Kanske mina barn"

Släktöden

Stenansikten

Avhoppare bekräftar

SILVER AWARD
OTHER
PAGE DESIGN
Dagens Nyheter
Stockholm, Sweden
Designers
Gunilla Peterson, Bo Holmstrom
Photographer
Leif Engberg

DAGENS NYHETER

SÖNDAG

DEL 2

Mahfouz på hemmaplan

Per Gahrton har mött Nobelpristagaren Naguib Mahfouz i Kairos färgstarka basarkvarter **4**

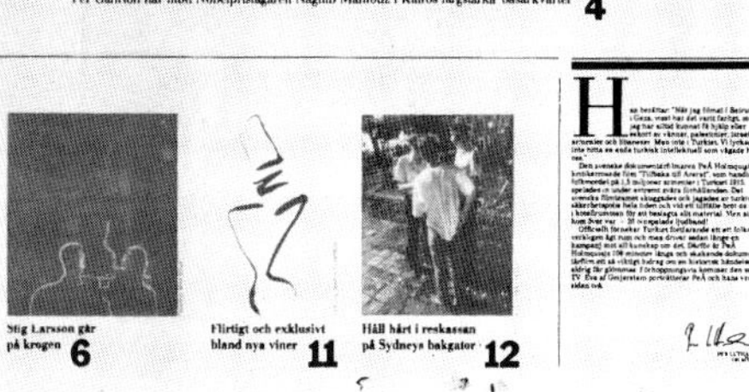

Stig Larsson går på krogen **6**

Flirtigt och exklusivt bland nya viner **11**

Håll hårt i reskassan på Sydneys bakgator **12**

AWARD OF EXCELLENCE
OTHER
PAGE DESIGN
Dagens Nyheter
Stockholm, Sweden
Designer
Bo Holmstrom
Photographer
Ulla Lemberg

AWARD OF EXCELLENCE
OTHER
PAGE DESIGN
The Financial Times of Canada
Toronto
Designer
Therese Shechter
Art Director
Therese Shechter

NOVEMBER 14, 1988 A1

FINANCIAL TIMES OF CANADA

Executive Autos

FYI: Smart cars, smart roads and the vanishing auto year A5 *The enduring appeal of the Corvette* A8 *Luxury carmakers fight for their niche* A9 *Getting the best price for your used car* A13 *Why I drive what I drive* A11 *John Maxwell's Jaguar collection* A18

Big is back

DOUG MACDONALD'S gut feeling that car buyers were about to end their love affair with small cars didn't prove out overnight. As owner of MacDonald Pontiac-Buick Ltd. in Moncton, N.B., it has been his business for 30 years to detect fundamental shifts in consumer psychology. And three years ago, his instinct told him that consumers were about to move to bigger autos. But it was not until this year that his prediction finally came true: small cars represent only 20% of his business so far in 1988, down from 30% a year before.

It's still another baby-boomer phenomenon. The Me generation is now the Us generation, with the desire and the wherewithal to move on to roomier, more luxurious automobiles. As PAGE A16

BY CLAYTON SINCLAIR

JANUARY 23, 1989 FINANCIAL TIMES OF CANADA A1

FINANCIAL TIMES OF CANADA

Mutual Funds

FYI: The worst of the lot, plus bullish hopes for '89 A3 *How seven managers saw their portfolios prosper despite the odds* A7 *High-flying rewards for high-grossing salespeople* A13 *Facts and fallacies explored at last* A11 *Our annual long-term performance checkup* A16

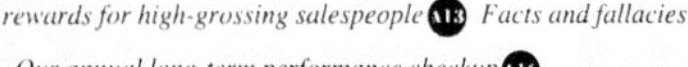

Riding out the storm

PATIENCE AND PRUDENCE — the search, if you will, for a sure bet — have traditionally governed mutual-fund investment. Most people, like marriage partners, commit themselves to have and hold through the market's richer or poorer patches. Lately, of course, the rough has overwhelmed the smooth. We know where we've been — blind-sided by Black Monday and saddled with galloping interest rates. It's where we're going that makes a horse race — and that depends on a number of variables. On the following pages we present a look at the track records of the best-performing funds over both the short and the long haul. We gauge a fund's volatility and examine the flexibility of its managers; demystify what funds can and cannot do; and aid you in establishing individual goals. PAGE A9

AWARD OF EXCELLENCE
OTHER
PAGE DESIGN
The Financial Times of Canada
Toronto
Designer
Therese Shechter
Illustrator
Emmanuel Lopez
Art Director
Therese Shechter

AWARD OF EXCELLENCE
OTHER
PAGE DESIGN
San Francisco Examiner
Designer
Gordon Studer
Illustrator
Gordon Studer

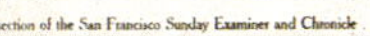
A section of the San Francisco Sunday Examiner and Chronicle

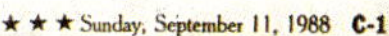
★ ★ ★ Sunday, September 11, 1988 C-1

EXAMINER SPORTS PREVIEW

X X I V

S U M M E R G A M E S

OLYMPIAD

By Art Spander
OF THE EXAMINER STAFF

SEOUL — So the Summer Games move across the sea to a country where ginseng hardly is the root of all evil and the hope is the circles on the Olympic flag, which symbolize universal cooperation, finally have a ring of truth.

Four years have fled since the pride and glory in Los Angeles. It is again time to light our fire, a torch that burns brightly and, with luck, will illuminate human achievement.

A few days from the beginning of the XXIV Olympiad a peculiar blend of apprehension and anticipation hangs in the polluted air over the world's ninth-largest city.

For the first time since the 1972 Munich Olympics — which, of course, will live in infamy for another reason, the massacre of Israeli athletes — the Summer Games will not be disgraced by a major boycott of eligible nations.

The Americans, the Soviets, the East Germans and most Africans will be here. Among the strongest teams in the world, only the Cubans will be absent.

"No problems, no regrets, no recourse," says Mac Wilkins, the American discus thrower.

Yet that satisfaction is balanced by the threat of violence at a showcase sporting event in a place where students riot as often as they study and a spiteful enemy, North Korea, is only 35 miles away.

Surely, anything is possible at an Olympiad where there will be 17,000 athletes and 110,000 security personnel.

Mary Decker Slaney may make amends, earning a medal in the 3,000 meters, the race in which she tumbled ignominiously in '84.

Carl Lewis might make history, becoming the first man ever to repeat as a gold medalist in the sprints.

Terrorists could create chaos.

What others create depends on their political beliefs.

For U.S. advertisers, the Olympics, with some 179 hours on television, are an opportunity to sell their wares. "There's a spirit sweeping America," we're told in a Chevrolet commercial . . . A winning spirit you can feel now that games are here . . ."

For the Soviets and East Germans, the Olympics are an opportunity to sell their system.

To each his own, and if all goes smoothly — meaning we see a zone defense on the basketball court but no offense at the demilitarized zone — capitalism and socialism will be able to coexist without a worry.

Which is much more than you can say for North and South Korea.

For many Americans, certainly, Korea is not munchkins twirling on the parallel bars but GIs ducking into foxholes.

Another generation recalls names such as Pork Chop Hill and euphemisms such as "police ac-

[See SPANDER, C-10]

EXAMINER GRAPHIC / GORDON STUDER

Sports inside
The regular Sunday sports section begins after Seoul '88 / C-11

Golden boy
Moraga swimmer Matt Biondi has high expectations / C-2

SEOUL 1988

Nancy Ditz
A calm personality keeps her happy in the long run / C-3

Playing it safe
South Korea security system's plan to keep The Games safe / C-5

THE SEASON
H. VEGA
THE MIAMI HERALD
1988
NOVEMBER 10

AWARD OF EXCELLENCE
OTHER
PAGE DESIGN
The Miami Herald
Designers
Herman Vega, Rhonda Prast
Illustrator
Herman Vega
Director of Editorial Art and Design
Randy Stano

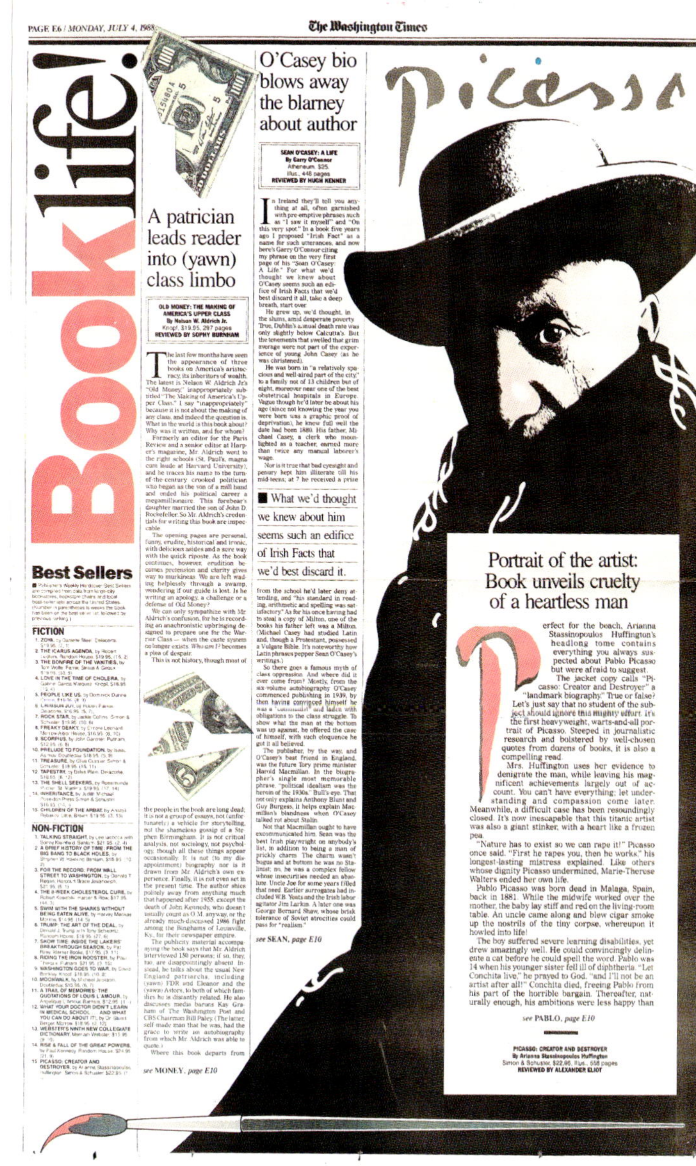
PAGE E6 / MONDAY, JULY 4, 1988
The Washington Times

Book life!

O'Casey bio blows away the blarney about author

SEAN O'CASEY: A LIFE
By Garry O'Connor
Atheneum, $25
illus., 448 pages
REVIEWED BY HUGH KENNER

A patrician leads reader into (yawn) class limbo

OLD MONEY: THE MAKING OF AMERICA'S UPPER CLASS
By Nelson W. Aldrich Jr.
Knopf, $19.95, 287 pages
REVIEWED BY SOPHY BURNHAM

■ What we'd thought we knew about him seems such an edifice of Irish Facts that we'd best discard it.

Best Sellers

FICTION

NON-FICTION

see MONEY, page E10

see SEAN, page E10

Picasso

Portrait of the artist: Book unveils cruelty of a heartless man

see PABLO, page E10

PICASSO: CREATOR AND DESTROYER
By Arianna Stassinopoulos Huffington
Simon & Schuster, $22.95, illus., 558 pages
REVIEWED BY ALEXANDER ELIOT

The Washington Times
MONDAY, OCTOBER 3, 1988 / PAGE E7

Book life!

The obscure composer of beloved concerto

MAX BRUCH: HIS LIFE AND WORKS
By Christopher Fifield
George Braziller, $30, 351 pages
REVIEWED BY PAUL MURK

Vann and Vietnam as seen through a '60s time warp

What we have here is two books in a single symbiosis. One book is a biography of the legendary John Paul Vann, the other is a history of the Vietnam War or at least major parts of it. "A Bright Shining Lie: John Paul Vann and America in Vietnam" will be bought and read, and probably will sell well as a biography. This is just as well, because what Neil Sheehan has produced here is good biography and bad history.

Best Sellers

FICTION

NON-FICTION

A BRIGHT SHINING LIE: JOHN PAUL VANN AND AMERICA IN VIETNAM
By Neil Sheehan
Random House, $24.95, illus., 861 pages
REVIEWED BY DOUGLAS PIKE

see VANN, page E8

see BRUCH, page E9

AWARD OF EXCELLENCE
OTHER
PAGE DESIGN
The Washington Times
Designer
John Kascht
Illustrator
John Kascht
Art Director
John Kascht

AWARD OF EXCELLENCE
OTHER
PAGE DESIGN
The Washington Times
Designer
John Kascht
Illustrator
John Kascht
Art Director
John Kasch

Chapter 5

Page-design portfolios: new rules, more participants

Judging of page-design portfolios underwent massive changes for the Tenth Edition. The category was broken into four sections based on page content and was divided into seven newspaper circulation levels.

The intent was to ensure that each portfolio was judged in context, that it be seen with other portfolios of similar content from a publication of about the same size.

Participation in this category increased by more than 50 percent. There were 309 entries in this category, 113 more than in the previous contest. Twenty-two portfolios won awards, including four for news pages, 14 for features pages, three for magazines and one for a combination portfolio. Six of those awards went for work from newspapers with less than 100,000 circulation.

INSIDE:

SECTION C

BUSINESS MONDAY

Detroit Free Press

COMPANY OF THE YEAR

THE BEST OF THE BEST

CMS ENERGY CORP.

Prospects brighten for power company

J.P. INDUSTRIES INC.

Non-hostile takeovers are paying off

KELLOGG CO.

Cereal maker has another healthy year

KELLY SERVICES INC.

Temporary work continues to add up

FORD MOTOR CO.

Automaker has the pole for fiscal '88

SILVER AWARD

NEWS PAGE DESIGN PORTFOLIO
CIRCULATION 250,000 AND OVER

Detroit Free Press

Designers
Deborah Withey, Andrew Hartley, and Staff

Illustrators
Deborah Withey, John Green, and Staff

Art Director
Deborah Withey

PERSONAL FINANCE

12 WAYS TO SAVE ON YOUR 1988 TAXES

1. LATE PAY

2. EARLY BILLS

3. CHARITY BEGINS . . .

4. RETIREMENT PLANS

5. INFORMED INVESTING

6. STOCK STRATEGY

7. MARRIAGE

8. MAKE GIFTS

9. NEW ANNUITIES

10. HELP FROM HOME

11. INTERESTING INTEREST

12. CLAIM ALL DEDUCTIONS

BONUS: COLLEGE FOOTBALL

SPORTS

Detroit Free Press

SECTION C

9.79

Johnson stuns Lewis in record 100

FLASHES OF GLORY

Probert, Klima suspended; they'll miss Wings' opener

O's, no! Two-run 9th shocks Tigers, 5-4

Business/Monday

December 26, 1988 — The Miami Herald

IN THE NEWS

Business and Law

Laying down law for lie detectors

A law banning many businesses from using lie detectors takes effect Tuesday. But firms that use or offer polygraphs are finding other tests to grade employees / **7.**

Profile

The Breakers would ♥ a ☆

If the Palm Beach resort wins back the Mobil Travel Guide's star, it would attract customers, prestige and, perhaps, higher rates. The job falls to Thomas P. Wicky / **9.**

Reflections on '88

The Joanies and Shame

Columnists Rosalind Resnick and Joan Chrissos take a long look back at what 1988 meant for the professions and marketing — and bestowe a few awards. The Hall of Shame / **12.** The Joanies / **13.**

Personal Business

The extended warranty gamble

On many big-ticket items, like refrigerators and cars, you can buy a warranty that protects more than the manufacturer does. But should you? / **19**

INSIDE

AGENDA	27
BANK RATES	23
FLORIDA STOCKS	24
INSIDER TRANSACTIONS	27
INVESTOR FORUM	21
JOB TALK	29
LARRY BIRGER	3
MARKETING	13
MORNING LINE	4
MORTGAGE RATES	22
MUTUAL FUNDS	26
PERSONAL BUSINESS	19
PROFESSIONS	12
PROFILE	9
PROMOTIONS	17
REAL ESTATE	18
SEC	25
TAXES	28

FUNNY BUSINESS 1988

THE YEAR OF GREED

Money
It's a hit
Don't give me that
Do-goody-good bull(loney)

— Slightly altered version of a Pink Floyd song

By GREGG FIELDS
Herald Business Writer

IN 1988, greed not only overcame fear, it overtook logic and Greg Louganis to become *the* national hero. Who could blame us? Money in America is easy to get today if you're at the top of a corporation: Just sell your shares to the British, your real estate to the Japanese, and pull the rip cords on that golden parachute. Stockholders? Oh yeah, toss them a junk bond. Never mind tomorrow. It

Turn to **GREED / 14**

AWARD OF EXCELLENCE
NEWS PAGE DESIGN PORTFOLIO
CIRCULATION 250,000 AND OVER
The Miami Herald
Designer
Ana Maria Lense
Illustrator
Ana Maria Lense
Director of Editorial Art and Design
Randy Stano

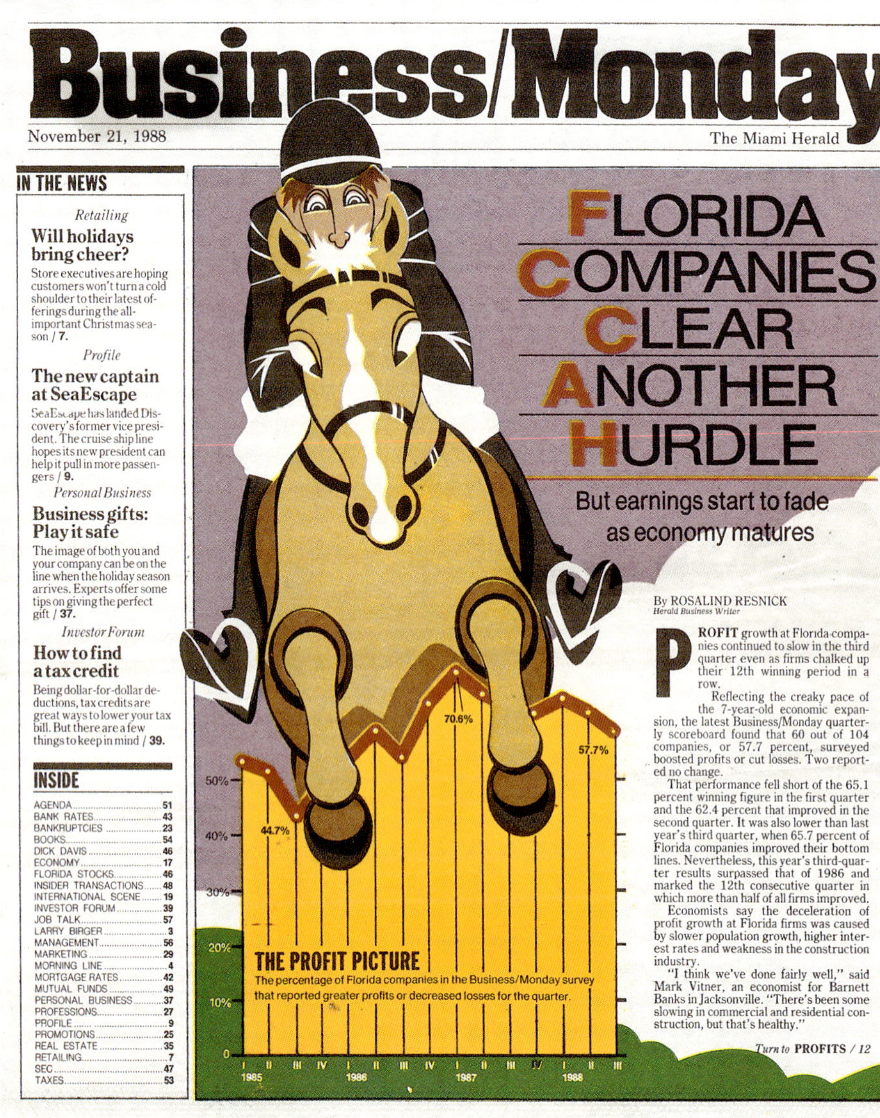

Business/Monday

November 21, 1988 — The Miami Herald

IN THE NEWS

Retailing

Will holidays bring cheer?

Store executives are hoping customers won't turn a cold shoulder to their latest offerings during the all-important Christmas season / **7.**

Profile

The new captain at SeaEscape

SeaEscape has landed Discovery's former vice president. The cruise ship line hopes its new president can help it pull in more passengers / **9.**

Personal Business

Business gifts: Play it safe

The image of both you and your company can be on the line when the holiday season arrives. Experts offer some tips on giving the perfect gift / **37.**

Investor Forum

How to find a tax credit

Being dollar-for-dollar deductions, tax credits are great ways to lower your tax bill. But there are a few things to keep in mind / **39.**

INSIDE

AGENDA	51
BANK RATES	43
BANKRUPTCIES	23
BOOKS	54
DICK DAVIS	46
ECONOMY	17
FLORIDA STOCKS	46
INSIDER TRANSACTIONS	48
INTERNATIONAL SCENE	19
INVESTOR FORUM	39
JOB TALK	57
LARRY BIRGER	3
MANAGEMENT	56
MARKETING	29
MORNING LINE	4
MORTGAGE RATES	42
MUTUAL FUNDS	49
PERSONAL BUSINESS	37
PROFESSIONS	27
PROFILE	9
PROMOTIONS	25
REAL ESTATE	35
RETAILING	7
SEC	47
TAXES	53

FLORIDA COMPANIES CLEAR ANOTHER HURDLE

But earnings start to fade as economy matures

THE PROFIT PICTURE
The percentage of Florida companies in the Business/Monday survey that reported greater profits or decreased losses for the quarter.

By ROSALIND RESNICK
Herald Business Writer

PROFIT growth at Florida companies continued to slow in the third quarter even as firms chalked up their 12th winning period in a row.

Reflecting the creaky pace of the 7-year-old economic expansion, the latest Business/Monday quarterly scoreboard found that 60 out of 104 companies, or 57.7 percent, surveyed boosted profits or cut losses. Two reported no change.

That performance fell short of the 65.1 percent winning figure in the first quarter and the 62.4 percent that improved in the second quarter. It was also lower than last year's third quarter, when 65.7 percent of Florida companies improved their bottom lines. Nevertheless, this year's third-quarter results surpassed that of 1986 and marked the 12th consecutive quarter in which more than half of all firms improved.

Economists say the deceleration of profit growth at Florida firms was caused by slower population growth, higher interest rates and weakness in the construction industry.

"I think we've done fairly well," said Mark Vitner, an economist for Barnett Banks in Jacksonville. "There's been some slowing in commercial and residential construction, but that's healthy."

Turn to **PROFITS / 12**

AWARD OF EXCELLENCE
NEWS PAGE DESIGN PORTFOLIO
CIRCULATION 250,000 AND OVER
The Orange County Register
Santa Ana, California
Designer
Pam Marshak

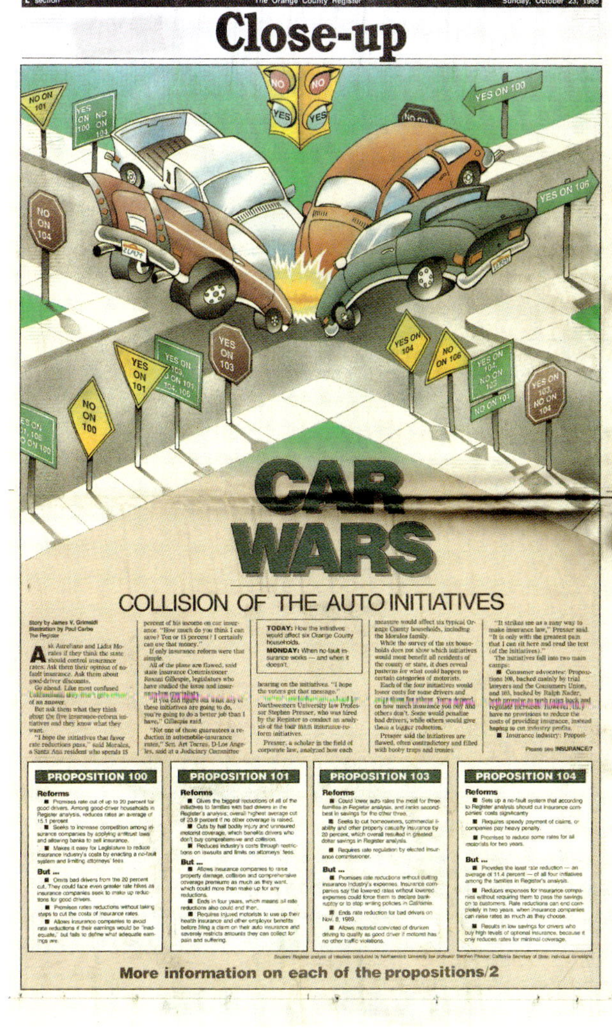
L section The Orange County Register Sunday, October 23, 1988

Close-up

CAR WARS

COLLISION OF THE AUTO INITIATIVES

PROPOSITION 100

PROPOSITION 101

PROPOSITION 103

PROPOSITION 104

More information on each of the propositions/2

REMEMBERING REAGAN: 25 YEARS IN HISTORY

1977 1978 1979 1980 1981 1982

Moments: Even red socks could convey Reagan humor

Moments: Rohrabacher camped on Reagans' lawn

AWARD OF EXCELLENCE

NEWS PAGE DESIGN PORTFOLIO

CIRCULATION 100,000-249,000

Gazette Telegraph

Colorado Springs, Colorado

Designer

Dan Cotter

SPORTS

Thursday, Oct. 20, 1988 — Gazette Telegraph — Section C

BASEBALL

Crippled LA one step from title

This time, Howell tames Oakland's bashers

The 1988 World Series

The Dodgers' Mike Davis, right, slides into second with a steal in the first inning Wednesday. Applying the late tag is Athletics shortstop Walt Weiss.

■ LA reliever goes from goat to hero/C6

■ Tudor's career jeopardized/C6

NFL

Kubiak to start Sunday

Elway's status still unknown

■ Steelers coach under fire from two sides/C5

COLLEGE FOOTBALL

No holiday for Holieway

Air Force guard Bell eligible for '89 season

Line can't afford any mistakes against Irish

Flirting with No. 1

VOLLEYBALL

Japan sweeps U.S. women in exhibition match

INSIDE

Business begins on C9

SPORTS

Sunday, Jan. 1, 1989 — Gazette Telegraph — Section C

NFL

Bears leave Philly in a fog

Chicago ends playoff drought with victory

Bears free safety Maurice Douglass (37) sprints off the field after intercepting Eagles quarterback Randall Cunningham late in the fourth quarter of Saturday's NFC semifinal at fogged-in Soldier Field in Chicago. The play allowed the Bears to run out the clock.

Bengals stick to ground, pound Seattle

■ Bills welcome Oilers to Buffalo/C2

■ 49ers out to end hex/C2

■ Philly can't stop McKinnon/C3

■ Wilson glad he's with Bengals/C3

FOOTBALL

Early outburst helps Wolfpack beat Hawkeyes

ONE LAST LOOK

Ari Vatanen, driving a Peugeot, roars into Glen Cove on his way to a record run in the Pikes Peak Auto Hill Climb last July.

The Colorado Springs Sky Sox, with general manager/president Fred Whitacre and owner Dave Elmore, right, await the opening of their home season April 29 at Spurgeon Stadium.

The Top Ten

1. Sky Sox
2. Andrew Maynard
3. Mike Bertsch to Brad Buetow
4. Pikes Peak Auto Hill Climb
5. Air Force Falcons
6. James Hill and Burnie Legette
7. Harvey Schiller-USOC
8. Sarah Schwald
9. Olympic Trials
10. Jill Trenary

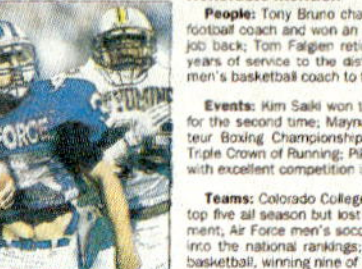

Senior fullback Andy Smith gets tops toward the end zone in a loss to Wyoming in September. Smith led 5-7 Air Force in rushing with 1,040 yards.

Honorable mention

INSIDE

Outdoors/C14

AWARD OF EXCELLENCE

FEATURE PAGE DESIGN PORTFOLIO
CIRCULATION 250,000 AND OVER

The Boston Globe
Boston

Designer
Rena Sokolow
Illustrator
Various
Photographer
Various
Art Director
Rena Sokolow

THE BOSTON GLOBE WEDNESDAY, AUGUST 24, 1988 **37**

FOOD

TV & Radio 44,45

Vegetables fresh from the sea

By Judith Barrett
Special to the Globe

A 6-year-old who was picked up from day camp recently, got into the car that was taking her home, opened her backpack and took out a snack. What was unusual was that her snack was crisp, thin sheets of nori, the seaweed that's used as the wrapping for sushi. "This is delicious," she said as she offered some to her 7-year-old friend who was sharing the back seat. "Try some."

Nori is delicious, as are many other types of seaweed, but with the exception of sushi most of us would never consider eating it, let alone on its own as a snack. Seaweed is an important culinary staple to vegetarians and natural-food devotees because of its high nutrient content and to people in other parts of the world. The Japanese consume tons of nori along with other seaweeds and the Irish, Scotch and Welsh have long been accustomed to eating a seaweed they call "laver" which is also known as "dulse." However, seaweed has never been popular with adults or children or widely available in the United States.

However, with the recent interest in American food, and more specifically with the emphasis by chefs on utilizing locally grown ingredients, seaweeds may be on Boston restaurant menus sooner rather than later.

According to Shepard Erhart, whose company, Maine Coast Sea Vegetables has been harvesting, drying and distributing four types of seaweed from the area around Franklin, Maine, since the early 1970s, seaweed offers a deliciously salty sea taste that can enhance soups, vegetables, grains and even popcorn. "Americans think of seaweed as the decomposing stuff you find on the beach," Erhart said. "Seaweed that's taken straight from the ocean beds where it grows has a fresh taste and aroma that's like a breath of salt air."

In addition to their fresh sea taste, seaweeds, which are low in sodium, have valuable vitamins and nutrients. "Seaweed is high in all the minerals. Calcium, magnesium, phosphorus, iron, potassium, iodine, zinc, and other trace minerals are all represented," Erhart said. In all the seaweeds there are Vitamins A, B1, B2, B6 and some B12, which is hard to find in vegetable sources, according to Erhart. In addition, kelp has glutamic acid (like msg) which helps tenderize protein.

Currently, Erhart's company harvests approximately 12 dry

SEAWEED, Page 38

KERNEL KNOWLEDGE

GREEN FORAY

DINNERS OF DESPERATION

By Sheryl Julian
Globe Staff

The muggiest, stickiest summer on record has reduced the dinner hour to desperate measures: In weather that makes graham crackers bend neatly and soggily, robs taco chips of their crunch, and leaves a pool of water around the glass minutes after the ice goes in, the whole world spent the summer eating without pleasure.

"Some nights," says Pam Hatchfield, an objects conservator at the Museum of Fine Arts, known among her friends as a splendid cook, "the best dinner in the world is popcorn at the movies."

When Hatchfield arrives home, she spends a certain amount of time "in front of the open fridge pretending I'm looking for something to eat. Really I'm in there to keep cool."

Psychologist Diana Ronell longs for take-out cooked chicken somewhere in her neighborhood where she could stop on the way home at night. Then she would serve chicken, cole slaw and potato salad, and follow that with fruit and ice cream. Alas, no shops exist nearby so the family meal is "fresh fruit and Haagen-Dazs."

"I do nothing," continues this former New Yorker. "Everything's rotting in my refrigerator. There's no ventilation in our house and we haven't done anything intelligent like put in attic fans."

What this city lacks, she says, is shops that sell cooked chickens. When she lived in Manhattan, there was a shop on every other corner (and everyone delivered!).

There is such a shop in Newtonville. The demand at The Boston Chicken for rotisserie-roasted birds has the little store bursting at the seams. Twenty-five customers were waiting for cooked chicken one steamy Friday afternoon with a line formed outside. "I don't know whether we could be any busier," said owner Arthur Cores.

HEAT, Page 40

FRIGID AIR

WASH AND LIE

COOK OUT

MOB SEEN

READING FREEZE

Chris Reed illustrations

Paula Munck illustration

Trout finds its place on the menu

By Claire Hopley
Special to the Globe

When looking at sheeny streamlined trout in supermarket cases, the mind imagines clear mountain waters, shady pools and artful anglers. But that is not the lifestyle of the trout we buy in the store or those served in restaurants.

These trout live out their lives on farms. They start as tiny thread-like wiggles hatched from yellow eggs stripped from females in late summer and fall. They grow quickly until at 18 months, at 12 inches long and weighing 10 ounces, they are ready for harvest.

Virtually all commercially produced trout are rainbow trout, easily recognizable by their silky blue skin shot with streaks of pink. Sold either fresh or frozen, most come from Idaho. Locally-raised rainbow trout are also available. They are sold fresh, often as fillets or live from tanks.

The other local trout making its way onto menus and into markets is brook trout. These handsome fish come from Kenneth Bergstrom's Red Wing Meadow Farm in Sunderland, Mass. Bergstrom raises brook trout because, as he says, "It's the gourmet fish. Much better eating." Brown-skinned with silvery highlights and elegant spots, brook trout have tender peachy-colored flesh, and a mild distinctive flavor. "They're a distinctive local product," said Bergstrom, "with freshness and flavor that you can't get from fish brought in from Idaho or other states."

Many anglers claim that the best trout comes straight from water into waiting frying pan. Some fishermen claim a trout that has fought hard before being pulled

TROUT, Page 43

THE BOSTON GLOBE WEDNESDAY, JANUARY 11, 1989 **41**

FOOD

Classified 47

CHEF FOR HIRE

Globe staff photo/David Ryan

Globe staff photo/[illegible] Greene

Globe photo/Craig Line

From left: Terry Endow, chef of Michela's; Tony Ambrose, chef of Julien, and Harry Daniels, who heads an employment registry in Vermont.

When it's time to get a job, the rumor mill and agencies are efficient

By Sheryl Julian
Globe Staff

It might start with a mysterious telephone call or a request for an unscheduled day off. The first symptoms are hardly noticeable. Then at the busiest time of day, there might be a screaming match. Mistakes are made. Things slide just a little.

Sometimes remarks from conversations caught in passing begin to make sense. Or the owner might be asked, "What time will you be in tomorrow?" which always signals that something is about to happen.

So it isn't ever a complete surprise when a chef gives notice. But when it actually happens, even mindful of the warnings, the owner almost always hits the wall.

"When the chef walks out, I go completely hysterical at first," said one employer. "I want to murder them. Then I get a hold of myself." In the kitchen, meanwhile, uncertainty and anxiety begin to permeate the work stations: people are worrying about their status.

CHEFS, Page 42

Patrick Blackwell illustration

Savory pies served hot and cold

By Nina Simonds
Special to the Globe

During the winter season, when the kitchen windows are frosted and the soul craves something hearty, few dishes are as satisfying, heartening or convenient as a main-dish pie. A pork, chicken or vegetable pie straight from the oven is a perfect New England winter's dish.

"Basically, pies are wonderful main-dish meals," says London Cordon Bleu-trained Sue Small, who owns the Peacock Restaurant in Cambridge. "During the winter, we make the traditional steak and kidney pie here once a month or so, and we've been doing it seasonally almost since the restaurant opened 12 years ago. One of our customers comes in just to eat it, and then he takes one home.

"Of course, steak and kidney pie is the most traditional hot main-course pie in England, but growing

Joel Pepadire illustration

up in Southampton in southern England, we put almost anything in pies. My mother knew for sure that one way to get us kids to eat almost anything was to put it in pastry. She did make wonderful pastry and she'd put almost everything in – chicken with vegetables, lamb, sometimes with potatoes and vegetables, and she'd just put a crust over it. That was our big favorite."

In England, Small says, savory pies are served hot and cold and some of the most popular are pork pies, which are made individually in miniature shapes in small bakeries. Larger pork pies are served for lunch in pubs and simple restaurants. But she adds, there are also ham, egg and veal pies – all served hot and cold.

Pies have been served all over the western world for centuries. According to "Food of the Western World" by Theodora Fitzgibbon (Quadrangle/The New York Times Book Co., 1976), "In fourteenth-century England, pie dishes were called 'coffins', which suggests that the shape was long and thin like that of a loaf tin. In the fifteenth and sixteenth centuries, pies made from globe artichoke bottoms mixed with raisins, currants, butter, herbs and

PIES, Page 42

Keeping food bacteria-free

By Gail Perrin
Globe Staff

Ten years ago, we may have passed off the symptoms as "a touch of the flu."

But today, more and more of us are aware that a stomachache, upset stomach, fever or diarrhea may be more food-related than influenza influenced.

Take, for instance, the recent publicity that has focused on eggs and chickens, both of which can have relatively high counts of salmonella bacteria.

Both industry and government agencies alike are working on ways to reduce the instances of this particular bacteria, but the fact is that salmonella is widely prevalent in the environment and there is no way to wipe it out altogether.

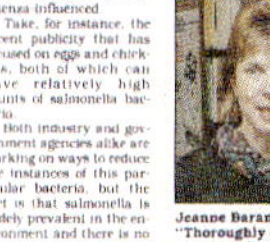

Jeanne Baranek: "Thoroughly cook your eggs."

Salmonella can be found in water, in soil and in the intestinal tract and on the skin of humans and virtually all other animals and birds.

SAFETY, Page 45

SILVER AWARD
FEATURE PAGE
DESIGN PORTFOLIO
CIRCULATION 250,000 AND OVER
The Boston Sunday Globe
Boston
Designer
James Pavlovich
Art Director
James Pavlovich

MAY 8, 1988 — Boston Sunday Globe

Arts Etc.

Books Section
'Quinn's Book,' William Kennedy's latest novel, is set in Albany (where else?)
103

MOVIES / MUSIC / LIFESTYLES / VIDEO / THEATER / ART / BOOKS

Bruce Wells at a Boston Ballet rehearsal.

dance

Ballet's Wells going out with a grand finale

Departing choreographer's 'Midsummer Night's Dream' to end season

portrait

Irving Berlin: an American original

The composer of 1,500 songs to mark his 100th birthday

conversations / marian christy

Larry King 'shapes up'

The talk-show host pulls no punches, gets audiences to respond

Talk show host Larry King.

INSIDE

GUIDE TO FEATURES

JANUARY 29, 1989 — Boston Sunday Globe — A Section

Arts Etc.

Books Section
Jay Cantor reviews Salman Rushdie's 'The Satanic Verses.'
A14

MOVIES / MUSIC / LIFESTYLES / VIDEO / THEATER / DANCE / BOOKS

architecture

The beauty-and-beast syndrome

By Robert Campbell, Globe Correspondent

Stubbins Associates has produced a clumsy giant (above) at 150 Federal St., and a tactful structure at 745 Atlantic Ave.

music

New Garden to be band-friendly

Design with concerts in mind could lure acts from Worcester and Providence

By Steve Morse, Globe Staff

Arena rock: Joe Perry (left) and Steve Tyler of Aerosmith.

interview

A crusader for black concert music

By Richard Dyer, Globe Staff

Composer T. J. Anderson

INSIDE

'Hotel Terminus' — **A6** Marcel Ophuls' documentary about Klaus Barbie has no pretense of impartiality.

'American Ceramics Now' — **A4** It's an engaging show at the DeCordova Museum, although it casts too wide a net.

High concept — **A2** Hollywood likes movies that can be summed up in 10 words or less. Paulina Porizkova (below) stars in "Her Alibi," an example of the genre.

GUIDE TO FEATURES

ART	A4-A5
MOVIES	A2, A6
MARQUEE	A7
RECORDINGS	A3
LETTERS	A8
LIFESTYLES	A12
WEDDINGS	B93, A24
LANDERS	B96
CHAT	B96

AWARD OF EXCELLENCE
FEATURE PAGE
DESIGN PORTFOLIO
CIRCULATION 250,000 AND OVER
The Dallas Morning News
Dallas

Designer
Bob Shema
Art Director
Ed Kohorst

The Dallas Morning News   Section E —   ....   Wednesday, June 15, 1988

This Ford always has a new model. **Interview**, page **2**.

A hot pace demands a cool face. **Cosmetics Bag**, page **8**.

A real estate agent gets a new lease on looks. **Makeover of the Month**, page **3**.

Fashion ! Dallas

Setting the styles for the new Southwest

LA MODA LATINA

A FIESTA OF FASHION FOR SASSY, SULTRY, SUMMER SEASONING

BY TAMMY THEIS

In summer, fashion rules are stretched to the breaking point. What's proper isn't as important as what's fun. And nothing exemplifies that mood more than the season's newest trend, imported directly from south of the border.

In the past, fashion's globe-trotting obsession with ethnic cultures has brought us influences from countries as far-flung as India, Africa and Turkey. This season, a distinctly Latin seasoning provides the flavor for many spring-summer '88 designer collections.

It's a melting pot of cultures that blends the spiciness of Mexico with the hot-blooded romance of Spain, adding a dash of tough Puerto Rican street style for good measure.

Recent movies glorifying the dance styles and steamy sexiness of Latin culture have added impetus to the trend. Modern variations of *West Side Story*, such as

Continued on page 5

Left: Rifat Ozbek's Aztec-embroidered bolero tops a high-waist skirt and white pique shirt, all from Stanley Korshak. Silver hoop earrings and yellow flower from Contempo Casuals. Orange rose from H.D.'s Women's.

Above: Folkloric fling: Workers for Freedom white cotton shirt with colorful floral appliques paired with Rifat Ozbek navy matador trousers, sidelined with silver coins, from Stanley Korshak. Mexican serape from Emeralds to Coconuts. Etched silver earrings from Cotton Island. Location: Tropical Fever.

Shoulder smolder: Benetton's hot pink off-the-shoulder cotton sweater with Mexican motif from Benetton Valley View. Diane Beaudry cotton/spandex toreador pants from Stanley Korshak. Straw gaucho hat and bright yellow flower from Contempo Casuals. Location: G&M Mexican Imports.

Salsa sizzle: Cotton tank dress with bright rickrack (left) and blanket-print cotton skirt/shorts (right) from Contempo Casuals. Off-the-shoulder black cotton top from Benetton Valley View. Rose earrings (left) from Cotton Island. Floral drop earrings (right) from J.C. Penney. Location: G&M Mexican Imports.

PHOTOS: BRIAN BARNAUD
STYLING: TAMMY THEIS
HAIR AND MAKEUP: MAX McBETH/L'ENTOURAGE

Makeover ! Fashion Calendar ! Cosmetics Bag ! Interview ! Bookshelf

The Dallas Morning News   Section E —   ....   Wednesday, December 28, 1988

There she is, Queen of the Nightlife. **FID Fax**, page **2**.

1988: the year the bubble burst. **Something Different**, page **6**.

Victor Costa captures a Quayle in Bush country. **FID Fax**, page **2**.

Fashion ! Dallas

Setting the styles for the new Southwest

IF FID RULED THE WORLD

Oh, the things we'd love to do!

MORE ON PAGE 6

Something Different ! Glossary ! Reliable Source ! Fashion Calendar

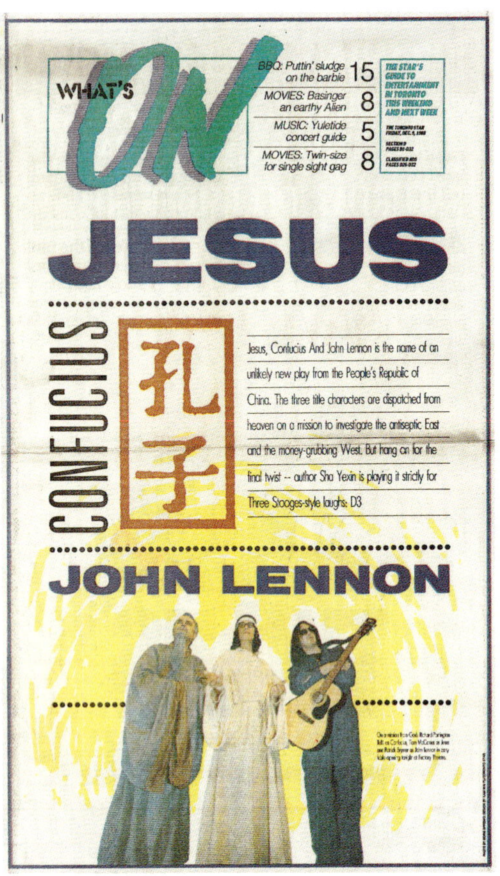

WHAT'S ON

BBQ: Puttin' sludge on the barbie 15
MOVIES: Basinger an earthy Alien 8
MUSIC: Yuletide concert guide 5
MOVIES: Twin-size for single sight gag 8

THE STAR'S GUIDE TO ENTERTAINMENT IN TORONTO THIS WEEKEND AND NEXT WEEK

THE TORONTO STAR FRIDAY, DEC. 9, 1988

SECTION D PAGES D1-D32

CLASSIFIED ADS PAGES D26-D32

JESUS

CONFUCIUS

孔子

Jesus, Confucius And John Lennon is the name of an unlikely new play from the People's Republic of China. The three title characters are dispatched from heaven on a mission to investigate the antiseptic East and the money-grubbing West. But hang on for the final twist -- author Sha Yexin is playing it strictly for Three Stooges-style laughs: D3

JOHN LENNON

AWARD OF EXCELLENCE
FEATURE PAGE
DESIGN PORTFOLIO
CIRCULATION 250,000 AND OVER
The Toronto Star
Toronto, Canada
Designer
Kam Wai Yu
Photographers
Boris Spremo, Dick Loek

WHAT'S ON

MOVIES: Quebec's slice of reel-life 9
STAGE: Love, hate & Wooster Group 10
MUSIC: Country's uneasy new hero 14
Classified section 20-32

THE STAR'S GUIDE TO ENTERTAINMENT IN TORONTO THIS WEEKEND AND NEXT WEEK

THE TORONTO STAR FRIDAY, JAN. 27, 1989

SECTION D PAGES D1-D32

PUT ON YOUR DANCING SHOES AND JOIN TORONTO'S BOOMING SALSA MUSIC SCENE: D3

LATIN

Salsa in the City

AWARD OF EXCELLENCE
FEATURE PAGE
DESIGN PORTFOLIO
CIRCULATION 250,000 AND OVER
The Washington Post

Designer
Carol Porter
Illustrators
Various
Photographers
Various
Art Director
Michael Keegan

Sunday, June 12, 1988 — The Washington Post — Editorials/Columnists C1

OUTLOOK

Commentary and Opinion

A HYMN TO THE SUMMER

Sometimes Even the Parish Outings Are No Picnic

By Peter J. Daly

A Parish Diary

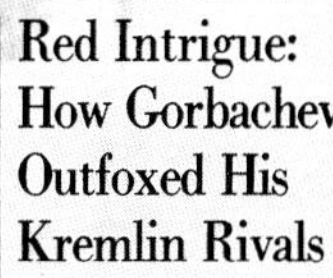

Red Intrigue: How Gorbachev Outfoxed His Kremlin Rivals

By Robert G. Kaiser

Let's Wake Up on Trade

Tokyo Knows We're Suckers—Why Don't We?

By Clyde V. Prestowitz, Jr.

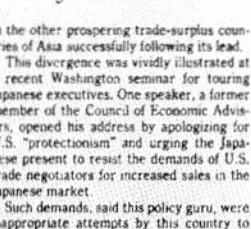

MARY McGRORY

So Who Will Run With Mike?

The Stubborn Triumph Of Michael Dukakis

By Linda Wertheimer

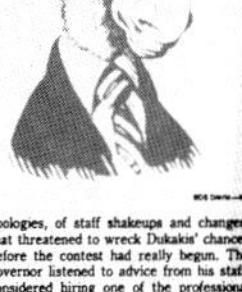

Sunday, November 27, 1988 — The Washington Post — Editorials/Columnists D1

OUTLOOK

Commentary and Opinion

THE SAD, STRANGE MIND OF COL. NORTH

An NSC Colleague Explains Why Ollie Met His Waterloo

By Constantine C. Menges

Tip for Bush: Go Outside The Beltway For Talent

By David Osborne

Living the Alzheimer's Nightmare

The Disease Is Cruel—But Our Policies For Dealing With It Are Crueler

By Timothy Saasta

Sorry, Comrades—You're In History's Dustbin Now

By Henry Grunwald

MARY McGRORY

is on vacation. Her Outlook column will resume next Sunday.

SILVER AWARD

FEATURE PAGE
DESIGN PORTFOLIO
CIRCULATION 250,000 AND OVER

The Washington Post

Designer
Alice Kreese

Illustrators
Alice Kreese, George Price, Peter Hoey

Photographer
Lisa Trei

Researcher
Bettmann Archives

Art Director
Alice Kreese

The Washington Post

TUESDAY, JULY 19, 1988

A WEEKLY JOURNAL OF MEDICINE,
HEALTH
SCIENCE AND SOCIETY

SHOULD JUVENILE KILLERS BE EXECUTED? THE STORY OF PAUL MAGILL

Growing Up on Death Row

DEATH WARRANT
STATE OF FLORIDA

WHEREAS, PAUL EDWARD MAGILL, did on the 23rd day of Dec
murder Karen Sue Young; and
WHEREAS, PAUL EDWARD MAGILL was found guilty of murder
st degree and was sentenced to death on the 25th day
; and resentenced to death on the 26th day of Jan
0th day of March 1983, the Florida Sup
imposed upon PAUL EDWARD MA
denied on the 3r

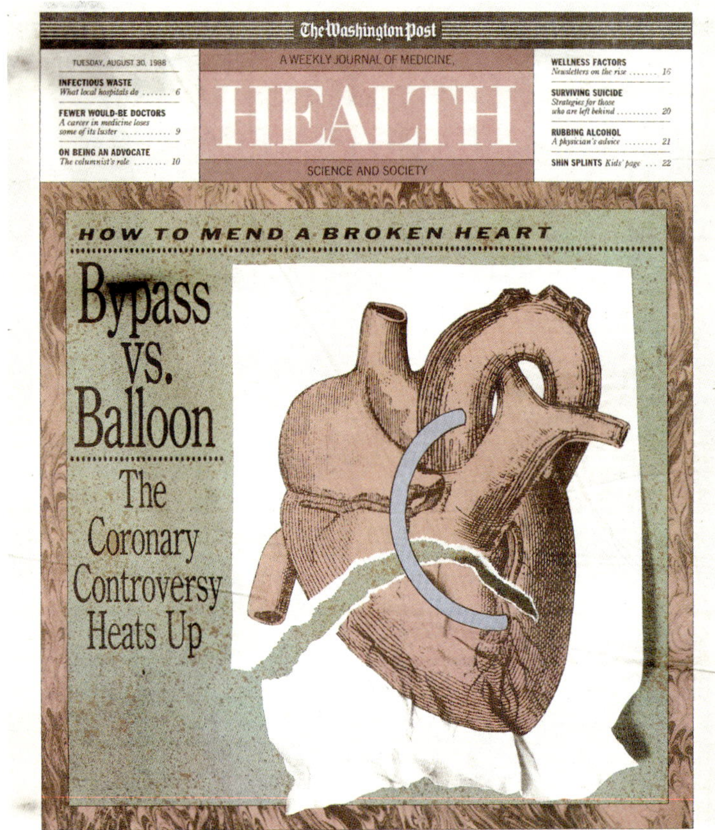

The Washington Post

TUESDAY, AUGUST 30, 1988

A WEEKLY JOURNAL OF MEDICINE,
HEALTH
SCIENCE AND SOCIETY

HOW TO MEND A BROKEN HEART

Bypass vs. Balloon

The Coronary Controversy Heats Up

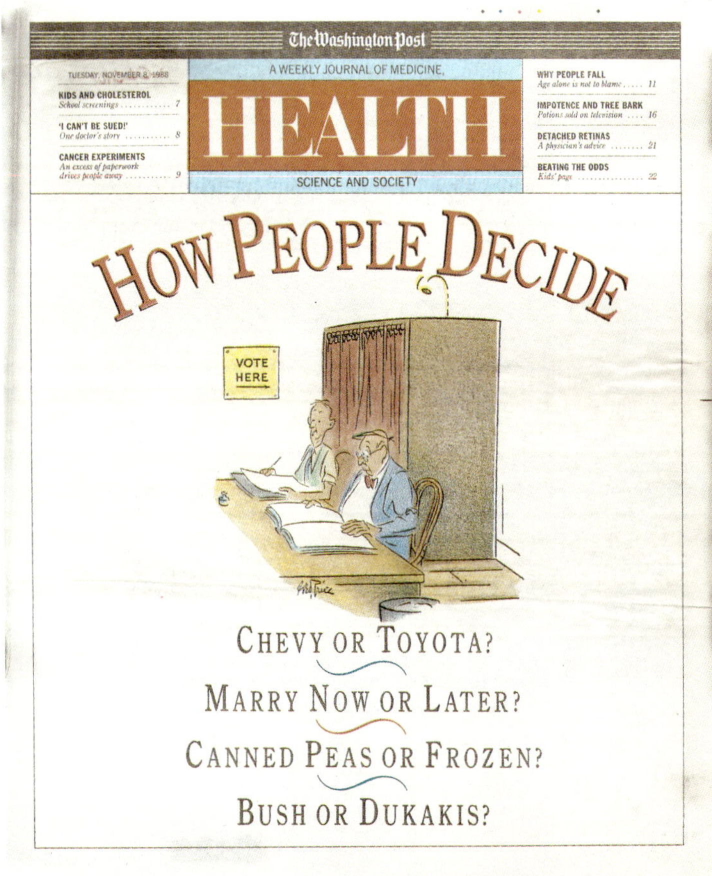

The Washington Post

TUESDAY, NOVEMBER 8, 1988

A WEEKLY JOURNAL OF MEDICINE,
HEALTH
SCIENCE AND SOCIETY

HOW PEOPLE DECIDE

CHEVY OR TOYOTA?

MARRY NOW OR LATER?

CANNED PEAS OR FROZEN?

BUSH OR DUKAKIS?

GAIL MEADOWS/8G
HELP YOURSELF/6G
ELAN, TOO/7G
ACTION LINE/11G

Living Today

Sunday, December 11, 1988 The Miami Herald Section G

IT'S A SEDUCTIVE, SUNNY, RICH, DANGEROUS, CHALLENGING PLACE THAT THOUSANDS OF TEENS CALL HOME.

By PEGGY LANDERS

THE SERIES

ORDINARY TEENS IN AN EXTRAORDINARY PLACE

Determining your values

GALERIA

POR DENTRO
TELEVISION Y RADIO. 3C
NOVELA. 5C
TIRAS COMICAS. 6C
WALTER MERCADO. 6C

C

MARTES 2 DE AGOSTO DE 1988 / EL NUEVO HERALD

CIENCIA AL DIA

Encuesta dice mamografías son indoloras

Nueva droga para tratar lupus severo

Más que enseñarles a moverse sobre la pasarela, esta modelo argentina ayudó a hacer realidad los anhelos de chicas que ansiaban formar parte de un mundo glamoroso

Por MARTA MENDEZ
Redactora de El Nuevo Herald

Pasa a la página 4C

Página diseñada por NURI DUCASSI / El Nuevo Herald

El nuevo "opio" del pueblo...

Por ENA NAUNTON
Redactora de El Nuevo Herald

Hemos llegado al punto que debemos salir y comprar a alguien que escuche nuestro dolor porque en casa, con un historial de ficción de televisión, nadie escucha a nadie.

Pasa a la página 2C

El factor hispano del antiguo Hollywood

Por JUAN PANDO
Agencia EFE

Pasa a la página 4C

AWARD OF EXCELLENCE

FEATURE PAGE
DESIGN PORTFOLIO
CIRCULATION 250,000 AND OVER

el Nuevo Herald
Miami, Florida

Designer
Nuri Ducassi

Feature Design Editor
Rhonda Prast

Director of Editorial Art and Design
Randy Stano

SILVER AWARD

FEATURE PAGE
DESIGN PORTFOLIO
CIRCULATION 250,000 AND OVER

The Washington Post

Designer
Nancy Brooke Smith

Illustrators
Jo Ellen Murphy, Cary Henry,
Patrick Blackwell, Gary Head,
Joe Teodorescu

Art Director
Nancy Brooke Smith

Feeding Our Future

The Elderly: Getting The Nutritional News

Making Their Way In a Difficult Marketplace

Depending on Others For More of Their Meals

Microwave Magic

Ten Tips That Keep The Kitchen Cool

Be Aware of Greeks Bearing Gifts

A Tasty Cuisine Rides in on Dukakis' Coattails

Knowing Your Oats

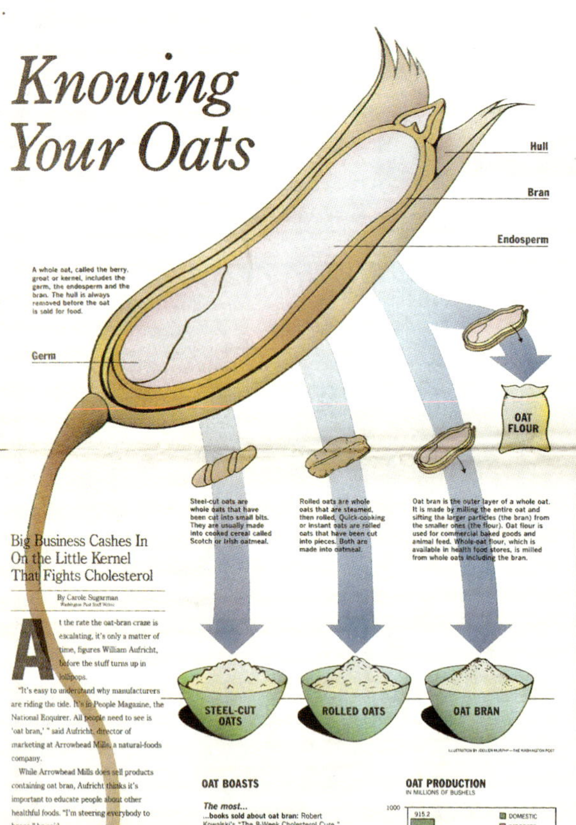

ILLUSTRATION BY JOELLEN MURPHY—THE WASHINGTON POST

Big Business Cashes In On the Little Kernel That Fights Cholesterol

By Carole Sugarman
Washington Post Staff Writer

At the rate the oat-bran craze is escalating, it's only a matter of time, figures William Aufricht, before the stuff turns up in lollipops.

"It's easy to understand why manufacturers are riding the tide. It's in People Magazine, the National Enquirer. All people need to see is 'oat bran,'" said Aufricht, director of marketing at Arrowhead Mills, a natural-foods company.

While Arrowhead Mills does sell products containing oat bran, Aufricht thinks it's important to educate people about other healthful foods. "I'm steering everybody to beans," he said.

Beans apparently don't have the marketing appeal of oat bran, the innocuous outer layer of an oat kernel. Oat bran has become a magic bullet for cholesterol-conscious consumers and they can't seem to get enough of it.

Neither can retailers. Signs in local supermarkets warn that "due to production difficulties" at Quaker Oats, some of its oat and oat bran products may be "periodically" out of stock. The company can't process it fast enough.

In fact, it has been 25 years since researchers first identified the cholesterol-lowering properties of oats, but only recently that oat bran has been added to everything from Health Valley animal crackers to Giant Food muffins to Sutton Place Gourmet bread.

See OAT BRAN, E8, Col. 1

OAT BOASTS

The most...

...books sold about oat bran: Robert Kowalski's "The 8-Week Cholesterol Cure," which recommends eating three oat bran muffins a day, has sold almost one million copies.

...eye-popping oat-bran sales data: The Quaker Oats Co. estimates that sales of Mother's Oat Bran have increased 600 percent since last year. Kowalski's book helped create that demand.

...unnecessarily huge oat-bran muffins: The recipe on Kellogg's new Common Sense Oat Bran cereal creates one mammoth muffin that contains 470 calories.

...ridiculous name for an oat-bran product: R.W. Frookie's Oat Bran Muffins. Not only is oat bran the seventh ingredient listed on the outside of the box, but inside are cookies, not muffins.

...difficult challenge facing an oat-bran fanatic: In research studies, says the back panel of Health Valley Oat Bran Graham Crackers, 3½ ounces of oat bran per day lowered cholesterol by as much as 30 percent in people with elevated levels. What the back panel doesn't say is that to get that amount of oat bran from the crackers, you'd have to eat 175 of them. They're good, but four boxes at a sitting?

OAT PRODUCTION

IN MILLIONS OF BUSHELS

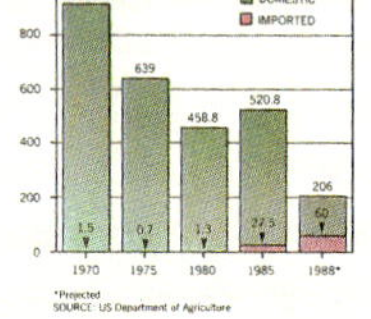

Year	Total	Imported
1970	915.2	1.5
1975	639	0.7
1980	458.8	1.3
1985	520.8	27.5
1988*	206	60

*Projected
SOURCE: US Department of Agriculture

American farmers are sowing fewer oats at a time that American consumers are demanding more. The result is an increasing dependence on imports, primarily from Canada, Scandanavia and Argentina. Several developments account for the decrease in American production.

1. Most oats are fed to animals, which have found greener pastures in cheaper, more efficient grains (although race horse owners will still pay top dollar to feed their animals oats).
2. The farm program has attracted farmers to crops that command higher subsidies than oats.
3. Add a devastating drought and it's no wonder that there aren't enough domestic oats to fill America's breakfast bowls.

What's For Lunch?

This is National School Lunch Week and a good time to consider where school lunches fit in the state of national health. You could start by comparing your child's school lunches with those in Japan and France, each of which has a higher life expectancy and a lower rate of death by heart disease.

In Tokyo, Meticulously Balanced School Meals

By Margaret Shapiro

See TOKYO, E14, Col. 1

In Paris, the Emphasis Is on Tradition

By Edward Cody

See PARIS, E14, Col. 1

RICHMAN'S TABLE

Rethinking A Classic

Vitello Tonnato Reborn

By Phyllis C. Richman

See TABLE, E13, Col. 1

RISING EXPECTATIONS

The Delicious, Nutritious Basics of Making Homemade Bread

TRUCKPATCH

Beauty Is Only Skin Deep

Battling Bacteria

Who's Winning the War Against Food Poisoning?

Quit Stewing Over a Taboo

It's Into the Microwave With the Aluminum Foil

Going With the Spirit

A Literary Cook Cherishes the Classics

■ **REVIEW:** India's dances delightful / C-3 ■ **COMICS:** And today in history / C-4 ■ **TELEVISION:** Today's highlights / C-6

IMPULSE

MONDAY
SECTION C Jan. 30, 1989

DUSTING OFF DISCO

There is reason to believe that the new year in music will look and sound strangely like a dusty repeat of the old NBC late-night show "Midnight Special." That's because 1989 promises to be the year in which the 1970s return with a vengeance. Is it time to put back on our boogie shoes?

The revival of the 1970s, which really began some time in late 1988, will, according to a consortium of independent sources, reach its nadir in 1989, with the re-emergence of the music from that decade being the most tangible proof.

There is much evidence to buttress this admittedly bizarre and, for some, probably frightening claim. Here is just a partial foreshadowing of what we have to look forward to in 1989:

● More reunions of seminal 1970s rock 'n' roll bands such as the Doobie Brothers, Steely Dan and Led Zeppelin. And further reminders of that decade from such acts as Yes, Jethro Tull, Pink Floyd, Boston, Aerosmith, Little Feat, the Steve Miller Band, the Moody Blues, Heart, Bachman Turner Overdrive, The Little River Band and Peter Frampton, all of whom plan to tour and/or release new material in the coming year.

● Escalating interest among new artists in covers of some of the 1970s' most identifiable hits. It has of course already begun — witness Shriekback's loyal rendition of KC and the Sunshine Band's "Get Down Tonight." In the video for that new/old tune, KC himself makes a brief, self-deprecating cameo appearance.

And look at the recent chart-topping "Baby I Love Your Way/Free Bird Medley" by Will to Power. According to Paul Grien of Billboard Magazine, this hit marks the first time in the rock era that a medley of two old hits has topped the Billboard Hot 100 singles chart. Frampton's original "Baby I Love Your Way" peaked at No. 12 in 1976, says Grien, and Lynard Skynard's "Free Bird" hit No. 19 in 1974.

● Booming media focus on the music of the 1970s, and of the decade in general. The trendy Los Angeles fashion and art magazine Exposure recently devoted nearly an entire issue to recapping the decade. Spy magazine, the New York monthly that some call the new purveyor of hipdom, called its December issue "seventies-something," and devoted much of it to "a return to the decade of mood rings, ultrasuede, sideburns and disco sex machine Tony Orlando." Spy called the 1970s the century's most embarrassing decade, but still acknowledge that the country is in the midst of a 1970s revival.

● And last, but probably most significant and terrifying, the revival of the most "'70s" of musical and cultural styles, disco. Yes, disco is

Please see Page E-2, DISCO

'Embarrassing decade' and its music return

Story by Jamie Reno • Los Angeles Times Syndicate

Tickets

Dance fever: Act now if you want to see the Alvin Ailey American Dance Theater, which performs Feb. 17-19 at the Alaska Center for the Performing Arts. Tickets go on sale today at the ACPA box office, and at Aurora, Huffman and Muldoon Carrs. They cost $15, $22, $30 and $40, half-price for seniors and youths.

Music

Get back: Twenty years ago today, the Beatles made their last public performance together. Well, sort of public: they did five songs from atop the Apple Records office building. Paul McCartney, it seemed, wanted to do a concert again (the band had quit touring in 1966) but the others didn't miss live shows at all. This rooftop serenade was a compromise.

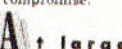

At large

Reach out and rap someone: Diehard fans of rappers D.J. Jazzy Jeff and Fresh Prince have dialed a special 900 number more than 2 million times since June. The message changes daily, and phone royalties provide extra income "well into the six figures," says a spokesman. We don't doubt it: the calls cost $2 for the first minute and 45 cents for each additional minute. And OK, we'll tell you: The number is 900-909-5333.

'Working Girl,' 'Rain Man' honored by foreign press

By JOHN HORN
The Associated Press

BEVERLY HILLS, Calif. — "Working Girl" and "Rain Man" took top Golden Globes honors to emerge as top Oscar prospects while the miniseries "War and Remembrance" dominated weekend awards for television excellence.

Tom Hanks, Dustin Hoffman, Melanie Griffith, Shirley MacLaine, Jodie Foster and Sigourney Weaver, who won twice, walked away with Golden Globes during Saturday night's Beverly Hilton Hotel ceremony.

But unlike those winners, there were also surprises in the event that signals the beginning of Hollywood's awards sweepstakes.

Actor-turned-director Clint Eastwood got the directing trophy for "Birds," beating out "Working Girl's" Mike Nichols and "Rain Man's" Barry Levinson.

Other pre-Oscar favorites were Golden Globe losers. The civil-rights film "Mississippi Burning" and the Australian melodrama "A Cry in the Dark" each went into the ceremony with four nominations but left empty-handed.

"Running on Empty" went in with five nominations but got only one, a screenplay award to Naomi Foner, and acclaimed "The Accidental Tourist" and the top hit of 1988, "Who Framed Roger Rabbit," got none.

The Golden Globes, presented annually by the 80-member Hollywood Foreign Press Association, is viewed as a barometer for movies in contention for Academy Awards. Oscar nominations will be announced Feb. 15.

"Rain Man," the chronicle of a scheming car salesman who learns to understand his autistic brother, won two film awards, as best dramatic motion picture and for top dramatic actor to Hoffman. "You are everything an actor could ever hope for," Hoffman said in an emotional acceptance speech giving special thanks

Please see Page C-2, GOLDEN GLOBES

'Arsenic and Old Lace' goes down well with audience

By ELIZABETH PULLIAM
Daily News theater reviewer

REVIEWS

"Arsenic and Old Lace" is to theater what the Model T was to the auto industry — a reliable assemblage that could survive the roughest roads. Amateur theater companies have repeatedly put "Arsenic" to the test, and it's always emerged, if not unbattered, at least intact.

That's why Anchorage Community Theatre's production of the play turns out to be a pleasant surprise. Not only does it survive, it flourishes, thanks to a quartet of talented amateur actors whose comedic gifts keep the action on course despite occasional lapses.

The play concerns two dotty old ladies who practice their own lethal brand of hospitality on lonely, elderly men. Their beloved nephew Mortimer discovers the women's secret in the form of a body cached in a window seat. The plot thickens further when Mortimer's evil brother Jonathan shows up, on the lam from the law and with an alcoholic plastic surgeon named Einstein in tow.

The play overflows with dry witticism, sly jabs at theater critics and tossed-off lines that pull gales of laughter from the audience. Explaining to his

Please see Page C-3, 'ARSENIC'

■ **MUSIC:** Rhode Island blues? Strange but true / D-5 ■ **TELEVISION:** Today's highlights / D-7 ■ **COMICS:** And puzzles / D-8

IMPULSE

FRIDAY
SECTION D Dec. 9, 1988

By STEVE MCKERROW
The Baltimore Evening Sun

Good golly, Miss Molly, what is happening to MTV? The brash 7-year-old cable television network that once basically offered non-stop rock 'n' roll music videos has slowly begun to look more like a conventional network.

In its 168 hours of weekly programming, MTV has scheduled 19 non-video hours, such as a movie preview show, a weekend news show, a half-hour stand-up comedy series, a dance show, a daily game show, comedy repeats and now even a nightly talk show.

"Mouth to Mouth," a live hour Monday through Thursday evening, is the latest edition: a talk show that premiered on Halloween and is hosted by affable stand-up comic Steve Skrovan. Interviews with guests, live musical performances and some audience interaction are supplemented by incoming telephone questions to guests from viewers across the United States.

The rock-oriented tone would not fit, say "The Tonight Show With Jonny Carson," but it still sounds like a talk show of fairly familiar format.

And "Remote Control," a kicky nightly game show now in production for its second season, is even being talked about as a potential syndicated product

See Page D-2, MTV

From clapper to gaffer: They all get credit

BW Feature

NEW YORK — The movie's over. The popcorn's gone. Now comes the really fun part — that's right, the credits!

If you've ever wondered what separates the "best boys" from the "script girls" (but were afraid to ask), you're about to find out.

According to Ann Foley Plunkett, senior vice president of Creative Services for The Movie Channel, the credits can be as interesting as the movie — if you know what you're looking at.

As part of its between-the-movies programming, The Movie Channel recently took on the task of explaining what all those people in the movies with funny sounding jobs actually do. Here's a look at what it came up with.

GAFFER: While Webster defines this as "an old man," Hollywood types know that on a movie or TV set, the gaffer is the person in charge of all things electrical — lights, fans and anything else that has "juice" running through it.

BEST BOY: Never really a youngster (but in some instances a woman, in which case the credit may read "bester"), the best boy is the gaffer's first assistant. "That means he has the privilege of being bossed around and generally abused by the gaffer," explains Plunkett. "It's considered quite an honor."

KEY GRIP: Here's one that almost makes sense. The key grip is in charge of the grip

See Page D-3, CREDIT

Music

Words and music: The words surround you at Cyrano's, the funky downtown bookstore. But music will surround you, too, when the Ibanez Brothers take the floor. The band plays jazz and blues from 8 to 11 tonight and Saturday at the bookstore, 413 D St.

Theater

Colorful musical: Alaska Light Opera Theatre sponsors performances of "Joseph and the Amazing Technicolor Dreamcoat" through Dec. 20. For show times and ticket information, call the Alaska Center for the Performing Arts at 263-2787.

Movies

Romantic notions: Marcello Mastroianni stars in the lush, hopelessly romantic "Dark Eyes" tonight at the Z.J. Loussac Library. The film, part of the Friends of the Library series, shows at 7 and 9 p.m. in the Wilda Marston Theatre. Tickets are available at the door.

Tickets

Dance fever: Want tickets to the January performances by Rudolf Nureyev? You and everybody else. Better get over to the Center for the Performing Arts *fast*, because that's how the tickets are going. Shows with Nureyev and stars of the Paris Opera Ballet are 8 p.m. Jan. 4 and 5. Information: 263-2787.

Pop stardom a two-edged sword for Dylan

By STEPHEN HOLDEN
The New York Times

NEW YORK — In "Dylan," a scrappy, unauthorized new biography of Bob Dylan by the journalist and former rock manager Bob Spitz, one of the few scenes in which the secretive star is shown pouring his heart out describes an evening Dylan spent in 1975 with a young writer named Madeline Beckman.

COMMENT

"Bob romanticized his brother's modest life style in contrast to his own public spectacle," the author writes. 'David's got it all,' Bob told Madeline, 'a good marriage and a family and . . . anonymity.

"Wish I had some of what he had — especially privacy. In the music business, everybody wants a piece of you until there's nothing left to give.'"

Throughout the book, Dylan is pictured as a figure imprisoned by the poet-genius mystique that he created for himself in the early 60s and has shrewdly exploited ever since.

The star's 1966 motorcycle accident, the author suggests, was an apocryphal event devised to camouflage the shaking of a drug habit.

His lunge into fundamentalist Christianity is portrayed as the capricious contortion of a rudderless artist grasping for instant moral authority.

Treated like a king for the last 25 years by an adoring entourage, Dylan is shown playing games of mental cruelty on his family and followers.

Because the author finds much to admire in Dylan's work, his biography isn't a character assassination like Albert Goldman's hate-filled hatchet job on John Lennon.

But along with Goldman's book, it reveals the destructiveness of a certain kind of fame on its recipient.

No matter how much Dylan may loathe fame, he has never turned his back on it for long. Being lonely at the top may be hell, but God forbid he should ever have to face being happy at

See Page D-4, DYLAN

Bob Dylan: a rock 'n' roll survivor

AWARD OF EXCELLENCE

FEATURE PAGE
DESIGN PORTFOLIO
CIRCULATION 50,000-99,999

Anchorage Daily News

Designer
Susan Berry
Art Director
Dee Boyles

De eerste berichten over een onbekend virus waaraan honderden zeehonden in de Deense wateren ten slachtoffer vielen, verschenen eind mei van dit jaar. Het heeft er nog even op geleken dat de zeehondenziekte niet tot de Nederlandse Waddenzee zou doordringen, maar drie weken later werden de eerste (vijftien) slachtoffers gemeld aan de zeehondencrèche van Lenie 't Hart in Pieterburen.
Meer dan tweehonderd slachtoffers voor de Deense kusten waren op dat moment aanleiding voor een congres van een groot aantal deskundigen in Kopenhagen. Een hele generatie was volgens de bioloog Paul Mortensen al omgekomen omdat de zieke moeders spontaan aborteerden en de klok dreigde teruggezet te worden naar 1975 toen de zeehond tot beschermde diersoort werd verklaard omdat de soort met uitsterving bedreigd werd. Er leefden toen nog 350 zeehonden in het Nederlandse deel van de Waddenzee.

Onbekend virus bedreigt zeehonden in Oostzee

Hoogtijdagen voor Lenie 't Hart in Pieterburen

Virus onder zeehonden bracht Europa verwarring

NO 25
WC 25
EC 28
HO 25
AC 25

Drents Groningse Pers

Zaterdag 31 december 1988

ZZ Mei

AWARD OF EXCELLENCE
FEATURE PAGE
DESIGN PORTFOLIO
CIRCULATION 50,000-99,999
Drents-Groningse Pers
Netherlands
Art Director
Jan Van Kooten

Zaterdag en zondag
Weekendbijlage van de Drents-Groningse Pers

ZZ

NO 19
WC 19
EC 21
HO 19
AC 19

Drents Groningse Pers

Zaterdag 31 december 1988

Voorspoedig 1989!

1988 ligt weer achter ons. Volgens sommigen een jaar dat snel zal worden vergeten. Anderen daarentegen beweren dat 1988 als het 'jaar van de vrede' de geschiedenis in zal gaan. Zeker is dat er een golf van vredesbesprekingen de wereld is rondgegaan. Het Gorbatsjov-effect? Dichter bij huis werden wij ook dit jaar weer geconfronteerd met een groot aantal bezuinigingen van het kabinet Lubbers II. Studenten, bejaarden, jongeren, ziekenhuizen en uitkeringsgerechtigden - om slechts een paar groepen te noemen - hadden ook dit jaar weer te maken met de bezuinigingsplannen van de regering.
Uiteraard kende 1988 weer een groot aantal rampen. Die van Armenië ligt nog vers in ons geheugen. Droogte, overstromingen, cyclonen en andere natuurrampen teisterden de wereld. Het milieu ging wéér verder achteruit. En verder...stortte in Ramstein een straaljager in het publiek en een Boeing 747 op het Schotse dorpje Lockerbie, brak er onder de zeehonden een ernstige ziekte uit, loste de politie de 'Zaak Heyn' op, behaalde Yvonne van Gennip drie gouden medailles in Calgary en werd het Nederlandse voetbalelftal Europees kampioen....

Brief aan een verre broer op Mars

In deze ZZ- bijlage:

De hoogtepunten van het afgelopen jaar per maand voor u op een rij gezet:
januari: Yvonne van Gennip
februari: bejaardenhuizen
maart: vrouwen tegen seksueel geweld
april: de zaak Heyn
mei: zeehonden worden ziek
juni: Nederland wint de finale EK
juli: werkdruk justitie te groot
augustus: doden bij vliegshow
september: pitbull-terriers in opspraak
oktober: burgemeesters op stap
november: nepjournaal op tv
december: voorstellen tot ontwapening

Beste Hans,
Wanneer het vannacht helder is moet je vanaf jouw planeet onze jaarwisseling kunnen zien. We hebben met zijn allen voor miljoenen vuurwerk gekocht en dat gaat om twaalf uur tegelijk de lucht in.

AWARD OF EXCELLENCE
FEATURE PAGE
DESIGN PORTFOLIO:
CIRCULATION 50,000-99,999

el Nuevo Herald
Miami, Florida

Designer
Herman Vega
Illustrator
Herman Vega

GUSTO/GALERIA C

JUEVES 1 DE SEPTIEMBRE DE 1988 / EL NUEVO HERALD

GEORGE CHILDS

¿Cómo es la vida en Cuba?

BATE que BATE

Deliciosos, nutritivos, ideales para aplacar la sed veraniega: batidos y refrescos que se preparan de mil maneras con pulpa de frutas.

Por MARIA ELENA CARDENAS

La primera batidora eléctrica

Pasa a la página 4C

Bocaditos

LA MANTEQUILLA SABE MEJOR

MARGARA DI PERSA-MAESTRA Y MAESTRO

DELE DOLE

CAMI'S SEASHELLS

FOLLETO DE FOLLETOS

EL BUZON GOLOSO

GALERIA C

POR DENTRO

MARTES 29 DE NOVIEMBRE DE 1988 / EL NUEVO HERALD

CIENCIA ESPACIAL

Por Rolando Millas

Telescopio y robots espaciales

LA VISION DE UN PACIENTE

En Miami se encuentra uno de los principales centros oftalmológicos del mundo —y el mayor del sureste norteamericano—, el 'Bascom Palmer Eye Institute', cuya labor abarca todas las fases de esta rama de la medicina.

BASCOM PALMER

Pasa a la página 4C

La historia de un virus bueno que se transformó en malo

"Un lobo con ropa de oveja", es como The Hearing Journal se refirió al papel del B.cat en la otitis media, una común infección del oído.

Pasa a la página 4C

Beatifican mártires de Guerra Civil Española

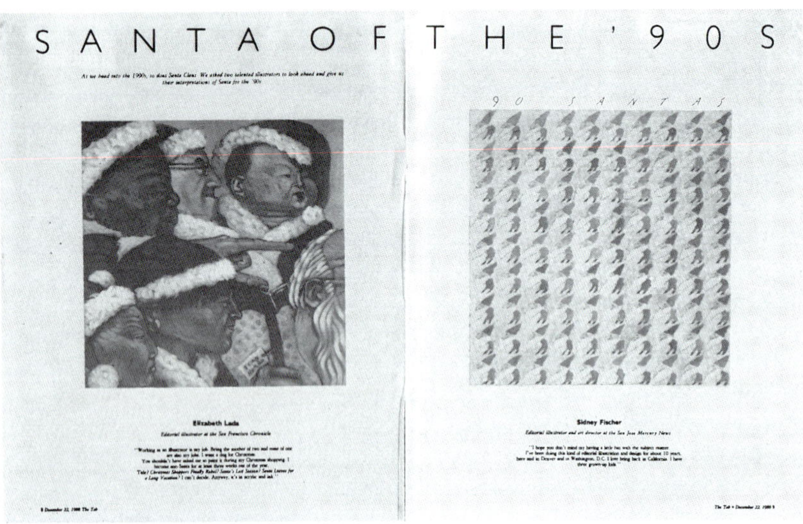

S A N T A O F T H E ' 9 0 S

As we head into the 1990s, so does Santa Claus. We asked two talented illustrators to look ahead and give us their interpretations of Santa for the '90s

9 0 S A N T A S

Elizabeth Lada

Editorial illustrator at the San Francisco Chronicle

Sidney Fischer

Editorial illustrator and art director at the San Jose Mercury News

AWARD OF EXCELLENCE
FEATURE PAGE
DESIGN PORTFOLIO
NON-DAILY CIRCULATION
The Tab
Palo Alto, California
Designer
Stephen Sedam-Stone
Art Director
Stephen Sedam-Stone

MARCH 11, 1988 ISTHMUS PAGE 23

SECTION 2

Nothing.
Nothing.
Nothing.

Performance artists rebel against traditional art, but what have they offered in its place?

BY BRUCE MURPHY

"People in Asia and Africa are starving for personality—we should be ashamed to have it all."
—Anatole Broyard

With the demise of Hart, Biden and Ginsburg, we have seen the other, less appreciated side of Andy Warhol's dictum that everyone will be famous for 15 minutes. If the media giveth, it taketh away just as fast. A quarter-hour of fame may be all that can be sustained in the face of a "vigilant press" in search of character flaws. Warhol, of course, helped turn the celebrity sausage grinder with his Interview magazine: After one of its endless, uncut interviews with the latest star, the readers had been given their fill of that personality and were ready to feast on another.

If every age requires its own kind of art, the age of personality would appear to have it in the form of performance art. Recent movies have been built around the work of performance artists like Spalding Gray (*Swimming to Cambodia*) and Laurie Anderson (*Home of the Brave*). Anderson also has a multi-album contract with Warner Brothers, while another practitioner, Eric Bogosian, moved on to Broadway with his *Drinking in America*. Less obvious has been the creative cross-fertilization between performance artists and the avant-garde in all the other art forms. Madison has spawned its own group of performance artists, and has also been visited by performers like Anderson and Meredith Monk.

Whatever the impact of performance art on American culture, it remains an ill-defined movement—partly by design. If performance art reflects the craze for naked personalities, it remains coy about its own esthetic anatomy. A big part of the avant-garde esthetic is to avoid tradition and elude definition. And so performance art has remained a bit of a mystery to observers, even as it has developed a tradition and an audience of its own.

In a narrow sense, performance art was created when certain visual artists rebelled against the stifling confines of the museum and began *performing* their art on (or off) stage. More broadly, it overlaps the entire avant-garde tradition in this century. Beginning in the early 1900s, a variety of artists—poets, painters, dancers and musicians—offered some deliberately informal performances (often held outdoors or in cabarets) that aimed at a new esthetic. From the Italian and Russian Futurists of the 1900s, to the French and German Dadaists of the World War I years, to the German Bauhaus artists of the 1920s, to the New York happenings of the 1960s, the general goal was to create art with a vital connection to real life, forcing audience members to think and react and perhaps change their lives.

To accomplish this, artists worked to break through the limits of a given art form and close the distance between art and audience. Thus, when Dadaist Walter Serner declaimed such lines as "the queen is an armchair and a dog is a hammock," he was, for better or worse, stretching the language of poetry and provoking audiences (who were suitably outraged) to respond. When John Cage composed his "chance music," which came out differently each time it was performed, he was assuring that both listeners and performers of his compositions would continually confront the new.

While the performance artists of the 1970s and '80s descend from this tradition, their work has not always retained that free-form unpredictability. Ironically, the unconventional has developed its own conventions, and "performance," as it is often called, has itself become a recognizable art form, albeit a hybrid one. Certain elements recur in much of performance art, including the following:

Charged imagery. Sex, violence and obscenity loom large. In 1918, artist George Grosz urinated on an Expressionist painting at the first Berlin Dada gathering. In 1971, Chris Burden had an assistant with a rifle shoot him in the arm. In the same year, Vito Acconci offered "Seedbed," where he masturbated under a ramp on which the audience walked. In the early 1980s, Rachel Rosenthal had herself stripped naked by assistants, who tried to repair her "imperfections" with masking tape and then covered her with frosting and nuts.

Genre crossing. As a famous Dadaist manifesto declared, "No more painters, no more musicians, no more sculptors. No more of these idiocies. Nothing. Nothing. Nothing."

Put more prosaically, performance artists rebelled against the idea of art as a demonstration of pure technique by virtuosic painters or violinists. They believed it was content and the process of creating art that should be emphasized. As the barrier of technique was broken down, there was nothing to prevent dancers from singing or painters from acting.

At its best, genre crossing has yielded a fresh vision of an art form: An actress turned choreographer like Yvonne Rainer helped to define postmodern dance, and her choreography, in turn, influenced avant-garde theater. At its worst, the concept of the untrained or "naive" artist has resulted in work marked by more naivete than artistry: Laurie Anderson's shows (or her recent movie) amply demonstrate that the former sculptor is a limited singer, so-so composer and banal poet.

Perhaps no artists have tested their versatility more than Meredith Monk, who has worked in theater, music, film and dance. And her "Songs from the Hill" (performed at her recent show in Madison) suggest the problems that occur as artistic boundaries are stretched. The music consistently defeats the listener's expectations, not so much because of Monk's surprising repertoire of sounds (microtones, vocal swoops, nasal screams and nonsense words), but because her songs have no rhythmic pattern. Their emotional flatness ultimately illustrates Ezra Pound's dictum that "music begins to atrophy when it departs too far from the dance." (A strange irony, given Monk's training in dance.)

Technological trappings: Unlike high art, which hides its technology, performance art consciously makes it part of the show: Taped voices, telephones and slide machines are forever popping up. (It is not uncommon for audiences to be left waiting for an unplanned technical screw-up to be resolved in a piece that intends to make a commentary on our technological era.) The peculiar juxtapositions of every technology from the telegraph to the TV have also affected the storytelling style of performance art. Just as the words "Now this" indicate that your television will present something with no relation to the thing before it, performance art has often used associative imagery or fragmented narrative rather than straight chronology. Finally, the growth of technology has become part of the content of a show—in the form of allusions to nuclear holocaust, industrial pollutants or TV images.

Indeed, the inevitable mention of some kind of global destruction has become a cliche in performance art. Rachel Rosenthal has sometimes managed to avoid this problem with her mother earth persona, whose visceral rejection of all the industrial pollutants buried in the earth becomes an arresting image. But even a thoughtful artist like Spalding Gray gets tripped up here. In *Swimming to Cambodia*, he describes some feuding Manhattan

Continued on Page 25

SECTION 2

AWARD OF EXCELLENCE
FEATURE PAGE
DESIGN PORTFOLIO
NON-DAILY CIRCULATION
Isthmus
Madison, Wisconsin
Designer
Christine Dehlinger
Art Director
Christine Dehlinger

The Washington Post Magazine

ALL THE

PRESIDENT'S GUESTS

After 3½ years and 2,150 yards of new carpeting, Blair House is ready to receive the nation's most honored visitors

Photographs by Kari Haavisto
Text by Judith Weinraub

OPPOSITE PAGE
The double drawing room and dining room suite at Blair House opens onto newly planted gardens, designed by the landscape firm Innocenti & Webel. In the rear drawing room, decorator Mark Hampton patterned the curtains on styles popular in England, on the Continent and on the East Coast in the early 19th century.

16 THE WASHINGTON POST MAGAZINE

AWARD OF EXCELLENCE
MAGAZINE PAGE
DESIGN PORTFOLIO
CIRCULATION 250,000 AND OVER
The Washington Post Magazine
Designer
Brian Noyes
Art Director
Brian Noyes

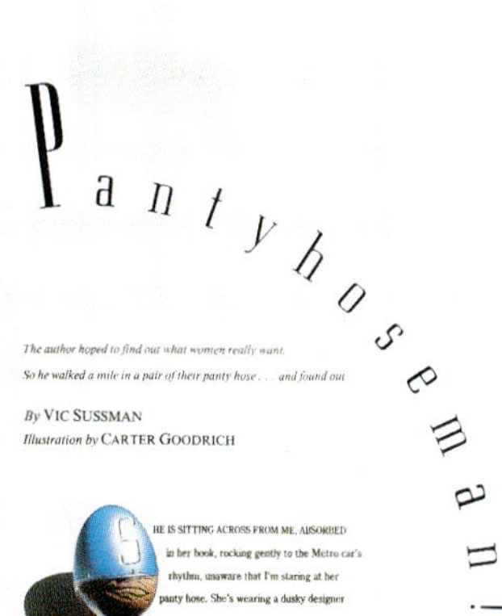

Pantyhoseman!

The author hoped to find out what women really want.
So he walked a mile in a pair of their panty hose . . . and found out

By VIC SUSSMAN
Illustration by CARTER GOODRICH

SHE IS SITTING ACROSS FROM ME, ABSORBED in her book, rocking gently to the Metro car's rhythm, unaware that I'm staring at her panty hose. She's wearing a dusky designer style peppered with tiny decorative diamonds. A poor choice, I think. The dots make her look as if she's suffering from a skin disease. I'm your basic kind of guy, so I'm wearing sheer support panty hose. It's not terribly comfortable under my tropical wool suit, but it's a more conservative choice for the business day.

I could explain this to her and we could commiserate about how my control top is killing me and how I can't wait to go home and change into something comfortable, but I don't think she'd understand. She'd probably wonder why a happily married

70 THE WASHINGTON POST MAGAZINE PHOTOGRAPH BY DAN MURANO

The Washington Post Magazine

NO ONE DIES ALONE

Peggy Gee was only the first victim of a savage murder. Two years later, her family is torn by tension, fear, nightmarish memories, an insatiable hunger for justice and revenge—and outrage that the District of Columbia doesn't have a death penalty or even a life sentence

By JUAN WILLIAMS

THE PHONE RINGS AT 5:40 A.M., AND JACK RUSSELL stirs from his sleep. It's a cousin, telling him there's a fire at his sister's house. "Okay, I'll be there," he mutters with resignation. He gets up, pulls on a pair of jeans and thinks of all the times he's told Peggy to get the darn furnace fixed—before it starts a fire. He gets in his old Toyota and leaves his quiet home in Potomac, heads toward the Beltway and his sister's house on 18th Street in Northeast. He worries as he drives—Peggy's basement is full of clothes and papers, a fire waiting to happen. Nearing the house he is swept by a sense of relief—no flames, not even any smoke, and the firemen are just standing around. But then he notices the plainclothes policemen and realizes that the grim-faced men in yellow slickers are federal agents. Something is very wrong.

Illustrations by MATT MAHURIN
Photographs by NIGEL DICKSON

14 THE WASHINGTON POST MAGAZINE

AWARD OF EXCELLENCE
MAGAZINE PAGE
DESIGN PORTFOLIO
CIRCULATION 250,000 AND OVER
The Washington Post Magazine
Designer
Michael Walsh
Illustrators
Denise Crawford, Carter Goodrich,
Michael Walsh, Matt Mahurin
Photographers
Dan Murano, Charles Griffin
Art Director
Brian Noyes

AWARD OF EXCELLENCE
MAGAZINE PAGE DESIGN PORTFOLIO
CIRCULATION 250,000 AND OVER
The Washington Post Magazine
Designer
Brian Noyes
Art Director
Brian Noyes

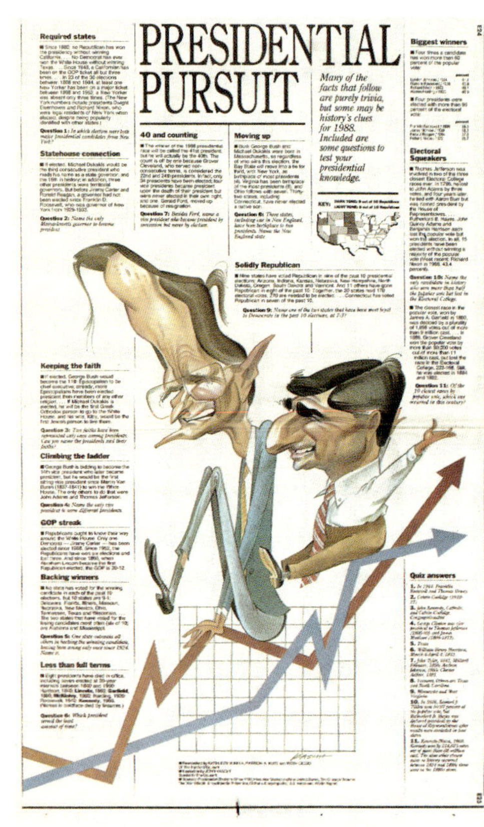

AWARD OF EXCELLENCE
INSIDE NEWS, SPORTS OR BUSINESS SECTION PAGE DESIGN
The Hartford Courant
Designer
Randy Cox

AWARD OF EXCELLENCE
MAGAZINE PAGE DESIGN PORTFOLIO
CIRCULATION 100,000-249,999
The Washington Times
Designer
David Bartlett
Art Director
David Bartlett

WashingtonWeekend

Out & About

A GUIDE TO INEXPENSIVE FAMILY FUN

Horse-pitality

The Prince George's Equestrian Center, at the intersection of Routes 301 and 4 in Upper Marlboro, is the site of the 1988 Maryland Horse Fair and Trade Show this weekend. More than $10,000 will be given away as prize money in various competitions, not including the jousting tournament and the Maryland's Best Barbecue Cookoff. The Uptown Rhythm Kings will perform. Admission is $3 for adults and $1 for children, with those 6 and under admitted free. For more information call (301) 952-4740.

Photo Courtesy of the Martin Luther King Memorial Library

Jackie Gleason's "Honeymooners" character, Ralph Kramden (left), is the subject of a Museum of American History program this Saturday.

The scenic route

The mules are in gear and the C&O Canal boat rides are again under way. The Canal Clipper docks at the Great Falls Tavern in Potomac and leaves at 10:30 a.m. and 1 and 3 p.m. Saturdays and Sundays. A 5 p.m. trip is added on Sundays. The Georgetown, which docks between Thomas Jefferson and 30th streets NW, a half block south of M Street, leaves at 1 and 3 p.m. Wednesdays, Thursdays and Fridays, at 10:30 a.m. and 1, 3, and 5 p.m. Saturdays and at 10:30 a.m. and 1 and 3 p.m. Sundays. The fare is $4 for adults, $3 for seniors and $2.50 for children. For more information call The Georgetown at 472-4376 and The Canal Clipper at 299-2026.

Highlights and hot sites

✔ The George Mason University Student Art Guild is sponsoring "Eat Your Art Out," an edible art competition, from 11:30 a.m. to 12:30 p.m. Friday in the school's Student Union Place Gallery, on the second floor of Student Union I. Admission is $1.50; after judging is completed, all entries will be eaten. For more information call 323-2138.

✔ The 100-voice Arlington Metropolitan Chorus performs a concert of works by American composer Aaron Copland at 3 p.m. Sunday in Kenmore Auditorium, 200 S. Carlin Springs Road, Arlington. A highlight of the concert will be his cycle "Old American Songs," which includes children's songs, square dance tunes and love ballads. Since the 90-minute concert is so appropriate for families, admission for children under 12 is free. However, admission for adults is $8 and for students over 12, $6. For more information call 739-2922.

✔ The Great One lives on. The National Museum of American History devotes an afternoon to Ralph Kramden, Jackie Gleason's character on "The Honeymooners," as a symbol of working-class life in the 1950s. The program includes a discussion at 1 p.m., the screening of two of the show's episodes at 2:30 and a tour of the "Symbols and Images of American Labor" exhibition at 3:30 p.m. Saturday. Admission is free with no reservations needed. For information call 357-2700.

Gardens in bloom

Anne Arundel County opens Maryland's 51st annual House and Garden Pilgrimage with a tour of seven waterfront homes, an Episcopal chapel and three 18th century mansions, including the Chase-Lloyd House, the William Paca House and the Hammond-Harwood House. The houses will be open from 10 a.m. to 5 p.m. Saturday. Tickets are $12 for all of the houses and $4 for a single house. For more information and a schedule of the week's activities call (301) 821-6933.

This is the weekend of the 61st annual Georgetown House Tour, featuring 14 houses, as well as high tea. The houses are open from noon to 5 p.m. Saturday and Sunday, with different houses featured on each day. Tea is served at St. John's Church, 3240 O St. NW. Tickets are $12 for each day and available at the church. For more information call 338-1796.

— Merrie Morris Hammons

Best of the crafts

Arts and crafts connoisseurs always eagerly await the Washington Craft Show, since it is one of the largest juried shows in this area. This year the show, sponsored by the Women's Committee of the Smithsonian Associates, will feature 100 artisans from 32 states. The show is open from 10 a.m. to 8 p.m. Friday, from 10 a.m. to 6 p.m. Saturday and from 10 a.m. to 5 p.m. Sunday in the Departmental Auditorium, 1301 Constitution Ave. NW. Admission is $5 for adults and $4 for seniors and children under 12. For more information call 357-2700.

At the Washington Craft Show this weekend (clockwise from left): Glass vessel by Wes Hunting, "Metalmorphosis" by Ron Hinton, vase by Laney X. Oxman

THE WASHINGTON TIMES — WASHINGTON WEEKEND APRIL 21, 1988 M3

AWARD OF EXCELLENCE
INSIDE NEWS, SPORTS OR BUSINESS SECTION PAGE DESIGN
The Hartford Courant
Designer
Randy Cox
Photographer
Brad Clift

AWARD OF EXCELLENCE
COMBINATION PAGE
DESIGN PORTFOLIO
CIRCULATION 100,000-249,999
The Hartford Courant
Designer
Randy Cox

Sunday Travel on Pages G10 to G12

The Hartford Courant

ARTS/ENTERTAINMENT

SECTION G
SUNDAY DECEMBER 25, 1988

Television

Performance

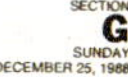

Music

Oh, sure.

You could ask for that hi-fi VCR, or Nintendo or, at the very least, a Dustbuster.

But if you were a *responsible* person, if you were a *cultured* person, if you were in charge of an arts or entertainment organization, perhaps you'd ask for something just a little bit more useful.

So we asked area arts and entertainment leaders what they would like to receive as a holiday gift this year. Not surprisingly, strike-free seasons, bigger audiences and larger corporate contributions were on their minds. So were some more whimsical wishes.

The art of WISHFUL THINKING

Compiled by Courant Staff Writers
Illustrations by MERLE NACHT / Special to The Courant

Dance

Film

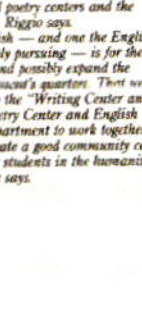

Theater

Literature

The Hartford Courant

ARTS/ENTERTAINMENT

SECTION G
SUNDAY NOVEMBER 27, 1988

Arts community rejoices at musicians' decision to play for 'Nutcracker'

Tchaikovsky Chestnut

By STEVE METCALF

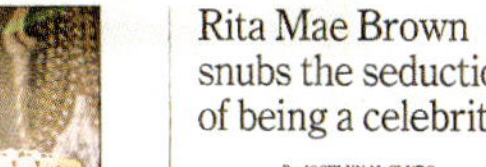

PERFORMANCE DATES
FOR MAIN COMPANIES

Rita Mae Brown snubs the seduction of being a celebrity

By JOCELYN McCLURG

Economic constraints force film industry to reel in projections

By MICHAEL CIEPLY

Chapter 6

Single-subject series, special sections and reprints

If any work should reflect the results of careful planning, it should be the design of series, special sections and reprints. Winning entries were well-edited. They showed careful attention to content. The photographs, illustrations and graphics helped drive the stories and complemented the reports. The designer was an inconspicuous guide who organized the presentation to give readers clear direction through volumes of information.

A Silver Award for series presentation went to the *St. Petersburg Times* for its thorough report of a woman's cruel murder: "It was one of the best things I saw. It's very simple. There was a lot of text and a lot of little devices to help you understand the story and what was going on," said judge John Rumbach.

The Dallas Morning News received a Silver Award for its special section on the Kennedy assassination. An outstanding job of photo editing and photo research, news judges said.

AWARD OF EXCELLENCE

SINGLE SUBJECT SERIES

Detroit Free Press

Designers

Randy Miller, John Goecke

Photographer

David C. Turnley

SPECIAL REPORT

Two cities talking:
About peace and politics, values and daily lives and how we see each other

MOSCOW & MOTOWN

DETROIT FREE PRESS
SPECIAL REPORT
JAN. 29-FEB. 2, 1989

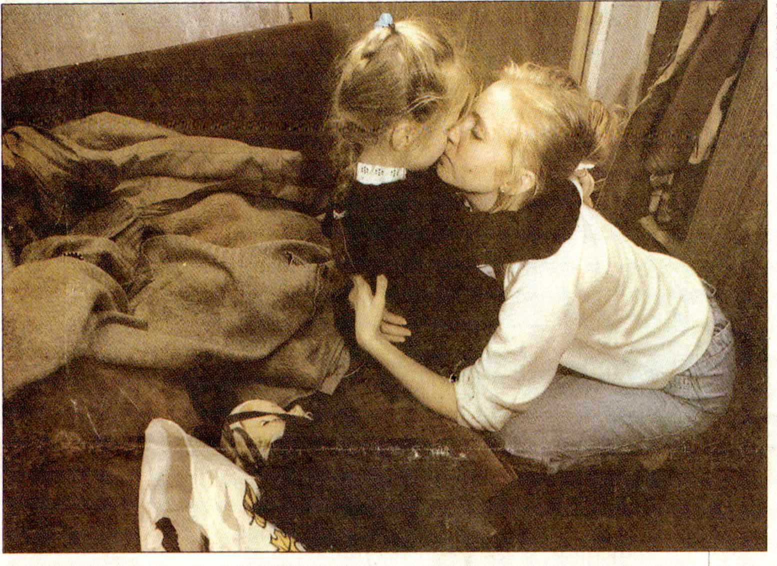

Greta Leontieff, 32, consoles her daughter, Nastia, 6, who has come home upset from school.

Moscow family finds love helps make ends meet

BY KAREN SCHNEIDER
Free Press Staff Writer

MOSCOW — The smell of a chicken roasting in the oven fills the small apartment. Greta Leontieff washes dishes and puts them to dry in a rack beneath the tiny wall-mounted refrigerator. Vadim Leontieff chops boiled eggs into a bowl of peas — a rare contribution to what Soviets consider women's work.

Six-year-old Anastasia, called Nastia, is still at day care at school, and won't be home until after 6 p.m. Eight-year-old Daria, called Dasha, tinkers on the piano. Vadim's grandmother Nina, 83, watches television in her room.

From the window of their apartment, on the 16th floor of a prefabricated concrete high-rise, they can see rows and rows of look-alike buildings, distinguished only by the laundry that flutters from the balconies.

Greta, a teacher, and Vadim, a theatrical set builder, both 32, share the problems and dreams of thousands of people in the Soviet Union's bustling capital.

They have little money for even simple luxuries. Greta sometimes despairs at the hardships they face, and Vadim laments his lost career as an actor.

But their souls stir with a warmth and a richness that make up for the material goods they lack.

"There are not many families that live like us," says Greta, a slender woman with soft blond hair. "Many families live without love."

See FAMILY, Page 8

2 cities, 2 nations – but often now we think as one

BY KAREN SCHNEIDER, KITTY MCKINSEY, PATRICIA CHARGOT AND ROGER CHESLEY
Free Press Staff Writers

As Moscow basked in the mildest January in a century, Kapitolina Batrakova, 64, served tea and cakes in her two-room apartment and talked about a book she had enjoyed — a collection of speeches by Ronald Reagan.

"I don't see any difference between what Reagan is talking about and our socialist system," she said. "Democracy, *glasnost* — everything we have right now — is the same as what Reagan is talking about."

Batrakova, an army nurse in World War II, once had been leery of Americans.

"But now we understand that they are just as open as we are," said the grandmother. "I like their straightforwardness, bravery, their friendly attitudes and their good-heartedness."

In Detroit, where an unusually sunny January lifted the pall of winter, Anita Flanagan, 38, a self-employed court reporter, remembered the fear of Russians that she felt each time she took cover during air raid drills in grade school in the 1950s, the height of the Cold War.

"As a child, I remember hearing a plane and having a phobia that maybe it was the Soviet Union coming to drop a bomb," she said.

Her attitude has changed dramatically since Soviet President Mikhail Gorbachev took office in 1985.

"I don't take such a dismal view," said Flanagan, who lives near Indian Village. Though she doesn't approve of the Soviet system, she conceded, "Now, with the arms talks, they've made progress.

"Gorbachev is very suave, very stylish. Probably one of the most broad-minded leaders they've had. I think he's willing to come to the table," she said.

Their governments once raced each other to stockpile nuclear weapons and dueled over Cuba. But Batrakova and Flanagan are among a majority of Americans and Soviets who now hold no Cold War animosities.

The attitudes are revealed in a new poll, cosponsored by the Free Press, that also provides a window into the lives of Soviets at an apparent turning point in their history.

The poll compared attitudes of people in Moscow, the Soviet Union's cosmopolitan capital, with those of metro Detroit and three

See CHANGE, Page 12

Detroiter Bradley Alexander, 25, thinks Soviets "never have time for fun." Muscovite Kapitolina Batrakova, 64, wears her war medals.

WHAT WE FOUND

- 73 percent of Detroiters gave a favorable rating to Soviet President Mikhail Gorbachev. In Moscow, 59 percent viewed Ronald Reagan favorably and 23 percent gave George Bush a favorable rating.
- 10 percent of Muscovites and 90 percent of metro Detroiters said they believe in a God.
- 64 percent in both cities approved of pre-marital sex.
- Nearly 6 of 10 in both cities said the woman in their family does most of the housework.
- More than 60 percent of Detroiters said the United States was wrong to send troops to fight in Vietnam. Similarly, more than 60 percent of Muscovites said the Soviet Union was wrong to send troops to fight in Afghanistan.
- Soviets say the economy and peace and disarmament are the most urgent problems facing their country. Detroiters list drugs and the federal deficit.

PHOTOS BY DAVID C. TURNLEY

DETROIT FREE PRESS

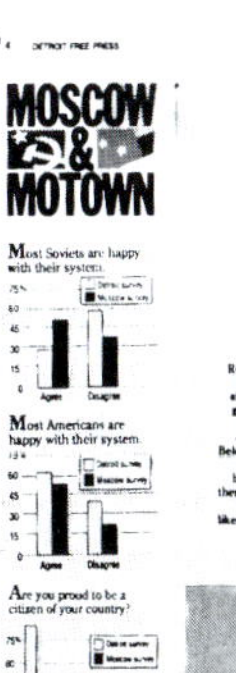

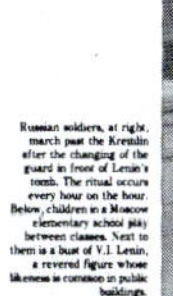

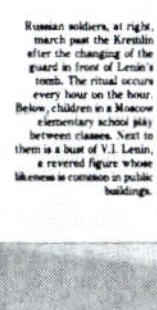

Russian soldiers, at right, march past the Kremlin after the changing of the guard in front of Lenin's tomb. The ritual occurs every hour on the hour. Below, children in a Moscow elementary school play between classes. Next to them is a bust of V.I. Lenin, a revered figure whose likeness is common in public buildings.

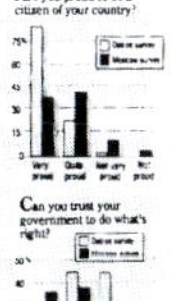

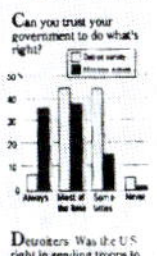

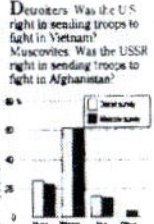

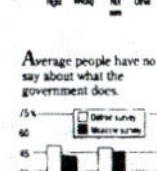

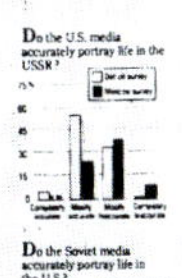

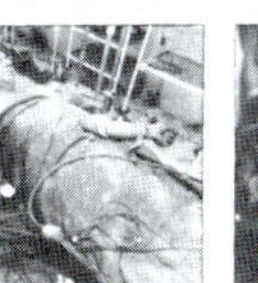

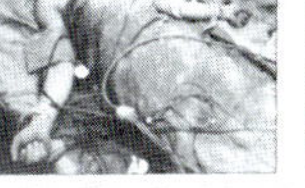

At Moscow Narcological Hospital No. 17, where alcohol and drug abusers are treated, a man is prepared for shock treatment that is part of therapy for alcoholism.

At Moscow School No. 45, which specializes in teaching English to children between ages 7 and 17, a student listens to her teacher in a grammar class.

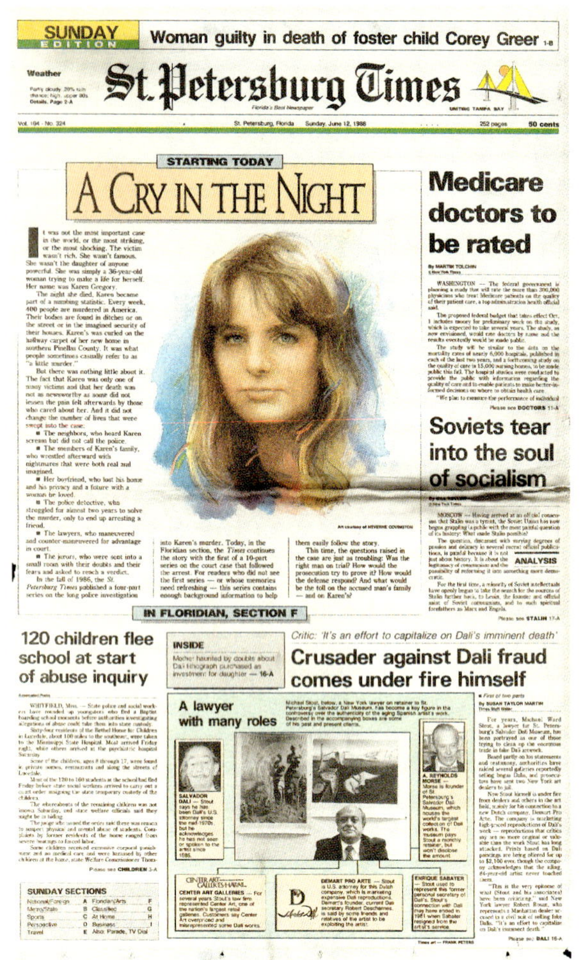

SUNDAY EDITION

Woman guilty in death of foster child Corey Greer

St. Petersburg Times

STARTING TODAY

A CRY IN THE NIGHT

Medicare doctors to be rated

Soviets tear into the soul of socialism

IN FLORIDIAN, SECTION F

120 children flee school at start of abuse inquiry

Crusader against Dali fraud comes under fire himself

A lawyer with many roles

SUNDAY SECTIONS

floridian/arts

PART ONE

A CRY IN THE NIGHT

Karen Gregory during a vacation to Jamaica in the early 1980s, before she moved from New Hampshire to Pinellas County.

Ghosts

As the oldest child, Karen reigned over her sister and two brothers. She wrestled with them and bossed them and held them at night when they were afraid. They thought she was indestructible.

A note to readers

By THOMAS FRENCH / Times Staff Writer

INSIDE

True to his art

Fears and phobias

What's a kid worth?

PART FOUR

A CRY IN THE NIGHT

"It's difficult for people who are not used to being in courtrooms," Judge Walker told the woman who'd been sitting patiently in the jury box. "You have to change your thinking in a lot of ways."

Principal figures

How the series was written

THE SERIES

SILVER AWARD

SINGLE SUBJECT SERIES

St. Petersburg Times

Designer

Rick Holter

GALLUP: A LETTER TO OUR READERS

The Albuquerque Tribune

GALLUP

The Killing season

Alcohol blurs line between a way of life, a way of death

Alcohol-related deaths

INSIDE

AWARD OF EXCELLENCE

SINGLE SUBJECT SERIES

The Albuquerque Tribune

Designers
Mike Davis, Brian Harrah, Randall K. Roberts, Dave Carlson

Illustrator
Charlotte Tongier

Photographer
Joe Cavaretta

Picture Editor
Mike Davis

Info-art
Marcia Cubra

AWARD OF EXCELLENCE

SINGLE SUBJECT SERIES

The Detroit News

Designers
Pegie Stark, Robert Graham

Illustrators
Marty Westman, Patrick Sedlar, Robert Graham

Researcher
Michele Fecht

Art Directors
Pegie Stark, Robert Graham

Editor
Dierck Casselman

GALLUP

The Killing Season

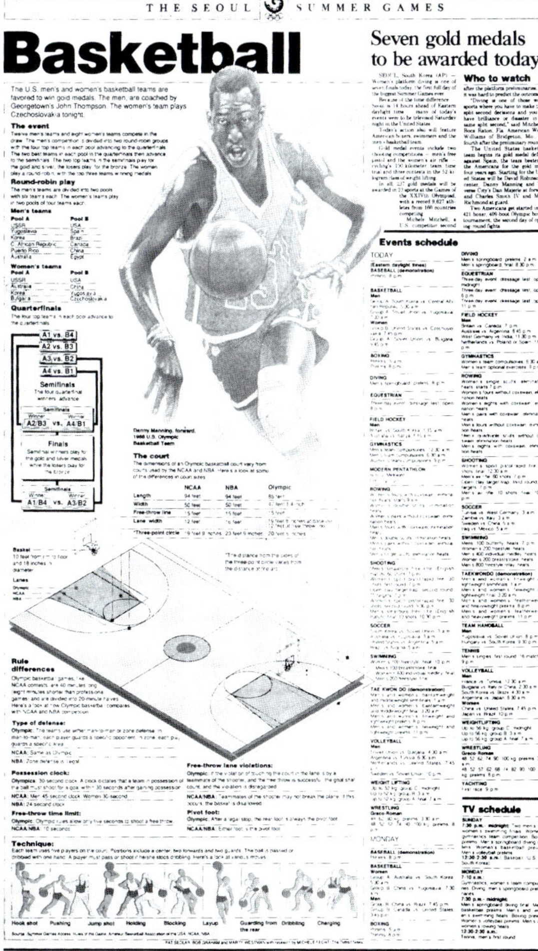

THE SEOUL SUMMER GAMES

Basketball

Seven gold medals to be awarded today

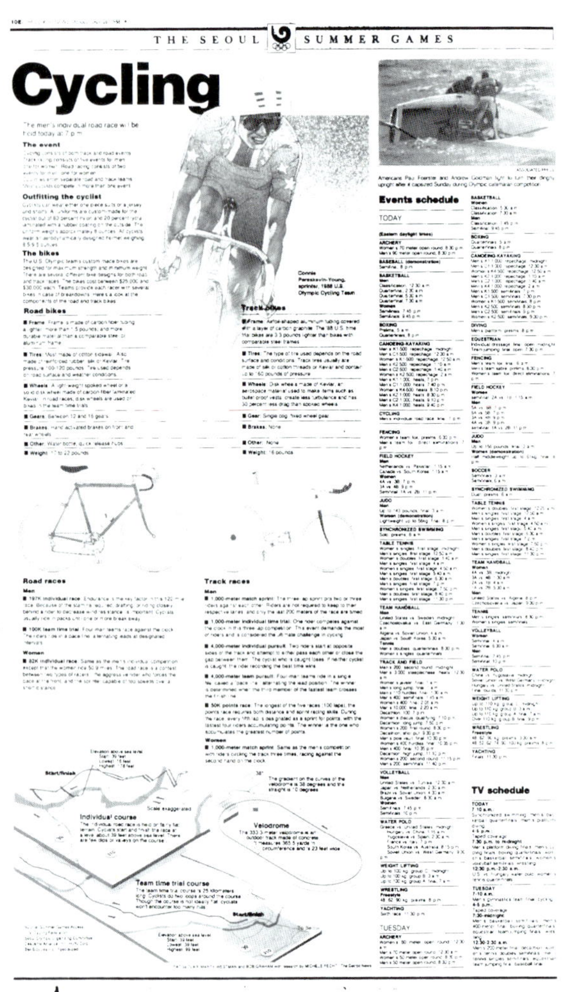

THE SEOUL SUMMER GAMES

Cycling

Events schedule

Road races

Track races

Individual course

Velodrome

Team time trial course

TV schedule

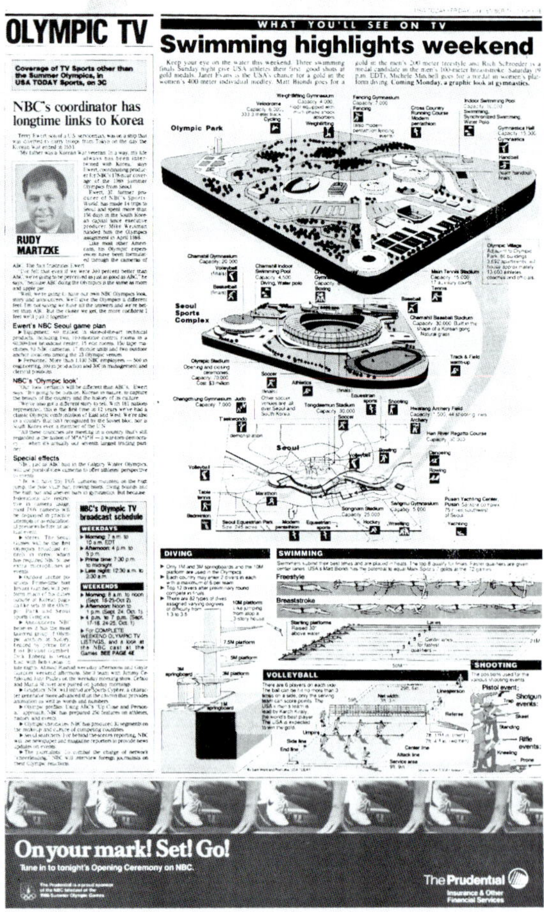

OLYMPIC TV

WHAT YOU'LL SEE ON TV

Swimming highlights weekend

NBC's coordinator has longtime links to Korea

RUDY MARTZKE

On your mark! Set! Go!

Tune in to tonight's Opening Ceremony on NBC.

The Prudential

AWARD OF EXCELLENCE
SINGLE SUBJECT SERIES
The Detroit News

Designers
Pegie Stark, Robert Graham
Illustrators
Marty Westman, Patrick Sedlar, Robert Graham
Researcher
Michele Fecht
Art Directors
Pegie Stark, Robert Graham
Editor
Dierck Casselman

Continued from page 149

Close-up

Orange County's beaches

Beaches: Crime is often a problem, especially when alcohol is allowed

LIFE AT LAND'S END

OC beaches riding a wave of change

AWARD OF EXCELLENCE
SINGLE SUBJECT SERIES
The Orange County Register
Santa Ana, California

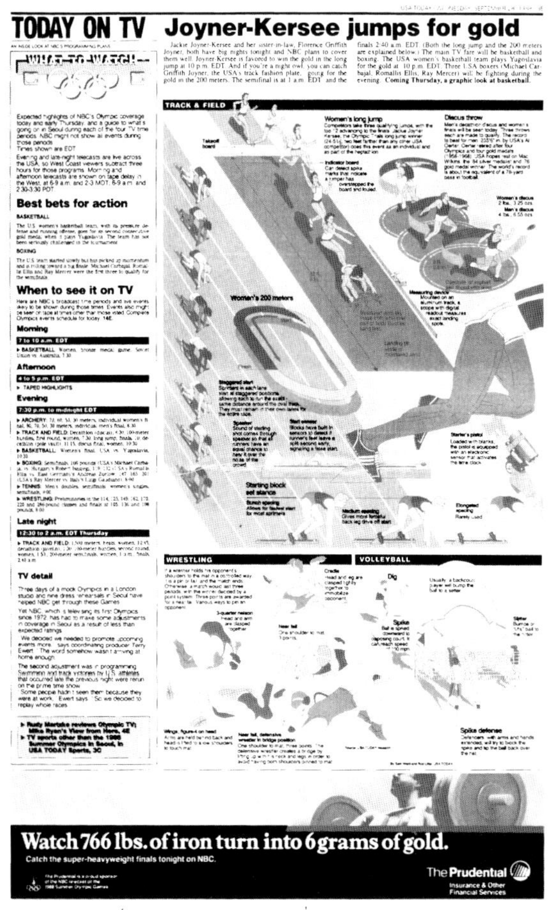
TODAY ON TV

Joyner-Kersee jumps for gold

Best bets for action

When to see it on TV

TRACK & FIELD

WRESTLING

VOLLEYBALL

Watch 766 lbs. of iron turn into 6 grams of gold.

Catch the super-heavyweight finals tonight on NBC.

The Prudential

AWARD OF EXCELLENCE

SINGLE SUBJECT SERIES

USA Today

Designer

Richard Curtis

Illustrators

Bob Laird, Sam Ward,
Rod Little, Webb Bryant

Art Director

Lynne Perri

Campaign '88

BUSH

DUKAKIS

SENATE

Senate seems in Democrats' grip

HOUSE OF REPRESENTATIVES

Few in House face a challenge

AWARD OF EXCELLENCE

SPECIAL SECTIONS
WITHOUT ADVERTISEMENTS

The Washington Times

Designer

Dolores Motichka, Paul Woodward

Illustrator

Paul Compton

Art Director

Joe Scopin

AWARD OF EXCELLENCE
SPECIAL SECTIONS
WITHOUT ADVERTISEMENTS
The Hartford Courant
Designers
Randy Cox, Jim Farrell

Olympics

Sunday
Sept. 11,
1988

Section
K

A Hartford Courant Sports Special Report

The Olympics are the world's greatest sporting summit. And for the first time since 1976, the Summer Games will include both the United States and the Soviet Union. That will make these 17 days in Seoul, South Korea, special.

Fast track
Florence Griffith Joyner, world record holder in the 100-meter dash, sets the pace with her speed . . . and may set trends with her racy outfits.

Day is night
Seoul is 6,825 miles from Hartford, which translates into a 14-hour time difference.

On the spot
John Thompson, coach of the U.S. basketball team, may be under more pressure than any athlete.

Record hop
Bob Beamon's 29-foot 2½-inch long jump record has withstood challenges for 20 years. Will it last past Seoul?

Inside
The U.S. selection process is in need of repair.
Page K2.
From Athens to Los Angeles, the Games in review.
Page K2.
Residents of Seoul put on a happy face.
Page K3.
State coaches, competitors analyze the events.
Page K4.
NBC will get good ratings, but wants good reviews.
Page K5.
A capsule look at some of the stars on display.
Page K6-7
Five unheralded athletes share a dream.
Page K8-9
Daily schedule of events.
Page K15.

State athletes
Karen and Sarah Josephson, twins from Bristol, have pooled their energies for most of their 24 years and may at last attain the ultimate reward — a gold medal in synchronized swimming. They lead the Connecticut contingent of 14 that is competing in South Korea.

Keeping the peace
A bomb could be left in an airport locker. A fire could be set in a crowded hotel. The threat of terrorism is real in South Korea, but the host country is determined to keep the Games safe.

Photos by
Joe Tabacca
Of The Hartford
Courant
and
Associated Press

THE SACRAMENTO BEE • WEDNESDAY, NOVEMBER 23, 1988

Book of DREAMS

KIMBERLY DOOLEY CAN TELL YOU SOMETHING ABOUT GRIEF. AND PAIN. AND WAITING. THAT'S A LOT FOR AN 8-YEAR-OLD TO CARRY AROUND. BUT, HAPPILY, SHE CAN ALSO TELL YOU ABOUT HOPE. AND SECOND CHANCES. AND DREAMS. HER DREAM, ALONG WITH 24 OTHERS, CAN COME TRUE THIS HOLIDAY SEASON — ALL BECAUSE OF YOU.

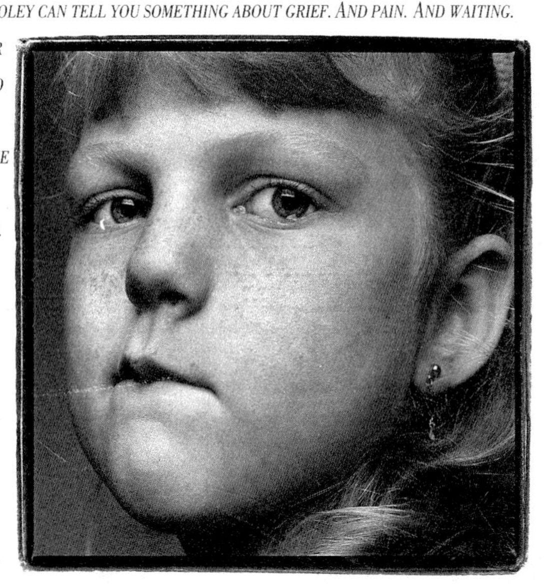

AWARD OF EXCELLENCE
SPECIAL SECTIONS
WITHOUT ADVERTISEMENTS
The Sacramento Bee
Designer
Howard Shintaku, J.D. Lasica
Photographer
John Trotter
Art Director
Howard Shintaku

PASSION AND PROMISE

The legacy of John F. Kennedy

By Carl P. Leubsdorf

President John F. Kennedy was often photographed sitting in a rocking chair. He found such chairs were the most comfortable for his back, which was injured during World War II. The injury, suffered when a Japanese destroyer sliced in half the PT boat he was commanding, plagued him the rest of his life.

Joseph P. Kennedy (center) is flanked by his sons Joseph P. Kennedy Jr. (left) and John F. Kennedy. The senior Kennedy had groomed Joseph Jr. for a political career leading to the presidency, but the role fell to John after his older brother was killed during World War II.

SILVER AWARD
SPECIAL SECTIONS
WITHOUT ADVERTISEMENTS
The Dallas Morning News
Designer
Marilyn Glaser
Art Director
Ed Kohorst

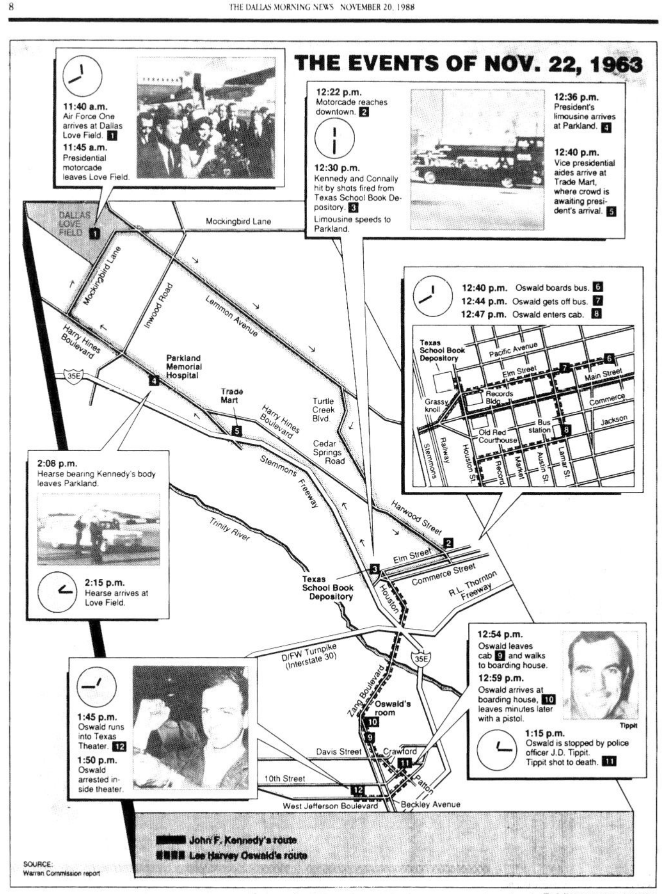

THE EVENTS OF NOV. 22, 1963

SPECIAL REPORT

MAC TOMORROW

MACS ON MAIN STREET: ARE THEY MAKING IT?

- The Fortune 1,000 challenge
- Is connectivity the key?
- Penetrating the government
- The DEC connection
- Will dealers get left out?

AUGUST 8, 1988 COMPUTERWORLD SR/1

AWARD OF EXCELLENCE
SPECIAL SECTIONS
WITH ADVERTISEMENTS
Computerworld
Designer
Nancy Kowal
Illustrator
Scott Baldwin
Art Director
Nancy Kowal
Editor
Glenn Rifkin

Detroit Free Press SPECIAL SECTION FRIDAY, SEPT. 30, 1988 SECTION B

REQUIEM OR REBIRTH?

Archdiocese plan has Detroit parishioners reeling

Planned closings send message on city neighborhoods

BY DAVID CRUMM AND JACK KRESNAK
Free Press Staff Writers

Archdiocesan leaders predicted a solid future for the Roman Catholic Church in greater Detroit Thursday as city parishes reeled from news of a planned shake-up unprecedented in U.S. Catholic history — one that would close 43 parishes serving 7,800 members and providing an array of neighborhood services.

"I don't think you could find a single historical parallel to this," said Msgr. John Tracy Ellis of Catholic University of America in Washington, D.C., widely regarded as the nation's pre-eminent Catholic historian.

"Closings are occurring, of course, in other dioceses. They're closing up parishes and there will be more of them in the future if the present conditions continue — but not anywhere near these numbers."

In a televised broadcast Wednesday night, the archdiocese said it would recommend shutting 43 churches — more than one-third of its 112 urban parishes — to shore up dwindling resources caused by the exodus over three decades of Catholics to the suburbs.

As priests, parishioners and civic leaders debated whether the plan represents a requiem or a rebirth for the church in Detroit, there was little question the plan sends another powerful message about collapsing neighborhoods.

Forty-two of the affected churches are in Detroit and one in River Rouge. Twenty of the churches would be closed outright, affecting 2,190 members, a church representative said Thursday. The rest would merge with neighboring parishes.

In televising the announcement Wednesday night, Cardinal Edmund Szoka said, "There has never been any question about our commitment to what has often been referred to as the church in the city."

He said the plan would create stable, active parishes that will serve the city. "Our bottom line is we want alive, vibrant parishes that really make a difference in the community."

Many pastors across the city, however, said Thursday that they did not share the optimism of their leaders.

The Rev. Norman Thomas, pastor of Sacred Heart Church, site of a

See CHURCHES, Page 7B

INSIDE

- Cardinal Szoka's personal touch was lacking. Page 7B.
- Closings deal another blow to a city losing people, businesses, institutions. Page 2B.
- Profiles of churches proposed to close, Page 3B.

Virginia Book, 68, wipes away a tear Thursday after morning mass at St. Stanislaus, which is scheduled to close and merge with St. Hyacinth Church, under the reorganization plan.

Deacons of St. Bernard Catholic Church Allen McNeeley, left, and Peter Schlesser, at the church scheduled to merge with St. Catherine-St. Edward.

St. Bernard's keeps the neighborhood alive

BY PATRICIA CHARGOT
Free Press Staff Writer

See ST. BERNARD, Page 8B

"The plumbing and cleaning are done by the parishioners. The teens cut the grass and clean the grounds. This all instills a sense of pride."

DEACON ALLEN MCNEELEY

AWARD OF EXCELLENCE
SPECIAL SECTIONS
WITH ADVERTISEMENTS
Detroit Free Press
Designers
John Goecke, Randy Miller

The Season's FOUR

Boosters, pundits and politicians always laud South Florida's biggest and best cultural events as having the potential to "put us on the map." This season, South Florida should get there at least four times.

November offers a chance to page through the world's latest and greatest writing — and meet some of the people responsible for it — at Miami Book Fair International. December has New Music America, which will turn Miami into a center for cutting-edge sounds.

In January, South Florida will welcome fans for Super Bowl XXIII weekend with countless entertainment events. Finally, there's the Miami Film Festival, which turns 6 in February and promises a long list of productions and filmmakers from around the world.

Put us on the map? With so many guests and parties, one map might not be big enough.

JUAN CARLOS COTO

TOM DOLPHENS / Miami Herald Staff

MIAMI BOOK FAIR

Open your eyes — and mind — to the Miami Book Fair International, on tap Nov. 13-20. Miami-Dade Community College's Wolfson Campus hosts the event, which offers the latest from international authors and booksellers. The "Evening with" program features talks by Norman Mailer and Hunter Thompson and a tribute to Isaac Singer. At the street festival (Nov. 18-20), cookbook authors will sign their works on Epicure Row, kids will romp at Children's Alley and collectors will have a chance to purchase rare books at the Antiquarian Annex.

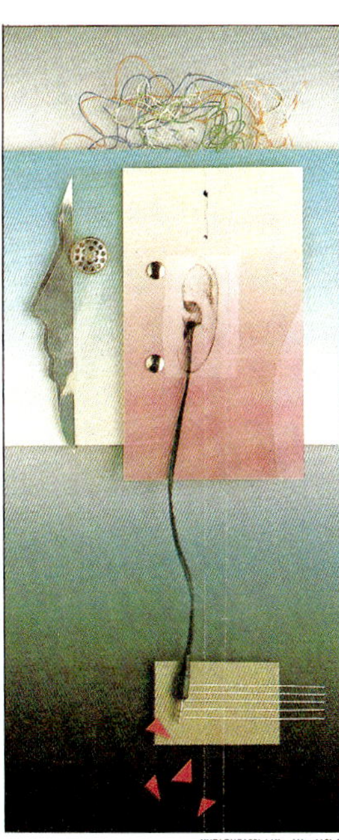

NURI DUCASSI / Miami Herald Staff

NEW MUSIC AMERICA

A high school band playing on a moving escalator? Concerts in Metrorail stations? Those are some of the more unusual offerings of New Music America, which checks into Miami Dec. 2-11. New Music America will mix the more traditional with the offbeat, and will involve many of the most creative musicians, artists and composers on the planet. Festival guests include Laurie Anderson, the Kronos Quartet, Sonic Youth, zydeco wizard Terrence Simien and the Mallet Playboys and Ornette Coleman. (See the classical music calendar for details).

PHILL FLANDERS / Miami Herald Staff

SUPER BOWL XXIII

You'll need some quick moves to keep up with the estimated 200 "community-sanctioned" concerts, festivals and tournaments surrounding Super Bowl XXIII weekend, Jan. 20-22. The biggest will be Super Miami Extravaganza, an open-air ethnic festival at Bayfront Park and Bayside featuring entertainment and loads of international foods. (For details, call 573-4300). Added attractions for the big weekend: Robin Williams at the Sunrise Musical Theatre and Frank Sinatra, Liza Minnelli and Sammy Davis Jr. at the Miami Arena.

ANA LARRAURI / Miami Herald Staff

MIAMI FILM FESTIVAL

"It looks as though this is going to be an exciting year for quality Spanish-language films," says Nat Chediak, director of the Miami Film Festival. The sixth festival "for the love of film" will take place Feb. 3-12 at Gusman Center for the Performing Arts. Titles haven't been confirmed, but festival scouts have been sighted in New York, Cannes and London, and Chediak is planning trips to Madrid and Paris. "We hold out as long as we possibly can to get the freshest product," Chediak says. It's one of South Florida's major events. Don't miss a frame.

20 Season Preview, November 10, 1988

Season Preview, November 10, 1988 21

AWARD OF EXCELLENCE
SPECIAL SECTIONS WITH ADVERTISEMENTS
The Miami Herald
Designers
Rhonda Prast, Herman Vega
Illustrators
Phill Flanders, Nuri Ducassi, Tom Dolphens, Ana Marie Lense
Editor
Ileana Oroza
Director of Editorial Art and Design
Randy Stano

AWARD OF EXCELLENCE
SPECIAL SECTIONS
WITH ADVERTISEMENTS
The Wall Street Journal
Designer
Joe Dizney
Design Director
Gregg Leeds
Art Director
Joe Dizney

THE WALL STREET JOURNAL REPORTS.

FRIDAY, JANUARY 20, 1989 — THE WALL STREET JOURNAL R1

THE INAUGURATION

BUSH ASSUMES COMMAND

He finally has the helm. What course will he steer?

Mark Summers

CHALLENGES FOR THE NEW CHIEF:

THE ECONOMY **16** THE RUSSIANS **26** THE DEMOCRATIC CONGRESS **30**

AWARD OF EXCELLENCE
SPECIAL SECTIONS
WITH ADVERTISEMENTS
The Washington Post
Designer
Wendy Ross
Art Director
Michael Keegan

The Washington Post — FRIDAY, JANUARY 20, 1989 — F1

THE INAUGURATION

OF THE 41st PRESIDENT OF THE UNITED STATES

'I, George Herbert Walker Bush, do solemnly swear that I will faithfully execute the office of president of the United States, and will to the best of my ability, preserve, protect and defend the Constitution of the United States.'

THE PRESIDENT'S FIRST TEST	3	THE PRESIDENCY'S CHALLENGES	4
THE INAUGURAL PARADE MAP	8	THE LEGACIES OF RONALD REAGAN	10
THE FESTIVITIES SINCE 1789	12	THE AVENUE'S NEW LOOK	17
THE VIEW FROM ABROAD	24	THE NEW FIRST LADY	34

B1

THE CHRISTIAN SCIENCE MONITOR

Special Report

A G E N D A

2000

The world is on the threshold of a new century, filled with expectations of new beginnings, new promise – a clean slate. But unless we begin right now to solve the most serious problems on the next century's agenda, how bright can the future be? How can we know where to begin unless we first find ways to establish clear, specific goals along the path of global progress?

Report by Rushworth M. Kidder *Illustrations by David Suter*

AWARD OF EXCELLENCE

REPRINTS

The Christian Science Monitor

Designer

Robin Jareaux

Illustrator

David Suter

gaged in because of the promise of future profit – and when the promise of future profit is low because the prices of fuel are low, we have no incentive to do the R&D."

Despite increasing global interdependence and an increasing recognition that environmental problems transcend national boundaries, however, most environmental decisions are still made by individual nations. "We do not have institutional forums appropriate to this increasingly interdependent world," says former World Bank president Robert McNamara, who calls for a strengthening of such institutions as the United Nations Environment Program.

That will not be easy. "There will clearly be enormous conflicts about whose rights and whose responsibilities are going to be put in," says Radcliffe College president Matina Horner. She sees a need for "an interdependent arena" that could "redefine rights and responsibilities and the appropriate balance between them."

On one point, however, most observers agree: There is a sense of urgency about the problem. No longer does humanity have the luxury of waiting until the causes of environmental degradation are wholly understood. "If you wait until causality is established," quips Harvard University sociologist Amitai Etzioni, "we will be dead – environmentally and otherwise."

Instead, says Mr. McNamara, we need to "buy insurance" against "potentially irreversible" damage to the environment – even though we may not have established the ultimate cause of the problem.

At the same time, says former Colorado Gov. Richard Lamm, the problems chosen for attack must be the most pressing ones – and not simply the ones easiest to identify. Otherwise environmental policy misses the mark – becoming, he says, "like looking for your keys under the lamppost even though that isn't where you lost them, because that's where the light is."

Whatever efforts are taken, however, many observers see potential benefits for global interdependence.

"Maybe," concludes Joan Abrahamson, a lawyer and community activist, "the identification of the common threat to the world through the environment is another way to unify us – as sad as that is. Maybe by developing appropriate technology to combat this threat, we can learn how to do cooperative problem solving that might even be related to security issues and other issues that face us." ■

2

THE NORTH-SOUTH AFFLUENCE GAP

CONFERENCE STATEMENT:

THE PROBLEM: Per capita gross national product (GNP) has been the traditional means of measuring national progress. The goal of raising per capita GNP has guided international development programs. Such programs have failed. The gap between rich and poor countries has grown, and within many countries the gap between rich and poor groups has widened. Absolute poverty has increased.

Development efforts can be refocused to address human well-being more directly. Data increasingly available can be used to provide more useful measuring criteria. These must include clear, easily understood descriptions of the human condition so that programs can be designed and improvement in the human condition can be easily assessed and compared from nation to nation.

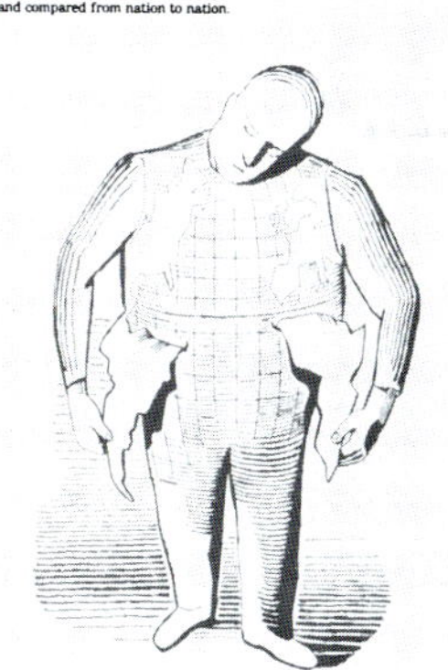

GLOBAL economic development simply isn't working. That's a stark assessment. But that's where Rodrigo Botero begins his analysis of the yawning gulf that separates the wealthy, consumer-oriented industrial nations from the impoverished, developing nations.

"If I were to make one recommendation for the the year 2000," says Mr. Botero, a journalist, author, and former finance minister of Colombia, "it would be simply to drop the goal of closing the gap – understood as it has been understood in the past 30 years."

That last phrase is crucial. Botero wants the gap closed. He's not arguing for the status quo. Nor is he calling for "zero growth" economies. Instead, he's seeking a new method of measurement.

Traditionally, the gap between North and South, the developed and the developing world, has been measured in a number of ways. The commonest is by charting gross national product (GNP) per capita. This measure shows the breadth of the gap in no uncertain terms: According to World Bank figures for 1985, the United States has a GNP per capita of $16,690, while Ethiopia (for example) has $110.

But there are other ways to assess the differences in well-being among the world's nations:

- Population. In 1950, one-third of the world's people lived in industrialized nations. By the early decades of the 21st century, that number will be less than one-sixth, as population pressures intensify in the developing world.
- Age. In the large group of developing nations that lie within the tropics, says Peter Raven of the Missouri Botanical Garden, an average of 40 percent of the population is under 15. The corresponding figure for industrial nations: 22 percent. Result: a built-in certainty of much more rapid growth rates in the tropics, as this young population reaches child-bearing age.
- Poverty. The World Bank estimates that about 40 percent of the 2.7 billion people in tropical and subtropical regions outside China live in absolute poverty – unable to count on adequate food, clothing, and shelter from day to day. In those regions, according to UNICEF, more than 14 million children under age 5 starve to death or die of disease each year.
- Delivery of services. Despite some cases of positive rates of growth in per capita income, many countries are falling behind in meeting the demand for clean water, adequate nutrition, education, medical services, and transportation and communication. Fewer and fewer children are going to school in Nigeria, reports Gen. Olusegun Obasanjo, that country's former head of state. "More people are not able to go to hospital because there are no facilities, no drugs, in the hospital," he says. "All these things are going down, and then we are told that GNP is going up."

That point is an example of what Botero calls "an idea that led us in the wrong direction" – the idea that the growth of per capita GNP measures real development.

For the last four decades, he says, the industrial world's answer to the challenges of global development has been the same: money. "Well-intentioned, intelligent people looked at the [developing] world and said, 'If the conditions are set whereby they're supplied with the necessary capital, then the rest will follow.' " As a result, he notes, a developing nation's progress was usually measured by charting per capita GNP.

The result has been bitter disappointment on the part of many developing nations – not simply because their lot has not improved, but because the promised goal of narrowing the differences in income among the world's people appears unreachable.

If GNP is the only measure of progress, says former World Bank president Robert McNamara, "it's absolutely impossible – mathematically and economically – to significantly close the gap [for most nations] within the next 50 years. There's no way."

Estimates based on World Bank figures confirm his point: If current rates of growth continue, the closing of the income gap with the industrial nations would take Thailand 365 years, China 2,900 years, and Mauritania 3,224 years.

Yet there are bright spots in the picture. In China, Sri Lanka, and the Indian state of Kerala, for example, per capita GNP is still low by Western standards. But other indicators – infant mortality, life expectancy, literacy, nutrition, employment, numbers living in poverty – show real progress.

Such indicators, in fact, may provide sounder measures of a developing nation's progress than per capita GNP. They chart what Botero calls "levels of human welfare, levels of well-being, that are relatively simple [and] not necessarily ethnocentric – [in that] they don't necessarily imply the values of one society."

For many developing nations, that centuries-old question of values remains a crucial one. The very kind of development that could lift them out of poverty might also destroy their cultures and traditions. Nazir Ahmad, a graduate student from Bangladesh, warns against "an element of interventionism" that comes when development projects bring Western values with them. "Maybe we need to create a little bit more isolationism in the West – to give us breathing room," he says.

Filmmaker Vineet Narain agrees. "The focus of our attention should be human," he says. It should center on the people themselves – "their welfare, their pleasure, their joy, and their spiritual and mental development. So far, it seems that most of the attention within the West has been on improving the material lot," under the mistaken assumption that "this increases human welfare and joy." What is needed, he says, is "to restore people's faith in things which are traditional."

Kenyan Patrick Mungai notes the bad impression left by cash-heavy development projects that failed. "We have in the third-world countries what are now popularly called 'white elephant projects' – projects that have been financed by Western donors, where a lot of money has been poured in, but that can't function."

All of which supports the case for measuring progress by something more meaningful than income. "Lowering the infant mortality rate," says Botero, "means much more to the ordinary man and woman of a developing country than obtaining an X percentage of growth in the GNP per capita, which to the majority of [those] people is an absolutely abstract and mysterious concept."

But there is another important reason for changing the way the gap is measured: Income figures can distort the overall condition of a nation. A small country where the majority lives in poverty, but where a thin layer at the top possesses extravagant wealth, may show a high per-capita income. But that, says Botero, "does not necessarily mean development."

"The $12,000 of income per capita of Saudi Arabia does not mean that Saudi Arabia's a developed country," he adds by way of example, noting that Saudi levels of literacy, infant mortality, and life expectancy are still well below the Western standards.

The issue, then, is not one of *total* benefit as much as *distribution* of that benefit across the entire society. When a country's progress is measured by something other than wealth, the results cannot mask a lack of distribution.

"You cannot lower the infant mortality rate," says Botero, "unless you offer to *all* of the population a minimum of medical service – instead of offering it to the 10 percent wealthy urban elite. You cannot achieve 70 years of life expectancy at birth unless you extend to *all* of your population, to all social classes, minimum conditions of hygiene, nutrition, education, and literacy."

Zhang Yi, from the Institute of American Studies in Beijing, agrees – although he notes that the issue of distribution applies differently to different nations. "For some countries," he says, "where there is a high degree of wealth polarization, there should be an effort to redistribute the wealth. But in countries where there is too much equality – which I think there is in China – there should be more stratification, there should be people who should be richer."

He also raises an issue of high concern to those seeing new measurements: whether the developing nations will embrace a different

RODRIGO BOTERO
Colombia

'Lowering the infant mortality rate means much more to the ordinary man and woman of a developing country than obtaining an X percentage of growth in the GNP per capita.'

KATHARINE WHITEHORN
Britain

'We are trying to look for something which you can measure – and most of the things that matter cannot be measured. The reason we've grasped GNP is because it's so easy to measure.'

CONFERENCE STATEMENT:

ACHIEVABLE GOALS *for the year* 2 0 0 0

While each nation must set its own goals, a developing country that achieves the following will have closed the gap with the developed world in satisfying basic needs:

- An infant mortality rate of less than 25 deaths per thousand live births.
- A population growth rate of less than 1 percent per year.
- An adult literacy rate of 85 percent.
- Life expectancy of 70 years.
- Meaningful employment of the greatest number possible.

HOW *it could be done:*

- Redirect the development strategies of the developing countries, as well as the policies of the bilateral and multilateral development institutions, away from primary reliance on economic factors.
- Design, implement, and track development programs using these new criteria.
- Continue to emphasize the obligations of the developed nations to help improve economic growth and overall economic performance in the developing countries. Each nation's internal development effort, as well as cooperative international efforts, should target fulfillment of the non-economic goals.
- Recognize that this new way of thinking about development will require a major effort on the part of developing countries, as well as significant increases in and transfers of resources from the developed countries.

The Christian Science Monitor B6

The Christian Science Monitor B7

Chapter 7

Magazines: rewards for new tricks (but where's the headline?)

It's Christmas morning. Packages, wrapping paper, and — something's a little strange here — dog collars are strewn about the room. Amid the clutter sits a dog, relaxing in an easy chair next to the Christmas tree.

"Oh great," the mutt growls, opening the last package, "another collar."

The illustration is funny, the style familiar. Gary Larson's offbeat schtick never fails to amuse or amaze on the comics page.

Comics page?

The New York Times doesn't have a comics page. You know the *New York Times*. Staid. Respected. Inscrutable. Humorless. Gray.

So what's a color cartoon doing on the cover of the Sunday magazine?

Making readers laugh.

Inviting them to read.

Making their day.

Larson's cartoon also made the day of judges in the magazine category. They awarded it a silver medal.

A silver medal for a cartoon? Where's the story? Where's the photo? Where's the graphic? Where's the design? WHERE'S THE HEADLINE?

So many entries, so few awards. Three hundred newspapers submit their best work — only to be overshadowed by a cartoon.

"How are we going to explain this to the *words* people?" asked features judge David Griffin.

For starters, tell them to look closely at *The New York Times*, *The Boston Globe* and *The Washington Post* magazines. They'll recognize the qualities in design that also distinguish good reporting: originality, content, editing and execution.

Maybe they won't notice the headline. ...

SILVER

OVERALL MAGAZINE DESIGN

Toronto Magazine,
Toronto Globe and Mail

Designer
Fernanda Pisani
Illustrator
Frank Viva
Photographers
Johnny Eisen, Chris Nicholls
Art Director
Lindsay Beaudry

AWARD OF EXCELLENCE

OVERALL MAGAZINE DESIGN

The Washington Post Magazine

Utterly Humiliated On National TV

My kids talked me into going on 'Jeopardy!' My ego will never be the same

By PETER PERL
Illustrations by STEVEN GUARNACCIA

I AM NOT QUITE SURE WHEN THE MADNESS began—the "Jeopardy!" Madness. I suppose I should have recognized the signs of it—in the puzzled faces of those around me, in the awkward reactions of my close friends who humored me, in the eyes of my wife and sons. But by the time I really tried to get a grip on myself, by the time I actually realized what had happened to my mind, it was too late. I was lost. A once-vibrant human brain had been transformed into something strange, something compulsive, something you wouldn't necessarily want to go fishing with or take to a movie.

Looking back on it now, sure, it's easy to pinpoint a few of the moments when it was clear that I was losing my grasp on reality. Like when I mumbled "What is Tegucigalpa?" to myself. Or when

10 THE WASHINGTON POST MAGAZINE AP PHOTOGRAPH

AWARD OF EXCELLENCE
OVERALL MAGAZINE DESIGN
The Washington Post Magazine
Designers
Brian Noyes, Michael Walsh, Richard Baker
Illustrators
Various
Photographers
Various
Art Director
Brian Noyes
Photo Editor
Molly Roberts

Continued from page 159

SHEAR & SOLITUDE

PHOTOGRAPHY BY CHARLES FOX

They seem a perfect complement to the pastoral splendor of Maine's offshore islands. To see them shrouded in fog, grazing on a granite-spined promontory, framed by towering pines, high above the crashing surf, is to experience a moment of natural beauty almost religious in its intensity. There was a time, back in the last century, when as many as 20,000 sheep wandered the rocky heaths of these islands, and Maine wool was especially prized for its quality. But as New England agriculture began to falter, the sheep-raising industry went the way of the Yankee clipper.

Today, on several of Maine's 3,000 islands, the sheep are back. About 2½ miles off the coast of the Down East town of South Addison, for example, shepherd Jenny Cirone, 76, a lighthouse keeper's daughter, maintains a flock of about 160 sheep on two islands. From long experience, she knows that an island is an ideal grazing ground: no expensive fencing, a minimum of predatory animals such as dogs and coyotes, plenty of forage during winter because of the moderating influence of the sea. Since the sheep feed off the island grass, their fleece is especially clean, with no interwoven hay or chaff, and while the wool is a little coarser, it is excellent for outer wear.

And if the islands are good for sheep, the sheep are good for the islands. Properly managed, the animals can turn overgrown woodland into open meadow, creating more ecologically varied open space and making the Maine coast even more spectacular.

continued on next page

CHARLES FOX is an Inquirer staff photographer.

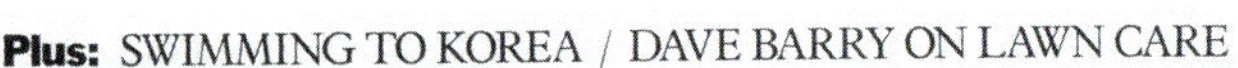

Plus: SWIMMING TO KOREA / DAVE BARRY ON LAWN CARE

AUGUST 7, 1988
The Philadelphia Inquirer Magazine
INQUIRER

TROUBLE IN PARADISE

The endless war that is destroying Sri Lanka.

Text by C.S. Manegold
Photography by Michael S. Wirtz

AWARD OF EXCELLENCE
OVERALL MAGAZINE DESIGN
The Philadelphia Inquirer Magazine
Designer
Bert Fox
Art Director
David Griffin
Photo Editors
Bert Fox, Tom Gralish

AWARD OF EXCELLENCE

OVERALL MAGAZINE DESIGN

A-Magasinet, Aftenposten
Oslo, Norway

Designers
Nina Holmsen, B. Johannessen, J. Mikalsen, H. B. Bang Ellingsen, A. Beu

Art Director
Ashley Booth

Utsynet: Skotsk i farve og fasong — fjell og daler kledt i grønt, et intenst grønnsvær som glinser i soldisen.

Og så navnene, på skiltene langs veien: Edinburgh, Balmoral, Hamilton, Blairlomond . . .

Sjåføren ler godt, han er en livat kar: — Vi sier som så: Gi en skotte bind for øynene og slipp ham løs her oppe. Da vil han tro han er hjemme i Skottland!

Langt fra sannheten ville *det* være. Vi er i høylandet — telandet — i det indre av Sri Lanka, verdens største te-eksportør. Ceylon-teens rike.

Veien slynger og slanger seg, flankert av te-terrasser. Plantasjene brer ut sitt grønne teppe oppover dalsidene, opp til samme høyde som vår hjemlige Galdhøpiggen — et nettoareal av tebusker større enn Vestfold fylke.

Skottene var te-pionérene. Men plantasjeskiltene har også engelske navn, mange med den samme aristokratiske slengen: Sandringham, Palmerston, Clarendon . . . Somerset — det er hit vi skal.

«Big Boss» prøvesmaker dagens vare — alle koppene. Tesmaking er like finjustert som vinsmaking.

TE — en drikk med stil

Tekst og foto: Gunnar Filseth

Et lite stykke England eksportert til det indre av Sri Lanka. Der man holder på tradisjonene. Og dyrker verdens mest eksklusive te.

— Avkolonialisere navnene? Nei, hvorfor det? De har med tradisjon å gjøre, og i denne bransjen holder vi på tradisjonene. Te og tradisjon, ja, de tingene hører jo sammen . . . Pran Dias snakker, bestyreren på Somerset Estate, grunnlagt i 1862. En plantasje av normalstørrelse: Dias råder over 3850 dekar, har 1262 på lønningslisten. Årsproduksjon: 550 000 kilo *high-grown* te, fineste høylandskvalitet. Over 99 prosent til eksport.

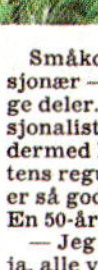

Småkonge og statsfunksjonær — Pran Dias er begge deler. Plantasjen ble nasjonalistert for 13 år siden; dermed havnet han på statens regulativ. Men makten er så godt som ubeskåret. En 50-åring med selvtillit.

— Jeg er tradisjonalist, ja, alle vi *planters* (bestyrere) er det . . . Vi har en paternalistisk tradisjon her oppe. Arbeiderne ser opp til oss som farsskikkelser . . .

Periya Dorai — «Big Boss». Slik tituleres han av sine 1262 undersåtter, akkurat som før i tiden. Som nestsjef på plantasjen har han en yngre mann, «Small Boss». De to «bosser» er hele bedriftsledelsen.

— Her er jeg *raj* (konge), sier han (en smule selvironisk?), men kall meg gjerne altmuligmann. Jeg må ha oppsyn med alt, alt som rører seg. Ja, det er jeg som skriver fødselsattesten når noen blir født her på godset. Dødsattestene også.

Hva tjener «Big Boss»? Vel 10 000 rupier i månedsgasje. Ikke så mye i norske penger, cirka 2200 kroner, dog 15 ganger mer enn en arbeider . . . Vi sitter på verandaen i det som er frynsegode nr. 1: bungalowen i britisk kolonistil, rammet inn av myke gressplener, roser, staudebed. Engelskmennene hadde for vane å ta godt i: 15 rom og en ballsal attpåtil. Og så flust med tjenerskap for å holde styr på herligheten: kokk, to boy'er, gartner, vaktmann, sjåfør . . .

Herfra har han panoramautsikt over sitt rike, og flere av naborikene med. Eller *estates*, som plantasjene kalles her.

Te, bare te, så langt øyet rekker — et hav av grønn frodighet som bølger omkring oss. Og hist og her ligger *factories* — te-fabrikkene. Av bare bølgeblikk — som skinnende hvite fartøyer i tehavet.

Vi drar til den nærmeste. Tid for prøvesmaking av dagfersk vare. →

To blader og en knopp . . . Livets refreng for Sunitra, teplukkerske med rappe fingre.

20 | 21

AWARD OF EXCELLENCE
MAGAZINE SPECIAL SECTION
The Boston Globe
Designer
James Pavlovich
Illustrators
Karen Barbour and Others
Photographers
Various
Art Director
Holly Nixholm

AWARD OF EXCELLENCE
MAGAZINE SPECIAL SECTION
The New York Times
Designer
Richard Weigand
Cover Art
Dennis Ziemienski
Art Director
Richard Weigand

AWARD OF EXCELLENCE
MAGAZINE SPECIAL SECTION
The Boston Globe
Designer
Aldona Charlton
Illustrators
Various
Photographers
Various
Art Director
Holly Nixholm

AWARD OF EXCELLENCE
MAGAZINE SPECIAL SECTION
The New York Times Magazine
Designer
Nancy Kent
Cover Photo
Nora Scarlett
Art Director
Nancy Kent

luciano
SOPRANI
A FLAMING TODDY AND THE WEARING OF WOOL FROM COLLAR TO ANKLE HELP KEEP THE STYLISH MAN TOASTY, TOP LEFT. SOPRANI TOSSES TOPCOAT AND JACKET IN DIFFERENT PLAIDS OVER A STRIPED, TABBED SHIRT AND GRAY TWEED TROUSERS.

jean-paul
GAULTIER
LIGHT UP THE NIGHT IN A BROWN DOUBLE-BREASTED JACKET WITH COVERED BUTTONS, BURGUNDY FLEUR-DE-LIS SWEATER AND GRAY TROUSERS, LOWER LEFT.

ronaldus
SHAMASK
STEP INTO THE EVENING IN CLASSIC STYLE WEARING BLACK STRIPED, DOUBLE-BREASTED JACKET OVER WHITE TUXEDO SHIRT AND BLACK TROUSERS, RIGHT. BLACK PATENT LEATHER LACE-UP SHOES ARE BY STREGA.

MATSUDA
AN UPDATED FORMAL LOOK IS HIGHLIGHTED BY EMBROIDERED BLACK EVENING JACKET AND EMBROIDERED SHIRT, WORN WITH BLACK TROUSERS AND STREGA'S VELVET EVENING SLIPPERS, FAR RIGHT.

AWARD OF EXCELLENCE
MAGAZINE SPECIAL SECTION
The Philadephia Inquirer
Designer
Robin Fogel
Photographer
J. Kyle Keener
Art Director
Robin Fogel
Photo Editor
Bert Fox

AWARD OF EXCELLENCE
MAGAZINE SPECIAL SECTION
The Washington Post Magazine
Designers
Brian Noyes, Michael Walsh, Richard Baker
Art Director
Brian Noyes
Photo Editor
Molly Roberts

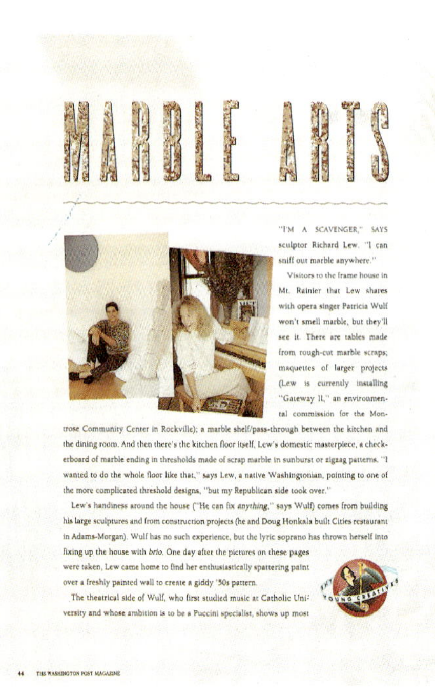

MARBLE ARTS

"I'M A SCAVENGER," SAYS sculptor Richard Lew. "I can sniff out marble anywhere."

Visitors to the frame house in Mt. Rainier that Lew shares with opera singer Patricia Wulf won't smell marble, but they'll see it. There are tables made from rough-cut marble scraps; maquettes of larger projects (Lew is currently installing "Gateway II," an environmental commission for the Montrose Community Center in Rockville); a marble shelf/pass-through between the kitchen and the dining room. And then there's the kitchen floor itself, Lew's domestic masterpiece, a checkerboard of marble ending in thresholds made of scrap marble in sunburst or zigzag patterns. "I wanted to do the whole floor like that," says Lew, a native Washingtonian, pointing to one of the more complicated threshold designs, "but my Republican side took over."

Lew's handiness around the house ("He can fix *anything*," says Wulf) comes from building his large sculptures and from construction projects (he and Doug Honkala built Cities restaurant in Adams-Morgan). Wulf has no such experience, but the lyric soprano has thrown herself into fixing up the house with *brio*. One day after the pictures on these pages were taken, Lew came home to find her enthusiastically spattering paint over a freshly painted wall to create a giddy '50s pattern.

The theatrical side of Wulf, who first studied music at Catholic University and whose ambition is to be a Puccini specialist, shows up most

44 THE WASHINGTON POST MAGAZINE

OPPOSITE PAGE: Richard Lew sits next to one of his sculptures, "The Four Horsemen of Palenque." Patricia Wulf is shown in her music studio. The lyric soprano sang her first professional role in June as Mimi in the Prince George's Opera Company production of "La Bohème." THIS PAGE: The kitchen combines Lew's construction skills and Wulf's flea-market savvy.

THE NEW SEASON

THE NEW YORK TIMES MAGAZINE/PART 2
SEPTEMBER 11, 1988

COVER BY AL HIRSCHFELD

Editor
MICHAEL J. LEAHY
Deputy Editor
JODY ALESANDRO
Art Director
DAVID BARNETT
Photo Editor
HADAS DEMBO

4 THE NEW SEASON

SILVER AWARD
MAGAZINE SPECIAL SECTION
The New York Times Magazine
Designer
David Barnett
Illustrator
Al Hirschfeld
Art Director
David Barnett

AWARD OF EXCELLENCE
MAGAZINE COVER DESIGN
BLACK AND WHITE
The Boston Globe Magazine
Designer
Lucy Bartholomay
Art Director
Lucy Bartholomay

The Boston Globe Magazine
SEPTEMBER 4, 1988

DEATH OF A FAMILY

MARTIN GAFFNEY, MOURNING HIS WIFE AND YOUNG SON, IS LIVING UNDER A DEATH SENTENCE HIMSELF. ONLY HIS DAUGHTER HAS BEEN SPARED THE A I D S VIRUS. NOW THE MARINE CORPS OFFICER HAS BUT TWO DESIRES: TO PROVIDE FOR HIS DAUGHTER'S FUTURE AND TO EXTRACT AN APOLOGY FROM THE US GOVERNMENT, WHICH HE ACCUSES OF DESTROYING HIS FAMILY.

BY DANIEL GOLDEN

SILVER AWARD
MAGAZINE COVER DESIGN
TWO OR MORE COLORS
A-Magasinet, Aftenposten
Oslo, Norway
Designer
Ashley Booth
Art Director
Ashley Booth

AWARD OF EXCELLENCE
MAGAZINE COVER DESIGN
TWO OR MORE COLORS
Computerworld
Designer
Nancy Kowal
Illustrator
Seymour Chwast
Art Director
Nancy Kowal

AWARD OF EXCELLENCE
MAGAZINE COVER DESIGN
TWO OR MORE COLORS
Detroit Free Press Magazine
Designer
Patrick Mitchell
Photographer
Tony Spina
Art Director
Patrick Mitchell

AWARD OF EXCELLENCE
MAGAZINE COVER DESIGN
TWO OR MORE COLORS
San Jose Mercury News, West Magazine
Designer
David Armario
Illustrator
Elwood Smith
Art Director
David Armario

SILVER AWARD
MAGAZINE COVER DESIGN
TWO OR MORE COLORS
The Boston Globe Magazine
Designer
Lucy Bartholomay
Illustrator
Gary Baseman
Art Director
Lucy Bartholomay

AWARD OF EXCELLENCE
MAGAZINE COVER DESIGN
TWO OR MORE COLORS
Los Angeles Times Magazine
Designer
Donald Burgess
Photographer
George Rose
Art Director
Donald Burgess

AWARD OF EXCELLENCE
MAGAZINE COVER DESIGN
TWO OR MORE COLORS
The Boston Globe Magazine
Designer
Lucy Bartholomay
Art Director
Lucy Bartholomay

AWARD OF EXCELLENCE
MAGAZINE COVER DESIGN
TWO OR MORE COLORS
The Baltimore Sun
Designer
Donna Crivello
Illustrator
Terry Allen
Art Director
Donna Crivello

AWARD OF EXCELLENCE
MAGAZINE COVER DESIGN
TWO OR MORE COLORS
The New York Times
Designer
Justine Strasberg
Photographer
Jeanne Strongin
Art Director
Janet Froelich
Photo Editor
Kathy Ryan

AWARD OF EXCELLENCE
MAGAZINE COVER DESIGN
TWO OR MORE COLORS
The New York Times Magazine
Illustrator
Wiktor Sadowski
Designer
Janet Froelich
Art Director
Janet Froelich

AWARD OF EXCELLENCE
MAGAZINE COVER DESIGN
TWO OR MORE COLORS
The Washington Post Magazine
Designer
Brian Noyes
Photographer
Brian Smale
Art Director
Brian Noyes
Photo Editor
Molly Roberts

SILVER AWARD
MAGAZINE COVER DESIGN
TWO OR MORE COLORS
The New York Times Magazine
Illustrator
Gary Larson
Designer
Janet Froelich
Art Director
Janet Froelich

THE MENSWEAR LOOK

Hot

What better way to chase the winter chill than stepping into a suit that says "sizzle!"

Looking to heat up your wardrobe? Try Ronaldus Shamask's fire-engine-red blazer.

For evening go for icy heat with Philadelphia designer Nathan Townsend's sleek tuxedo of ebony Chinese silk. Or designer Larnell Baldwin's black wool tuxedo.

The silhouette for the fall calls for a tapered look; jackets with padded shoulders, longer lapels and nipped in at the waist. Look for single-breasted suits with three buttons or double-breasted with six.

For shirts — again, the tapered look is preferred.

The trousers, pleated, of course, are slightly fuller from the thigh down than last year's, sometimes tapered at the ankle.

Lace those pants with a razor-thin reptile-skin belt and you're set to face the frosty fall with style.

ronaldus SHAMASK

WARM UP THE WINTER WITH A RED-HOT BLAZER, COMPLEMENTED BY BLACK-AND-WHITE STRIPED SHIRT, DARK STRIPED TIE AND CHARCOAL PANTS.

AWARD OF EXCELLENCE
MAGAZINE DESIGN
TWO OR MORE PAGES
The Philadelphia Inquirer
Designer
Robin Fogel
Photographer
J. Kyle Keener
Picture Editor
Bert Fox
Art Director
Robin Fogel

THE COLORS OF

Fall

COLOR is what you see first in virtually every New York and Paris designer's ready-to-wear collection for fall. REAL COLOR. Hot, bright, pure color borrowed from a paint box or a grocer's display of tropical fruits. Mango, lime, tangerine, hot pink, purple, grass green, bright blue, and lots and lots of strong, true red.

This is not to say that black has disappeared from the scene. In fact, one way to handle fall's brights is to add a shot of strong, enlivening color to a background of basic black — the way Norma Kamali puts her short scarlet swing jacket over all-black, or Stephen Sprouse adds a shot of neon green to a high-rise black skirt, black stockings, black shoes. One bright new piece — an emerald-green sweater or a shocking-pink blazer — can update all the black clothes in your closet the same way.

All-one-color is another workable approach: Add red to red to more red, the way Michael Kors tops off his red wide-legged jersey jumpsuit with a curly red Mongolian lamb jacket, the way Marc Jacobs puts hot-pink pants and a pink halter under a hot-pink jacket — punctuated with black buttons a la Norman Norell.

IT'S GOING TO BE A COLOR-COATED AUTUMN, WITH BRIGHT OUTER WEAR LIKE PATRICIA CLYNE'S ORANGE DOUBLE-BREASTED WOOL REEFER TOSSED OVER HER CHARCOAL PANTS AND CREWNECK TOP.

FASHION 9

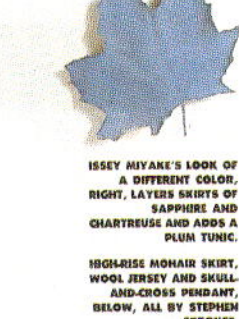

ISSEY MIYAKE'S LOOK OF A DIFFERENT COLOR, RIGHT, LAYERS SKIRTS OF SAPPHIRE AND CHARTREUSE AND ADDS A PLUM TUNIC.

HIGH-RISE MOHAIR SKIRT, WOOL JERSEY AND SKULL-AND-CROSS PENDANT, BELOW, ALL BY STEPHEN SPROUSE.

Mizrahi proved equally adept at still another approach to real color: using several at once — say, a bright-pink coat over a yellow jumpsuit. And he wasn't the only one. Issey Miyake's plum-colored turtleneck layered over two uneven-hemmed skirts of different lengths and hues — one sapphire-blue, one chartreuse — is another example of the toss-on-a-few-colors-and-see-what-happens school.

COLORS

12 September 11, 1988

AWARD OF EXCELLENCE
MAGAZINE DESIGN
TWO OR MORE PAGES
The Philadelphia Inquirer
Designer
Robin Fogel
Photographer
J. Kyle Keener
Picture Editor
Bert Fox
Art Director
Robin Fogel

AWARD OF EXCELLENCE
MAGAZINE DESIGN
TWO OR MORE PAGES
The New York Times Magazine
Designer
Janet Froelich
Photographer
Nathan Farb
Photo Editor
Kathy Ryan
Art Director
Janet Froelich

UP FROM THE ASHES

PHOTOGRAPHS BY NATHAN FARB

TEXT BY ANDREW H. MALCOLM

ONCE,

RIVER BLINDNESS

CONQUERING AN ANCIENT SCOURGE

By Erik Eckholm

ON THIS BRIGHT NOVEMBER morning the mood is anything but gloomy in Sikoroni, Mali, a mud-hut village of the vast West African savanna. The summer rains were generous for the first time in years, and today 10-foot sorghum stalks are bowed by heavy heads of grain. True to protocol, the chief of this village of 400 has called in the elders to exchange ceremonial words with arriving visitors. As boys run to fetch them, we wait to the quotidian music of rural Africa: the ancient booming cadence of women pounding grain, the laughs and cries of children and the discordant crows of wandering roosters. The women's extravagant cotton prints are welcome flares of color against the drab landscape.

Only as the men begin trickling in does Sikoroni's awful curse become apparent. One man, then another and another, is led to the meeting place by a small boy who holds one end of the elder's walking stick. The men, most of them in their fifties or sixties, are the picture of dignity in their long loose tunics and Muslim skullcaps. But as they stumble into place under the veranda, I make the astonishing count: of the 14 men here, a dozen have lifeless scarred-over eyes.

They are victims of onchocerciasis — river blindness, so named because the tiny black flies that spread the pernicious disease breed in fast-moving water. An estimated 18 million people in Africa and parts of Latin America and the Middle East carry in their bodies the parasitic worms that cause river blindness, according to the World Health Organization. Many suffer agonizing itching and disfigurement of the skin. More than 300,000 have been blinded.

The West African environment inflicts many miseries on its rural poor, which a world full of medical miracles has done little to alleviate. Neglect, bureaucracy, a paucity of funds can all be blamed. But in this case — the centuries-old torment of river blindness — developments have world health authorities cheering. In what will surely rank as one of the century's great medical triumphs, a dreadful scourge is coming under control.

Two remarkable developments have loosened the stranglehold of the disease. The first is a cooperative international effort, carried out in the face of enormous logistical obstacles for a decade and a half, to suppress the insect that spreads the worm. The Onchocerciasis Control Program, run by the World Health Organization, has strategically applied insecticides to curb the disease in large areas of West Africa.

And now those fighting river blindness have been handed an unexpected new weapon: a safe, effective drug. Ivermectin, developed in the 1970's for use against livestock parasites, has been shown in a swift series of human trials in the 1980's to be something doctors had scarcely dared hope for. Taken, in pill form, as seldom as once a year, it protects infected people

A dose of ivermectin, Merck's surprisingly effective new drug against river blindness, being distributed in Guinea. More than 300,000 people in West Africa have been blinded by the disease, including this man from Guinea, on the facing page.

Erik Eckholm is science and health editor of The New York Times.

PHOTOGRAPHS BY EUGENE RICHARDS

20

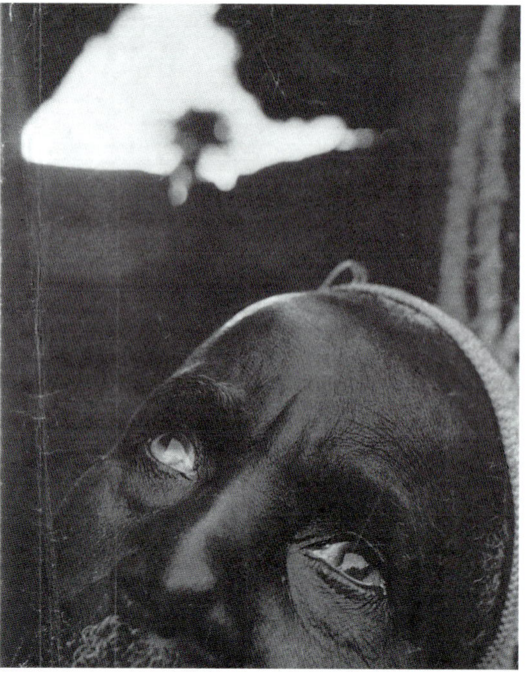

SILVER AWARD
MAGAZINE DESIGN
TWO OR MORE PAGES
The New York Times Magazine
Designers
Janet Froelich, Justine Strasberg
Photographer
Eugene Richards
Photo Editor
Kathy Ryan
Art Director
Janet Froelich

SILVER AWARDS
MAGAZINE DESIGN
TWO OR MORE PAGES
and
TYPOGRAPHY
The Washington Post Magazine
Washington, D.C.
Designer
Michael Walsh
Photographer
Charles Griffin
Photo Editer
Molly Roberts
Art Director
Brian Noyes

FASHION

at ease

By JEAN-FRANÇOIS BIZALION

Photographs by CHARLES GRIFFIN

MEN ARE KIND OF FUNNY ABOUT clothes. Sometimes the merest suggestion of "style" is enough to send them diving back into their pin stripes. But they look so great in classics that it's hard to blame them for passing their conservative instincts from father to son. Besides, calling something a classic doesn't mean it's without style or image. Some of the clothes shown here are evocative of the '30s, reminiscent of "Tennis, anyone?" and sportswear before sweat suits. One recalls boyhood as lived in the '50s. And maybe that's what men want in their clothing, after all—a kind of shorthand communication. In a language that only fathers and sons understand.

FOR SHOPPING INFORMATION, SEE PAGE 37.

THE TENNIS SWEATER, RIGHT, LOOKS AS GOOD ON TODAY'S DAD AS IT DID ON THE '30s GENERATION. AT FAR RIGHT, THE SON TEAMS A LINEN SUIT WITH HONEST-TO-GOODNESS WHITE BUCKS. OPPOSITE, A BLAST FROM THE MORE RECENT PAST—'50s-STYLE DUNGAREES AND A STRIPED POLO SHIRT.

AWARD OF EXCELLENCE
MAGAZINE DESIGN
TWO OR MORE PAGES
The Courier Journal
Louisville, Kentucky
Designer
Barbara Barry
Art Director
Barbara Barry

"Happy"?

Continued

Perhaps he was. It's instructive to recall that when the Civil Rights Act of 1964 was passed Chandler was 66 years old. The last time he held public office was in 1959, when he was governor.

In the nearly 30 years since he left office, legends clung to him the way lint collects on other mortals. He came to be regarded as the state's good-luck charm, a colorful and benign token of cantankerous cheer. It was as if, having nourished himself on his love of Kentucky for nearly 90 years, he had finally swallowed the state whole. And vice versa.

Occasionally, intemperate pronouncements would billow forth from him like the puffy captions in a comic book. His intimates — a cast of thousands — would shrug and say, "Oh, that's just Happy."

People who were not his intimates still imagined they knew him. Happy was always turning up somewhere, singing "My Old Kentucky Home." As his old political enemies died or softened, Happy seemed to be enveloped in a warm, blue, tear-shaped bubble.

He crustily resisted this characterization; it made him seem powerless. "He doesn't want to be a symbol of anything," said his wife, Mildred. "He wants to be *it*."

So perhaps he felt compelled to make his voice heard by his fellow trustees. Its raucous echo reached to every corner of the state, making him a contemporary figure again.

As in days of old, he stubbornly fought off his critics and kept his seat on the UK board. By the light of contemporary sociology (consider Al Campanis and Jimmy the Greek), this was fairly remarkable.

In light of some of the other storms Chandler had weathered, though, this one must have seemed like a day at the beach. When he sent in the National Guard to enforce school integration in 1956, the response was voluminous and venomous. His more benign critics sought his impeachment; others thought only hanging would do.

So it fell to his wife, who has been scarred, saddened and strengthened by Happy's scrapes, to put some perspective on the Zimbabwe controversy.

"This," she said feistily, "was a *nothing*-burger."

And then she added, "This came as close to breaking his heart as anything ever has."

•

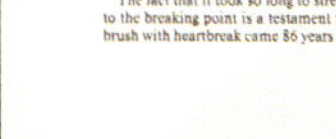

The fact that it took so long to stretch Albert Benjamin Chandler's heart to the breaking point is a testament to his legendary resilience. His first brush with heartbreak came 86 years ago. His mother, Callie, deserted him.

Continued

Below, Chandler with Virginia Gov. Thomas B. Stanley and celebrities Dean Martin and Jerry Lewis at the 1956 National Governors' Conference.

Left, 20 years after his first inauguration, Chandler was sworn in for a second term as Kentucky's governor in 1955. Above, with his wife at the 1956 inaugural ball.

Chandler, left waving his hat, campaigning as a favorite-son candidate for president at the 1956 Democratic National Convention in Chicago.

"In the nearly 30 years since he left office, legends clung to him the way lint collects on other mortals."

AWARD OF EXCELLENCE
MAGAZINE DESIGN
TWO OR MORE PAGES
The Columbus Dispatch
Columbus, Ohio
Designer
Scott Minister
Illustrator
Maurice Sendak
Writer
George Myers, Jr.
Art Director
Scott Minister

MAURICE SENDAK

Child's play is father to the man

. . . His mother called him
"WILD THING!"
and Max said
"I'LL EAT YOU UP!"
– from
Where the Wild Things Are

¶ COLOR him a lighter shade of blue. Sadness, loss and even death are as much a part of his world as laughter, Mozart and great horned beasts. So, shade his thinking a little on the frightful, fanciful side. The side where the wild things are. ¶ HE is illustrator Maurice Sendak, the nation's preeminent chronicler of childhood and its unruly, undomesticated fantasies. ¶ YOU know his characters if you've stood before a fun-house mirror and seen a stubby, short body with overly large feet and head staring back. You understand his themes first-hand if childhood is within memory's reach, because it is the childlike in us – the unknowing – that knows him best.

¶

BY GEORGE MYERS JR.

From *Where the Wild Things Are*

AWARD OF EXCELLENCE

MAGAZINE DESIGN
TWO OR MORE PAGES

The Columbus Dispatch
Columbus, Ohio

Designer
Scott Minister

Photographers
Staff

Year-End Photo Issue

As I RECALL, the picture was of some kind of a hunting dog, lying beneath some kind of a bush that was bearing some kind of berries that may well have been rare for central Ohio. ¶ THE POINT of this picture I do not remember. It had been submitted by a veteran outdoors reporter to illustrate a story he had written that might have been about hunting dogs, bushes or berries. I do remember that I looked at the photo along with several other members of the then *Dispatch* sports department, and the best anyone could come up with was: "Well, it looks like it might be some kind of dog under some kind

P H O

T O S

of bush." None of us suspected the berries. ¶ THE PHOTO was tossed aside, and somebody later used it to take a phone message. When the paper hit the streets the next day, the reporter could not hide his hurt feelings. He shook his head sadly and said, "Fellas, I can't take a better picture than that one." You could have heard a pin drop. Which is a roundabout way of saying that one person's idea of great art is another's scratch pad. Which is a roundabout way of saying that this is our annual year-end photo issue showing some of what we feel is the best work by the *Dispatch* photo department. No dogs. No bushes. No berries. Just moments that made us laugh, cry or just hold on. – *Jim Massie*

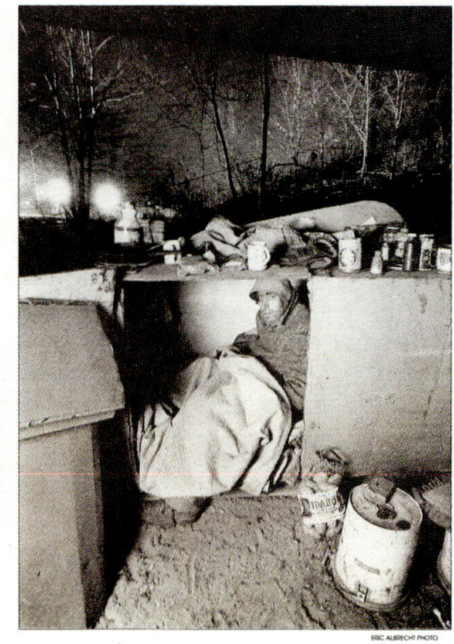

ERIC ALBRECHT PHOTO

THE ISSUE OF THE HOMELESS IN AMERICA WAS GRAPHICALLY CAPTURED ON FILM SEVERAL TIMES BY *DISPATCH* PHOTOGRAPHERS IN 1988. THERE ARE AN ESTIMATED 140,000 HOMELESS PEOPLE IN OHIO ALONE AND MORE THAN 600 IN COLUMBUS. ONE OF THOSE PEOPLE IS STEVE DEVOE, TAKING SHELTER FROM LAST JANUARY'S BITTER COLD IN A CARDBOARD BOX. THE YEAR 1989 FINDS THE PLIGHT OF THESE DISPLACED PEOPLE STILL AWAITING A SOLUTION.

Capital Magazine—Jan. 1, 1989 6

Capital Magazine—Jan. 1, 1989 7

IN ONE OF THE MOST DRAMATIC *crime stories of any year, the alleged handcuff-rapist was captured as a result of a yearlong stakeout by the mother and father of one of his victims. Robert Biddings, 34, of Columbus was apprehended by police shortly after an attempted assault on the mother. The incident occurred at the same bus stop where the woman's daughter was assaulted a year earlier. Her husband chased the assailant to his car and got the license number. Police later arrested Biddings and charged him with 102 counts of rape, kidnapping, felonious assault and aggravated robbery, involving 30 victims ages 6 to 46 since 1984. The family, which has remained anonymous, met the press at a news conference. The three were silhouetted against a screen during the interview, and their names not revealed. The daughter held the hand of Det. James Demming of the sexual abuse squad.*

MIKE MUNDEN PHOTO

RAMON OWENS PHOTO

AFTER A YEARLONG SEARCH, *Ronald Etheridge, 45, was hired in April to be the 15th superintendent of Columbus Public Schools. Etheridge, seen jogging past Central High School, found the disposal of this school property one of the major issues facing him and the school board when he took the job. The 17.5-acre site eventually was sold to the city for $15 million.*

TOM DODGE PHOTO

JEFF HINCKLEY PHOTO

AT 9:05 P.M. ON MAY 28, *the strains of* Shine On You Crazy Diamond *emanated from a stage in Ohio Stadium, and 64,000 fans celebrated the arrival of the rock superstar band Pink Floyd. It was the first rock concert in the 66-year-old stadium's history and was termed a success by the university, the police and, most of all, the fans. It may lead to more.*

THE 1988 PRESIDENTIAL CAMPAIGN *ran hot and heavy in Ohio. It started with a July 28 visit to Cleveland by Democratic candidate Michael Dukakis; and it didn't end until the day before the election, when both Dukakis and his Republican counterpart, Vice President George Bush, made last-ditch stops. In all, the candidates crisscrossed Ohio 27 times in quest of the state's 23 electoral votes. Bush and his running mate, Indiana Sen. Dan Quayle, stumped through Ohio the most – 15 times. Quayle demonstrated a vintage political move on Oct. 20 when he picked 4-month-old Joseph Lavelle out of the crowd in Reynoldsburg and held him up to the cameras. Joseph is the son of Kimberly Lavelle of Columbus.*

A PAIR OF GOLDEN MONKEYS *began the spring by captivating audiences at the Columbus Zoo. The rare monkeys, on loan from the People's Republic of China at a cost of $40,000, went on display May 4 for 100 days. Zoo attendance was up for the first two months of their visit, but the summer drought kept crowds down in July and August. In the end, the zoo broke even on the venture.*

Capital Magazine—Jan. 1, 1989 14

Capital Magazine—Jan. 1, 1989 15

FRIDAY, MAY 13, 1988 — SPENDING IT — BORN TO SHOP — THE WALL STREET JOURNAL

GREAT MOMENTS IN SHOPPING

Celebrating some deals–good, bad and otherwise–that didn't get away

By MARIA BRADING

There is run-of-the-mill spending, and then there is SPENDING: the two-handed, world-class, Hall-of-Fame-caliber conspicuous consumption that involves the purchase of luxury goods for sums that would keep a mid-sized army in the field for a month or two. Participants often have needlework declarations over the hearth saying things like: "Money is the root of all evil, and everyone needs roots." Some Great Moments in Spending:

Playtime

Real Estate

Dogdom

Dressing Up

Getting Around

AWARD OF EXCELLENCE

MAGAZINE DESIGN
SINGLE PAGE

The Wall Street Journal
New York

Designer
Joe Dizney

Illustrator
Peter Kuper

Design Director
Greg Leeds

Art Director
Joe Dizney

AWARD OF EXCELLENCE
MAGAZINE DESIGN
TWO OR MORE PAGES
The Boston Globe Magazine
Designer
Lucy Bartholomay
Photographer
Michele Clement Studio
Art Director
Lucy Bartholomay

Kronos QUARTET

By Fred Kaplan

SPINNING AND TWISTING THE WORLD OF MUSIC INTO NEW ORBITS

They amble onto stage, decked in spandex jackets, leather suits, medieval gowns, spike hairdos, anything but standard-commission string-quartet tux and bow tie. Their audiences, a mix of devoted fans and curious first-timers, applaud wildly or nervously. The players sit down, flex their bows, and dive into a concert that might include anything from Bela Bartok's Fourth Quartet to Alfred Schnittke's Third to Thelonious Monk's "Round Midnight" or Ornette Coleman's "Lonely Woman" to some newly commissioned work by Terry Riley, Astor Piazzolla, or such otherwise obscure composers as Kevin Volans, Thomas Oboe Lee, Ben Johnston, or Jon Hassell.

The players are the Kronos Quartet, and for the past few years they have been spinning and twisting the world of classical music into more orbits than anyone previously knew existed.

They play nothing but 20th-century music, usually a box-office nightmare for concert-hall bookers. But Kronos dates consistently sell out, and their last two albums — ***Kronos Quartet*** and ***White Man Sleeps*** (both on Elektra/Nonesuch) — stayed on ***Billboard***'s charts for nearly a year and peaked well inside the top 10. Moreover, they have earned nearly unanimous plaudits from classical-music critics, possibly a first for post-modernism.

David Harrington, Kronos' first violinist, says people often ask him why the group never plays Mozart, Schubert, Brahms, Ravel, the classics. "The only thing I can think of to say to that is: Would anyone ask the Beastie Boys to sing Stephen Foster?

From left, David Harrington, Joan Jeanrenaud, John Sherba, and Hank Dutt.

18

19

SILVER AWARD
MAGAZINE DESIGN
TWO OR MORE PAGES
The Boston Globe Magazine
Designer
Lucy Bartholomay
Illustrator
Gary Baseman
Art Director
Lucy Bartholomay

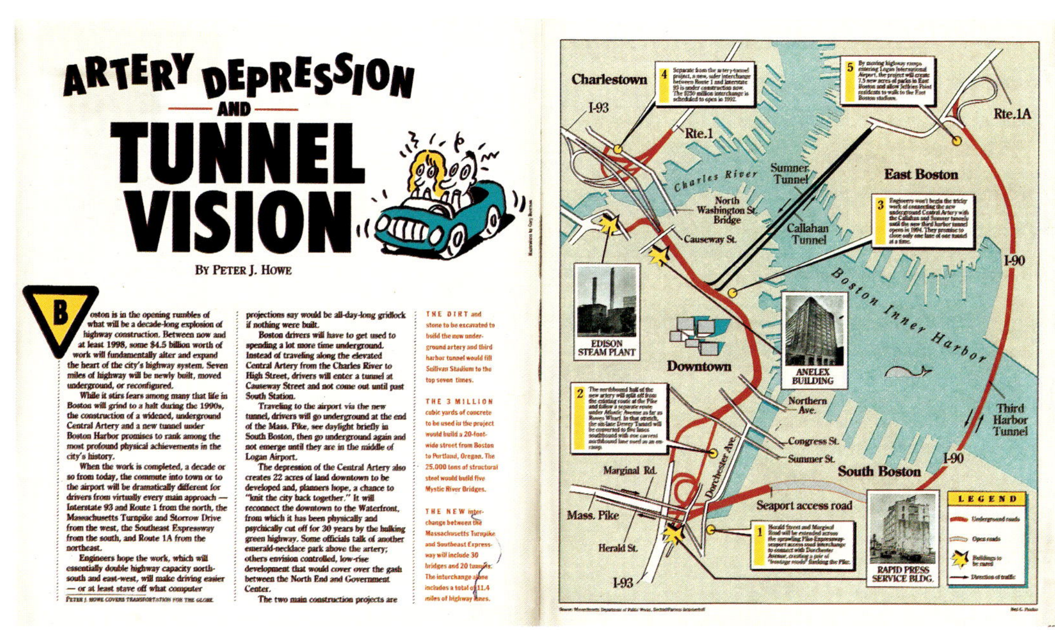

ARTERY DEPRESSION AND TUNNEL VISION

By Peter J. Howe

Boston is in the opening rumbles of what will be a decade-long explosion of highway construction. Between now and at least 1998, some $4.5 billion worth of work will fundamentally alter and expand the heart of the city's highway system. Seven miles of highway will be newly built, moved underground, or reconfigured.

While it stirs fears among many that life in Boston will grind to a halt during the 1990s, the construction of a widened, underground Central Artery and a new tunnel under Boston Harbor promises to rank among the most profound physical achievements in the city's history.

When the work is completed, a decade or so from today, the commute into town or to the airport will be dramatically different for drivers from virtually every main approach — Interstate 93 and Route 1 from the north, the Massachusetts Turnpike and Storrow Drive from the west, the Southeast Expressway from the south, and Route 1A from the northeast.

Engineers hope the work, which will essentially double highway capacity north-south and east-west, will make driving easier — or at least stave off what computer projections say would be all-day-long gridlock if nothing were built.

Boston drivers will have to get used to spending a lot more time underground. Instead of traveling along the elevated Central Artery from the Charles River to High Street, drivers will enter a tunnel at Causeway Street and not come out until past South Station.

Traveling to the airport via the new tunnel, drivers will go underground at the end of the Mass. Pike, see daylight briefly in South Boston, then go underground again and not emerge until they are in the middle of Logan Airport.

The depression of the Central Artery also creates 22 acres of land downtown to be developed and, planners hope, a chance to "knit the city back together." It will reconnect the downtown to the Waterfront, from which it has been physically and psychically cut off for 30 years by the hulking green highway. Some officials talk of another emerald-necklace park above the artery; others envision controlled, low-rise development that would cover over the gash between the North End and Government Center.

The two main construction projects are

PETER J. HOWE COVERS TRANSPORTATION FOR THE GLOBE.

THE DIRT and stone to be excavated to build the new underground artery and third harbor tunnel would fill Sullivan Stadium to the top seven times.

THE 3 MILLION cubic yards of concrete to be used in the project would build a 20-foot-wide street from Boston to Portland, Oregon. The 25,000 tons of structural steel would build five Mystic River Bridges.

THE NEW interchange between the Massachusetts Turnpike and Southeast Expressway will include 30 bridges and 20 tunnels. The interchange alone includes a total of 11.4 miles of highway lanes.

AWARD OF EXCELLENCE
MAGAZINE DESIGN
TWO OR MORE PAGES
The Columbus Dispatch
Columbus, Ohio
Designer
Scott Minister
Photography
Courtesy of Cinncinnati Art Museum
Researcher
Jacqueline Hall
Art Director
Scott Minister

By Jacqueline Hall

CINCINNATI – *In the closing decades of the 19th century, when American museums were scrambling to acquire European paintings and Greek and Roman sculpture, the Cincinnati Art Museum was not afraid to show a taste for the exotic.* ¶ *It was a time when most art museums had not heard of African art and were consigning the*

EXOTIC ELEGANT ART
American Indian & African Collections Find Themselves In OHIO

works of American Indian cultures to natural history museums. Yet, in Cincinnati something different was happening. Along with works from the Italian Renaissance and 17th-century Dutch masterpieces, the Cincinnati museum accepted donations of American Indian material and the extensive African art collection of Carl Steckelmann of Columbus, Ind.

RAVEN RATTLE
wood,
British Columbia;
19th century

TWIN FIGURE
wood;
Yoruba people,
Nigeria, Africa;
20th century

PHOTOS COURTESY CINCINNATI ART MUSEUM

CANTEEN
clay;
Acoma people,
New Mexico

Chapter 8

Art and illustration; photography; informational graphics; redesign

Art and illustration

The powerful statement — strong intellectually and visually — is the common theme among the 45 award winners in the art and illustration category.

The judges avoided work of a whimsical nature and rewarded serious concepts and technique. They were seeking a fresh vision, a fresh approach, and they found themselves bypassing ideas that seemed familiar.

"You keep seeing clones, what was hot a year ago," said judge Bonnie Timmons.

"In a business that depends upon cliches, it's shocking to see so many — but it's also shocking to see how many you've done yourself," judge Russ Ball said. "The strong works just jump right out."

Photography

The moment — Greg Louganis' head hitting the rebounding diving board. The striking image, fresh in concept, treated with respect. Evocative images of stunned earthquake survivors and of a young man's journey through the court system. The gutsy page-one play for a photo of a drunk frozen to death, snow and ice on his body, the lead picture in a series on a city's pervasive alcohol problems.

These medal-winning entries typify the criteria that arose during judging: Winners were clean, well-edited and well-printed; presentation did not interfere with photography.

One judge found a pleasant surprise: "I was happy to see that the photo essay is alive and well. I was amazed at the number of newspapers that are willing to devote significant amounts of news space to these essays," said Judy Griesedieck.

Some sins common to the bulk of the entries:

■ Loose editing. (Of a picture-story entry denied a Silver, one judge said, "There was a subtractive factor to some of the photos. They take away from the story instead of making it complete.")

■ Poor use of stronger photos.

■ Tight, shoehorned displays.

■ Rambling, bigger-is-better displays.

■ Design gimmicks that hurt the photos' "readability."

■ Photo essays masquerading as photo stories ("An essay is a collection of pictures on a topic. A picture story has a beginning, a middle and an end," Griesedieck said.)

Informational graphics

Take a look at info-graphics '89. Content. Detail and execution. Realism.

Judges applied the same standards to informational graphics that editors should apply to news stories. "Informational graphics should tell stories," judge Bob Giles explained.

Winning entries shared these qualities of a compelling news story:

■ Clarity and function. In news stories, it's called a lead or a hook. In informational graphics, judge Mario Garcia called it "a clear path." "The best infographics were simple," Garcia said. "Those that tried to be encyclopedic were confusing or overwhelming." ("Just because you can do it doesn't mean it's the way to go," said judge Ken Raniere.)

■ Accuracy. Graphics should portray events as they occur. "The function of an informational graphic is to explain a news event, not to astonish or amaze," said judge Rob Covey.

■ Detail. Scale, perspective, frame of reference, execution. And this observation about the entries from Raniere: "Three seemed to be little regard for the reader in the use of type in infographics. In some instances, type was laid over illustrations or on dark patches of color, making the information impossible to read. Type was too small in some graphics. ... I wouldn't go less than 8 points."

Redesigns

Winning redesigns had one thing in common: They responded to editors' decisions to take a fresh look at the way they packaged their news.

The seven award-winners did more than change type and rule systems; they built upon changes in editorial philosophy about the best way to organize and present content.

"I think I saw only a few real redesign projects," said judge Mario Garcia. "The basic question that has to be asked here is: 'Did this newspaper really need to be redesigned, or is the newspaper just following a trend?' I think that is has become the trendy thing to do to redesign the paper. ... It's the Ivana Trump approach to newspaper design — clean out the closet every season for a new look!"

Said judge Steve Rice, "I thought some papers really cleaned some things up well." But others, he said, added too much color and too many gimmicks. "Some people designed them to be more difficult to read, and then they entered the more complex one as the redesign. The 'before' version was actually the cleaner presentation."

"I look for energy that continues off the front of the section inside, and I'm not seeing that happen," said judge Rob Covey.

That idea was echoed by Robert Giles, who said editors and art directors should redirect their energies. Jurors agreed with Giles when he said he saw redesigns of section fronts that looked terrific, while inside pages received little attention.

"Even on big papers where you have designers on the desks, there are people working with A1," he said. "But, the inside is left to copy editors. I think the industry has to find some way to bring those skills up.

"Even if we can't hire specialists to design inside pages, we can make a case for upgrading skills, for training young copy editors who might have an interest in makeup. Papers must have stylebooks so that everyone knows how to use type."

AWARD OF EXCELLENCE
ART AND ILLUSTRATION
BLACK AND WHITE
Los Angeles Herald Examiner
Designer
Ed Herch
Illustrator
Kathryn Blackmun
Art Director
Mike Gordon

AWARD OF EXCELLENCE
ART AND ILLUSTRATION
BLACK AND WHITE
The Christian Science Monitor
Illustrator
Brian Lies
Art Director
Cynthia Hanson

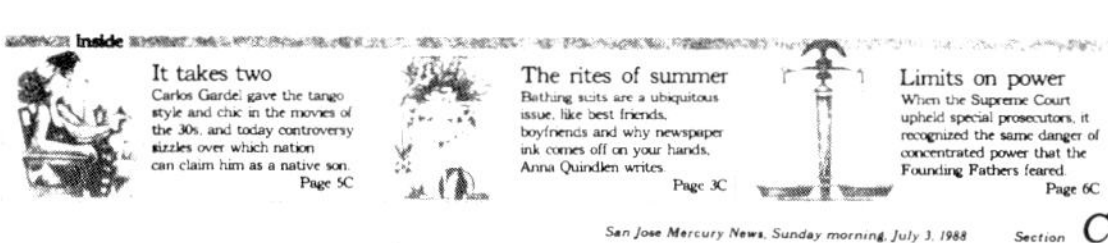

Inside

It takes two
Carlos Gardel gave the tango style and chic in the movies of the 30s, and today controversy sizzles over which nation can claim him as a native son.
Page 5C

The rites of summer
Bathing suits are a ubiquitous issue, like best friends, boyfriends and why newspaper ink comes off on your hands, Anna Quindlen writes.
Page 3C

Limits on power
When the Supreme Court upheld special prosecutors, it recognized the same danger of concentrated power that the Founding Fathers feared.
Page 6C

San Jose Mercury News, Sunday morning, July 3, 1988 Section C

Perspective

Analysis • Commentary • Editorials

AMNESIA IN LITTERIS

The books I have read (I think)

By Patrick Süskind

HOW does the question go? Oh, yes: Which book has most impressed, impacted upon, stamped and dented me, or even "put me on track" or "thrown me off course"?

But this sounds rather like a violent shock or trauma of the kind one remembers only in nightmares, never in a waking state, let alone in writing or in the glare of publicity, as was, I believe, very correctly pointed out by an Austrian psychologist (whose name escapes me at the moment) in a highly commendable essay, the title of which I cannot recall with any assurance, except to say that it was published in a little volume under the omnibus title "You and I" or "We and It" or even "I" or something like that, and was reissued recently by one or another of the major northern German publishers in a greenish white or yellowish pale blue or conceivably greenish gray-blue jacket.

Well, perhaps the question is not aimed at soliciting examples of psychotraumatic reading experiences, after all, perhaps what is being sought is that rousing experience of art described in the famous poem "Fair Apollo" . . . no, I don't think its called "Fair Apollo," it has a different title, something archaic, "Young Torso" or "Ancient Fair Apollo" or something like that — anyway, as described in that famous poem by . . . by . . . I can't seem to remember his name at the moment, but he is really a very famous poet with cow's eyes and a pendulous mustache, and he found an apartment in the Rue de Varenne for this fat French sculptor — what's his name? But apartment is hardly the word; it's more like a *palazzo*, with a park that takes more than 10 minutes to cross (Which raises the question, by the way: Where did people get the money to pay for these things?) Anyway, as described and expressed in that marvelous poem, which I would not be able to quote in its entirety, but whose last line remains ineradicably engraved in my memory as a constant moral imperative: "You must change your life."

So, what about those books of which I could say that reading them has changed my life?

To shed light on this issue, I approached my bookshelf (this was just a few days ago) and let my gaze wander along the spines of my books. As always happens on such occasions — that is, when too many members of a species are assembled in one spot and the eye gets lost in the mass — I first

See AMNESIA, Page 4C

Patrick Süskind is the author of "Perfume." He wrote this article for Harper's Magazine.

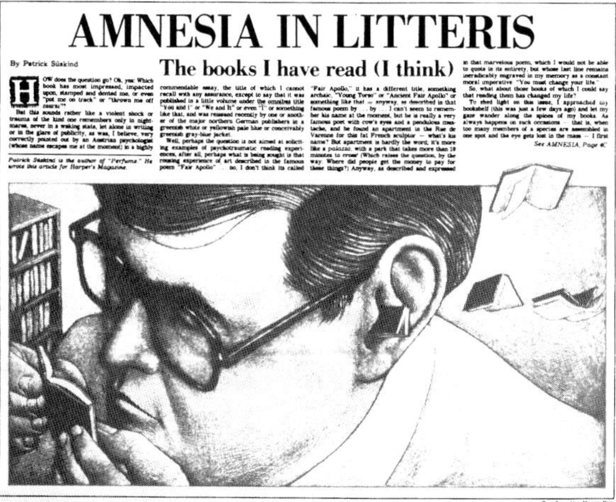

Doug Griswold — Mercury News

What it meant to be a McGovern Democrat in '72

By George McGovern

MY NAME is back in the news these days, and it occurred to me that it's being used in a way that might puzzle my four grandsons, who were either infants or not yet born when I ran for president in 1972. What follows is in the form of a letter to them and others of their generation.

I know you are aware of the frequent press references these days to "McGovern Democrat." It stems, I guess, from George Bush's decision to label Michael Dukakis "a McGovern Democrat." Apparently not to be outdone, Dukakis aides were quoted as stating that the purpose of their candidate's recent foreign policy speech was to demonstrate that Dukakis is "not another George McGovern."

I've been told that it is a compliment I am still discussed 16 years after I was a presidential nominee. But I've been wondering what you think about me when you hear my name used as a kind of swearword. Let me tell you first of all not to get too agitated about this. The political epithets thrown at far greater men than I — George Washington, Thomas Jefferson and Abraham Lincoln — make "McGovern Democrat" seem pretty polite stuff by comparison.

But let me tell you what I think this McGovern Democrat business is about. It goes back to 1972, when I was supposedly so liberal and

See MCGOVERN, Page 4C

Former Sen. George McGovern was the Democratic candidate for president in 1972. He wrote this article for the Washington Post.

How not to choose a running mate

By Mark Bowden

FOUR years ago, Walter Mondale was in the position Michael Dukakis and George Bush are in today. Weeks before his party's national convention, he had clinched the nomination. The only contest left was for vice president.

In Mondale's case, the choice would be historic. On July 4, 1984, 10 days before the convention, he decided to name a woman as his running mate. It was a conscious effort to bring excitement and novelty to what had been a highly predictable march to the nomination. But the move was historic for another reason as well: Mondale had sought, from the beginning, to make his selection the most carefully considered such choice ever made.

Months in advance, his staff had begun compiling detailed dossiers on several potential running mates, including the woman who was to become his first choice for the job. On the day Mondale finally made up his mind, two members of his staff were dispatched to closely examine the personal and financial history of this woman.

But problems developed. The woman was a prominent and successful politician, and her husband was prominent and successful in his own right. He had spent a lucrative career dealing in real estate. Mondale's men knew that, unfair as it might be, the business practices of a running mate's husband would suffer the same public scrutiny and be held up to the same high standards as her political career. And her husband's real estate dealings were complex.

They found nothing to suggest any wrongdoing, but they kept getting bogged down. Mondale's men realized that if they were having problems now, with both the candidate and her husband eagerly cooperating, then later on, the media and their political opponents would create even bigger problems. And if there was one thing Walter Mondale didn't need in his desperate, uphill campaign against a popular incumbent

See FERRARO, Page 4C

Mark Bowden is a Philadelphia Inquirer reporter.

A grand renovation

Medico-Dental Building reborn as apartments

Architecture
Alan Hess

THE recipe for any livable city calls for a blend of the new and the old. San Jose learned that lesson the hard way. Too many gracious old buildings were urban renewed out of existence in the 1960s and 1970s.

But the lesson has been learned, and the proof is the soon-to-open Vintage Tower at Sixth and East Santa Clara streets. This superb conversion of the 1927 Medico-Dental office building into apartments shows how a little investment in imagination can pay handsome dividends.

Demolishing the old Medico-Dental building would have been a tragedy. It's a gateway to downtown from the east side. Today, when much of the San Jose skyline is easily mistaken for refrigerator crates, its stepped-back silhouette, accented with pinnacles and statuary, is a delight. Already a city of San Jose landmark, it is also on its way to being listed on the National Register of Historic Places.

But the welcome surprise is that the 59 apartments in the old building are better designed than 95 percent of the new apartments on the market today.

See HESS, Page 5C

Alan Hess is a Bay Area architect whose column appears every other week in Perspective.

HARPER'S INDEX

- Value of the arms that Warsaw Pact members have bought from NATO countries since 1982: $35,000,000
- Value of the arms that NATO members have bought from Warsaw Pact countries since 1982: $165,000,000
- Amount the Pentagon spent last year on foreign-made parts and equipment: $21,000,000,000
- U.S. military spending during the Reagan administration, per second: $8,607
- Portion of all arms sales worldwide, since 1982, that went to the Middle East: 2/5
- Percentage of Jewish settlers on the West Bank who consider themselves "religious": 8
- Price of a box of Cheerios in Japan: $7.20

AWARD OF EXCELLENCE
ART AND ILLUSTRATION
BLACK AND WHITE
San Jose Mercury News
San Jose, California
Designer
Doug Griswold
Illustrator
Doug Griswold
Art Director
Bob Reynolds

Grandfather Lived in Heaven

by James Fadiman

AWARD OF EXCELLENCE
ART AND ILLUSTRATION:
BLACK AND WHITE
Palo Alto Weekly
Palo Alto, California
Illustrator
Stephen Sedam-Stone
Art Director
Patricia Hardenberger

Not a crook
Special prosecutor's report sheds new light on poor maligned Ed Meese, Donald Kaul writes.
Page 3C

Driving crazy
Staying alive is the major rule of road in Malaysia, where something happens to gentle people when they get behind the wheel.
Page 5C

Duped on pensions?
In San Jose 85 percent of police and firefighters retire on disability. Does that indicate the danger of their jobs, or a sweetheart retirement deal?
Pages 6C and 7C

San Jose Mercury News, Sunday morning, July 31, 1988 Section C

Perspective

Analysis • Commentary • Editorials

For Latinos, a key step toward power

By Bill Flores

A population nightmare

Global crisis wasn't gone, just forgotten

U.S. policy toward Asia: a new reality

By Paul H. Kreisberg

Leaving Atlanta? Use the time machine

By David E. Early

HARPER'S INDEX

AWARD OF EXCELLENCE
ART AND ILLUSTRATION
BLACK AND WHITE
San Jose Mercury News
San Jose, California
Designer
David Miller
Illustrator
David Miller
Art Directors
Bob Reynolds, David Miller

AWARD OF EXCELLENCE
ART AND ILLUSTRATION
BLACK AND WHITE
The Miami Herald
Illustrator
Tom Dolphens
Editor
Rick Barb
Director of Editorial Art and Design
Randy Stano

BONNIE TIMMONS

SILVER AWARD
ART AND ILLUSTRATION
BLACK AND WHITE
The New York Times Magazine
Designer
Nancy Harris
Illustrator
Bonnie Timmons
Art Director
Janet Froelich

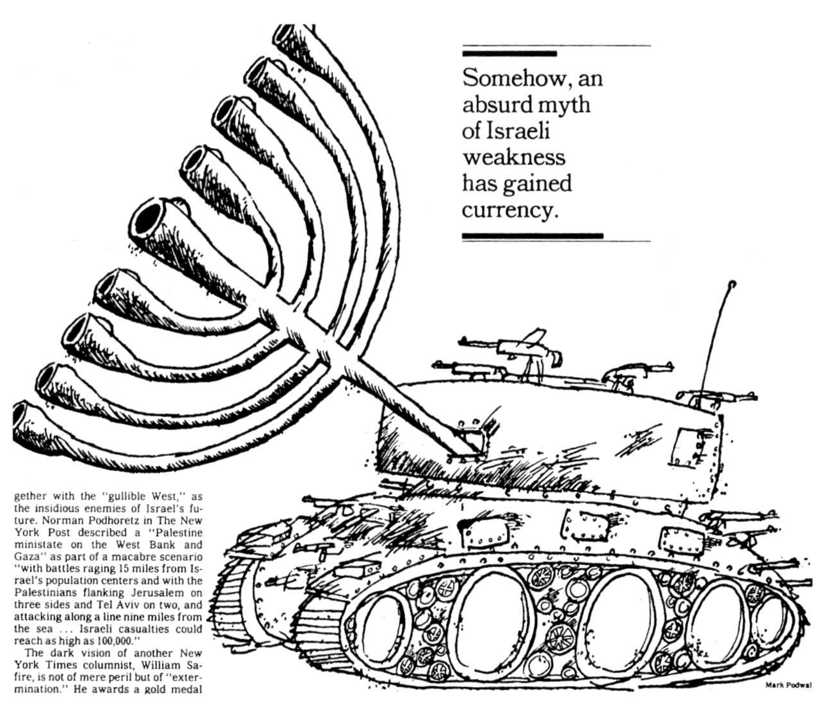

Somehow, an absurd myth of Israeli weakness has gained currency.

gether with the "gullible West," as the insidious enemies of Israel's future. Norman Podhoretz in The New York Post described a "Palestine ministate on the West Bank and Gaza" as part of a macabre scenario "with battles raging 15 miles from Israel's population centers and with the Palestinians flanking Jerusalem on three sides and Tel Aviv on two, and attacking along a line nine miles from the sea . . . Israeli casualties could reach as high as 100,000."

The dark vision of another New York Times columnist, William Safire, is not of mere peril but of "extermination." He awards a gold medal

Mark Podwal

AWARD OF EXCELLENCE
ART AND ILLUSTRATION
BLACK AND WHITE
The New York Times
Designer
Jerelle Kraus
Illustrator
Mark Podwal
Art Director
Jerelle Kraus

AWARD OF EXCELLENCE
ART AND ILLUSTRATION
BLACK AND WHITE
The New York Times
Designer
Jerelle Kraus
Illustrator
Horacio Fidel Cardo
Art Director
Jerelle Kraus

THE NEW YORK TIMES, MONDAY, JULY 11, 1988 A17

ESSAY
William Safire

Ergo Propter Hoc

Ed Meese and the priority of loyalty.

The Curse of Campaign Fund Raising

By John Frederick Martin

Ceaseless communion with the big money givers.

Avoiding United States Unilateralism

By Brian Urquhart

The World Bank's Growing Irrelevance

By Roger Altman

Debt relief, not business as usual.

AWARD OF EXCELLENCE
ART AND ILLUSTRATION
BLACK AND WHITE
The Financial Times of Canada
Toronto
Illustrator
Emmanuel Lopez
Art Director
Therese Shechter

JANUARY 23, 1989 FINANCIAL TIMES OF CANADA A1

FINANCIAL TIMES OF CANADA

Mutual Funds

FYI: The worst of the lot, plus bullish hopes for '89 *How seven managers saw their portfolios prosper despite the odds* *High-flying rewards for high-grossing salespeople* *Facts and fallacies explored at last* *Our annual long-term performance checkup*

Riding out the storm

PATIENCE AND PRUDENCE — the search, if you will, for a sure bet — have traditionally governed mutual-fund investment. Most people, like marriage partners, commit themselves to have and hold through the market's richer or poorer patches. Lately, of course, the rough has overwhelmed the smooth. We know where we've been — blind-sided by Black Monday and saddled with galloping interest rates. It's where we're going that makes a horse race — and that depends on a number of variables. On the following pages we present a look at the track records of the best-performing funds over both the short and the long haul. We gauge a fund's volatility and examine the flexibility of its managers; demystify what funds can and cannot do; and aid you in establishing individual goals. PAGE A9

SILVER AWARD
ART AND ILLUSTRATION
BLACK AND WHITE
The New York Times
Designer
Jerelle Kraus
Illustrator
Stasys Eidrigevicius
Art Director
Jerelle Kraus

AWARD OF EXCELLENCE
ART AND ILLUSTRATION
BLACK AND WHITE
The New York Times
Designer
Jerelle Kraus
Illustrator
Rafal Olbinski
Art Director
Jerelle Kraus

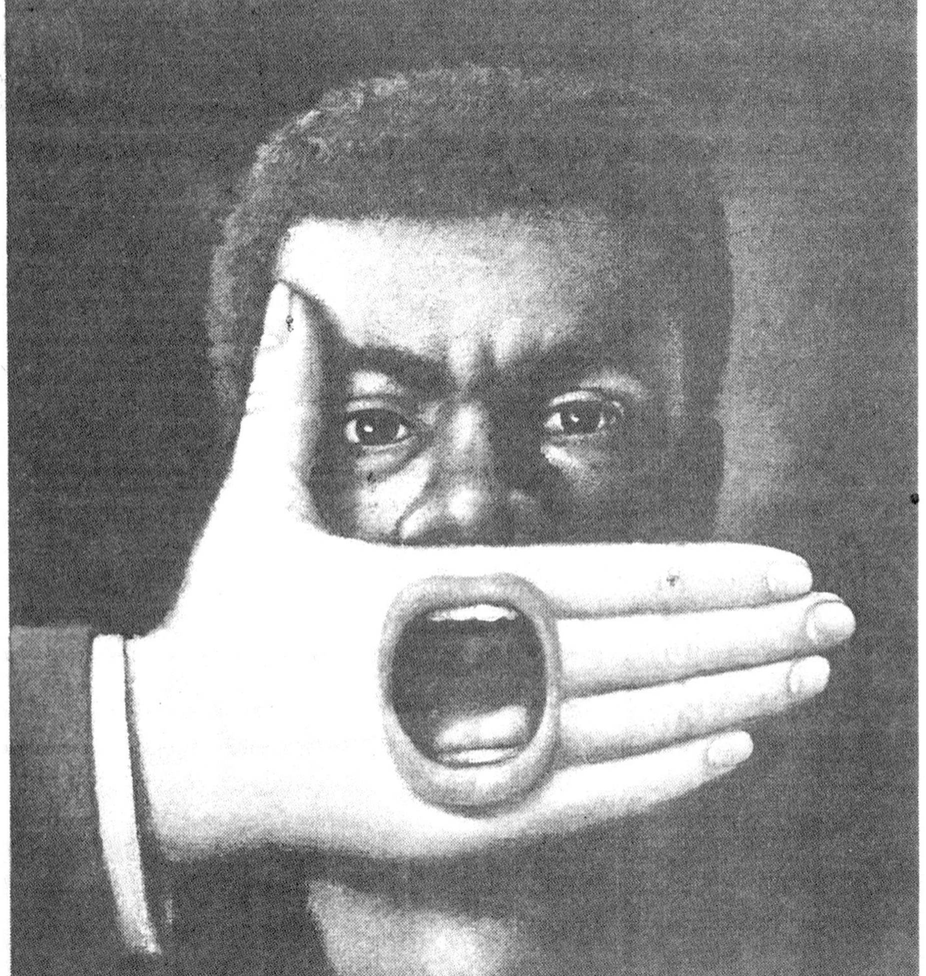

AWARD OF EXCELLENCE
ART AND ILLUSTRATION
BLACK AND WHITE
The New York Times
Designer
Steven Heller
Illustrator
Mark D. Summers
Art Director
Steven Heller

A Book Fair That Transports Voyagers to Faraway Places

By JOHN GROSS

"BOOKS are for traveling," proclaims this year's New York Is Book Country fair (to be held this Sunday on Fifth Avenue). Yes indeed. But it isn't necessarily travel books that we want to take on our travels.

Quite the contrary, many people would say: the last thing we want to read when we are in Ruritania is somebody else's impressions of Ruritania. Before we set out, perhaps, and after we come back; but not while we are actually there.

On the whole I agree. But then how do we decide what books to slip into our luggage or take down to the beach? In my experience, choices fall into three categories, none of them without their drawbacks.

First, books we've been planning to read for a long time — perhaps for as long as we can remember. The thought of a vacation expands the spirit: now at last we have a chance to catch up with ourselves, to stand back, to breathe the air of the great spacious classics.

And quite often the plan works. When else, after all, are most of us going to have time to tackle Gibbon or Cervantes? But quite often it doesn't work. We can't concentrate, or we are in the wrong mood, or it's too much like hard work — we are on vacation, after all.

My own books bear witness to some sad failures. A deck chair ticket marks the place where I gave up on Robert Musil's "Man Without Qualities" (and another ticket marks the place where I gave up the following year). There is an Ambre Solaire stain on page 31 of "The Golden Bowl" — and no evidence that I ever got as far as page 32.

Second, at the other extreme, there are the books we pick up while we are in transit, or when we reach our destination. Paperbacks, for the most part, which means that at least they have the virtue of being disposable: we don't have to cart them back.

But we are leaving things to chance, and the choice at the average airport or drugstore tends to get narrower and narrower. "The Ludlum Memorandum," "The Follett Conspiracy," Judith Bradford, Barbara Taylor Krantz, last year's best seller about low cholesterol or Japanese management techniques, a row of Agatha Christies that we've probably read before.

Third, I find I can't make up my mind, and I grab a book from the shelves at the last minute, just before leaving home. Here again, there is

Continued on Page C22

Maurice Sendak

AWARD OF EXCELLENCE
ART AND ILLUSTRATION
BLACK AND WHITE
The New York Times
Designer
Richard Aloisio
Illustrator
Maurice Sendak
Art Director
Richard Aloisio

AWARD OF EXCELLENCE
ART AND ILLUSTRATION
BLACK AND WHITE
The New York Times
Designer
Michael Valenti
Illustrator
Bob Gale
Art Director
Michael Valenti

The New York Times
Travel
Sunday, October 9, 1988
Section 5

SPECIAL EUROPEAN ISSUE

The Off-Season's On

The 12th-century bronze head of Kaiser Friedrich Barbarossa.

Coping With Rising Prices
The dollar's value has increased about 10 percent this year, but European inflation has more than wiped out the gain. Still, there are ways to trim costs. By Steve Lohr. Page 15.

Long Weekends For Short-Timers
Tour operators and airlines are trying to make a three- or four-day jaunt or shopping spree a welcome break at the right price for a wider range of people. By Janet Piorko. Page 14.

Highlights Of the Season
A guide to fall and winter events in 16 countries, from a show of 120 Henry Moores in London to the premiere of a rock ballet in Hanover. By Carol Plum. Page 14.

A Spirited Germany
Schnapps and steeples in Westphalia. By Nicholas Fox Weber. Page 8.

Italy's Valtellina
From vineyards to high peaks. By Beth Archer Brombert. Page 19.

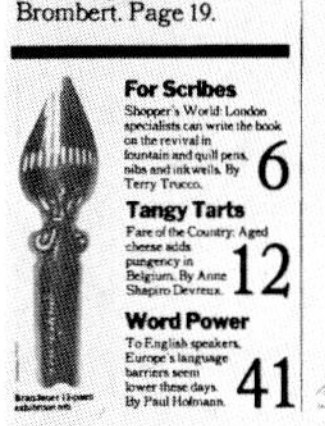

For Scribes 6
Shopper's World: London specialists can write the book on the revival in fountain and quill pens, nibs and inkwells. By Terry Trucco.

Tangy Tarts 12
Fare of the Country: Aged cheese adds pungency in Belgium. By Anne Shapiro Devreux.

Word Power 41
To English speakers, Europe's language barriers seem lower these days. By Paul Holmann.

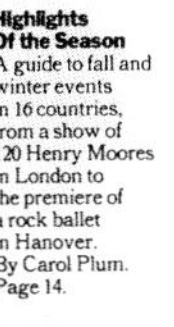

SILVER AWARD
ART AND ILLUSTRATION
BLACK AND WHITE
The New York Times
Designer
Jerelle Kraus
Illustrator
Jean-Jacques Sempe
Art Director
Jerelle Kraus

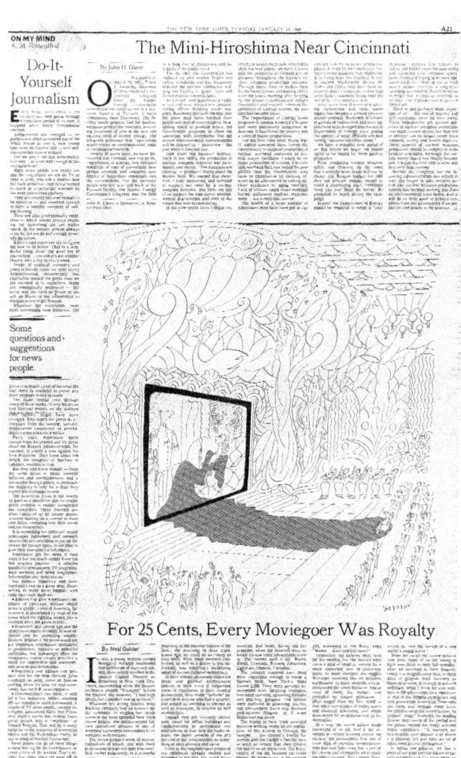

ON MY MIND
A. M. Rosenthal

The Mini-Hiroshima Near Cincinnati

Do-It-Yourself Journalism

Some questions and suggestions for news people.

For 25 Cents, Every Moviegoer Was Royalty

AWARD OF EXCELLENCE
ART AND ILLUSTRATION
BLACK AND WHITE
The Plain Dealer
Cleveland, Ohio
Illustrator
John Backderf

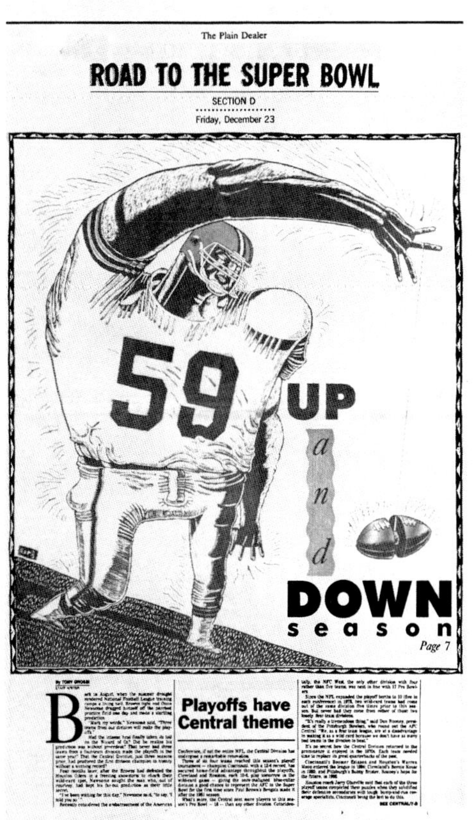

The Plain Dealer

ROAD TO THE SUPER BOWL

SECTION D

Friday, December 23

Page 7

Playoffs have Central theme

NURI DUCASSI / El Nuevo Herald

AWARD OF EXCELLENCE
ART AND ILLUSTRATION
TWO OR MORE COLORS
el Nuevo Herald
Miami, Florida
Designer
Nuri Ducassi
Illustrator
Nuri Ducassi

AWARD OF EXCELLENCE
ART AND ILLUSTRATION
TWO OR MORE COLORS
El Nuevo Dia
San Juan, Puerto Rico
Designer
Jose L. Diaz de Villegas, Jr.
Illustrator
Jose L. Diaz de Villegas, Jr.
Art Director
Jose L. Diaz de Villegas, Jr.

AWARD OF EXCELLENCE
ART AND ILLUSTRATION
TWO OR MORE COLORS
Chicago Tribune
Designer
Margret Carsello
Illustrator
Cynthia Torp
Art Director
Margret Carsello

UNCLE JOHN

She thought her uncle "made" racehorses. He was really making a tradition of courage and willingness to take risks.

By Bridgett Davis
Illustration by Jeff Jackson

I WAS BARELY SEVEN, and my cousin Jewel was six, when my Uncle John began taking us to work with him. We would rise before dawn and dress quickly in layers of undershirts, our daddies' white cotton socks and too-big rubber boots. Then we would slip into the darkest portion of morning and into the front seat of his '66 Plymouth, its headlights leading the way to Detroit Race Course.

There, rubbing our eyes, we would find a barn full of horses: stalls and stalls of strong brown ones with white-tipped noses and towering black ones who swished their tails and whinnied as we walked by. We sipped our coffee like adults from Styrofoam cups, and we marveled at the contrast between this world and ours — places where factory smoke drifted across the skyline outside our bedroom windows.

On some mornings, Uncle John would let us mount his pony, Bill, and ride around the back track, near the sheds. He taught us that to ride a horse, you had to trust it. Then it would trust you.

Back then, in 1967, Jewell loved to clean the horses' drafty stalls and feed them their hay. I was content to pet the colts on the nose and watch those long, delicate legs kick at imaginary intruders.

Thanks to the undershirts, I felt warm. Thanks to Uncle John, I felt safe.

We would watch as he exercised the horses. One by one, Uncle John would mount the young, high-strung thoroughbreds, speaking to them softly, caressing their necks. He was teaching each horse how to run and how to react.

SILVER AWARD
ART AND ILLUSTRATION
TWO OR MORE COLORS
Detroit Free Press Magazine
Designer
Patrick Mitchell
Illustrator
Jeff Jackson
Art Director
Patrick Mitchell

2. premie i A-Magasinets nordiske novellekonkurranse

Egil Haxthow er født i 1924 og jurist av utdannelse. I det daglige er han forhandlingssjef i Forsikringsfunksjonærenes Landsforbund.

Haxthow debuterte som romanforfatter i 1964 og har ialt skrevet seks romaner. En av disse — «Kjære Brams» — ble valgt ut som en av «Norwegian Books 1976». Han har laget en rekke radioprogrammer og kåserier for radio, publisert endel noveller og forfattet artikler og kronikker i dagspresse og tidsskrifter. En av hans kronikker er blitt premiert (innkjøpt) i en tidligere kronikkkonkurranse i Aftenposten.

Haxthow har også noen dramatiske arbeider bak seg. Et skuespill fra hans hånd er oppført på Scene 7, og flere hørespill av ham er sendt i Radioteatret. Ett av disse — «Polsk visitt» — representerte Norge på Biennalen for «Prix Italia» i Siena for noen år siden.

Haxthow er Spania-elsker. En av bøkene hans — «En skål med oliven» (Solum, 1984) — utspiller seg der, på sydkysten. Det samme gjelder denne novellen.

26

Calamaritos

Novelle av Egil Haxthow
Illustrasjon: Vera Felokowsky

De satte seg ved det lille bordet ytterst mot *paseo'en*. Han tok frem et blått lommetørkle og tørket seg over den blanke skallen, mens han studerte spisekartet. Efter en stund sa han: —*Calamaritos*.

— Hva? Hun la fra seg spisekartet og så på ham.

— Blekksprut, forklarte han.

— Blekksprut! Du vil alltid ha blekksprut.

— Det er fordi jeg liker blekksprut, sa han. Stemmen hans var flat som en sandstrand og uten klang, som om noe var blitt slitt bort av den.

Hun skjøv menyen fra seg. — Det er bare noe du tror, sa hun.

— Tror . . . gjentok han og så utover sjøen. — Hva er det jeg tror?

— At du liker blekksprut.

Han la sin egen meny oppå hennes. — Jeg trodde vi var enige om at vi skulle spise, sa han.

Hun satte blikket i ham. — Du skal alltid gjøre sånt som andre ikke gjør, sa hun. — Det skal du alltid når du kommer ned her.

Han så omkring seg. — Folk her spiser blekksprut, sa han. — Bare se selv.

— Det kommer av at de er spaniere, sa hun.

«Du, som er så interessert i alt fordi det er spansk, har du noengang tenkt over hva slags liv det er å være katt her nede? spurte hun.»

— Det kan ikke jeg noe for.

— Jo, du kan noe for det. Du går alltid der spanierne går, for det gjør ingen av de andre som ikke er spaniere og som er sånn som oss.

Han tok opp menyen igjen. — De har biff her også, sa han. — Men jeg tror den er seig, og dessuten er den dobbelt så dyr som blekkspruten.

— Alltid skal du snakke om penger, sa hun. — Jeg trodde vi skulle ha

27

SILVER AWARD
ART AND ILLUSTRATION
TWO OR MORE COLORS
A-Magasinet, Aftenposten
Oslo, Norway
Designer
Nina Holmsen
Illustrator
Vera Felskoesky
Art Director
Ashley Booth

AWARD OF EXCELLENCE
ART AND ILLUSTRATION
BLACK AND WHITE
The Wall Street Journal
New York
Designer
Joe Dizney
Illustrator
David Small
Design Director
Greg Leeds
Art Director
Joe Dizney

R30 THE WALL STREET JOURNAL — A WSJ REPORT — THE INAUGURATION — FRIDAY, JANUARY 20, 1989

AFTER YOU...

Democrats say they'll let Bush take the lead in risky initiatives

By DAVID SHRIBMAN

THE DEMOCRATS are playing defense again.

As the Bush era dawns in the capital, Democrats are talking a very modest game. In the cloakrooms and corridors of Congress and in the consultants' suites downtown, there are very few grand plans, only shards of an agenda and nary a hint of an aggressive strategy.

"The price of Bush's victory," says Democratic Rep. Mike Espy of Mississippi, "is that he has to go first."

On the budget deficit, on national security, on virtually every major issue, the Democrats are calculating that they bat best by batting last. This attitude reflects more than propriety; it reflects a careful political calculation.

"The Republicans got the mandate to lead, and we ought to turn the field over to them and let them provide the leadership," says Greg Schneiders, a Democratic political strategist. "There are a lot of mines in the field, and there's no reason for us to be out front."

Adds former Rep. James Jones of Oklahoma, one of the early candidates to succeed Paul Kirk as party chairman: "They have the burden, and we'd be foolish not to let them go first and set out their vision for America."

Eight years ago, Ronald Reagan took office facing a badly shaken Democratic opposition that had just lost control of the Senate for the first time in a generation and was wondering if it might be headed in the same direction in the House. The party George Bush faces is in a very different mood. With its 85-seat advantage in the House and 10-seat margin in the Senate, the Democratic Party shored up its position on Capitol Hill even as a Republican captured the White House for the fifth time in the last six elections. Now, content with their suzerainty in the legislative branch, the Democrats are groping to find a way out of the executive wilderness.

Despite their familiarity with this position, the Democrats have developed no consistent strategy to confront their predicament. After Jimmy Carter failed in 1980 to win a second term, a chunk of congressional Democrats followed Mr. Reagan's lead and supported the new president's plans for large budget and tax cuts. After Walter Mondale suffered an ignominious defeat in 1984, the party underwent a lengthy self-examination that often took on a self-conscious and self-indulgent character.

"The Democrats have to decide whether this is a good time to fight for the heart and soul of the party, or whether they want to be a united opposition," says Stephen Hess, a Brookings Institution analyst. "How they resolve that question will tell us how successful they are in offering an alternative to George Bush."

This time, few Democrats seem to have much taste for another round of deep introspection.

"We had a lot of intense analysis and soul-searching," says Sen. Albert Gore of Tennessee, who ran for president in 1988 and is likely to try again in 1992. "This time we're apt to make more progress by concentrating singlemindedly on substance without worrying about the politics until the political season rolls around. The soul-searching makes everything unnecessarily complicated."

The Democratic Leadership Council, which sought to push the party into taking more moderate positions on social questions and more strenuous positions on national-security issues, is planning another conference this March in Philadelphia. But the group seems more interested in trumpeting new ideas such as a national-service program and a reexamination of the War Powers Act than in embracing what its critics once called "Republican ideas."

If leaders of the council are shying away from questioning the underlying philosophy of the party, though, they still hope Democrats will rethink a fundamental element of the party's political character: Its tendency to approach politics as a game of blocs where the goal is to rebuild the structure that Franklin Roosevelt assembled in 1932.

"The Democrats need to concentrate on developing some defining ideas around which we can rebuild a coalition," says Alvin From, the DLC's executive leader. "Clearly, the idea of appealing to blocs of the old coalition is not working. That kind of politics—putting interest groups together—is getting us nowhere. Instead of interest groups, we need ideas that convince people we really are on their side."

That notion, rejected for so long by Michael Dukakis's strategists, was finally embraced with desperation in the final month of the 1988 presidential election. Once Mr. Dukakis made that message—"on your side"—part of his election appeal, he began to regain some of the Democrats who, in the Reagan years, had wandered into the Republican column.

But Democrats must do more than recapture the sense that they are the party of the great mass of Americans who make the country work. They also believe they must convince voters that they can be entrusted with making government work.

"People share our hopes for the country," says Sen. Joseph Biden of Delaware, who cut short his presidential campaign in 1988 but who may make another bid in 1992. "But they do not trust our

Please turn to page R32

MR. SHRIBMAN COVERS POLITICS FROM THE WALL STREET JOURNAL'S WASHINGTON BUREAU.

AWARD OF EXCELLENCE
ART AND ILLUSTRATION
TWO OR MORE COLORS
Chicago Tribune
Designer
Kevin Fewell
Illustrator
Dave Calver
Illustrations Director
Judie Anderson
Art Director
Kevin Fewell

TempoWoman

Section 6 — Chicago Tribune Sunday, May 29, 1988 — N

Why • women • CHEAT

Affairs of the '80s alter the myth of marital bliss

By Laurance R. Stains

'Infidelity is the ultimate touchy subject—a subject your marriage vows were supposed to put to rest.'

See Cheat, pg. 4

Out of Africa

Ancestry that includes royalty and slavery has shaped the life of Nigeria's Ayo Vaughan-Richards. Page 3.

Special delivery

For mothers over 35, science poses difficult questions, observes Anna Quindlen. Page 5.

Person studies

How a bookstore displays the elements of culture arouses debate in Alice Kahn's neighborhood. Page 5.

ILLUSTRATION BY BECKY HEAVER

AWARD OF EXCELLENCE
ART AND ILLUSTRATION
TWO OR MORE COLORS
The Baltimore Sun, Sun Magazine
Designer
Donna Crivello
Illustrator
Becky Heaver
Art Director
Donna Crivello

AWARD OF EXCELLENCE
ART AND ILLUSTRATION
TWO OR MORE COLORS
The Baltimore Sun, Sun Magazine
Designer
Donna Crivello
Illustrator
Terry Allen
Art Director
Donna Crivello

AWARD OF EXCELLENCE
ART AND ILLUSTRATION
TWO OR MORE COLORS
The Washington Post, National Weekly Edition
Washington, D.C.
Designer
Marty Barrick
Illustrator
Tom Herzberg
Art Director
Michael Keegan

AWARD OF EXCELLENCE
ART AND ILLUSTRATION
TWO OR MORE COLORS
The Virginia-Pilot and The Ledger-Star
Norfolk, Virginia
Designer
Sam Hundley
Illustrator
Sam Hundley
Art Directors
Bob Lynn, Bill Pitzer
Editor
Marian Anderfuren

AWARD OF EXCELLENCE

ART AND ILLUSTRATION
TWO OR MORE COLORS

The Kansas City Star, Star Magazine

Designer
Bill Gaspard
Illustrator
Eric Dinyer
Art Director
Bill Gaspard

AWARD OF EXCELLENCE

ART AND ILLUSTRATION
TWO OR MORE COLORS

The Virginia-Pilot and The Ledger-Star
Norfolk, Virginia

Designer
Sam Hundley
Illustrator
Sam Hundley
Art Directors
Bob Lynn, Bill Pitzer
Editor
Marian Anderfuren

SUNDAY NOVEMBER 27, 1988 The Virginian-Pilot THE LEDGER-STAR SECTION J

Tidewater Living

■ DAVE BARRY/J4
■ RAISING CHILDREN/J6

MILKING VIETNAM

Pistols, plaques, poetry, you name it. Merchandisers are cashing in on the burgeoning popularity of our most unpopular war.

Please see **VIETNAM,** *Page* J2

PERSONALITIES

Martina Navratilova finds that she still hasn't tired of the racket

By Vicki Croke
Boston Globe

MARTINA NAVRATILOVA and her longtime companion Judy Nelson approach an interview like an experienced doubles team. Navratilova stays far back and lets Nelson approach the net for all the personal questions.

Ask Navratilova about the stability of her personal life vs. the two-year instability of her career, and she launches into a litany of recent injuries and talks about being back on track with her career.

Ask her what she thinks the biggest misconception about her is, and she says, "I don't know what the average person thinks I'm like. I get 'You're taller than I thought' or 'You're shorter than I thought.' Some say, 'You're better looking in person than you are on TV.' People don't say that much to me."

Ask about the tabloid frenzy that ensued when Nelson (a former beauty queen from Texas, and married at the time) showed up at Wimbledon in 1984 to watch Navratilova play, and Nelson takes over. "I tried to ignore it," she says. "You can't avoid some of the things — especially in what we think of as quality magazines. You see things that really are not true and it hurts.

"I was concerned with how all that affected my boys. I certainly had to be willing to accept that kind of exposure — I knew it would happen and I had to deal with it. But I was an adult and I could deal with it.

"I've always contended that if you're honest with yourself and like who you are, then whatever is written about you or whatever people think about you really doesn't make any difference."

Navratilova and Nelson now live together in Fort Worth with Nelson's two sons, who are 15 and 17. But Navratilova says she is not an authority figure. She says she's a friend to the boys.

Nelson says, "Martina's not their parent. I'm their parent and their father is their parent and we're probably doing a better job now. Martina doesn't have to be anything but Martina."

And just who is Martina?

"Whoever I was 20 years ago — I'm still that person," says Navratilova, who once lived in Virginia

Please see **MARTINA,** *Page* J3

"Whoever I was 20 years ago — I'm still that person," says Martina Navratilova, who turned 32 last month. "I still try to do the right thing."

AP photo

Navratilova on the court: She says her best tennis is yet to come.

SILVER AWARD

ART AND ILLUSTRATION
TWO OR MORE COLORS

The Virginia-Pilot and The Ledger-Star
Norfolk, Virginia

Designer
Sam Hundley
Illustrator
Sam Hundley
Art Directors
Bob Lynn, Bill Pitzer
Editor
Debbie Armstrong

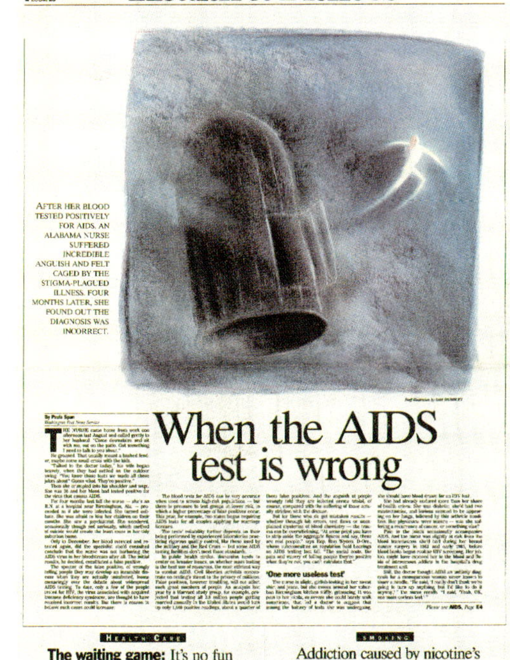

WEDNESDAY MAY 25, 1988 The Virginian-Pilot THE LEDGER-STAR SECTION E

Health & Fitness

■ SCIENCE/E5
■ ZOOM/E6

AFTER HER BLOOD TESTED POSITIVELY FOR AIDS, AN ALABAMA NURSE SUFFERED INCREDIBLE ANGUISH AND FELT CAGED BY THE STIGMA-PLAGUED ILLNESS. FOUR MONTHS LATER, SHE FOUND OUT THE DIAGNOSIS WAS INCORRECT.

When the AIDS test is wrong

By Paula Span
Washington Post News Service

'One more useless test'

Please see **AIDS,** *Page* E4

HEALTH CARE

The waiting game: It's no fun having to be a patient patient

By Victor Cohn
Washington Post News Service

Please see **WAIT,** *Page* E3

SMOKING

Addiction caused by nicotine's effect on central nervous system

By Danielle A. Fouquette
Special to Health and Fitness

Please see **NICOTINE,** *Page* E2

AWARD OF EXCELLENCE
ART AND ILLUSTRATION
PORTFOLIO OF WORK
Detroit Free Press Magazine
Illustrator
Bonnie Timmons
Art Director
Patrick Mitchell

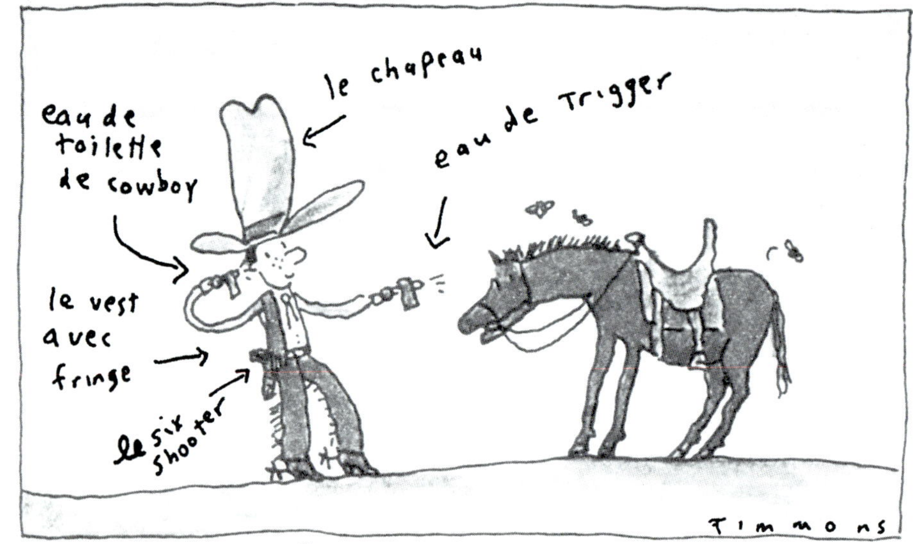

FALL FASHION

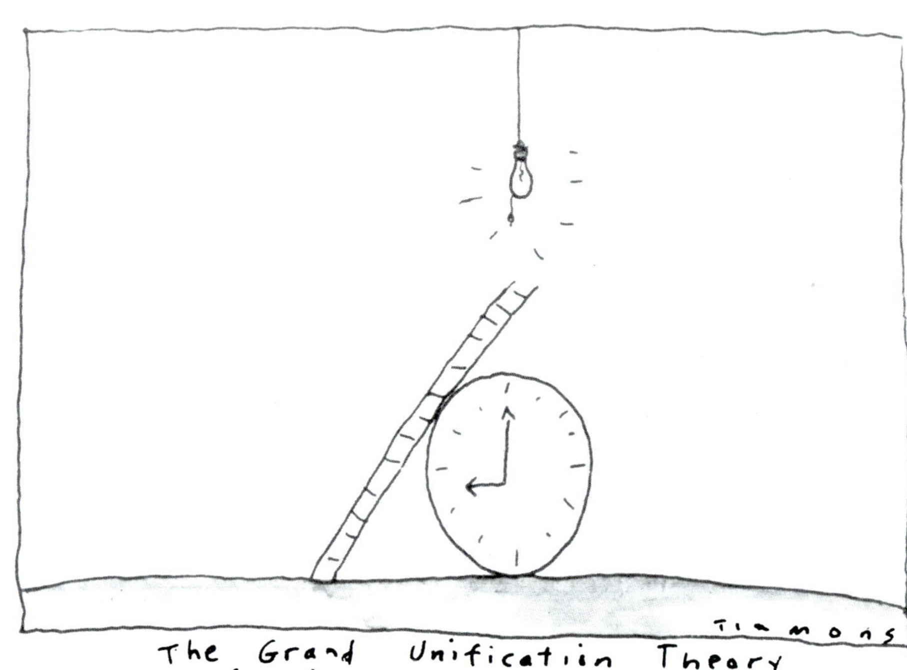

The Grand Unification Theory of the ENTIRE UNIVERSE

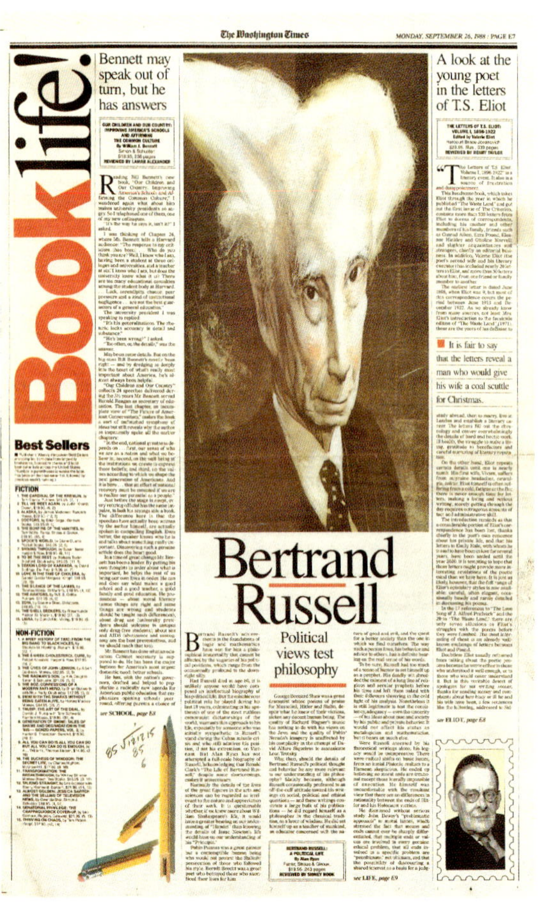

The Washington Times — MONDAY, SEPTEMBER 26, 1988 / PAGE E7

Book life!

Bennett may speak out of turn, but he has answers

A look at the young poet in the letters of T.S. Eliot

It is fair to say that the letters reveal a man who would give his wife a coal scuttle for Christmas.

Bertrand Russell

Political views test philosophy

Best Sellers

SILVER AWARDS
ART AND ILLUSTRATION
TWO OR MORE COLORS
and
PAGE DESIGN
OTHER FEATURE FRONT
The Washington Times
Washington, D.C.
Designer
John Kascht
Illustrator
John Kascht
Art Director
John Kascht

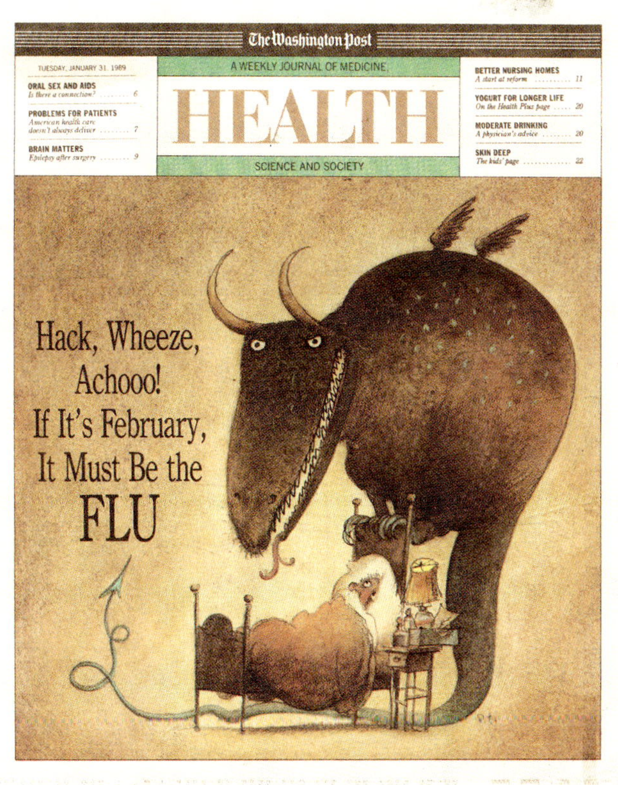

The Washington Post

TUESDAY, JANUARY 31, 1989

ORAL SEX AND AIDS
Is there a connection? 6

PROBLEMS FOR PATIENTS
American health care doesn't always deliver 7

BRAIN MATTERS
Epilepsy after surgery 9

A WEEKLY JOURNAL OF MEDICINE

HEALTH

SCIENCE AND SOCIETY

BETTER NURSING HOMES
A start at reform 11

YOGURT FOR LONGER LIFE
On the Health Plus page 20

MODERATE DRINKING
A physician's advice 20

SKIN DEEP
The kids' page 22

Hack, Wheeze, Achooo! If It's February, It Must Be the FLU

AWARDS OF EXCELLENCE

ART AND ILLUSTRATION
TWO OR MORE COLORS
and
PAGE DESIGN
SCIENCE/TECHNOLOGY

The Washington Post
Washington, D.C.

Designer
Alice Kresse

Illustrator
Richard Thompson

Art Director
Alice Kresse

A special edition of The Washington Times featuring essays by Ambassador Alan Keyes, Lt. Gen. Colin Powell, the Rev. James Bevel, and others.

The Vision

Where must we go from here?

AWARD OF EXCELLENCE

ART AND ILLUSTRATION
TWO OR MORE COLORS

The Washington Times
Washington, D.C

Designer
John Kascht

Illustrator
John Kascht

Art Director
John Kascht

MODE

Naturen sätter färg på hösten

Medeltida modedockor

På Orkney klagar britterna på vädret

AWARD OF EXCELLENCE

ART AND ILLUSTRATION
PORTFOLIO OF WORK

Gotesborgs-Posten
Gothenburg, Sweden

Designers
Hans Norrby, Karin Johansson,
Mats Widebrant, Karin Teghammar

Illustrator
Ulf Sveningson

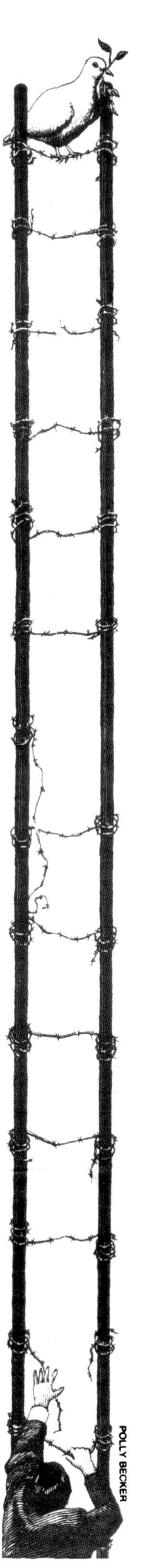

AWARD OF EXCELLENCE
ART AND ILLUSTRATION
PORTFOLIO OF WORK
Christian Science Monitor
Illustrator
Polly Becker
Art Director
Cynthia Hanson

AWARD OF EXCELLENCE
ART AND ILLUSTRATION
PORTFOLIO OF WORK
The New York Times
Designer
Jerelle Kraus
Illustrator
Rafal Olbinski
Art Director
Jerelle Kraus

THE NEW YORK TIMES, SATURDAY, NOVEMBER 26, 1988

Defiance on Latin Debt

By Marlene Nadle

Peru's President, Alan García Pérez, may have run into deep economic troubles recently but that hasn't discouraged politicians in the major Latin American countries from following his populist defiance of debt repayment.

All over the region, populist candidates are gaining widespread support. Among the most prominent are the following:

- Cuauhtémoc Cárdenas, who ran a strong second in the still disputed Mexican presidential election in July.
- Carlos Andrés Pérez, a strong favorite in Venezuela's presidential elections on Dec. 4.
- Carlos Menem, who is favored to succeed Raúl Alfonsín as president of Argentina in May.
- Leonel Brizola, a leading candidate for the Brazilian presidency, which will be decided in November 1989, unless the military intervenes.

Populist victories could cut one of two ways, either leading to greater confrontations with Washington and increased strains on fragile Latin democracies or finally forcing the United States to develop a more rational debt policy.

The populists repudiate their governments' current, United States-backed debt policies that give billions to bankers each year while driving Latins deeper into economic crisis. They are striving to build their mandates with appeals to the middle

mer Governor Brizola in unease over the weak leadership of President José Sarney and out of fear that their economy and country are out of control and their democracy threatened.

Despite a strong industrial base, the Brazilian economy is edging toward a situation as bad as Argentina's, with an annualized inflation rate of more than 700 percent in October. Mr. Brizola is developing a plan that would restructure payment terms on the country's $121 billion debt, which

Horacio Fidel Cardo

ON MY MIND
A. M. Rosenthal

The Murder of Rosa Urena

Zapping The Myth Of TV's Power

By Douglas Davis

The 'global village' is just a flashy fantasy.

Aggressive, educated viewers are rising in revolt.

Good News on the Trade Deficit. But ...

By Lawrence H. Summers

How about the Federal deficit?

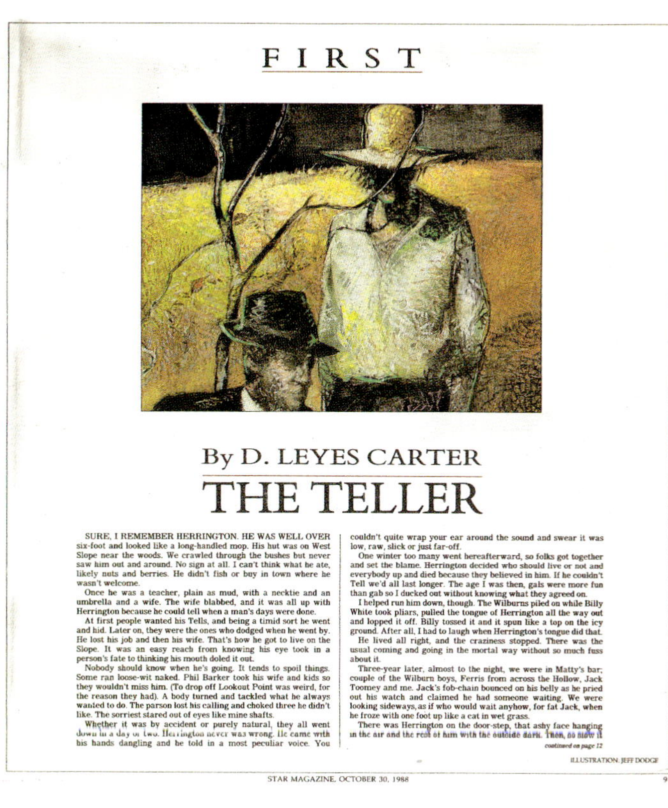

FIRST

By D. LEYES CARTER

THE TELLER

SURE, I REMEMBER HERRINGTON. HE WAS WELL OVER six-foot and looked like a long-handled mop. His hut was on West Slope near the woods. We crawled through the bushes but never saw him out and around. No sign at all. I can't think what he ate, likely nuts and berries. He didn't fish or buy in town where he wasn't welcome.

Once he was a teacher, plain as mud, with a necktie and an umbrella and a wife. The wife blabbed, and it was all up with Herrington because he could tell when a man's days were done.

At first people wanted his Tells, and being a timid sort he went and hid. Later on, they were the ones who dodged when he went by. He lost his job and then his wife. That's how he got to live on the Slope. It was an easy reach from knowing his eye took in a person's fate to thinking his mouth doled it out.

Nobody should know when he's going. It tends to spoil things. Some ran loose-wit naked. Phil Barker took his wife and kids so they wouldn't miss him. (To drop off Lookout Point was weird, for the reason they had). A body turned and tackled what he always wanted to do. The parson lost his calling and choked three he didn't like. The sorriest stared out of eyes like mine shafts.

Whether it was by accident or purely natural, they all went down in a day or two. Herrington never was wrong. He came with his hands dangling and he told in a most peculiar voice. You couldn't quite wrap your ear around the sound and swear it was low, raw, slick or just far-off.

One winter too many went hereafterward, so folks got together and set the blame. Herrington decided who should live or not and everybody up and died because they believed in him. If he couldn't Tell we'd all last longer. The age I was then, gals were more fun than gab so I ducked out without knowing what they agreed on.

I helped run him down, though. The Wilburns piled on while Billy White took pliars, pulled the tongue of Herrington all the way out and lopped it off. Billy tossed it and it spun like a top on the icy ground. After all, I had to laugh when Herrington's tongue did that.

He lived all right, and the craziness stopped. There was the usual coming and going in the mortal way without so much fuss about it.

Three-year later, almost to the night, we were in Matty's bar; couple of the Wilburn boys, Ferris from across the Hollow, Jack Toomey and me. Jack's fob-chain bounced on his belly as he pried out his watch and claimed he had someone waiting. We were looking sideways, as if who would wait anyhow, for fat Jack, when he froze with one foot up like a cat in wet grass.

There was Herrington on the door-step, that ashy face hanging in the air and the rest of him with the outside dark. Then, so slow it

continued on page 12

ILLUSTRATION: JEFF DODGE

STAR MAGAZINE, OCTOBER 30, 1988 9

THE KANSAS CITY STAR.

ELECTION 88

Hayden-bashing in season for GOP candidates, too

Democrats see chance to make gains

INSIDE

FEATURES

THE ELECTION

THE CANDIDATES

POLLING

QUESTIONS

Bush, Dukakis survived, but voters have suffered

Even if not pleased about the choices, we shouldn't boycott the ballot box

Rich Hood

Challengers decry unfair advantage of incumbency in election years

AWARD OF EXCELLENCE
ART AND ILLUSTRATION
PORTFOLIO OF WORK
The Kansas City Star and Times
Illustrator
Jeff Dodge

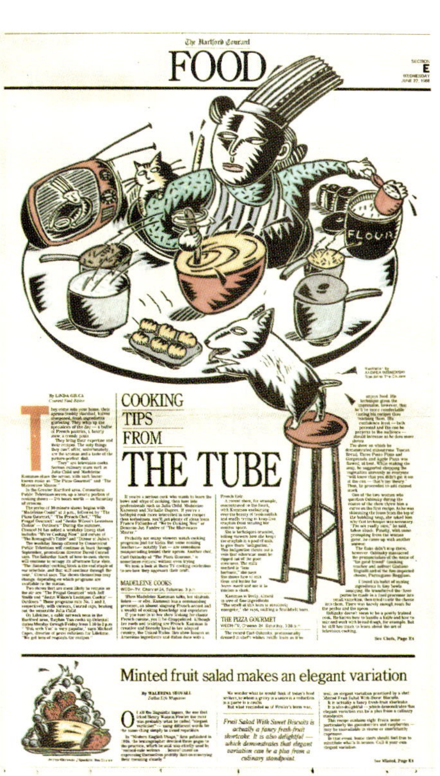

The Hartford Courant

FOOD

COOKING TIPS FROM THE TUBE

Minted fruit salad makes an elegant variation

AWARD OF EXCELLENCE
ART AND ILLUSTRATION
PORTFOLIO OF WORK
The Hartford Courant
Hartford, Connecticut
Designers
Linda Shankweiler, Chris Butler
Illustrator
Andrea Wisnewski
Art Directors
Patti Nelson, Richard Aloisio

ON MY MIND
A. M. Rosenthal

The Arafat Murder Threat

IN THE NATION
Tom Wicker

The Right Goal

Is the Underclass Beyond Help?

By Richard P. Nathan

It's not enough to end poverty.

Why won't the Israelis negotiate with the P.L.O.?

Confessions of a Lottoholic

In Deep Russia, the Camp at the End of the Road

By A. M. Rosenthal

ON MY MIND

Moscow permits the first visit to Perm 35.

A message from a locked ward.

Democrats Dare Not Deny Jackson

IN THE NATION | Tom Wicker

Epitaph for a Cycle

The end of the Reagan years.

SILVER AWARD
ART AND ILLUSTRATION
PORTFOLIO OF WORK
The New York Times

Designer
Jerelle Kraus
Illustrator
Horacio Fidel Cardo
Art Director
Jerelle Kraus

Rafal Olbinski

AWARD OF EXCELLENCE
ART AND ILLUSTRATION
PORTFOLIO OF WORK
The Seattle Times
Designers
Fred Birchman, Robert Massa
Illustrator
Fred Birchman
Art Director
Marian Wachter

Fred Birchman / Seattle Times

AWARD OF EXCELLENCE
PHOTOJOURNALISM
SPOT NEWS PHOTOGRAPHY
Houston Chronicle
Photographer
Richard J. Carson
Art Director
Jim Townsend

AWARD OF EXCELLENCE
ART AND ILLUSTRATION
PORTFOLIO OF WORK
The Washington Times
Washington, D.C.
Designer
John Kascht
Illustrator
John Kascht
Art Director
John Kascht

AWARD OF EXCELLENCE
PHOTOJOURNALISM
SPOT NEWS PHOTOGRAPHY
Democrat and Chronicle
Rochester, New York
Photographer
Burr Lewis
Designers
Joe Gibbs, Joette Riehle
Art Director
Joe Gibbs

Tango master's tale dramatized/3

Advice: TV hoax raises questions/5

life!

Books: Alexander on Bill Bennett/7

Books: Hook on Russell/7

The Washington Times

The Groucho days of T.S. Eliot

ART / Jane Addams Allen

The lesson of Lichtenstein? Art is more than what meets eye

TELEVISION / Don Kowet

'Politics of Privacy' puts news media's policies on trial

"The question is, has the press gone too far? Or are media critics simply reacting with a 'kill the messenger' syndrome?"

MOVIES / Tom Breen

Toon in to best of international animation at the Biograph

The Washington Times

Fashion life!

Karl Lagerfeld

The savior of Chanel introduces his own line to America

A la Chanel, bob haircut is 'in' again

Lagerfeld's Chanel look for spring: Feminine, flattering and very wearable

Democrat and Chronicle

WINDY, COLDER

Bush, Dukakis tie in polls

Democrat's negative rating rises; Quayle hurts GOP ticket

REGIONAL EDITION

Dodgers take 3-2 lead in NL series

'18 Wheels' wins top single at country music awards

VA medical official ordered researchers to alter finding

Univ. of Maryland students volunteer for AIDS tests

CAMPAIGN '88

2 children die playing with fire

Third boy, 14 months, in guarded condition after Berlin St. blaze

'Couch potato' warning to air on ABC, CBS

QUOTE OF THE DAY

INSIDE

Nuke weapon plants are unsafe

U.S. cites 'pattern,' closes 2nd operation

Pork-barrel projects focus of N.Y. probe

AWARD OF EXCELLENCE
PHOTOJOURNALISM
SPOT NEWS PHOTOGRAPHY
News Sun-Sentinel
Ft. Lauderdale, Florida
Photographer
Ursula Seemann

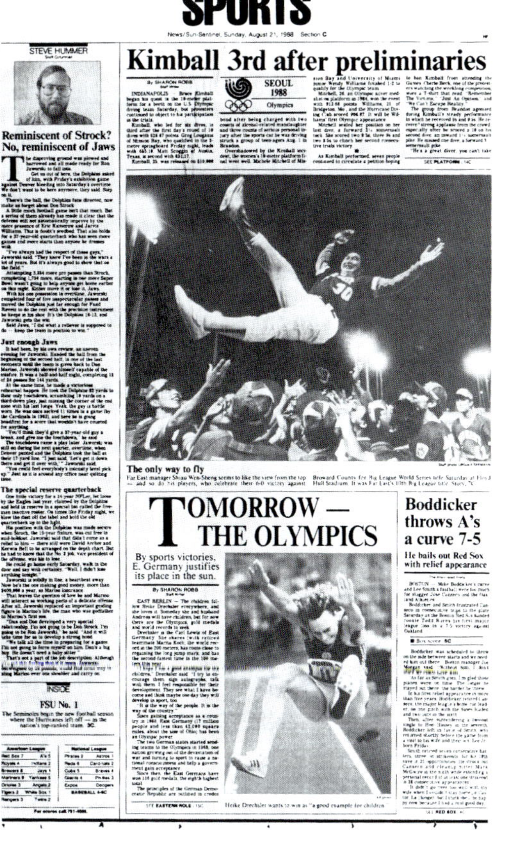

SPORTS

News/Sun-Sentinel, Sunday, August 21, 1988

Kimball 3rd after preliminaries

SEOUL 1988 Olympics

Reminiscent of Strock? No, reminiscent of Jaws

Just enough Jaws

The special reserve quarterback

The only way to fly

TOMORROW — THE OLYMPICS

By sports victories, E. Germany justifies its place in the sun.

Boddicker throws A's a curve 7-5

He bails out Red Sox with relief appearance

INSIDE

FSU No. 1

TAMPA EDITION

Summer Olympic Games begin tonight in Seoul

St. Petersburg Times

Texas runs for cover

Gilbert leaves Yucatan in ruins: more color photos 12-A, 13-A

Tourists feel like refugees in Cancun

Residents prepare for knockout blow

MORE ON GILBERT

INDEX

House rejects proposal for handgun waiting period

AWARD OF EXCELLENCE
PHOTOJOURNALISM
SPOT NEWS PHOTOGRAPHY
St. Petersburg Times
St. Petersburg, Florida
Photographer
Ricardo Ferro
Designer
Ron Reason

Why 'Little Dorrit' is worth six hours of your time and a trip to Los Angeles 6

Sixteen years older, three Byrds reunite for a soaring performance in San Juan Capistrano 33

P section The Orange County Register Friday, January 6, 1989

Show

LOOKING OUT FOR WHALES

PAGE 4

Travel

TRAVELING WITH 2 BIG DUMB DOGS

Hyatt survey checks in on business travelers, gets mixed bag of reactions

AWARD OF EXCELLENCE
ART AND ILLUSTRATION
PORTFOLIO OF WORK
The Seattle Times
Designers
Fred Birchman, Robert Massa
Illustrator
Fred Birchman
Art Director
Marian Wachter

Continued from page 189

BEST BETS

ON THE STREETS

ON THE RADIO

ON THE HOUSE

The Albuquerque Tribune

INSIDE: PEOPLE

OPTIONS

By George, 2
TV listings, 13
Comics, 14

A Cowboy's Christmas Prayer

S. Omar Barker

Blend of cultures stirs the holiday heart in the Southwest

ARIZONA PYRACANTHA JELLY

SILVER AWARD
PHOTOJOURNALISM
FEATURE PHOTOGRAPHY
The Albuquerque Tribune
Photographer
Pat Davison
Picture Editor
Mike Daivs

Potatoes: Jason 'Pete' Peckham, above and at left (with daughter Elyssa), is one of Rhode Island's last potato farmers. His land is worth millions, but he won't sell out.

Photographs and Story by Lane Turner

SUNDAY JOURNAL MAGAZINE, OCTOBER 23, 1988 7

AWARD OF EXCELLENCE
PHOTOJOURNALISM
FEATURE PHOTOGRAPHY
Sunday Journal Magazine
Providence, Rhode Island
Photographer
Lane Turner
Designer
Mike Duval
Picture Editors
Scott Sines, Michael Delaney

AWARD OF EXCELLENCE
PHOTOJOURNALISM
FEATURE PHOTOGRAPHY
The Providence Journal and Sunday Journal Magazine
Providence, Rhode Island
Photographer
Bob Breidenbach
Designer
Christian Potter Drury
Picture Editors
Bill Ostendorf, Dick Benjamin

AWARD OF EXCELLENCE
PHOTOJOURNALISM
FEATURE PHOTOGRAPHY
Reno Gazette-Journal
Photographer
Jean Dixon Aikin
Designers
Mike Blackwell, Lance Iversen

AWARD OF EXCELLENCE
PHOTOJOURNALISM
SPOT NEWS PHOTOGRAPHY
The Albuquerque Tribune
Photographer
Pat Davison
Picture Editor
Mike Davis

LOCAL/STATE

Women increasingly are fearing for their lives

Student's death focuses attention

FOR HELP

WOMEN HOMICIDE VICTIMS

UPDATE

Two charged with murder

WHAT HAPPENED?

CORRECTIONS

AWARD OF EXCELLENCE
PHOTOJOURNALISM
SPOT NEWS PHOTOGRAPHY
The Bakersfield Californian
Photographer
Casey Christie
Art Director
Ron Cioffi

Cold-blooded thrillers
Exotic reptiles take roost in Tulare, E1

STARTING ALL OVER
Raider lineman learns a new way to play, D1

The Bakersfield Californian

SATURDAY HEADLINES

Vincennes crew cleared

WORLD-NATION

STATE

LOCAL

BUSINESS

ON THE GO

FAITH

SPORTS

FOR THE RECORD

INDEX

Stranded

Stars to join Chavez for end of fast

On 111th birthday, oldest man gives credit to honey and song

Land mine blast kills seven soldiers in Northern Ireland

Hospital curtails gathering of infant organs for transplants

SILVER AWARD
PHOTOJOURNALISM
SPOT NEWS PHOTOGRAPHY
The Miami Herald
Photographer
Brian Smith
Photo Editors
Steve Rice, Dennis Copeland

Sports News

Boxing just gets curiouser and curiouser

U.S. holds on in basketball

SEOUL '88

Louganis gashed, golden

Diver overcomes accident to win springboard

Pagel leads Browns; Colts (0-3) lose QB

Gary gets off to a start that UM hopes he'll finish

Detroit Free Press

Sunday, June 26, 1988 Section J

SPECIAL SECTION

A CLASS ACT

The life and times of Southwestern High School

WORDS AND PHOTOS BY MANNY CRISOSTOMO

a CLASS ACT

ANGIE DELGADO, JUNIOR

AWARD OF EXCELLENCE
PHOTOJOURNALISM
PHOTO STORY
Detroit Free Press
Photographer
Manny Crisostomo

AWARD OF EXCELLENCE
PHOTOJOURNALISM
FEATURE PHOTOGRAPHY
The Tallahassee Democrat
Tallahassee, Florida
Photographer
Mark Wallheiser
Designer
Chris Norman

SILVER AWARD
PHOTOJOURNALISM
FEATURE PHOTOGRAPHY
The Providence Journal and Sunday Journal Magazine
Providence, Rhode Island
Photographer
Bob Breidenbach
Designer
Christian Potter Drury
Picture Editor
Scott Sines

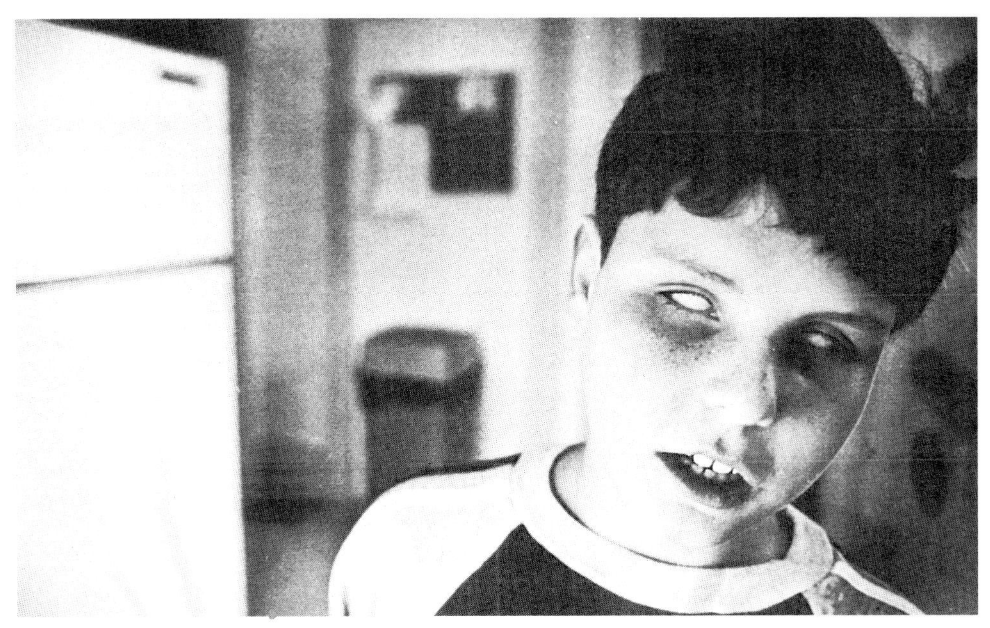

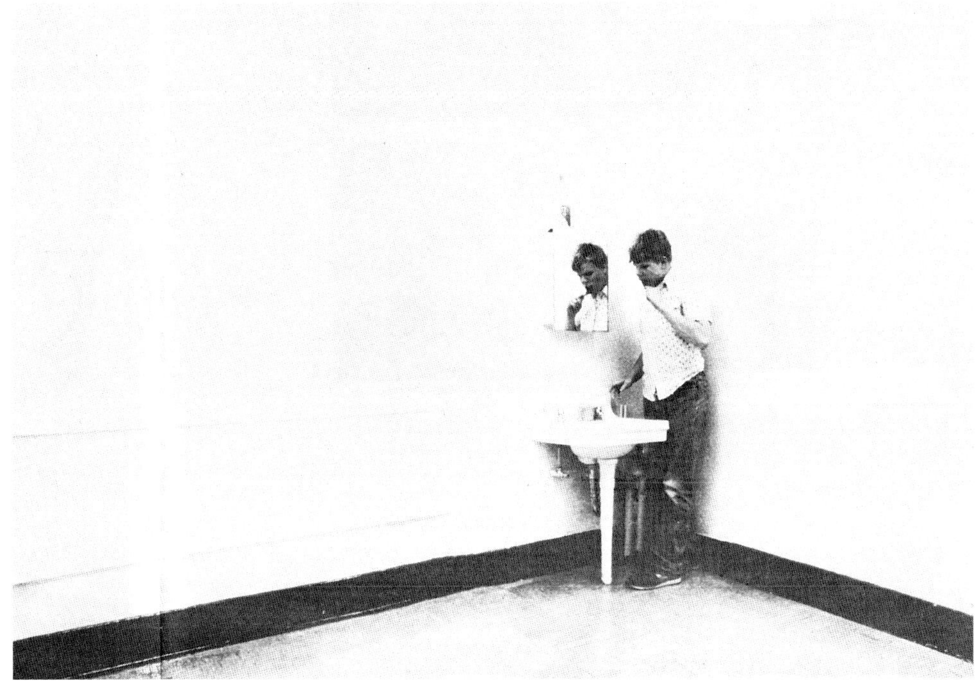

AWARD OF EXCELLENCE
PHOTOJOURNALISM
PHOTO STORY
Gazette Telegraph
Colorado Springs, Colorado
Photographer
Mark Reis

AWARD OF EXCELLENCE
PHOTOJOURNALISM
FEATURE PHOTOGRAPHY
The Seattle Times
Photographer
Alan Berner

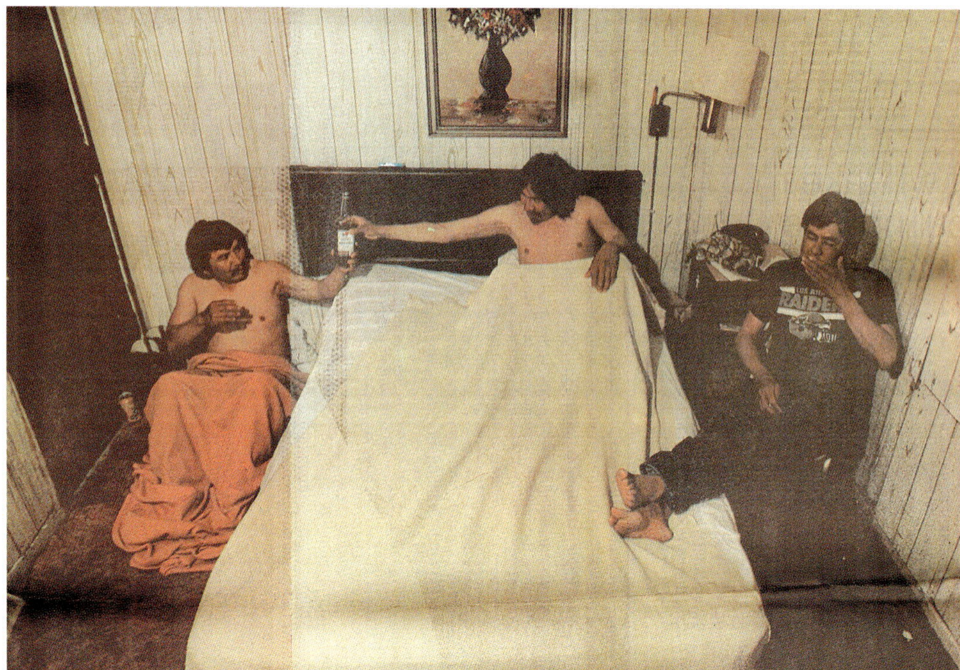

SILVER AWARD
PHOTOJOURNALISM
PHOTO STORY
The Albuquerque Tribune
Photographer
Joe Cavaretta
Designers
Brian Harrah, Mike Davis,
Randall Roberts, Dave Carlson

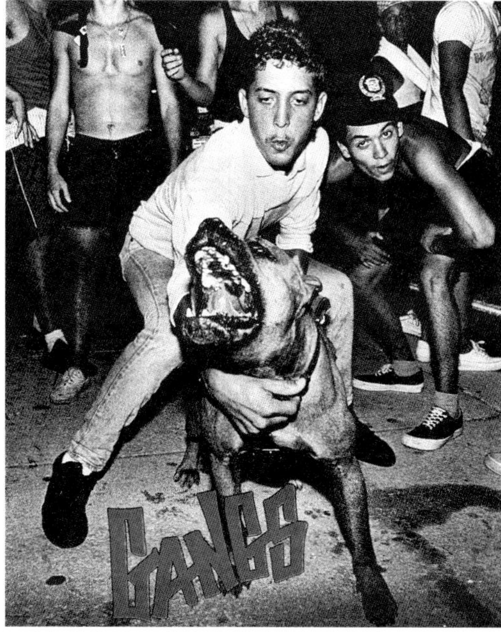

AWARD OF EXCELLENCE
PHOTOJOURNALISM
PHOTO STORY
The Miami Herald, Tropic Magazine
Photographer
Jon Kral
Designer
Phillip Brooker
Photo Editors
Steve Rice, Dennis Copeland

SILVER AWARD
PHOTOJOURNALISM
PHOTO STORY
The Miami Herald, Tropic Magazine
Photographer
Pete Cross
Designer
Phillip Brooker
Photo Editors
Steve Rice, Dennis Copeland

PHOTOGRAPHS BY PETE CROSS

Boot camp, first week: Inmate Michael Hancock, 17, sentenced to 2½ years for burglary, makes an obscene gesture at officer David Smoak while he turns his back to yell at another inmate. Hancock was kicked out after two weeks, which were spent fighting with inmates, arguing with guards and — finally — yelling obscenities at a prison secretary.

LAST CHANCE U.

Can the method that makes Marines unmake criminals?

James McDonald is running.

The rain is driving now, stinging his face, blinding him.

"HIT IT!!"

His legs stiffen. His arms fly straight up, as though a cop had screamed, *Reach for the sky.* He is falling, falling face down into the stinking water and muck that covers the prison yard. He closes his eyes and holds his breath.

The mud is everywhere. It seeps into the nostrils, the ears, under the lips, between the buttocks. Socks fill with it. Eyelids crust over. When you push yourself up, the muck sucks at your wrists; when you run, it is up to the laces on your brogans.

"DON'T WALLOW AROUND DOWN THERE, YOU PUKES!! MOVE IT!! ON YOUR BACK!! ON YOUR STOMACH!! ON YOUR FEET!! ON YOUR STOMACH!! ON YOUR FEET!! WE'RE RUNNING!!"

James McDonald is running. He — and the rest of the hard-core punks in the second platoon — have been doing these grass drills for more than an hour: running in place, dropping flat, rolling over, jumping up and starting over again on command. It is a Sunday afternoon in August. A billowing thunderstorm has been belting the place since just after noon. The punks failed room inspections. The punks are being punished.

It is Day 26 at boot camp on the soaking grounds of Sumter Correctional Institution, a maximum security state prison set in the boondocks 60 miles north of Tampa. This is Florida's great hope in prison reform: a program designed to turn street hoods into law-abiding young men.

The deal, offered to selected criminals under the age of 24, is simple: Survive 90 days of boot camp and the rest of your sentence — up to 10 years — is commuted to probation. Blow it, and you're back in prison for the full ride.

NEELY TUCKER is a Herald staff writer. For this story, he spent 24 days as a member of the second platoon.

The camp's directors say the 4 a.m. exercises, the six-mile runs, the classes on rational behavior and drug abuse combine to have an overwhelming impact. They say the physical discipline gets drug-softened bodies in shape; the mind is to follow. It's the Marine blueprint: Strip away the garbage with adversity and humiliation; build a new man from the ground up.

This is the newest program born of the simple conviction that there must be a better alternative to simply warehousing convicted felons. It's nothing new, in principle. A host of similar rehabilitative programs flourished in the '70s, ranging from wilderness training to music therapy to the "Scared Straight" project in California that became a book and a film and two years of TV documentaries. Most of these programs have been canceled because of their cost and because of their track record. Lots of repeat offenders. They tend not to work.

Florida prison officials predict this one will. They're high on it for a lot of reasons, not the least of which is that it's not very expensive, hardly more than traditional incarceration, and it is very quick. In and out. The men of the second platoon have only 64 days to go.

They are a brutal menagerie of losers, drug dealers, gunmen, thieves and thugs. Their lives are stories of illegitimate children, street fights, a robbery, a high, a gun. Work means fast-food restaurants, laying power lines and mindless construction labor. Dead-end grunt work. These kids can imagine only one way to achieve the glitzy life of fast cars and easy riches, the world they worship on television. Stealing it. And maybe, if the take is that good or you're that high, pulling a trigger for it.

Everybody here has been arrested five, six times. Been put in and thrown out of every juvenile program Florida has to offer. Counseling centers, drug rehabilitation programs, halfway houses — forget it. They've been there.

So now they've come to one last shot at

BY NEELY TUCKER

AWARD OF EXCELLENCE
PHOTOJOURNALISM
PHOTO STORY
Philadelphia Inquirer Magazine
Photographer
Ed Hille
Art Director
David Griffin
Photo Editors
Bert Fox, Tom Gralish

Continued from page 197

AWARD OF EXCELLENCE
PHOTOJOURNALISM
PHOTO STORY
Philadelphia Inquirer Magazine
Photographer
Charles Fox
Designer
Bert Fox
Art Director
David Griffin
Photo Editor
Tom Gralish

AWARD OF EXCELLENCE
PHOTOJOURNALISM
PHOTO STORY
Philadelphia Inquirer Magazine
Photographer
Michael Wirtz
Art Director
David Griffin
Photo Editors
Bert Fox, Tom Gralish

SILVER AWARD
PHOTOJOURNALISM
PHOTO STORY
Philadelphia Inquirer Magazine
Photographer
Akira Suwa
Designer
Bert Fox
Art Director
Bert Fox
Photo Editor
Tom Gralish

SUNDAY JOURNAL

MAGAZINE

October 23, 1988

SPECIAL TRAVEL SECTION INSIDE

BURIED TREASURE

IMAGES OF A TIVERTON FARM ON PRIME REAL ESTATE

ALSO: ARLENE VIOLET ON HOLLYWOOD

AWARD OF EXCELLENCE
PHOTOJOURNALISM
PHOTO STORY
The Providence Journal, Sunday Journal Magazine
Providence, Rhode Island
Photographer
Lane Turner
Designer
Mike Duval
Photo Editors
Scott Sines, Michael Delaney

AWARD OF EXCELLENCE
PHOTOJOURNALISM
PHOTO STORY
The Seattle Times
Photographer
Alan Berner

SECTION J
Sunday, December 25, 1988
The Seattle Times
Seattle Post-Intelligencer

Scene

Books, J 3, J 8
Dear Abby J 2
Troubleshooter J 9

AFGHANISTAN is their Vietnam, a hidden war for thousands of Soviet soldiers. The parallels are there – in pain, in injury and in rejection. Into their midst comes a group of Vietnam veterans, to meet their counterparts, to listen to their stories, to try to make some sense of things. To try to find some . . .

Common ground

VICTOR NOSATOV, an Afghan War veteran, is comforted by Vietnam vet Peter Mahoney, left, Donna Germano, Randy Richard and Marianne Clarke at the grave of a comrade killed in Afghanistan.

A YOUNG PIONEER stands guard at a memorial in Alma-Ata that honors 28 guardsmen who stopped Nazi tanks from entering Moscow during World War II.

One mother tries to alter the pattern of abuse

by Elizabeth Rhodes
Times staff reporter

Please see GROUND on J 8

Please see FUND on J 2

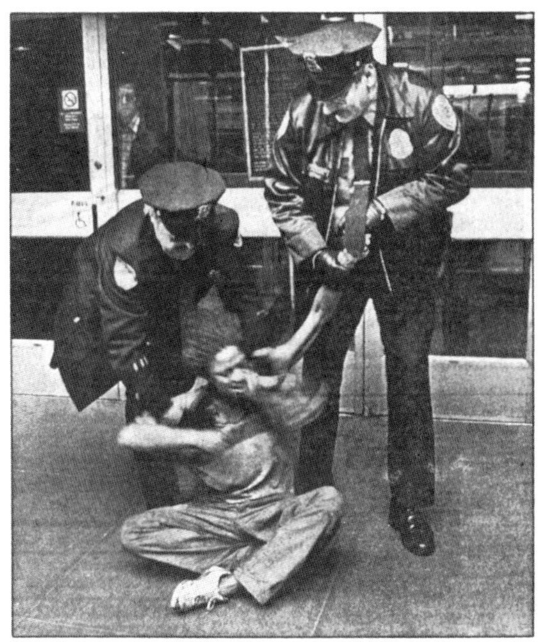

AWARD OF EXCELLENCE
PHOTOJOURNALISM
PHOTO STORY
The Seattle Times
Photographer
Jimi Lott
Designers
Marian Wachter,
Rob Kemp
Art Director
Marian Wachter
Photo Editor
Cole Porter

THE DARK SIDE OF LIGHT

Photographed by
Lois Bernstein
The Sacramento Bee

Kim and Jim Harrison take Jaime to a dermatologist in San Francisco, a tiring, frustrating trip. They wait a long time at the office, and learn nothing new.

Vallejo pediatrician Shanee Martin, left, gives Sherry a routine checkup. The younger girl hasn't had to endure the extensive testing that her older sister, Jaime, has, and doesn't share her fear and dislike of doctors.

Sherry wears a helmet, right, with reflective film to screen out UV radiation from her face during a daytime trip. This cuts her vision, so her mother must guide her. Below, Jaime screams, "Get her out of the window," as Robert reaches for Sherry, who has tried to sneak a look at the world outside the prison of her home.

'I'd just like my kids to be able to play with a hose on a summer day.'
—Kim Harrison

A nightmare that won't end

Sun is the enemy, night a friend

Sunlight, above, causes Robert and his mother to squint as they emerge from their dark home with the girls. Jaime is wrapped in a blanket to protect her. Left, Robert keeps a watchful eye on Jaime during a trip to the doctor.

'It didn't turn out the way it does on TV.'
—Kim Harrison

Her parents let Sherry peek at a world she'll never explore during a trip to the doctor. The van's windows are covered with a reflective film and dark curtains.

THE SERIES

AWARD OF EXCELLENCE
PHOTOJOURNALISM
PHOTO STORY
The Sacramento Bee
Sacramento, California
Photographer
Lois Bernstein
Designer
Richard Perry

AWARD OF EXCELLENCE
PHOTOJOURNALISM
PORTFOLIO OF WORK
The Pittsburgh Press
Photographer
John Kaplan

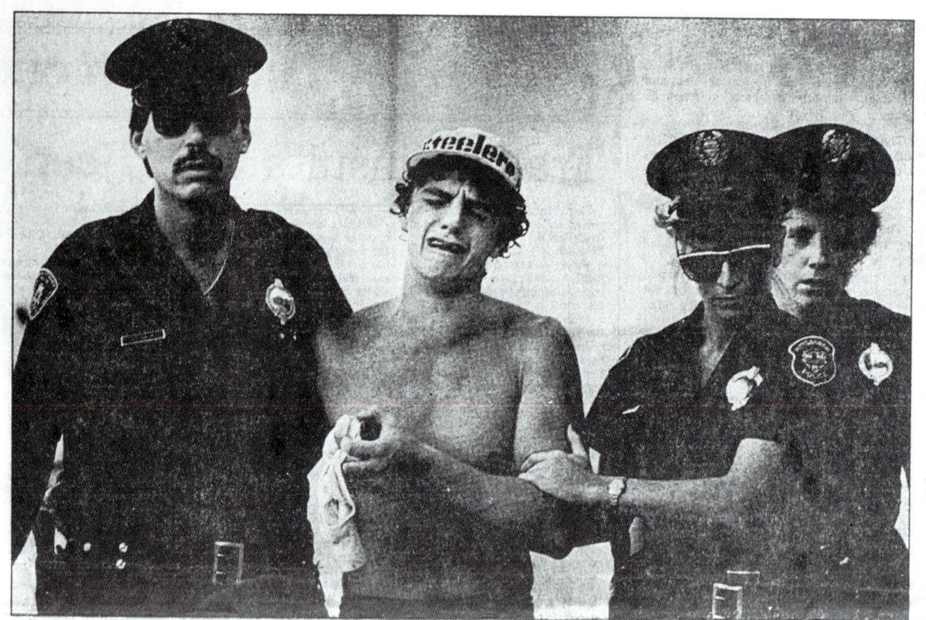

John Kaplan/The Pittsburgh Press

AWARD OF EXCELLENCE
PHOTOJOURNALISM
PORTFOLIO OF WORK
Gazette Telegraph
Colorado Springs, Colorado
Photographer
Mark Reis

SPORTS

• SECTION C

BASEBALL

Cardinals' Smith, A's Canseco are fans' favorites

LEADING VOTE-GETTERS

NBA

Nuggets sign Davis, release Dunn, Evans

GOLF

Saiki rallies to win second Ladies title

Smith can't shake early round, opponent's putter

■ Chip Beck chases million-dollar mark/C7

A CLOUD OF DUST

INSIDE

FOOTBALL

Broncos plan around two starters

Air Force tackle has leg amputated

SKY SOX

Rain can't dampen Springs' zany show

Zuvella, Lovell hit first homers

Mark Reis/Gazette Telegraph

Anthony Romero holds a pistol to his head during a standoff with police at his Colorado Springs home Monday. He holds a box containing a phone that police left outside the front door.

AWARD OF EXCELLENCE
BREAKING NEWS
INFORMATION GRAPHICS
BLACK AND WHITE
The Detroit News
Illustrators
Daivid Pierce, Robert Richards,
Felix Grabowski
Researchers
Michele Fecht, Laura D. Varon,
Pegie Stark
Art Deirector
Felix Grabowski
Graphics Editors
Dierck Casselman,
Felix Grabowski
Assistant Graphics Editor
Laura D. Varon

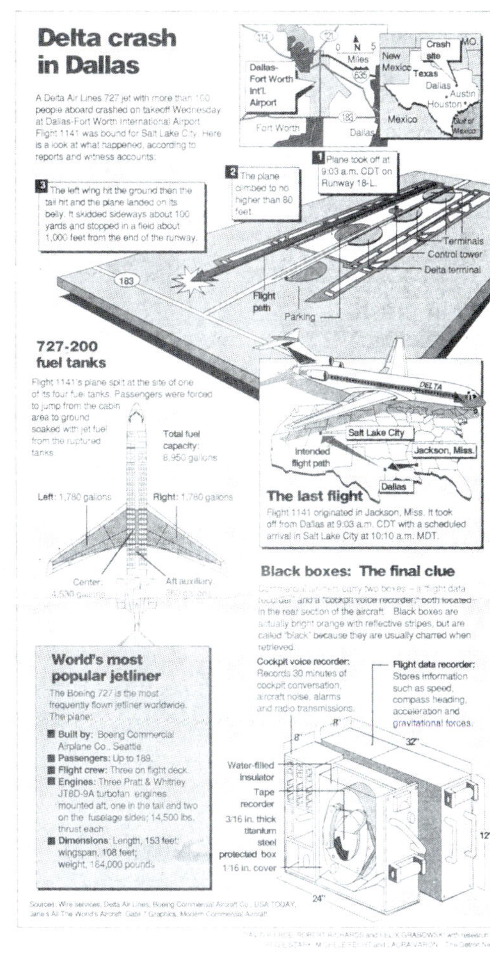

SILVER AWARD
PHOTOJOURNALISM
PORTFOLIO OF WORK
The Seattle Times
Photographer
Alan Berner

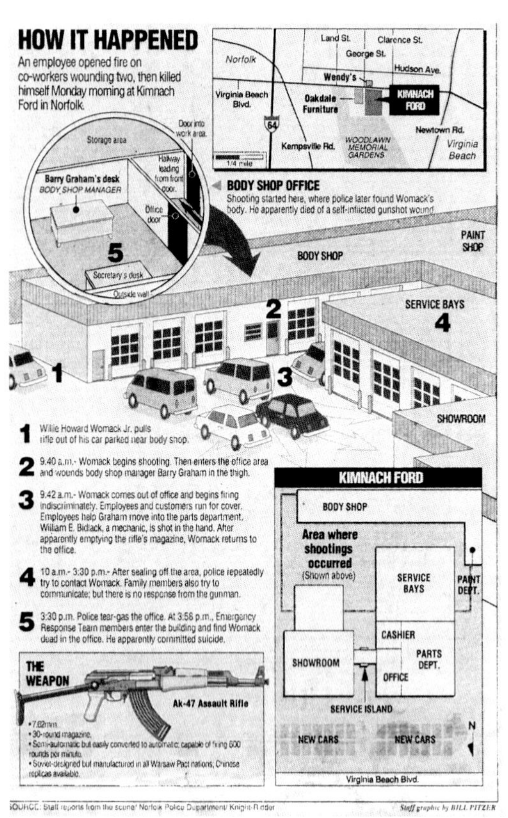

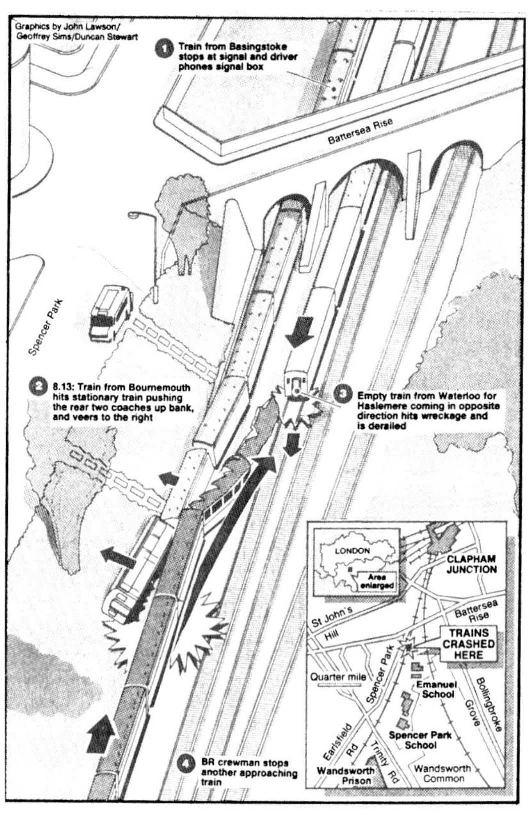

AWARD OF EXCELLENCE
BREAKING NEWS
INFORMATIONAL GRAPHICS
BLACK AND WHITE
The Times
London, England
Illustrators
Geoffrey Sims, J. Lawson, D. Stewart
Head of Graphics
Geoffrey Sims

AWARD OF EXCELLENCE
BREAKING NEWS
INFORMATIONAL GRAPHICS
BLACK AND WHITE
The Virginian-Pilot and The Ledger-Star
Norfolk, Virginia
Illustrator
Bill Pitzer
Designer
Bill Pitzer
Art Director
Bob Lynn

AWARD OF EXCELLENCE
BREAKING NEWS
INFORMATION GRAPHICS
BLACK AND WHITE
The Orange County Register
Santa Ana, California
Illustrator
Jeff Goertzen
Designer
Jeff Goertzen
Art Director
Bill Dunn

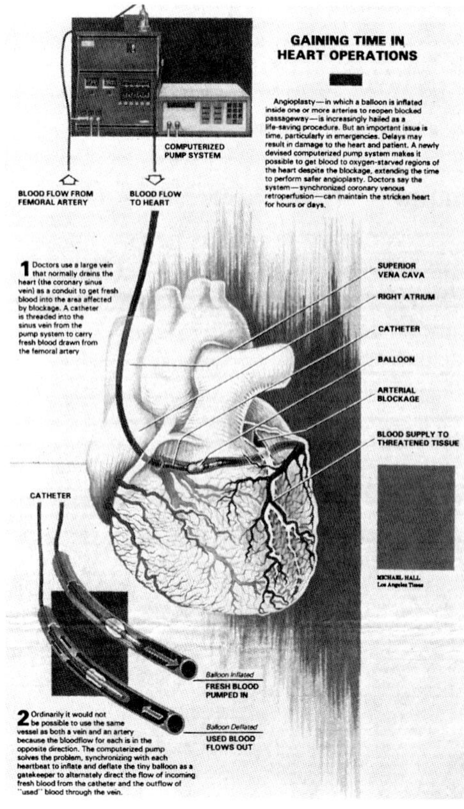

AWARD OF EXCELLENCE
INFORMATIONAL GRAPHICS
BLACK AND WHITE
Los Angeles Times
Illustrator
Michael R. Hall
Editor
Terry Schwadron

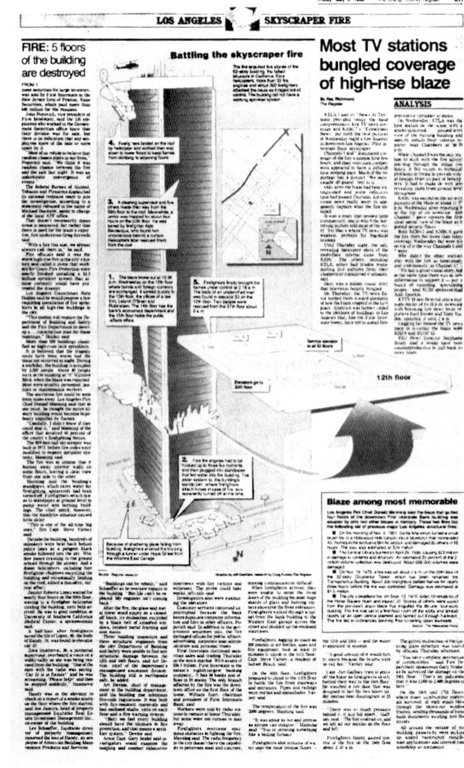

SILVER AWARD

BREAKING NEWS
INFORMATIONAL GRAPHICS
TWO OR MORE COLORS

USA Today

Illustrators
Bill Baker, Jeff Dionise, John Sherlock, Sam Ward, Julie Stacey
Designer
John Sherlock
Art Director
Lynne Perri

AWARD OF EXCELLENCE

BREAKING NEWS
INFORMATION GRAPHICS
BLACK AND WHITE

The Orange County Register
Santa Ana, California

Illustrator
Paul Carbo
Designer
Paul Carbo
Researcher
Paul Carbo
Art Director
Bill Dunn

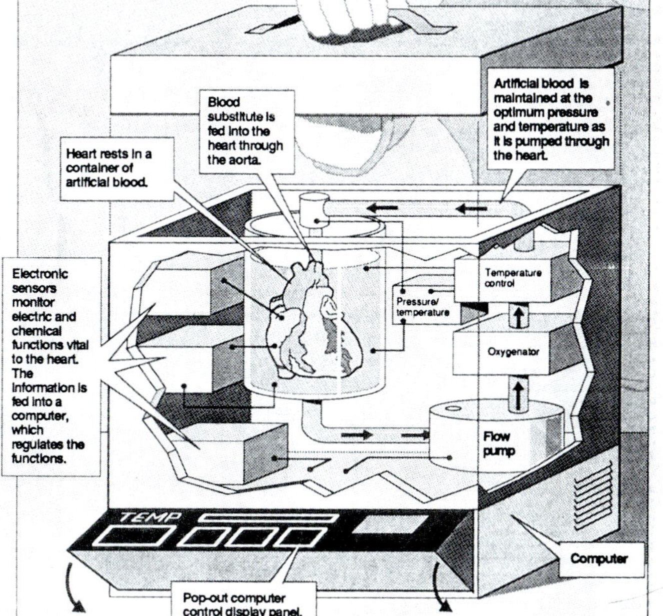

AWARD OF EXCELLENCE

BREAKING NEWS
INFORMATIONAL GRAPHICS
TWO OR MORE COLORS

The Detroit News

Illustrators
Marty Westman, David Pierce
Researchers
Michele Fecht, Richard Egan
Art Director
Felix Grabowski
Graphics Editors
Felix Grabowski, Laura Varon

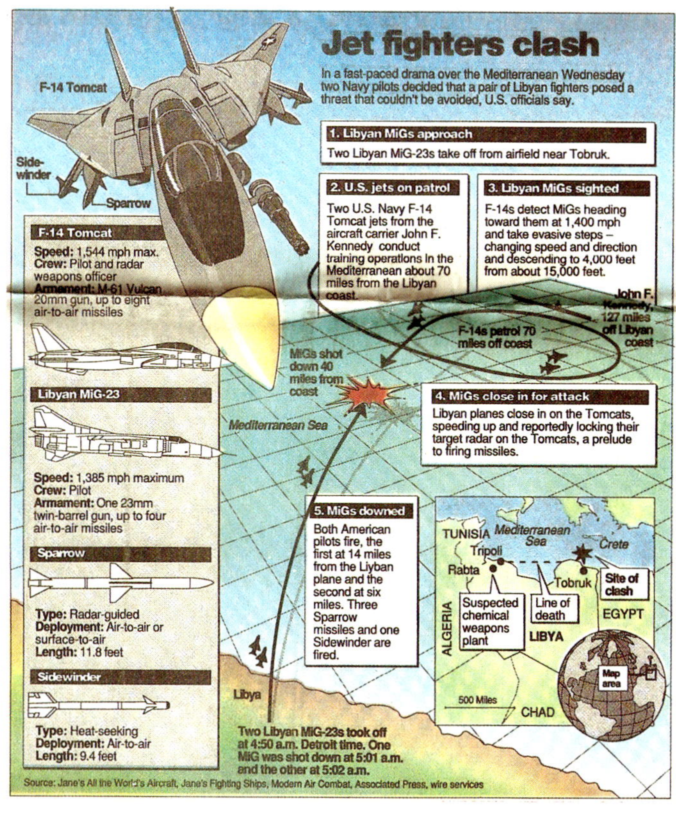

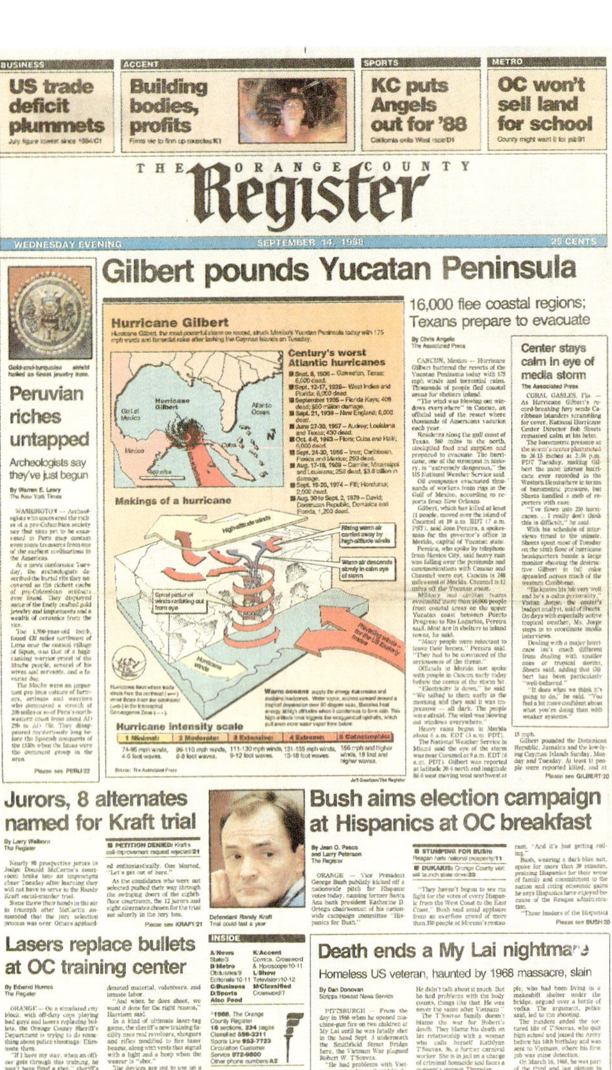

BUSINESS
US trade deficit plummets

ACCENT
Building bodies, profits

SPORTS
KC puts Angels out for '88

METRO
OC won't sell land for school

THE ORANGE COUNTY **Register**

WEDNESDAY EVENING — SEPTEMBER 14, 1988 — 25 CENTS

Gilbert pounds Yucatan Peninsula

16,000 flee coastal regions; Texans prepare to evacuate

Hurricane Gilbert

Century's worst Atlantic hurricanes

Makings of a hurricane

Hurricane intensity scale

Center stays calm in eye of media storm

Peruvian riches untapped

Archeologists say they've just begun

Jurors, 8 alternates named for Kraft trial

Bush aims election campaign at Hispanics at OC breakfast

Lasers replace bullets at OC training center

INSIDE

Death ends a My Lai nightmare

Homeless US veteran, haunted by 1968 massacre, slain

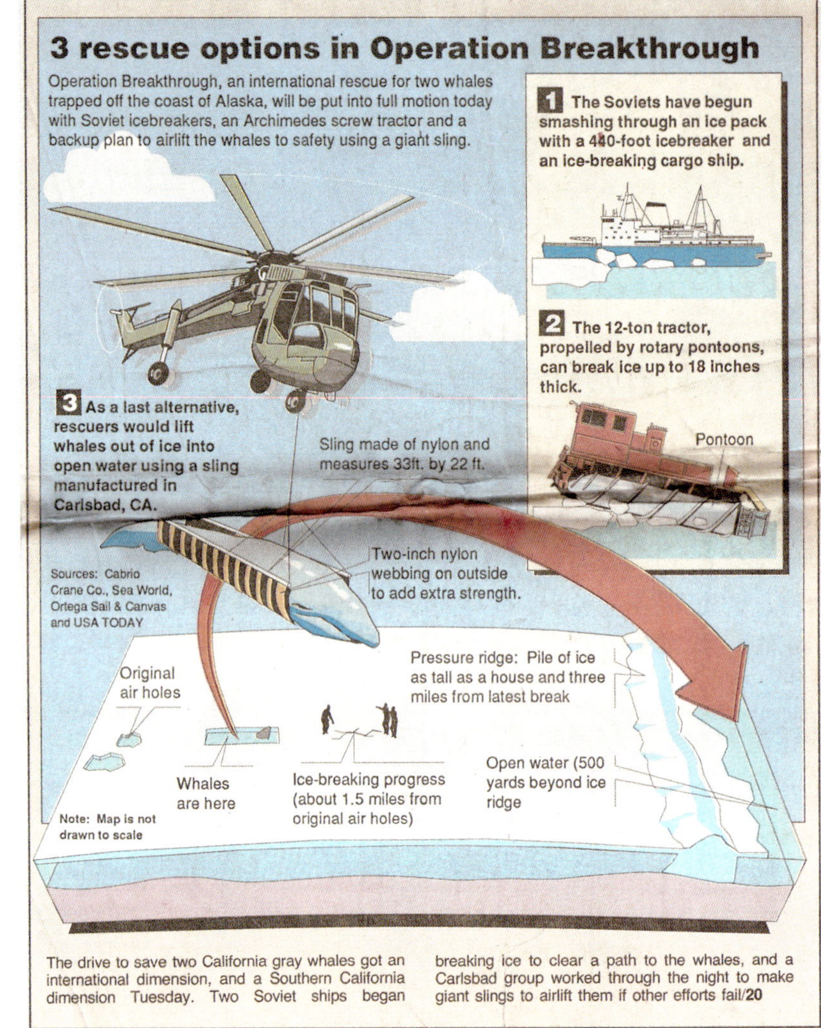

Jeff Goertzen and Nancy Ward/The Register

AWARD OF EXCELLENCE
BREAKING NEWS
INFORMATIONAL GRAPHIC
PORTFOLIO OF WORK
The Orange County Register
Santa Ana, California

Illustrator
Jeff Goertzen
Designer
Jeff Goertzen
Art Director
Bill Dunn

AWARD OF EXCELLENCE
INFORMATIONAL GRAPHICS
BLACK AND WHITE
The Detroit News

Illustrators
Marty Westman, Robert Graham
Designers
Pegie Stark, Robert Graham
Researcher
Michele Fech
Art Director
Pegie Stark, Robert Graham
Editor
Dierck Casselman

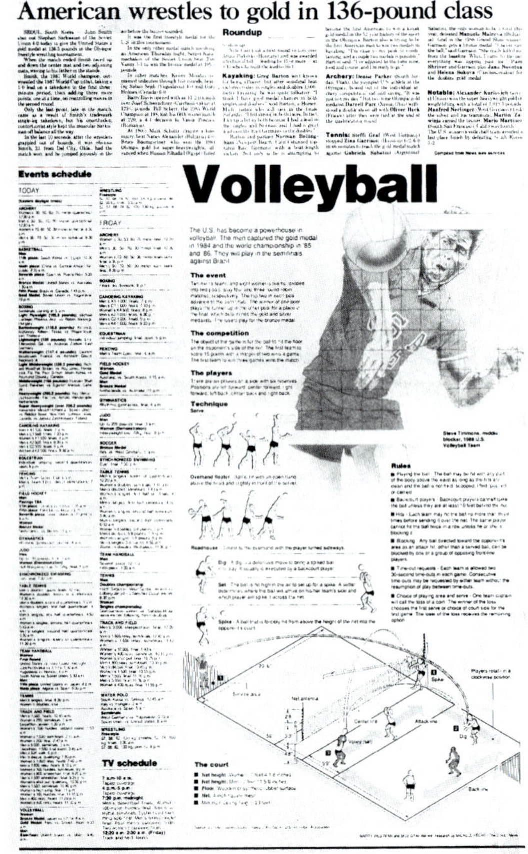

THE SEOUL SUMMER GAMES

American wrestles to gold in 136-pound class

Roundup

Events schedule

Volleyball

The U.S. has become a powerhouse in volleyball. The myth captured the gold medal in 1984 and the world championship in '85 and '86. They will play in the semifinals against Brazil.

The event

The competition

The players

Technique

Rules

The court

TV schedule

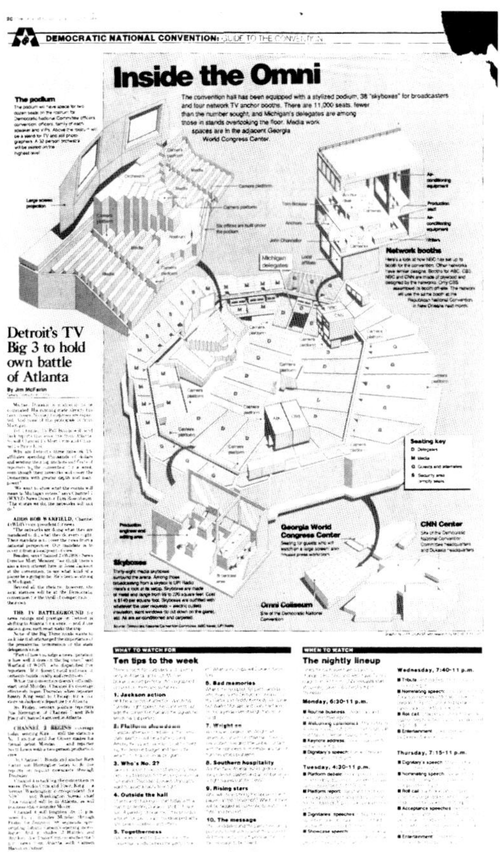

DEMOCRATIC NATIONAL CONVENTION

Inside the Omni

Detroit's TV Big 3 to hold own battle of Atlanta

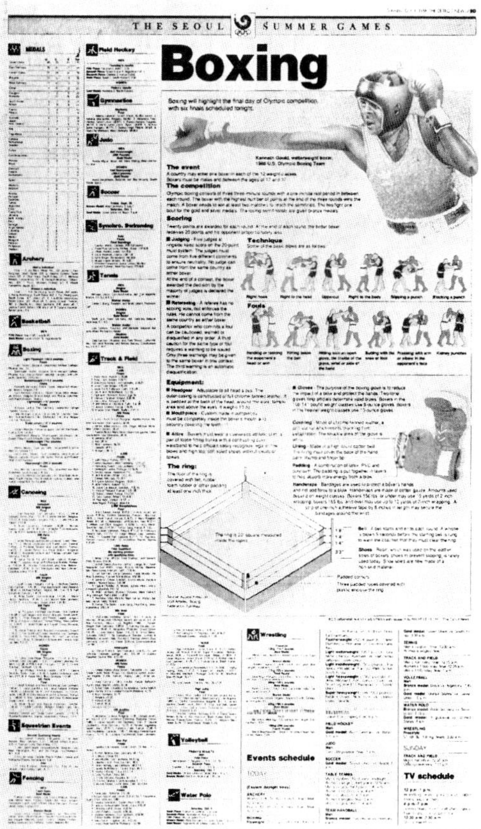

THE SEOUL SUMMER GAMES

Boxing

AWARD OF EXCELLENCE
INFORMATIONAL GRAPHICS
BLACK AND WHITE
The Detroit News
Illustrators
Marty Westman, Robert Graham
Designers
Pegie Stark, Robert Graham
Researchers
Michele Fecht, Pegie Stark
Art Director
Pegie Stark, Robert Graham
Editor
Dierck Casselman

AWARD OF EXCELLENCE
INFORMATIONAL GRAPHICS
BLACK AND WHITE
The Detroit News
Illustrator
Jeff Dionise
Researcher
Michele Fecht
Editors
Pegie Stark,
Dierck Casselman

AWARD OF EXCELLENCE
INFORMATIONAL GRAPHICS
BLACK AND WHITE
The Detroit News
Illustrators
Marty Westman, Robert Graham
Designers
Pegie Stark, Robert Graham
Researchers
Michele Fecht
Art Director
Pegie Stark, Robert Graham
Editor
Dierck Casselman

AWARD OF EXCELLENCE
INFORMATIONAL GRAPHICS
BLACK AND WHITE
The Detroit News
Illustrators
Marty Westman, Patrick Sedlar,
Robert Graham
Designers
Pegie Stark, Robert Graham
Researcher
Michele Fecht
Art Director
Pegie Stark, Robert Graham
Editor
Dierck Casselman

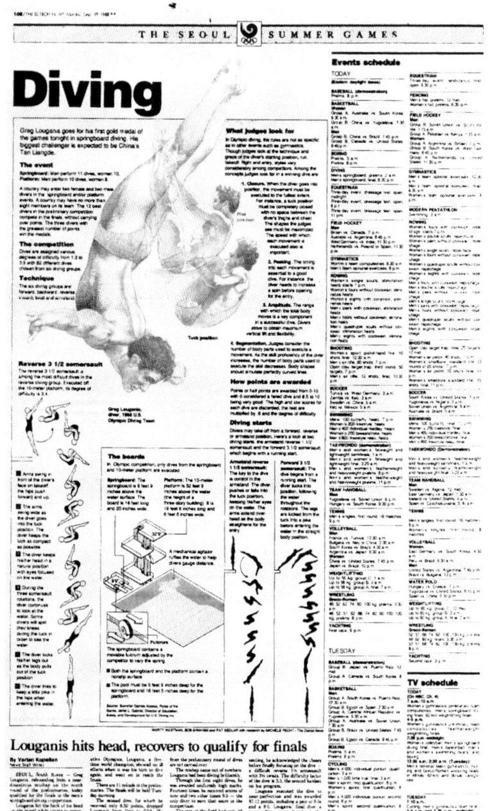

THE SEOUL SUMMER GAMES

Diving

Louganis hits head, recovers to qualify for finals

THE SEOUL SUMMER GAMES

Track and field

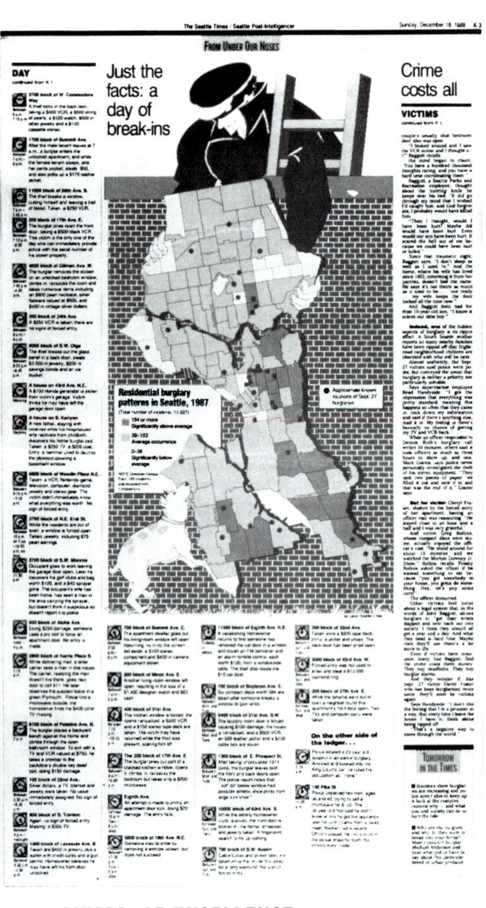

From Under Our Noses

Just the facts: a day of break-ins

Crime costs all

Residential burglary patterns in Seattle, 1987

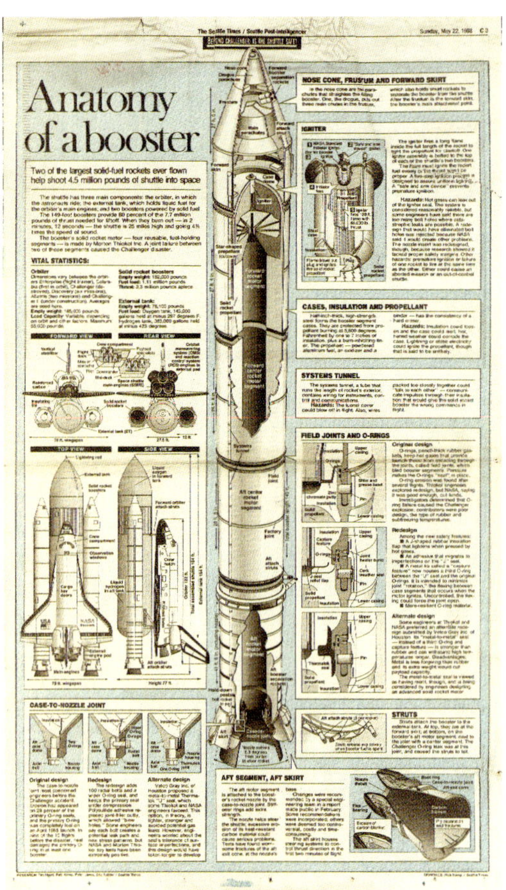

Anatomy of a booster

Two of the largest solid-fuel rockets ever flown help shoot 4.5 million pounds of shuttle into space

SILVER AWARD

INFORMATIONAL GRAPHICS
BLACK AND WHITE
WITH ONE COLOR

The Seattle Times

Illustrator
Rob Kemp
Designer
Rob Kemp
Art Director
Marian Wachter
Researchers
Tim Hyatt, Eric Nalder, Peter Lewis
Project Editor
Kathleen Triesch Saul

AWARD OF EXCELLENCE

INFORMATIONAL GRAPHICS
BLACK AND WHITE

The Seattle Times

Illustrator
Bo H. Cline
Designer
Bo H. Cline
Art Director
Marian Wachter

AWARDS OF EXCELLENCE

INFORMATIONAL GRAPHICS
TWO OR MORE COLORS
and
PAGE DESIGN
INSIDE NEWS PAGE

Chicago Tribune

Illustrator
Megan Jaegerman
Designer
Megan Jaegerman
Researcher
Megan Jaegerman
Art Directors
Stephen Cvengros, Tony Majeri

REAGAN AND GORBACHEV: ROUND FOUR

Guide to Moscow summit

TV brings it home

Ambassador's host at Spaso House

THE SUMMIT

Kremlin: Center of attention

AWARD OF EXCELLENCE

INFORMATIONAL GRAPHICS
BLACK AND WHITE

USA Today

Illustrators
Sam Ward, Web Bryant,
Jeff Dionise, Bob Laird,
Rod Little, Suzy Parker,
John Sherlock, Marcia Stamier
Art Director
Lynne Perri

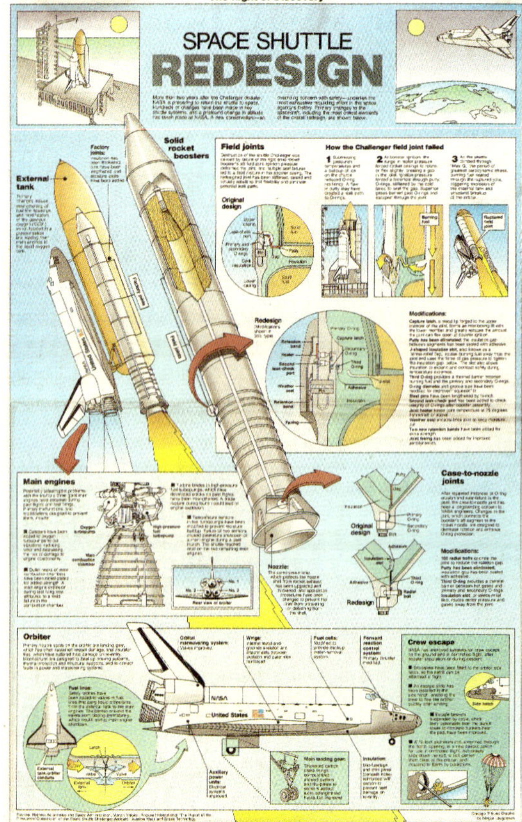

The flight of Discovery

SPACE SHUTTLE REDESIGN

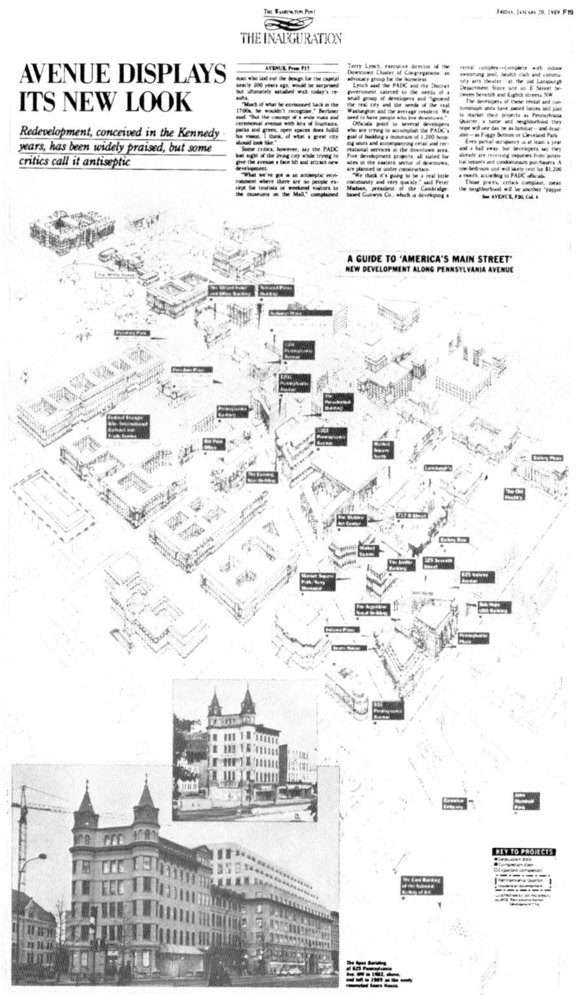
THE INAUGURATION

AVENUE DISPLAYS ITS NEW LOOK

Redevelopment, conceived in the Kennedy years, has been widely praised, but some critics call it antiseptic

AWARD OF EXCELLENCE
INFORMATIONAL GRAPHICS
BLACK AND WHITE
The Washington Post
Illustrator
Joe Passoneau
Designer
Michael Drew
Researcher
Jane Ashley

AWARD OF EXCELLENCE
INFORMATIONAL GRAPHICS
BLACK AND WHITE
USA Today
Illustrators
Sam Ward, Web Bryant,
Jeff Dionise, Bob Laird,
Rod Little, Suzy Parker,
John Sherlock, Marcia Stamler

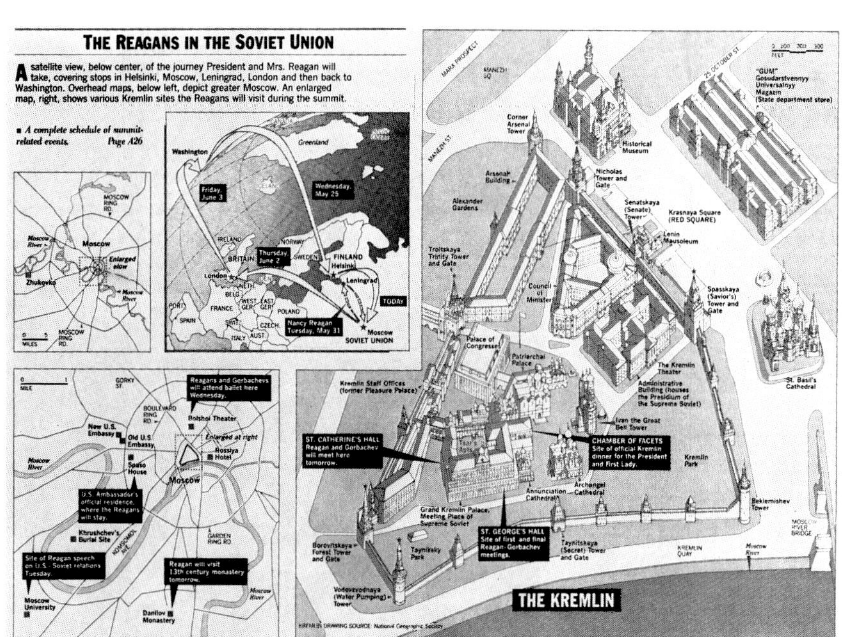

AWARD OF EXCELLENCE
INFORMATIONAL GRAPHICS
BLACK AND WHITE
The Washington Post
Illustrator
Larry Fogel
Researcher
James Schwartz
Art Director
Michael Keegan

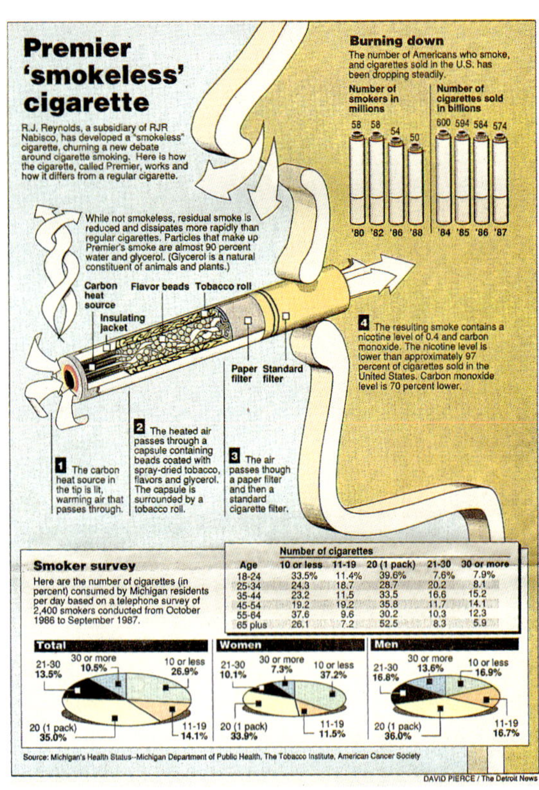

	Number of cigarettes				
Age	10 or less	11-19	20 (1 pack)	21-30	30 or more
18-24	33.5%	11.4%	39.6%	7.6%	7.9%
25-34	24.3	18.7	28.7	20.2	8.1
35-44	23.2	11.5	33.5	16.6	15.2
45-54	19.2	19.2	35.8	11.7	14.1
55-64	37.6	9.6	30.2	10.3	12.3
65 plus	26.1	7.2	52.5	8.3	5.9

AWARD OF EXCELLENCE

INFORMATIONAL GRAPHICS
TWO OR MORE COLORS
The Detroit News

Illustrator
David Pierce
Art Director
Laura D. Varon
Graphics Editor
Laura D. Varon

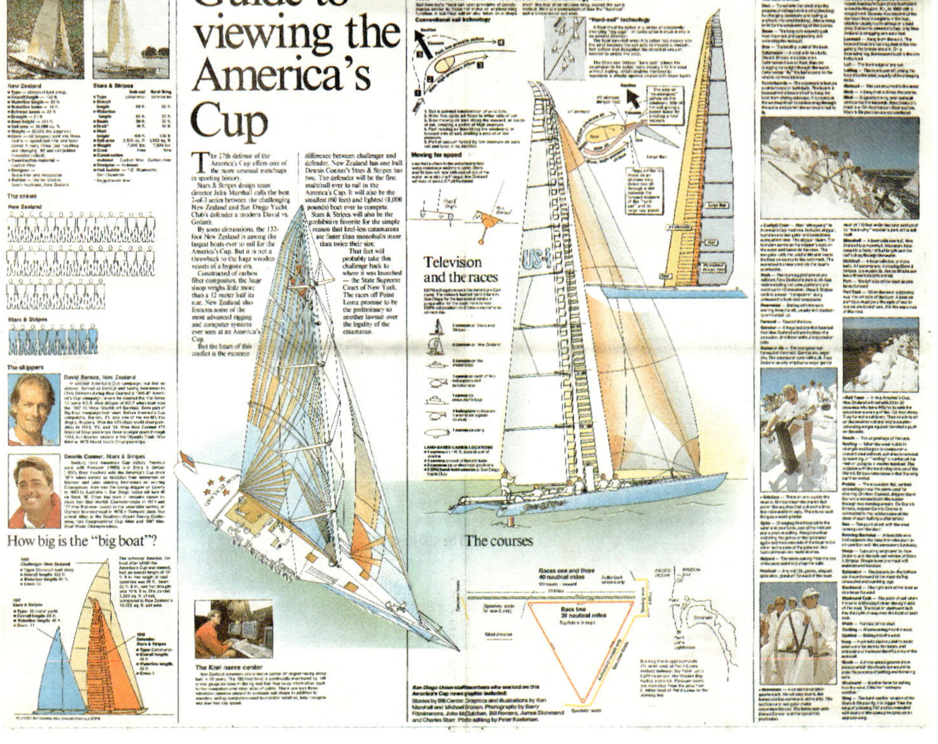

AWARD OF EXCELLENCE

INFORMATIONAL GRAPHICS
TWO OR MORE COLORS
The San Diego Union

Illustrators
Ken Marshall, Michael Cronan
Designer
Ken Marshall
Photographers
Barry Fitzsimmons, John McCutcheon, Bill Romero, James Skovmand, Charles Starr
Researchers
Ken Marshall, Bill Center
Art Director
Randy Wright
Picture Editor
Peter Koeleman

AWARD OF EXCELLENCE

INFORMATIONAL GRAPHICS
TWO OR MORE COLORS
The New York Times

Illustrator
Anna Walker
Designer
Nicki Kalish
Photographer
Walter Wick
Researcher
Madeline Jaynes
Art Director
Nicki Kalish
Graphics Editor
Richard J. Meislin

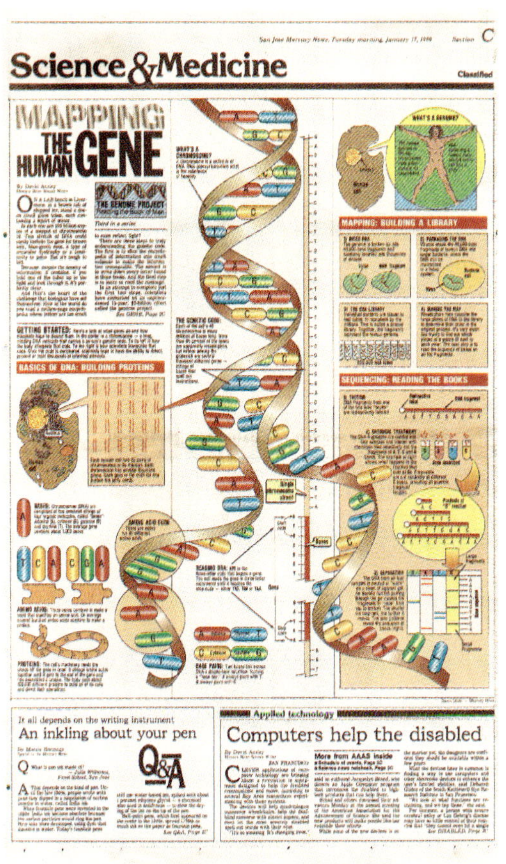

Science & Medicine

MAPPING THE HUMAN GENE

It all depends on the writing instrument

An inkling about your pen

Q&A

Applied technology

Computers help the disabled

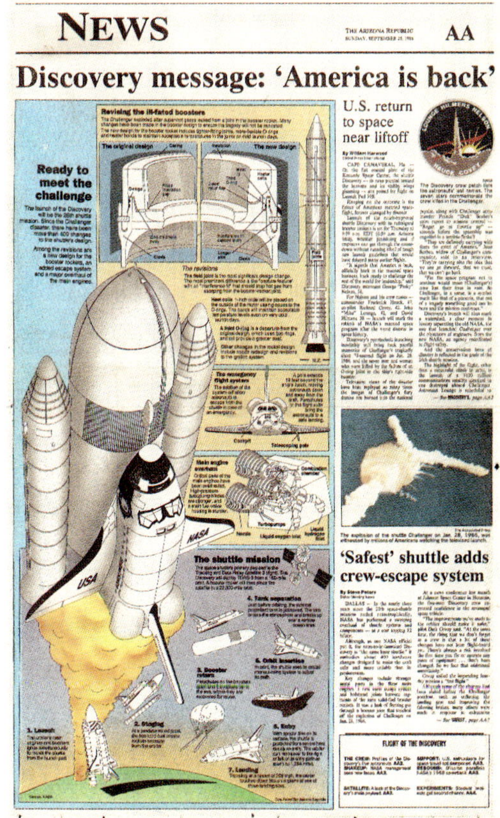

NEWS

Discovery message: 'America is back'

U.S. return to space near liftoff

Ready to meet the challenge

'Safest' shuttle adds crew-escape system

AWARD OF EXCELLENCE
INFORMATIONAL GRAPHICS
TWO OR MORE COLORS
The Arizona Republic
Phoenix, Arizona
Illustrator
Joe Willie Smith
Designer
Joe Willie Smith
Researcher
Joe Willie Smith
Art Director
Patti Valdez

AWARD OF EXCELLENCE
INFORMATIONAL GRAPHICS
TWO OR MORE COLORS
San Jose Mercury News
Illustrator
David Miller
Designer
David Miller
Researchers
David Ansley, David Miller
Art Directors
Bob Reynolds, David Miller

AWARD OF EXCELLENCE
INFORMATIONAL GRAPHICS
TWO OR MORE COLORS
The Orange County Register
Santa Ana, California
Designer
Paul Carbo
Illustrator
Paul Carbo
Researcher
Paul Carbo
Art Director
Bill Dunn

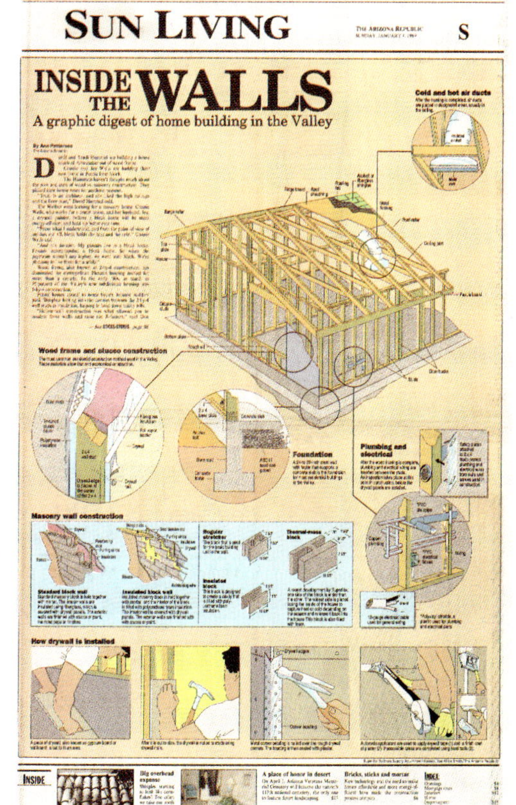

SUN LIVING

INSIDE THE WALLS

A graphic digest of home building in the Valley

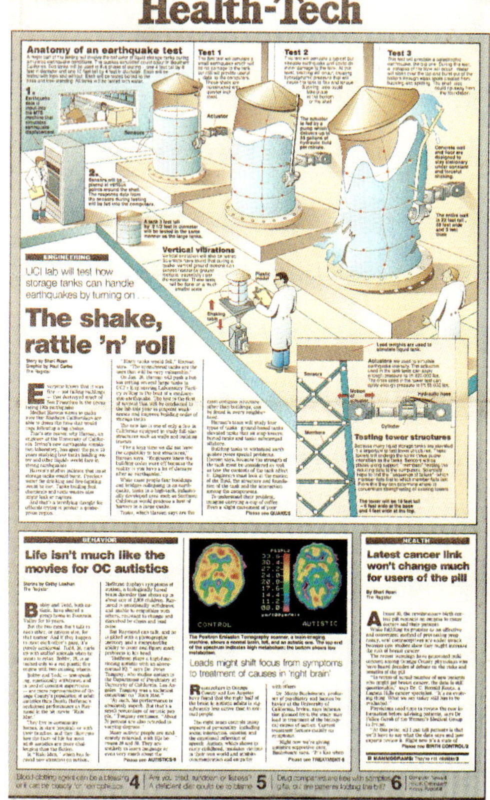

Health-Tech

Anatomy of an earthquake test

UCI lab will test how storage tanks can handle earthquakes by turning on

The shake, rattle 'n' roll

Life isn't much like the movies for OC autistics

Latest cancer link won't change much for users of the pill

AWARD OF EXCELLENCE
INFORMATIONAL GRAPHICS
TWO OR MORE COLORS
The Arizona Republic
Phoenix, Arizona
Illustrator
Don Foley
Designer
Don Foley
Researcher
Don Foley
Art Director
Patti Valdez

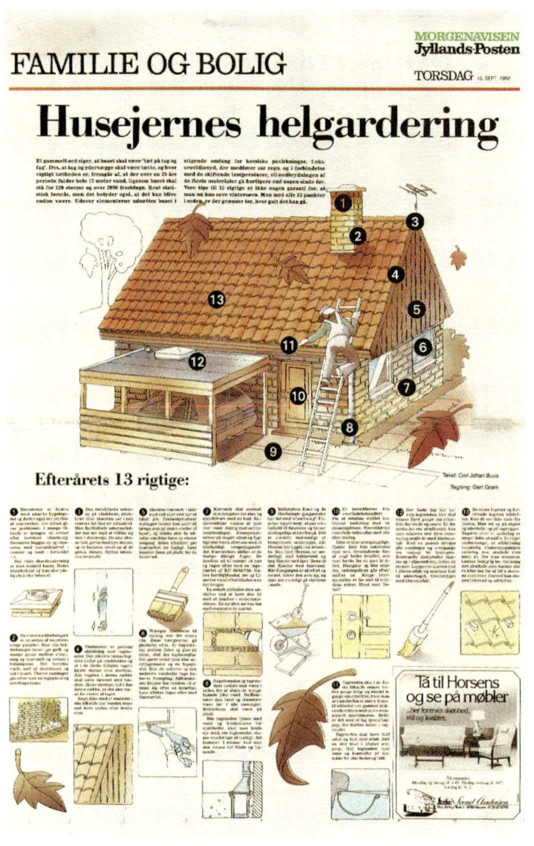

FAMILIE OG BOLIG

MORGENAVISEN Jyllands-Posten

TORSDAG

Husejernes helgardering

Efterårets 13 rigtige:

Tekst: Carl Johan Buus

Tegning: Gert Gram

Tå til Horsens og se på møbler

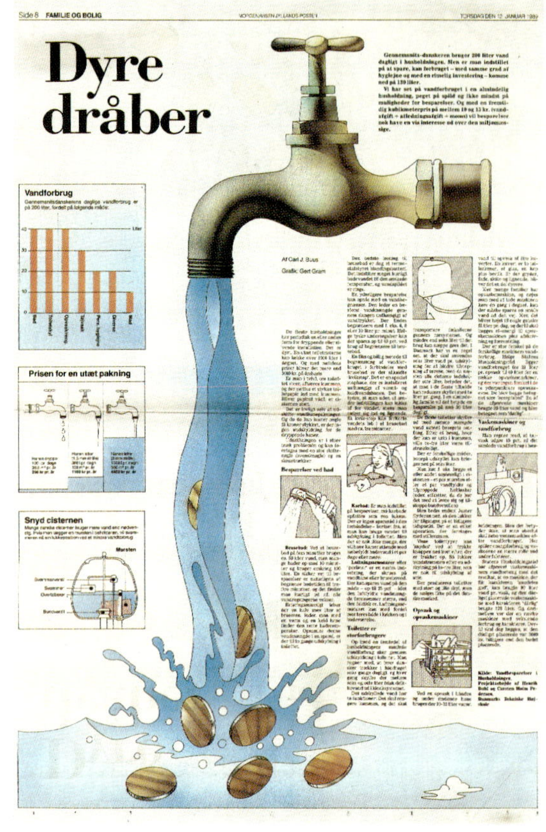

Dyre dråber

Vandforbrug

Prisen for en utæt pakning

Snyd cisternen

Af Carl J. Buus

Grafik: Gert Gram

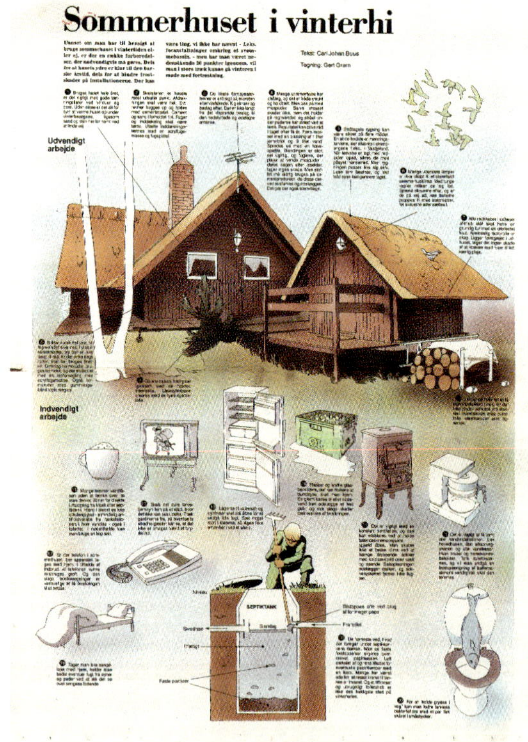

Sommerhuset i vinterhi

Tekst: Carl Johan Buus

Tegning: Gert Gram

Udvendigt arbejde

Indvendigt arbejde

SILVER AWARD

INFORMATIONAL GRAPHICS PORTFOLIO OF WORK

Morgenavisen Jyllands-Posten

Aarhus, Denmark

Illustrator

Gert Gram

Designer

Gert Gram

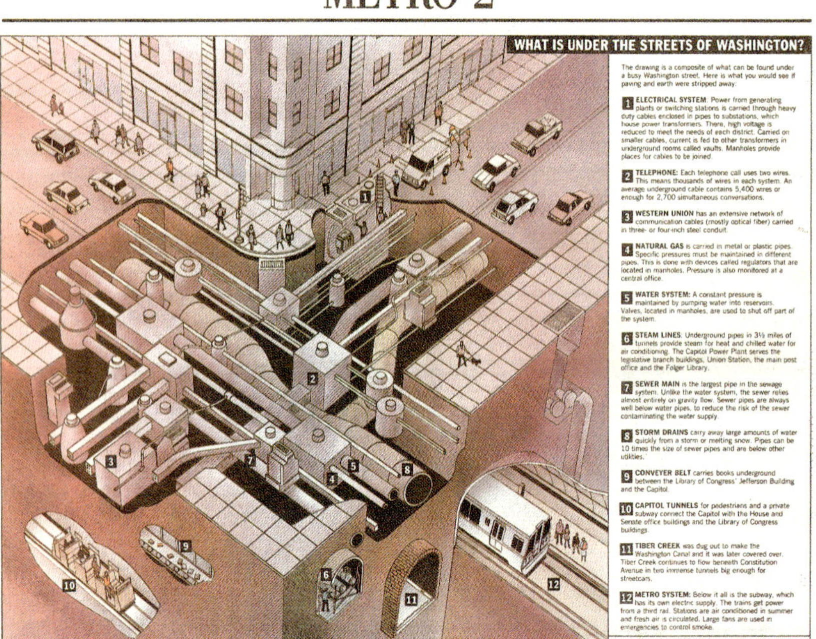

FRIDAY, NOVEMBER 11, 1988 THE WASHINGTON POST DR. GRIDLOCK/COMICS E1

METRO 2

WHAT IS UNDER THE STREETS OF WASHINGTON?

The drawing is a composite of what can be found under a busy Washington street. Here is what you would see if paving and earth were stripped away:

1 **ELECTRICAL SYSTEM**: Power from generating plants or switching stations is carried through heavy duty cables enclosed in pipes to substations, which house power transformers. There, high voltage is reduced to meet the needs of each district. Carried on smaller cables, current is fed to other transformers in underground rooms called vaults. Manholes provide places for cables to be joined.

2 **TELEPHONE:** Each telephone call uses two wires. This means thousands of wires in each system. An average underground cable contains 5,400 wires or enough for 2,700 simultaneous conversations.

3 **WESTERN UNION** has an extensive network of communication cables (mostly optical fiber) carried in three- or four-inch steel conduit.

4 **NATURAL GAS** is carried in metal or plastic pipes. Specific pressures must be maintained in different pipes. This is done with devices called regulators that are located in manholes. Pressure is also monitored at a central office.

5 **WATER SYSTEM:** A constant pressure is maintained by pumping water into reservoirs. Valves, located in manholes, are used to shut off part of the system.

6 **STEAM LINES**: Underground pipes in 3½ miles of tunnels provide steam for heat and chilled water for air conditioning. The Capitol Power Plant serves the legislative branch buildings, Union Station, the main post office and the Folger Library.

7 **SEWER MAIN** is the largest pipe in the sewage system. Unlike the water system, the sewer relies almost entirely on gravity flow. Sewer pipes are always well below water pipes, to reduce the risk of the sewer contaminating the water supply.

8 **STORM DRAINS** carry away large amounts of water quickly from a storm or melting snow. Pipes can be 10 times the size of sewer pipes and are below other utilities.

9 **CONVEYER BELT** carries books underground between the Library of Congress' Jefferson Building and the Capitol.

10 **CAPITOL TUNNELS** for pedestrians and a private subway connect the Capitol with the House and Senate office buildings and the Library of Congress buildings.

11 **TIBER CREEK** was dug out to make the Washington Canal and it was later covered over. Tiber Creek continues to flow beneath Constitution Avenue in two immense tunnels big enough for streetcars.

12 **METRO SYSTEM:** Below it all is the subway, which has its own electric supply. The trains get power from a third rail. Stations are air conditioned in summer and fresh air is circulated. Large fans are used in emergencies to control smoke.

DR. GRIDLOCK is on page 2

BY JOHNSTONE QUINAN—THE WASHINGTON POST

AWARD OF EXCELLENCE

INFORMATIONAL GRAPHICS TWO OR MORE COLORS

The Washington Post

Illustrator

Johnstone Quinan

Art Director

Michael Keegan

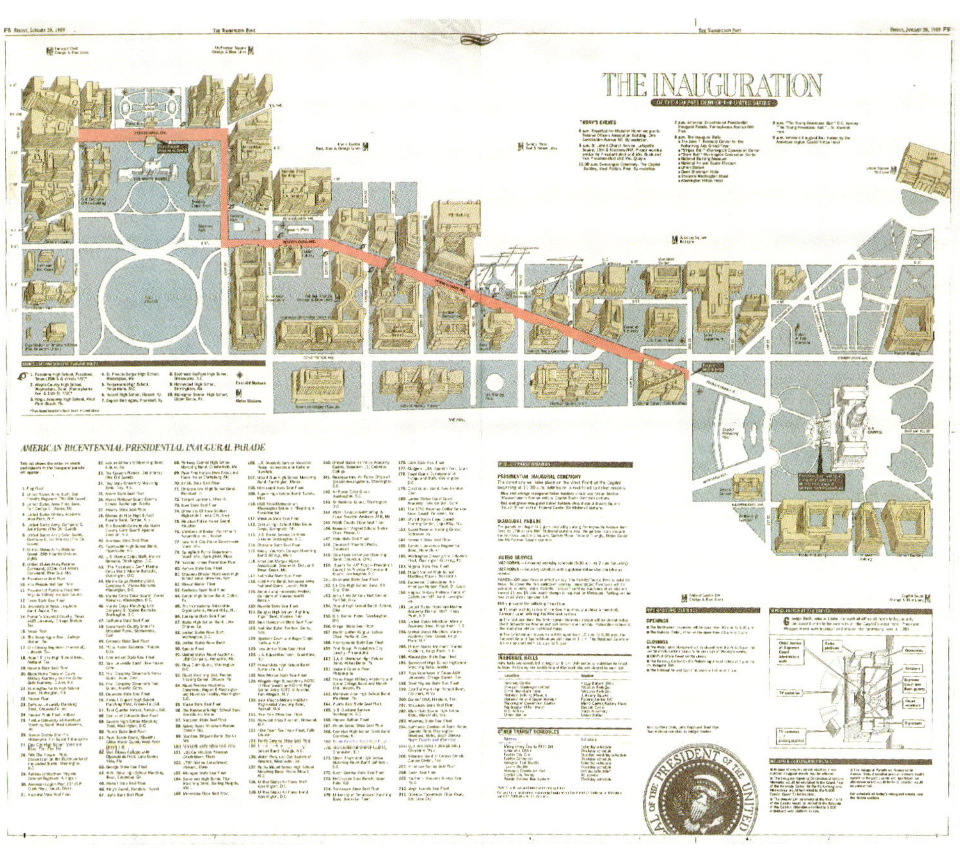

THE INAUGURATION

AMERICAN BICENTENNIAL PRESIDENTIAL INAUGURAL PARADE

AWARD OF EXCELLENCE
INFORMATIONAL GRAPHICS
TWO OR MORE COLORS
The Washington Post
Researcher
Bridget Roeber
Cartographers
Dave Cook, Brad Wye,
Larry Fogel
Art Director
Michael Keegan

AWARD OF EXCELLENCE
INFORMATIONAL GRAPHICS
TWO OR MORE COLORS
Tribune Newspapers,
Mesa Tribune
Mesa, Arizona
Illustrator
Michelle Wise
Designer
Michelle Wise
Art Director
Dave Seibert

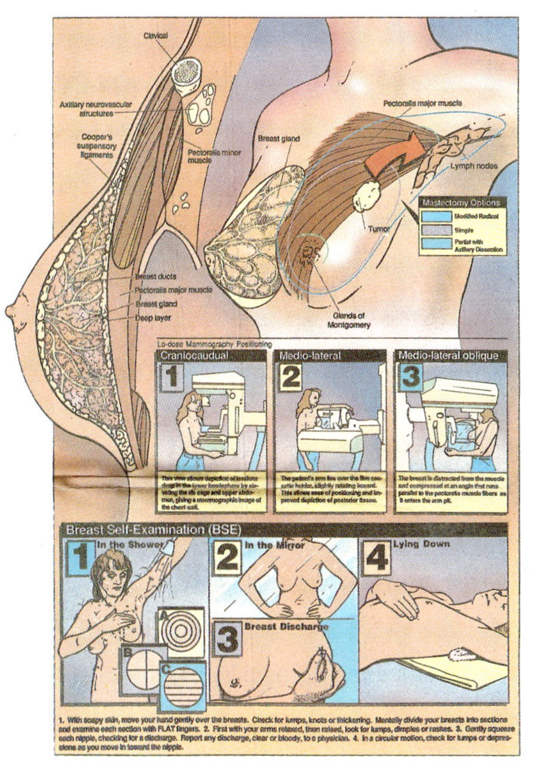

AWARD OF EXCELLENCE
INFORMATIONAL GRAPHICS
TWO OR MORE COLORS
The Seattle Times,
Pacific Magazine
Illustrator
Christine Cox
Researchers
Mary Ann Gwinn, Christine Cox
Art Director
Robert Massa

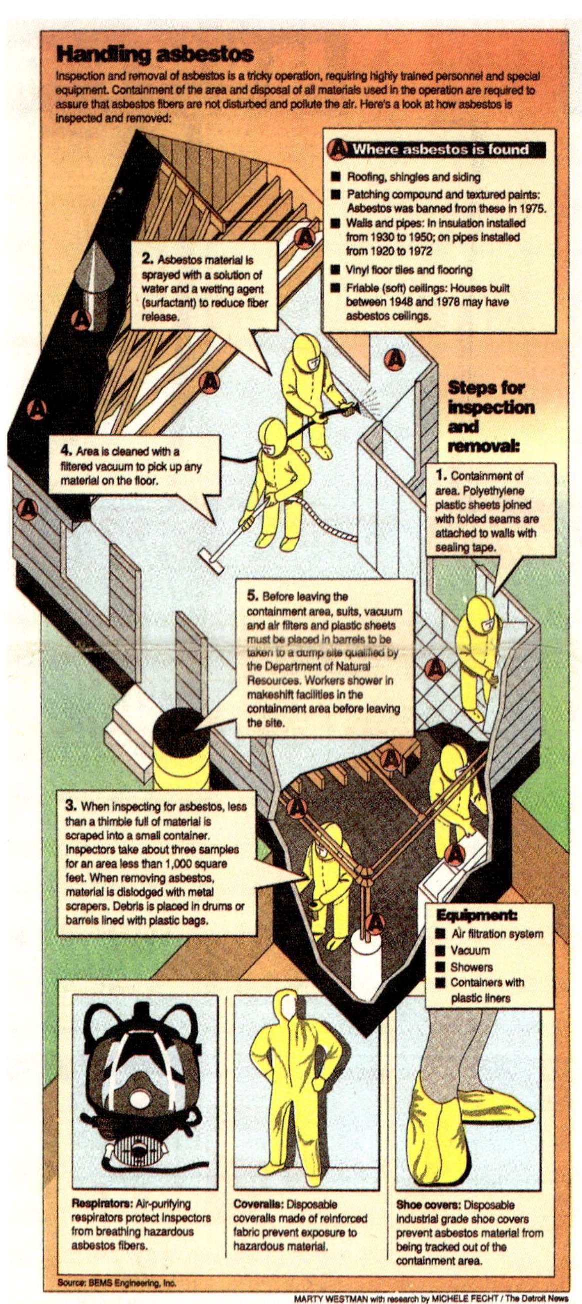

SILVER AWARD

INFORMATIONAL GRAPHICS
PORTFOLIO OF WORK
The Detroit News
Illustrator
Marty Westman

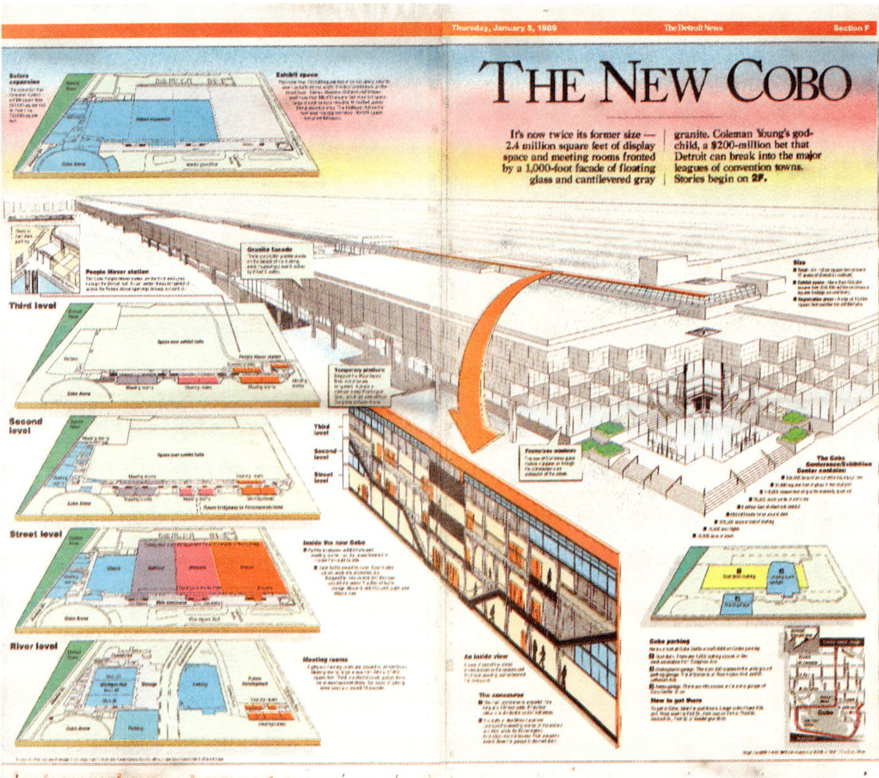

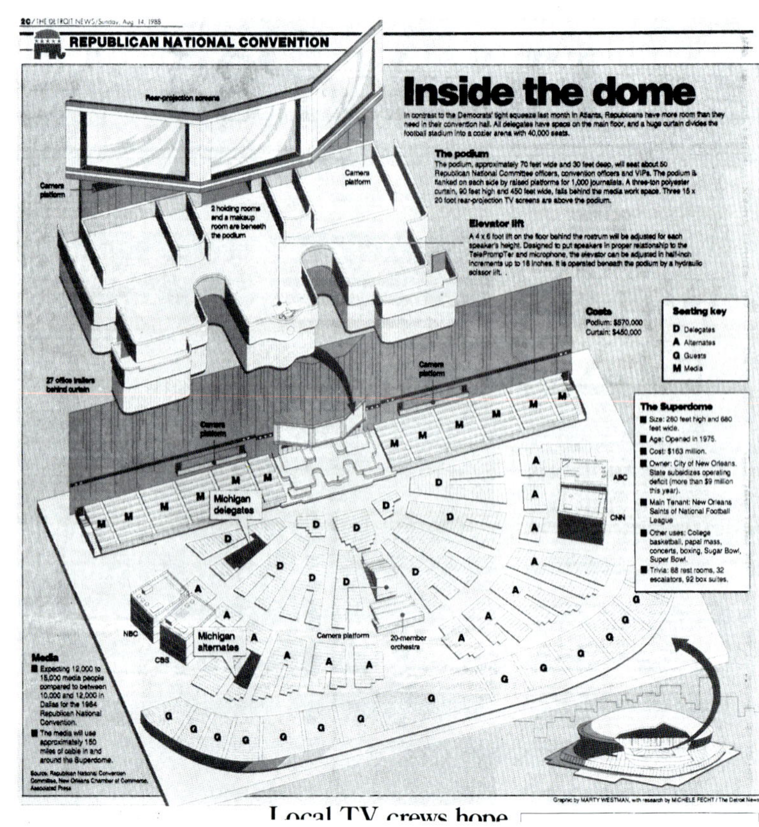

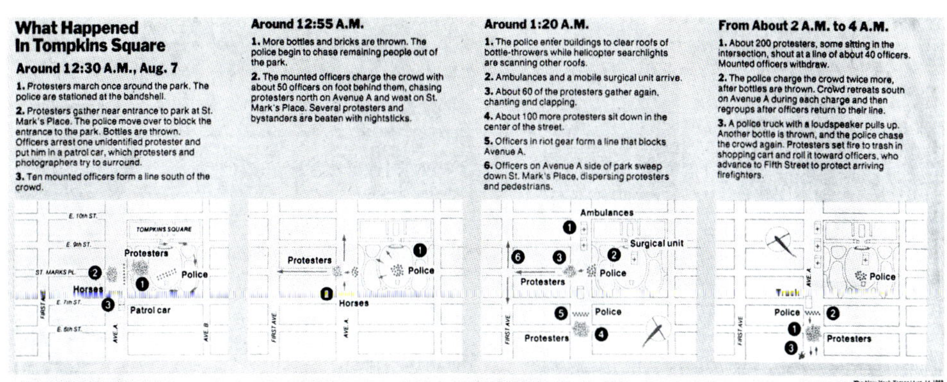

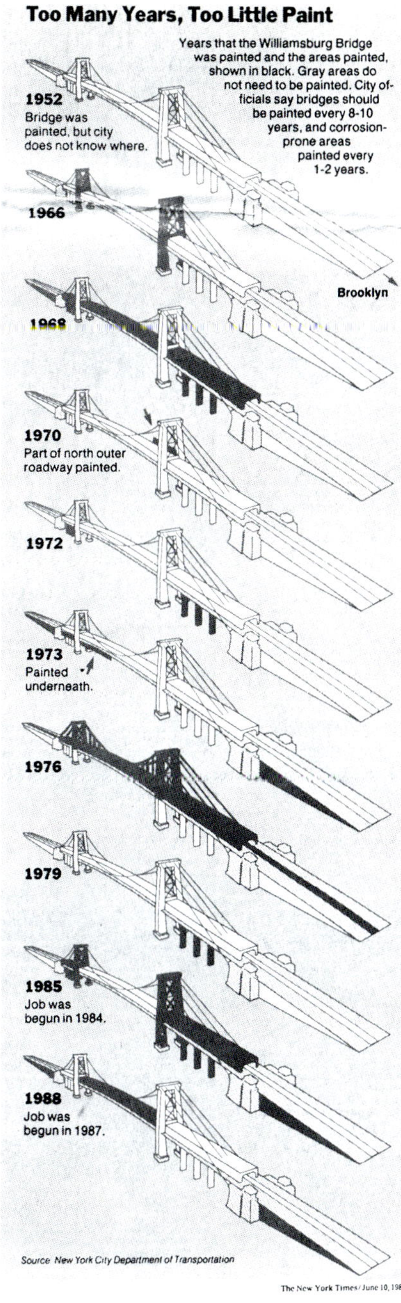

AWARD OF EXCELLENCE
INFORMATIONAL GRAPHICS
PORTFOLIO OF WORK
The New York Times
Graphics Editor
Anne Cronin

AWARD OF EXCELLENCE
INFORMATIONAL GRAPHICS
PORTFOLIO OF WORK
The New Paper
Singapore
Illustrator
Peter Sullivan
Designers
Peter Ong, Mario Garcia, Chantal Nair
Art Director
Peter Ong, Peter Sullivan

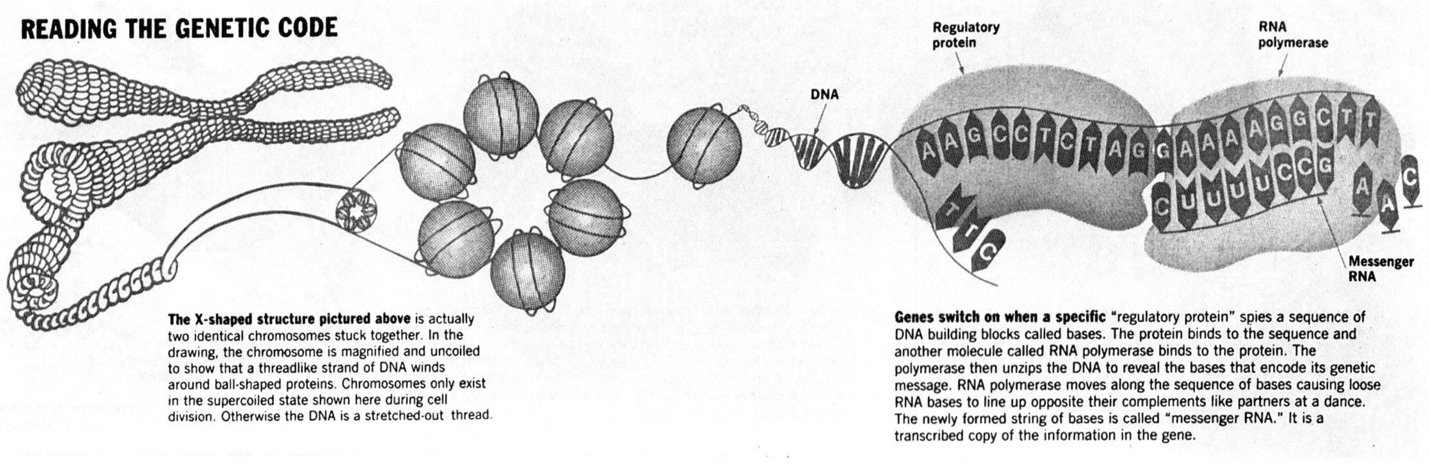

READING THE GENETIC CODE
Regulatory protein
RNA polymerase
DNA
Messenger RNA
The X-shaped structure pictured above is actually two identical chromosomes stuck together. In the drawing, the chromosome is magnified and uncoiled to show that a threadlike strand of DNA winds around ball-shaped proteins. Chromosomes only exist in the supercoiled state shown here during cell division. Otherwise the DNA is a stretched-out thread.
Genes switch on when a specific "regulatory protein" spies a sequence of DNA building blocks called bases. The protein binds to the sequence and another molecule called RNA polymerase binds to the protein. The polymerase then unzips the DNA to reveal the bases that encode its genetic message. RNA polymerase moves along the sequence of bases causing loose RNA bases to line up opposite their complements like partners at a dance. The newly formed string of bases is called "messenger RNA." It is a transcribed copy of the information in the gene.

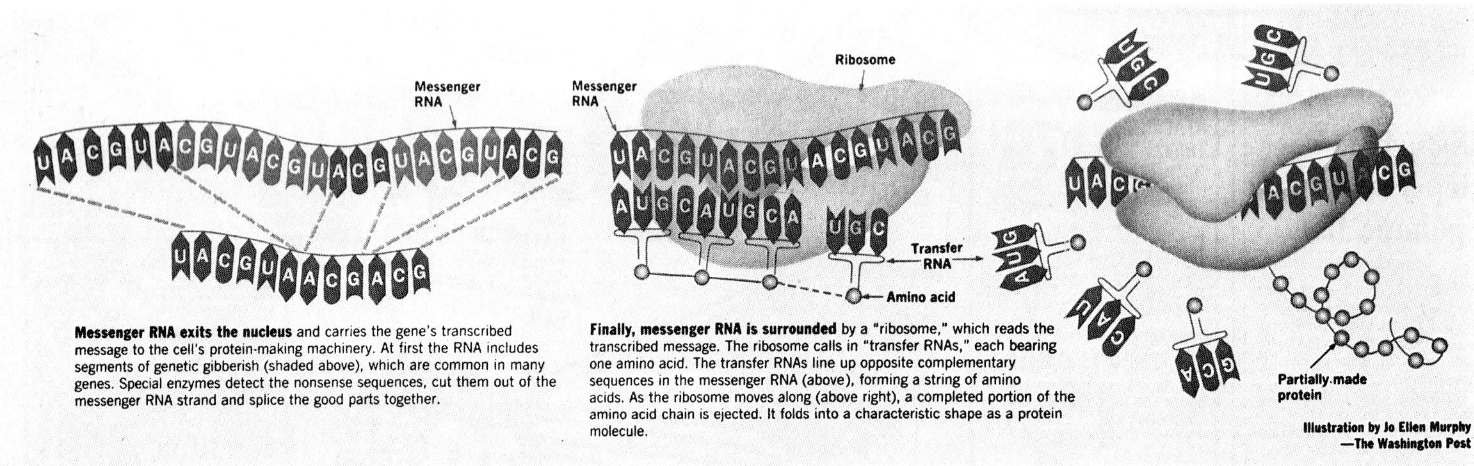

Messenger RNA
Messenger RNA
Ribosome
Transfer RNA
Amino acid
Partially made protein
Messenger RNA exits the nucleus and carries the gene's transcribed message to the cell's protein-making machinery. At first the RNA includes segments of genetic gibberish (shaded above), which are common in many genes. Special enzymes detect the nonsense sequences, cut them out of the messenger RNA strand and splice the good parts together.
Finally, messenger RNA is surrounded by a "ribosome," which reads the transcribed message. The ribosome calls in "transfer RNAs," each bearing one amino acid. The transfer RNAs line up opposite complementary sequences in the messenger RNA (above), forming a string of amino acids. As the ribosome moves along (above right), a completed portion of the amino acid chain is ejected. It folds into a characteristic shape as a protein molecule.
Illustration by Jo Ellen Murphy —The Washington Post

AWARD OF EXCELLENCE
INFORMATIONAL GRAPHICS
PORTFOLIO OF WORK
The Washington Post
Illustrator
Jo Ellen Murphy
Researcher
Boyce Rensberger
Art Director
Michael Keegan

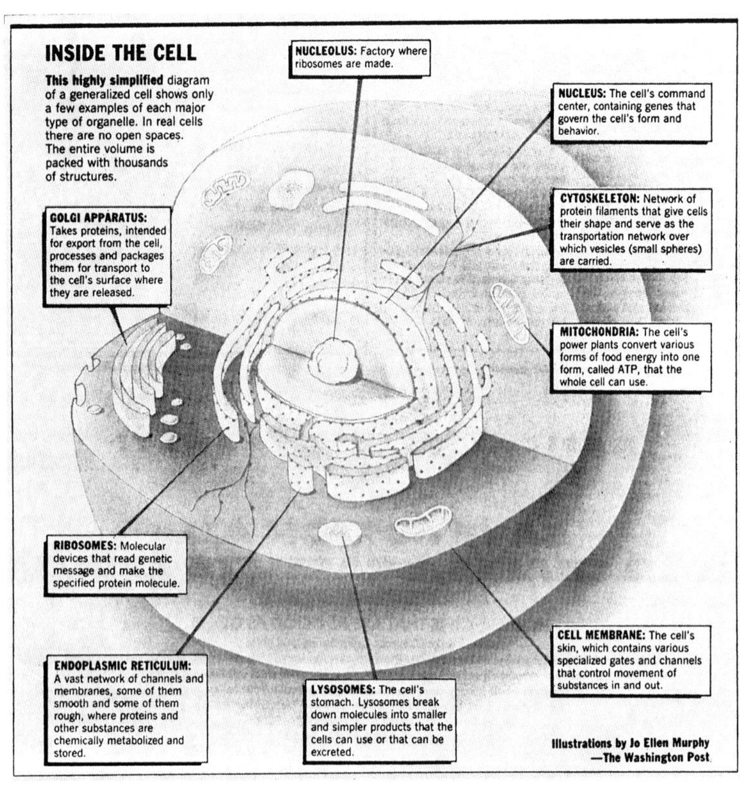

INSIDE THE CELL
This highly simplified diagram of a generalized cell shows only a few examples of each major type of organelle. In real cells there are no open spaces. The entire volume is packed with thousands of structures.
NUCLEOLUS: Factory where ribosomes are made.
NUCLEUS: The cell's command center, containing genes that govern the cell's form and behavior.
GOLGI APPARATUS: Takes proteins, intended for export from the cell, processes and packages them for transport to the cell's surface where they are released.
CYTOSKELETON: Network of protein filaments that give cells their shape and serve as the transportation network over which vesicles (small spheres) are carried.
MITOCHONDRIA: The cell's power plants convert various forms of food energy into one form, called ATP, that the whole cell can use.
RIBOSOMES: Molecular devices that read genetic message and make the specified protein molecule.
CELL MEMBRANE: The cell's skin, which contains various specialized gates and channels that control movement of substances in and out.
ENDOPLASMIC RETICULUM: A vast network of channels and membranes, some of them smooth and some of them rough, where proteins and other substances are chemically metabolized and stored.
LYSOSOMES: The cell's stomach. Lysosomes break down molecules into smaller and simpler products that the cells can use or that can be excreted.

AWARD OF EXCELLENCE
INFORMATIONAL GRAPHICS
PORTFOLIO OF WORK
The Washington Post
Illustrator
Jo Ellen Murphy
Art Director
Jo Ellen Murphy

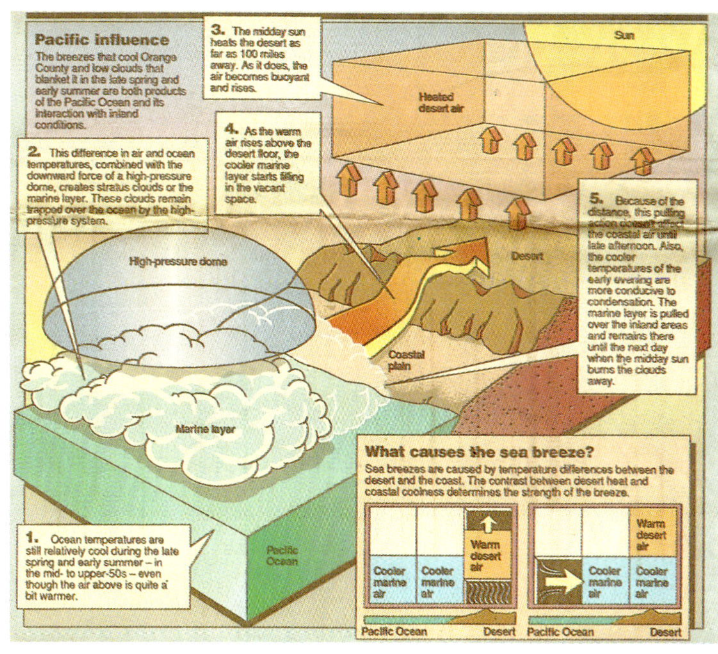

AWARD OF EXCELLENCE

INFORMATIONAL GRAPHICS

PORTFOLIO OF WORK

The Orange County Register

Santa Ana, California

Illustrator

Paul Carbo

Designer

Paul Carbo, Neil Werthiemer

Researchers

Paul Carbo,

Kim Christensen, Business Department

Reporter

Boyce Rensberger

Art Director

Bill Dunn

TUESDAY, MARCH 22, 1988 THE CHRISTIAN SCIENCE MONITOR 31

Treasure or not

Kathryn N. Hardin

THE CHRISTIAN SCIENCE MONITOR'S DAILY RELIGIOUS ARTICLE

A lesson we keep on learning

DAILY BIBLE VERSE

The Lord hath appeared of old unto me, saying, Yea, I have loved thee with an everlasting love: therefore with lovingkindness have I drawn thee. Jeremiah 31:3

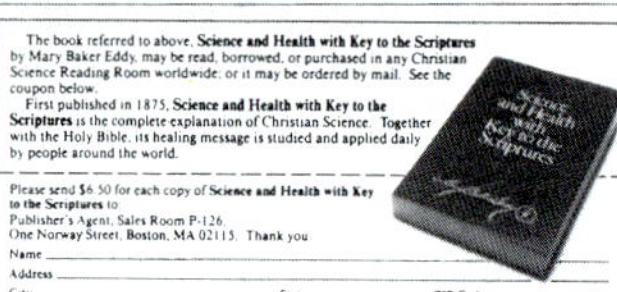

AN INTERNATIONAL DAILY NEWSPAPER Tuesday, January 31, 1989

THE CHRISTIAN SCIENCE MONITOR

GREAT WALL: Series debunks reverence for wall, saying it represents timidity.

MONEY AND POLITICS

Lawmakers Try to Nudge Election-Spending Reforms

Although the public seeks changes, Congress is reluctant to act

By John Dillin

ASSAILING ANCIENT TRADITIONS

Television: a Tool for China's Reformers

By Ann Scott Tyson

Panama Canal Treaties

Robert Brustein's Provocative Theater

Teen-age Gamblers

INSIDE

AWARD OF EXCELLENCE
REDESIGNS
OVERALL NEWSPAPER
The Christian Science Monitor
Designer
Greg Paul
Design Consultants
Brady and Paul Communications

NORGES STØRSTE MORGENAVIS

Aftenposten

Ap. snur - bot for promille

NRK vil drive butikk

LO vil ha øket avgift på aksjer

Høy bot bedre enn Ilseng

Bi-erverv i register

Bach hjem på 1. klasse

LEIEBIL

Vårruller

Aftenposten

Imot forsvars-kutt

Svensker bak børs-oppgang

Siktet for korrupsjon i Bergen

Mye ros til Kåre Willoch

Bush til Det hvite hus idag

Skatt uten strev

Snill vind i test-tunnel

Pensjon med høyrentekonto

AWARD OF EXCELLENCE
REDESIGNS
OVERALL NEWSPAPER
Aftenposten
Oslo, Norway
Art Director
Tor Bugge

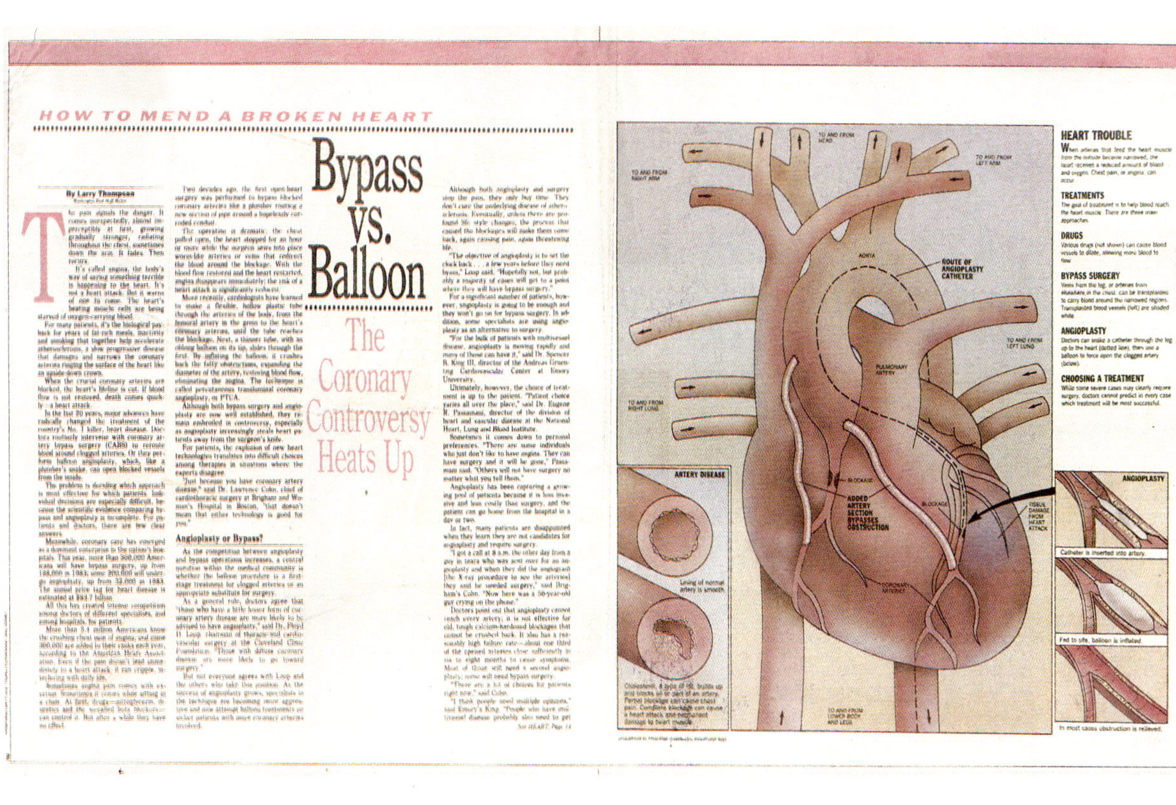

HOW TO MEND A BROKEN HEART

Bypass vs. Balloon

The Coronary Controversy Heats Up

By Larry Thompson

Angioplasty or Bypass?

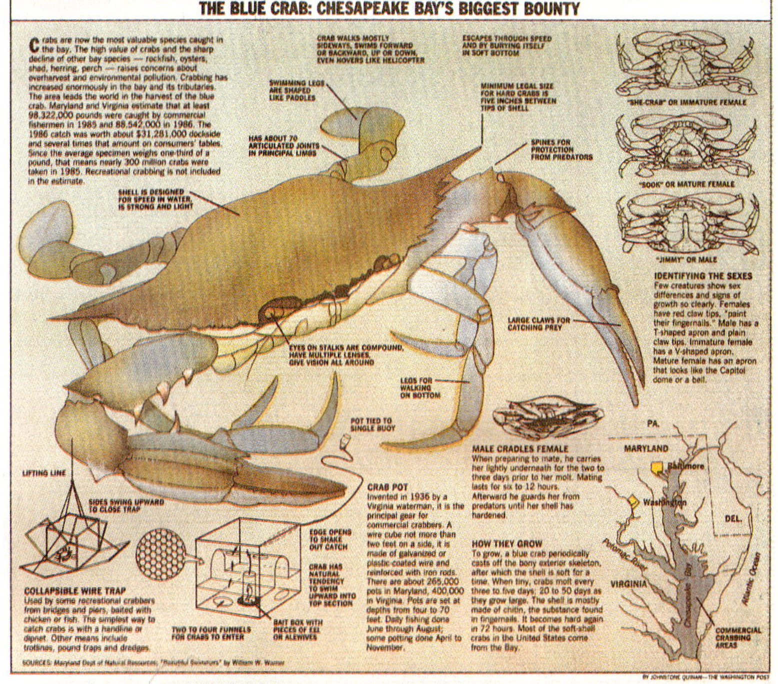

THE BLUE CRAB: CHESAPEAKE BAY'S BIGGEST BOUNTY

Crabs are now the most valuable species caught in the bay. The high value of crabs and the sharp decline of other bay species — rockfish, oysters, shad, herring, perch — raises concerns about overharvest and environmental pollution. Crabbing has increased enormously in the bay and its tributaries. The area leads the world in the harvest of the blue crab. Maryland and Virginia estimate that at least 98,322,000 pounds were caught by commercial fishermen in 1985 and 88,542,000 in 1986. The 1986 catch was worth about $31,281,000 dockside and several times that amount on consumers' tables. Since the average specimen weighs one-third of a pound, that means nearly 300 million crabs were taken in 1985. Recreational crabbing is not included in the estimate.

IDENTIFYING THE SEXES
Few creatures show sex differences and signs of growth so clearly. Females have red claw tips, "paint their fingernails." Male has a T-shaped apron and plain claw tips. Immature female has a V-shaped apron. Mature female has an apron that looks like the Capitol dome or a bell.

MALE CRADLES FEMALE
When preparing to mate, he carries her lightly underneath for the two to three days prior to her molt. Mating lasts for six to 12 hours. Afterward he guards her from predators until her shell has hardened.

CRAB POT
Invented in 1936 by a Virginia waterman, it is the principal gear for commercial crabbers. A wire cube not more than two feet on a side, it is made of galvanized or plastic-coated wire and reinforced with iron rods. There are about 265,000 pots in Maryland, 400,000 in Virginia. Pots are set at depths from four to 70 feet. Daily fishing done June through August; some potting done April to November.

HOW THEY GROW
To grow, a blue crab periodically casts off the bony exterior skeleton, after which the shell is soft for a time. When tiny, crabs molt every three to five days; 20 to 50 days as they grow large. The shell is mostly made of chitin, the substance found in fingernails. It becomes hard again in 72 hours. Most of the soft-shell crabs in the United States come from the Bay.

COLLAPSIBLE WIRE TRAP
Used by some recreational crabbers from bridges and piers, baited with chicken or fish. The simplest way to catch crabs is with a handline or dipnet. Other means include trotlines, pound traps and dredges.

SOURCES: Maryland Dept of Natural Resources; "Beautiful Swimmers" by William W. Warner

BY JOHNSTONE QUINAN—THE WASHINGTON POST

SILVER AWARD
INFORMATIONAL GRAPHICS
PORTFOLIO OF WORK
The Washington Post
Illustrator
Johnstone Quinan
Art Director
Michael Keegan

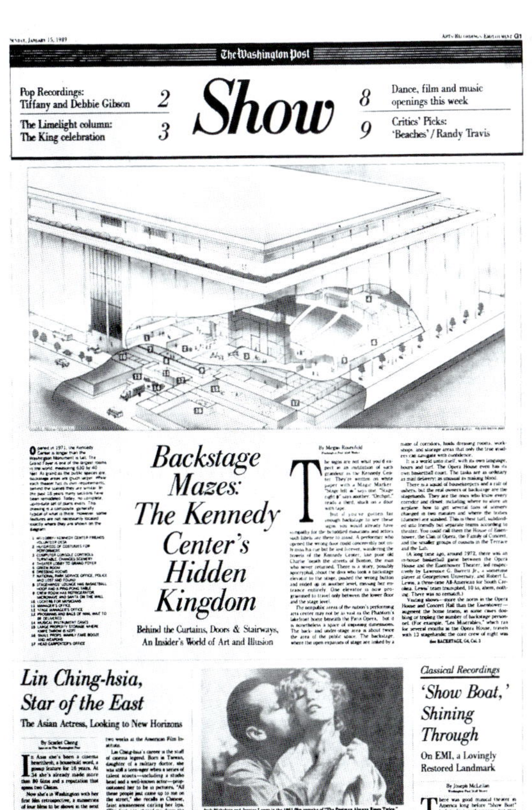

The Washington Post

Pop Recordings: Tiffany and Debbie Gibson 2

The Limelight column: The King celebration 3

Show

Dance, film and music openings this week 8

Critics' Picks: 'Beaches' / Randy Travis 9

Backstage Mazes: The Kennedy Center's Hidden Kingdom

Behind the Curtains, Doors & Stairways, An Insider's World of Art and Illusion

Lin Ching-hsia, Star of the East

The Asian Actress, Looking to New Horizons

Opera Meets the Auto Age

Stephen Paulus' 'Postman,' Updating an Ancient Art

Classical Recordings

'Show Boat,' Shining Through

On EMI, a Lovingly Restored Landmark

SILVER AWARD
INFORMATIONAL GRAPHICS
PORTFOLIO OF WORK
The Washington Post
Illustrator
Johnstone Quinan
Art Director
Michael Keegan

THE SAN FRANCISCO BAY
GUARDIAN
NOVEMBER 30, 1988/VOL. 23/NO. 8
THE NEWS, ARTS AND ENTERTAINMENT WEEKLY

ON THE COVER:
MADE IN SAN FRANCISCO
A guide to locally made gifts and 50 holiday crafts fairs. . . Part I of the Bay Guardian's five-part holiday guide

A LONG WAY FROM HOME PORT
Despite the passage of Prop. S, the Missouri battle is far from over

IS PRODIGY AHEAD OF ITS TIME?
Sears and IBM are investing millions in a bold attempt to bring computer networking to a broad market. But will it work?

AWARD OF EXCELLENCE
REDESIGNS
OVERALL NEWSPAPER
The San Francisco Bay Guardian
Designer
John Schmitz
Art Director
John Schmitz

FREE
THE DISTRICT ELECTIONS TIME BOMB
SF's mayoral candidates scramble for position
UP AGAINST THE WALL!
A tour guide's guide to travel to China
THE SAN FRANCISCO Bay Guardian
PUBLISHED WEEKLY EVERY WEDNESDAY VOL. 21, NO. 29, MAY 6-13, 1987.
THE PLEX PERPLEX
Two more screens for the Castro, the whirlwind arrival of the Kabuki 8-plex and other tales of the art-house wars

SINCE 1966, THE LARGEST CIRCULATION NEWSWEEKLY IN NORTHERN CALIFORNIA

AWARD OF EXCELLENCE
SECTION
REDESIGN
Detroit Free Press
Designers
Andrew Hartley, John Van Pelt
Art Director
Deborah Withey
Editor
Jack Seamonds

business monday
Monday, Jan. 25, 1988
D
Luther Jackson
Michigan's economy
Saginaw seeks new focus for job-retention effort
Tough dose for chronic absenteeism
GM, union prescribe treatment for no-shows
The hopes of a hybrid
Chrysler, Mitsubishi are working to get Diamond-Star on the road
Taking leave from a job may save your senses

BUSINESS MONDAY
Detroit Free Press
SECTION C
INSIDE INFORMATION
PRIX VIEWS
Even if race is not as grand, it'll be red, white and blue
TAKING THE CHECKERED, GETTING THE GREEN
HIGH PROFILE
Agencies crave Reagan on the after-dinner menu

AWARD OF EXCELLENCE
SECTION
REDESIGN
Syracuse Herald American
Syracuse, New York
Designer
Gary Visgaitis
Art Director
Gary Visgaitis
Managing Editor
Tim Atseff

AWARD OF EXCELLENCE
SECTION
REDESIGN
San Francisco Examiner
Designers
Bill Prochnow,
Josephine Rigg-Parik
Design Consultant
Roger Black
Art Director
Josephine Rigg-Parik

AWARD OF EXCELLENCE
MISCELLANEOUS
San Francisco Chronicle
Illustrator
Ron Chan